THE
INSTANT
HOROSCOPE
READER

THE
INSTANT
HOROSCOPE
READER
Planets by Sign, House, and Aspect

Julia Lupton Skalka

Barnes & Noble Books
BOOKS
NEW YORK

This edition published by Barnes & Noble, Inc.,
by arrangement with Llewellyn Worldwide, Ltd.

2000 Barnes & Noble Books

ISBN 0-7607-1767-2

Printed and bound in the United States of America

00 01 02 03 04 MC 9 8 7 6 5 4 3 2 1

BVG

DEDICATION

For Nana, who makes the world a better place

ACKNOWLEDGEMENTS

In the course of its creation and multiple reincarnations, *The Instant Horoscope Reader* became much more than the single effort of its author. For this book and any work I accomplish as an author, I will always be in debt to Julia A. Wagner, former Editor-in-Chief of *Horoscope Magazine*, who gave me an opportunity to write about astrology twenty years ago. Special indebtedness goes to Dennis Haskell of Time Cycles Research who encouraged me to write text for his remarkable astrological software. His *Io* series of astrology programs contains the natal report writer on which *The Instant Horoscope Reader* is based. The astrological fonts used in the book are one of many innovative font styles available from Time Cycles. I am truly grateful to Dennis, along with Elaine Tyropolis, Bob Stuller, Joshua Jewell, and Chuck Weigand at Time Cycles for their treasured friendship and support.

I am profoundly appreciative of the intelligence and editorial skills of Lauren Crasco and Gloria Freemire who patiently read and reread the manuscript. Their corrections and suggestions were insightful and somehow managed to keep my words and ideas from collapsing under their own weight. Grateful thanks must go to my family—Stan, David, Karen, and Aaron, who, despite my preoccupation and frequent absences, have unaccountably remained affectionate and loyal to me. The valuable suggestions they made, necessary tasks they performed, and many personal favors they granted contributed in no small measure to the writing process. Never one to take things for granted, I also offer thanks to the gods of the reliable Xerox and the clever Macintosh.

Any creativity and originality in this book reside solely in the presentation of the material—the success or failure for which I accept responsibility as well as blame. The content of its information belongs to astrology itself and to the generations of astrologers who have recorded its ideas and observations since the beginning of history.

CONTENTS

ILLUSTRATIONS

TABLES

Preface

Introducing people to astrology is an exhilarating experience for me. I confess it isn't always easy to decide where to begin. Some people are intrigued with astrology's long and colorful history. Some want to know if it's like the daily horoscope columns they read in newspapers. Others are interested in how a horoscope is cast. There is one thing everyone always wants to know. "How," they invariably ask me, "did you become interested in astrology?" To readers who may also wonder, let me reply that I began to study astrology for the same reason that motivated you to read this book—it's a fascinating subject. Whether you want a little information or you want to become a serious student, learning about astrology also happens to be a lot of fun.

What exactly is astrology? Let me begin by saying what it is not. Astrology is not a religion. It does not require blind faith. Astrology is not magic. It does not involve secret knowledge or occult techniques. Although certain of its signs and symbols originated in mythology, astrology is not myth. Religion, magic, and mythology arose from the need to understand ourselves and to explain the world in which we live. So did astrology. One of the worst misconceptions people have about astrology is that it proposes that the planets and/or their movements actually cause things to happen. This is not true. Let's say, for example, an astrologer observes a planetary pattern that is, among other things, associated with war. Let us suppose that, indeed, such a catastrophe occurs. Does the astrologer believe the planets were responsible for the war? No. The principle of cause and effect

has no part in astrological thinking. One event (the planetary pattern) is used to recognize the potential of another event (the war). The first event is only a connection or association with but certainly not the cause of the second event.

Astrology began as the simple observation of the Sun and Moon. To early observers the supreme lord of the celestial realm was the Sun; he whose fiery countenance appeared each morning and disappeared over the horizon each evening, plunging the world again into darkness. The Moon, though she lacked the warmth and splendor of the Sun, also inspired appreciation and adoration. Gradually changing from a slender crescent to a wondrous silver bubble afloat in the starry mists, she was the undisputed goddess of the night. Ancient art and architecture stand as mute testimony that observation and worship of the Sun and Moon are far older than recorded history. How and when astrology developed will never be known for certain, but it is not difficult to understand how early societies learned to recognize a correlation between celestial cycles and earthly events, such as the seasons and the annual flooding of rivers. If such vital, life-sustaining events were connected with the movements of heavenly bodies, why not with everything else? This essential question was the seed from which astrology sprang. And out of astrology's womb came the science of astronomy.

From ancient times the practice of using planetary positions as favorable and unfavorable indicators in the lives of nations as well as individuals was fairly widespread throughout the regions of the Middle East, especially in Mesopotamia. About one hundred and fifty years ago, before the age of archaeology, Europeans began digging in the desolate, forsaken sands of what is now modern Iraq. Prompted by desire to locate the lost cities of the Bible, they had barely disturbed the earth when the remains of a ziggurat, or temple tower, were uncovered. Excavations continued, and in the capitals of the world excitement grew as the discoveries became known. Royal palaces, along with enormous statues of winged bulls, long-dead kings, warriors, and horses, slowly emerged from what had been nothing more than rubbish heaps. There was little doubt that the ancient city of Nineveh had been found when reliefs depicting the story of the Assyrian people who "delighted in war" began to appear. This was the biblical nation that the prophets of Israel had cursed for their barbaric deeds. English and French excavators pried centuries-old stonework and other Assyrian artifacts out of dusty graves and sent them off to museums in a world undreamt of by those who had created them. Thrilled with their success, the excavators did not yet recognize their most amazing discovery. They did not know the buried treasures they had

found would lead to far more ancient times and peoples than those of their Bible.

One of the most impressive of the Assyrian palaces that was discovered belonged to Ashurbanipal, 668-627 BC, the last of the great kings of Assyria. As frightful as he was to his enemies, Ashurbanipal nevertheless possessed at least one redeeming trait; he had a thirst for knowledge. Unlike many of his predecessors, this monarch could read and write, and, most significantly, he was devoted to preserving records from earlier millennia. Much as Alexander would do when building his famous library hundreds of years later, Ashurbanipal sent for all the texts that were stored in private collections throughout his kingdom. He employed many excellent scribes, who recorded the texts in ancient Akkadian, side by side with their translation in the still older language of Sumer. In 612 BC, Nineveh and the people that Ashurbanipal had led into a last burst of prosperity were completely destroyed by the Medes. Ashurbanipal and his great kingdom vanished for two thousand five hundred years.

When excavators uncovered Ashurbanipal's palace early in the nineteenth century, they found lying within its chambers hundreds of clay tablets with strange cuneiform inscriptions. This was all that remained of the royal library. The tablets, later thought to be only a small portion of the royal archives collected by Ashurbanipal at Nineveh, were shoveled into bushels and sent to the British Museum. When the cuneiform code was finally broken and the text could be deciphered, the modern world was astounded. The writing on the clay tablets made it obvious that stories and ideas thought to have originated in biblical times could be traced back to the Sumerians, a civilization that had existed two thousand years earlier. The tablets found in Ashurbanipal's library and elsewhere contained the historical roots of biblical lore, and they also contained evidence that astrology, too, has a very ancient history. A particular group of these tablets, referred to by scholars as omen texts, contain many one-line entries that describe the movements of the Sun, Moon, and planets. The descriptions further associate the celestial movements with the welfare of the king or the nation.

"The royal art of astrology is the method of divination for which Mesopotamia is famed,"[1] wrote the distinguished Assyriologist A. Leo Oppenheim in his book, *Ancient Mesopotamia*. In an essay published posthumously in 1975, Professor Oppenheim focused his attention on the astrologers of ancient Assyria. According to Professor Oppenheim, the study of the rise of astrology has hardly begun. Because of the time-consuming, highly specialized scholarship required, many of the cuneiform tablets have still not been translated. Until they

are, we cannot have a true history of astrology. The science and art of astrology, as it is still practiced in modern times, does not come directly from the Chaldeans or Babylonians, but from fourth- and fifth-century Hellenistic Greeks. The translated cuneiform texts reveal, however, that astrology inherited much material from the Babylonians and far earlier cultures.

The rational thought of Greek philosophers and writers embraced the notion of a cosmos so well ordered that no part is independent of the other parts. They believed enthusiastically in a correspondence between planetary patterns and the lives of people, and they developed the mathematics necessary to calculate a horoscope. The greatest of the Greek astronomers, Ptolemy and Hipparchus, were astrologers, and the cosmological teachings of Plato and Aristotle embodied astrological ideas. To Mesopotamian literature, the Greeks added their knowledge of geometry, philosophy, and rational thought. By the second century BC, they had given astrology the definite shape and structure it has retained from generation to generation in Western thought and culture, attracting along the way the interest of respected scholars and charlatans alike.

In 2000 BC, the basis of the emerging art of astrology was the association of celestial cycles with events on the earth. As a modern twentieth century astrologer, I benefit from being able to use accurate mathematical calculations and a more enlightened understanding of the world. However, the basis of my astrology is the same as it was for those who practiced it almost four thousand years ago.

Chapter One

Introduction to Astrology

One of the main purposes of an introduction is to acquaint readers with some of the material they will encounter in the book. I decided that for me the best introduction might be simply to answer questions about astrology that people frequently ask.

What is astrology?
Astrology is the study of cycles. The Sun, Moon, and planets move in their own time and space according to specific cycles. Each planet faithfully follows its individual orbit around the Sun. In turn the Sun follows its own path through the galaxy, and the galaxy inexorably moves through the endless universe. Although science has made some progress, we are still in the formative stages of understanding the great cosmic entity of which the Earth and those who dwell upon her are such a tiny part. We have gained much of our knowledge about the universe from studying the various cycles of animate and inanimate matter within it. Above, the Earth, the Sun, Moon, and planets move according to their individual cycles. On the surface of the Earth, man, beast, and plant live according to their biological cycles. The Earth itself has many cycles—weather cycles, geological cycles, and so on. Human society experiences economic, political, and social cycles. Since the time of the learned Greeks, we have known that everything in

I

nature is related to everything else in uniquely integrated and observable patterns. The planetary cycles observed in the heavens are related to the cycles observed on the Earth—as surely as one season follows another. Astrologers are by no means the only ones who continue to believe in the correlation between people and the universe. On Sunday, October 3, 1993, the *New York Times* printed an article on mathematics in which Simon Kochen, Mathematics Department Chairman at Princeton University, was quoted, "We evolved from this universe, and our brains work in some kind of conformity with the universe. There must be some kind of harmony between the way we think and the way the universe works."[1]

Why is the Sun's position so important in astrology?

Compared to other stars with respect to size and brilliance, our Sun is not an impressive specimen. However, in a universe incalculably cold and dark, it is fortunate for us that the Earth unfailingly continues to circle around this little spark of warmth and light. Otherwise, there would be no life. During the year it takes to make one orbit around the Sun, the Earth receives life-giving solar rays from continually changing angles. The changing angles of the Earth's position as it moves around the Sun produce the four seasons. Birth, growth, maturity, and death are the patterns within the cycle of the seasons, a cycle ordained by the Earth's relationship with the Sun. Every life that is created is an imitation of this pattern.

As the Earth moves along her path, we who watch from her surface keep track of our solar journey by observing that the Sun appears in a slightly different section of the sky each day. In a year's time, the Earth has come full circle, and the Sun can be seen at approximately the same point in the sky. We know the Earth moves around the Sun, but because the Sun is in a slightly different position each day, it appears to us as though he is the one slowly tracing a circular path in the heavens. This "apparent" path of the Sun through the sky is called the zodiac. Since the path of the zodiac is a circle, it is divided into 360 degrees. The circle is further divided into twelve sections of thirty degrees, one section for each sign of the zodiac. The twelve signs always appear in the same order. They are as follows: Aries, Taurus, Gemini, Cancer, Leo, Virgo, Libra, Scorpio, Sagittarius, Capricorn, Aquarius, and Pisces. Dividing the sky into twelve sections, or zodiacal signs, makes it easy to state the position of the Sun throughout the year. The zodiacal year begins on March 20 or 21, when the Sun is seen in the sky at zero degrees Aries, which is the first degree of the first sign of the zodiac. Choosing this point to start may seem arbitrary; after all, who is to say when a

circle begins or ends? The reason is that when the Sun appears at zero degrees Aries, the Sun's vertical rays extend equally from the North Pole to the South Pole. This phenomenon, known as the vernal, or spring, Equinox (*equinox* is Latin meaning "equal nights"), results in making day and night equal all over the Earth, twelve hours of day and twelve hours of night. Now the days start to become longer until September 23 when the Sun has reached a second point in the sky known as the autumnal equinox. We are halfway through our solar journey. The Sun's vertical rays extend equally from the North Pole to the South Pole, once again resulting in twelve hours of day and twelve hours of night. From this date it is the nights that begin to grow longer. The exact reverse occurs in the southern hemisphere. When days in the northern hemisphere begin to grow longer, the days in the southern hemisphere begin to grow shorter. When nights in the northern hemisphere begin to grow longer, the nights begin to grow shorter in the southern hemisphere.

The Sun enters Aries each year on the 20th or 21st day of March. On March 22 the Sun is in one degree Aries. The next day it is in two degrees Aries, and so on, moving approximately one degree each day. On the 20th or 21st of April the Sun has traveled through thirty degrees of Aries and enters zero degrees Taurus. The date on which the Sun leaves one sign of the zodiac and enters the next sign varies a day or two, occurring between the 20th and 23rd each month. The astrological sign of those born during the one day in the month when the Sun changes signs can only be determined by the time of their birth. Let us say, for example, that in a given year the Sun enters Taurus April 20 at 2:00 o'clock in the afternoon. Babies born on April 20 before 2:00 p.m. are born in the sign Aries, while those born the same day but at 2:00 p.m. or later are born in the sign Taurus. People born on the date the Sun changes signs often say they were born "on the cusp." What they are really saying is that they don't know when the Sun changed signs on the day of their birth. If the time of birth is known, the confusion can easily be remedied. Many calendars and almanacs list the time as well as the date when the Sun enters a new sign each month.

What is the difference between one's astrological sign and one's horoscope?

A person's astrological sign describes in which sign of the zodiac the Sun was located at birth. A person's horoscope, or natal chart as it is also called, is literally a map of the heavens, showing the exact position of the Sun, Moon, and planets at birth. The natal chart is mathematically calculated using the exact date, hour,

and location of an individual's birth. Many people are born on the same date but at a different hour. Many are born on the same date and in the same hour, but not in the same place. An accurate horoscope requires all three variables: date, time, and location. Every four-minute interval produces a slightly different chart, and even twins are rarely born within such a narrow space of time. The horoscope is a totally unique chart; no two individuals have the same one. This is why an astrologer can define an individual's nature and temperament in a most subtle and personal manner.

Why don't some people seem to fit their astrological sign?

There are two reasons why some people don't think they fit their astrological sign. The first is that they may not really understand the entire astrological description of their sign and are basing their opinion on a few generalities. A more thorough explanation often reveals that they *do* exhibit characteristics of their Sun sign.

The second explanation of why some people don't seem to fit their astrological sign is more complex. Astrological interpretation is based on an individual's complete horoscope, which indicates where all the celestial bodies were positioned at the time of birth. The entire array of planetary positions in a horoscope defines how strongly an individual is apt to exhibit the traits associated with his or her Sun sign. For example, let's take Aries individuals. They are all born when the Sun is in Aries, but in what sign is the Moon? Some Aries people are born when the Moon is also in Aries, but since the Moon spends about two and a half days in each sign during a month's time, she could just as easily be in another sign. The astrological sign of the Moon is significant in describing an individual's emotions. The emotional nature greatly influences how individuals will handle the traits indicated by their Sun sign. An Aries person born with the Moon in a sign that indicates great cautiousness or a tendency to worry, for example, will not be so apt to fit the description of someone who enjoys taking risks and is always looking for new adventures. If other factors in the horoscope, in addition to the Moon, also indicate a tendency for caution, it is even less likely the individual will exhibit the risk-taking, aggressive characteristics usually described for Aries.

Doesn't astrology recognize that we all share similar character traits?

Astrology reflects the principle that nothing in the universe is at once so simple and so complicated as people themselves, from the simple human traits inherent in everyone to the complex personality and behavior patterns of a single individual.

Desirable and undesirable characteristics repeat themselves in countless generations. Describing specific traits for one astrological sign does not deny that these traits can also be found in people born in any of the other eleven signs. What it means is that hundreds of years of recorded astrological observations have shown that certain traits are more prominent in the personality and temperament of those born in certain signs than in others. No single trait is prominent in only one sign. Certain signs share certain traits, but these traits are specific. Moodiness, for instance, is a trait associated with some signs and loquaciousness is the hallmark of others.

There are a number of psychological and philosophical methods that match groups of traits to different personality types. Such methods result in personality profiles which are used to help people choose the type of work for which they are best suited, understand how they interact with others, and find the kind of environment they need to be happy and productive. Astrology does the same thing. The twelve astrological signs are divided into two classifications: the elements and the qualities. The elements place the twelve signs into four groups: fire signs, earth signs, air signs, and water signs. The qualities place the twelve signs into three groups: cardinal signs, fixed signs, and mutable signs. Listed separately, elements and qualities indicate characteristics shared by certain signs. Listed together, elements and qualities describe the true nature of each sign as it is distinct from the others. This may sound complicated to the beginner, but it is a simple method that provides an excellent overview of the astrological signs.

What are the traits described by elements and qualities, and on what are they based?

THE ELEMENTS
There are four elements: fire, earth, air, and water. The elements are based on temperament, as it is seen in a person's primary response to situations, relationships, and most things in general. Each astrological sign is matched with one of the elements according to whether the primary response associated with that sign is basically to act (physical), to gain something (purposeful), to analyze (intellectual), or to feel (emotional). An individual's primary response is not always obvious, especially since it may be followed immediately by other influences. Although it is an oversimplification to be sure, one example may illustrate how primary responses affect attitude and behavior. Suppose there is a large, angry bee in the room. To avoid being stung, an earth-sign person either kills it

FIRE SIGNS	EARTH SIGNS	AIR SIGNS	WATER SIGNS
Aries	Taurus	Gemini	Cancer
Leo	Virgo	Libra	Scorpio
Sagittarius	Capricorn	Aquarius	Pisces

Table 1: The Elements

or leaves the room, advising anyone allergic to bee stings to come along. An air-sign person asks how the bee got into the room, starts to discuss the best way to get rid of it, or injects humor into the situation by inquiring if it belongs to anyone. A water-sign person becomes upset or feels sorry for the bee and tries to protect it. The fire-sign person swats it.

Fire—The first element is fire. Aries, Leo, and Sagittarius are the astrological fire signs. The primary response of fire-sign people is action. They are the ones most likely to "shoot first and ask questions later." They do not stop to consider the reality of a situation, nor do they take time to get the facts or try to understand. They do not consider feelings. The moment their interest is aroused, they act on it. The passion of the moment can lead them into battle unarmed and unaware. In their haste, important details may be forgotten or disregarded. The animated fire-sign nature includes great courage and vitality. They are inspired as well as inspiring. They are willing to take risks. Their accomplishments are legendary when they learn to channel their energy constructively and develop the patience to complete projects they initiate. Fire-signs are the most active. They seek the greatest number and variety of physical experiences. On a primary level, Arians seek to release the physical energy of the body. On a primary level, Leos seek to release the creative energy of the ego. On a primary level, Sagittarians seek to release the mental and spiritual energy of the intellect.

Earth—The second element is earth. The astrological earth signs are Taurus, Virgo, and Capricorn. The initial response of earth-sign people is invariably of a practical nature and seldom without a purpose. They do not want to waste time or resources. They do not seek information or facts that may thwart their goal, nor do they allow sentimentality to confuse them. Earth signs assess everything

in terms of goals and expect tangible rewards as a result of tangible efforts. At times it is hard to convince earth-sign personalities that everything cannot be measured in terms of material worth. The pragmatism of the earth-sign nature is not always self-directed. Earth signs recognize intrinsic value that may not be apparent to others. Their great contribution in the world is to provide structure, form, and solidity. Earth signs are the most opportunistic. They seek to achieve a sense of their own worth in some physical way. On a primary level, Taureans identify their worth with personal possessions or accomplishments. On a primary level, Virgos seek personal identification through service and responsibility to others. On a primary level, Capricorns equate who they are with the respect, gratitude, or recognition they get from others.

Air—The third element is air. Gemini, Libra, and Aquarius are the astrological air signs. Before taking action that might be unnecessary, before practical considerations can distract their attention, and before emotionalism can blur the facts, air-sign people form mental perceptions. Unfortunately, they can get sidetracked by endlessly analyzing or looking for some lesson to be learned. Caught up in their intellectual approach, they fail to realize that no matter how rich the world of ideas and imagination is, there is no substitute for experiencing the physical and emotional realities of life. In personal relationships, they have to remember that high-mindedness is no excuse for lack of sentiment or physical demonstrations of affection. In practical matters, air signs must learn that what works in theory may not work in reality. Air-sign people provide the world with knowledge, humor, and inspiration. They are the ones who prove that worlds can be conquered with words just as well as with wars. Air-sign people seek to experience the greatest number and variety of communications with others. On a primary level, the endlessly curious Geminis seek to gather as much information as possible. On a primary level, Librans seek mental stimulation and inspiration from personal interactions. On a primary level, Aquarians seek mental stimulation from disseminating information and ideas to society as a whole.

Water—The fourth element is water, represented by the signs Cancer, Scorpio, and Pisces. Those born in a water sign always lead with their hearts. Before taking action that might have undesirable consequences, before practicality imposes a limit on sentiment, and before the facts can undermine their position, water-sign people express their feelings. Emotions dominate their decisions, and they can retard their own growth and development with self-pity, guilt, or

CARDINAL SIGNS	FIXED SIGNS	MUTABLE SIGNS
Aries	Taurus	Gemini
Cancer	Leo	Virgo
Libra	Scorpio	Sagittarius
Capricorn	Aquarius	Pisces

Table 2: The Qualities

hysteria. Their willingness to act is largely a matter of how they are feeling at the time. When they curb sentimentality, their amazing instincts and intuition are sharpened. Their emotions can inspire remarkable achievements but can also lead to degradation and despair. Water-sign people are the most sensitive. They seek constant reassurance and emotional satisfaction of one kind or another. On a primary level, Cancerians seek emotional satisfaction from being needed. On a primary level, Scorpios seek emotional satisfaction from being in control. On a primary level, Pisceans seek emotional satisfaction from being loved.

The Qualities

There are three qualities: cardinal, fixed, and mutable. Each astrological sign is placed under one of the three qualities according to the basic approach to life associated with that sign. Here the term "basic approach" is meant to describe how people achieve their goals. It also considers the way people solve problems and how they adjust to the environment in which they find themselves.

Cardinal—Cardinal signs are Aries, Cancer, Libra, and Capricorn. Cardinal signs are strong-willed and ambitious. They are the doers, the movers and shakers in the world. Problems and obstacles that stand in their way are eliminated one way or another. They like to be involved in major projects, take charge, and decide what and how things should be done. If they don't like their environment, they either change it to suit themselves or leave.

Fixed—Taurus, Leo, Scorpio, and Aquarius are fixed signs. There is great cautiousness and a formidable stubbornness in the fixed signs. They cling tenaciously to a comfortable, nonthreatening environment. When forced to accept a

Cardinal Fire: Aries	*Fixed Fire:* Leo	*Mutable Fire:* Sagittarius
Cardinal Earth: Capricorn	*Fixed Earth:* Taurus	*Mutable Earth:* Virgo
Cardinal Air: Libra	*Fixed Air:* Aquarius	*Mutable Air:* Gemini
Cardinal Water: Cancer	*Fixed Water:* Scorpio	*Mutable Water:* Pisces

Table 3: The Elements and Qualities

new environment or situation, they need more time than most to adjust. They resent the unexpected and resist that which is imposed. Their stamina and strength are impressive, and they will stick with a problem or situation until success is attained.

Mutable—Mutable signs are Gemini, Virgo, Sagittarius, and Pisces. Adaptability best describes the approach of mutable signs. Willingness to constantly adapt ultimately makes them survivors. It also makes it easy for others to live and to work with them. One form of their adaptability is imitation. In some it emerges as remarkable talent. In others it may only mean lack of imagination. Duality in the nature of mutable signs allows them to be all things to all people. They need only to avoid being trapped by their own versatility and cleverness.

Putting the Elements and Qualities Together

Adding the elements and qualities together gives us a unique personal profile for each astrological sign (Table 3).

Cardinal Fire—Aries is the cardinal fire sign. Arians need to keep busy. Their typical urge is to take on more projects than they can handle. Although they need to learn how to make constructive use of their time and energy, they accomplish many things simply because their restlessness keeps them on the go. The sheer force of their passion and vitality is also responsible for marvelous achievements. It may be difficult to keep pace with them physically, but the spirit and enthusiasm of Arians inspire others to try.

9

Cardinal Earth—Capricorn is the cardinal earth sign. Capricorns are willing to handle any task if it helps them get what they want. Many accomplishments are the result of their long and patient efforts. Tradition, rules, and regulations provide the structure of their life-styles. They are very competitive, but not always openly aggressive about it. Ambition makes them highly goal-oriented and successful. It can also give them a too-ready willingness to believe the end justifies the means.

Cardinal Air—Libra is the cardinal air sign. Librans evaluate what they want to accomplish, plan the best method, and decide who and/or what is needed to help them succeed. Then, with as little fuss as possible, they get it done. By unselfishly sharing their success with those who helped them attain it, Librans continue to engender the cooperation and affection of others. Fear of hurting others and avoiding hostile situations can keep them from pursuing their goals.

Cardinal Water—Cancer is the cardinal water sign. Cancerians initially tackle a problem or pursue a goal in a quiet or circumspect manner. When they are sure of success, however, they move aggressively forward. Cancerians are motivated, as well as inspired, by emotional needs. The emotional energy they possess is the powerful force that helps them attain their goals. Cancerians also succeed quite often because they know how to appeal to the emotions of others. Moodiness of Cancerians can sometimes make it hard to live and work with them.

Fixed Fire—Leo is the fixed fire sign. Leos use imagination and enthusiasm to get things going and to keep things going. Where they often run into problems is not completing the things they start. A big obstacle to their success, and even to their happiness, is stubborn pride. Generous in spirit they are, but nevertheless they do not see there is little virtue in giving only what they want to give. When others need inspiration and a good friend, there is no one as wonderful as a Leo.

Fixed Earth—Taurus is the fixed earth sign. The basic approach of Taureans is simply to hang on. If they can't solve a problem, they are prepared to wait until it solves itself. Nothing stays the same forever, and no one knows this better than Taureans. If a goal does not appear to be within their grasp, they work around it and patiently wait until conditions change in their favor. Taureans are loathe to accept new ideas or situations if they are not convinced there is a practical

advantage to doing so. However, no one acts with more speed and efficiency than Taureans who know what they want.

Fixed Air—Aquarius is the fixed air sign. The basic Aquarian approach is to find the lowest common denominator. They find the biggest problems, what is attracting the most attention, or where most of the people are heading, and they gravitate in that direction. They have an uncommon instinct for understanding and attracting other people. Aquarians are excellent communicators. When motivated to pursue a goal or work with other people, no one is more successful. Their problem in life is trying to find something that can stimulate and sustain their interest.

Fixed Water—Scorpio is the fixed water sign. The incredible psychological power that Scorpios develop is the key to their success. Their approach is to observe, assess, and, if possible, control. Scorpios find it hard to forget or forgive, a self-defeating trap that can undermine their lives. Some of the world's most amazing achievements have been the result of Scorpios who have rechanneled their negative feelings and experiences.

Mutable Fire—Sagittarius is the mutable fire sign. Restless energy and need for personal independence keep Sagittarians moving in many directions. Myriad interests and talents are responsible for their accomplishments. Always ready to travel for business or pleasure, they effortlessly adapt to wherever they happen to be. Sometimes an overwhelming urge to escape (either figuratively or literally) makes them all too willing to bypass responsibility and work.

Mutable Earth—Virgo is the mutable earth sign. Highly competent as well as highly critical, Virgos readily accept problems and an imperfect environment, if only so they can spend their lives solving the problems and perfecting everything and everyone around them. This is what they do best. Their minds and their hands are always occupied, and they are well-meaning and helpful in spite of an ungrateful world willing to exploit their service-oriented nature.

Mutable Air—Gemini is the mutable air sign. The Gemini approach to life and to problem-solving is so multifaceted as to be virtually impossible to predict. Clever, flexible, and alert, they adapt to any situation they encounter. Geminis collect information. They are experts at networking and at transporting ideas,

people, and material goods. Their biggest problems stem from trying to do too many things at one time, failure to get all the facts, and, in personal relations, the inability to demonstrate passionate feelings others may require.

Mutable Water—Pisces is the mutable water sign. Emotional vulnerability has a lot to do with the Piscean approach to life. Some overcompensate by taking on the riskiest of activities. Others may hide their vulnerability by being very public in their professions, and by representing something or someone other than themselves. The duality of Pisceans is represented by incredible strength and ability on the one hand, and weakness and self-pity on the other. Physical laziness, lack of confidence, and inability to face reality can undermine their happiness and success.

I hope you can see from this brief introduction that astrology is not about the stars. It is about people. It is a science and an art. Those who subject astrology to statistics and the scientific method produce disappointing results and say astrology doesn't work. They are wrong. Science counts and measures and categorizes human beings. It observes and records their thinking and behavior. But what of you and me? What can be said of the totally unique combination of traits and talents we each possess? Science cannot tell us who we are as individuals. We must learn this for ourselves. Astrology has its categories and its scientific measurements; these are the structures upon which it is based. But these structures are secondary to a much older art that has been used for thousands of years, an art that seeks to understand and interpret the nature of a single individual within the context of his or her personal place and time. As you learn more about astrology, do not be underwhelmed by what seems too simplistic or overwhelmed by what seems complex. This book includes some of the science and history of astrology. Its main purpose, however, is to present the information that is the basis for its art. That is, after all, what makes astrology so interesting.

Chapter Two

The Zodiac

The best place to start learning about astrology is the zodiac. What is the zodiac? Where did it come from, and how is it used? In our space age society of calendars and atomic clocks, it is hard to imagine life with no means of telling the time and date, or even the month and year. Early civilizations turned to the heavens for guidance. Above the Earth could be seen the Sun, Moon, and a vast panorama of stars. Moving "stars" in the sky were eventually recognized as planets, and individual as well as certain groups of stars were identified. The most obvious period of time was the twenty-four hours between one sunrise and the next. Days were grouped into months by observing the phases of the Moon. Many of the first calendars were lunar. Today the Islamic and Hebrew calendars are still based on the Moon.

Lunar calendars are not sufficient, however, to keep track of longer periods such as the dry and rainy seasons in tropical climates or the seasonal changes that occur in temperate climates. All seasons, no matter what their description, are solar events. In antiquity, those whose task it was to track the Sun's cycle began by observing all the constellations through which the Sun passed. They

could not view the stars during the day, of course, but all they had to do was observe the stars that rose in the east just after sunset to know which constellation must then be in the west with the Sun. When a year had passed and the same stars began to reappear once again in the east after sunset, it signaled the beginning of another solar cycle. Year after year, the Sun could be seen to trace a circular path in the heavens through the same series of constellations.

This circular path of the Sun is known as the ecliptic, or what we call the zodiac. The zodiac then was originally devised as a way to measure the apparent time it took the Sun to pass through the constellations. We are aware it is really the Earth that is moving around the Sun, but from the Earth it appears to us as though it is the Sun that is moving. Imagine yourself sitting on a moving train. From your position, you can observe only what is passing, or appears to be passing, outside your window. The Earth is like a train traveling on a track around the Sun, and from the Earth's window, the part of the sky you observe is called the zodiac. Astrology is based on celestial movements as they appear from the Earth. Until we take up residence on other planets, the Earth is the only place where we are able to observe the correlations between planetary cycles and earthly events.

Like all circles the zodiac is divided into 360 degrees. The zodiac divides the sky into twelve sections of thirty degrees, each representing one of the astrological signs. The Sun appears in each sign at approximately the same time each year. In astrology, each sign and the particular section of the sky it represents has special significance. Let me introduce the signs, their symbols, and the dates when the Sun appears in each sign (Table 4, page 15).

Observing the yearly cycle of the Sun through the zodiac presents the problem of where to mark its beginning. Since a circle has no natural beginning or end, we must choose a place to start. Although there is some controversy about which point should be chosen, most astrologers begin the year at the vernal equinox, the point at which the Sun appears at zero degrees Aries. Since the equinox never occurs in exactly the same spot, the zero degree mark of Aries is recalculated each year. The earliest zodiac was devised by men who were unable to calculate the equinox, so their zodiac had to be determined by the more or less fixed position of certain stars.

It has been the practice since the time of Ptolemy in the second century AD to calculate exactly when the equinox occurs (March 20/21) each year, using this point as zero degrees Aries to mark the start of the Sun's cycle, a cycle we know

ARIES	♈	MAR. 20/21–APR. 19/20
TAURUS	♉	APR. 20/21–MAY 20/21
GEMINI	♊	MAY 21/22–JUN. 20/21
CANCER	♋	JUN. 21/22–JUL. 21/22
LEO	♌	JUL. 22/23–AUG. 22/23
VIRGO	♍	AUG. 23/24–SEP. 22/23
LIBRA	♎	SEP. 23/24–OCT. 22/23
SCORPIO	♏	OCT. 23/24–NOV. 21/22
SAGITTARIUS	♐	NOV. 22/23–DEC. 20/21
CAPRICORN	♑	DEC. 21/22–JAN. 19/20
AQUARIUS	♒	JAN. 20/21–FEB. 19/20
PISCES	♓	FEB. 18/19–MAR. 19/20

Table 4: The Sun's Entry into the Signs

in reality is the year it takes the Earth to complete one revolution around the Sun. As I describe the Earth's journey, some readers will already understand the more complicated aspects of what I am outlining. While I do not in any way wish to minimize the importance of these concepts, my purpose here is simply to limit my description. Experience has taught me that the students of astrology are far more receptive to learning the details of astronomy after they have satisfied their desire to learn at least some of the astrology connected with it.

Each year around March 20, the Sun is at zero degrees Aries and the Earth lies "flat" in her orbit. That is, neither of her poles is tilted into or away from the Sun. During the next twenty-four hours, the Earth will rotate once on her axis. As she does so, the Sun's vertical rays strike her surface evenly from the North Pole to the South Pole, resulting in twelve hours of day and twelve hours of night. This is the vernal equinox.

15

As another twenty-four-hour period passes, the Earth rotates once on her axis, and at the same time moves forward approximately one degree along her path around the Sun. The Earth's forward movement changes the angle at which the Sun's rays hit the Earth. Her North Pole is now tilted slightly into the Sun, while the South Pole is tilted slightly away from it. Instead of equal hours of day and night, the period of daylight is a little longer. As the Earth continues to move forward one degree each day, the hours of daylight gradually become longer until they reach their maximum length (the longest day of the year) on June 21. The North Pole is now tilted its maximum angle into the Sun. The Sun's position in the zodiac is zero degrees Cancer. This is called the summer solstice.

The days grow shorter until the Earth reaches the halfway point in her annual journey on September 23. Once again the Earth lies "flat" with neither pole tilted toward the Sun. The Sun's vertical rays extend equally from the North Pole to the South Pole, resulting in twelve hours of day and twelve hours of night. This is called the autumnal equinox, and the Sun's position in the zodiac is zero degrees Libra. However, now it is the South Pole that begins to tilt more and more toward the Sun each day, as the North Pole tilts away from it.

As the Earth continues to move, the nights grow longer until they reach maximum length (the longest night of the year) on December 21. The South Pole is now tilted at its maximum angle toward the Sun. This is called the winter solstice, and the Sun's position in the zodiac is zero degrees Capricorn. After December 21 the nights become shorter until the end of the journey, around the 19th of March, when the Sun is in the last degree of Pisces. The next day when the Sun reappears in zero degrees Aries, he will find the Earth poised and ready to begin another journey.

Looking at Figure 1 on page 17, you can see why the changing length of daylight we observe in the Northern Hemisphere during the year is exactly reversed in the Southern Hemisphere. At the time of the equinox in March, the North Pole faces into the Sun, and as the Earth moves forward, the hours of sunlight are increased in the Northern Hemisphere. When the equinox occurs in September, the South Pole faces into the Sun, so the periods of sunlight are increased in the Southern Hemisphere.

Before we begin to concentrate on the astrological signs, it is important to understand that there are really two zodiacs. Though they share some common mythological references, the zodiac and each of its signs that we use in

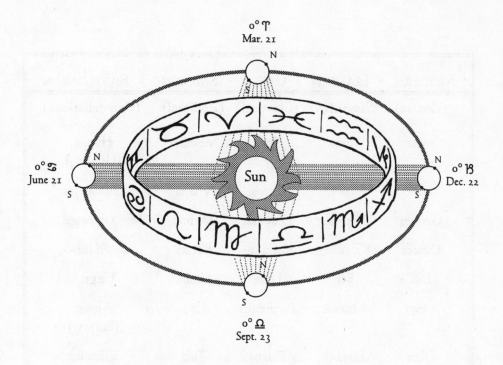

Figure 1: The Earth's Yearly Orbit Around the Sun

astrology do not correspond to the constellations of the same name. The constellations Aries, Taurus, Gemini, Cancer, Leo, Virgo, Libra, Scorpio, Sagittarius, Capricorn, Aquarius, and Pisces take up large sections of the sky and do not fit neatly into the thirty-degree sections of the tropical zodiac, which is the narrow band of sky astrologers use. The zodiac is the basic structure on which we build astrological study. We study individuals by observing the patterns of their attitude and behavior in their environment which is the Earth. If we want to study the meaning of the planetary cycle, we have to study the planets in their environment which is the zodiac. Finally, it is through careful study of both environments that we begin to understand the correlation between planetary cycles and mankind.

MODERN	IRANIAN	GREEK	SANSKRIT	BABYLONIAN
(Zodiac)	(Sassanian)	(Classical)	(Zodiacal)	(Constellations)
Aries	Varak	Krios	Mesham	Hunga (Hireling)
Taurus	Tora	Taros	Vrisha	Gud.an.na
Gemini	Do-patkar	Didemoi	Mithna	Mas.tab.ba.gal.gal
Cancer	Kalakang	Karkinos	Karata	Al.lul
Leo	Ser	Leon	Simba	Ur.gu.ll
Virgo	Khusak	Parthenos	Kanya	Ab.sin (Furrow)
Libra	Tarazuk	Zugos	Tula	Zibanitu (Horn?)
Scorpio	Gazdum	Skorpios	Vrischika	Gir.tab
Sagittarius	Nemasp	Toxotes	Dhanus	Pa.bil.sag
Capricorn	Vahik	Aigokeros	Makara	Suhur.mas (Goat-fish)
Aquarius	Dul	Hydroxous	Kumbha	Gu.la (Giant?)
Pisces	Mahik	Ichthys	Mina	Sim.mah (Swallow?)

Table 5: Corresponding Zodiacs

Chapter Three

The Signs

Y ou might want to practice drawing the astrological symbols so that you will eventually recognize each sign by its symbol. (The astrological signs and their symbols are shown in Table 6 on page 20.) The twelve signs did not spring all of a piece from the imagination or the observations of a few men. They evolved at different times and from different places, eventually developing into the ideas and expressions with which they are associated today. Whatever their original derivation or their connection to constellations, the various zodiacs share common mythological and other interpretative attributes. The *Arkana Dictionary of Astrology* lists some corresponding zodiacal signs from different ages and cultures and is the resource consulted for constructing Table 5 on page 18.

The whole of the zodiac represents the cycle of evolution as well as current existence, each sign being a unique field of energy in which that existence is actualized. It is important to understand the environment of each sign, that is, the type of action and energy that characterizes it. The following paragraphs present a brief summary of the history and ideas associated with each sign and its symbol. The symbols, like the zodiac, did not all appear at the same time. Some of them have very ancient origins, while the development of others occurred much later. They also have more than one meaning. As a general reference, however, each

ARIES ♈	LIBRA ♎
TAURUS ♉	SCORPIO ♏
GEMINI ♊	SAGITTARIUS ♐
CANCER ♋	CAPRICORN ♑
LEO ♌	AQUARIUS ♒
VIRGO ♍	PISCES ♓

Table 6: Signs and their Symbols

symbol is regarded as a stylized depiction of the parts of the body ruled by a particular sign. The most important aim of these paragraphs is to acquaint the reader with the primary cycle of existence that each sign represents and the description of its environment.

ARIES

Aries is the first sign. The environment in this part of the zodiac is raw, undifferentiated energy. Action that feeds on itself—action for action's sake. Think of New York, Hong Kong, and other places where there is constant activity. Everywhere there is change, one building is going up while another is being torn down. Everything is available on the spot—instant gratification, no questions asked. Everyone is in motion, and work or play is attacked with equal enthusiasm. Imagine a crowded sports arena. There is so much commotion it is hard to tell the players from the spectators. Think of the courage, energy, and sometimes foolhardiness of those who are the first to venture into wild and hostile territory. Their actions allow others to come and settle the land that has been conquered. There is great passion here, a sponta-

neous outpouring of feelings and ideas turned into actions. As the first stage in the cycle of existence, Aries is the energy of the life force at the moment of its inception. It is the initial impulse through which the potential becomes actual, and is therefore associated with the beginning of any cycle.

The astrological image for Aries is the Ram. Rams were sacred in Egypt and were associated with many of their gods. Perhaps the most appropriate god with which to associate Aries is the ram-headed Khemenu. The first member of a triad of gods of the first Cataract, Khemenu became incarnate as the Ram. He wears the White Crown and was known as one of the creators of the universe. The papyrus of ANI describes him as "the father in the beginning." Babylonian zodiacs do not feature the Ram, its place being given to Hunga, or "The Hired Hand," not an altogether inappropriate image given the association of Aries with keeping busy. The Greek god Hermes gave the gifts of reason and speech to a ram. Recovering the Golden Fleece of this magic ram later became the quest of Jason and the Argonauts. The symbol for Aries is viewed as a depiction of the ram's horns. Aries governs the head, so its symbol also represents the eyebrows and nose of the human face.

TAURUS

Unlike the pulsating, primal energy of the Aries environment, the second sign is a quiet atmosphere of focused energy. The fire of life that was generated in Aries is given opportunity to grow in Taurus, the second astrological sign. It is the energy of green pastures and fields of growing wheat or corn. It is the energy of heavy trucks carrying dirt out of great holes in the earth where buildings and homes will rise. Taurus is development and growth; its activity and energy are never random. There is also possession. Material goods are counted, weighed, and measured. Imagine storehouses of food and goods, Fort Knox and other stockpiles of gold and silver. Think of the bank-lined Bahnhofstrasse where the "gnomes of Zurich" guard the secret bank accounts of the world's wealthiest people. Feel the comfort of goosedown, the warmth of wool, and the softness of fine leather. As a stage in the cycle of existence, Taurus is the energy of physical contact, of form and structure.

The traditional image for the second sign is the Bull and, by most accounts, Taurus is a translation of the Babylonian "Bull of Heaven." Featured prominently

in early cave drawings, the bull was an important part of life long before history recorded his significance as a deity. The bull was universally regarded as a symbol of great strength and sexual potency. The story of the Babylonian Bull of Heaven comes from the legend of Gilgamesh, the oldest epic in history. Other legendary bulls include Apis, the sacred bull of Egypt presumed to be the incarnation of Ptah, the monstrous Minotaur of Minos confined in a labyrinth, and the Greek god Zeus who changed himself into a snow-white bull to attract the affections of Europa. Four thousand years ago the ancient civilization of Crete celebrated spring each year with a spectacular running of the bulls, ending with the death of the bulls in the arena—a ritual that still continues in Spain and other parts of the world. The symbol for Taurus is the head and horns of a bull. It also represents the human ears and throat to connect Taurus with its rulership of those areas of the body. The symbol, a circle (the Sun) and a crescent Moon, is perhaps a link with the fact that bulls were lunar as well as solar gods.

GEMINI

As the third stage in the cycle of existence, Gemini is the mental energy of ideas, understanding, and communication. Borrowing from Descartes, the environment in Gemini might be described as "Cogito Ergo Sum"—I think therefore I am. The life force arises in Aries, develops physically in Taurus, and in Gemini it is focused on awareness. Language is learned, communication takes place. Information is acquired, processed, and traded. It is not the mental energy that creates libraries or universities. It does not seek wisdom. It wants to inform. It is energy turned to cleverness and imitation. It is the education of elementary school, and the trade school where basic skills are developed into arts or crafts. It is newspapers, magazines, and record-keeping. Think of community activities, neighbors, gossip. Think of the postal system, business offices, meetings, and sales. It is local transportation: bicycles, taxicabs, and buses. It is physical and mental energy in a constant state of busyness—traffic in the streets, people running errands. Think of the energy of the wind that ripples the water and carries aloft the seeds of plants, the seeds of ideas, and the seeds of change from place to place in short bursts.

The image for Gemini is the Twins. The mythological twins Castor and Pollux are most often used for this sign. In Egyptian zodiacs Gemini is Two Stars,

while in Babylonia it was known as "Great Twins." The twins that are found in mythology are siblings, lovers, deities, and sometimes the guardians of doors. They can also be associated with the pillars of Hercules. Their stories vary but twins usually represent either the polarity of good and evil, or they signify contradictions or opposites as in masculine and feminine, old and young, and so on. The symbol for Gemini may be viewed as the Roman numeral two, linking it with the duality the sign represents. It is also said to be two people holding hands in friendship or, by some accounts, two people joined in the sharing of ideas. The symbol depicts the lungs or the arms, areas of the human body governed by Gemini.

CANCER

The fourth astrological sign is Cancer, an environment totally dominated by emotional energy. The life force of Aries adapts to the physical world in Taurus, attains awareness in Gemini, and is focused on need and desire in the environment of Cancer. As a stage in the cycle of existence, the emotional energy introduced in Cancer is, after the creation of life itself, the strongest force of all. However, it is energy that requires nurturing before it can function and, therefore, constantly seeks to feed itself. It is immature and uncontrolled, bouncing back and forth between extremes. Protective, self-serving, and intolerant, it is strong enough to destroy whatever threatens it. It is also the positive energy of putting down roots, building strong foundations, raising families, bringing together those who share similar beliefs and common goals. It is sentimental, grasping, and amazingly successful. Because it does not exist outside the human spirit, it is the energy of all that is good and all that is evil. Emotional energy is, in fact, what gives us our unique place in the cosmos.

The traditional image for Cancer is the Crab, although early zodiacs often used the crayfish. The Egyptian equivalent is translated as scarabaeus, but apparently it was not intended to mean the sacred scarab beetle since their image for the sign is shown as either a crab, or more familiarly, the Two Turtles. Hard-shelled aquatic creatures employed as images are suggestive of the Cancerian emotional nature that protects its vulnerability inside a hard, impervious shell. In Greek mythology, the crab pinched Heracles in the toe and was promptly stomped to death. The goddess Hera rewarded the crab's courage by placing him in the heavens. The symbol for Cancer represents two female breasts, linking the

sign with its rulership of that part of the body as well as its association with food and nurturing in general. The symbol is also seen as the crab's claws. If viewed as two moons turned inward to form a closed system, the symbol may be a reference to the Cancerian tendency for keeping what they have within their grasp.

LEO

The environment of Leo, the fifth sign of the zodiac, is akin to the atmosphere of Aries. There is great stimulation and vitality in this energy, but it does not promote action for its own sake as it does in Aries. Leo is sustained and motivated activity. As part of the cycle of existence, Leo is energy that seeks to experience itself through re-creation. Beginning in Aries, the life force develops on a physical, mental, and emotional level. What was once the Aries spark has become a flame in Leo that adds new dimensions to the stages that preceded it. Leo's energy seeks to achieve great physical accomplishment and physical pleasure, to add humor and imagination to mental awareness, and to increase emotional capacity for enjoyment and inspiration. The energy in Leo requires recognition; it demands an audience. Uncontrolled, it is capable of consuming everything in its path. It is the energy of adventure and amusement, of noble gestures and grandiose schemes. It seeks freedom from the mundane in order to pursue the fantastic.

The Lion is the image for Leo, although the sign has also been called the Great Dog or the Noble Dog. Egyptians worshiped the lion since the waters of the Nile rose when the Sun entered Leo. Sekhmet was the terrible Egyptian war goddess who is represented as a woman with the head of a lioness. The Babylonian name for the Lion was Great Light. The lion frequently appears in the role of guardian. Throughout the world in widely separated cultures, lions stand or lie as great stone sentinels of strength and power at the gates of royal palaces and other buildings. Sometimes, as in the familiar tale of Androcles and the Lion, the king of beasts represents noble generosity, an appropriate characterization of Leo. The symbol for Leo is a drawing of the lion's tail. The symbol also represents the human heart, which is the part of the body governed by the sign.

VIRGO

The environment in Virgo, sixth sign of the zodiac, is much more subdued than Leo, though no less active in its own way. As part of the cycle of existence, Virgo is energy focused on gathering what has been gained and putting it to some higher purpose. Crops are harvested, skills are developed, information is organized, and desire is sacrificed in the line of duty. In this segment of the zodiac, virtue is its own reward. It is energy directed to the ordinary, to the carrying out of tasks, to weaving the fabric of life. It is the energy of household gods dedicated to the glory of the lint trap and the clean bathroom. It is the overseer of goods and provider of services. It is the necessary, that which is taken for granted and immediately missed when absent. Think of the pharmacy, the school, the local newspaper, the grocer, the tailor, and the traveling salesman. This is the energy of cleverness, competence, and expectation. It is energy that can too easily be inhibited by stronger forces and trapped by its own standards.

The Virgin is the image for the sixth sign. Virgo's image has changed from time to time. Its oldest references can be traced as far back as history itself when Virgo was not a virgin at all but a Sumerian corn goddess. In medieval times, Christianity associated her with the Virgin Mary. In most of her images, Virgo holds sheaves of wheat or an ear of corn to signify her role as a goddess of fertility or of the harvest. Sometimes she holds flowers, which may be a reference to her Babylonian name Mi, which means cluster of flowers. Virgo's symbol is viewed as a combination of the letters MV for Maria Virgo or Virgin Mary. It also depicts the female sexual organs to associate it with the part of the body governed by the sign.

LIBRA

Libra is the seventh sign. The mental energy that dominates Libra makes the environment in this part of the zodiac deceptively quiet. Physical and emotional activity are carefully weighed and measured. It is energy directed outward as well as inward in equal measure. Extremes are avoided. The middle course is always taken because when it is off balance, this energy is paralyzed. The maturity gained in previous cycles is the energy in Libra focused on civility of behavior and attitude. Somewhat akin to the environment of Gemini, there is also an emphasis on communication and ideas here. In Libra,

however, the energy is not as concerned with ideas and information as it is with the means by which they are shared, cooperation and interaction. Refinement and considered judgment hide the formidable strength of its strategy and manipulation. This is the environment of the general, not the foot soldier; the designer, not the builder; the judge, not the executioner. In the cycle of existence, Libra is the energy that sustains the balance between the physical and mental, between spiritual and nonspiritual, and between the individual and society.

The traditional image for Libra is The Scales. In many images, a female, mythologically identified as the blindfolded Venus, holds the scales of justice in one hand and the sword of Mars in the other. In antiquity, the constellation that governed this month was connected with the judgment of the living and dead. In Hebrew tradition, it is Rosh Hashanah in the month of Teshrit. Laws and principles of justice have continued to be associated with Libra. The symbol for Libra may be viewed as a depiction of its image, a pair of scales. It is also described variously as sunset or sunrise. In either case, it is an appropriate indication since Libra begins its rule at the autumnal equinox, which equally divides the hours of day and night as well as the Sun's yearly cycle. Although Libra has some link to the kidneys, its symbol is viewed as the diaphragm which separates the lower half of the body from the upper half.

SCORPIO

From the mentally energized environment of Libra, we pass into the watery realm of Scorpio, the eighth zodiacal sign. Emotional energy is the ruling force here. It is not the obvious or wildly emotional environment of Cancer. Scorpio uses the balance acquired in Libra to exert control over the expression of its energy. It is more intense and more patient. It is the energy of observation, analysis, and penetration. It seeks to recognize its own motivation and behavior. It separates the relevant from the trivial, fathoms the depths, and unlocks the secrets. It is instincts and resourcefulness. As a stage in the cycle of existence, Scorpio is focused on emotional control as a means of becoming more powerful. The inclination to protect that prevails in Cancer is expanded in Scorpio's environment to the ultimate preservation which is regeneration. It is the energy of transformation. It is development, conservation, and use of basic resources. Think of urban renewal, recycling, and waste management. Think of the cook, the butcher, the gardener, and the renovator.

The Scorpion is the image of Scorpio. Babylonian zodiacs called this constellation "The Stinger." Its Egyptian image was a snake. Scorpio is associated with
life and death, with great power that is gained or lost. In Greek mythology, a scorpion was sent to kill the mighty hunter Orion after he threatened to kill all the
wild beasts of Crete. The Bible uses a snake to tempt Eve with an apple, thereby
causing mankind to lose the power God had bestowed. The symbol for Scorpio
depicts the male sex organ, linking it with the part of the body ruled by the sign.
It represents sexual potency and the power of the life force. The symbol is also
viewed as the scorpion's tail.

SAGITTARIUS

Sagittarius is the ninth sign. The environment in this part of the zodiac
is active, restless: an energy focused on the physical, intellectual, and
emotional attainments acquired in previous stages. It seeks the total
experience. Everything is the biggest and the boldest. It is adventure and passion,
joy and spiritual development. It turns information into knowledge and knowledge into truth. It is the creative force so dynamic and unique as to be almost a
religious experience. It cannot or will not function when it is limited or confined.
It is independent. The energy here is abundance, the grand gesture, exaggerated
pageantry. Imagine a storm, thunder, and lightning. Think of universities and
libraries, theaters, and museums. Think of publishers and art dealers. It is status-
seeking, righteous, and fanatic. It is inspiring and prophetic. It is energy
constantly reaching beyond its own environment. As part of the cycle of existence, Sagittarius is the spirit seeking its outer limits.

The Archer is one image for Sagittarius. Older versions picture Sagittarius as
The Centaur, half horse and half man, or show him as a centaur with the human
half aiming a bow and arrow. Classical mythology relates the story of Chiron, the
wise centaur who taught the practice of healing. The image for Sagittarius is more
ancient than the Greeks. In Egypt, he is pictured as a centaur, and in Babylonian
contexts, he is the Scorpion man designated as "The Strong One." The symbol
for Sagittarius is the archer's arrow. It is a depiction of the upper part of the leg or
thigh as a link with the part of the body governed by this sign. Others have
described the symbol as the path of aspirations, its energy pointed upward into
the spiritual realm.

CAPRICORN

The energy of life has grown heavy by the time it reaches the tenth stage in the cycle of existence. Nothing is better suited to provide the proper focus at this stage than Capricorn, the zodiacal guardian of time and space. In this environment, the energy is focused on the big picture, the structure that contains the parts that make up the whole. It is the foundation. Imagine the bones that support the flesh and the walls that support the building. Think of the clock and the calendar, bound by the units of the time that they measure. The energy of Capricorn is the energy of limits, rules, and regulations that must be observed in order to be stable and to endure. It is the energy of authority, and control. It is ambitious. Devious. Cunning. It is the end that justifies the means. It is longevity. The rewards of dedication and hard work. Its natural inclination is serious, formal, and never random. It is the energy of experience. It never assumes. It must merit what it attains, or suffer the consequences. It is patient. There is great and earthy passion, but never pleasure without responsibility. It is energy focused on the long term. Think of a virgin forest in awesome maturity, the pleasure of wine that has aged. Think of the richness of tradition and the legacy of remembrance.

The Goat is the symbol for Capricorn. Many of the oldest zodiacs employed the Goat-Fish as the image for Capricorn. The modern association for the sign is the sure-footed goat carefully working its way up the mountain. Other associations connect it with the lusty goat-figured Pan or Bacchus. The symbol for Capricorn is a depiction of the human knee to connect it with the part of the body governed by the sign. The symbol is also the face and horns of the goat. The curvature on the bottom of the symbol may also be seen to resemble a fish tail associating it with its ancient image of the Goat-Fish.

AQUARIUS

From the mountains of Capricorn, the cycle of life passes into the ethereal environment of Aquarius, dominated by the energy of ideas and communication. The energy of the eleventh sign is focused on taking all that has been learned in previous cycles and making it function for all mankind. In this stage of existence, knowledge is transformed into principles and ideals. It

is the energy of universal language and communication. This is a strange environment to the uninitiated because the principle force represents society, but does not become society. Its task is to retain the many without sacrificing the one. If the uniqueness of one is lost, so is the uniqueness of all. It is energy unbiased, singular, and independent. It is communication that seeks the widest possible audience. Think of the radio, the telephone, the telegraph. Think of science, technology, and the computer. It is democratic and liberal. Conservative and traditional. It is stability being upset by the unpredictable, and the unpredictable being made stable. It is the energy of groups and organizations who share the same interests and goals.

The Water Bearer, a man pouring water from a jug or urn, is the traditional image for Aquarius. The Babylonian constellation Shabatu meant "Curse of the Rain." Aquarius is also linked with the "God of the Storm." Because of the depiction of water in its image as well as in its related mythology, Aquarius is sometimes confused with the astrological water signs. Aquarius is nonetheless an air sign. The water depicted in its image is meant to convey the dissemination of knowledge. The symbol for Aquarius has been traced to the Egyptian hieroglyph for running water. It is also a depiction of the lower leg and ankles as well as the circulatory system linking it to the parts of the body governed by the sign.

PISCES

The twelfth sign of the zodiac is Pisces. As the last stage in the cycle of existence, Pisces is the energy of the subconscious, and the power of spiritual and emotional ideals. It is an environment ruled by emotional energy; energy of a remarkable kind. Easily consumed by the action of fire, overwhelmed by the responsibility of earth, blown away by the air of confusion, and drowned in the water of need, it is able to survive them all. It is energy that must, however, devote itself to this task or risk its own destruction. Illusion is reality and reality is illusion in this environment. It is inner strength and unseen power. It is the energy of inner struggles and hidden dreams. Think of the fragile beauty and the incredible strength in a spider's web. Think of a flower growing out of a rock, and the world reflected in a rain drop.

The image for Pisces is Two Fish. The fish are usually connected by a cord because the constellation itself consists of two lines or ribbons of stars joined at

one end by the star Al Rescha, which means "the Cord." Regarding the fish as sacred is a very ancient practice. Three thousand years before Christianity adopted the fish as a symbol, Sumerian legends relate that the first fish to rise from the primordial waters became the teacher of the arts of civilization to men. A Babylonian name for the constellation Zib Me means "tails" and was associated with the Tigris and Euphrates. Another image for Pisces was the swallow-headed fish, which Babylonians regarded as an expression of psychic regeneration. The fish found its way into classical mythology in the story of Venus and Cupid who were chased into the Euphrates by Typhon. They were saved by two fish, who were then rewarded with a place in the heavens. The symbol for Pisces depicts two fish connected with a cord. It also signifies the feet since they are the part of the body governed by the sign.

Chapter Four

The Horoscope

Consider the circle, measure it please,
All its three hundred and sixty degrees.
Wasn't that fun, and haven't you found
You can do it again, the other way round?

Now that we know how many degrees,
Must be accounted for nice as you please
Here come astrologers, what do they say?
Divide the degrees in precisely this way.
Take thirty degrees for each of the signs
It makes a nice wheel divided by lines.

Chris Angelino

The zodiac was devised to measure the period in which the Earth makes one revolution around the Sun. We use another perspective of the zodiac to measure the twenty-four-hour period it takes the Earth to rotate once on its axis. This is how the horoscope is derived. The horoscope is based on the zodiac as it is related to the hours of the day, not the twelve months of the year. Just as the zodiac is divided into twelve sections, one section for each sign, the horoscope is also divided into twelve sections. These sections, as you will see in the next chapter, become the "houses" of the horoscope. In the yearly cycle of the zodiac, the Sun is in the middle as the Earth revolves around it. In the

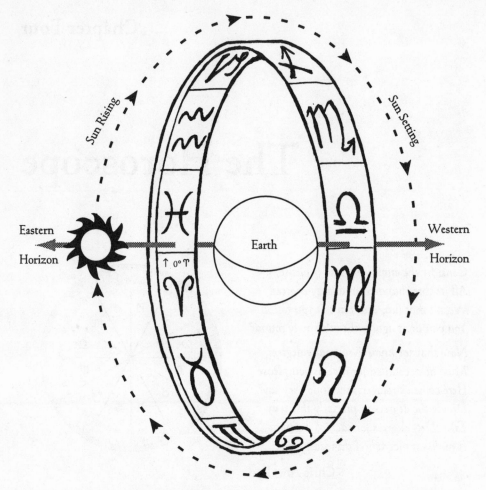

Figure 2: The Zodiac's Twenty-Four-Hour Movement

daily zodiac from which we derive the horoscope, the Earth is in the middle and the zodiac is a circle that surrounds it.

The horoscope is actually a map of the sky for a particular date, time, and location. In looking at a sky map, the first thing to realize is that the positions of east and west are reversed, E–W. Figure 2 pictures the Sun rising over the eastern horizon on March 20, and on that date the Sun's position in the sky is 0° Aries. As the Sun rises over the eastern horizon, so does 0° Aries. And right behind the Sun at 0° Aries, in an unbroken line, the rest of the 360 degrees of the

zodiac will continue to rise, one degree at a time. Between sunrise March 20 and sunrise March 21, the entire circle of the zodiac will rise over the eastern horizon following the Sun. However, the next morning, when the Sun rises, it will not be at 0° Aries. Remember that in a day's time the Earth has also advanced one degree farther along its path around the Sun. Therefore, on March 21 the Sun will rise at 1° Aries. On March 22 it will rise at 2° Aries and so on.

Every twenty-four-hour period, while the Sun is advancing one degree in its forward motion, all 360 degrees of the zodiacal circle rise over the eastern horizon following the Sun. Let's take a closer look at what happens during a twenty-four-hour period. There are 1,440 minutes in one day. (60 minutes [one hour] multiplied by twenty-four hours is 1,440). Divide 1, 440 minutes by 360 (degrees of the zodiac) and you get four. This means that every four minutes one degree of the zodiac rises over the eastern horizon.

Let's say the time the Sun rose March 20 was exactly 6:00 AM and the Sun's position at that time was exactly 0° Aries. Using Figure 3 on page 34, let's calculate what has happened by 6:00 PM. Twelve hours of clock time have elapsed (half the twenty-four-hour period), and the Sun has progressed half a degree to 0° Aries 30'. Don't confuse these minutes with minutes of clock time. There are 60 minutes in a degree, so half a degree is 30 minutes. What degree and sign would be rising over the eastern horizon at 6:00 PM? During the twelve hours it took the Sun to move forward, the zodiac was right behind it, rising approximately one degree every four minutes. A twelve-hour period (6:00 AM to 6:00 PM) is 720 minutes. Every four of those minutes represent one degree of the zodiac. Divide 720 minutes by 4 and you get 180. The zodiacal circle has risen 180 degrees. In other words, the 180th degree of the zodiac, which happens to be 0° Libra, is rising over the eastern horizon.

The zodiacal circle is divided into the twelve astrological signs, and the horoscope is a circle divided into twelve houses. As we have seen, the zodiacal circle begins at 0° Aries, but how do we find the beginning of the horoscope? The degree of a sign that is rising over the eastern horizon at the moment for which the chart is calculated marks the beginning of the horoscope.

This point begins the first house, and the other eleven houses follow in counterclockwise order. The point or line that indicates the beginning of a house is called the cusp. The cusp of the first house is special and is called the Rising Sign or the Ascendant (either term is correct). For purposes of this discussion we will make each house exactly thirty degrees. A chart for 6:00 AM with Sun rising

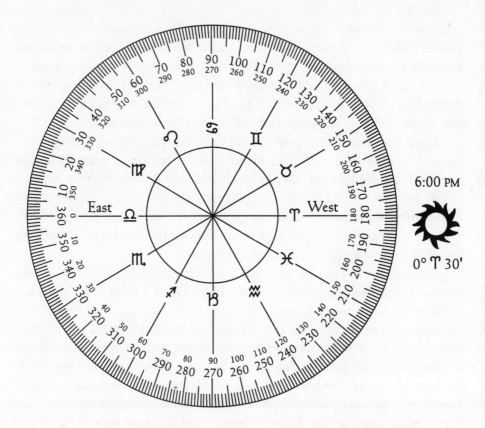

Figure 3: The Twelve-Hour Movement of the Zodiac with the Sun

at 0° Aries tells you that 0° Aries is also the Rising Sign. If the chart is cast for 6:04 AM, however, the first house begins at 1° Aries. A chart for 6:08 AM begins the first house at 2° Aries, and so on. In 120 minutes, or two hours time, the sign Taurus begins to rise. A chart for 8:00 AM would begin the first house at 0° Taurus. Study Figure 4.

The charts in Figure 4 are drawn for March 20 with the Sun at 6:00 AM, noon, 6:00 PM, and midnight. Notice how the astrological sign for each house changes according to the time of day. Each house represents approximately two hours of clock time. The sign rising over the eastern horizon along with the Sun at 6:00 AM is Aries. People born between 6:00 AM and 7:59 AM not only have Sun in Aries, they also have Aries as their Rising Sign or Ascendant. Now look at the chart for noon. People born between noon and 2:00 PM also have Sun in Aries,

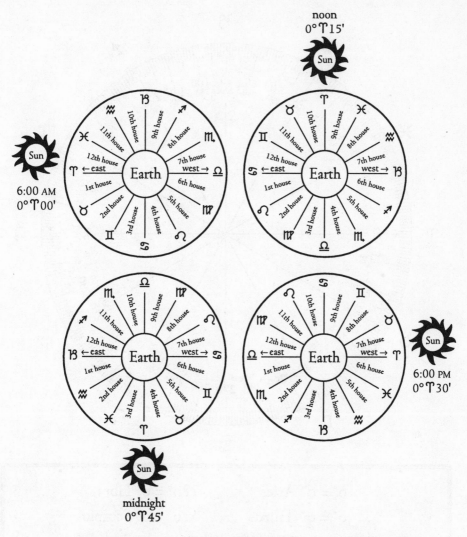

Figure 4: The Twenty-Four-Hour Movement of the Sun

but their Rising Sign is going to be Cancer. Arians born between 6:00 PM and 8:00 PM have a Libra Ascendant. Those born between midnight and 2:00 AM the next day have Capricorn Ascendant.

The next morning the Sun, having progressed through 0° Aries during the preceding twenty-four hours, now rises at 1° Aries and the whole cycle begins again. The Sun rises in each successive degree of Aries until about April 20,

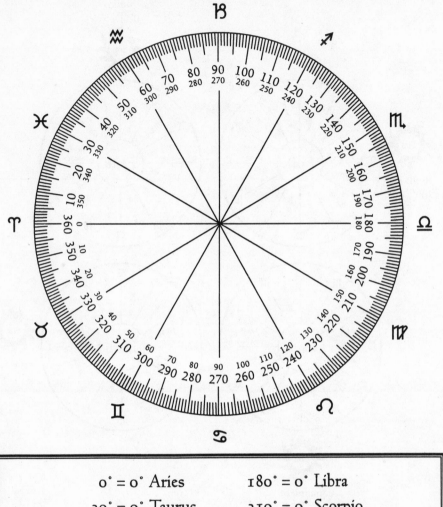

Figure 5: The Degrees of the Horoscope

when it enters Taurus. The daily and monthly cycles move in tandem like this until the following March, when it begins all over again at 0° Aries.

All horoscopes begin with the time because the time is what marks the first house. Not everyone is born at sunrise or, for that matter, at noon, 6:00 PM, or midnight. If you know what time you were born, it is not hard to figure out approximately what your Ascendant might be. First, you need the approximate degree of the Sun for the date of birth. Use the zodiacal circle in Figure 5 for assistance.

FINDING THE SUN'S DEGREE ON A GIVEN DATE

We know that the Sun's yearly cycle begins on March 20 or 21 at 0° Aries. Even though we know the Sun travels approximately one degree every day, we can't start at 0° Aries on March 20 and simply count around the zodiac one degree at a time. The year is 365 days while the zodiacal circle only has 360 degrees. The Sun travels faster on some days than others, which accounts for this discrepancy. Some days it will only travel 57 minutes of a degree instead of 60. We can eliminate some of the margin of error by dividing the year into quarters.

The first quarter is between March 20 and June 21. The second quarter is between June 21 and September 23. The third quarter is between September 23 and December 22. The fourth quarter is between December 22 and March 20. From the discussion of the zodiac and the Sun's yearly cycle, we know that the Sun starts out on March 20 at 0° Aries and by June 21 at the summer solstice its position is 0° Cancer.

For any date in the first quarter of the year, say April 1, count forward (use the wheel in Figure 5) from March 20 one degree per day. There are twelve days between March 20 and April 1. The twelfth degree on the zodiacal wheel is 11° Aries. Use an average movement (since the Sun doesn't move exactly 60 minutes each day) and make it 11–12° Aries. Suppose the birth date was April 26. There are 37 days between March 20 and April 26. Counting around the zodiacal wheel from 0°Aries, the 37th degree belongs to 6° Taurus. For birth dates during the second quarter of the year between June 21 and September 23 (the autumnal equinox) start counting from 0° Cancer on June 21 since you know that's the position of the Sun on that day. Let's say the birth date was August 8. There are 49 days between June 21 (when the Sun was at 0° Cancer) and August 8. Counting from 0° Cancer and going 49 degrees brings you to 17–18° Leo. For

births during the third quarter between September 23 and December 22, start counting from 0° Libra since that was the Sun's position on September 23. Finally, for birth dates during the fourth quarter between December 22 (the winter solstice) and March 20, use the position of the Sun at 0° Capricorn on December 22 to count forward.

FINDING YOUR ASCENDANT

Having figured out the approximate degree of the Sun for a given date, use that as the degree of the zodiac rising with the Sun at 6:00 AM just as we did earlier in this chapter. Count forward from that degree until the correct time of birth. Let's use the birth time of 2:00 PM on December 22. Knowing that the Sun rose December 22 at 6:00 AM at 0° Capricorn, keep moving the Ascendant from 0° Capricorn one degree for every four minutes of clock time. Divide 480 minutes of clock time (between 6:00 AM and 2:00 PM) by 4, and that tells you that 120 degrees have elapsed. Counting around the zodiac 120 degrees from 0° Capricorn brings you to 0° Taurus. For January 1 at 2:00 PM, the Rising Sign starts at 11° Capricorn at 6:00 AM and counts forward 120 degrees. This gives an approximate Rising Sign of 11° Taurus. For a 2:00 PM birth time on February 8, the 6:00 AM count will start at 18–19° Aquarius and move forward 120 degrees to get an Ascendant at 18–19° Gemini. The Ascendant is an important part of the horoscope. It describes some of the strongest characteristics in an individual's personality and mannerisms.

At first glance, it would seem that calculating a horoscope using the degree of the Sun as it rises on any given day is fairly simple, and, in fact, it can give most people at least a rough idea of what sign they have rising. However, the time at which the Sun rises as well as the number of hours between sunrise and sunset varies from one place to another on the surface of the Earth. A chart calculated for New York City is going to be different than a chart cast for Los Angeles, London, or Moscow. Each sign is always exactly thirty degrees, but the number of degrees in the houses as well as which sign appears on the house cusps will change not only according to the time but also because of the location for which the chart is cast.

All students of astrology learn how to calculate horoscopes. Many of them are not fond of this task. Although the mathematics is not difficult, the calculations can be very tedious. With the advent of computers in the late 70s and early

80s, we were all liberated—students and professionals alike—from the time-consuming chore of chart calculations. As a teacher, I strongly urge anyone serious about learning astrology to take some time to learn how to calculate a horoscope. There are two texts with excellent chapters on chart calculation listed in the bibliography. Calculated birth charts can also be obtained from Llewellyn, the author, and other chart services listed in Appendix B. In the meantime, it is not difficult for readers to get started on their own. Finding the approximate position of the Ascendant has already been described above. The approximate position of the Sun, Moon, and planets for any date may be looked up according to the ephemeris in Appendix A.

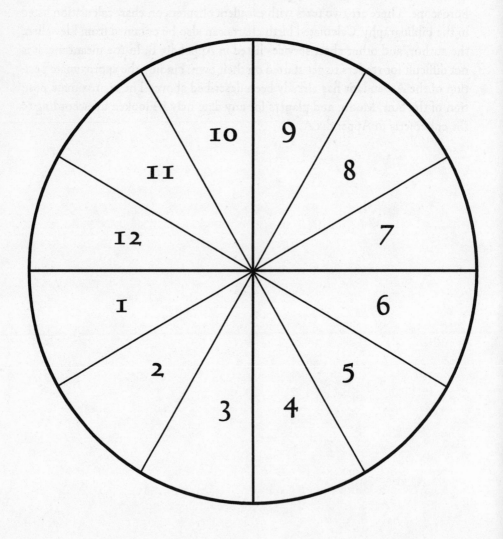

Figure 6: Houses of the Horoscope

Chapter Five

The Houses

The zodiac consists of twelve sections of the sky, each section being one of the astrological signs. Each sign is a special field of energy. There are also twelve sections or houses of the horoscope (Figure 6), and, as we saw in the previous chapter, each house is ruled by one of the astrological signs. The sign that rules a house in a given horoscope is determined by the Rising Sign, which rules the first house. The rest of the signs, following in their natural order, rule each of the remaining eleven houses. The function of each house is to direct the energy of the sign that rules it. In other words, the house indicates where the energy of the sign will be used. The ideas I am trying to convey might be better understood if I explain them in the context of a play.

The play is performed on a stage with twelve sets, one for each house of the horoscope. Each house or "set" contains special props and scenery that depict the ideas and the physical locations where the action takes place. Each set also has supporting actors and actresses who have a role to play in that set. The scenery, props, and people that belong to each set never change, but the signs that govern the sets change with each play. The play is a human life. The individual whose life is being performed is the star of the play. The plot may turn out to be a comedy, a tragedy, or perhaps a mystery. No one knows for sure until the play has ended. Now let us go into the theater and look around. The sets have all been erected in twelve sections on the stage. There is no action in any of them because the signs that dictate the energy in each set cannot be designated until the play actually begins. For now we will walk around and see what each set is like.

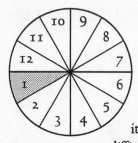

FIRST HOUSE

There is no scenery in Set One. The only actor that ever appears here is the star. This is the most important set since it is where the play begins—where the star makes his or her grand entrance. What kind of an entrance will it be? There may be obstacles that make an entrance very difficult, even perilous. Perhaps the star will not be able to make an entrance after all. The play cannot begin and those who waited for his or her entrance leave the theater. The most frequent scenario, however, is one in which the curtain rises just as the star gives a loud cry and steps out into the spotlight, front and center. The play begins. The only prop in Set One is a large mirror. During the play the star returns again and again to this set; trying on different costumes, experimenting with different kinds of make-up and mannerisms, all the while watching his or her image in the mirror. This is the first house of the horoscope. It describes the outer personality, physical appearance, to a certain extent the physical health of the body, and the beginning of life.

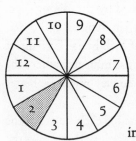

SECOND HOUSE

The scene in Set Two is a bank vault. It may be filled or it may contain very little. Money and other valuables are stored here by the star. As the play continues, certain nonmaterial assets that the star has earned may show up in the vault: education, development of skills, social and professional status. There are supporting actors and actresses in this scene. Some of them may be totally inanimate, simply stored here like other possessions with no human role to play. They have been bought and paid for. Others may be lively and animated, and they are the people whom the star values. The second house of the horoscope describes income and assets. It is attitude and behavior related to money. It describes some of the ways in which income may be earned, how it is managed, and how it is spent. The second house represents values and priorities which an individual establishes.

THIRD HOUSE

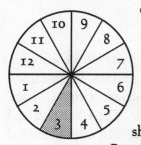

Set Three contains scenes of the local environment. A neighborhood. Places where the star goes to school, shops, takes care of business, and visits friends and relatives. It is not only *where* he or she goes but *how* he or she goes, the transportation used to get from place to place. Broader scenes include towns or cities within the distance of a short journey. Actors and actresses that appear are familiar faces: the postman, grocer, librarian, gas station attendant, neighbors. If the star has brothers or sisters, they appear in this set. Set Three also represents another environment, the star's mental state. In this inner environment, information is received, learning takes place, methods are devised, and ideas and opinions are formed. The third house of the horoscope is the mind. It is the manner in which an individual communicates, how understanding and ideas are physically expressed. It describes physical actions, basic physical skills, and speech. This is the house of short trips, elementary school experiences, and activities within the community.

FOURTH HOUSE

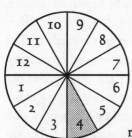

The main scene in Set Four is home and the domestic environment. It may be splendid or squalid. It may change constantly, or change only once or twice throughout the play. Actors and actresses in this set are related to the star. The principal supporting actress is the star's mother, and most of the relatives that appear are from her side of the family. Other scenes for Set Four will be used as needed to depict the beginning of new cycles and the end of old ones. In the broadest sense, Set Four represents the beginning and the end of the play. It does not include the birth of the star since that occurs in Set One. It is the star's forebearers, the roots from which the drama arose, and it depicts the end of the drama. The fourth house of the horoscope is home and family. It is family activities and domestic chores. It is real estate, family business, and domestic possessions.

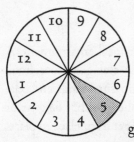

FIFTH HOUSE

Set Five contains scenes of a party and other social gatherings. There may be a gambling casino, dog races, or a game of poker. The set may include a circus, movie house, carnival, or a county fair. There are toys and games, arts, crafts, and other hobbies. The main actors and actresses who play a major role in this set are either the lovers or the children of the star. The fifth house of the horoscope describes the capacity for enjoyment, for humor and imagination. It is indulgence. The pursuit of pleasure, entertainment, luxury, physical comfort, and ease. This is the house of speculation and willingness to take risks. It is the creative expressions of special talent and skills. It is the house of romance and children.

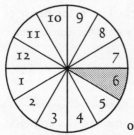

SIXTH HOUSE

There are two separate areas in Set Six. One area includes a gymnasium, health club, health food store, drug store, barber shop or beauty salon, and the offices of a doctor, dentist, and other health care specialists. The other area of the set includes a business office, factory, retail store, hotels, and any place where the star carries out responsibilities and tasks on a daily basis. Those who have a role to play in Set Six are people who work for or with the star. If the star owns a pet or works with animals, they appear in this set. The sixth house of the horoscope describes the status of health and physical fitness. It also describes the type of work in which an individual might be engaged, the behavior and attitude related to work. It is service an individual provides to others as well as the services he or she receives.

SEVENTH HOUSE

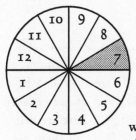

Set Seven is the opposite of Set One. In Set One, the star is always alone. In Set Seven, other people share the spotlight with the star. One scene for this set may be a wedding ceremony. Another may be a lawyer's office where contracts and legal matters can be initiated or they can be dissolved. Special props include a teeter-totter, a balance, and a bicycle built for two. The seventh house of the horoscope is partnership. It is joint ventures and all cooperative efforts to attain common goals. It is interactions with other people in general. It is the house of legal agreements, negotiations, and debates. It is how the individual is viewed by others.

EIGHTH HOUSE

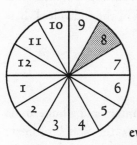

The scene in Set Eight is a duplicate of the bank vault in Set Two. The difference is that the star is never the one who puts things in this vault. It is other people who bring money, possessions, and nonmaterial assets. Whatever the star gains from others through inheritance, marriage, or other partnership is contained in this vault. The eighth house of the horoscope is joint income. It is the house of all that is inherited—monetary assets, genetic traits, and the values and priorities others establish for the individual. It is funds received as tax rebates or insurance benefits. This is the house of debts that must be paid, as well as debts that are collected. It is the self-worth gained as a result of developing innate talents, abilities, and resourcefulness.

NINTH HOUSE

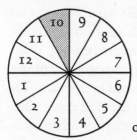

There are many and varied scenes in Set Nine. They include a university, cathedral or synagogue, museums, a zoo, a theater, a courtroom. There may also be a concert hall, a publishing house, and an advertising company. There is pageantry and ritual. There are many actors and actresses with roles to play. Some of them may speak a foreign language. Some of them may be related to the star through marriage. If there is a second marriage, the star's second spouse will appear in this set. Set Three is learning, communication, and transportation in the local community. Set Nine is the opposite set, and it is the world beyond the star's immediate environment. The ninth house of the horoscope is higher education, advanced training, court decisions, spiritual growth, and cultural pursuits. It is the growth and expansion of the ideas and experiences of the individual. It is writing, publishing, and international travel or trade.

TENTH HOUSE

Scenes in Set Ten include a mountain and a huge arena or stadium. This set represents the star's ultimate destiny, public position, and reputation. The star may never attain the top of the mountain. He or she may fall off the mountain into a deep valley and remain lost forever, or perhaps struggle to regain a former position with eventual success in attaining the pinnacle. The principal supporting actor in Set Ten is the star's father, and relatives that appear are from his side of the family. Set Four is the opposite set, being the home and the roots from which the star has come. Set Ten represents the notable or public achievements of forebearers. Set Four contains the family circle, Set Ten contains the public at large. Other people in this set are those with influence and authority in the life of the star; those who play an important role in his or her destiny. The tenth house of the horoscope is career (as distinct from a job) and other important long-range ambitions. It is the house that describes one's largest achievements in life. This house is the government and other agencies under which the individual resides. It represents the supervisor to whom the individual is responsible.

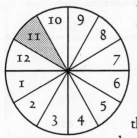

ELEVENTH HOUSE

There are more people than scenery in Set Eleven. It contains all the people who form the personal network surrounding the star. In particular, Set Eleven represents the kind and quality of roles that the star plays in the lives of others. Though the focus on roles is intimate, the scenes depicted tend to be more of a public nature. The action in this set usually involves more than two people at a time. Scenes in this set depict the establishment of business contacts, activities of special clubs and organizations, and social activities with friends and relatives. Children of the star may be found here as well as in the opposite Set Five. If the star has ties with other children that are not biological offspring, they appear in Set Eleven. The eleventh house of the horoscope describes the recognition an individual receives. It describes money or rewards derived from a profession. The main focus of this house is to describe what an individual gains (or fails to gain) from projecting energy and talent outwardly through other people.

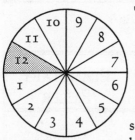

TWELFTH HOUSE

The light is very dim in Set Twelve. The star is isolated. Other people may be here, but the star either does not see them or does not recognize them. The main prop is a mirror in which only the past is reflected. The star may sense dark shapes here or there, but they remain elusive and just out of reach. Not all in Set Twelve is unknowable and invisible. The star can become the master instead of the victim in this set. It may take some time, but eventually he or she can learn to negotiate the concealed passages and read the hidden messages. The twelfth house of the horoscope is the subconscious mind, it is resentment, loss, and disappointment. It is the past. It is that which is hidden from the individual as well as that which the individual deliberately hides. It is secrets and secret or unobserved activity. The twelfth house describes confinement, despair, and deprivation. It is the occult, hidden power, and psychic energy.

PLANET	GREEK	ROMAN
Sun	Helios	Sol
Moon	Selene	Luna
Mercury	Hermes	Mercury
Venus	Aphrodite	Venus
Mars	Ares	Mars
Jupiter	Zeus	Jupiter
Saturn	Kronus	Saturn
Uranus	Hephaestus	Vulcan
Neptune	Poseidon	Neptune
Pluto	Hades	Pluto

Table 7: Corresponding Planets and Deities

SIGN	PLANETARY RULER	SIGN	PLANETARY RULER
Aries	Mars	Libra	Venus
Taurus	Venus	Scorpio	Pluto/Mars
Gemini	Mercury	Sagittarius	Jupiter
Cancer	Moon	Capricorn	Saturn
Leo	Sun	Aquarius	Uranus/Saturn
Virgo	Mercury	Pisces	Neptune/Jupiter

Table 8: Astrological Signs and their Planetary Rulers

Chapter Six

The Planets

All the world's a stage,
And all the men and women merely players;
they have their exits and their entrances...

Shakespeare

S etting up the basic structure of astrology is a three-step process. The first step is to map the heavens by dividing the sky into the twelve astrological signs. This is the zodiac. Astrology uses the zodiac as a blueprint—twelve different fields of energy—in which the cycle of life is outlined. The second step is to construct a more intimate map from the zodiac. This is the horoscope. This map takes the cycle of life reflected in the heavens and connects it to the Earth, which is where life actually exists. The third step in the process is to put a human being into the picture. This is the function of the planets. How and why the planets came to symbolize human beings is a fascinating part of our history.

There are certain experiences all people share. No human being escapes the real world's physical pain and pleasure, and its emotional sorrow and joy. There has never been a time when there were no earthquakes, floods, famines, fires, and plagues. The only difference between the earliest civilizations and our own, is that we understand more about what causes these things. People who survive the

horrors of a natural catastrophe or live through the terrors of a war may escape with their lives, but they cannot erase the experience from their memory.

Each of us retains the memory of our personal experiences and we also have a collective memory. This concept, developed by the Swiss psychiatrist Carl Jung, is that everything humanity has experienced since the beginning of our existence is retained. These experiences become part of a collective memory bank, indelibly imprinted in each human being that comes into the world. As civilization struggled to establish itself along the ancient banks of the Tigris and Euphrates rivers, floods periodically occurred that destroyed all but a few fortunate souls who lived to tell the tale. And tell the tale they did, from one generation to the next. Cataclysmic deluge was a theme of legend long before the story of Noah and the ark found its way into the Old Testament. It is recounted in many different cultures and is still alive in our collective memory.

In antiquity, the only comprehension that humankind possessed to cope with the awesome forces of nature came from observation and imagination. Observing the cycles of the Sun, Moon, and planets, people began to correlate these cycles with the cycle of human existence. Why should life on Earth not be as regulated and orderly as that which existed above it? And if this is so, who or what might be responsible? From these imaginings, there arose the pantheon of gods and goddesses who controlled the universe, the forces of nature, and the lives of human beings. And where would such beings exist but in the heavens, far above the reach of ordinary man.

The Sun, Moon, and planets were considered to be either the gods themselves or at least the messengers of the gods. People need only observe them to understand what was being communicated from celestial masters. But this is an oversimplification. The fact that along with immortality, gods were also endowed with many human traits suggests the subconscious desire of human beings to be masters of their own fate and able to control the forces that threatened their survival. To further suggest this possibility, superheroes were created who represented the link by which man might cross the bridge to immortality. Heroes were often killed and, for their courage, were given the gift of immortality. Whether god, goddess, hero, or heroine, all these fictional characters are archetypes, primordial images of human existence. To the astrologers of antiquity, they were the planets, and the heavens became the theater in which they performed.

The horoscope is the theater in which man exists, so the planetary symbols in the horoscope are the embodiment of human traits. While it is true that we no

longer view the planets as gods and goddesses, it does not invalidate the human traits they once represented. Life still brings death, and the human experiences that occur in between have not changed since humankind first appeared on the face of the Earth. This is why we do not abandon the lessons of astrology that began four thousand years ago.

Mythology, arising as it does from the imagination of the earliest cultures, constitutes a considerable population of fabulous beings. Attempts to compare deities from the pantheon of one culture and age to similar deities in the pantheon of another is to invite controversy. The reason for taking such a risk is to provide the reader with a method for associating the qualities and traits of the various deities with the appropriate planets (see Table 7 on page 48).

Before we take a closer look at each planet, it is important to note that when astrologers refer to the "planets," they include the Sun and Moon. This is done merely for the sake of convenience. There are some other things to know about the planets in general. Each of the astrological signs is given a planetary ruler. Since there are twelve signs and only ten planets, some of them share the same planetary ruler (see Table 8 on page 48). Each planet, in conjunction with the sign that it rules, governs a part of the human anatomy. Some of the planetary symbols have Egyptian or Babylonian origins and some are very modern. For the most part, however, they are derived from Greco-Roman prototypes. Each symbol embodies certain esoteric ideas related to spirit, matter, and energy. Although the planets have other meanings in a horoscope which will be mentioned, taken together, they represent the individual. In your own horoscope, that individual is you.

SUN

The Sun is the individual, without personality and habits, without the influence of environment and background. It is an individual's potential and uniqueness. It is ego, the main direction and focus a person wants to take. It is the power of the will, the determination to attain goals. The Sun is personal honesty and integrity. The ability to command respect and authority, and to impress and influence others. The Sun is physical vitality, and rules the heart. In a natal chart, the Sun also represents those with great influence in the individual's life. It is the boss or supervisor at work, the government and other

similar agencies. In a male's natal chart, the Sun is the father, and in a female's chart it is the husband. The astrological sign Leo is ruled by the Sun.

MOON

☽ The Moon represents feelings and sensitivity. How an individual responds emotionally to others and to situations and experiences. It describes attitude and behavior related to nurture—the ability to give and to receive physical and emotional nurturing. It describes the rhythm and flow of an individual's daily life and functions: physical, emotional, and mental. It describes fickleness and changeable moods. It is habits, needs, and desires. It is the subconscious mind, memory, intuition, and instincts. The Moon is personality, although personality is more clearly indicated by the Ascendant or Rising Sign. The Moon is passive. It reflects and motivates, but does not act on its own. The breasts and digestive system are ruled by the Moon. The Moon also signifies one's home and domestic environment. It is babies and young children, and the individual's mother. The astrological sign Cancer is ruled by the Moon.

MERCURY

☿ Mercury governs perceptions. It is the mental state, intellectual endeavors, the way an individual thinks and communicates. It is the way information is received and interpreted, how learning takes place. It represents a person's ideas and opinions, and the methods that are devised and used. It is perception and thought without judgment. It describes innate cleverness, the ability to imitate as well as originate. Mercury rules the hands and thus manual dexterity and mechanical skills. It governs the physical response of the nervous system and the senses' response to stimuli. It also rules the respiratory system. Mercury describes travel and transportation, how an individual goes from one place to another—mentally as well as physically. Is it accomplished with great speed or a slow amble with many detours along the way? The astrological signs Gemini and Virgo are ruled by Mercury.

VENUS

Venus rules social attitudes and behavior. It is aesthetic tastes and inclinations. It is physical beauty and gracefulness. It is artistic talent. Venus represents values and priorities, and thus describes an individual's judgment and moral sensitivities. It is the cooperative spirit. Venus is romance and love. It is marriage and other partnerships. The manner of merriment and pursuit of physical ease and sensual pleasure. It rules the kidneys. It also describes the general harmony and attractiveness of the physique. Venus represents female relationships and social interactions at every level. The astrological signs Taurus and Libra are ruled by Venus.

MARS

Mars represents physical energy and efforts, the physical power and action of an individual. It describes the strength and direction of the physical force that drives the ego, fires the emotions, and encourages mental endeavors and communicative skills. Mars rules the head and face. It is risk-taking inclinations and physical challenges that are encountered. It is aggressiveness and the combative spirit. It is sexual drive, and in a male's horoscope, it is the sexual potency. Mars represents all male relationships and associations in general. The astrological sign Aries is ruled by Mars. Before Pluto was discovered, Mars also ruled Scorpio.

JUPITER

Jupiter describes the potential for growth and expansion on many levels: physical, intellectual, spiritual, and cultural. It is the potential of an individual to reach beyond the ordinary and basic experiences in life. The ability to exaggerate and enlarge. It is the accumulation of material assets, power, and status. It describes the capacity for enjoyment and optimism, and the development of aspirations. It represents the father and his position in society. Jupiter rules the upper legs. The astrological sign Sagittarius is ruled by Jupiter. Before the discovery of Neptune, Jupiter also ruled the sign Pisces.

SATURN

♄ Saturn describes responsibilities, restrictions, and limitations that an individual is apt to encounter. It represents the lessons that must be learned in life. It describes the areas where the individual may experience the greatest stability and longevity. Saturn is endurance and practicality. In a horoscope, Saturn represents elderly people or those who represent an authoritative, strict, or austere presence in the individual's life. The astrological sign Capricorn is ruled by Saturn. Before the discovery of Uranus, Saturn was also the ruler of Aquarius.

URANUS

♅ Uranus rules freedom and independence. It indicates originality of thought and expression. In society as a whole, it rules radical ideas and people, as well as revolutionary events that upset established structures. Uranus takes approximately seven years to transit one sign, taking about 84 years to complete all twelve signs. People with Uranus in the same sign are separated by 84 years, so it is easier to describe conditions in society at the time when Uranus transited a given sign. The personal implications of Uranus are described by its house position and the aspects it makes with other natal planets in an individual's horoscope. It describes areas of unpredictability, and where a person or their life-style may be different from other people. Uranus relates to the unusual or unique. Friends and the clubs or associations to which an individual belongs are also indicated by Uranus, as is their potential involvement with science and technology, computers, and the media. The astrological sign Aquarius is ruled by Uranus.

NEPTUNE

♆ Neptune is in one sign for approximately thirteen years, taking about 164 years to complete its cycle through all twelve signs. Since 164 years separate people born with Neptune in the same sign, the significance of Neptune in a given sign is described from a generational or historical point of

SUN ☉	JUPITER ♃
MOON ☽	SATURN ♄
MERCURY ☿	URANUS ♅
VENUS ♀	NEPTUNE ♆
MARS ♂	PLUTO ♇

Table 9: Planets and their Symbols

view. Neptune rules those who are oppressed or abandoned, the misfits of society. Neptune also rules visionaries, and those who are glamorous and charismatic. It represents the growth or suppression in society of spiritualism, mysticism, and certain ideals. The interpretation of Neptune in an individual's horoscope is related to its house position and the aspects it makes with other natal planets. Neptune represents a person's spirituality, abstract thinking, illusions, and disillusionment. It describes areas of an individual's life where things aren't always what they seem. It is despair, derangement, guilt, persecution. It is sensitivity, psychic awareness, and compassion. Neptune describes the potential for experiences related to confinement, abandonment, addiction, or physical intolerance to drugs. The astrological sign Pisces is ruled by Neptune.

PLUTO

Pluto takes approximately 248 years to make one cycle through all twelve signs. Due to the eccentricity of its orbit, the period that Pluto spends in each sign can vary from twelve years to thirty-two years. Like atomic energy, a force ruled by Pluto, the presence of Pluto's energy is never obvious until it is used. Pluto's influence in a given sign is described by conditions in

society at the time it transited that sign. On a personal level, Pluto's significance is interpreted from its house position and the aspects it makes to other natal planets in a person's horoscope. Pluto represents intense energy. It describes areas in which an individual consciously or subconsciously seeks to exercise power or control. Pluto is also linked to karmic responsibility, and, in this respect, it describes the areas where a person must gain the deepest level of understanding. The astrological sign Scorpio is ruled by Pluto.

Chapter Seven

Planets in the Signs

Before you start to read and to study the meaning of the Sun, Moon, and planets in each sign, let's review some things. Recall that the planets symbolize the individual as a whole, and that each planet is a different part of that individual. Each astrological sign represents a special energy that a planet will encounter. Reread Chapter Three to familiarize yourself with the kind of energy associated with each sign. The meaning of each planet never changes, but the planet exhibits its characteristics in different ways according to the energy of the sign it is in. For example, the Sun always represents the ego, but the disposition and tendencies of the ego are different in each sign. Although the meaning of each planet is mentioned throughout this chapter, it may help to review Chapter Six for a description of the planets.

By this time you have learned the twelve signs and their symbols. You also know that one sign always follows another in the same order. The natural wheel, a chart that is drawn with Aries as the first house and ending with Pisces as the twelfth house, is shown in Figure 7. Notice that in each house is the planet that rules the sign. For example, Mercury is found in the third house because it is the ruler of Gemini, and it is also in the sixth house because it rules Virgo. Venus is found in the second house and in the seventh house because it rules both Taurus

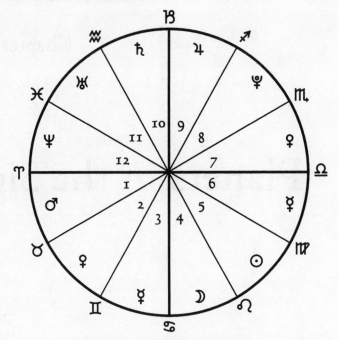

Figure 7: The Natural Wheel

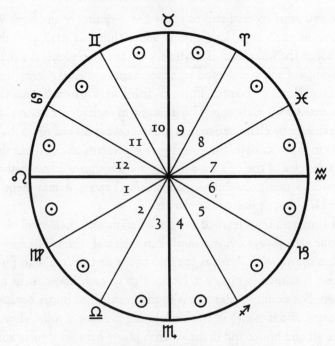

Figure 8: The Natural Houses of the Sun

58

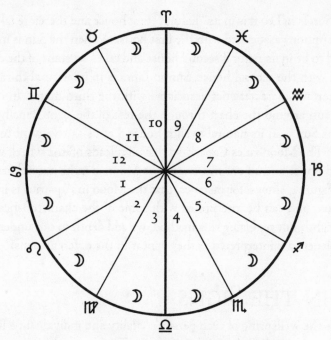

Figure 9: The Natural Houses of the Moon

and Libra. Practice making the wheel. As you draw it, think about the meanings for each of the twelve houses, and as you draw the symbols for the signs and planets, think about their meanings as well. Study the natural wheel. It represents what you have learned in the previous chapters.

Interpretation is the heart and soul of astrology. There are many contributing factors behind a description of a planet in a certain sign or in a certain house. It is only by long and careful study that one learns the reasons behind interpretation. Little by little the student gradually starts to piece these reasons together. At the end of each of the following interpretations, there is a short paragraph that explains how the natural wheel can be turned to emphasize and describe further the Sun, Moon, and planets in the signs.

The natural wheel always has Aries on the Ascendant with Mars as the first house ruler. Suppose we want to study the Sun. The Sun is the ruler of Leo so we turn the wheel to make that sign the Ascendant and the other signs (in their correct order) are then placed on the rest of the houses. Virgo becomes the second house, Libra is the sign on the third house, and so on as illustrated in Figure 8. What does this tell us? It tells us that since the Sun is the natural ruler of Leo,

when the Sun is in Leo it is in its "natural" first house and therefore takes on some of the descriptions associated with the first house. When the Sun is in Virgo, it is considered to be in its natural second house and takes on some of the descriptions associated with the second house. Sun in Libra is in its natural third house and takes on certain characteristics associated with the third house. In this way we move the sun around the chart through the rest of the signs. Finally arriving at Cancer, the Sun is in its natural twelfth house. Let us say we want to emphasize the Moon. The Moon rules Cancer, so that sign leads off the wheel, with Leo on the second house and so on. In Cancer, the Moon is in its natural first house. A glance at Figure 9 shows, for instance, that the Moon in Aquarius is in its natural eighth house and can be interpreted with some of the characteristics associated with the eighth house. Using this method, we add depth to our understanding of how the planets are interpreted as they appear in the different signs.

SUN IN THE SIGNS

The Sun is the wellspring of each person's vitality and individuality. It is the ego, the will, the essential energy of the life force. The Sun is the center of the solar system; the ego is the center of the individual.

SUN IN ARIES (March 20–21/April 19–20)

⊙♈ People born with Sun in the environment of Aries are high-spirited individuals, ready to try anything at least once. Lively participants in the everyday bustle of life, Arians maintain a frantic pace that others find difficult to match. In the environment of Aries, the ego becomes a primitive force, raw and uncomplicated as a baby newly born. When hungry or in pain, babies cry until their demands are satisfied. Reverting to demanding and infantile behavior, Arians can be very self-centered. They want what they want, when they want it. This kind of selfishness is not attractive certainly, but it is often mitigated by the fact that Arians are also very generous and not intentionally mean-spirited. It is careless disregard for others that is usually at fault in Arians rather than deliberate unkindness or unwillingness to share. Refreshingly open and direct, they do not understand the need or desire for endless and complicated physical, mental, or emotional maneuverings.

Fiery Mars, the planet of physical action, rules the environment of Aries. Mars gives the Sun strength and combativeness. Most of all, Mars encourages

physical action. So it is that Arians are invariably given to react physically to everything. Feelings and ideas are immediately translated by the ego into actions. Constant physical activity helps to work off excess energy, which is why Arians are always in motion. Abundant energy is the basis for prodigious physical accomplishments, and the fuel that feeds their intellectual and creative endeavors. Cut off from the physical activity so necessary to their essential nature, Arians become depressed, unproductive, and overweight.

Arians are nearly always friendly, but they are not necessarily outgoing or gregarious. They are very hard workers and easy to get along with. Generous with their time and energy, they are happy to help others. They don't mind being asked to do something, but they resent being told what to do. Arians are ideal-istic and courageous. Theirs is the astrological sign of the soldier, and they are instantly ready to battle against insult or injustice. In their haste, however, they often forget the practicality of being adequately armed before rushing headlong into physical or verbal combat. Frustration and anger lie close to the surface, but once released these reactions do not last long. Arians don't want to waste time dwelling on whatever caused them to be angry or upset. They want to move along to other things. They are doers.

To Arians, success is a just a matter of getting out and doing what needs to be done. They are willing to start projects others would be afraid to tackle. They approach situations with confidence and the attitude that challenges or obstacles can be overcome. Sometimes they have to learn the difference between being confidently aggressive, a responsible "take-charge person" on whom others rely to get things moving, and being rudely aggressive, a "know-it-all" who is insensi-tive to the feelings as well as the wisdom of others. They may fail to finish what they start when too many details slow them down.

Arians are eager athletes and generous players. They enjoy the challenge of a tough contest. Combative by nature, they are attracted to boxing, wrestling, and team sports. Most Arians are mechanically inclined, adept at arts and crafts, typing, working with machinery, playing musical instruments, or performing magic tricks. They do have a tendency to allow their enthusiasm to exceed their actual ability. Before taking something apart, for instance, they don't often stop to wonder if they can put it back together.

Aries colors are red and white. Vulnerable parts of the body are the head and face. As a sign of this celestial association, many Arians are born with a birth mark on their head or face. Headaches, black eyes, nose bleeds, and insect bites

are common Aries complaints. The birthstone for Aries is the diamond. The tremendous heat and pressure that nature exerts in turning carbon into hard, brilliant diamonds represent the strength and physical force in the Aries-born. Flowers for Aries include the poppy (red), geranium, honeysuckle, and hollyhocks.

In Aries, the Sun is in its natural *ninth house*. If you think of Aries ego and drive in ninth-house terms, you may be able to see why ...

Arians like to identify themselves with ideals, with some higher purpose. They may seek careers in religion or higher education. They are good at sales and advertising, and become publishers or involved in theater or the arts. Many Arians are skilled with languages, or involved with foreign trade and travel, the judicial system, or international law.

SUN IN TAURUS (April 20–21/May 20–21)

In the focused energy that dominates the environment of Taurus, the ego, like an egg attached to the womb, seeks a protected position where it can grow and develop. Those born in Taurus are not meant to be cast adrift aimlessly in the world. They are driven to cling like barnacles to a solid rock that represents reality. Broken promises and betrayal by others threaten their security. Taureans do not react well to disappointment, and it can cause them to behave in a manner completely in conflict with their own best interests. Socially, they may either retreat from the world or go in the opposite direction and become promiscuous. Whichever direction is taken, they end up sacrificing the meaningful, enduring relationships they really need in order to feel emotionally secure. Other values may also be sacrificed. Becoming totally materialistic, Taureans may accumulate wealth and either refuse to spend it or recklessly squander it. In either case, they do not improve the quality or enjoyment of life for themselves or anyone else.

Taureans need a definite purpose for the things they do, and they need solidity in their relationships. Their initial reaction to whatever they experience is to assess its worth. Before they take action, they want to ascertain what tangible advantages can be gained. What appears too abstract or vague fails to attract more than their passing interest. Their natural cautiousness saves them

from making mistakes, but it can also prevent them from taking advantage of valuable opportunities.

Taureans can concentrate their energy and attention for incredible periods of time. They do not want to be rushed or forced into anything. The bull is the well-known image for Taureans, but perhaps a turtle would be just as appropriate. Friends, relatives, and everyone else waits for the Taurean. Stubborn and impervious to changes not of their own making, Taureans are more comfortable when allowed to follow their planned agenda and when they are given sufficient time to prepare for new activities or situations. They are often highly successful because of their tenacity in sticking to projects. Taureans are loving and patient. Their quiet strength and determination inspire others to trust them. Because they want to be able to rely on others, they are usually dependable themselves.

Venus is the planetary ruler of Taurus. Venus prompts a keen eye for beauty as well as value, and encourages the pursuit of comfort and physical pleasure. As a result of their addiction to personal pleasure and comfort, Taureans can become very lazy and vulnerable to the consequences of overindulging in rich food and other physical pleasures. Venus inspires love of music and art, and many Taureans have considerable talent in these areas. In particular, many of them have pleasant speaking or singing voices. Although Taureans are usually soft-spoken and subdued, they have a lively humor and enjoy socializing.

Taureans love nature and natural things. To stay in harmony with themselves, Taureans need to be close to the earth. They admire fine wood and other beautiful materials. They love the colors and the sensualness of vivid flowers and the luxurious green of shrubs and other plants. Taureans are natural architects, builders, and developers. As a rule, Taureans are physically strong and solidly built. Even those who are not fat may be physically more dense per pound of body weight. Many of them favor weight lifting or other body-building routines as a way to keep in shape. They enjoy participating in sports that require strength and endurance.

Taurus colors are brown, russet, and turquoise. Vulnerable parts of the body are the neck, throat, shoulders, and upper torso. Stiff necks, sore throats, and earaches are common Taurean complaints. The emerald, a variety of beryl and as costly as a diamond, is the Taurus birthstone. The emerald's rich green is suitably Taurean since it is the color of money, green pastures, and serenity. The emerald has a six-sided geometric form. Six is the number assigned to Venus, the planetary ruler of Taurus. Flowers for Taurus are the rose (red), daisy, lily, and daffodil.

In Taurus, the Sun is in its natural *tenth house*. If you think of the Taurus ego and drive in tenth-house terms, you can see why …

Taureans can be very ambitious and involved with their career or destiny in life. They seek public positions or those in which they deal with the public. They may be concerned with their public reputation, and attaining positions of great influence. Taureans can be excellent managers and administrators. Their ego development may be profoundly affected by their father or the main authority figure in their life.

SUN IN GEMINI (May 21–22/June 20–21)

In the mentally charged environment of Gemini, the ego is energized by communication. People born in this sign are compelled to occupy themselves with the expression of ideas and the communication of information. The mature Gemini becomes a serious scholar and careful researcher. The immature Gemini turns into a gossip and the proverbial "jack-of-all-trades and master of none." Although it is generally not an accurate assessment, the singular mental orientation of Geminis can make it appear to others that they are unfeeling or emotionally superficial.

Mercury, the planet of the intellect and communication in general, rules Gemini. Mercury enhances intellectual curiosity and talkativeness. It also favors those born in Gemini with quick-witted humor and clever mechanical skills. Geminis are always busy with projects, errands, meetings, and other matters that keep them on the go. They are the embodiment of the White Rabbit in Louis Carroll's classic tale, *Alice in Wonderland*.

Natural versatility and ever-changing interests contribute to a youthfulness that Geminis retain throughout life. It is difficult for them to concentrate on one thing at a time. Easily jumping from one thing to another, Geminis forget that others are not so nimble. They often have to be reminded to slow down and let others catch up. They also have to be reminded to stop talking once in a while and listen. Sometimes they neglect to get all the facts before repeating information. Although Geminis can often be secretive about themselves, they are very interested in learning about what's going on in the lives of others. They are especially fond of secrets and intrigue and don't mind becoming involved in behind-

the-scenes antics of one sort or another. Always wanting to know everything, they amass quite a store of information, which in turn makes them very interesting to others. Add to that their cheerful, friendly dispositions and it isn't surprising that they get along so well in the world.

Geminis readily adapt to changing ideas, different people, and whatever situation they are in. Such flexibility is no doubt useful in some situations, but it perplexes those around them. Geminis instinctively seem to know what others are thinking, and they also possess great talent for imitation. Like their adaptability, these skills can be used in many ways. Certainly Geminis are successful when it comes to salesmanship, but they are often tempted to say what others want to hear instead of the truth. How their talent or fondness for imitation will be demonstrated is difficult to predict. For instance, miniaturization, which is a form of imitation, fascinates Gemini, and many of them collect or create miniatures of all kinds. They are adept at copying the handwriting of others, and their own writing tends to be small and cramped.

Since they are apt to spend more time talking than eating, Geminis usually stay fairly slim. As a rule they are physically flexible and agile, and they enjoy gymnastics, bicycling, and swimming. Other favorite sports are tennis, racquetball, and similar games in which they can participate with a partner. Most Geminis are skillful with mechanical devices or doing repair work. Their manual talents also include design, interior decoration, arts and crafts, magic and illusion, and playing musical instruments (usually more than one).

Gemini colors are yellow and light blue. Vulnerable parts of the body are the arms, hands, fingers, lungs, and nervous system. Respiratory problems and various nervous conditions are common Gemini complaints. Agate is the traditional Gemini birthstone. Appropriate to the multifaceted Gemini personality, this mineral is streaked with many colors. It may seem that Geminis are scattered and thus weakened by their wide range of interests and abilities, but the steel-like hardness of agate is a reminder that the Gemini personality and character can be just as strong as it is varied. Gemini flowers include the lilac, azalea, lily of the valley, and miniature varieties of flowers and shrubs.

In Gemini, the Sun is in its natural *eleventh house*. If you think of the Gemini ego and drive in eleventh-house terms, you can see why ...

Geminis identify strongly with their friends but not necessarily on an emotional level. They involve themselves with meetings and organizational activities. They are stronger and more successful when they work with groups than when they act alone. Geminis are experts at networking.

SUN IN CANCER (June 21–22/July 21–22)

In the emotional sea of Cancer, the ego is a ship that is borne aloft on mighty waves but is in perpetual danger of drowning in its treacherous waters. Cancerians react emotionally to everything. Their biggest struggle in life is to avoid becoming prisoners of their own emotions. Unlikely to suffer in silence, everyone around them is made aware that something is wrong. On the other hand, they are also caring and considerate. Cancerians are always willing to help others when they are down. Emotional insecurity makes them hang on to things. They hate to throw anything away, and many of them are avid collectors, conservators, and savers of string. It is equally difficult for them to give up on failed relationships, and still harder for them to learn the difference between caring and possessiveness. Highly sensitive, Cancerians tend to take criticism, even constructive criticism, as a personal indictment. Although they can be outwardly gregarious, most Cancerians are shy. However, when they feel comfortable in a situation or relationship, they relax and open up completely. Their emotional sensitivity is troublesome to be sure, but it also gives rise to remarkable intuition.

The Moon, celestial guardian of fertility and nurture, rules Cancer. The lunar emphasis encourages a strong identification with home and family. Cancerians are born ready to mother anyone who appears to be in need of such nurture. They are not necessarily good cooks or efficient housekeepers, but they are attached to home and hearth, or at least to the concept of belonging somewhere, to having roots. As an offshoot of their natural interest in family, they often develop a passion for genealogy and history in general. Food is important to them. They enjoy feeding others as much as they enjoy feeding themselves. When upset, Cancerians tend to use food as consolation which often results in excess weight.

Cancerians are doers. In spite of their emotional sensitivity, they are very strong-willed and determined. They have no trouble expressing what they want

or finding a way to get it. Many Cancerians succeed in life because their genuine concern for the welfare of others inspires loyalty as well as cooperation. The Crab is their astrological symbol, and certain crab-like gestures are associated with the behavior of Cancerians. Just as the crab walks sideways instead of straight ahead, Cancerians use an indirect approach in accomplishing their goals. Rather than direct confrontation or request, they are more apt to resort to using emotional appeal. At the slightest provocation, the crab quickly hides in the sand or retreats into a shell until safer times are at hand. Cancerians who feel threatened or suspect that their attempts may be unsuccessful often hide their true ambitions until a more comfortable situation occurs.

Participation in physical fitness or sports activities becomes an important, often vital way for Cancerians to work off emotional stress. They are especially comfortable with team sports, since they view team members as a family-like group. Favorite Cancerian sports are swimming, fishing, sailing, skiing, and mountain climbing. Cancerians are creative. Even those who may not have a particular talent can use some type of involvement with art, music, or writing as another method of emotional release instead of indulging in eating binges or other destructive habits. Living or spending time near the water is a relaxing, as well as creatively stimulating environment for Cancerians.

Cancer colors are white, silver, and pale yellow. Vulnerable parts of the body are the breasts and stomach. Stomach aches, food allergies, and hysterics are the usual afflictions of Cancerians. Cancer rules silver. The emotionally sensitive nature of Cancerians tends to reflect the people and circumstances surrounding them in the same way as the shiny, polished surface of silver. The ruby as well as the pearl are Cancerian birthstones. The ruby, a variety of corundum, is one of the hardest minerals known, while the pearl is soft and easily scratched. These gems uniquely illustrate the two contrasting sides of the Cancerian personality, hard and determined as well as soft and vulnerable. Cancerian flowers are the water lily (lotus), iris, poppy (white), carnation (white) and southern magnolia.

In Cancer, the Sun is in its natural *twelfth house*. If you think of the Cancerian ego and drive in twelfth-house terms, you can see why ...

Cancerians can be very shy about their private lives. They identify strongly with the past and their childhood conditioning. They may devote their lives to

helping minority groups, and those who are ill, abandoned, or in other desperate circumstances. Cancerians become involved with those who are confined in prison or mental institutions. Their work may involve secret or highly confidential material or activities.

SUN IN LEO (July 22–23/August 22–23)

⊙ ♌ The grandiloquent energy in the environment of Leo makes the ego vital, full-blown, and glorious. Those born in this sign are driven to seek confirmation of their individuality, to enjoy it, to gain strength and purpose from it. They perform great deeds. They become leaders. They attract and amuse others. When their egos are turned inward, Leos are self-centered and tyrannical. Seeking attention (consciously or subconsciously), they play the hero. At times this gesture is noble, but they may neglect to learn what assistance is actually wanted and their misguided generosity is worthless to those they sought to help. Leos envision grandiose schemes, and many of them possess considerable talent to turn their ideas into reality.

The Sun is the ruler of Leo, and it inspires a true zest for life and its pleasures. Imbued with this solar spirit, Leos are genial hosts and natural entertainers. They derive much pleasure out of helping others enjoy life as much as they do. Their sunny dispositions inspire the affection of many friends and admirers. Though usually full of ambition and enthusiasm, Leos also have a lazy streak. If given the opportunity, they will take the easy way out of things, especially when a situation offers little fun or glory.

For all their wit and fun-loving spirits, Leos are very stubborn. Stubbornness is most often exhibited when their egos are involved. They are likely to suffer far less from a broken heart than from wounded pride or the loss of attention. Attempts to back them into a corner, or demands that they change their thinking or behavior, will reveal the extent of their intractable nature. Even when confronted with irrefutable evidence of its unworthiness, Leos may cling to a bad relationship or idea because their egos simply will not allow them to admit being wrong. However, their tenacity is also a valuable asset. It gives them steadfast loyalty, patience, and determination to succeed. Leos generally have opinions about everything, and not a bit of reluctance in expressing them. They must have the last word and, as far as they are concerned, it is the only one that counts. This kind of arrogance may be hard to take for more timid souls, but those who know Leos well also know how generous they are in helping others to believe in themselves.

Leos tackle projects others would not attempt, though they cannot help calling as much attention as possible to their efforts. Their penchant for exaggeration and overreaction works well in theater, advertising schemes, and other situations where a "bigger than life" approach is desirable. Leos are often guilty, however, of habitually turning a minor problem or fairly routine situation into an overblown crisis, much to the confusion and annoyance of those around them. Their sociable nature makes it hard to stick to boring or solitary physical fitness routines, but they may not mind dressing up in flashy gym outfits and joining an exercise class. Dancing, swimming, and tennis are favorite activities. When engaged in team sports, they can make too many grandstand plays, forgetting that they are just part of a team. Arts and crafts, theater groups, philanthropic societies, and religious organizations attract their interest and participation. It is easy for pleasure-loving Leos to become addicted to rich food and, as they get older, they may find themselves putting on weight. Vulnerable parts of the body are the back and the heart. Overexertion, heart murmur, and various types of back pains are the usual Leo complaints.

Leo colors are gold, royal blue, purple, and red. Leo rules gold, and the birthstone for this sign is the sardonyx. An appropriate inspiration for Leo's unique personality, the intriguing sardonyx is a variety of agate that can be cut in many dramatic ways. Flowers for Leo include dahlia, yellow lily, poppy (red), marigold, sunflower, and heliotrope.

In Leo, the Sun is in its natural *first house*. If you think of Leo's ego and drive in first-house terms, you can see why ...

Leos are powerful personalities. They seek to attain personal influence and to call attention to themselves and their uniqueness as individuals. Leos seek to improve themselves and are concerned with their physical appearance. They are sensitive to personal criticism. They involve themselves on a very personal level with many of the things they do.

SUN IN VIRGO (August 23–24/September 22–23)

The ego in Virgo is directed to the development of potential. In this environment, few egos waste time in fiery demonstrations of their own power. So it is that those born in Virgo are not encouraged toward extravagant

or dramatic gestures. They are inclined to measured pace and practical purpose, driven to strive not for glory but for perfection. Virgos are most excellent critics. They seem unable, however, to resist the urge to improve everything and everyone, which is a fatal undertaking, guaranteed not only to fail but to place a severe strain on their relationships. Some Virgos use their own inability to achieve perfection as an excuse for idleness and unproductiveness. Sloppy, disorganized, and irresponsible Virgos are contradicting their true nature. It is unlikely that even Virgos with such bad habits will refrain from criticizing others for the same behavior. Virgos need to think that what they do is of a practical and helpful nature. To this end, many of them pursue careers in health related fields or in other areas such as teaching, labor relations, environmental protection, social work, or religious counseling. Though most of them do have altruistic motives in helping others, it must be said that Virgos have a tendency to act the martyr. It is not unheard of for them to use their self-sacrificing efforts as a weapon to arouse feelings of guilt in others.

Mercury, the planet of information and communication, rules Virgo. Mercury enhances analytical ability and mechanical skills, and it promotes an interest in business and trade. Virgos are natural teachers, librarians, secretaries, bookkeepers, and retailers. They are also among the most highly skilled craftsmen and designers. Communication is important to Virgos, aptly demonstrated by the fact that many of them are very talkative. They are effective negotiators and salesmen. They love books, magazines, writing, and are very fond of traveling. Virgos are very busy people who are always occupied with one project or another, meetings, errands, and a variety of business or household chores.

Like a virgin waiting to give herself to the perfect lover, Virgos are also idealistic. When they allow idealism to get out of hand, nothing is accomplished. The virgin becomes a bitter spinster and talents die on the vine. Virgos instinctively respond to the needs of others. They make themselves so useful it leaves them vulnerable to exploitation. They are friendly and outgoing, but the truth is they are apt to be shy or inhibited in intimate contacts. One way they deal with this is to work quietly in the background while the attention is focused on others. Although intensely personal situations may be difficult for them, there are other situations when Virgos can be very dynamic. For example, when the spotlight is not directly on them but on a product or a service they offer, they are excellent salespersons. They patiently endure endless details and responsibilities, if convinced their efforts are justified.

Virgos are health conscious and, as a rule, they make an effort to stay physically fit. They don't mind tedious exercise routines, and they also enjoy tennis, racquetball, swimming, sailing, fishing, and biking. As athletes, Virgos may not be overly competitive, but they will attempt to perfect whatever skills they possess. Virgo colors are blue, yellow, gray, tan, navy, and lilac. Vulnerable parts of the body are the sinuses, respiratory system, and bowels. Colds, flu, allergies, and constipation are common Virgo complaints. The sapphire, which is a variety of the mineral corundum, is Virgo's birthstone. This gem was considered by ancient societies to be a love charm. Though they come in a variety of colors and can even be transparent, the most valuable sapphires are blue. Blue is also the principal color associated with Virgo. Flowers and plants for Virgo include aster, chrysanthemum, ivy, and fern.

In Virgo, the Sun is in its natural *second house.* If you think of Virgo's ego and drive in second-house terms, you can see why ...

Virgos are concerned with finance and are excellent bookkeepers and treasurers. They may be concerned with establishing values and priorities. Virgos are more strongly motivated when they work in areas that deal with the real world, the world of material goods and the most valuable services.

SUN IN LIBRA (September 23–24/October 22–23)

The ego, created for the purpose of individual expression, is unable to achieve this purpose of or by itself in the environment of Libra. The energy and direction the ego needs in order to develop must come from within and without in equal measure. Librans need other people. They need to understand relationships and cooperation. They need to understand the balance between the individual and society, and they need to achieve a compromise between the passion and the intellect. The physical world must come to terms with the nonphysical world. The objectivity of judgment needed for these tasks is characteristic of the Libran temperament. Librans are meant to seek true objectivity by refusing to be knocked off balance by the burdens of emotional or physical attachments. Individual Librans may not achieve or even strive for the type of objectivity and balance they need. Those who do achieve these things are the happiest and most productive.

Librans are doers. In spite of their need to be liked and reluctance to face confrontations, they are surprisingly strong-willed. They find ways to succeed one way or another, most often by using their wit and charm. When such ploys are ineffective, they can become uncharacteristically aggressive and determined to solve the matter then and there. Their change of attitude in such situations is usually effective enough to catch others off guard, allowing the Librans to gain control. If convinced that nothing more is to be gained no matter what they do, they won't hesitate to walk away from a situation with no further explanation or thought of returning. Librans require balance in their lives. In relationships, they invariably give back in kind what they have been given. The mental orientation of Librans may cause others to think they lack passion. This is not the case. Their passion is not apt to be sustained, however, if their interest in someone does not include intellectual rapport as well as physical attraction.

Venus, the planet of beauty and social grace, rules Libra. Venus enhances emotional, physical, and psychological pleasure derived from beauty in all forms. Books, music, flowers, and perfume are typical Venus-inspired delights. If their environment is not aesthetically pleasing, Librans can become depressed.

For Librans, social grace begins with good manners, extends to high-level diplomacy, and ends with absolute abhorrence of disagreeable confrontations. When forced to endure a fractious atmosphere, they do not think or function efficiently. Although they need partnership and association with other people, Librans do not like crowds and attempt to avoid them whenever possible.

Librans can exert impressive physical energy, but their stamina tends to run in cycles. They work hard, play hard, and then collapse. Librans have a prominent lazy streak when it comes to physical exercise. Few of them walk if they can ride. Fondness for rich food (sugar is their biggest weakness) makes it necessary to get proper physical exercise. However, if they have not been thoroughly indoctrinated in the virtues of physical fitness from childhood, and if they are not inspired by some outside influence to stay in shape, they turn into marshmallows. Tennis, horseback riding, skating, and aerobics are a few activities with special appeal for those Librans who do get out once in a while.

Libra colors are ivory, pink (or rose), turquoise, and blue. Vulnerable parts of the body are the kidneys, lumbar region of the back, and ovaries. Lower back pain and the problems caused by too much sugar or rich food are common complaints. Libra's birthstone is the opal. This unique gem consists mostly of ordinary sand and water. Just as hidden water in opals causes the fire in the gem,

there is more emotional content than is immediately apparent behind the brilliant flashes of the Libran intellect. Libra rules flowers in general, but particularly appropriate blooms for Librans include rose (white or pink), daisy, violet, aster, and orchid.

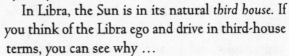

In Libra, the Sun is in its natural *third house*. If you think of the Libra ego and drive in third-house terms, you can see why ...

Librans are writers and communicators. They seek their life's work in some area that employs their mental ability and basic mechanical or design skills. They identify strongly on an intellectual level with siblings and those who occupy their neighborhood and daily environment. Librans frequently seek a career or job in their immediate neighborhood or with their siblings.

SUN IN SCORPIO (October 23–24 November 21–22)

The environment of Scorpio is dominated by emotional energy, the most deceptive power in the universe. It can easily be destroyed, but never conquered. It will rise like the mythical phoenix from its own ashes, stronger and more powerful than before. The ego that is born in the environment of Scorpio is not driven solely by need or desire. It is able to develop its own potential only through the mastery of these forces. As will be seen later in this description, the true Scorpio energy is rarely obvious until it is unleashed. For many Scorpios the compelling need to develop or use the power of their potential does not arise. This is why the easy-going, open personality of many Scorpios makes it difficult for them to identify with the intensity and secretiveness often described for their sign. Observed or not in a single individual, Scorpio traits are nevertheless always a Scorpio potential. There is the tendency, for example, to consciously or subconsciously dominate relationships. There is also reluctance to openly exhibit feelings. Even when Scorpios seem to be open, they always hold back something of themselves. They may not intend to be mysterious, but they manage to appear enigmatic anyway.

Scorpios are stubborn. Keys to their success are a strong will and the ability to get to the bottom of things. They want answers and doggedly persist until they get them. Though all Scorpios do not spend their lives pondering the mysteries of human emotions, most of them are inquisitive and probing individuals. They

are fascinated with how things work, especially people. They do not like being fooled or manipulated and react to such treatment with sarcasm and vengeful-ness. Their mental and physical powers of recuperation are remarkable.

Pluto, the planet of intensity and hidden power, rules Scorpio. Before the discovery of Pluto, Mars was considered to be the ruler of Scorpio. Both planets influence the nature of those born in this sign. The penetrating focus of their expressions and personality enhanced by Pluto can make Scorpios appear magnetic and powerful. The fiery energy of Mars is exhibited in their stamina and fierce determination. Their intensity can completely overwhelm others. The considerable energy of Scorpios is not aroused or employed just to have some-thing to do. They are not openly combative unless it becomes necessary. Privacy is tightly protected. Others know Scorpios only up to a certain point. They rarely show any sign of inner struggles. Scorpios are not arrogant or self-involved and, in fact, are quite interested in others and what others have to say.

Strong and competitive, Scorpios are exceptional athletes. They want real challenges and will not suffer would-be competitors who lack skills equal to their own. They enjoy body-building, soccer, hockey, hunting, swimming, scuba diving, and spelunking. Scorpios are resourceful. Recycling, rehabilitation, and renovating are typical activities for which they are well suited. Scorpios are immensely creative. They are outstanding cooks, writers, designers, and composers. Shrewd ability to assess the value of resources makes them excellent real estate agents and developers, bankers, stockbrokers, and financial planners.

Scorpio colors are red, black, midnight blue, and emerald green. Vulnerable parts of the body are the reproductive organs and excretory system. Headaches, infections, and fevers are Scorpio complaints. Topaz is Scorpio's birthstone. The Roman naturalist, Pliny the Elder, traced the name to the Island of Topazos, which in Greek means "to guess." This meaning fairly describes the inquisitive, mystery-loving nature of Scorpio. Topaz, one of the hardest minerals, cannot be cut with a knife. It is another representation of the impenetrable Scorpio nature. Scorpio flowers include the anemone, heather, and gardenia.

In Scorpio, the Sun is in its natural *fourth house.* If you think of the Scorpio ego and drive in fourth-house terms, you can see why ...

Scorpios identify with home and family, and many of them possess domestic talents as cooks, gardeners, interior designers. They are deeply interested in family origins and the psychology of family relationships. Scorpios work in real estate and others areas that involve domestic products and services, and they work for family finances and family businesses.

SUN IN SAGITTARIUS (November 22–23/December 20–21)

⊙♐ The ego in the environment of Sagittarius is restless and hungry to experience the full range of its own powers. It is driven to constantly overreach itself, to pounce on every opportunity that affords it a means of growth and recognition. Those born in Sagittarius seek higher levels of spiritual growth, more physical experiences, greater prosperity, higher intellectual achievements, advanced social and professional status, greater aesthetic appreciation and understanding. Sagittarians are natural politicians, interested in knowing everyone and in going everywhere. They possess intellectual curiosity that covers a wide range of subjects. Never try to present Sagittarians with facts because they already have an unlimited supply. They become bored when surrounded by people or circumstances in which they have no interest. They would rather learn things on their own through travel and personal experience than endure structured classroom environments and routine work assignments. Ironically, given opportunities to broaden their knowledge and gain experience on their own, they become excellent teachers and administrators in the very educational system they once found so restricting.

One of the hallmarks of the true Sagittarian is independence. Sagittarius is the sign of the bachelor. Even happily married Sagittarians seek to maintain some aspect of personal independence. Nothing will drive them away from a relationship or a situation faster than the threat of being confined or restricted. Sagittarians readily adapt to change. They feel comfortable and at home wherever they happen to be. They are very talkative and do not hesitate to give their honest opinions, a gesture which can seem tactless at times, though it is rarely their intention to be cruel.

Jupiter, the planet of bountiful fortune and good luck, rules Sagittarius. Jupiter promotes the spirit of generosity and optimism, and encourages merriment and humor. Addicted to all the good things in life, Sagittarians know how to get maximum enjoyment from them. Unfortunately too much of a good thing can be ruinous, and prudence is a difficult trait for most Sagittarians to acquire.

Their innate philosophy that "more is better" aptly describes their tendency to go overboard. Being overly spiritual or too philosophical, for example, they become too far out of touch with the real world. Making overblown efforts to be prudent in one area, they still manage to bankrupt themselves in other areas. Attempting to be prudent, they become misers.

Sagittarians are enthusiastic sportsmen. They enjoy physically challenging endeavors of all kinds. Archery, jogging, hang gliding, sailing, and fishing (especially for big sport fish, such as swordfish or blue marlin) are favorite activities. One of their biggest challenges may be the battle of the bulge when their fondness for great quantities of food and drink finally catches up with them. They are natural gamblers and often have the good fortune to come out on the winning side of their wagers, especially when they try their luck at horse or dog racing. Sagittarians are clever at imitation and mimicry, though how or if they will ever use this potential is hard to predict. For some it may be skill with languages, for others it may be acting ability or talent for photography. They love music, art, dance, and drama (theater), and many of them have considerable talent in these areas.

Sagittarian colors are maroon, tan, navy, orange, and cobalt blue. Vulnerable parts of the body are the thighs, hips, and, to some extent, the feet. Many of their physical complaints result from unrestricted eating habits or indulgence in other pleasures. Turquoise is the birthstone for Sagittarius. Turquoise, prized since antiquity, was believed to enhance wisdom and understanding. This is an appropriate association with Sagittarius, the sign of those who seek knowledge and truth. Because Sagittarius is associated with bigness in general, flowers for this sign include larger blooms such as hydrangea, dahlia, and peony.

In Sagittarius, the Sun is in its natural *fifth house*. If you think of the Sagittarius ego and drive in fifth-house terms, you can see why ...

Sagittarians identify strongly with creative talent, are devoted to unique and original projects, and concern themselves with the development and education of children. They see themselves as great adventurers and often seek their life's work in the field of art or entertainment.

SUN IN CAPRICORN (December 21–22/January 19–20)

☉ ♑ Born in the environment of Capricorn, the ego is controlled by structure and form. The energy it needs to develop comes from purpose and direction. Capricorns are therefore goal-oriented. It is their essential nature to establish and to be guided in life by goals. Their ambitious, pragmatic nature inspires them to learn how to get things done. Getting things done is what Capricorns do best. To get things done requires being in charge, being the one who controls what happens. And this is what Capricorns aspire to do. They seek positions of control and authority, and they admire others who attain such positions. The mountain goat is an appropriate astrological symbol for this sign since a sure-footed, methodical climb to the top is the main goal of Capricorn individuals. Initiative and willingness to accept responsibilities are keys to their success. Capricorns always want to know where they stand in situations, in relationships, and in society. They are not afraid to act but before they do, they want to plan their move, to assess what they will actually accomplish and what may be lost or wasted in the process. If they believe they can succeed in attaining a goal, they will persevere in their efforts for as long as it takes. However, Capricorns can be very lazy when they lack goals.

Even when they are outwardly aggressive and competitive, Capricorns can harbor an inner lack of confidence which makes them defensive. They fear rejection. Wanting to be admired and respected, they do not want to appear weak or ineffective. They have a good sense of humor but will not tolerate being ridiculed or teased on a personal level. Those who set out to so abuse a Capricorn will soon learn the error of their ways. As children, Capricorns possess unusual maturity. They are in a hurry to participate in the adult world and often prefer being with adults than with their peers. Capricorns look older or more mature when they are young, but when they reach middle age, they seem to defy the aging process, retaining a youthful appearance well into old age.

Saturn, the cosmic timekeeper and taskmaster, is the ruler of Capricorn. Saturn inspires the need to protect and preserve. Saturn encourages the love of tradition, ritual, propriety. It is the structure and formality of all these things that guide Capricorns through life.

Capricorns usually do not have a predisposition to be fat. Good dietary habits in their youth tend to stay with them as adults. Enthusiastic sportsmen, they enjoy jogging, running (especially cross country), golf, skating, hunting,

wrestling, boxing, martial arts, and body-building. Some Capricorns are so determined to win, it is difficult for them to be gracious when they lose. They make good team players as well as good team managers. Many Capricorns collect guns and other weapons, perhaps because these things are undeniable symbols of authority.

Capricorn colors are chocolate brown, royal and navy blue, dark green, charcoal gray, and red. Vulnerable parts of the body are bones and joints (especially the knees), teeth, and skin. Although sensitive skin, allergies, and broken bones are their most likely complaints, worrying too much can also result in physical problems. The garnet is Capricorn's birthstone. This gemstone is believed to keep its wearers from accidents and falls. In some ancient societies, garnets were worn only by royalty. Capricorn flowers include camellia, orange blossom, carnation (red), magnolia, and baby's breath.

In Capricorn, the Sun is in its natural *sixth house*. If you think of the Capricorn ego and drive in sixth-house terms, you can see why ...

Capricorns are workaholics. They are forever involved in taking care of business and are good employers as well as employees. They accept responsibility for others and don't mind taking care of mundane tasks and details. They are concerned with health and physical fitness.

Sun in Aquarius (January 20–21/February 19–20)

The mental energy that dominates the environment of Aquarius directs the ego to identify itself with ideas and concepts. The main concept for those born in Aquarius is to retain the expression of their own individuality even while thrusting themselves outward into society as a whole. Is the individual more important than the state, or should the individual live for the state? Is the individual more important than the family, or should the individual live for the family? That is the basic Aquarian issue. There are always going to be Aquarians who head for one extreme or the other. Those who go overboard one way react violently to any restrictions on the right to express themselves as they wish. Aquarians who go the other way give up their private lives and needs to work for the common good. Most Aquarians, however, become well integrated members of society.

Aquarians are the original "organization men" of the zodiac. They take on the role of making the organizations of society function as the people-oriented institutions they were intended to be. Aquarians are loyal, fair, and objective and, as a result, attract many friends and acquaintances. Though they are not above wanting to live well, many Aquarians are more interested in people than they are in amassing great wealth or taking on the responsibilities that invariably accompany such a life style. When they cannot afford some luxury, they rationalize why they didn't need it in the first place.

Aquarians are idealists who champion the highest principles to which humanity can aspire. However, they are also extremely independent thinkers. They don't mind being asked to do something, but they resent being told to do it. When confronted with authoritarian demands to which they do not subscribe, they rebel. They may hesitate to take the initiative at times, but once they decide a situation or idea is worthwhile, they become totally involved and aggressive in pushing it forward.

The independence and mental orientation of Aquarians can make them appear interested but not particularly passionate or possessive in close relationships. It does not necessarily mean they really do lack passion. When they fall in love, their passion can be as intense as it is inspirational.

The modern ruler of Aquarius is Uranus, planet of the unorthodox and eclectic. Before Uranus was discovered, Saturn was given rulership of Aquarius. Saturn is the planet of restriction and structure while Uranus is the planet of originality and freedom. Such different characteristics seem to contradict one another directly, but a close look at the Aquarian personality shows that both planets co-exist in a strangely compatible way. When Aquarians suddenly change course or do something unexpected, they are likely to do so for some very practical or advantageous reason. They favor the unique as well as the traditional. Sometimes they are so involved with the past (history and antiques) or so tuned in to the future (spaceships and neon clothes), they lose track of the present. Exhibiting the stability of Saturn, they may live unvaried, even boring lives, feeling very comfortable and secure in such an unchanging environment. Sooner or later, however, they are apt to encounter unexpected circumstances that make it hard to predict what they will be doing next. They often adopt life styles and ideas counter to current trends. The odd and unique fascinate them, and they are rarely caught off guard by abnormal situations and strange people.

Aquarians are not likely to miss any meals but most of them don't care what's on the menu. Unless they are reared in a home devoted to eating and preparing food, they are often indifferent when it comes to food. As a rule they are enthusiastic participants in sports that involve a partner or a team. Tennis, racquetball, and baseball are favorite activities. Science and engineering, international finance, writing, music, psychology, or social work are areas of special interest to Aquarians.

Aquarian colors are silver, aqua, purple, and the more electric shades of pink and blue. Vulnerable parts of the body are the shins, ankles, and circulatory system. Aquarians are apt to experience cramps, allergies, sudden illness, and freak accidents, though they may also suffer from various nervous disorders.

The birthstone for Aquarius is amethyst. This gem is believed to confer stability and mental poise on those who wear it. Flowers for Aquarians are the more unusual blossoms and include the gladiolus, tiger lily, trillium, bird of paradise, and jack in the pulpit.

In Aquarius, the Sun is in its natural *seventh house*. If you think of the Aquarius ego and drive in seventh-house terms, you can see why ...

Aquarians make good partners and they identify very strongly on an intellectual level with their partners and other allies. They are excellent at promotion, public relations, and organizing others in cooperative efforts. Aquarians champion equal rights and fairness for all people.

SUN IN PISCES (February 18–19/March 19–20)

☉♓ The ego must steer its course through the sea of need and desire in the emotionally dominated environment of Pisces. If the ego becomes burdened by desire for physical or mental achievements, it sinks like a millstone. It is spirituality and ideals that keep Pisceans afloat. Although not all Pisceans are concerned with lofty aspirations, the notion of perfection is a strong factor in their personality. They find it difficult to deal with people and situations that do not live up to their idealized images. It isn't that they can't see things clearly, they just don't want to accept them as they really are. Seeking greater perfection than the real world can produce, Pisceans often turn to religion or other spiritual and philosophical disciplines.

Pisceans are flexible, which makes them survivors. Because they so easily identify with others, Pisceans who lack a healthy ego risk exploitation and neglect of their own needs and talent. The opposite side of the coin is that Pisceans can exploit those they understand so intimately. Pisceans are so sensitive that it is easy for them to develop the attitude that they must hurt others before others can hurt them. The ultimate choice for Pisceans is either to be strong as well as sensitive, or to be a victim of their own vulnerability. An addictive nature makes it necessary for Pisceans to avoid habit-forming drugs and other harmful substances. To maintain their emotional equilibrium, they need a private place or a private time for daily retreat and relaxation. The most creative, stimulating, and soothing environment for Pisceans is near water. Pisceans are compassionate, fair-minded, and courageous. They are not afraid to bend rules if the situation demands a more humane approach. They are excellent judges, sensitive administrators, and inspirational teachers.

Neptune, the planet of spirituality and idealism, rules Pisces. Before Neptune was discovered, Jupiter was given rulership of this sign. Jupiter also represents spiritual growth and philosophical ideals, so both planets blend together to encourage an identification with all that is noble and perfect. Pisceans are often shy and would much rather impersonate someone else than be themselves. That's why so many are actors, artists, writers, and dreamers. Neptune's influence inspires vague and elusive qualities, so it is hard to predict how Pisceans will develop. Some of them are extremely neat and well organized, while others become slovenly and careless. Personal habits are often a direct reflection of emotional reactions to their environment. Pisceans have remarkable imaginations, which make some of them successful writers of fiction and turn others into pathological liars. Unique ability to understand the abstract makes them gifted mathematicians and theorists, or it can put them so out of touch with reality that they make no sense at all.

For Pisceans the vulnerable parts of the body are the feet and lymphatic system. Swelling, allergic reaction to drugs, and sore feet are common complaints, but they are also apt to experience psychosomatic illness. Emotional insecurity can make them compulsive eaters who face a lifelong battle of the bulge. As if to confront their own vulnerability, many Pisceans are daredevils, becoming race car drivers, aviators, explorers, and hunters. Sports and physical fitness routines help them stay in shape as well as reduce emotional stress. Horseback riding, dancing, skating, swimming, or sailing are favored activities.

Piscean colors are pale green, purple, rose, and gray blue. The Piscean birth-stone is the aquamarine. The sea-colored aquamarine becomes invisible when submerged in water. This is appropriate representation of the shy Pisceans who often wish they could disappear. Flowers for Pisces are orchid, lilac, wisteria, water lily (lotus), poppy (white), and pansy.

In Pisces, the Sun is in its natural *eighth house*. If you think of the Pisces ego and drive in eighth-house terms, you can see why …

Pisceans may be secretive or reluctant to reveal their inner struggles. They may seek work in areas that involve natural resources, insurance, taxes, or debt.

The development of their ego or sense of self-worth may be profoundly affected positively or negatively by the way they handle joint income or inherited property.

MOON IN THE SIGNS

The Moon is the changing kaleidoscope of an individual's feelings and moods. It describes emotional reactions and experiences. The Moon is personality, desire, and need. It is memory, instincts, and intuition.

MOON IN ARIES

There is bound to be a quickening of the emotional force in Aries, which is why those born with Moon in Aries immediately turn feelings into action. They want instant gratification. They go after what they want with passion and energy, and soon lose interest in people who don't demonstrate the same kind of enthusiasm. Many of these individuals find it difficult to settle down to responsibilities and the drudgery of daily routine. On a short-term basis, lunar Arians get passionately involved with people and projects, but until they reach an age or level of maturity that gives them a different perspective, they are not inclined to become involved in long-term commitments. Their easily aroused emotions can be dangerously misguided at times, especially when they act in haste or anger.

Aries Moon personalities are not easily put off when their efforts fail. If one approach doesn't work, they cheerfully try another. These individuals were

meant to be the masters of their own success or failure in getting what they want in life. Some relish this challenge. Others blame their mistakes and lack of progress on everyone else. The self-assertiveness of lunar Arians makes them resentful of authority and impatient with people who try to give them direction or advice, but personal forcefulness is also what helps them get ahead in the world. They may be guilty of being self-indulgent, overconfident, and foolhardy, but they are also inspired leaders and tireless in their efforts to help others. Their soul mates in life are often people with Libra Sun or Libra Ascendant.

Women with Aries Moon are too aggressive or competitive in romance and other situations that require a subtle approach. On the other hand, these ladies are admirably well suited to conquer many challenges that destroy more fragile females. Men with Aries Moon expect too much and give too little in romance. They may not particularly like women and feel ill at ease with them. These men may be jealous, but are never very devious.

In Aries, the Moon is in its natural *tenth house*. If you think of emotional needs and other Moon-related aspects of an individual's life in tenth-house terms, you may be able to see why ...

Aries Moon individuals act out their feelings in public or in a public way. Their popularity and public reputation are very important to them. Lunar Arians want to work for themselves, and they are more apt to pursue a career rather than be content with just a job.

MOON IN TAURUS

In the materially oriented environment of Taurus, the Moon is grounded in the physical world. Those born with Moon in Taurus don't want to give up one thing in order to get another unless they know it will be to their advantage. These individuals trade up, or they don't trade at all. Moon in Taurus people require tangible proof of affection from others, but they are also willing to show their affection in the same way. Strong physical appetites push them to gratify their desires whenever they have the opportunity. Material comforts and the advantages of wealth are important, and they can be overly concerned with social status. Although they enjoy and want the stability of a home and family, lunar Taureans are not necessarily homebodies. In fact, most of

them spend far more time on social activities than they do on household chores.

Taurus Moon personalities do not react well to being rushed or forced into commitments. Once these individuals decide to make a commitment, however, it is usually solid and they are faithful to it. These individuals possess calm and quiet temperaments that have a reassuring influence on others. It is not easy for lunar Taureans to accept when something goes wrong, and it may take a long time for them to adjust to or rectify a situation that has failed or disappointed them. People who break promises or do not keep their word eventually learn that Moon in Taurus individuals have long memories. They may forgive, but they rarely forget. They are often attracted in friendship and love to people with Sun or Ascendant in Scorpio.

Women with Taurus Moon are independent and self-reliant, although they frequently gain substantial material assets through marriage. Their nature is to spend lavishly in some areas and be surprisingly frugal in others. Men with Taurus Moon are charming and diplomatic in social situations, and considerate, sensual partners in romantic encounters. Although they can be very hedonistic when it comes to satisfying their personal needs, these men are unselfishly devoted to their children.

In Taurus, the Moon is in its natural *eleventh house*. If you think of emotional needs and other Moon-related aspects of an individual's life in eleventh-house terms, you may be able to see why ...

Moon in Taurus individuals form strong emotional attachments to friends. They enjoy participating in groups and associations, and they may be quite concerned about or involved with the recognition and popularity they gain as a result of their efforts in organizational activities.

MOON IN GEMINI

When the Moon is in Gemini, the emotions become conduits of information that are instantly processed and integrated into attitude and behavior. Lunar Geminis often respond to situations in a way they think others expect them to. Their reactions seem detached, as if whatever is going on is not really happening to them. They will deal with their feelings, of course, but the process is delayed while their minds are busy absorbing the facts. Moon in

Gemini people can sometimes take their intellectual approach too far. Constant analysis, rationalization, and acting as though they had already experienced a thing instead of just thinking or talking about it can prevent them from ever doing it. Talkative, mentally alert, and curious about everything, these individuals always seem to know what's going on around them. Continually looking for intellectual stimulation, they are easily bored with repetitive jobs and uninteresting people. Restless and impatient, they do not always get all the facts before repeating what they see or hear. As eager to share information as they are to receive it, many lunar Geminis are natural teachers, writers, and communicators. They love secrets, mysteries, and solving puzzles.

Gemini Moon personalities are emotionally flexible, which allows them to identify with both sides of an issue and with a very wide range of people. They instinctively understand what people want to hear and what it is that satisfies others, yet they don't always know how to make themselves happy. Because they can be so outwardly cheerful and optimistic, few people would guess that lunar Geminis can feel lonely and isolated. Though quite willing to discuss others, they can be secretive about themselves. Their closest relationships are often with people who have Sun or Ascendant in Sagittarius. They have highly sensitive nervous systems. A variety of tasks, frequent changes of scene, and alterations in their daily routine help these individuals maintain physical and mental health.

Women with Gemini Moon are talented with their hands. These ladies are efficient and organized, but restlessness makes it difficult for them to remain content with household chores. Men with Gemini Moon are quite charming, but their temperament is not particularly suited to sustaining passion in themselves and tolerating emotional hysteria in others.

In Gemini, the Moon is in its natural *twelfth house*. If you think of emotional needs and other Moon-related aspects of an individual's life in twelfth-house terms, you may be able to see why ...

Moon in Gemini individuals are interested in the occult, dreams, and the subconscious mind. Many of them possess remarkable instincts, but they also suffer from insomnia. Lunar Geminis are apt to engage in secret emotional attachments, desires, and fantasies. They have strong memories of the past and are emotionally tied to it. Lunar Geminis are uncomfortable in the company of strangers.

85

MOON IN CANCER

☽♋ The Moon is the ruler of Cancer and thus it is quite at home in this environment. The strong emotional orientation of the Moon in its own sign implies individuals with enhanced sensitivity, intuition, and artistic talent, or at least great appreciation for the arts. Lunar Cancerians are so receptive as to be unusually vulnerable to the influence of those with whom they spend the most time. It is sometimes hard to distinguish whether they are expressing their own opinions or merely reflecting those of someone else. They can be extremely passive when it comes to extricating themselves from unhappy emotional situations. They may cling to such situations even after they manage to find happiness elsewhere. Lack of motivation can make them lazy, disorganized, and sloppy. Moon in Cancer people hate to throw anything away. They are often too possessive or overly concerned, especially with children.

Cancerian Moon personalities may be soft-spoken and even shy, but they can become very aggressive when it comes to pursuing their desires and satisfying their emotional needs. Many of them, especially men with Cancer Moon, exhibit a certain awkwardness in their bearing and approach. Their nurturing nature makes them caring and compassionate, although at times their altruism is deceptively self-serving. Strong identification with the concept of family makes them treat everyone as part of the family, an approach they successfully employ in getting others to cooperate. As babies, lunar Cancerians tend to be finicky eaters or develop food allergies; as adults, they use food as an emotional pacifier. The partners and allies they frequently choose are people with Sun or Ascendant in Capricorn.

Women with Moon in Cancer are vulnerable, possessive, dependent, demanding, and at the mercy of their feelings. Emotionally they are their own worst enemy. These women are, however, highly intuitive and creative once they learn to control their emotional tidal waves. Men with Cancer Moon have a streak of domesticity, the potential of which includes gardening, cooking, or concern with household furnishings. It is often hard for them to act with sustained aggressiveness in emotional situations.

86

PLANETS IN THE SIGNS

In Cancer, the Moon is in its natural *first house*. If you think of emotional needs and other Moon-related aspects of an individual's life in first-house terms, you may be able to see why …

Moon in Cancer individuals have changeable personalities and tend to retain fluid in their bodies. Many of these individuals physically resemble their mother's side of the family. They view their offspring as extensions of themselves. Lunar Cancerians are highly sensitive to any sort of personal criticism.

MOON IN LEO

The environment of Leo animates and enlivens the Moon's creativity and emotional force. It is not surprising that people born with Moon in Leo are artistic, imaginative, and interested in art, architecture, and design. Lunar Leos are magnanimous and passionate in expressing their feelings. In the excitement of a particular moment, these individuals make promises they don't always carry out. Stubborn pride is their emotional downfall. They cannot separate their feelings from their ego, and it is ego that prompts them to dominate relationships. They have a jealous nature, although they are not particularly possessive. When a romance ends, they are more apt to suffer from a wounded ego than a broken heart. They are often attracted to those with Sun or Ascendant in Aquarius.

Their cooperation is gained by applying subtle flattery. On the other hand, they become completely intransigent when they are backed up against the wall. Although Leo Moon personalities are stubborn, they have great purpose, determination, and tenacity when it comes to getting what they want. Strongly idealistic, these individuals are capable of great personal sacrifice. They are very assertive when it comes to protecting not only their own freedom but also the rights and freedom of others.

Women with Leo Moon are forceful, materialistic, and preoccupied with status. However, they are also able to accept responsibilities as a matter of honor and behave with exceptional grace and dignity in the face of insult and adversity. Men with Leo Moon can be braggarts who always want the last word. They have endless schemes and grandiose plans, and seek all the

good things in life. When good fortune does come their way, these men are generous in sharing it with others.

In Leo, the Moon is in its natural *second house*. If you think of emotional needs and other Moon related aspects of an individual's life in second-house terms, you may be able to see why ...

Moon in Leo people are interested in business and finance, and have good instincts when it comes to handling money and material assets. These individual may tend to identify emotionally with wealth or status, or spend money to impress others. Their values and/or priorities may be very changeable.

MOON IN VIRGO

☽ ♍ The environment in Virgo imparts modesty to the Moon, which is why lunar Virgos are often so guarded about their feelings. They put up invisible barriers that prevent others from getting close to them. An over crit-ical or too analytical approach to emotional situations also makes it difficult for lunar Virgos to express their feelings freely or spontaneously. Serious minded, with common sense about most things, they are also idealists and, as a result, they can be surprisingly unrealistic when idealism interferes with their judgment. Creativity in these individuals always has some practical element. As writers or artists, for example, they take few risks, usually sticking to what they know best.

Virgo Moon personalities are emotionally adaptable. They instinctively seem to know what it takes to make others feel better. Their compassion can some-times be confused with passion. They make many friends because of their sympa-thetic nature, but it also leaves them vulnerable to exploitation. When it comes to intimate relationships, they are frequently attracted to people with Sun or Ascendant in Pisces. All lunar Virgos are not scholars, but many of them are avid readers, good writers, excellent teachers and communicators. Intellectual curiosity gives these individuals a proclivity for gathering information. This tendency can turn them to serious research endeavors, or merely develop into fondness for gossip. Moon in Virgo people can sometimes be overly fastidious or finicky, usually with regard to eating habits. Many of them have an interest in health and make some field of health care their life's work. On the other hand, preoccupation with their own health causes some of them to become hypochon-driacs or use maladies to attract sympathy.

Women with Virgo Moon may encounter sorrow through marriage. They can be dreadful nags themselves or become the victims of a nagging spouse.

These ladies are, however, the most faithful and responsible of guardians, perhaps best described as the salt of the earth. Men with Virgo Moon tend to idealize their wives, but may not be very passionate toward them.

Their quiet emotional nature tends toward domesticity, but these men often have a secret desire for flamboyancy and intrigue.

In Virgo, the Moon is in its natural *third house*. If you think of emotional needs and other Moon-related aspects of an individual's life in third-house terms, you may be able to see why ...

Moon in Virgo individuals reside in the same neighborhood all of their lives. They have a strong emotional attachment to siblings, and may also form strong attachments with neighbors. Their emotional needs are often expressed in letters or a diary.

MOON IN LIBRA

Balance and objectivity, the primary orientations of the energy in Libra's environment, are not easy for the emotional Moon to absorb. Individuals with Moon in Libra need to maintain emotional perspective or their mental and physical health suffers. For these individuals to establish a long-term relationship, they must share an intellectual rapport as well as physical attraction with their partner. They don't want to be emotionally compromised, preferring to let go of a relationship if their partner is not equally willing or enthusiastic. But neither are they inclined to live alone, so it becomes a crucial search for the right partner or at the very least an amiable companion. Lunar Librans are apt to be attracted to people who have Sun or Ascendant in Aries. Their accomplishments are often the direct result of the stimulation and encouragement they receive from other people.

Libra Moon personalities are excellent at planning and preparing projects, but most of the time they would rather charm others into physically carrying them out. Although they are excellent at strategy and problem-solving in their business or profession, they can be impractical, overindulgent, or inconsistent when it comes to handling personal situations. These individuals have strong attachment to home and family, even though it is not always obvious in their lifestyle. In one way or another, they encounter more than an average share of good

and bad experiences with partners, legal matters, and making choices. Their enhanced aesthetic tastes are demonstrated, for the most part, in dressing well and maintaining an attractively decorated home.

The emotional temperament of women with Moon in Libra inclines them more toward engaging financial matters, social activities, and intellectual endeavors than toward raising children and paying attention to household chores. Men with Libra Moon are interested in cooking, home furnishings, and gardening. There are apt to be one or two strong or influential females in their background. If their mate fails to keep them mentally stimulated, their physical attention tends to wander. Their mother may have been the primary guardian.

In Libra, the Moon is in its natural *fourth house*. If you think of emotional needs and other Moon-related aspects of an individual's life in fourth-house terms, you may be able to see why ...

Moon in Libra individuals are very interested in their family's history. Their work or hobby involves food preparation or dietary planning. Many of them are profoundly influenced by their mother and their homes provide emotional satisfaction. Their domestic environment can be unstable and family ties are vulnerable to change. They may reside in the same house or hometown all of their lives.

MOON IN SCORPIO

☽ ♏ There are many secret places for the Moon to hide in the watery depths of Scorpio. People born with Moon in Scorpio are not inclined to reveal or discuss their feelings, and especially so if they are subjected to emotional manipulation or deprivation in childhood. Their emotional isolationism can be deceptive, however, since most of them are outwardly easygoing and cheerful individuals. There is no denying that there is also a large potential for hedonism, possessiveness, jealousy, and revenge in lunar Scorpios, but not all of them are given to venting such destructive emotions. Those who do open themselves up to negative energies are likely to suffer accordingly, reaping their rewards in this life rather than the next.

Scorpio Moon personalities are stubborn. They resist changing their opinions and behavior and it is hard for them to break undesirable habits. Once they

make a commitment or establish a relationship, they tenaciously hang on forever, even to bad relationships. They often form their closest emotional bonds with people who have Sun or Ascendant in Taurus. Lunar Scorpios can develop an amazing ability to overcome adversity. Instinctive understanding of human motivation and behavior gives these individuals an emotional advantage, a conscious or subconscious way to control themselves as well as others. The mistake many of them make is being so intent on controlling others that they never learn to control themselves effectively.

Women with Scorpio Moon are apt to be shrewd, and, when they possess intelligence, it is likely to be brilliant. Their desires are not easily satisfied and their ambitions are rarely knocked off course by temporary distractions. Men with Scorpio Moon are very romantic and imaginative when properly stimulated. When forced to endure intimate relationships that are uninteresting and nonchallenging, they become sarcastic and sometimes cruel. In their work, however, these men are well suited to handling economic, human, and natural resources.

In Scorpio, the Moon is in its natural *fifth house*. If you think of emotional needs and other Moon-related aspects of an individual's life in fifth-house terms, you may be able to see why ...

Moon in Scorpio people love to have a good time. Their offspring may be their biggest emotional challenge. They seek an environment near water to truly relax, and may reside in a resort area. Moon in Scorpio individuals get the most emotional satisfaction from creative projects or from building their own home.

MOON IN SAGITTARIUS

The wide open spaces associated with Sagittarius allow the Moon to grow large in all directions, which is why those born with Moon in Sagittarius are emotionally expansive, idealistic, and romantic. Their adventurous natures and magnanimous generosity are a curse as well as a blessing. This combination of traits makes them vulnerable to exploitation, but it is just what they need to become enormously successful in life. Lunar Sagittarians are open and honest with a tendency to be too candid at times, especially in situations that require a more diplomatic approach. Impatience is frequently the biggest stumbling

block to getting what they want. They are not reluctant to make long-term emotional commitments, but relationships or situations that restrict their personal freedom too much eventually fall apart. Their most intimate relationships are apt to involve those with Sun or Ascendant in Gemini.

Sagittarius Moon personalities are emotionally adaptable to changing circumstances and different relationships. Emotional duality makes them fickle and insecure, and at the same time steadfast and independent. Concerned with making an impression on others, they may be guilty of inflating their own knowledge and importance. Attracted to architecture, art and design, many of them also have interest and talent for mimicry and acting. Lunar Sagittarians are happiest when their work involves writing, teaching, performing, sales, education, or communication.

Women with Sagittarius Moon make better friends than lovers, although their restlessness may lead to many sexual adventures. Friendship is very important to these ladies, and their temperament is not well suited to living a quiet domestic life. Men with Sagittarius Moon are inveterate chasers of the ideal woman. Their emotional nature is uncomplicated in love, loyal in friendship, and, at times, apt to make them amazingly prophetic.

In Sagittarius, the Moon is in its natural *sixth house*. If you think of emotional needs and other Moon-related aspects of an individual's life in sixth-house terms, you may be able to see why ...

Moon in Sagittarius people are always concerned with their health. They exhibit uneven work habits. Their employment may be in their home or in a family-owned business, and they become emotionally attached to those who work for or with them.

MOON IN CAPRICORN

☽ ♑ The rigid structure and purposeful energy in the environment of Capricorn greatly reduce the spontaneity, warmth, and imagination of the Moon's emotional force, although it does gain some needed stability. Those born with the Moon in Capricorn don't nonchalantly establish long-term relationships, and those who do invariably suffer for their haste. Most lunar Capricorns may hesitate to move at all unless they feel they are on solid ground. They are more than willing to fulfill what they perceive as their responsibilities in a

relationship, but they are often unable or unwilling to understand what the other person actually wants or needs. Their greatest tendency is to worry. To help reduce the need for worry, they seek structure and stability in their lives. They find it hard to relate to those who do not share their opinions and values. Reluctant or unable to discuss their own problems, lunar Capricorns are nevertheless quite willing to help others. It is never very easy for them to express their deepest emotions, or to feel relaxed and content inside themselves. Fear of rejection is strong. Anything vague or unspecified in a relationship, whether business or personal, makes them feel insecure. They must know where they stand. Everything must be proper and legal. When it comes to romance and marriage, it may take them longer to find someone they can trust as well as love. Their marriage or business partners are often people with Sun or Ascendant in Cancer.

Capricorn Moon personalities are ambitious and strong-willed. Their efforts are primarily directed to their own advancement, although they can also be very effective and generous in helping others to progress. They enjoy being in the spotlight, which prompts many of them to seek a public or prominent position in their work or other activities. They have great respect for knowledge and are often quite intelligent themselves. Tendency to harbor anger and resentment can cause physical maladies and depression.

Women with Capricorn Moon are likely to be ambitious at the expense of their personal life. More interested in gaining material wealth and status, or overburdened with too many responsibilities, they miss the joy and satisfaction of relationships. They are excellent administrators. Men with Capricorn Moon have difficulty relating to women. Relationships with females may be too formal to allow warmth and closeness, or the bond they share may be so tight as to be emotionally crippling. Their complicated emotional nature must be handled with considerable patience and understanding.

In Capricorn, the Moon is in its natural *seventh house.* If you think of emotional needs and other Moon-related aspects of an individual's life in seventh-house terms, you may be able to see why ...

Moon in Capricorn people demand much from their marriage partner. They need to express their feelings to other people, but this only extends to public matters and nonintimate matters. Lunar Capricorns tend

93

to identify strongly on an emotional level with their spouse, with their spouse's family, and with other partners and close allies. They have a fear of lawsuits.

MOON IN AQUARIUS

☽ ♒ The emotional force loses some of the intimate passion and unquali-
♒ fied compassion when the Moon encounters the nonpersonal envi-
ronment of ideas and communication in Aquarius. Those born with Moon in Aquarius appear emotionally cool, but they are loving and loyal in their own way. They can be very sympathetic without being sentimental. Rarely beset with moodiness themselves, they often fail to pay attention to it in others, giving the impression they don't care. Idealistic, optimistic, and friendly, they are unbiased and liberal in their treatment of people in general. Moon in Aquarius individuals are highly social and attract friends and acquaintances from all social and cultural backgrounds. They have trouble focusing attention on just one person. As far as they are concerned, "the more the merrier." In spite of whatever eccentricities show up in their personality, they are emotionally stable. Something in their emotional makeup gives them remarkable ability to calm those who are mentally disturbed or hysterical. When disappointed or unhappy, lunar Aquarians focus on their activities and chores with such aplomb that other people may not even realize they are upset.

Aquarius Moon personalities are stubborn and opinionated, and the more emotional they get the more recalcitrant they become. Once they make a commitment they are dedicated to it. They are attracted to people with Sun or Ascendant in Leo. Strong individualism and an eccentric nature can make marriage a chore. Marriage or raising a family rarely changes their way of thinking and doing things. Independent or not, however, their attitudes and opinions usually turn out to be pretty traditional.

Women with Aquarius Moon are often better friends and companions to their children than they are traditional nurturing mothers. Their interest in business or social affairs can distract them from ordinary domestic life. They may experience sorrow and disappointment in female relationships. Men with Aquarius Moon display little jealousy or possessiveness in romantic relationships, a tendency that is sometimes interpreted by their partners as lack of love.

Pursuing ideals and mental endeavors are often more important to them than amassing material wealth.

In Aquarius, the Moon is in its natural *eighth house*. If you think of emotional needs and other Moon-related aspects of an individual's life in eighth-house terms, you may be able to see why ...

Moon in Aquarius individuals are more emotionally involved than most people in matters related to joint income, debt, insurance, taxes, and inheritance. For the sake of their own happiness, they need to be independent in money matters. Their emotional stability is tied to their own resourcefulness. Many lunar Aquarians are excellent fund-raisers.

MOON IN PISCES

)☽ ♓ The emotional force of the Moon is easily cast adrift in the waters of Pisces, and those born with Moon in Pisces are at the mercy of their sensitive nature. Wounded by insults and beset with fear of rejection and other insecurities, they do not do well in relationships with people who are emotionally tough and independent. As a defense mechanism to protect their inner vulnerability, lunar Pisceans can turn into bullies. It is best for these individuals to adopt a religious or philosophical outlook that can provide them with an underlying strength their temperament does not naturally possess. In spite of their sensitive nature, they often have a strong outer personality. Adept at sales and promotion, they are not always as responsible as they should be when it comes to how much actual substance there is in what they sell.

Piscean Moon personalities are romantic, idealistic, and creative. Quite a few of them are gifted writers, actors, and illustrators. Remarkably imaginative and farsighted, the major flaw that prevents their projects from being successful is impracticality or lack of clarity, or both. Their excess emotions imply the almost certain potential for waging lifelong battles against overindulgence of every kind. Lunar Pisceans often choose a lover or marriage partner with Sun or Ascendant in Virgo.

Women with Pisces Moon are prone to developing anxiety complexes. They are also apt to be psychic, with a gift for healing. Their emotional nature is well suited for the comfort of a domestic life, though they may be unwilling or unable to efficiently manage the household. Men with Pisces Moon are vulnerable to being victimized in their personal lives, while at the same time they have great strength and wisdom to handle the affairs of others.

In Pisces, the Moon is in its natural *ninth house*. If you think of emotional needs and other Moon-related aspects of an individual's life in ninth-house terms, you may be able to see why ...

Lunar Pisceans become emotionally attached to those of a different nationality or culture. They may reside in a foreign country, or their mother or mother's family may be foreign. These individuals are highly spiritual or philosophical, and they seek their life's work in religious or charitable institutions. Sensitive lunar Pisceans are vulnerable to fanatic ideas and ideologies.

MERCURY IN THE SIGNS

Mercury is thought and ideas and the way they are developed and expressed. It is mental perceptions and learning. It also describes how an individual gets from one place to another, mentally as well as physically. It is transportation, methods, and cleverness.

MERCURY IN ARIES

In Aries, the mind is animated and eager, the decision-making process is immediate. Individuals born with Mercury in Aries want to give full and enthusiastic expression to thoughts and ideas. As soon as they think of a thing, it is likely to be done. They are not interested in protracted discussions or lengthy, detailed investigations, preferring to leave such time-consuming activities to others. Their minds are brilliant but their ideas, or the manner in which they express those ideas, may lack subtlety and refinement.

In some cases, they lack the organization necessary to explain or develop their thoughts. Mercury in Aries indicates acute senses, perhaps nervous tension, and frequently a very quick temper. Their learning, study habits, articulation, and modes of transportation tend to be rushed. They want to get where they are going as fast as possible.

In Aries, Mercury (as the ruler of Gemini) is in its natural *eleventh house*, and (as the ruler of Virgo) it is also in its natural *eighth house*. Imagine how an individual's thinking, communication, interests, and skills might be expressed in eleventh- and eighth-house terms, and you might be able to see why...

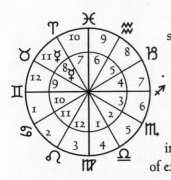

Mercury in Aries people may end up being the secretary or treasurer of organizations to which they belong. They may also edit newsletters or act as a spokesperson or lobbyist for an association. They may work with joint incomes, collection of debts, and taxes or insurance matters. They may be behavioral scientists, surgeons, researchers, and investigators. Their minds are sharp and their manner of expression may be intense.

MERCURY IN TAURUS

Thoughts and ideas must be related to some form of physical reality in the Taurus environment. The thinking process of those born with Mercury in Taurus is structured and conservative, and their ideas are usually of a practical and constructive nature. These individuals don't usually jump to conclusions, nor are they inclined to easily accept new ideas with nothing to recommend their merit. The patient and focused energy of Taurus implies the potential of great concentration. The most productive approach to learning for lunar Taureans is usually by practical application. Once they see the need or use for understanding something or developing a skill, they are motivated to learn. When it comes to handling information, communications, or getting around, they don't want to rush, but they also don't want to be distracted with side trips. They take the most practical and the most direct route that suits their needs.

In Taurus, Mercury (as the ruler of Gemini) is in its natural *twelfth house*, and (as the ruler of Virgo) it is also in its natural *ninth house*. Imagine how an individual's thinking, communication, interests, and skills might be expressed in twelfth- and ninth-house terms, and you might be able to see why ...

Mercury in Taurus people can be very religious or spiritually oriented. They may have a great interest in the occult or in secret societies. They may be involved in military or other forms of secret intelligence. They seek higher education. They are writers, publishers, advertisers, and judges. They travel or trade in foreign countries. They may keep their ideas and methods hidden.

MERCURY IN GEMINI

☿ ♊ The mental orientation in Gemini is very strong. It does not make scholars or sages of those born with Mercury in this sign, but they have a greater than average facility for information and communication. They deal with thoughts and ideas rather than feelings and attitudes. There is bound to be flexibility in their ideas and opinions, and they change their minds accordingly. Ideas flow with amazing rapidity. The worst potentials of Mercury in Gemini include lack of concentration and organization, while the best potentials can mean remarkable skill for handling and processing information. In Gemini, Mercury indicates those with great cleverness and persuasive articulation. However, it can also mean individuals who lack depth in their perception and have little patience for detailed analysis. Mercury in Gemini people may possess quick and merry wits, musical talent, mechanical skills, and the ability to mimic the characteristics of others. Wanting to keep busy (physically as well as mentally), they are constantly on the go, involved with a myriad of errands and projects all at the same time. Their approach to learning as well as the way they prefer to get from place to place is liable to be erratic and changeable.

In Gemini, Mercury (as the ruler of Gemini) is in its natural *first house*, and (as the ruler of Virgo) it is also in its natural *tenth house*. Imagine how an individual's thinking, communication, interests, and skills might be expressed in first- and tenth-house terms, and you might be able to see why ...

Mercury in Gemini individuals have a very personal or unique way of expressing themselves. They may tend to talk or write about themselves. They seek a public forum in which to express their ideas and opinions. Their careers often involve intellectual ability or mechanical skills.

MERCURY IN CANCER

☿ ♋ The enhanced emotional influence of Mercury in Cancer implies imagination and creativity or artistic talent. These individuals may find it difficult to separate their thoughts from their feelings. They are extremely susceptible consciously or subconsciously to absorbing the ideas and thoughts of those around them. This makes objectivity and originality hard for them to generate.

98

They can, however, inject valuable intuitive or instinctive elements into ideas or into the expression of ideas in order to make them more appealing and effective. Whatever their ideas may be, or however ideas may be generated, Mercury in Cancer individuals need to find some means of expressing them. They will not be content to let their thoughts go unnoticed or unappreciated. Methods and motivation for the way they tend to learn, the way they communicate, and the type of transportation they use to get around are all subject to the mood they are in at any given time.

In Cancer, Mercury (as the ruler of Gemini) is in its natural *second house*, and (as the ruler of Virgo) it is also in its natural *eleventh house*. Imagine how an individual's thinking, communication, interests, and skills might be expressed in second- and eleventh-house terms, and you might be able to see why …

Mercury in Cancer people may write about or study finance and real estate, and tend to make innumerable lists of their income, assets, and priorities. These individuals often value intellectual ability and education more than anything else. They are involved in groups and organizations, and play an active role as secretary or membership chairperson. They may be highly skilled at fund-raising.

MERCURY IN LEO

In the creative, lively environment of Leo, Mercury is given imagination and enthusiasm. Individuals with Mercury in Leo have no trouble forming their own opinions and ideas. Sometimes their success and personal growth may be stymied by refusal to accept ideas that disagree with their own. The tenacity of energy in Leo indicates the ability to concentrate, the patience to follow through with ideas, and the skill to organize information. These individuals often find unique and dramatic ways to communicate their message. In addition to the potential gift of oratory, they may also possess admirable talent in writing or research. It is mental enthusiasm that fuels their learning process, the way they communicate, and the transportation they choose. A flair for vivid demonstration and passionate expression lets others know they are coming even before they arrive. When they leave, everyone is sure to know they were there.

In Leo, Mercury (as the ruler of Gemini) is in its natural *third house*, and (as the ruler of Virgo) it is also in its natural *twelfth house*. Imagine how an individual's thinking, communication, interests, and skills might be expressed in third- and twelfth-house terms, and you might be able to see why ...

Mercury in Leo individuals make excellent salespeople and creative teachers. Their mechanical or design skills are very good, and many of them are interested in studying occult subjects or learning about dreams and the unconscious mind. They enjoy getting around in their own community and are often the unofficial mayor of their block or street. They may be reluctant to discuss their private affairs or ideas, and they keep projects secret.

MERCURY IN VIRGO

Mercury is the ruler of Virgo, which means this planet is strongly placed in Virgo's environment. There is bound to be a quickness of perception and widespread interests in those who are born with Mercury in Virgo. Many of them possess sharp analytical abilities. As a rule, they learn quickly, and most of them also derive pleasure from their education. They have organizational ability, but other factors in their natal charts must support a willingness to implement this skill. They may be prone to change their minds, especially when they are subjected to the persuasive power of others. They need to develop confidence in their own ideas and opinions. The perfection they seek is always in conflict with the less than perfect world. Sometimes they can be patient and accommodating in teaching or sharing information and ideas. At other times, they are too impatient and overly critical. They are excellent librarians, schoolteachers, and systems analysts. Other areas of interest and activity include health and human resources and labor unions. Their approach to learning as well as how they choose to get from one place to another can best be described as a variable but purposeful pace. Curiosity leads them down many paths, mentally as well as physically.

In Virgo, Mercury (as the ruler of Gemini) is in its natural *fourth house*, and (as the ruler of Virgo) it is also in its natural *first house*. Imagine how an individual's thinking, communication, interests, and skills might be expressed in fourth- and first-house terms, and you might be able to see why …

Mercury in Virgo people have very talkative personalities. Their favorite topics for discussion are apt to be themselves and their family. These individuals possess clever domestic skills such as sewing, decorating, home building and repair.

MERCURY IN LIBRA

☿ ♎ The mental energy requires harmony and balance when Mercury is in the sign Libra. Those who are born with Mercury in Libra do not do well with extreme ideas or opinions, since sooner or later they are forced to return to some sort of middle ground in order to maintain stability. Individuals with natal Mercury in Libra usually want to turn their ideas into money or other tangible rewards. Many of them seek to earn their living in mental, rather than physical, endeavors. Intellectual pursuits and communication can range from a fondness for gossip magazines to serious studies in literature and talent for writing. They often possess skills in music, art, or design. Interest in the law can turn them into court reporters, courtroom spectators, lawyers, or judges. Objectivity and an unbiased approach works well in their impersonal communications, but it can hamper some situations where they need to speak more from the heart and less from the brain. Their methods and approach to learning as well to transportation would tend to put them in the middle of the road traveling at an average speed.

In Libra, Mercury (as the ruler of Gemini) is in its natural *fifth house*, and (as the ruler of Virgo) it is also in its natural *second house*. Imagine how an individual's thinking, communication, interests, and skills might be expressed in fifth- and second-house terms, and you might be able to see why …

Those with Mercury in Libra possess creative skills and artistic talent. Their hobbies often involve writing, communication, and they almost always enjoy traveling. They may write or study about economics, and are highly organized when it comes to their financial and business records. Many of them are excellent teachers of young children.

MERCURY IN SCORPIO

☿ ♏ In Scorpio, the mental perceptions take on depth and intensity. Understanding is both instinctual and intellectual. Individuals with natal Mercury in Scorpio have sharp tongues as well as minds. The intensity of Scorpio indicates obsessiveness. These individuals are jealous or highly protective of their ideas, and, in some cases, there is a tendency for great secrecy. They equate knowledge and information with power. Once they form opinions, they stubbornly cling to them. Although there is emotional understanding to be sure, their mental powers are not bogged down by sentiment. The emotional element in Scorpio's energy sharpens their instincts, giving them the ability to read between the lines. It is difficult for others to deceive them. Analytical, with a healthy dose of skepticism, they are excellent investigators. What and how they choose to learn, and where or how they choose to get from one place to another, are variable, but rarely without design or purpose. Whether they move quickly or slowly with great care, they prefer their movements to be silent and undetected.

In Scorpio, Mercury (as the ruler of Gemini) is in its natural *sixth house*, and (as the ruler of Virgo) it is also in its natural *third house*. Imagine how an individual's thinking, communication, interests, and skills might be expressed in sixth- and third-house terms, and you might be able to see why ...

Those born with Mercury in Scorpio have jobs that involve their mental skills, communication, or the processing of information. They are involved in work related to public transportation, travel, or geography. Their work may be in the post office, or with newspapers or magazines. They are interested in minute details, interesting facts, puzzles, and other problem-solving activities.

MERCURY IN SAGITTARIUS

☿ ♐ In the active environment of Sagittarius, Mercury is stimulated to perform great feats of intellectual skill and imagination. Those with natal Mercury in Sagittarius have enthusiastic, adaptable intellects. Their interests are varied and they quickly learn what they want to know. If they don't have a natural inclination for a subject, or even for school in general, it is difficult for

them to remain content in the confining routine of formal education. Many of these individuals possess considerable gifts for mimicry and oratory. Very independent in their ideas and opinions, they learn best by traveling, circulating within various groups, and visiting new places. When communicating opinions and ideas, they have a tendency to be very direct, sometimes to the point of what others may consider tactless. They can be spiritually oriented, or become very involved in art or politics. When it comes to their method of learning and the way they prefer to get around, they are usually found rushing from place to place. However, they are also capable of ambling along, taking every interesting detour that catches their fancy.

In Sagittarius, Mercury (as the ruler of Gemini) is in its natural *seventh house*, and (as the ruler of Virgo) it is also in its natural *fourth house*. Imagine how an individual's thinking, communication, interests, and skills might be expressed in seventh- and fourth-house terms, and you might be able to see why …

Mercury in Sagittarius people study the law or work in public relations. They seek to establish strong lines of communication with others, especially with their partners and other allies. Their interests, skills, and work may be related to home building, real estate, or other areas that involve home, family, or domestic products. They have a particular interest in tracing family history.

MERCURY IN CAPRICORN

☿ ♑ Capricorn imposes structure and form on Mercury's orientation in this sign. Individuals with natal Mercury in Capricorn want to turn knowledge and ideas to some practical advantage, which is why many of them have a certain flair for organization, business, and administration. Unless other factors in their natal charts soften the sober Saturnine influence, their imaginations can be restricted to the pragmatic and material world. However, this is not always the case. They may be gifted musicians or poets, well able to understand and utilize the basic pattern of rhythm and measure that escapes less structured or disciplined thinkers. Too dedicated to espousing traditional ideas, or ideas that do not conflict with or threaten their own, they limit the scope of their intellectual

growth. Learning to relax and develop a sense of humor is important for their mental health. The pace and method they use in learning, developing skills, or getting from one place to another are strongly influenced by practical needs or advantages to be gained at the time.

In Capricorn, Mercury (as the ruler of Gemini) is in its natural *eighth house*, and (as the ruler of Virgo) it is also in its natural *fifth house.* Imagine how an individual's thinking, communication, interests, and skills might be expressed in eighth- and fifth-house terms, and you might be able to see why ...

Those born with Mercury in Capricorn are often quite interested in the stock market, commodities, banking, and investment. They are frequently the ones to handle joint income and matters related to taxes, insurance, or the collection of debts. These individuals may study psychology, or work as investigators and in the areas of intelligence and security. Their hobbies may be traveling, creative writing, or arts and crafts.

MERCURY IN AQUARIUS

In Aquarius, the energy is geared toward ideas and communication. Those with natal Mercury in Aquarius have a curious, but usually compatible mixture of characteristics associated with their thoughts and ideas and the expression of those ideas. These individuals are stimulated by unusual or unorthodox methods and ideas, which they are often successful at fitting into traditional systems. They have respect for tradition but are also able to express traditional ideas in an avant-garde or unorthodox manner. They can be very stubborn and opinionated, while also maintaining liberal, unbiased attitudes. They are inclined toward design, architecture, science, finance, and, in some cases, music or literature. They are unpredictable in the matter of how they approach learning and the way they choose to get from one place to another mentally as well as physically. Sometimes they are highly original and unique. Sometimes they perversely go against the popular trends. And sometimes they may be found hopelessly stuck in a rut.

In Aquarius, Mercury (as the ruler of Gemini) is in its natural *ninth house,* and (as the ruler of Virgo) it is also in its natural *sixth house.* Imagine how an individual's thinking, communication, interests, and skills might be expressed in

ninth- and sixth-house terms, and you might be able to see why ...

Mercury in Aquarius individuals are interested in journalism, writing, and publishing. They are likely to seek or be involved in higher education, religion, politics, and cultural pursuits. They enjoy travel. Many of them are excellent linguists. Their job may involve their intellectual or communicative ability or mechanical skills. They are effective labor negotiators.

MERCURY IN PISCES

☿ ♓ In the emotional environment of Pisces, Mercury is given remarkable intuition and instinct. Those born with natal Mercury in Pisces may, however, find it hard to separate emotions when clear thinking is needed. They allow passion and idealism to overrule logic. Their mental orientation can be unstable, unrealistic, and overly spiritual. They also possess remarkable sensitivity to beauty and design. If supported by other strengths, they have a photographic memory, mathematical ability, and sometimes more common sense than they are given credit for. When it comes to learning, development of skills, or the way in which they get from one place to another, they are hard to predict. It is apt to be their emotional strength or weakness that determines whether they forge straight ahead or amble aimlessly from place to place at a snail's pace.

In Pisces, Mercury (as the ruler of Gemini) is in its natural *tenth house*, and (as the ruler of Virgo) it is also in its natural *seventh house*. Imagine how an individual's thinking, communication, interests, and skills might be expressed in tenth- and seventh-house terms, and you might be able to see why ...

Those born with Mercury in Pisces seek a public forum in which to express their ideas and opinions. Their career may be related to public positions that use their intellectual ability or communicative skills. Many of them study and practice the law and are involved in public relations or marriage counseling. They seek strong lines of communication with their partner or other allies. They may seek to travel or write in partnership with another person.

VENUS IN THE SIGNS

Venus represents social attitudes and behavior. It is the spirit of cooperation, affection, and love. Venus indicates the pursuit of pleasures and the sense of beauty and harmony. It represents what is valued. Venus indicates the lucky breaks (or lack of them) that an individual experiences.

VENUS IN ARIES

In the enthusiastic environment of Aries, Venus picks up more passion but may suffer the loss of some refinements. Individuals with Venus in Aries rush enthusiastically to embrace relationships of all kinds. They enjoy having fun and their pursuits frequently involve an element of risk. Their passionate eagerness can be inspiring and contagious, but a penchant for undue haste sometimes results in rudeness. The combative nature of Aries also implies the potential that these individuals can be too aggressive in forcing their attentions or affections on others. Their social instincts are friendly and, most of the time, attractively uncomplicated. Unwilling to take the necessary time for proper evaluation, they are not very discriminating in their values and relationships. This is something, however, that can be overcome with maturity and guidance. They are not likely to seek a peaceful or mundane existence, preferring to be active and among people to find inspiration.

In Aries, Venus (as the ruler of Taurus) is in its natural *twelfth house* and (as the ruler of Libra) it is also in its natural *seventh house*. Think of the potential lover, marriage partner, friends, and other Venus-ruled situations in twelfth- and seventh-house terms, and it might help to explain why ...

The eagerness and haste of Venus in Aries individuals can make them their own worst enemy. They are outgoing and willing partners, and may be quite successful in joint ventures.

VENUS IN TAURUS

Venus may be no less amiable and fun-loving in Taurus, but it is also more directed and focused. Venus in Taurus individuals seek to develop the potential of relationships and material possessions. Though they

enjoy social gatherings, they are not likely to rush around slapping everyone on the back, spouting one-liners or the latest gossip. They are not particularly glib or talkative unless other factors in their nature support it. Most of the time they prefer to keep a low but friendly profile. Consciously or subconsciously, they tend to make practical use of social relationships. They are fond of music, art, food, and fine wine, as well as all the other sensual delights of life. They can also become overly influenced by the lure of wealth and status. Warm, charming, and romantic, their affections are deep and long-lasting. When they feel insecure in relationships, they can become possessive and jealous.

In Taurus, Venus (as the ruler of Taurus) is in its natural *first house* and (as the ruler of Libra) it is also in its natural *eighth house*. Think of the potential lover, marriage partner, friends, and other Venus-ruled situations in first- and eighth-house terms, and it might help to explain why …

Venus in Taurus individuals are preoccupied with their own appearance. They understand the value of beautiful things. They enjoy the pleasure and intense nature of sexual contacts, and may gain materially through marriage.

VENUS IN GEMINI

♀ ♊ Venus in Gemini is given great flexibility and charm in communicative skills. Individuals with Venus in Gemini are some of the most accomplished flirts in the zodiac. It would be a mistake to accuse them of being emotionally shallow because other factors in the horoscope more accurately account for the depth of their emotional commitment. However, in purely social situations, these individuals are remarkably adept. The influence of Gemini indicates that their physical pleasure in relationships is never as great as the intellectual stimulation derived from them. They are excellent salesmen, speakers, and ad-libbers. Their social instincts are geared more toward sharing ideas and picking up information than engaging in intense physical or emotional encounters. They find inspiration in maintaining a wide variety of relationships with people of different backgrounds and experiences.

In Gemini, Venus (as the ruler of Taurus) is in its natural *second house* and (as the ruler of Libra) it is also in its natural *ninth house*. Think of the potential

lover, marriage partner, friends, and other Venus-ruled situations in second- and ninth-house terms, and it might help to explain why ...

Those with Venus in Gemini may be lucky in earning a good income. They tend to spend money on entertainment, pleasure, and cultural pursuits. Many of these individuals establish friendships with foreigners and marry people of a different religion, culture, or nationality.

VENUS IN CANCER

The environment of Cancer causes Venus to lose objectivity in judgment but replaces it with greater emotional identification. Those born with Venus in Cancer are sensitive, although not particularly shy. They are often the ones to take the initiative in relationships. Most of them derive much enjoyment from domestic and family life, and meals are the focus of many of their pleasures. Even confirmed bachelors with this Venus position tend to keep cozy, well-managed homes in spite of the lack of a spouse or offspring. They are responsive to the needs and welfare of parents or siblings. They are warm and caring individuals, but they can be too possessive and jealous, driving away the very people for whom they care the most.

In Cancer, Venus (as the ruler of Taurus) is in its natural *third house* and (as the ruler of Libra) it is also in its natural *tenth house*. Think of the potential lover, marriage partner, friends, and other Venus-ruled situations in third- and tenth-house terms, and it might help to explain why ...

Venus in Cancer individuals may marry a friend of their brother or sister, or they may marry a neighbor. These individuals have many friends in their community. They usually enjoy great popularity within as well as outside of their family circle. Their career in life may involve caring for the social needs of people, and they become hotel owners and managers or restaurateurs.

VENUS IN LEO

♀ ☌ ♌ In Leo, Venus is given full rein to pursue the pleasures and enjoyment of life, and there is bound to be some artistic or creative association. The enthusiastic people-oriented qualities associated with Leo make it the most gregarious sign position for Venus. Individuals with Venus in Leo are friendly, outgoing, and magnanimous. They place great value on being sincere and loyal. It must not be forgotten, however, that there is sure to be a measure of ego involvement in the establishment of relationships. They tend to recognize a certain pecking order in social situations, and for the good of everyone around them, they had better not be placed at the bottom. Whatever the social situation happens to be, they like to play a leading role. Many of them possess special talent in art or design. There is tendency for exaggeration, and a certain flair for drama is likely to be exhibited in their mannerisms or some other aspect of their personality.

In Leo, Venus (as the ruler of Taurus) is in its natural *fourth house* and (as the ruler of Libra) it is also in its natural *eleventh house*. Think of the potential lover, marriage partner, friends, and other Venus-ruled situations in fourth- and eleventh-house terms, and it might help to explain why …

Many Venus in Leo people want to entertain at home. They attract many friends and tend to join, and perhaps become the leader of, groups and associations. Their marriage may be to a friend or to someone from their home town.

VENUS IN VIRGO

♀ ♍ In Virgo, Venus is bound to seek some sort of perfection. Individuals with Venus in Virgo are very communicative and sociable as long as interactions are confined to impersonal matters. They do, however, quickly warm to people who go out of their way to make them feel at ease, and they feel more comfortable with people with whom they share similar interests. Even if they are interested in pursuing a relationship (romantic or otherwise), they are not likely to be the aggressor. When they do go out of their way to form associations, it is usually for practical reasons. Close friendships may be few, but those they do establish are treasured. They can miss good times, good friends, and sometimes even romance because they wait too long for conditions to be perfect.

In Virgo, Venus (as the ruler of Taurus) is in its natural *fifth house* and (as the ruler of Libra) it is also in its natural *twelfth house*. Think of the potential lover, marriage partner, friends, and other Venus-ruled situations in fifth- and twelfth-house terms, and it might help to explain why …

Venus in Virgo individuals are shy in meeting new people. They like to have a good time, but are afraid of the consequences of being too uninhibited. They possess creative talent and are good at entertaining children. They may have secret lovers or friends.

VENUS IN LIBRA

Venus is strengthened in Libra. It is given strategy and diplomatic skills. Individuals with Venus in Libra approach relationships with a certain intellectual objectivity. They aren't particularly shy, but whether or not they go out of their way to grab the spotlight depends on other factors in their personality. In spite of their charm and romantic nature, these individuals can also be quite manipulative about selecting those with whom they wish to associate. In social situations, as well as in personal relationships, their deeper passions are not likely to surface very often. They enjoy the companionship of both sexes equally. Their social graces and mannerisms are flirtatious, but not obviously so. There is a great appreciation for music, art, and especially books.

In Libra, Venus (as the ruler of Taurus) is in its natural *sixth house* and (as the ruler of Libra) it is also in its natural *first house*. Think of the potential lover, marriage partner, friends, and other Venus-ruled situations in sixth- and first-house terms, and it might help to explain why …

Venus in Libra people are sociable with those who work for or with them, and may marry someone with whom they work. They need beauty and harmony in their work environment. These individuals enjoy dressing well and are often vain about their physical appearance.

VENUS IN SCORPIO

♀ ♏ Scorpio gives Venus increased ability to assess value, but may take away some light-heartedness and spontaneity. Social attitude and behavior of individuals with Venus in Scorpio are strongly influenced by their emotional needs. They are not usually shy and, in fact, many of them are quite gregarious. Their strong, passionate nature needs some measure of control or they can become possessive, obsessive, or jealous. Even those who seem outwardly easygoing will consciously or subconsciously seek to manipulate relationships. They are not ones to mince words or engage in idle flattery. Many of their interactions, even fleeting or superficial contacts, are apt to be tinged with a certain intensity. Social instincts can be remarkably keen, and their actions in this regard are direct and purposeful, although not always obvious or open. There are certain domestic talents or preferences in many of these individuals. They are, for example, excellent cooks and gardeners.

In Scorpio, Venus (as the ruler of Taurus) is in its natural *seventh house* and (as the ruler of Libra) it is also in its natural *second house*. Think of the potential lover, marriage partner, friends, and other Venus-ruled situations in seventh- and second-house terms, and it might help to explain why ...

People with Venus in Scorpio may advance their social status or gain monetarily through marriage. Increased social position and monetary assets may also come through a business partner or joint ventures.

VENUS IN SAGITTARIUS

♀ ♐ The expansive environment of Sagittarius increases the capacity for enjoyment and enhances all Venus-ruled attributes and situations. Those who are born with Venus in Sagittarius exhibit an honest straightforward approach in their social attitudes and behavior. Sometimes, however, they can be a bit too blunt in situations where they should have been more discreet. Those who know them well come to accept bluntness as part of their charm and appreciate the honesty with which their statements are intended, rather than the way they are expressed. Blunt or not, it is always best for them to stick to honesty in all things. It is hard for Venus in Sagittarius people to get away with falsehoods

since either their words, their mannerisms, or their failure to cover their tracks always trips them up. They are friendly, outgoing, and idealistic, and seek a wide variety of acquaintances. Uncomplicated friendships are much easier for them to handle than passionate entanglements that, more often than not, leave them hurt and confused.

In Sagittarius, Venus (as the ruler of Taurus) is in its natural *eighth house* and (as the ruler of Libra) it is also in its natural *third house*. Think of the potential lover, marriage partner, friends, and other Venus-ruled situations in eighth- and third-house terms, and it might help to explain why ...

Those born with Venus in Sagittarius receive benefits from taxes and insurance, inheritance, or joint income. They enjoy great popularity in their communities and cordial and merry relationships with siblings. They are excellent salesmen and communicators. Their marriage partner may come from their own community or from among their grammar school classmates.

VENUS IN CAPRICORN

In the environment of Capricorn, Venus takes on a certain formality and inhibition, although it also gains talent for artistic structure and form. No matter how easygoing or strong their outer personality may appear, it is likely that underneath they are insecure. Individuals born with Venus in this sign are apt to exhibit the restrictive influence of Capricorn in managing their romantic entanglements. Nor can their social attitudes and behavior be described as very glib or spontaneous. Although it may not be their intention to do so, they appear brusque or abrupt when dealing with people they do not know well. In spite of this, most of them really enjoy social gatherings. A cautious nature makes them feel more comfortable in relationships and social situations that are formal, purposeful, and, to some extent, calculated to remove the possibility of personal rejection, which is some-

thing they wish to avoid at all costs. Consciously or subconsciously, they want to make some practical use of their associations.

In Capricorn, Venus (as the ruler of Taurus) is in its natural *ninth house* and (as the ruler of Libra) it is also in its natural *fourth house*. Think of the potential lover, marriage partner, friends, and other Venus-ruled situations in ninth- and fourth-house terms, and it might help to explain why ...

Venus in Capricorn people enjoy socializing in religious, philosophical, or political groups. They enjoy travel, especially long-distance travel. They enjoy popularity in organizations to which they belong and may meet their marriage partner, friends, or lovers through participation in organizational meetings and activities.

VENUS IN AQUARIUS

♀ ♒ Individuals with Venus in Aquarius have wide-ranging social attitudes and behavioral patterns. For these egalitarian personalities, a restricted code of social acceptability does not exist. They welcome all types of people into their social circle. Extremely people-oriented, they have no trouble attracting many friends and acquaintances. They would suffer greatly if denied access to a telephone or other means of constant communication. Though they tend to have a less than passionate approach to romance and other close relationships, no one denies their essential loyalty. They tend to be passionate about humanitarianism and spiritual development that (for them) transcend mere social contacts or physical romance. Financial as well as people skills make them good fund-raisers. They are also excellent at organizing, teaching, and writing.

In Aquarius, Venus (as the ruler of Taurus) is in its natural *tenth house* and (as the ruler of Libra) it is also in its natural *fifth house*. Think of the potential lover, marriage partner, friends, and other Venus-ruled situations in tenth- and fifth-house terms, and it might help to explain why ...

Those born with Venus in Aquarius are natural entertainers, and many of them make their career in this area. They are excellent politicians and effective civic leaders. They are highly sociable. They are likely to meet friends, lovers, and marriage partners through social activities. They are adept at entertaining children.

VENUS IN PISCES

♀ ♓ The emotional energy in Pisces gives Venus added artistic and social sensitivity. Although the Piscean influence implies a certain level of shyness, this is not always the case. Individuals born with Venus in Pisces love to have other people around. They can be deeply hurt if a relationship does not go well, and, as a result, they may be very reluctant when it comes to making new associations. The compassionate nature of these individuals makes it difficult for them to be harshly judgmental and discriminating in their choice of companions. This is unfortunate since they attract people who take advantage of them. They often possess uncanny instincts about people. They may, for example, have remarkable skill when it comes to putting together the right people in the right situations.

In Pisces, Venus (as the ruler of Taurus) is in its natural *eleventh house* and (as the ruler of Libra) it is also in its natural *sixth house*. Think of the potential lover, marriage partner, friends, and other Venus-ruled situations in eleventh- and sixth-house terms, and it might help to explain why ...

Venus in Pisces individuals enjoy being part of group activities, and may find their marriage partner, allies, lovers, and friends either through group activities or through their job. They seek beauty and harmony in their work environment. Their work may involve art, music, law, as well as writing, reading, or illustrating books.

MARS IN THE SIGNS

Mars is the essential physical energy of the individual. It is the fuel that drives the engine. Mars describes physical expressions and mannerisms. It rules male relationships and male contacts.

MARS IN ARIES

♂ ♈ Strong in its own sign, Mars gains inspiration and enthusiasm. Individuals with Mars in Aries usually have a great deal of energy, but whether or not they will make productive use of it is determined by other factors.

It does seem certain that frustration occurs if their energy is not given some kind of physical outlet. If the typical Aries aggressiveness is prominent in their personality, they are in continual verbal or physical combat. Even if their outer personality is more subdued, they become courageous and forceful when there is need to evoke such passions. Most of these individuals are not as restless or outwardly feisty as such a strong Mars would indicate. They do, however, have incredible stamina and are always ready to go anywhere for work or fun.

In Aries, Mars (as the ruler of Aries) is in its natural *first house* but (as the old ruler of Scorpio) it is also in its natural *sixth house*. Think of how and where physical efforts and energy might be directed as well as other Mars-ruled situations in terms of the first and sixth houses, and you can see why ...

Those with Mars in Aries enjoy participating in sports and other physical activities. Vicarious pleasures are not for these individuals. They are hands-on people who get personally involved in projects and activities. Mars in Aries people are hard workers, and much of their energy is channeled into their job. They may have more male coworkers than female.

MARS IN TAURUS

The deliberately focused energy that Mars acquires in Taurus encourages efforts that have purpose and solidity. Individuals with Mars in Taurus are, therefore, not likely to waste their time or efforts. Whatever they seek to accomplish or to acquire is consciously or subconsciously linked to satisfying some goal. For most of them, the aim is usually money or other material assets. Even those who do not seek to amass material wealth become discouraged if their efforts and activities do not result in gaining some goal or tangible reward. Physical pleasures are often the object of their energetic pursuits. The Taurean influence gives these individuals patience and determination in whatever projects and activities they take on. Mars in Taurus is also an indication of artistic skills. These individuals possess physical strength and stamina, or at least have the capacity to develop these traits.

In Taurus, Mars (as the ruler of Aries) is in its natural *second house* but (as the old ruler of Scorpio) it is also in its natural *seventh house*. Think of how and

where physical efforts and energy might be directed as well as other Mars-ruled situations in terms of the second and seventh houses, and you can see why ...

Mars in Taurus people are inclined to expect monetary rewards for their efforts. They also regard physical energy itself as a valuable asset. They work well with a partner and put whatever physical efforts are required into making a partnership or joint venture succeed.

MARS IN GEMINI

Some of the energy of Mars is bound to be directed to the communication of information and ideas when Mars is in the environment of Gemini. For this reason, individuals with Mars in Gemini are usually well occupied with organizing, disseminating, and creating ideas and information. The varied and widely scattered interests that command their attention keep them quite physically active as they hop from one project to another. Doing more than one thing at a time is second nature to them, and they constantly attend meetings, write letters, chat on the phone, travel, or run errands. Organizing and limiting their activities can minimize their potential for nervousness and irritability. Many of them are avid readers, excellent teachers, mechanically inclined, or artistically skilled. They may be very interested in or work in areas that involve cars, trucks and other vehicles, transportation, traffic patterns, and travel.

In Gemini, Mars (as the ruler of Aries) is in its natural *third house* but (as the old ruler of Scorpio) it is also in its natural *eighth house*. Think of how and where physical efforts and energy might be directed as well as other Mars-ruled situations in terms of the third and eighth houses, and you can see why ...

Those born with Mars in Gemini often find work in their community. They may work with siblings, in the military, or in areas that involve security. Many of them are surgeons, investment brokers, bankers, barbers, and butchers. The sexual drive of these individuals is frequently stronger than Mars in Gemini would indicate.

MARS IN CANCER

♂♋ Fiery Mars has a hard time in the watery environment of Cancer since its energy is in constant danger of being drowned. Yet there is no doubt that people born with Mars in Cancer work up the energy to accomplish quite a lot. Their efforts can be spoiled and their motivation to work can disappear, however, when they allow themselves to be sidetracked by possessiveness or jealousy. The Cancerian influence implies a domestic streak, and these individuals may direct many of their physical efforts toward family or household activities. They are avid collectors and savers of everything. Many of them engage in such Cancer-ruled work as catering, agriculture, family counseling, and areas that involve women or children.

In Cancer, Mars (as the ruler of Aries) is in its natural *fourth house* but (as the old ruler of Scorpio) it is also in its natural *ninth house*. Think of how and where physical efforts and energy might be directed as well as other Mars-ruled situations in terms of the fourth and ninth houses, and you can see why ...

Mars in Cancer individuals like to initiate new beginnings. They work as home builders or real-estate developers. They enjoy long-distance travel or they may be quite active in religious or political activities.

MARS IN LEO

♂♌ The environment of Leo adds a dynamic character to the already active energy of Mars. Those born with Mars in Leo are inclined toward grandiose gestures and improbable schemes, and whatever they do is usually done in a big way. Sometimes their energy and enthusiasm are such inspirational forces that they actually accomplish some of the seemingly impossible things they set out to do. Strong determination is another important factor in their stunning accomplishments. If they allow stubborn pride to interfere, they can waste valuable time. Their efforts may be very creative, although they need to be reminded of practical considerations and assisted by those more attentive to mundane details. Mars in Leo individuals are very generous with their time and energy.

In Leo, Mars (as the ruler of Aries) is in its natural *fifth house* but (as the old ruler of Scorpio) it is also in its natural *tenth house*. Think of how and where physical efforts and energy might be directed as well as other Mars-ruled situations in terms of the fifth and tenth houses, and you can see why ...

Mars in Leo individuals enjoy having a good time, and they often engage in risky pursuits. Much of their physical efforts are put into a career or other long-range ambitions. Mars in Leo people are great agents and promoters.

MARS IN VIRGO

The detail-oriented energy of the Virgo environment encourages Mars toward a constant state of busyness. Individuals born with Mars in Virgo usually possess a number of different kinds of physical and mental skills that allow them to participate in a wide range of activities. Writing, teaching, health care, interior design, or fashion design are just a few areas in which these individuals may be involved. They can be very self-disciplined, organized people who have no trouble dividing their energy among several projects at the same time. The negative potential implies those who lack attention to detail and their efforts are disorganized and sloppy. Sometimes they use the impossibility of achieving perfection as an excuse for leading an idle and unproductive existence. Individuals with Mars in Virgo make determined efforts to perfect their physical skills, and many of them possess enviable technical talents.

In Virgo, Mars (as the ruler of Aries) is in its natural *sixth house* but (as the old ruler of Scorpio) it is also in its natural *eleventh house*. Think of how and where physical efforts and energy might be directed as well as other Mars-ruled situations in terms of the sixth and eleventh houses, and you can see why ...

Mars in Virgo people are excellent employees, and their work tends to be in areas that involve an element of risk. They may, for example, work for fire depart-

ments or other emergency groups. They participate in many physical activities with their friends or with groups and associations.

MARS IN LIBRA

♂ ♎ The balance and harmony needed in Libra are not easy for the energetic Mars to maintain, and so it is sometimes paralyzed in its effectiveness in this sign. However, what energy there is is usually devoted to expressing ideas and communication. People born with Mars in Libra can be strong and focused when they do act, but the motivational force behind their efforts often relies on interacting with other people. If they have limited opportunity to work in partnership or in cooperative arrangements with others, they find it difficult to get things accomplished or to develop their own potential. Their physical energy tends to run in definite cycles. If they go too fast and hard for too long, their bodies force them to slow down and rest in equal measure. These individuals are not inclined to waste energy in combative gestures, and will more than likely go out of their way to avoid direct conflict, at least on a physical level. They are good strategists, able to accomplish things through diplomacy and charm instead of physical force.

In Libra, Mars (as the ruler of Aries) is in its natural *seventh house* but (as the old ruler of Scorpio) it is also in its natural *twelfth house*. Think of how and where physical efforts and energy might be directed as well as other Mars-ruled situations in terms of the seventh and twelfth houses, and you can see why ...

Mars in Libra individuals make excellent partners. The energy and enthusiasm they put into a relationship are what they expect to be given in return. Their real strength is hidden, their work or physical efforts may often go unnoticed or unrecognized. The nature of their work may require that they work alone, and they may be involved in secret activities.

MARS IN SCORPIO

♂ ♏ Instead of drowning the energy of Mars, the watery environment of Scorpio is often brought to a boil by this fiery planet. The energy of

those with Mars in Scorpio is intense and focused. If their actions are prompted by emotional needs, it is not often obvious. In fact, consciously or subconsciously, they may hide or disguise their real reason for doing things. The formidable energy which they are capable of applying to their efforts is persistent, accurately directed, and usually successful. They can be misguided by possessiveness and jealousy, and waste their energy in pointless acts of revenge. These individuals are among the world's most remarkable researchers, investigators, writers, composers, renovators, and financial manipulators.

In Scorpio, Mars (as the ruler of Aries) is in its natural *eighth house* but (as the old ruler of Scorpio) it is also in its natural *first house*. Think of how and where physical efforts and energy might be directed as well as other Mars-ruled situations in terms of the eighth and first houses, and you can see why ...

Mars in Scorpio people are sexual and may be physically very active in that area. They put physical efforts into handling joint income, investments, property, or tax and insurance matters. Their work frequently involves great detail and depth. The potency of their physical energy may be evident in their personality and mannerisms.

MARS IN SAGITTARIUS

Mars takes on zeal and idealism in the environment of Sagittarius. The actions of individuals with Mars in Sagittarius are enthusiastic and inspired. Spurred on by the excitement of the moment, they act quickly and decisively. However, they can quickly lose interest and head off in a different direction, leaving others to finish their work. Their curiosity is easily aroused, and they enjoy absorbing, collecting, and sharing all kinds of information. Patience and organization must be developed, or the facts that these individuals accumulate become disconnected, and they end up repeating themselves and their efforts. They are apt to possess mechanical or artistic skills and the ability to mimic. Many of them are gifted actors, salespersons, clerics, writers, teachers, and musicians. They accomplish more if they are allowed a certain amount of latitude and independence in the performance of their tasks.

In Sagittarius, Mars (as the ruler of Aries) is in its natural *ninth house* but (as the old ruler of Scorpio) it is also in its natural *second house*. Think of how and

where physical efforts and energy might be directed as well as other Mars-ruled situations in terms of the ninth and second houses, and you can see why ...

Mars in Sagittarius people love to travel, especially long distances. They love sports and may be excellent athletes themselves. These individuals seek to turn physical efforts into monetary or other tangible rewards, and may not care to put forth any physical efforts unless it is important to them. They may work in publishing, politics, or the law.

MARS IN CAPRICORN

♂ ♑ In the formal and purposeful atmosphere of Capricorn, the energy of Mars is given to devising aspirations and schemes. Individuals with Mars in Capricorn are aggressively ambitious. They are even more decisive and confident when they act within the limits of what is legally and socially acceptable. They are also more effective when they know they are being observed, and when they know that what they are doing commands respect. Rejection in business or romance is not something they accept easily, and they continue to pursue their goals relentlessly in any way they think will work. The influence of Capricorn may mean a certain ruthlessness, but that is usually what is needed in order to succeed in the fiercely competitive situations they often pursue. These individuals are the ones responsible for bringing about greatly needed changes and establishing institutions and structures that ultimately benefit many people other than themselves.

In Capricorn, Mars (as the ruler of Aries) is in its natural *tenth house* but (as the old ruler of Scorpio) it is also in its natural *third house*. Think of how and where physical efforts and energy might be directed as well as other Mars-ruled situations in terms of the tenth and third houses, and you can see why ...

Mars in Capricorn people put much of their hard work into a career and other long-range goals. Their career may involve an element of risk. They are excellent at organizing and handling information. These individuals have a quick temper and tend to communicate with physical gestures.

121

MARS IN AQUARIUS

♂ ♒ Aquarius gives the energy of Mars a great deal of sociability so that its physical exertions are almost always carried out in company with others. Those born with Mars in Aquarius are, on the whole, more successful or at least happier when they do things with others. These individuals devote a lot of their energy to communicating ideas and information and to turning ideas into reality. Highly sociable, they are addicted to the telephone, and will rarely miss opportunities to participate in group activities and group discussions. Their efforts, as well as the results of those efforts, are as unpredictable as the rest of their life-styles. Totally unmotivated at times, they let themselves fall into a rut. At other times, their energy and enthusiasm flow in a steady stream of focused activity. Without warning, some unexpected circumstance can force or inspire them to execute a complete change of attitude and direction.

In Aquarius, Mars (as ruler of Aries) is in its natural *eleventh house* but (as the old ruler of Scorpio) it is also in its natural *fourth house*. Think of how and where physical efforts and energy might be directed as well as other Mars-ruled situations in terms of the eleventh and fourth houses, and you can see why ...

Those born with Mars in Aquarius enjoy sports and other physical activities with friends. They put their physical efforts into groups and organizations. These individuals also put much physical energy into domestic and family activities.

MARS IN PISCES

♂ ♓ The emotional atmosphere of Pisces adds inspiration and spirituality to Mars but submerges its physical energy in much the same way that an engine cannot start when it is flooded. Those born with Mars in Pisces often find themselves at the mercy of the environment in which they operate. They can easily be inspired as well as inspiring, and many possess outstanding creative and artistic talent. Their instinctive reactions are keen, as is their power of turning abstract concepts into reality. These individuals invariably find it difficult to accomplish things because they are too lazy or lack the necessary confidence to act. As a result, they waste their talents and skills for want of

a good push to get started. Many develop inner strength that is remarkable. As if to confront the potential of physical weakness, some of them engage in high-risk activities.

In Pisces, Mars (as the ruler of Aries) is in its natural *twelfth house* but (as the old ruler of Scorpio) it is also in its natural *fifth house*. Think of how and where physical efforts and energy might be directed as well as other Mars-ruled situations in terms of the twelfth and fifth houses, and you can see why …

Mars in Pisces people have to be content if their efforts fail to get noticed. By choice or circumstances these individuals often work alone and with as little distraction as possible. They enjoy the pursuit of pleasure, and sometimes this proclivity makes them their own worst enemy. They may engage in secret activities or romances.

*　*　*

When interpreting the planets in the signs, it is necessary to separate the so-called inner planets—Sun, Moon, Mercury, Venus, and Mars—from the outer planets—Jupiter, Saturn, Uranus, Neptune, and Pluto. (See Figure 10 on page 124). The inner planets move through all twelve astrological signs more rapidly than the outer planets. The Moon takes only 27 days to move through the zodiac. Mercury's zodiacal cycle is approximately 88 days, Venus takes 244 days, the Sun takes 365 days, and Mars takes about a year and a half to complete one cycle through the zodiac. The zodiacal periods of the outer planets are much longer. Jupiter requires 12 years to complete one cycle. Saturn completes the zodiac in about 27 years. Uranus needs 84 years for its cycle. Neptune pokes along the zodiacal circle for 164 years and, finally, Pluto begins and ends its zodiacal circuit in about 248 years. In the previous sections, I used the zodiacal wheel after each sign to illustrate one of the methods you can employ to improve your understanding of the twelve houses. I also used this method to help you understand where some of the meanings that are not obvious may be derived. This works well for the inner planets, but is not as useful when describing the outer planets in the signs. When interpreting an individual's horoscope, the sign position of an inner planet is associated with personal characteristics. The sign position of an outer planet, Jupiter through Pluto, is more general in nature and is used as a way to connect the individual with some of the experiences likely to be

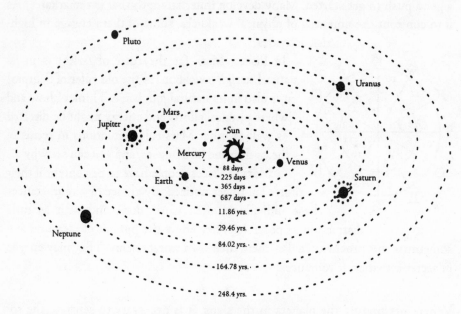

Figure 10: The Solar System

encountered in society. Although the sign position has some significance, the real influence of an outer planet in a person's horoscope is interpreted from its house position as well as the aspects it makes with other natal planets. The aspects between the natal planets are described in Chapter Nine.

JUPITER IN THE SIGNS

Jupiter represents the areas in which an individual is likely to experience growth, to expand understanding and knowledge, to gain economic prosperity, to attain a wider reputation, and to attain spiritual or cultural growth. It represents optimism, generosity, and abundance.

JUPITER IN ARIES

♃ ♈ It is not what is achieved but the act of achieving that often becomes the real purpose for Jupiter in Aries. Individuals with an Aries Jupiter find that the areas in which they grow or expand tend to get out of control. How efficient they are at regaining control when it has been lost is determined by

other factors in their natal chart. Although they have the good fortune to be wealthy, they may also have a tendency to spend what they have, which makes it hard for them to get ahead. They do not pay much attention to details or limitations and can easily lose sight of reality, but optimism and faith help make their dreams come true.

JUPITER IN TAURUS

♃ ♉ In Taurus, the natural optimism and generosity of Jupiter are not lacking, but these traits are likely to be of a more cautious nature. Those born with Jupiter in Taurus are bound to the material world in order to achieve growth and gain understanding and experience. These individuals are more than a little appreciative of the luxuries and physical pleasures of life, but they may be willing to forego these things in order to develop and preserve what they accumulate. The chances they take are calculated risks. They want whatever growth and success that they experience to be real and tangible to them, something they can measure or physically possess.

JUPITER IN GEMINI

♃ ♊ The environment of Gemini gives Jupiter mental and communicative energy. For those born with this Jupiter, it means growth and productivity are tied to the ebb and flow of information, ideas, and contacts with others. Jupiter in Gemini expands enthusiasm for selling messages, ideas, and methods. If fortune or circumstances restrict their formal education or opportunity to travel, these individuals become self-educated and are likely to correspond, trade, and have other contacts with far distant people and places.

JUPITER IN CANCER

♃ ♋ The expansive nature of Jupiter in the emotional environment of Cancer gives full expression to instincts and intuition. Individuals born with Jupiter in Cancer accomplish much personal growth and progress through their family or family connections. The concept of caring for others is a strong element in this Jupiter sign position. These individuals may be successful in activities that are related to feeding people, providing products and services for women or children, and the protection of human rights.

JUPITER IN LEO

♃ ♌ Jupiter is given added momentum to seek all that is bold and beautiful when it is in the extravagant environment of Leo. People who are born with this Jupiter often exhibit their facility for personal growth in creative areas such as art, design, and drama. Whatever direction their efforts take, however, it is liable to be somewhat overdone or exaggerated. A philanthropic spirit is to be expected as well as high ideals and principles. These individuals enthusiastically embrace the pomp and pageantry of traditional rituals.

JUPITER IN VIRGO

♃ ♍ In Virgo, Jupiter picks up the detail-conscious, perfection-seeking qualities of Virgo but may suffer the loss of some of its own spontaneous warmth and optimism. Individuals with Jupiter in Virgo run into problems when they get lost in petty concerns and unnecessary details and lose sight of the big picture. They jeopardize valuable relationships or other experiences when nothing seems good enough or perfect enough to suit them. The generosity of Jupiter is evident because these individuals are often as involved with the personal growth and success of others as they are with their own.

JUPITER IN LIBRA

♃ ♎ The balance and harmony that prevail in Libra's environment exert pressure on Jupiter's tendency to go overboard. Those born with Jupiter in Libra are required to strike a balance between excess and austerity in order to achieve personal growth and success. Jupiter in Libra implies that these individuals do well in partnerships, joint ventures, and other cooperative efforts. It also means an inspired sense of justice and affinity for the law and for writing.

JUPITER IN SCORPIO

♃ ♏ Jupiter is given increased emotional direction in the environment of Scorpio. Individuals with Jupiter in Scorpio have intense emotional desires and interests. Their capacity for growth and expansion is on an emotional level. Unfortunately, with Scorpio there is also a tendency for manipulation, and

they may engage in this practice without realizing its destructive potential. As Jupiter's zeal overwhelms moderation, they become fanatics. These individuals may be gourmets as well as gourmands.

JUPITER IN SAGITTARIUS

At home in the environment of its own rulership, Jupiter is given strength and encouragement. Individuals with this Jupiter achieve personal growth and success through travel, education, and communication. There is great generosity of spirit and attitude. However, if circumstances in their background or development force these individuals to turn inward, they are capable of going to the opposite extreme, becoming miserly and withdrawn. Jupiter in Sagittarius implies those who take risks, and it often includes the luck to come out ahead when they do.

JUPITER IN CAPRICORN

The structured, goal-oriented energy of Capricorn brings out the formal, traditional character of Jupiter. Individuals born with Jupiter in Capricorn are overly concerned with the way things are done. Lack of inspirational factors in their development and background forces many of them to gain understanding and wisdom primarily through their own experiences and maturity. Growth and success in life is rarely a matter of haphazard luck or whimsy. These individuals are forced to keep track of where they have been, where they are at present, and where they want to go.

JUPITER IN AQUARIUS

Jupiter picks up a more serious social conscience in the atmosphere of Aquarius. Individuals with Jupiter in Aquarius can successfully operate within traditional ideas and institutions, but they are also receptive to ideas and activities which threaten to upset the established order. They are apt to experience their greatest personal progress and growth by working for needed change without destroying what is still useful. These individuals are effective catalysts who inspire changes and other actions within various organizations and groups.

JUPITER IN PISCES

♃ ♓ The spirituality and prophetic nature of Jupiter awaken in the inspired waters of Pisces. People born with this Jupiter are required to develop spirituality, artistic talent, and psychic energy. Jupiter in Pisces also implies the potential for ruinous indulgence and delusion. The personal growth and success of individuals with this Jupiter are dependent on making prudent choices.

SATURN IN THE SIGNS

Saturn represents areas in which an individual is likely to experience limitations and restrictions. It signifies lessons to be learned and challenges that must be met and overcome if one is to merit the rewards that are sought.

SATURN IN ARIES

♄ ♈ The steadiness and measured pace of Saturn can be confused by the chaotic and restless energy of Aries. Individuals with Saturn in Aries are invariably faced with the consequences of their actions. They do not have the luxury of leaving their actions and reactions up to pure instinct. They are frustrated when they do not succeed because they acted spontaneously, and frustrated on other occasions when they deliberately move at a slower pace and still fail. Success becomes a matter of learning to control their physical, mental, and emotional reactions, an ability that can only be developed through maturity and experience.

SATURN IN TAURUS

♄ ♉ Saturn is well positioned in the focused energy of Taurus, but becomes too tied to the physical world. Individuals with Saturn in Taurus find it difficult to do something for nothing. They need tangible thanks and appreciation. They have to measure themselves: who they are, what they do, and what they have in relation to the rest of the world. One way or another, life presents them with situations in which they regret that a more spiritual or philosophical approach was not or could not be used in measuring their own worth or the relative worth of others.

SATURN IN GEMINI

♄ ♊ Saturn is not naturally inclined to the free association kind of atmosphere encountered in Gemini. Individuals with Saturn in Gemini find restrictions in communication. They may lack ability or opportunity to acquire or communicate information. In some cases, it may be the inability of others to communicate effectively that hampers their own efforts. Disorganization may be the reason that some of them cannot efficiently use information, or, being overly organized, they miss important details. Efforts to turn ideas into action are restricted. Many of them are too serious when a lighthearted approach would be more appropriate.

SATURN IN CANCER

♄ ♋ The nature of Saturn requires that all roads be clearly marked and each path must lead somewhere. In the unmarked and uncontrolled territory of Cancer where all is directed by instinct and emotion, Saturn is befuddled. Individuals with Saturn in Cancer find their home or domestic life limited in some way. Family responsibilities, for example, may interfere with their career, development of their talents, or other personal ambitions. Nurturing they received or their own ability to nurture may be inhibited. Relationships with women and young children are also liable to be restricted. The positive potential includes creative talents that are constructively developed and applied. The trust these individuals learn to have in others, whether too much or too little, is one of their important lessons in life.

SATURN IN LEO

♄ ♌ The gregarious and imaginative environment in Leo may not suit Saturn's more sober nature, but the focused and tenacious energy that is also present allows Saturn to find a comfortable niche to accomplish definite goals. Saturn in Leo people may encounter inhibitions of one kind or another in romantic encounters, relationships with children, and the development of creative talents. They may tend to approach these matters with a too heavy hand or too severe an attitude. Capacity for enjoyment may be limited. Their lesson in life is learning to accept responsibilities that go along with pleasure, but not to let responsibilities diminish enjoyment. The positive potential implies financial

astuteness in speculative ventures and the ability to bring reality and practicality to artistic projects.

SATURN IN VIRGO

♄ ♍ Saturn finds much to suit its nature and inclinations as it encounters the organizational and structured energy in the environment of Virgo. Saturn in Virgo individuals are able to efficiently accomplish things of a mundane character. They can and often do improve the lives of many people. These individuals may, however, be confronted with restrictions or limitations that involve matters of practicality or perfectionism. Too much pragmatism leaves no room for imagination or spiritual growth. Lack of practicality denies the solid base they need for progress and stability. Blind pursuit of perfectionism denies the reality of life, and they accomplish nothing. Their lack of idealism ends in mediocrity.

SATURN IN LIBRA

♄ ♎ Saturn does well in the less emotional and more objective atmosphere it encounters in Libra. Those born with Saturn in Libra are adept in nonpersonal situations. Skills they apply in nonpersonal circumstances include logic and strategy. Restrictions they encounter usually involve interactions with partners or in personal contracts they make. Interactions often become complicated, no matter how fleeting the association may be. These individuals tend to get more involved in situations than they had originally expected. If something in their development or background knocks them off balance, they may stay away from all relationships. On the positive side, Saturn in Libra indicates those who establish stable and long-lasting relationships.

SATURN IN SCORPIO

♄ ♏ Saturn recognizes immediately the control it encounters in the environment of Scorpio. Control is not always a desirable or easy thing to handle for those born with Saturn in Scorpio. The intensity associated with Scorpio and the rigidity of Saturn indicate that these individuals will encounter limitations imposed by the presence of too much control in some area of their lives, or the need to establish control without employing destructive forms of manipulation in order to gain it. Another potential for these individuals is respon-

sibility and restriction related to debts of one kind or another. Debts they incur may be of an emotional, physical, financial, or moral nature. On the positive side, these individuals are favored in many situations with the formidable stamina of Scorpio and the longevity of Saturn.

SATURN IN SAGITTARIUS

♄ ♐ The unrestricted exuberance of Sagittarian energy may temporarily stymie Saturn's need for a more legitimate and orderly progress, but in general, Saturn finds the atmosphere in Sagittarius compatible. Individuals born with Saturn in Sagittarius encounter limitations and responsibilities in their quests for higher education, increased professional status, or high positions in government or community service. But there is also the potential for these people to end up as acknowledged experts and authorities in their particular field of endeavor. Knowledge is not usually a luxury for them. It may be difficult to acquire purely for its own sake, and it must have structure and meaningful application. Their spirituality demands the highest standards, and those who become morally righteous are apt to suffer.

SATURN IN CAPRICORN

♄ ♑ In Capricorn, Saturn is at home. Its rulership of this environment adds stability and force to Saturn's goal-oriented nature. For individuals born with Saturn in its own sign, it usually means learning to interject structure and goals in almost every phase of life. They usually develop a high regard for tradition as well as the institutions and associations that make up the foundations of society. The work or avocation many of these individuals undertake involves eliminating or making necessary changes in situations that have grown weak through neglect or that no longer fulfill their original purpose. One of their problems is the struggle to get around the endless red tape of rules and regulations that they themselves may have helped to create.

SATURN IN AQUARIUS

♄ ♒ The energy of order and discipline inexplicably coexists with unpredictable and independent energy in the environment of Aquarius. This odd arrangement also inexplicably suits the character of Saturn. Individuals with

Saturn in Aquarius are often confronted with situations that need organization, dedication, and stability in order to be successful, yet must also have room for freedom and original thinking. These individuals find ways to deal effectively with the conflict between control and noncontrol. They are responsible for the wise use of freedom within the confinement of organization and discipline, both of which are necessary if anything worthwhile is to be accomplished and if it is to endure once it is accomplished.

SATURN IN PISCES

♄♓ The sentimental and imaginative energy in the atmosphere of Pisces is not compatible with Saturn's structured and purposeful nature. Individuals with Saturn in Pisces become very restricted by their inability to deal with or let go of the past. They may be denied the ability to learn from their past. Consequently, they are forced to rely on the understanding that comes from the development of maturity and the ability to accurately analyze relationships and situations in their present reality. The positive potential includes mathematical skill, musical talent, and the ability to turn theory into practical application.

URANUS IN THE SIGNS

Uranus is societal concerns and conditions that an individual is likely to encounter. It also describes areas of unstable or nontraditional circumstances.

URANUS IN ARIES

♅♈ The generation of individuals born with Uranus in Aries is given impetus to explore new fields of research and technology. They are prepared to accept change for its own sake as well as for other reasons. In turn, this readiness for new ideas and methods inspires progress. Caution is necessary, however, or in their haste they may destroy much that was worth keeping.

URANUS IN TAURUS

♅♉ The generation that comes into the world with Uranus in Taurus is not inclined to initiate or accept changes merely for the sake of making changes, nor do they accept originality just because it is different. For them,

change and innovation must have structure and purpose. Freedom is encouraged if its responsibilities are also accepted. The importance of theories is recognized but only to the extent that their practical application is considered feasible.

URANUS IN GEMINI

Uranus in Gemini is associated with a generation of individuals that seeks freedom of speech and communication. Research and development of innovative technology and better methods of communication are eagerly undertaken by these individuals. All new ideas are given attention and free access to information is emphasized. Community action groups become more prolific and forceful.

URANUS IN CANCER

New and nontraditional concepts of family and domestic issues are likely to be promoted by the generation of individuals born with Uranus in Cancer. These individuals may not have the traditional desire to own homes, or circumstances in society make it difficult for them to afford the same type of homes in which they were raised. New ways of sharing family responsibilities, as well as new ideas and methods concerning food and nurturing, emerge from this generation.

URANUS IN LEO

The generation of individuals born with Uranus in Leo is likely to be involved in the creative arts. They tend to introduce their ideas with innovative flair and great boldness, in defiance of traditional concepts. Leo is also associated with scientific research and humanitarian gestures, so these individuals may be expected to attack old problems with new energy, ideas, and methods.

URANUS IN VIRGO

The energy of Virgo does not necessarily promote the idea of changing things. Virgo inspires improvement and the ability to make better use of what is already at hand. It will therefore be up to the generation of individuals born with Uranus in Virgo to explore new methods, concepts, and

technologies that enable society to deal more efficiently with existing resources, products, and institutions.

URANUS IN LIBRA

♅♎ Concern with ideas and concepts that involve legal codes, particularly the issue of freedom, is likely to be one of the hallmarks of the generation of people born with Uranus in Libra. Individual liberties are reexamined and perhaps altered to meet the needs of the community. The reverse may also occur and freedom of the community may be restricted to protect the individual. Nontraditional partnerships, marriages, joint ventures, and other contractual arrangements may emerge from this group.

URANUS IN SCORPIO

♅♏ The generation of individuals born with Uranus in Scorpio is most likely to be concerned with psychology, mind control, and breakthroughs in medical and diagnostic research. They are also involved with such social issues as renovation and reclamation projects. They sanction movements and methods that protect and conserve natural resources, and find new ways to use resources more efficiently. Individual privacy and methods of surveillance are also strong public concerns.

URANUS IN SAGITTARIUS

♅♐ The spread of nationalism and the conflicts it causes among the nations of the world are apt to preoccupy the generation of individuals with Uranus in Sagittarius. Another of their concerns is to explore and provide new concepts of higher education. Many of them are in the forefront of new technology as well as different psychologies that affect publishing, advertising, and travel. They are the ones to initiate revolution within established religious institutions.

URANUS IN CAPRICORN

♅♑ The task of confronting revolutionary changes in traditional institutions and political ideologies, as well as major changes in business and industry may fall to the generation of individuals born with Uranus in Capricorn. Other factors will determine how far-reaching these changes will be, but these

individuals seek to reorganize in order to improve. They eliminate what they deem wasteful or mismanaged.

URANUS IN AQUARIUS

The generation of individuals born with Uranus in Aquarius is likely to have to deal with emancipation and independence. They seek to overcome restrictions imposed by traditional institutions and concepts. Individuals and institutions that fail to make changes to accommodate the new wave are discarded. However, that which is perceived as having enduring value will be treasured and lifted to new heights.

URANUS IN PISCES

Innovations and creative concepts appear among those born in the generation of Uranus in Pisces. The truly different and what older generations view as weird and unorthodox are commonplace manifestations of their talents and endeavors. They also contribute original methods that are undeniably farsighted and ingenious.

NEPTUNE IN THE SIGNS

In the horoscope, Neptune represents areas where an individual may experience enhanced sensitivity, spiritual awareness, and psychic development. It is also areas of deliberate as well as subconscious deception and illusion. Neptune can mean compassion as well as cruelty, glamor and charisma as well as disguise and charade. It signifies charlatans as well as visionaries. It is an interesting and valuable exercise for the student of astrology to study the various periods of history when Neptune transited each of the signs. In this book, I can only mention a few examples from the most recent transit which will serve as a model and stimulate readers to come up with additional ideas from their own readings in history.

NEPTUNE IN ARIES

Aries is the sign of action. Specific areas that Neptune represents are actualized during its transit in Aries. In the period 1862–1875, Neptune-ruled ideas were actively promoted. Emancipation was the Neptune-

ruled issue in the Civil War. The eroding effect of Neptune can be seen in the way that beliefs and traditions between the North and South bitterly divided the nation. The compassionate side of Neptune in the Mars-ruled sign of Aries was also evident. Clara Barton began the Red Cross, and the Salvation Army was also founded to bring assistance and comfort to the ill and the unfortunate. In 1866, Alfred Nobel invented dynamite and Robert Whitehead invented the underwater torpedo. Neptune rules chemistry and water, while Mars-ruled Aries is associated with weapons of destruction. The following table lists the AD periods in history when Neptune transited Aries.

— Ψ in ♈ —			
62–75	552–566	1043–1057	1534–1548
225–239	716–729	1207–1220	1698–1712
389–402	880–893	1371–1384	1862–1875

NEPTUNE IN TAURUS

Ψ ♉ The last transit of Neptune in Taurus occurred between 1875 and 1889. Taurus is associated with the earth and Neptune with water. Neptune can undermine the productivity of the earth and, indeed, throughout much of this period the world suffered from drought which caused widespread crop failure and famine. China suffered the worst famine in history in 1878 with the death toll exceeding 10 million people.

Business is ruled by Taurus, and many collapsed as the result of the economic depression that occurred during this period. Neptune's spirituality gained roots exhibited in the founding of two religious groups, Christian Science and Jehovah's Witnesses, as well as the establishment of religious-sponsored universities such as Hebrew University in Cincinnati and the Mormons' Brigham Young University in Utah.

The mimeograph (a Neptune-ruled process), an important tool for business, went on sale March 17, 1889, when the Sun was in the Neptune-ruled sign of Pisces. On April 22, 1875, when the Sun was in the sign of Taurus, Arbor Day was established to encourage the planting of trees (ruled by Taurus). Arbor Day is an idea that came from the imagination (Neptune) of agriculturalist J. Sterling Morton. The following table lists the AD periods in history when Neptune transited Taurus.

— ♆ in ♉ —			
75–88	566–579	1057–1070	1548–1561
239–252	729–743	1220–1234	1712–1725
402–415	893–906	1384–1397	1875–1889

NEPTUNE IN GEMINI

♆ ♊ The last occurrence of Neptune in Gemini was between 1889 and 1902. Gemini rules communication, and Neptune in this sign inspired the invention of the universal language Esperanto. However, the idea of having the world communicate in one language failed to gain support. John Gregg introduced his system of English shorthand which did succeed.

Neptune rules the ocean, gasoline, and imagination, and Gemini rules writing, communication, and transportation. The following description gives examples of the combination of Neptune in Gemini. *The Influence of Sea Power Upon History 1660–1783*, written by United States naval officer historian Alfred Thayer Mahen in 1890, inspired world powers to develop strong navies. The first volume of the fifteen-volume *The Golden Bough*, written by anthropologist James George Frazer, explored myths, legends, and the development of religion.

Most of the early development and introduction of gasoline-powered vehicles occurred in this period. In 1891, bicycle designer Charles Duryea invented a gasoline (Neptune) engine to power a road vehicle (Gemini) which was produced in 1892. Subsequently in 1895, the first U.S. motorcar was offered for public sale.

The Ocean Mail Subsidy Act passed by Congress authorized subsidization of the U.S. merchant marine. The first full service advertising agency was established March 15, 1891, in New York. The first delivery van (Gemini) powered by gasoline was produced by the French company Peugeot Freres in 1895. In 1895, Marconi pioneered wireless telegraphy, and in 1901 he received the first transatlantic wireless message. The following table lists the AD periods in history when Neptune transited Gemini.

— ♆ in ♊ —			
88–101	579–592	1070–1083	1561–1574
252–265	743–756	1234–1247	1725–1738
415–428	906–919	1397–1410	1889–1902

NEPTUNE IN CANCER

Ψ ♋ The most recent period of Neptune in Cancer occurred between 1901 and 1916. Cancer rules the stomach and food in general. In America in 1901, a deranged (Neptune) anarchist shot President McKinley in the stomach (Cancer). In 1909, the portly 300-pound William Taft was inaugurated as President. During this period, the United States Congress passed the Meat Inspection Act and the Pure Food and Drug Act. In 1902, a "Poison (Neptune) Squad" of young volunteers tested the safety of U.S. foods (Cancer).

The National Reclamation Act of 1902 encouraged family (Cancer) farms by limiting the size of land holdings to 160 acres. An epidemic of typhoid in 1903 was traced to Mary Mallon ("Typhoid Mary") who was a carrier of the disease. She took jobs handling food (Cancer) and often used assumed names (Neptune). Cancer rules women, and the inventiveness and idealism of Neptune in Cancer is evidenced by the creation of the elastic brassiere to replace the corset in 1914, the introduction of Mothers Day, and the growth of cosmetic entrepreneurs Helena Rubenstein and Elizabeth Arden. The following table lists the AD periods in history when Neptune transited Cancer.

— Ψ in ♋ —			
101–114	592–605	1083–1096	1574–1587
265–278	756–769	1247–1260	1738–1751
428–442	919–932	1410–1423	1901–1916

NEPTUNE IN LEO

Ψ ♌ The last period of Neptune in Leo was 1914–1929. Leo rules monarchy, entertainment, and art. Neptune rules photography and film-making. The Russian monarchy ended, largely because the Tsars refused to recognize (in typical Neptunian fashion) and deal with the troubled conditions that existed in that country. The same can be said of the Ottoman empire, which ended during this period. The hidden tomb of a long-dead Egyptian king, Tutankhamen, was discovered by Howard Carter in November 1922. In America, the total failure of Prohibition is an example of misguided ideals that sought to forbid alcohol (Neptune) as one pursuit of pleasure (Leo).

Neptune in Leo witnessed luxurious, glamorous, and entertaining activities that also became very lucrative. The ideal American beauty selected in the first Miss America contest was chosen in Atlantic City in 1921. Beauty met the camera on professional terms when the first modeling agency was opened by John Powers in 1926.

The movie industry saw its greatest growth and development during this period, and the first full-length talking picture, *The Jazz Singer*, was released in 1927. The avant-garde nature of Leo combined with Neptune produced the Dada artistic and literary movement, which in turn led to Surrealism. The following table lists the AD periods in history when Neptune transited Leo.

— Ψ in ♌ —			
114–128	605–619	1096–1109	1587–1601
278–291	769–782	1260–1273	1751–1764
442–455	932–946	1423–1437	1914–1929

NEPTUNE IN VIRGO

Ψ ♍ The last time Neptune transited Virgo was in 1928–1943. Virgo rules idealism, work, the labor force, public health, and welfare. Neptune rules minority groups and those who are ill, abandoned, orphaned, poor, and disabled. The first Blue Cross tax-exempt, nonprofit health insurance was organized in 1929 to benefit schoolteachers in Dallas, Texas. The Blue Cross trademark of the American Hospital association (blue is a Virgo color) was soon used by similar health insurance agencies throughout the country. The erosion of Neptune on the work force during this period was the worst in history. United States unemployment passed 4 million in 1930, 8 million in 1931, and by the end of 1932, 34 million Americans had no income at all.

The influence of Neptune in Virgo was not confined to the United States. A general depression in the 1930s caused worldwide trade to decline, production to drop, and unemployment to rise.

The combination of Neptune, which is associated with water, and Virgo, which is an earth sign, is not conducive to productive agriculture as witnessed in the unprecedented drought that parched the U.S. South and Midwest.

After Adolf Hitler came to power in Germany in 1933, Neptunian madness combined with Virgo's idealism resulted in the most monumental tragedy in the history of civilization. In 1935, Nazi leader Heinrich Himmler, following Hitler's plans, started a state breeding program to produce an Aryan "super race" and at the same time, leaders of the Third Reich put into motion other plans to eradicate all Jews and other people that were considered inferior. Until the Allied victory in 1945 brought an end to World War II, the world at large remained unaware of the horrors of the degradation and loss of lives that took place in Germany and its occupied countries during the 30s and early 40s. The following table lists the AD periods in history when Neptune transited Virgo.

— Ψ in ♍ —			
128–141	619–632	1109–1123	1601–1614
291–305	782–796	1273–1287	1764–1778
455–469	946–959	1437–1450	1928–1943

NEPTUNE IN LIBRA

Ψ ♎ When Neptune transited Libra in 1942–1957, World War II came to an end. The establishment of the United Nations was typical of the Libran effort to establish peace. Neptune's association with illusions was evident since the U.N. had minimal effect in accomplishing its ideals and goals. Equality (Libra) for minorities (Neptune) gets attention, and throughout the intervening years since its founding, many such issues have been the subject of debate in the United Nations. But real and lasting solutions prove illusive.

Neptune is religion. Libra is communication, writing, and law. The Dead Sea scrolls were discovered in the late 40s and 50s during Neptune's transit of Libra. Scholars and clerics felt that once the religious observances and biblical writings of antiquity were disseminated and studied, the current historical and religious understandings would be immeasurably enhanced. Neptune, however, undermined this hope and for more than forty years (until 1993) these precious documents were kept "hidden" from public view, studied only by a handful of privileged scholars.

Libra's energy does not want to be burdened by emotionalism. In 1953, the Church of Scientology was founded by L. Ron Hubbard, who promoted the idea that man can achieve his true nature only by freeing himself of emotional

encumbrances of the past through counseling. The following table lists the AD periods in history when Neptune transited Libra.

— Ψ in ♎ —			
141–155	632–646	1123–1137	1614–1628
305–319	796–810	1287–1301	1778–1792
469–482	959–973	1450–1464	1942–1957

NEPTUNE IN SCORPIO

Ψ ♏ The last period of Neptune in Scorpio was 1955–1970. Sexual codes (Scorpio) prior to the 60s dissolved (a Neptunian influence). Sexually explicit material invaded the media and everyday life. Drugs and the creation of a counterculture eroded the family and traditional values.

Spying and secret surveillance (Scorpio) increased in public and private life. Scorpio's energy seeks to get to the bottom of things, but Neptune can obscure true motivations for investigations as well as the results. In 1954, Senator Joseph McCarthy conducted televised senate hearings referred to as "witch hunts" for Communists in the United States. Many innocent and highly intelligent and talented people suffered unnecessary disgrace and loss of their professions as a result of McCarthy's misguided hysterics. His accusations became so destructive that he was censured. His career ruined, he declined into alcoholism and obscurity until he died in 1957.

Another example of Neptune in Scorpio was the release of the highly classified Pentagon Papers by Defense Department official Daniel Elsberg. These documents revealed that the U.S. government lied to the American people about its involvement in Vietnam. In the 60s, Dr. Martin Luther King, Jr., President John F. Kennedy, and Robert Kennedy were assassinated (Scorpio), but those responsible or the true conspirators behind these killings will never be known for sure (Neptune). The following table lists the AD periods in history when Neptune transited Scorpio.

— Ψ in ♏ —			
1–6	482–497	973–987	1464–1478
155–169	646–660	1137–1151	1628–1642
319–333	810–824	1301–1315	1792–1806

NEPTUNE IN SAGITTARIUS

Ψ ♐ Neptune was in Sagittarius from 1806–1820, and more recently from 1970–1984. Sagittarius rules optimism, but Neptune introduces mistaken judgments. During the early 1800s, Napoleon conducted his disastrous Russian expedition. At the same time, in the mistaken impression that Britain would not yield to their demands for neutral shipping, President Madison and the United States Congress declared war.

Sagittarius is the sign of higher education. Neptune has undermined the purpose of higher education with its latest transit through Sagittarius. The exorbitant cost of a college degree has put most students and their families in great debt, and put the attainment of a college degree out of reach for many others unable to even consider such a financial burden.

Evangelists (ruled by Sagittarius as well as Neptune) gained widespread popularity on television in the 70s and 80s. Some of the biggest of these religious personalities became involved in great scandals that occurred after Neptune had entered Capricorn. The following table lists the AD periods in history when Neptune transited Sagittarius.

— Ψ in ♐ —			
6–20	497–511	987–1002	1478–1493
169–183	660–674	1151–1165	1642–1656
333–347	824–838	1315–1329	1806–1820
			1970–1984

NEPTUNE IN CAPRICORN

Ψ ♑ Neptune's last period in Capricorn was 1820–1834, and its current transit is 1984–1998. Capricorn rules conservatism, and Neptune brings extremist tendencies. The 1800s witnessed the "era of Metternich," the powerful, very conservative Austrian statesman. Conservative tendencies in France were also accentuated when Charles X ascended the throne. In Great Britain, the conservative Tory faction maintained control.

The conservative mood in America under Ronald Reagan continued under George Bush, evidence of the current influence of Neptune in Capricorn. The administration of President Clinton, though not of the conservative bent of the

previous administrations, will nevertheless be stymied time after time by the strongest conservative elements in society. As this is written, the greatest thrust of the Clinton administration is to correct health-care problems in the United States. Since Neptune is associated with hospitals and the ill as well as with minority groups, the administration's choice of where to focus their major efforts is a wise one.

In Capricorn, there is a need to structure, protect, and conserve, but Neptune is spiritual and illusive. The ideals are there to be sure, but implementing them in a balanced and realistic way is difficult. The crumbling of the Soviet Union may mean great freedom but also great confusion and turmoil. The following table lists the AD periods in history when Neptune transited Capricorn.

— ♆ in ♑ —

20–34	511–525	1002–1016	1493–1507
183–198	674–688	1165–1179	1656–1671
347–361	838–852	1329–1343	1820–1834
			1984–1998

NEPTUNE IN AQUARIUS

♆ ♒ Neptune's last transit in Aquarius occurred in 1834–1848. American and European literature and philosophy gave rise to the Romantic period, a reaction against the conventions and restraints of classicism. It was the dominant note in the artistic and intellectual life of Europe. Aquarius promotes the concept of society rather than the individual, but with Neptune's influence this concept was dissolved and completely reversed as Romanticism emphasized the glorification of the individual.

Aquarius rules new technology and Neptune can undermine or distort the purpose behind a thing. An example of this can be seen in the circumstances surrounding the calculator on which Charles Babbage worked and which was improved and promoted by Augusta Lovelace in England in 1841. This calculator was no doubt a step forward in the world of punched card systems, but both Babbage and Lovelace sustained heavy losses when they used the calculator as the basis for what they believed was an infallible system for betting on horse races (Neptune).

In 1843, the British launched the first iron-hulled, screw-propeller steamship, a combination of technical advancement in a Neptune activity. The ship served until 1937. Aquarius is communication and writing, and the tales of Charles Dickens are descriptions of society (Aquarius) as he chronicled the woes of the poor and unfortunate (Neptune) masses in England. The following table lists the AD periods in history when Neptune transited Aquarius.

— Ψ in ♒ —

34–48	525–539	1016–1030	1507–1521
198–212	688–702	1179–1193	1671–1684
361–375	852–866	1343–1357	1834–1848
			1998–2012

NEPTUNE IN PISCES

Ψ ♓ The last period of Neptune in Pisces was 1848–1862. Neptune is in its own sign in Pisces. It is associated with religion, spiritualism, drugs, illusion, and confusion. In the mid 1800s, Bernadette Soubirous of Lourdes announced her visions of the Virgin Mary. At the same time Horace Wells, a pioneer in anesthesia, was jailed while under the influence of chloroform, and later committed suicide in a fit of despondence.

On the other hand, the British nurse, Florence Nightingale, became a heroine of the Crimean War, and an American president, Abraham Lincoln, became a martyr to the cause of slavery. The issue of slavery (Neptune) chipped away at the foundations of the United States throughout this period, although it would not be until Neptune entered Aries that war resulted. The first U.S. state prohibition law was passed in Maine in 1851.

In 1861, the California State Legislature authorized the importation of wine grapes, inaugurating the modern era of wine production in California. Neptune and Pisces rule the feet. The Bally Shoe factories, founded in 1851, developed into a worldwide shoemaking company.

Chemistry and oil are ruled by Neptune and Pisces. The first fractional distillation of crude petroleum was made in 1854. In 1859, petroleum production began in Pennsylvania, which in turn reduced the demand for whale oil, coal gas, and lard. The sometimes total misguidedness and futility of Neptune is evidenced

in one example, the Wabash and Erie Canal. The canal, which opened in 1856, took 24 years to construct at the cost of many lives lost to cholera and a great deal of money lost to embezzlers. The 458-mile canal was the largest ever dug in America. After only four years, one section was closed, and by 1874, the rest of the canal was closed because railroads made it obsolete. The following table lists the AD periods in history when Neptune transited Pisces.

— ♆ in ♓ —			
48–62	539–552	1030–1043	1521–1534
212–225	702–716	1193–1207	1684–1698
375–389	866–880	1357–1371	1848–1862

PLUTO IN THE SIGNS

Discovered in 1930, Pluto is still being studied by modern astrologers. Some ideas about the influential patterns associated with this planet have been proposed and for the most part seem to fit. Pluto is the crucible in which complete transformation occurs. It is related to the areas in which an individual cannot hide from reality—the past, the present, and the future. Like the other outer planets, Pluto in the signs is significant only in terms of how society reacted during those transits. But in an individual horoscope, Pluto's significance has more to do with the house it occupies and the aspects it has with the other natal planets.

PLUTO IN ARIES

♇ ♈ Pluto's last period in Aries was 1823–1853. Introducing a new cycle of actions and reactions, Pluto's transit in Aries witnessed many revolutions in Europe as liberal forces rebelled against the repression of the conservatives. Pluto is exploration and Aries is the pioneering instinct. In 1830, the first covered wagon train traveled from the Missouri River to the Rockies. Pluto is energy, research, and development, and when Pluto was in the fast-paced sign of Aries, scientific advance was rapid as new understanding and methods were developed in thermodynamics, optics, magnetism, and electricity. Pluto is the ultimate form of preservation which is transformation from one form to another. Eventually from this transit came the understanding that energy can neither be

created nor destroyed. The greatest transformation of this Pluto transit in Aries was the industrial revolution.

— ♇ in ♈ —			
112–144	601–632	1090–1120	1579–1608
356–388	845–876	1334–1364	1823–1853

PLUTO IN TAURUS

♇ ♉ The most recent period of Pluto in Taurus was 1853–1884. Taurus is pragmatic and materialistic. During the period of Pluto in Taurus, the scientific principles that were learned and the machines that had been invented when Pluto was in Aries now made the development of industrialization possible. The meteoric rise of capitalism during this time was fueled by an unprecedented growth of industry and finance. During this period, vast fortunes were created. Men that included John D. Rockefeller, the Vanderbilts, Chicago meatpacker (Pluto and Taurus activity) Gustavis Swift, Andrew Carnegie, and Meyer Guggenheim were embodiments of the term plutocrat.

— ♇ in ♉ —			
144–174	632–663	1120–1151	1608–1640
388–419	876–907	1364–1396	1853–1884

PLUTO IN GEMINI

♇ ♊ Gemini rules communication and transportation. During Pluto's long transit in this sign, between 1884 and 1914, there were many changes and improvements in these areas. The Linotype typesetting machine revolutionized newspaper composing rooms. The first subway was built in London, the first automatic telephone switchboard was introduced, Marconi invented radio telegraphy, and Zeppelin built his airship.

— ♇ in ♊ —			
174–200	663–690	1151–1179	1640–1669
419–445	907–935	1396–1424	1884–1914

PLUTO IN CANCER

♇ ♋ When Pluto transits Cancer, the most obvious targets of transformation are women and the family. This transit would especially affect the United States, which happens to be a Cancerian country, founded July 4, 1776. The most recent transit of Pluto occurred between 1914–1938. During the 20s, the attitudes and roles of women were transformed. Women demanded and got greater freedom in society and release from the drudgery of domestic chores. As a result of the increasing number of women seeking employment outside of the home, family life also changed dramatically.

— ♇ in ♋ —			
200–219	690–710	1179–1202	1669–1693
445–465	935–956	1424–1447	1914–1938

PLUTO IN LEO

♇ ♌ Pluto's last period in Leo was 1938–1956. Leo rules the king or representative government and it also rules individual rights and freedoms. During Pluto's transit of Leo in the late 1600s and early 1700s, John Locke, philosopher of the English Revolution and American Revolution, wrote his famous essays stating that governments existed by virtue of voluntary agreements and their function was to protect the rights of individuals. The generation of individuals born between 1938 and 1956 will witness the end of all monarchies. In maturity, these individuals will be instrumental in setting up global governments and institutions.

— ♇ in ♌ —			
219–233	710–726	1202–1218	1693–1710
465–479	956–972	1447–1464	1938–1956

PLUTO IN VIRGO

♇ ♍ Virgo rules health, practical applications of science and technology, and the work force. During the period of Pluto's last transit in Virgo, between 1956 and 1971, the general state of America's health and welfare

systems experienced unprecedented changes, computers came of age, the once powerful labor unions experienced great loss of influence and vitality, and in 1970 the Environmental Protection Agency was established.

— ♀ in ♍ —			
233–245	726–738	1218–1231	1710–1724
479–491	972–985	1464–1478	1956–1971

PLUTO IN LIBRA

♇ ♎ Pluto transited Libra between 1971 and 1983. Libra demands equality, and Pluto is power. Pluto's transit in Libra indicates great shifts of world power to favor a more equitable balance. During the recent transit, there were increasing demands by Third World nations for their fair share of the Earth's resources. World sentiment was also developing against South Africa's policy of apartheid.

— ♀ in ♎ —			
1–9	491–503	985–996	1478–1490
245–256	738–749	1231–1243	1724–1736
			1971–1983

PLUTO IN SCORPIO

♇ ♏ Pluto's current transit in Scorpio is between 1983 and 1995. In Scorpio, Pluto is in its own sign. Emotional transformations that occur can produce violent conflicts and ultimately bring about great change. The Great Awakening during Pluto's Scorpio transit in the 1700s increased the number of church participants, but also resulted in serious internal conflict as it divided the church between those of the old order and the new members who demanded change. Scorpio rules sex and abuse. Public outcry against child abuse and the worldwide spread of AIDS are examples of Pluto's current transformation of society.

— ♇ in ♏ —

9–22	503–515	996–1008	1490–1502
256–268	749–762	1243–1255	1736–1748
			1983–1995

PLUTO IN SAGITTARIUS

♇ ♐ Pluto will begin transiting Sagittarius in 1995. Its great energies were seen in the period of the Enlightenment which occurred during Pluto's last Sagittarian transit in 1748–1762. During that era, great advances were made in scientific knowledge and political thought, there was a proliferation of newspapers, and higher education became available to a wider spectrum of social classes.

— ♇ in ♐ —

22–37	515–530	1008–1023	1502–1515
268–284	762–776	1255–1269	1748–1762
			1995–2008

PLUTO IN CAPRICORN

♇ ♑ Pluto's last period in Capricorn was 1762–1778. Pluto will not transit Capricorn again until the next century. Capricorn rules structure, form, and legality. During Pluto's last transit, its powerful energies can be associated with the men who wrote the Declaration of Independence, a document granting America her freedom as a new nation with her own form of government.

— ♇ in ♑ —

37–57	530–549	1023–1040	1515–1532
284–303	776–795	1269–1286	1762–1778

PLUTO IN AQUARIUS

♇ ♒ Aquarius rules the common man and it also rules rebellions against the status quo. Pluto's last period in Aquarius was 1778–1798, and it will not appear in this sign again until the next century. During Pluto's transit in the late 1700s, Americans went from a government run by the elite to the more democratic form advocated by Jefferson. America's victory over the British also encouraged the French Revolution in 1789.

— ♇ in ♒ —

57–82	549–572	1040–1063	1532–1553
303–327	795–817	1286–1308	1778–1798

PLUTO IN PISCES

♇ ♓ Pluto's last period in Pisces was 1798–1823. Pluto will not transit Pisces again until the next century. Pluto rules investigation, power, and intense energy. Pisces rules the ocean, medicine, and chemistry. Pluto's transit in the early 1800s inspired appropriately associated events. Robert Fulton produced the first submarine. John Dalton introduced the atomic theory in chemistry. Egyptian hieroglyphics were deciphered.

— ♇ in ♓ —

82–112	572–601	1063–1090	1553–1579
327–356	817–845	1308–1334	1798–1823

Chapter Eight

Planets in the Houses

In this chapter, you will learn the meaning of the Sun, Moon, and planets in each of the twelve houses of the horoscope. Before you start putting the planets in the houses, take some time to review Chapter Five for the meaning of the houses, and in particular the special areas that are associated with each house. Recall the meaning of each planet, and that taken as a whole the planets represent the total individual. The meaning of the planets never changes, but the characteristics of each planet will be focused in different areas according to the house the planet is in. For example, the Sun always represents the ego, but the disposition and tendencies of the ego are expressed primarily in the special areas that are described by the house where the Sun is located. It may be helpful to review Chapter Six for a detailed description of the planets.

NATAL SUN IN THE HOUSES

SUN IN THE FIRST HOUSE

Strong involvement with one's own personality and influence is emphasized when the Sun is in the first house. It indicates those who want to leave their

mark. Whether or not they successfully impress others with expressions of their individuality is another matter, since the urge to do so is developed and guided by the strength of their ego. If the ego is weak and complacent, the personality is not likely to be bold or assertive. No matter what the world may think of them, it is meaningless compared to what these individuals think of themselves. Pride can make it difficult for solar first-house people to accept advice or personal criticism. Although much of their enthusiasm and efforts is directed inward to the greater glory of the self, they can exhibit great generosity toward others and admirable loyalty toward their friends. The energy and vitality these individuals radiate attract and inspire others.

SUN IN THE SECOND HOUSE

The ego's identification with material wealth and with the personal prominence that accompanies money or power is characteristic when the Sun is in the second house. Individuals born with this solar house position are not, however, totally selfish or materialistic. Their goals often benefit others as well as themselves, as in the case of those who seek public recognition through charitable and philanthropic endeavors. How these individuals handle the money and assets that they eventually gain or lose, or even if they succeed in getting what they want, is signified by the strength and direction of their ego. Monetary goals they seek, priorities they establish, and values they embrace all tend to be what these individuals decide is important to them, not what others dictate.

SUN IN THE THIRD HOUSE

Sun in the third house indicates those who are compelled to establish their individuality in some form of mental and/or physical expression. Characteristically, solar third-house individuals are in continuous contact and interaction with others: writing letters, talking on the telephone, and attending one meeting or another. They are bound to assert thoughts and opinions, although it does not

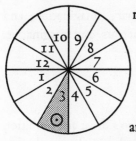

necessarily mean they will seek a public forum in which to express themselves. Some are content with keeping personal diaries while others find self-expression through artistic endeavors. Much depends on their particular personality and background. The Sun's third-house position implies creativity and enthusiasm in ideas and communication, and not infrequently the inclination to engage in theatrics and hyperbole.

SUN IN THE FOURTH HOUSE

Childhood conditioning has a crucial effect on the development of the ego in those born with Sun in the fourth house. Their willpower and drive are guided by and focused on their home and family. Sometimes these individuals dominate and manipulate their family and domestic environment. Whether their home life is associated with positive or negative circumstances is not the issue. The point of this solar house position is that they are never quite free of family relations and influence. Their energy and creativity may, for example, be directed to a family-owned business. Even the most dedicated world travelers in this group invariably end up back home. One expected pattern of a fourth-house solar position is individuals who rise to prominent positions as a direct result of their family or family connections.

SUN IN THE FIFTH HOUSE

While it does not necessarily herald unbridled hedonism, those who are born with Sun in the fifth house do possess an enhanced appetite for the pursuit of pleasure. They frequently find it difficult to develop a level of maturity with regard to enjoyment and indulgence. As a rule, these individuals are very fond of children and animals. Those who become parents do not always make the best disciplinarians, for they are apt to over-indulge children without establishing a counterbalance of limitations, correct behavior, and attitude necessary for proper development. They love to entertain and be

entertained. The ego's ambition identifies with creativity, imagination, and artistic talent. Solar fifth-house people are romantic, generous, and imaginative. They are vital if not always strong; noble if not always wise.

SUN IN THE SIXTH HOUSE

Work, health, and physical fitness are the focus of the ego's drive and ambition when the Sun occupies the sixth house. This is not enough to indicate whether solar sixth-house individuals will be workaholics, or whether they will spend their lives avoiding work, or constantly finding fault with their job, coworkers, and every other aspect of their employment. Other factors in their individual personality and background magnify and qualify their behavior and attitude toward work and health. The positive potentials imply robust health and a willingness to handle tasks with dedication and pride. Some of them exaggerate the importance of their job, while others refuse to accept any work they think is beneath them. Health and physical fitness are important, but it is hard to say if they will be too stubborn or proud to admit when they are ill or so preoccupied they spend every waking moment concerned about their health and physical appearance. Those with Sun in the sixth house should protect their heart with proper diet and exercise.

SUN IN THE SEVENTH HOUSE

Sun in the seventh house suggests that the ego is developed and manipulated by partnerships, cooperative efforts, and other people in general. Individuals born with this Sun position constantly measure themselves in terms of other people and in terms of how others react to them. Even if these individuals are very independent in other ways, they are likely to find their best achievements occur with a partner or partners. To suggest that solar seventh-house people are unable to succeed on their own is a fallacy. The seventh-house Sun merely implies success through opportunities or assistance that others provide, but not because others have done their work for them. Strongly supportive of fairness and equality in all levels of society,

they may, nevertheless, exhibit actions or a life-style that conflicts with such high-minded principles. Some of these individuals are not above choosing a marriage or business partner merely to gain a higher economic or social standing.

SUN IN THE EIGHTH HOUSE

Sun in the eighth house indicates people whose ego is bound inescapably to the depth of their sense of self-worth. They have inner containment and depth others do not often penetrate. There is little urge here for self-promotion merely for its own sake. The behavior and attitude of solar eighth-house individuals are motivated by their own standards and requirements and rarely by any need to impress others. Many of them are skilled in handling resources and material assets. No matter what they gain from other sources, it is ultimately the development and use of their own talent and skills that provide the personal independence and success that truly satisfy them. Family connections or legacies, as well as the absence of these things, can play a significant part in the shaping of their life-style and goals.

SUN IN THE NINTH HOUSE

The ego's ambition and drive identify with the world at large when the Sun is in the ninth house. To find ego satisfaction, solar ninth-house individuals must go beyond their immediate environment, reach for broader experiences and understanding, and establish contact with the many rather than the few. Theirs is a generous, risk-taking nature with the capacity to enjoy the best that life offers. Professional status can become overly important to them, and sometimes they become bombastic and morally righteous. Solar ninth-house people appreciate knowledge even if they are not scholars, are enthusiastic about sports even if they are not good athletes, and are spiritually oriented even if they are not religious. There is increased potential for linguistic skills and acting talent.

SUN IN THE TENTH HOUSE

Magnified and strengthened when the Sun is in the tenth house, the ego seeks a public forum for expression as well as recognition. Very few solar tenth-house individuals are satisfied with staying quietly at home. Those who choose such an unobserved life-style or are forced into it, are apt to be miserable. Even if their main focus is home and family, sooner or later they are compelled to accomplish their personal goals through a career or other activities. The father is emphasized when the Sun is in the tenth house. These individuals feel his influence more than most, especially with regard to their ego development. Their accomplishments may be the direct result of his help, or may be motivated by the lack of it. They frequently bear a strong physical resemblance to the father and to his side of the family. These individuals seek to attain public positions, work for themselves, or occupy an elevated position in the companies that employ them.

SUN IN THE ELEVENTH HOUSE

Sun in the eleventh house indicates people who identify who they are with whom they know—friends, social contacts, and organizations to which they belong. They may be excellent managers of organizations, but inattentive when it comes to managing their personal affairs. Business acumen can bring them wealth and status, but they often prefer to remain in humble or temporary surroundings that do not require their attention or care. Wide-ranging goals supersede the desire to be confined by too many material possessions. However, they can never have too many friends or amusements. Their ego is thrust outward into society, which means their activities and talents must be expressed in that direction. Solar eleventh-house individuals are natural promoters and fund-raisers.

SUN IN THE TWELFTH HOUSE

When the Sun is in the twelfth house, the development and direction of the ego are not affected nearly as much by what these individuals gain in life as they are

by what is lost. Other people may never really come to know or fully understand the real ambitions and nature of solar twelfth-house individuals. The truth is that they often find it difficult to understand themselves. They can surprise others (as well as themselves) with just how strong and determined they can be. Many of them possess keen interest in psychic energy, the occult, dreams, and the subconscious mind. They may also be deeply and adversely influenced by superstition or their past. A twelfth-house Sun ego is strong implication of those who prefer exerting their real control or influence behind the scenes. Even individuals who have a life-style or work that necessitates involvement with the public at large may go out of their way to avoid interactions with people on a personal level.

NATAL MOON IN THE HOUSES

MOON IN THE FIRST HOUSE

Moon in the first house indicates individuals with personal magnetism as well as powerful personal aspirations. In spite of this, they are emotionally vulnerable and can be greatly influenced by others. They are highly sensitive about their looks and the impression they make on others. Their personality and even their physical appearance are subject to constant change. They may, for example, adopt the latest fashions or mode of behavior merely to assure themselves of being accepted. To cover up any real or perceived weakness in themselves, they usually follow one of two paths. Either they work twice as hard as anyone else, often becoming very successful in the bargain, or they avoid failure by not doing anything at all. Even those who seem successful and competent need continual reassurance on an emotional level. They constantly seek advice from one source or another. Lunar first-house people are apt to be guided and influenced in life by women, or one female in particular.

MOON IN THE SECOND HOUSE

Equating money or personal assets with emotional security is characteristic of those born with Moon in the second house. As a result of the tendency to pin their happiness on inanimate treasures, these individuals exhibit certain behavior patterns. Lack of money causes them to feel insecure and vulnerable, so they react by being extremely conservative or even miserly. The more usual behavior, however, is for them to engage in impulse buying, spending money as a means of emotional consolation. These individuals may use money or status to obtain the affections or cooperation of others, or allow themselves to be bartered in this way. The Moon in the second house implies a certain flexibility when it comes to priorities. What is important to these individuals today may not be so important tomorrow. Many lunar second-house people have to assume financial responsibility for the family. They may derive income or property through a woman or as a result of inheritance.

MOON IN THE THIRD HOUSE

Third-house Moon indicates individuals with a singularly strong emotional identification with primary education, siblings, and their neighborhood or community. They are deeply affected by positive or negative circumstances and relationships they encounter in these areas. Lunar third-house people need to express their feelings, although they may prefer to do it in a circumspect manner, especially if they are shy to begin with. They may possess a good bit of intellectual curiosity, but these individuals have to be firmly prodded along intellectual paths or they remain content to reflect the ideas of others rather than generating or asserting their own. The potential to be accident-prone, have limited memory, or lack mechanical and communicative skills causes some of them to live by sheer instinct. For those who escape this potential, there is frequently a strong desire to write or teach. Third-house Moon implies those who like to keep busy in their own communities and prefer working close to home.

MOON IN THE FOURTH HOUSE

Emotional ties to home and family are greatly strengthened in those who are born with the Moon in the fourth house. Researching their family's genealogy and preserving family heirlooms are strong characteristic patterns. Lunar fourth-house people tend to fantasize about their family or family background, but there is no telling exactly how this sort of tendency may be actualized. If these individuals possess mechanical or artistic skills, they use their talents to enhance their home. There are apt to be frequent changes of residence. Either these individuals are raised near the water or will reside near water as adults. Many of them prefer to work or run a business from their home. The mother is the most likely parent to play a dominant role in shaping the desires and needs of fourth-house Moon individuals. They often bear a strong physical resemblance to the mother or to her side of the family. They may receive special assistance from the mother or be profoundly affected by her death or absence.

MOON IN THE FIFTH HOUSE

Fifth-house Moon individuals are sensitive, romantic, and apt to be quite fertile, either literally, figuratively, or both. They tend to be rather lax disciplinarians when dealing with children or pets, but they more than make up for it with affection, concern, and patience. Unless other factors in their personality interfere, they attract a large number of friends and social acquaintances. Their most enjoyable times are likely to be experienced at home and with family members. The pursuit of pleasure is problematic for lunar fifth-house individuals. With concentrated efforts they can be very prudent and self-controlled. However, when they cannot engender self-discipline, they open the door to weight gain, promiscuity, wasted talents, and addiction to habit-forming substances. Fond of the arts and entertainment, many of them possess a fair amount of imagination and creative talent of their own.

MOON IN THE SIXTH HOUSE

Vulnerability to a continuing variety of medical complaints, especially stomach or digestive disorders, is a common pattern when the Moon is in the sixth house. The ailments of these individuals are not usually major threats, but their maladies can disrupt work and routine schedules. As a result, their work habits are inconsistent as is their ability to remain employed. Their general health and psychological outlook are strongly affected by their job, and when the work environment or responsibilities upset them, they lapse into inefficiency and frequent absences. Many lunar sixth-house people operate a business from their home or seek jobs related to homes, food, family life, women, or children. They develop mothering instincts and other strong emotional identification toward those who work for or with them. They often work better with women than with men.

MOON IN THE SEVENTH HOUSE

Individuals who are born with Moon in the seventh house are apt to be the beneficiaries of help or assistance from others, whether or not they have asked for such assistance. They engender strong protective or nurturing instincts in others, and may achieve success solely through the help they receive. Moon in the seventh house is indicative of the emotional nature of the marriage and marriage partner. A man with seventh-house Moon, for example, will often select a wife who physically resembles or exhibits characteristics of his mother. He may marry a very young woman or a woman willing to play the role of mother as well as wife to him. A woman with Moon in the seventh house exhibits strong emotional identification with her husband. She is apt to be dominated in marriage, either by marrying a man with a forceful nature or by the authority or status her husband represents. Even if she divorces her husband, there is the potential she will have difficulty finding psychological release from the failed marriage.

MOON IN THE EIGHTH HOUSE

People who know exactly what they want and go about satisfying their desires with remarkable tenacity describes those born with Moon in the eighth house. These individuals are not apt to be glib or open concerning their emotional needs until what they want is in front of them, and then they become very frank and explicit in expressing themselves. It may be difficult for others to fathom the true feelings of eighth-house lunar people because they so often appear emotionally self-contained or satisfied even when they are not. They are excellent researchers and investigators. They can be very competitive on an emotional level which often results in jealousy and possessiveness. These individuals have some special emotional involvement with legacies or concern with death. The income of marriage partners may be derived from family trusts or from work related to women, children, homes, food, nursing, and family.

MOON IN THE NINTH HOUSE

Moon in the ninth house indicates those who tend to idealize relationships, which can mean they are very romantic but not very realistic. These individuals invariably possess a strong emotional identification with higher learning whether or not they obtain degrees, with cultural pursuits whether or not they have artistic talent, with publishing whether or not they are writers, with travel whether or not they go anywhere, with religion whether or not they are religious, or with politics whether or not they run for public office. Many lunar ninth-house people are adept at foreign languages, promotion, and public relations. Their residence may be close to or associated with a church, university, or in a foreign country. They may marry a foreigner, or their mother may be from a foreign country or of a different race than their father.

MOON IN THE TENTH HOUSE

There is bound to be desire for public acclaim when the Moon is in the tenth house. Individuals born with this Moon position often end up in very prominent public positions or attain public attention for their actions or some particular talent. Someone in their family may achieve fame (or at least notoriety). Although all tenth-house Moon individuals may not gain widespread fame, they often achieve limited public recognition as lecturers, clerics, business leaders, local politicians, or public officials. At the very least, these individuals have considerable concern with their popularity or public repu-tation. They may care more about keeping up appearances than they do about what happens to them privately. Tenth-house Moon implies emotional satisfaction derived through a career or long-range goals. It also includes those who participate in a family business or follow the same career as that of a parent. Even lunar tenth-house people who devote themselves to quietly tending home and family derive renewed energy, inspiration, and enthusiasm from being out in public.

MOON IN THE ELEVENTH HOUSE

Emotional networking is the key factor in describing the Moon in the eleventh house. It is difficult for lunar eleventh-house people to invest their entire concen-tration in one person. They need continuing contacts and a variety of roles to play in the lives of others. These indi-viduals are apt to be well-liked, optimistic, and idealistic. However, even those with a strong personality of their own may tend to rely too heavily on what their friends and associates think. In turn, they are endlessly involved with the many confidences entrusted to them by these people. The Moon in the eleventh house suggests that the aspirations of these individuals can be so changeable that it becomes difficult for them to establish definite commitments, practical plans, or long-range goals. Other potentials for those born with Moon in the eleventh house include living with friends, friends living with them, and that family

members may be among their closest friends. Lunar eleventh-house people may accomplish their successes in life through the assistance or guidance of friends.

MOON IN THE TWELFTH HOUSE

Reality and unreality can become woefully confused when the Moon is in the twelfth house. Those with this Moon position are going to have to work harder than most to avoid the emotional pitfalls of guilt, self-pity, depression, and the idea that there is loss connected with emotional commitment. Some will resist these tendencies while others become victims of their own emotions. What they have to understand is that they do have a choice in the matter. These individuals are not likely to discuss their feelings or fantasies, at least not very often or with too many people. Others find it hard to fathom what they are feeling. It is almost certain that these individuals will experience secret or clandestine attachments. With them the past is never quite over. People and events from their past always seem to reappear. The intuitive powers of lunar twelfth-house individuals is quite remarkable, and many of them are interested in the occult, the subconscious, dreams, and psychic energy. Their nature may be quiet but, nevertheless, they are surprisingly social. Instinctively understanding what is wanted by others, they unobtrusively supply it, thereby gaining appreciation and affection. Many of these individuals prefer to live near the sea.

NATAL MERCURY IN THE HOUSES

MERCURY IN THE FIRST HOUSE

People with Mercury in the first house are very talkative and very busy. Ideas and projects seem to take up their every waking moment. Not only do they eagerly communicate their own ideas and information, most of these individuals are continual conduits of information and news from and about everyone else. Even first-house Mercury individuals who are not inclined to engage in constant chatter possess intellectual curiosity and absorb all sorts of

information that they are happy to share. No matter what the true depth of their understanding may be, those with first-house Mercury are able to give an impression of intelligence, or at least mental alertness. These individuals find it easy to adapt their words and mannerisms to almost any situation. They are quick-witted and clever manipulators. Adept at knowing what other people are thinking, they are often tempted to say what others want to hear. The favorite topic of their conversation is themselves.

MERCURY IN THE SECOND HOUSE

Mercury's mental and mechanical gifts are translated into money and assets by those who are born with this planet in the second house. As a result, these individuals are likely to derive their income through communication, sales, education, writing, publishing; travel, transportation, or the design, installation, and repair of machinery. Second-house Mercury people are adept at picking up on the priorities and values of others, which can make them successful opportunists, although not necessarily manipulators or exploiters. Devising and using networks of all kinds is often their most valuable asset. These individuals deal with the paperwork involved with various aspects of income and money. This includes people who cut out coupons from newspapers to those who work as cashiers, accountants, and bank tellers.

MERCURY IN THE THIRD HOUSE

The emphasis on information, ideas, communication, and transportation is considerably magnified when Mercury occupies the third house, which is why many of those born with third-house Mercury are natural writers, teachers, salespersons, and secretaries. They are the ones most likely to be involved with community projects, mail delivery, telephones, travel, design, and engineering. These individuals are constantly busy with meetings, errands, and continual contact with siblings and neighbors. They always know what's going on around them. Third-house Mercury people have very keen instincts, not ESP exactly, but what may seem like ESP. They may suffer from nervousness, irritability, inattentiveness, and a short attention span.

MERCURY IN THE FOURTH HOUSE

There is likely to be a sizable collection of books, magazines, and other written material in the homes of people who are born with Mercury in the fourth house. If these individuals happen to be more mechanically inclined than intellectually oriented, their homes become the repository of a wide assortment of appliances and other machinery from clocks to cars. Fourth-house Mercury people often prefer to work at home as bookkeepers, writers, researchers, and teachers. Many possess artistic and mechanical skills that enable them to make household repairs and do interior decorating. These individuals may end up living with a sibling or in the same neighborhood as their siblings. Their homes are favorite gathering places for neighbors. Other potentials for fourth-house Mercury people include residing in a mobile home, many changes of residence, frequent alterations to their residence, or more than one residence at a time. These individuals may buy and sell real estate and write about or teach real estate.

MERCURY IN THE FIFTH HOUSE

Creative talent is combined with intellectual and communicative skills when Mercury occupies the fifth house. For this reason many people born with fifth-house Mercury possess talent for creative writing, acting, imitation, and impersonation. Though not above taking a chance on one throw of the dice, these individuals are just as apt to enjoy learning the real mechanics of gambling or trading stocks and commodities. They may devise unique systems of their own for gambling and other speculative ventures. They are most likely to be romantically attracted to those with intellectual ability. Mercury's presence in the fifth house suggests fickleness and the tendency to indulge in more than one romance at a time. Fifth-house Mercury people can be overly critical of a romantic partner or too analytical regarding romance. They know all the right words to say but may not always follow them up with actions. They take pride in children's intellectual accomplishments and enjoy helping them with their studies, which is the reason many fifth-house Mercury individuals are excellent teachers.

MERCURY IN THE SIXTH HOUSE

Mercury in the sixth house indicates those who keep busy whether they work at an outside job or in their home. These individuals are usually employed in Mercury-ruled jobs and professions. They are writers, librarians, researchers, teachers, trainers, physical-fitness experts, and computer or communications experts. They operate or work in employment agencies and in social or health-related agencies and services. Whatever their work happens to be, people with Mercury in the sixth house are sure to generate a lot of paperwork, reports, memos, and lists. Some of them are so preoccupied with unnecessary details or needless tasks, their work is never caught up. Unwilling or unable to delegate tasks to others, they end up exhausted, overworked, and frustrated. Other sixth-house Mercury individuals may have so many things going on that it is difficult for others to assist them. Mercury's link with the sixth-house also implies a preference for working in one's own neighborhood and those who work with or for a neighbor or sibling.

MERCURY IN THE SEVENTH HOUSE

Ideas and intellectual stimulation derived from interactions with others is vital to people born with Mercury in the seventh house. This house position of Mercury also suggests individuals who may have more than one marriage partner, more than one business partner, or several partnerships concerning different enterprises. These individuals may also form partnerships or have contractual agreements of one kind or another with siblings or with aunts and uncles on the mother's side of the family. Seventh-house Mercury people usually have a great deal of communication with their partners, and the partners themselves are apt to be very talkative, intellectually curious, and mechanically skilled. These individuals frequently possess an excellent memory for names, faces, and facts about others.

166

MERCURY IN THE EIGHTH HOUSE

Expressing their ideas and opinions is not apt to be a way of merely passing the time for people born with Mercury in the eighth house. They are often serious-minded individuals who do not enjoy pointless small talk. 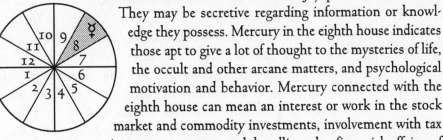 They may be secretive regarding information or knowledge they possess. Mercury in the eighth house indicates those apt to give a lot of thought to the mysteries of life, the occult and other arcane matters, and psychological motivation and behavior. Mercury connected with the eighth house can mean an interest or work in the stock market and commodity investments, involvement with tax or insurance matters, and handling the financial affairs of others. Many of these individuals are pathologists, researchers, and investigators. Eighth-house Mercury also indicates that satisfactory sexual experiences may require mental as well as physical stimulation, and that these individuals may spend more time talking and thinking about sex than they do participating in it.

MERCURY IN THE NINTH HOUSE

There is bound to be intellectual curiosity in those born with Mercury in the ninth house. These individuals may not end up with college degrees or Pulitzer prizes, but they are eager to communicate their ideas and opinions and to improve their understanding and gain new experiences beyond their basic education and immediate environment. Many of these individuals are motivated to learn what they need or want to know on their own if a formal education is not possible. They are avid readers and collectors of books and magazines. Ninth-house Mercury indicates the potential for traveling to foreign countries, receiving advanced education or training in a foreign country, or earning advanced degrees in more than one subject.

MERCURY IN THE TENTH HOUSE

Public recognition is what those born with Mercury in the tenth house are looking for. Even if they do not seek attention for themselves, these individuals

seek a public forum in which to express their ideas, opinions, and information. Some tenth-house individuals write speeches for others or become city planners and engineers. Others enjoy carrying out mental pursuits in public places, such as chess matches in the park or writing letters to the editors of newspapers. Mercury in the tenth house implies the potential for more than one career, or there is a dual-natured quality connected with the career. Other tenth-house Mercury implications include much communication and/or travel with the father or other authority figures, and individuals whose career or profession demands a great deal of traveling, or involves writing, communications, transportation, networking, and areas of teaching or medicine that involve hearing, speech, or sight.

MERCURY IN THE ELEVENTH HOUSE

Mercury in the eleventh house indicates individuals who use friends and acquaintances as sounding boards as well as inspiration for their thoughts and ideas. Whatever their mental pursuits, they enjoy doing them in the company of friends. These individuals may spend a lot of time analyzing and discussing the roles they play (or think they should play) in the lives of others. Mercury in the eleventh house also implies individuals who are interested and active in clubs and associations and are often the ones who write and publish newsletters or handle the paperwork for organizations. They are experts at networking. Because they generally do a lot of circulating, eleventh-house Mercury people often end up with more acquaintances than real friends. This may also have to do with the fact that many of their friendships are based on mental rapport rather than deep emotional commitment. Their best friends are apt to be siblings or neighbors, and they may develop special or secret forms of communication with them.

MERCURY IN THE TWELFTH HOUSE

Those born with Mercury in the twelfth house tend to keep many of their ideas and thoughts to themselves. They are able to think better when they are alone or

in quiet places, and they are apt to be interested in studying dreams, the subconscious, and ESP. Their thinking may not be in the least bit faulty but it is often likely to be based as much on instinct or intuition as it is on logic or reasoning. Sometimes this type of thinking works, and sometimes these individuals need to get a clearer sense of reality. They spend a lot of time thinking about and analyzing their failures and disappointments, their hidden fears and worries, and their past. They often suffer from insomnia. Twelfth-house Mercury implies the potential of a photographic memory or the ability to become a master of disguise. The work that twelfth-house Mercury people do may involve something normally hidden or out of sight, or it may be in areas related to hospitals, prisons, or charitable institutions. These individuals may deal with secret communications, ciphers, or other forms of code.

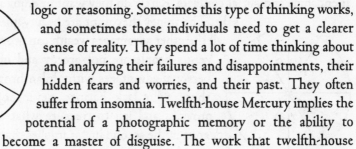

NATAL VENUS IN THE HOUSES

VENUS IN THE FIRST HOUSE

All the charm and social grace of Venus are applied to the personality and, in many cases, the physical appearance of those who are born with this planet in the first house. As a rule their physical features, especially facial features, are evenly balanced. Even when they are not beautiful, first-house Venus people can and do employ their charming personality and mannerisms to enhance their physical appearance. They enjoy dressing well, and use cosmetics and other beauty aids with desirable results. At times some of these individuals become avant-garde as a social statement of sorts, but most of them rarely go to extremes in either their looks or personality. When Venus is knocked off balance by other factors in the background or character, it can mean individuals who are either totally and constantly absorbed with their own appearance and social status or those who are totally negligent of how they look or behave.

VENUS IN THE SECOND HOUSE

Second-house Venus implies individuals who place a high premium on their friendships and social contacts. Rarely do they want or enjoy money for its own sake. The things they want are beauty, pleasure, luxury, and all the other advantages wealth can provide. Second-house Venus people are not greedy and often balance their personal advantages with philanthropic endeavors, but those who lack balance never enjoy what money provides and fail to treasure what should be valued. Venus in the second house implies that income is derived from such areas as law, art, music, jewelry, design, or beautification. Money and assets may come to these individuals through joint ventures or a partner.

VENUS IN THE THIRD HOUSE

Communicative skills and social instincts are enhanced when Venus occupies the third house. Individuals born with Venus in this house are very sociable, especially within their immediate environment. Relations with their siblings and with their neighbors are usually very cordial, and there is apt to be continuous visiting back and forth. These individuals may be quite active in efforts to beautify their community, and they play the role of arbitrator in neighborhood disputes. If Venus is knocked off balance by some factor in their character or background, these individuals can experience difficulty in getting along with relatives and neighbors, or they may be rude and antisocial in their attitudes and expressions. Third-house Venus people frequently form partnerships or joint ventures with a sibling, neighbor, or classmate. Venus also implies that much enjoyment may be derived from vehicles (especially luxury vehicles) and from travel.

VENUS IN THE FOURTH HOUSE

Venus in the fourth house indicates individuals who feel more sociable and romantic when they are in the comfort of their own home, and as a result enjoy

entertaining in this environment. They seek a beautiful, harmonious home. Books, art, and music are prominent features of the decor as well as the activities in their home. Fourth-house Venus people enjoy presenting musical programs at home or extend the hospitality of their home to literary or art organizations. These individuals may be involved in real estate, architecture, interior or landscape design. They may come from a wealthy or luxurious background or inherit wealth or beauty from the mother or mother's side of the family. Venus also suggests a marriage partner from their home town. Negative potentials of fourth-house Venus include lack of enjoyment and harmony in the home and domestic life. These individuals may only use home as a place to camp out, when they bother to come home at all. It can also indicate difficult relationships with parents and other family members.

VENUS IN THE FIFTH HOUSE

The capacity for enjoyment is enhanced when Venus occupies the fifth house. These individuals frequently have the ability to raise socializing and the pursuit of pleasure to an art form. They have such merry, generous natures that others don't notice or become offended if they overindulge themselves. They can be such thoughtful lovers that their amorous conquests don't seem to mind being in a long line of other romantic partners. Fifth-house Venus people enjoy expensive clothes and other luxury items. Venus also implies artistic and other creative talents which is why quite a few of them work in stage and costume design, music, writing, or illustration. They are apt to have special rapport with children, understanding what sort of activities amuse and entertain them. There is no doubt that their tendency to go overboard makes it necessary for these individuals to keep their appetites under control, curb the desire to overindulge children and romantic partners, and confine gambling instincts within safe limits.

VENUS IN THE SIXTH HOUSE

Preference for working with others, in partnership, or in small groups is a good indication of those with Venus in the sixth house. These individuals are apt to be very sociable and cooperative in their working environment and may play the role of peacemaker when disagreements occur. Sixth-house Venus individuals find it difficult to work efficiently in an atmosphere of disharmony. They want to get out of their work an equal measure of what they put into it. They become discouraged by insufficient wages, lack of promotion or recognition, and assignments that have nothing to do with their skills or the reasons for which they were hired. Venus in the sixth house implies the potential for marriage with a coworker or with someone they meet through their work. Jobs that attract these individuals are related to health, beauty, fashions, books, law, counseling (especially marriage counseling), art, design, jewelry, flowers, and public relations. Rich foods, especially sweets, must be limited or their health will suffer. When it comes to keeping physically fit, these individuals do best if they have a partner to encourage and motivate them.

VENUS IN THE SEVENTH HOUSE

The sociable, people-oriented energy of Venus is emphasized in those with Venus in the seventh house. These individuals are charming and polite to everyone they meet. Without constant exposure to other people, they can become withdrawn and unmotivated because they depend on such interactions for inspiration and feedback. However needful seventh-house Venus people are for the company of others, it usually has to be on a one-to-one basis, since they dislike waiting in line and hate to get caught in crowds. They have the capacity to derive much enjoyment from marriage, although Venus in the seventh house is no guarantee of wedded bliss. Whether or not they are married, these individuals achieve some of their greatest successes through partnerships and cooperative efforts of one kind or another. If Venus is knocked off balance because of other factors in their char-

acter or background, these individuals experience difficulty in finding the right partner, or they lack ability to get along with other people in general.

VENUS IN THE EIGHTH HOUSE

Venus in the eighth house indicates people who tend to be quiet but intense in social environments. They do not relish superficial small talk for which they usually have limited ability and less patience. Although it may not be deliberate on their part, eighth-house Venus people often seem enigmatic or intriguing to others. Venus in the eighth house includes the potential that financial gain as well as increased social status can come through marriage. They frequently possess remarkable ability to understand the psychology of human motivation and relationships. These individuals can become jealous and possessive in their sexual attachments even if they do not exhibit such traits with regard to other matters. Negative factors in their personality or background can cause them to marry for money, experience loss of money or status through marriage, contact sexually transmitted disease, or develop neurotic social tendencies.

VENUS IN THE NINTH HOUSE

Appreciation for art, music, and other cultural pursuits is almost always enhanced in those who are born with Venus in the ninth house. These individuals like to think of themselves as citizens of the world and, indeed, many of them fit this description very well. Ninth-house Venus suggests the potentials for romance, marriage, partnership, and other joint ventures in foreign countries or with those of a different nationality or race. Ninth-house Venus people seek work related to art, museums, writing, broadcasting, advertising, diplomacy, foreign trade, or the judicial system. If Venus is knocked off balance by other factors in their character or background, these individuals can develop antisocial attitudes, have difficulty with in-laws, and experience unfavorable court judgments.

VENUS IN THE TENTH HOUSE

Venus in the tenth house indicates people who tend to get noticed because of their talent, looks, charming personality, or all three of these assets. They are very popular and have friends or a partner in prominent positions. Tenth-house Venus also suggests the potential that the father may be especially handsome or he may possess artistic talent. Most tenth-house Venus individuals derive a great deal of pleasure from performing in public. They are excellent ad-libbers, impromptu speakers, and toastmasters. When Venus is knocked off balance, they become overly dramatic and nonappeasable seekers of the spotlight who selfishly use relationships to further their own career or goals. They experience difficult relationships with the father and other authority figures.

VENUS IN THE ELEVENTH HOUSE

Impressive networking skills and innumerable friends and social acquaintances are some of the gifts of those who are born with Venus in the eleventh house. They almost always have a full schedule of social activities, organizational meetings, and other interests that keep them in constant contact with others. These individuals enjoy the companionship of beautiful, charming people, especially those who are musical or artistic. When marriage or romance ends for these individuals, they are often able to remain friends with their partners. Eleventh-house Venus suggests the potential for marrying someone who started out to be just a friend. These individuals are excellent membership chairpersons, fund-raisers, diplomats, and international finance experts. On the negative side of Venus, these individuals can become antisocial and rude, exploit their friends for personal gain, and lack discrimination in choosing friends.

VENUS IN THE TWELFTH HOUSE

Venus in the twelfth house indicates those who are shy in social situations. Their shyness may develop into lack of confidence, and, as a result, they fall in love with

anyone who pays them the slightest attention. They can become victims of relationships with those who threaten "suicide or worse" should the affair be broken off. These individuals may themselves be guilty of using this destructive ploy in order to hold on to partners who threaten to abandon them. The positive side of Venus includes potential for remarkable artistic talent that appeals to others on a subliminal or unconscious level. They also have uncanny intuition about people as well as relationships. Venus implies those who are wise, compassionate judges or counselors, creative writers, or gifted poets. They are almost certain to have secret fantasies and, perhaps, a secret romance or marriage. Twelfth-house Venus implies the potential that their lovers or marriage partners may be dancers, reside near the ocean, have disabilities, or belong to a minority race or culture.

NATAL MARS IN THE HOUSES

MARS IN THE FIRST HOUSE

Red hair, ruddy complexions, or the tendency to wear red hats or other clothing are characteristic trademarks of people who are born with Mars in the first house. Unless other factors in their personality or background subdue such traits, these individuals are often impatient and aggressive. They may not appear openly combative, but with very little provocation they confront situations openly and with force. They want to convey an impression of physical force, or at least their physical presence wherever they go. Most of these individuals have a distinctly masculine approach to things. Females as well as males with first-house Mars can be described as hard drinkers, hard workers, and hard players. Once motivated, they seldom hesitate and go after what they want with energy and enthusiasm. Although a prominent Mars position implies energy and action, there is often too little thought or organization behind what they do and as a result valuable time and talent is needlessly wasted. Those who possess a quieter personality may not be as openly aggressive or impatient. However, they too have an underlying energy and stamina that keeps them going long after others have run out of steam.

MARS IN THE SECOND HOUSE

The physical energy and efforts of Mars are focused on income and assets when this planet occupies the second house. Second-house Mars suggests that physical efforts are likely to be equated with money or with gaining something equally valuable, which is why these people are not inclined to put much work into anything that doesn't pay. They don't usually have much preoccupation with amassing wealth for its own sake, but those who do have a tendency to become passionately dedicated to the accumulation of money never stop to spend it or enjoy any of the advantages it can provide. Second-house Mars people are more likely to be enthusiastic spenders than savers. Their assets may come through men or a particular male influence. Income may also be derived through Mars-ruled enterprises such as sports, armed forces, manufacturing, fire fighting, and physical labor. Mars represents energy. Whether or not these individuals are conscious of it, they value energy and vitality as desirable assets and are attracted to these qualities in others.

MARS IN THE THIRD HOUSE

Mars in the third house speeds the thought process, communication, and mannerisms. It indicates individuals with short attention spans. They have intellectual curiosity so they want to know many things, but unfortunately they usually want to know everything at once. Their impatience makes the procedure of formal education very confining. Third-house Mars people learn best through actual physical experience. Although they dislike long-winded lectures and convoluted thinking in other people, they are not above engaging in these activities themselves. Taking care of details and organization presents too much of a task, and if they are obliged to pay attention to such matters, they resort to hiring or cajoling others to do it for them. They are most physically active in their own neighborhood and community, so much so that many of them never venture too far away from it. These individuals are compelled to turn thoughts and ideas into action. A too quick or volatile temper and the tendency to engage in ill-considered acts are negative

potentials, along with being accident-prone, especially with cars and while traveling within a short distance of home. On the positive side, Mars suggests mechanical ability, impressive oratory, and inspired ideas.

MARS IN THE FOURTH HOUSE

A great deal of physical energy and vitality is likely to be focused on family activities and various aspects of home and domestic life when Mars occupies the fourth house. This has a wide range of potentials for individuals born with fourth-house Mars. It may mean, for example, that their occupation involves real estate, interior design, architecture, family counseling, a family business, or business operated in their home. Fourth-house Mars is a strong indication of an active domestic environment. There may be so much physical activity it is difficult for these individuals to generate a serene and quiet atmosphere when the need arises. Their residence is apt to be designed and/or decorated with a distinctly masculine orientation using bold colors (perhaps a lot of red, which is a favorite Mars color). There is potential that the mother may be overly domineering or that she may be forced by circumstances to play the role of father as well as mother. The negative potential includes a volatile, perhaps violent domestic environment, as well as the danger of accidents or fire in the home.

MARS IN THE FIFTH HOUSE

Creative projects, children, romance, social activities, and the pursuit of amusement and pleasure are primary targets for the physical efforts of individuals with Mars in the fifth house. This Mars position indicates love of children, and further it implies individuals with a high potential for procreation. Long on passion, fifth-house Mars people can be short on patience when it comes to the more subtle intricacies of romance. Those whose life-style does not include bearing children or engaging in romantic adventures themselves may deal with these subjects on a professional or impersonal level, or they may sublimate their energy into other creatively satisfying activities.

The energy of fifth-house Mars suggests those with a gambler's heart. They are also likely to be sports enthusiasts as well as participants. Physical pleasures are pursued with enthusiasm, and their sense of humor may extend to playing practical jokes. This position of Mars relies heavily on the maturity of those who inherit it. If there are negative factors in their personality or background, they can be grossly self-indulgent and egotistical or waste their skills and talent.

MARS IN THE SIXTH HOUSE

Mars in the sixth house indicates those who put a lot of their energy and vitality into their work. It indicates mechanical skills, and many of these individuals are inventors, surgeons, tailors, machinists, engineers, builders, and inveterate tinkerers. Those with managerial skills are tireless administrators who know how to extract maximum efficiency from their staffs. Sixth-house Mars individuals often choose a line of work that involves an element of risk. The risk could be physical, economic, or it could be emotional as in the case of those who work with very ill or disturbed people. Their work may involve manufacture or sale of knives, weapons, explosives, or firefighting equipment. Whatever their job, these individuals are happiest in an active environment that offers a wide variety of challenges and tasks. Mars in the sixth house also suggests enthusiasm for maintaining health and physical fitness. If other factors contribute to giving these individuals a high level of energy, they engage in a variety of strenuous activities that keep them in shape. They must guard against high blood pressure, fever, headaches, and strain.

MARS IN THE SEVENTH HOUSE

Marriage, business partnerships, joint ventures, contractual negotiations or other legal matters, and dealing with other people in general are the focus for the physical efforts of those born with Mars in the seventh house. They enthuse and encourage others to be sure, but seventh-house Mars people also rely on others to inspire energy and vitality within themselves. Seventh-house Mars implies physical contacts with others, but whether they are hostile confrontations or cooperative efforts is not described simply by Mars in the seventh house.

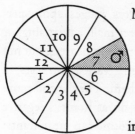

Marriage or business partnerships may not always be easy for them to establish. Their energy and activities can be sapped or overshadowed by an overly aggressive partner. Negative factors in their personality or background can mean argumentative and even violent encounters, and loss of a partner through accident. Seventh-house Mars individuals may seek a career in law and contract negotiation or marry someone who works in these areas.

MARS IN THE EIGHTH HOUSE

Energy and stamina are given intensity when Mars occupies the eighth house. Where the energy is applied is not determined solely by Mars in the eighth house, but aggressiveness and focus are connected with almost every physical effort. Individuals who are born with Mars in the eighth house have specific desires and no hesitation about gratifying them. They may be secretive or circumspect in their movements and activities, or at least give others that kind of impression. The negative potential of this Mars position includes those who are deeply possessive or vengeful. Mars in the eighth house suggests an active sex life, concern with sexual matters, and intense attitudes and mannerisms toward the opposite sex. Many of these individuals develop remarkable ability to understand sexuality from a psychological as well as physical point of view and to do research or counseling in this field. Eighth-house Mars people are physically resourceful and frequently are able to do more than one thing extremely well. They are likely to possess mechanical and/or artistic skills that are especially valuable in renovation and remodeling.

MARS IN THE NINTH HOUSE

Mars in the ninth house indicates those who concentrate energy and physical efforts in areas related to higher education, specialized training, politics, sports, philosophy, art, religion, sociology, music, publishing, foreign studies, and travel. Even though these individuals may not be involved professionally in any of these areas, they are likely to pursue some type of active involvement in them. Mars in

the ninth house also indicates lawyers, judges, spokespersons, and those who work in direct mail, advertising, or broadcasting. Home may be where their heart is, but not necessarily where the many and varied interests of ninth-house Mars people take them. They spend more time running around than they do at home. Negative factors in their personality or background can mean frantic actions and fanatic zeal. It also signifies problems related to higher education, unfavorable court decisions, and confrontations with in-laws. The positive ninth-house Mars potential suggests a lively, risk-taking nature that urges these individuals to seek higher levels of understanding, new adventures, and experiences beyond their immediate environment.

MARS IN THE TENTH HOUSE

Those who are born with a tenth-house Mars enjoy carrying out their work or other activities in a public place. These individuals are very ambitious and are excellent promoters. For the most part it is themselves or their own efforts that they promote, but they can become enthusiastic about seeking public attention for someone else or a cause in which they have great interest. Some people may work as tirelessly as they do, but few will match the aggressiveness and persuasive force of tenth-house Mars individuals. Some people may be content to work quietly behind the scenes, but tenth-house Mars people want their efforts to be noticed. They are apt to work better alone and prefer to operate their own business rather than work for anyone else. The life-style they choose is not apt to be tranquil or ordinary. Mars in the tenth house suggests difficulty attracting a marriage partner. This is principally because their attention is so often focused on their career or other goals that they don't have time for anyone else or they are so aggressive that a potential marriage partner feels threatened. The negative potential of this Mars position implies a father who is domineering or disagreements with superiors and other authority figures.

MARS IN THE ELEVENTH HOUSE

Those who put energy and vitality into social relationships and who constantly devise schemes for attaining what they want are likely to have Mars in the eleventh house. The rashness and passion associated with 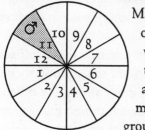 Mars also mean they work very hard for something but once they get it, they want something else. These individuals often have many acquaintances but few friends, there being more energy applied to participating in activities with friends than in making emotional commitments. Negative factors in their personality or background increase potential for hostile confrontation with friends and acquaintances. It can also mean they are so irascible and contentious that they are unable to attract anyone with enough patience to put up with them. Mars in the eleventh house indicates that most friendships are formed either with men or with people of either sex who have an Aries type of nature and energy, such as sports enthusiasts, hunters, or daredevils.

MARS IN THE TWELFTH HOUSE

The activities of those with Mars in the twelfth house are not carried out in places of high visibility. The things these individuals do may go unrecognized or undetected. They may deliberately attempt to be secretive, or sometimes it is a case where the nature of their work or 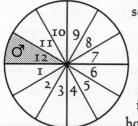 activities requires clandestine movements. Twelfth-house Mars suggests individuals whose job or profession may not be connected with what they would really like to do. It is also an indication that they work in charitable organizations or in places of confinement such as hospitals and prisons. The twelfth-house position of Mars indicates those who have an interest in the occult, dreams, or the unconscious mind. The negative potential includes the loss of a partner, being cheated or deceived by a partner, or unrealistic ambitions and undertakings. The real energy, depth of passion, and power in these individuals are not readily apparent to others.

NATAL JUPITER IN THE HOUSES

JUPITER IN THE FIRST HOUSE

A people-oriented personality, independence, optimism, and flair for exaggeration and dramatic gestures are characteristic of people born with Jupiter in the first house. They possess intellectual curiosity and a quick wit. Whether or not they are serious scholars, these individuals respect knowledge. They want to surround themselves with all the good things in life and to give others the impression that they have such things. Enjoyment of food and drink causes many of them to gain weight, but bigness may be an element of their personality and spirit rather than their physical girth. First-house Jupiter people frequently have talent for acting and impersonation. As a rule, they never miss an opportunity to travel, have new experiences, or embark on new adventures. They are very open and honest, and their too-candid remarks can be misinterpreted as rudeness. They are apt to resemble their father in looks and personality.

JUPITER IN THE SECOND HOUSE

People who like to succeed on their own is one way to describe those with Jupiter in the second house. These individuals thrive on the challenge of making their own money. Second-house Jupiter does not guarantee wealth or luck in monetary matters, but it invariably means generosity and the potential for spending money lavishly. There is potential for travel or trade that is related to foreign goods and services as a means of livelihood. Other possible sources of income for second-house Jupiter people include consulting, publishing, theater, sports, education, or religion. These individuals usually place a high priority and value on knowledge even though they may not be scholars themselves. Jupiter also implies they may receive financial help in attaining higher education and/or they may be the ones to come to the aid of others in this respect.

JUPITER IN THE THIRD HOUSE

Jupiter in the third house indicates very talkative people, born communicators and salesmen. Although this Jupiter position implies that they are very bright and anxious to learn new things, it doesn't mean they will become scholars. If these individuals have trouble with school, it's because they prefer to learn on their own, following their interests and curiosity rather than plodding through repetitious lessons. They constantly seek to expand their intellectual horizons, even if it is only by reading the daily newspaper. Jupiter in the third house implies mechanical ability, artistic skills, or writing talent.

They and/or their father may work in sales, advertising, drama, dance, publishing, travel, promotion, politics, education, or religion. These individuals tend to get involved with community actions and projects. Jupiter's third-house presence implies generosity to family members as well as to neighbors. Negative factors in their personality or background can mean inability to settle down, physical awkwardness (sometimes to the point of being accident-prone), disorganization, procrastination, unwillingness to take responsibility, and tendency to shade the truth or exaggerate facts.

JUPITER IN THE FOURTH HOUSE

The nature of the background and upbringing of people who are born with Jupiter in the fourth house might be described as an environment that encourages independent thinking and personal growth and emphasizes religion, education, or cultural pursuits. As a rule, these individuals enjoy warmth, merriness, and generosity in their home and family. Their residence, either as children or adults, may be quite grand or opulent, evidence of the best advantages that life has to offer. The negative potential can mean those who suffer from the effect of an environment that is too permissive, or one that places too much importance on material wealth or status and not enough on developing personal character and loving relationships. There is also potential that these individuals are born in a foreign country or their parents are of foreign birth. More than one language may be spoken in their

home. The fourth house of the horoscope represents the beginning as well as the end of things. No matter what happens to these individuals, they always seem to land on their feet.

JUPITER IN THE FIFTH HOUSE

Jupiter in the fifth house indicates those with a strong sense of their own creative spirit. It is more than an expression of artistic talent, vivid imagination, or abundant procreation. These individuals want to feel somehow set apart from the world while still a part of it; they want to associate themselves with higher spiritual or intellectual levels. However, even those who aspire to the highest planes of spirituality and creativity are likely to possess a merry disposition that is not above enjoying the pleasures and delights of the physical world. Jupiter in the fifth house implies those who are likely to be very generous to romantic partners, having the ability to be a friend as well as a lover to them. They are most attracted (romantically or platonically) to people with a high degree of intelligence, enthusiasm, spirituality, and a flair for excitement and drama. Whether or not fifth-house Jupiter individuals become parents themselves, their attitude toward children is warm and caring, although perhaps a bit too indulgent at times. Likely to be fond of animals, they treat their pets with the same doting affection as their children. The negative potentials of this Jupiter house position include the possibility of disappointment in romance and speculative ventures, gross exaggeration, and reckless indulgence.

JUPITER IN THE SIXTH HOUSE

People who require a lot of independence and latitude in their work are characteristic of those born with Jupiter in the sixth house. Many of them prefer to operate their own businesses. When they are employed by others, however, they are happiest when they can work without too much supervision, when they can proceed at their own pace and make their own deadlines, and when they are allowed to take some liberty in changing the tasks and projects they are given. These individuals often prefer working with the public and

184

in highly visible areas. Travel or publishing may be related to their job. They may be employed by relatives from their mother's side of the family. Although sixth-house Jupiter people have a tendency to exaggerate their own importance at times, they are cheerful and optimistic toward those who work for or with them. The negative potentials include those who are chronically disorganized in their work and those who experience health problems that result from overindulgence.

JUPITER IN THE SEVENTH HOUSE

Marriage and business partnerships require a certain amount of independence when Jupiter is in the seventh house. People born with this Jupiter position cannot let their alliances become burdened by possessiveness or emotional dependency. Marriage, joint ventures, and partnerships are likely to broaden their intellectual horizon, increase their economic or social status, and expand their life-style. Their marriage or business partner may tend to propose big ideas and grandiose schemes, and/or be physically above average in size. Seventh-house Jupiter individuals may be regarded by others as scholarly, influential, generous, or spiritual, some-times without much justification for such opinions. Females with seventh-house Jupiter often marry men that resemble or characterize their father. The negative potentials include those who marry solely to improve their wealth or status and those who take their partner too much for granted.

JUPITER IN THE EIGHTH HOUSE

People who feel that a vital part of their independence and importance as an individual depends on their material and nonmaterial resources often have Jupiter in the eighth house. These individuals may be very interested in the stock market, handle property and investments for others, or be involved with taxes, insurance, and estate planning. Jupiter in the eighth house is also an implication of remarkable recuperative powers. The potential involves more than recovery from physical illness; it includes emotional upheavals, financial setbacks, and other disappointments or failures. Eighth-house Jupiter

implies the possibility of a wealthy marriage partner, and it also suggests that a partner's income may be derived through writing, publishing, politics, law, foreign trade, or education. The negative potential is that expansiveness and optimism can waste resources and monumental debt may be incurred.

JUPITER IN THE NINTH HOUSE

Intellectual curiosity, independent attitudes, idealism, and quickness of mind are associated with Jupiter in the ninth house. People born with this Jupiter house position have great respect for knowledge. There is no guarantee they will pursue higher education, but they generally have a talent for getting the latest news as well as gossip. Avid readers of newspapers and magazines, these individuals are usually very well informed about political and social issues. Ninth-house Jupiter suggests potential talent for languages, diplomacy, and arbitration. These individuals enjoy traveling, cultural pursuits, gambling, sports, and other activities that offer intellectual and physical challenge. Many of them have a strong religious or spiritual nature, a wonderful sense of humor, and a gift for storytelling. Negative potentials can mean mental laziness, disorganization, dishonesty, exaggeration, and overestimation.

JUPITER IN THE TENTH HOUSE

Jupiter in the tenth house indicates those who consciously or subconsciously seek a public forum to exhibit their intellectual skills, artistic talent, or specialized training. Their knowledge and skills must be transmitted to others, and so they seek work or other activities that put them directly in touch with the public. Jupiter's association with the tenth house suggests individuals with special interest or a career in such areas as promotion, entertainment, politics, art, sales, broadcasting, education, or religion. They effortlessly attract the attention of those with power and influence, and just as effortlessly achieve such positions themselves. A tenth-house Jupiter implies wealth, honor, and status related to the father. It also suggests the father is a generous parent who broadens his offspring's intellectual horizons and gives

valuable assistance and advice. The negative potentials of Jupiter in the tenth house include difficulty or loss related to the father, restrictions imposed by superiors, and frustration or delay in attaining promotions or other personal goals. It can also mean individuals who are put in situations for which they are not adequately prepared or for which they lack the necessary skills.

JUPITER IN THE ELEVENTH HOUSE

People who are born with Jupiter in the eleventh house derive much happiness and joy through friends, children, and social contacts. They are very optimistic and enjoy everything life has to offer. These individuals are likely to gain personal growth and advancement through their network of friends and acquaintances. When circumstances or lack of motivation leaves no opportunity to make friends or join groups and associations, their progress may suffer accordingly. Sometimes these individuals collect more friends and acquaintances than a single lifetime can handle. Eleventh-house Jupiter people feel they are someone's friend even though the association consists of nothing more than a single meeting. The negative potential includes those who never settle for anything less than the best and seek to attain the highest social status, no matter what the cost or whether it is obtained at the expense of more important values. It also implies people who are never content, always wanting more than what they have.

JUPITER IN THE TWELFTH HOUSE

Jupiter in the twelfth house indicates those who possess remarkable inability to worry. They may never even get that far in their thinking. They simple forge ahead. In troubled or risky situations that make most people uneasy, twelfth-house Jupiter individuals seem to have a vague sense that they will somehow be saved, even if the rescue usually occurs at the eleventh hour. For better or worse they are encouraged in such notions since, in fact, they are often rescued. Sometimes they are saved by unexpected or unknown sources, and sometimes their savior is a marriage partner or other relative. These

187

individuals are often very generous themselves when it comes to helping others. Jupiter represents expansive thinking, and the twelfth house does not present a clear sense of reality. As a result, they may never be certain of their own limitations or have a true idea of what is and what is not possible. These individuals can achieve astounding success simply because no one told them they couldn't. Many of them possess a highly developed intuition and are interested in occult subjects, the subconscious mind, and the interpretation of dreams. Jupiter's twelfth-house position implies fondness for gambling, theater, art, and dancing. The ocean or marine life may also have particular appeal.

NATAL SATURN IN THE HOUSES

SATURN IN THE FIRST HOUSE

For those with Saturn in the first house, the biggest lessons in life involve self-image. It doesn't matter what circumstances life presents, the biggest challenge for these individuals is always themselves. First-house Saturn indicates difficult circumstances surrounding birth and the early years of life. Whatever their childhood was like, these individuals are consciously or subconsciously disappointed by it and with themselves as well. Such inner negativity may result in their denying themselves any personal success or happiness, or they may completely abandon themselves to pleasure and other indulgences as a form of self-destruction. They feel they are unworthy, unattractive, and undesirable, no matter what the mirror reflects or what others may tell them. At every turn, they are confronted by their fears and insecurities. How well they learn to deal with such personal conflict becomes a mark of their strength and success as an adult. First-house Saturn may indicate inner turmoil but by no means does it suggest a somber or colorless personality. On the contrary, these individuals usually overcompensate by developing a cheerful demeanor. They are willing to accept hardship and responsibilities, which, in most cases, they feel they were born to endure.

SATURN IN THE SECOND HOUSE

Whether they are rich or poor, people born with Saturn in the second house worry about money. Concern with money, however, is usually their motivation to acquire it, and few of them ever experience the poverty they fear. The biggest lessons in life for these individuals involve material assets as well as values and priorities. These are not easy lessons because the struggle is not necessarily lack of wealth or lack of values but a question of development and use of these things. Second-house Saturn individuals can, for example, be foolishly extravagant when they should be cautious and too prudent when they should be generous. They may be so wary about being taken advantage of that they refuse to help deserving people or causes. Some of them overcompensate for such unworthy suspicions by being too generous, with the result that people do take advantage of them. Grappling with values, priorities, and money—and in the process, learning what is really important in life—is the key to their happiness and success.

SATURN IN THE THIRD HOUSE

Learning, communication, and the development or use of basic skills are going to present some problems or limitations somewhere along the line for those with Saturn in the third house. Circumstances may prevent or greatly restrict their early education, or they may simply be uninterested students. Later in life, however, these individuals are more receptive, even eager to learn and to communicate their thoughts and ideas. Saturn implies the potential for learning disabilities and sight, hearing, or speech impediments. It also suggests those who suffer from depression or are overly cautious and pessimistic. Other areas of concern can involve siblings, and there are several possibilities regarding them. Third-house Saturn people may be deprived of such relationships by being an only child. A generation gap may exist that limits their contacts or understanding with much older siblings. They may have to assume responsibility for younger brothers and sisters. Relationships with neighbors and schoolmates can be stable and long-lasting, but loss of privacy or

other burdens can sometimes complicate these associations. Travel may be restricted, or accommodations while traveling may be austere. These individuals own few cars or other vehicles, and the standard, practical models they choose give them many years of dependable service. Saturn suggests a stable, practical (if unimaginative) mind. Third-house Saturn individuals are able to present well-organized and structured ideas and information, and they can develop and make good use of basic mechanical, design, or computer skills. Many of them become the soul of authority, reliability, and strength to their family and neighbors.

SATURN IN THE FOURTH HOUSE

Learning to accept and to handle family relationships, hardships, and responsibilities is what Saturn in the fourth house is all about. For those born with this Saturn, there is an austerity and strictness that may apply to the personality of one or both of their parents, to the emotional content of their home, or to physical aspects of their surroundings. It can mean those who are deprived of a parent early in life. Whatever their actual childhood circumstance or family history may be, these individuals harbor great concerns about it. As adults they may be strict and inflexible in their own domestic environment or so fearful as to dismiss any notion of establishing their own home or family. Saturn's positive association includes those who maintain very stable family relationships. Many of these individuals live their entire life in the same house or hometown. In some cases they may become homebound, unable through illness or for other reasons to leave their residence.

SATURN IN THE FIFTH HOUSE

People born with Saturn in the fifth house find that their biggest restrictions and other obstacles in life involve romance, the pursuit of pleasure, speculative ventures, the development and use of creative talent, and children. For fifth-house Saturn individuals there is often a fear of rejection that makes them hesitant in matters of the heart. Spontaneity is out of the question. Their romantic attachments are burdened by commitment or other inhibitory factors somewhere along the line. Self-indulgence and the pursuit of pleasure are sure to be penalized.

Social activities are often undertaken as much for business purposes and obligatory reasons as for simple enjoyment. Gambling is not wise. When good luck does come along, it must never be taken for granted. The best philosophy for these individuals is to take the money and run. Their artistic or creative talent may be limited or nonexistent. Those who do possess such talent may have difficulty developing or gaining recognition for it. Saturn's connection with restriction does not necessarily indicate lack of offspring. It implies that relationships with young children may be burdened with too much somberness or formality. However, as their children mature, relationships with them may become more satisfying. Fifth-house Saturn individuals may have to assume the entire parental responsibility for their children. Maintaining a healthy, balanced perspective and determined attitude in all that has just been described brings these individuals well-earned joy.

SATURN IN THE SIXTH HOUSE

Saturn in the sixth house suggests those who tend to be overly concerned about their job. They are often workaholics who suffer stress from overwork. Whether they work at home or at a job, they are required to make a total commitment to their tasks. Other people may not be penalized if they refuse to accept unpleasant chores, take shortcuts, or get others to do their work, but sixth-house Saturn individuals rarely succeed in such attempts. Part of their responsibilities may require supervising or giving extra assistance to coworkers. These individuals do well in an occupation that involves definite methods and procedures. Other potentials include those who stay in the same job for many years. Longevity of service may also apply if these individuals hire others to work for them. Others may be able to get away with neglecting themselves year after year, but when sixth-house Saturn individuals fail to maintain their health and physical fitness, they suffer accordingly. Illnesses that they experience are apt to be lingering or of a chronic nature.

SATURN IN THE SEVENTH HOUSE

It is hard for people born with Saturn in the seventh house to establish quick or lighthearted contacts with others. Whether or not these individuals encourage it, others find them to be rather serious and often regard them as an authority figure or at least very competent in some area. As a result, seventh-house Saturn people either keep themselves in a constant state of turmoil trying to live up to what they think others expect of them, or fearing such responsibility, they may totally avoid making commitments to others. These individuals are apt to constantly encounter restrictions when trying to get others to cooperate. For them, marriage will not be without heavy responsibilities. They may not succeed should they marry in haste, or their spouse may be sickly or a burden in some other way. Other potentials include those for whom marriage is a means of security, those who marry someone much older, and those who develop such negative opinions about marriage that they avoid it altogether. In spite of these possibilities, Saturn does not doom the prospects for wedded bliss. Many of these individuals enjoy stable, long-lasting unions. If adversity does come along, it can make the alliance even stronger. Others may look upon these individuals as having gained little or nothing by marriage. However, these individuals, as well as their spouses, may not share or be the least bit adversely influenced by such outside opinions.

SATURN IN THE EIGHTH HOUSE

Saturn in the eighth house indicates those who should not expect to gain financially through marriage. Their spouse may have nothing in the way of assets to contribute, or these individuals suffer because of their partner's attitude and behavior with regard to joint income. If they marry for money or status, they will come to regret such a venture. Other potentials include those unlikely to receive an inheritance and those whose legacy is lost or becomes more of a burden than a boon. Their genetic inheritance contains the potential for chronic illness or other physical defects. When it comes to financial matters, eighth-house Saturn individuals either fear debt so much that

they refuse to seek loans of any kind, or they incur debt that leads to bankruptcy and other situations from which they are forced to slowly and painfully extricate themselves. Aversion to insurance can cause them to avoid it or have so little that they are inadequately protected. Some of them worry about it so much they end up paying for expensive premiums far in excess of what is necessary. These individuals also fear death and the tax collector. Although Saturn's description seems harsh, it also implies those who develop solid values, trustworthiness, and the ability to manage resources responsibly.

SATURN IN THE NINTH HOUSE

Ninth-house Saturn people must reach beyond their immediate environment to gain the experiences and understanding they are required to have in life. And most of them are apt to be forced by choice or circumstance to be extremely practical about how they do it. Advanced training and higher education, for example, cannot be undertaken as a mere whim or luxury, or they may have to wait until later in life to accomplish these things. Sooner or later, ninth-house Saturn individuals realize the importance of taking a serious approach to such matters when they come to rely heavily on whatever knowledge and skills they have attained. Living in a foreign country or dealing with those of another race or culture is apt to present some difficult or burdensome situation for them. Religion can impose severe limitations rather than spiritual freedom. These individuals may have significant responsibilities concerning the job or health of a parent. Circumstances related to in-laws or a second marriage may be long-lasting and stable, although the negative potential suggests added responsibilities are also likely.

SATURN IN THE TENTH HOUSE

A strong tendency to worry a great deal about appearances and what others think of them is characteristic of those born with tenth-house Saturn. Saturn's association with the tenth house also indicates special concerns related to the father, as well as supervisors and other authority figures in general. These individuals may be separated at a young age from their father. The father may be austere, strict, or overburdened with responsibilities. They may have to assume responsibility

for the father. The strongest motivations these individuals have in life is related to the positive or negative paternal relationship they experience. Tenth-house Saturn suggests those with strong career goals. They seek positions of authority and are dedicated to pushing themselves relentlessly forward. As a result, they usually accomplish much of what they set out to do, although it takes them longer to succeed. Success or good fortune that these individuals gain is accompanied by heavy responsibilities. Those willing to accept their rewards on this basis will do well in life. Those who waste what they attain or abuse any authority or power with which they are entrusted are invariably disgraced and forced to start over.

SATURN IN THE ELEVENTH HOUSE

Eleventh-house Saturn individuals can expect heavy responsibilities related to the role they play in the lives of others, especially friends, children (not necessarily their biological offspring), and others who make up their personal network. Saturn's association here does not imply lack of people in their life, and, indeed, they may enjoy solid, long-lasting relationships. Even with many friends, these individuals frequently harbor the notion that they are friendless and unappreciated. Many of them have an aversion or little motivation to join societies. Those who do become a member of a club are often given or take on responsibilities in the organization. Saturn's association with the eleventh house suggests that income or promotion from a career or profession may be limited, delayed, or prove to be unrewarding. The father is apt to have few assets, and, if he has wealth, it may be of little use to them. Real happiness and enjoyment will be hard won and perhaps not achieved until later in life.

SATURN IN THE TWELFTH HOUSE

The past can impose severe burdens on the present as well as the future when Saturn occupies the twelfth house. It indicates those who must overcome failure, disappointment, loss, and confinement or other severe limitations. These

individuals have to confront any of these unpleasant situations. They must learn from them, let them go, and move forward with determination. They may be helped in their endeavors by others who have the love and patience to guide them slowly through the labyrinths of fears and misgivings. Great personal success in life is possible for twelfth-house Saturn people, although gaining recognition for what they accomplish may be difficult. Curiosity about psychic phenomena and the occult may be keen, but areas that involve superstition can pose a serious threat to their peace of mind. Attempts at secrecy may work at times, but they often lack the necessary guile, imagination, or luck to carry it off successfully. Saturn in the twelfth house suggests their marriage partner may suffer from chronic illness or have a job that entails heavy responsibilities.

NATAL URANUS IN THE HOUSES
URANUS IN THE FIRST HOUSE

People born with Uranus in the first house tend to be argumentative and enjoy playing devil's advocate. They think of themselves as being different and unique, or at least they want to give the appearance of being so. It is one reason they love to take the opposing side in discussions. The personality and appearance of these individuals are often somewhat off-beat or out of step with current fashion. They are capable of such unexpected behavior and reactions that it is difficult to predict with certainty what they will do in any given situation. Although they require a certain amount of personal independence, marriage is not usually a problem unless their partner becomes too dependent or too possessive. They can get restless if there isn't enough in their immediate environment to stimulate them, but whether or not they will seek to actually change a boring existence or just keep roaming around in the same places depends on their individual personality and background. First-house Uranus people are fascinated by strange and unusual things or people. Intrigued by futuristic topics and technologies, they also have great interest in history and politics.

URANUS IN THE SECOND HOUSE

Income and material assets are vulnerable to sudden change when Uranus occupies the second house. This implies the improvement of monetary circumstances for those with little wealth, and the danger of loss for those with many assets. The spending attitudes and habits of second-house Uranus individuals can vary considerably from one time to the next. Unlikely to be dedicated to earning money for its own sake, they are more interested in the personal freedom that money can buy. Their income may be related to a fraternal organization or earned through the help and influence of friends. Their livelihood may also be derived from an unorthodox or unusual line of work or through more mundane areas that involve computers, research and development, antiques, international finance, medicine, television, or social work. Other potentials for Uranus in the second house include those whose priorities and values are unorthodox or radical, and those whose established values and priorities are altered by an unexpected event or change in their life. Among the things these individuals value the most are freedom and friendship.

URANUS IN THE THIRD HOUSE

A keen and original intellect is a characteristic pattern of those with Uranus in the third house, although how their intellect will be manifested is unpredictable. It is difficult for these individuals to use or communicate what they learn unless they practice retention, develop organization, and eliminate distractions. Taking tests can also be difficult for them. They want to learn and to convey what they actually know rather than what others require them to know. Likely to be very adept and self-taught, these individuals enjoy interesting trivia and knowledge of odd and unusual subjects. Their intellectual and physical reactions to stimuli are immediate. It is difficult for them to maintain consistency and a steady rhythm in their mental processes as well as physical mannerisms and habits. Unpredictable, jerky movements can make them very clumsy, and, in some cases, accident-prone. In the structured routine of the classroom, they soon become restless. It is not easy

for them to sit quietly for long periods, even when being entertained. If subjected to long-winded sermons or boring lectures, they head for the nearest exit. For all their jumpiness and unpredictability, third-house Uranus people have remarkable mental poise. Rarely frightened or upset by unusual situations or people, third-house Uranus individuals have a very calming influence on others who are mentally distressed or hysterical. Eagerly receptive to new ideas and methods, they also come up with ingenious ideas and clever solutions of their own. Separation from siblings is a likelihood. Plans often develop complications or go awry for one reason or another, usually due to circumstances for which these individuals are not responsible. As if to make up for being unable to plan ahead, they do things spontaneously or at the last minute with very little fuss or dislocation.

URANUS IN THE FOURTH HOUSE

Unpredictable, unusual, or unorthodox circumstances regarding home and family are likely to be experienced by those who are born with Uranus in the fourth house. These individuals adopt a very different life-style or reside in a much different type of place than the one in which they were brought up. Choosing a dramatically different life-style or environment may be deliberate on their part, but it occurs more often as a result of circumstances over which they have no control. Other potentials associated with a fourth-house Uranus include sudden separation from a parent or from home and family, and circumstances that necessitate living for a time under abnormal or unusual conditions. Fourth-house Uranus also suggests those who tend to favor odd or unusual designs and architecture in their home and its furnishings. These individuals mix the very old with the very new in eclectic arrangements. Their home is likely to be the favorite gathering place for friends and groups or organizations to which they belong.

URANUS IN THE FIFTH HOUSE

Unusual romantic attachments, romance encountered in unexpected places, and romance that begins or ends suddenly or unexpectedly are some of the patterns that occur when Uranus occupies the fifth house. Fifth-house Uranus people

often possess highly unique artistic or creative talent. It is also possible that their children may be quite unusual or distinguished in some way. Women with Uranus in the fifth house may have difficulty conceiving children. They may choose not to bear children at all, preferring to concentrate their creative energies elsewhere. People with Uranus in the fifth house seek unusual amusements, and they enjoy taking very unique vacations or they vacation in off-beat places. Some of these individuals may devise unusual methods for gambling or speculation.

URANUS IN THE SIXTH HOUSE

Uranus in the sixth house indicates those who seek a job that allows maximum personal freedom. The ideal situation is to work for themselves. If that isn't possible, the next best thing is to be able to select their own schedule and work at their own pace. They dislike being saddled with repetitive, uninteresting tasks. If the challenge of the job fades, sixth-house Uranus people may either quit and go on to something else or find ways to make their work more exciting. These individuals usually experience many changes of employment. Their job may unexpectedly or abruptly be terminated, but they are just as likely to leave on their own out of boredom and restlessness. They may be attracted to unusual lines of work. More traditional areas in which they are likely to be employed include medicine, computers, sales, social work, international finance, fund-raising, electronics, or teaching. Although these individuals may be very healthy most of the time, the association of Uranus in the sixth house implies that illness tends to occur suddenly or unexpectedly and at highly inconvenient times. These individuals may adopt unorthodox or unusual methods to maintain health and physical fitness.

URANUS IN THE SEVENTH HOUSE

If people born with Uranus in the seventh house manage to accomplish a long and stable marriage, they can count themselves fortunate. Seventh-house Uranus

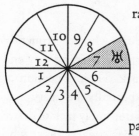

rarely allows such peaceful or uninterrupted alliances. There is likelihood of more than one marriage or, in some cases, too much personal independence discourages marriage altogether. There is also the possibility they may marry suddenly and unexpectedly or that marriage may be abruptly terminated. Their marriage partner, or the marriage itself, may be unusual or unorthodox, or at least be considered unusual in their particular society. Seventh-house Uranus individuals possess natural poise and ability when it comes to relating well to others. Strangers usually feel so comfortable on meeting them that they feel they have known these individuals for a long time. The potential of Uranus in the seventh house suggests those who, for one reason or another, appear unusual or different to others. In turn, these individuals can expect to encounter more than their own share of strange or unusual people. Cooperative efforts, joint ventures, and partnerships may be established in unorthodox ways or for unusual reasons.

URANUS IN THE EIGHTH HOUSE

Uranus in the eighth house indicates those who seek to understand the deeper mysteries of life and death. They want to know where they individually fit into the universal landscape. These individuals may have unpre-

dictable or unorthodox attitudes and behavior when it comes to sex. They can be rigid when prevailing notions accommodate laxity in sexual behavior and liberal when society imposes too many restrictions. Whatever their stated views, they are apt to have keen interest in sex. These individuals may indulge in or deal in some other way with unorthodox sexual encounters. Their marriage partner's income is vulnerable to sudden change, or it may be earned in some unusual or unorthodox line of work or derived from a more conventional job that involves computers, communications, medicine, social services, or international finance. Debts may suddenly occur or just as suddenly be wiped out. Eighth-house Uranus suggests those who may devise ingenious methods for handling debt, taxes, and insurance. They may receive an unusual or unexpected legacy.

URANUS IN THE NINTH HOUSE

Uranus in the ninth house indicates witty, clever individuals who are frequently self-taught. Those who do receive higher education or special training may end up not using it in their career or work. Their education or training may suddenly or unexpectedly be disrupted. Uranus in the ninth house does not imply lack of desire to pursue higher education. It does suggest those who are too restless to endure lectures and instructions. Left to their own devices and motivations these individuals become expert at things that interest them. With little or no training they develop their mechanical skills and artistic talents to a high level of competence. Religious and philosophical views of ninth-house Uranus people are unpredictable. Some of them lean so far toward the traditional as to become ultraconservative. Others will be attracted to more radically liberal points of view. Even if they do not actually adopt radical ideas, they often rebel against tradition if only to experience the difference. They make friends everywhere they go. Unless other factors in their personality or background prevent the desire or opportunity, these individuals are highly stimulated by travel in foreign countries or dealing with those of another race or culture. Relations with in-laws, a second marriage, court decisions, and the job or health of a parent are all vulnerable to sudden and unexpected change when Uranus occupies the ninth house.

URANUS IN THE TENTH HOUSE

One of the strongest implications of Uranus in the tenth house is that at some point, usually after they have embarked on a particular career or life-style, tenth-house Uranus individuals are apt to go off in a completely different direction. Even if they do not initiate such a switch, some momentous circumstance over which they have no control can turn their life around. Uranus in the tenth house also implies that their career or activities may be unorthodox, dealing with an unusual subject or requiring unusual skills. Those who follow a more traditional career are usually attracted to medicine, music, communication, teaching, social work, computers, or the

200

media. These individuals may suddenly or unexpectedly be separated from their father, or he may be unusual or unorthodox in some way. Tenth-house Uranus people are likely to rebel against authority and restriction, but when it suits their long-range goals, they happily embrace more traditional ideas and methods. These individuals may also have unusual or unorthodox supervisors. Uranus in the tenth house indicates those who may unexpectedly attract public attention. Noteworthy activities that bring these individuals into the spotlight are likely to be connected with some impact they make on society, which can mean anything from criminal acts to humanitarian projects.

URANUS IN THE ELEVENTH HOUSE

People who can pick up with friends they have not seen or talked to in years as though no time has passed depict those with an eleventh-house Uranus. This ability is really an asset since instability and separation are potential patterns in their friendships. These individuals usually have a tendency to consciously or subconsciously organize their friends into a loose fraternity. Many of them exhibit an egalitarian approach that attracts friends and acquaintances from all walks of life, social levels, and cultural backgrounds. They are also apt to establish friendships with people involved in occult or other unorthodox subjects, as well as with those in more traditional areas involved with computers, music, electronics, medicine, finance, social work, or communications. Eleventh-house Uranus individuals value their place as a child, parent, friend, lover, spouse, and whatever role they play in the lives of others. However, they also value their own independence and do not want to confine all their attention to one individual. They may find themselves playing highly unusual or unexpected roles in the lives of other people.

URANUS IN THE TWELFTH HOUSE

Those who are born with Uranus in the twelfth house may have trouble sleeping, or their job and other circumstances require them to sleep at odd hours. These individuals must learn to properly relax, and many of them develop an interest in Transcendental Meditation or other methods that help them achieve inner peace and tranquility. The job and health of a marriage partner are vulnerable to sudden

or unexpected change. Their spouse may also introduce them to unconventional or unorthodox ideas and methods regarding health and physical fitness. Other potentials of twelfth-house Uranus include hidden friendships or clandestine activities with friends, membership in a secret society, and illegal activities that may or may not represent a subconscious need to rebel against authority.

NATAL NEPTUNE IN THE HOUSES
NEPTUNE IN THE FIRST HOUSE

There is an element of glamor or mystery in the personality or appearance of those who are born with Neptune in the first house. How the various facets of their looks and behavior will turn out is hard to pin down. They may, for example, photograph so well that they look much better on film than in reality, or their likeness on film is so poor they hate to be photographed. Neptune's association with the first house includes those who are prone to anxiety, especially about their health or appearance, which can result in hypochondria or addiction to habit-forming substances. First-house Neptune indicates those with very little understanding of how their personality, looks, and behavior affect others. Consciously or subconsciously, they give an impression of such vulnerability that others instinctively want to protect them, sometimes going to great lengths to avoid hurting their feelings. These individuals often harbor fear of abandonment. No matter how many people surround them, first-house Neptune people tend to feel left behind or unwanted. They frequently use guilt as a weapon for eliciting the affections and cooperation of others, but they are also apt to be the victims of others who use the same ploy. In spite of their apparent sensitivity, these individuals are definitely survivors. They are very compassionate and possess enormous strength that can sometimes take others by surprise. Many people born with Neptune in the first house are very spiritual, able to see and appreciate the beauty of the soul. These individuals can inspire others to a remarkable degree. There is danger, however, that they will insist others accept their ideals.

NEPTUNE IN THE SECOND HOUSE

Individuals born with Neptune in the second house must preserve what they value or it may be lost, sometimes before they even realize that such a danger exists. These individuals may never quite figure out what it is they truly value. Attuned to a higher plane of consciousness, they may put far more value on their soul than on their bank account. A second-house Neptune suggests the strong potential for bankruptcy or a steady erosion of assets. It can mean individuals who pay little heed to their financial status and, as a result, they always live on the edge of debt. Some of these individuals go in the opposite direction and become paranoid about losing their assets. They suspect everyone of trying to cheat them. Neptune associated with the second house indicates the potential for income derived through Neptune-related areas such as photography, movies, chemicals, oil, boats, religion, water (maritime industries or activities), dancing, theater, or work involving handicapped, confined, or underprivileged people. These individuals have a difficult time setting or sticking to priorities. They may get sympathy, understanding, or money from the father, but whatever he provides is not likely to be what they may need the most.

NEPTUNE IN THE THIRD HOUSE

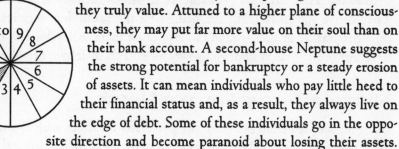

There is often a high degree of intelligence when Neptune occupies the third house, but there is also apt to be mental laziness, an unwillingness to explore thoughts and ideas that appear to be too much work. Those with Neptune in the third house are often uneasy with strangers. They enjoy watching others while remaining hidden or unobserved themselves. Neptune's third-house potential may mean that the father's occupation is the navy, maritime industry, chemistry, photography, footwear, religion, medicine, or it may involve minorities and people who are disabled or institutionalized. The father may suffer from hypochondria or hard-to-diagnose illnesses. Third-house Neptune individuals form sensitive, perhaps clairvoyant relationships with siblings, neighbors, or childhood friends. They may also experience

loss or failure of these relationships, or their siblings, neighbors, or childhood friends may be involved with drugs or other illegal activities. Third-house Neptune people may suffer from mental confusion or rely too heavily on alcohol or other drugs to stimulate their interest or to overcome problems in expressing themselves. They often use pet names or aliases for themselves and their friends. They derive special benefit from being near the ocean, but negative factors in their personality or background can also cause them to develop fear of water or fears that prevent them from going very far outside their own neighborhood.

NEPTUNE IN THE FOURTH HOUSE

Being an adopted child is one of the potentials for those with Neptune in the fourth house. Childhood experiences can make these individuals feel they were deprived or abandoned, even if it is not true. They may have a very spiritual, sensitive, or even psychic relationship with their mother. She may be deeply spiritual, intuitive, or psychic. The mother may suffer from the use of drugs, or there may be secrets, scandal, or mystery surrounding her or her family. Other potentials for fourth-house Neptune individuals include a home and family life that is vague or disjointed. Their domestic environment can also be very spiritual or highly artistic and imaginative. Whatever their home or family is like, there are certain elements of illusion or confusion surrounding it. It is necessary for them to be able to retreat to their home and family in order to restore their mental and physical energies. However, they have to avoid the tendency to hide at home, refusing to face the reality of the outside world. These individuals may reside near the water. Negative factors of fourth-house Neptune include danger of drowning and the possibility that the home may be damaged by water or gas.

NEPTUNE IN THE FIFTH HOUSE

Illusion, confusion, or some kind of mystery connected with romance, children, speculative ventures, social activities, pursuit of pleasure, and artistic or creative projects are characteristic when Neptune occupies the fifth house. Fifth-house Neptune individuals may find romance with dancers, artists, or people involved

with religion or the occult. Their children and/or lovers may possess artistic talent or psychic ability, or they are spiritual. "Love is blind" is an apt description for fifth-house Neptune. The negative potential includes deception in romance or a romantic partner who is confined, disabled, or addicted to drugs. These individuals may care for a child who is not their own. Their children may suffer from mental confusion, physical disability, or adverse reaction to drugs. Fifth-house Neptune can mean remarkable intuition in speculative ventures, but deception and loss are also possible. These individuals may have to rely on the opinion of others to evaluate their artistic talent since their own judgment (whether it is positive or negative) may be clouded or unrealistic. In the pursuit of pleasure, they may become dangerously overindulgent. Vacations are frequently taken on or near water, especially the ocean.

NEPTUNE IN THE SIXTH HOUSE

Working in isolated environments and jobs related to secrecy, deception, or fraud are some of the possibilities for people born with Neptune in the sixth house. These individuals may become involved with coworkers in secret activities. Sixth-house Neptune people develop idealistic or unrealistic notions concerning their job. Other people may not be quite sure what these individuals do for a living, but then they may not be so sure themselves since there is also potential for confusion related to job assignments. They may fail to get recognition for the work they do. Neptune's association with the sixth house suggests employment in the navy or maritime industries, religion, photography, chemistry, psychology, and medicine (especially homeopathy or cosmetic surgery). The work these individuals do may involve the feet, which could mean anything from selling shoes to being a dancer or a podiatrist. Many of them also find jobs working with the handicapped, minorities, and people in prison or confined for other reasons. Sixth-house Neptune is also associated with health and physical fitness. The self-discipline of exercise and other methods needed to stay in shape is difficult for sixth-house

Neptune individuals to develop. Although some of them become fanatic about physical fitness, most of the time their approach is more metaphysical than physical. They are vulnerable to hypochondria and illnesses that are difficult to diagnose or treat. Caution is necessary with drugs since they are apt to have negative reactions to medicine as well as anesthetics.

NEPTUNE IN THE SEVENTH HOUSE

People born with Neptune in the seventh house have a hard time being understood by their marriage or business partner, by those with whom they share joint ventures or cooperative efforts, and by other people in general. Whether or not they intentionally project such images, something about seventh-house Neptune individuals seems glamorous, illusive, or mysterious to others. Whatever the case, their true personality and physical appearance are difficult for others to recognize clearly, remember, or accurately describe. On the other hand, these individuals themselves may find it difficult to recall names or appearances of people they meet. They can unwittingly arouse feelings of fear or jealousy in others. However, they also establish highly sensitive or spiritual relationships with a partner and other close allies. The negative potentials include the possibility of the untimely loss of a partner or a marriage partner who is emotionally disturbed, disabled, from a minority group, or addicted to habit-forming substances. There may be deception or unrealistic expectations in partnership, although there is no certainty about which partner is at fault in this respect. Their marriage partner may possess highly developed intuition or psychic ability and considerable artistic sensitivity or talent.

NEPTUNE IN THE EIGHTH HOUSE

Difficulty collecting debts is one of the associations made with Neptune in the eighth house. When they lend money or favors, those with eighth-house Neptune should do so with the idea of never realizing a return on their investment. Just as likely are misunderstandings or unclear ideas where debts are concerned. Eighth-house Neptune people may distort facts concerning taxes or insurance matters, or they can be falsely accused of such practices. Neptune can also imply erosion or loss of joint income. The income of the marriage partner, as well as that of a sibling, may be derived from maritime industry, footwear,

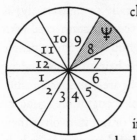

chemistry, religion, photography, medicine, or working with those who are disabled, institutionalized, or minorities. Eighth-house Neptune individuals may be cheated of an inheritance, or their inheritance may be wasted. There may be mystery surrounding their genetic inheritance. These individuals often possess remarkable instincts about human motivation and behavior. They read body language very well. Many of them are intuitive, shrewd, and highly resourceful. Sex is a very spiritual experience for some of them, while others prefer a certain amount of mystery and charade in their sexual activities.

NEPTUNE IN THE NINTH HOUSE

Neptune in the ninth house indicates those who are highly intelligent but who are also vulnerable to mental confusion, fanaticism, and misplaced idealism. These individuals can be totally organized and efficient in some areas, while appallingly inattentive to facts and details in other areas. They can be dangerous masters of deception or highly successful promoters. Interest in religion, spiritualism, or philosophy is characteristic of these individuals. Neptune's negative association includes disillusionment, deception, or illegal activities in a foreign country or involving foreigners. On the positive side, it can mean highly inspirational or spiritual experiences with those of another race or culture. Ninth-house Neptune implies interest in writing and publishing occult or religious material. These individuals are compassionate judges and sensitive teachers. A parent or a sibling's spouse may suffer from disabilities, drugs, or alcohol. He or she may be employed in a job that involves maritime industry, religion, photography, medicine, psychology, footwear, or those who are institutionalized, disabled, or minorities. Relations with in-laws and with a second marriage partner can be undermined by deception or misunderstandings.

NEPTUNE IN THE TENTH HOUSE

A glamorous or mysterious public image is one of the strongest associations of Neptune in the tenth house. It can also mean scandal or disgrace, which in turn implies the necessity for tenth-house Neptune people to guard their reputation.

The possibility of abandonment by a parent (either literally or figuratively) is present, as are misunderstandings, secrets, mystery, or scandal connected with the father or father's family. Tenth-house Neptune people often have difficulty relating to or being understood by supervisors and other authority figures, and, as a result, they may fail to get the kind of recognition (good or bad) that they deserve. Whether or not it involves their actual profession, it is often part of their destiny to help others less fortunate than themselves. The career or long-range goals of those with Neptune in the tenth house are apt to involve photography, film industries, the arts, religion, drugs, chemicals, and the navy or maritime industry.

NEPTUNE IN THE ELEVENTH HOUSE

Undermining influences and elements of illusion, confusion, or mystery surround the role eleventh-house Neptune people play in the lives of others. These individuals may not understand the true nature of the people with whom they live and socialize. They may adopt a child or marry someone with children. Other associations of Neptune in the eleventh house include those who have difficulty in getting a true or realistic picture of their own happiness. When they attain what they thought would make them happy, they often discover it doesn't. They are never content with their achievements or with the money, possessions, and relationships they have. Some of them, however, become so content with whatever comes their way that they never succeed in realizing their full potential. Their friends are apt to be artists, poets, and dreamers. They may also share affection and friendship with mathematicians, dancers, clerics, and sailors. Eleventh-house Neptune people must develop discretion in their choice of companions since they frequently attract people who can do them absolutely no good. Negative associations of eleventh-house Neptune can mean friends who are addicted to drugs or alcohol or involved in illegal activities, the untimely loss of a friend, and the infidelity of a marriage partner. Though friendships can be afflicted by deception, this is not always the case. Neptune also implies highly inspirational, perhaps even clairvoyant, friendships.

NEPTUNE IN THE TWELFTH HOUSE

Neptune in the twelfth house indicates hidden vulnerability. Individuals born with this Neptune house position can be heavily influenced by dreams, feelings of guilt, and the past. Encompassed herein are those who struggle with despair, those who isolate themselves from society, and those who must be confined for one reason or another. Communication with the father may be undermined by lack of awareness, fear, or misunderstanding. The marriage partner of those who have Neptune in the twelfth house may suffer from hypochondria and hard-to-diagnose illnesses. Their partner's job may involve secret or illegal activities, naval or maritime industry, religion, photography, drugs, or charitable institutions. Positive twelfth-house Neptune associations include remarkable intuition, artistic talent, sensitivity, vivid imagination, and spirituality. The ability to float in and out of reality with ease makes these individuals masters of disguise.

NATAL PLUTO IN THE HOUSES

PLUTO IN THE FIRST HOUSE

An intense self-awareness is to be expected in people with Pluto in the first house. There is hardly anything others can tell them about themselves that they don't already know. They can be very controlling and manipulative, but these tendencies can also be entirely directed toward themselves. Surprisingly, those born with Pluto in the first house do not seek to project a powerful self-image as much as might be expected. These individuals like being surrounded by very powerful people, even when they show little evidence of wanting to be identified with a similar image. Most first-house Pluto people may be quiet and unassuming, but they also possess a certain amount of personal magnetism, the essence of which is often exhibited in their deep and hypnotic eyes. Some choose to develop their personal magnetism to great advantage, while others allow it to lie dormant, but it is nevertheless there to be tapped.

They are usually so pleasant and accommodating that, unless others make a serious attempt to probe beneath the surface, the intensity and depth of their personality stay hidden. When they are strongly motivated, however, they can exert an incredible influence. First-house Pluto people are highly resourceful and can develop impressive powers of recuperation and survival.

PLUTO IN THE SECOND HOUSE

Those born with Pluto in the second house can focus so intently on attaining something that everything and everyone else becomes meaningless. They find it difficult, if not impossible, to give up one thing in order to attain another. Consciously or subconsciously, they tend to equate wealth or status with control or power. No matter how much or how little their income and assets, it is best for second-house Pluto individuals to control their own finances; how money is spent and how it is handled in other ways. Whether they mismanage this responsibility and lose their assets or become very wealthy as a result, it is their karma to experience this part of life. The real power of these individuals is understanding that money and material possessions may be attained but never really owned. The entire thrust of second-house Pluto is not just money. Those born with Pluto in the second house encounter circumstances that require uncompromising values and definite priorities. There may be secrecy associated with the income or assets of these individuals. Other associations with second-house Pluto include complete regeneration of assets and those who are more likely to leave an inheritance than to receive one.

PLUTO IN THE THIRD HOUSE

When Pluto occupies the third house, information that is gathered and methods that are chosen are used to gain control or a more powerful position. The development of mental powers and basic mechanical, computer, or design skills leads third-house Pluto people to their ultimate karmic experiences. The old saying "mind over matter" is particularly true for these individuals. Although they may not choose to develop it, they possess remarkable mental ability to persuade themselves (as well as others) that something is true, whether it is or not. Singular powers of concentration make them keen observers, and they miss very

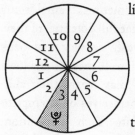

little of what goes on around them. Ability to concentrate their attention does not guarantee that they will apply it to scholarly pursuits or that they have any real understanding of what they observe. It implies that they can present incredibly detailed descriptions of their observations. These individuals are often very intense in the way they express their thoughts and opinions. They enjoy secrets, mysteries, and intrigue. By choice or circumstance, there may be secrecy, manipulation, or power struggles connected with communications, travel, siblings, neighbors, their primary school experiences, and their father's work or health.

PLUTO IN THE FOURTH HOUSE

Pluto in the fourth house indicates those who may experience trauma in childhood, most likely as the result of the death of someone in the family or because

of their physical or mental abuse by a family member. Whatever may have actually happened, or how they may have felt about it, childhood experiences ultimately leave these individuals with a sense that they have no control over things. They have difficulty as adults in relinquishing any control over themselves or their home. Some of them may never seek to own a home of their own. They may be reluctant to marry or find it difficult to stay married to a spouse who insists on dominating their domestic environment. An element of secrecy may be connected to their home or family background. Pluto in the fourth house also implies individuals who may not experience the full potential of their power and energy until later in life. There are definite periods (especially after the age of thirty) when they may have to start over again in some new enterprise or life-style. Although they may or may not attempt to escape their childhood home or its circumstances, they find themselves returning to it again and again.

PLUTO IN THE FIFTH HOUSE

The intensity associated with Pluto makes a decided mark on the creative impulses and talent of those who are born with this planet in the fifth house.

These individuals have a healthy ego involvement (sometimes vainglorious pride) in what they produce, and most of them develop the full potential of their skills and talents. Those who lack creative ability may focus their energy and ego on procreation. If these individuals are emotionally immature, they may regard their children merely as extensions of themselves or attempt to manipulate their offspring into such a position. Romantic encounters are apt to be intense, and fifth-house Pluto individuals have a tendency to dominate these relationships. They are romantically attracted to people who are intellectually superior or have positions of power and status. Learning to understand and exercise proper control with respect to children, creative talent, and the pursuit of pleasure is the karmic responsibility of those with fifth-house Pluto. By choice or circumstance, secrecy or wrongful manipulation can creep into creative projects, romantic attachments, or speculative ventures.

PLUTO IN THE SIXTH HOUSE

Those who seek to control their daily environment is one way to describe people with Pluto in the sixth house. If these individuals work at home, they are compelled to control their domestic environment. If there is too much chaos at home, they may seek to work elsewhere, staying out of the house as much as possible. It is not a good idea to visit sixth-house Pluto individuals unannounced. These individuals prefer to work for themselves, but if their daily environment is in an office, they work better without interference from coworkers or supervisors. They are capable of completely reorganizing their work environment and revising job assignments, often with highly successful results. Many of them possess great power of concentration, attention to detail, and formidable research and investigative skills. Another potential for sixth-house Pluto people is enormous physical strength and stamina. When afflicted with illness, they can exhibit astounding recuperative power. Being of service to others is one of the karmic responsibilities of those born with sixth-house Pluto.

PLUTO IN THE SEVENTH HOUSE

There is a compulsion to control and manipulate partnerships and other close alliances when Pluto occupies the seventh house. If these individuals happen to be aggressive by nature, they are often compelled to interfere with other peoples' relationships as well as their own, not always with happy results. Seventh-house Pluto individuals, consciously or subconsciously, want to gain the advantage where other people are concerned. They do not have a strong sense of cooperation or fair play unless factors in their individual personalities or backgrounds encourage them to develop a more even-handed approach in dealing with others. Pluto does, however, imply justice in the form of eventual retribution. Sooner or later, they are likely to receive the kind of treatment they deserve from their relationships, both good and bad. Whether or not they make a conscious effort to do so, seventh-house Pluto individuals attract partners who are intellectually superior or who have more power or status than themselves. Other potentials for seventh-house Pluto include marriage that becomes a continual contest of wills and joint ventures or other cooperative efforts that turn into endless power struggles.

PLUTO IN THE EIGHTH HOUSE

Pluto in the eighth house indicates individuals who possess formidable strength and endurance, a truly remarkable life force. However, Pluto in the eighth house also indicates those with a dark side to their nature, a side that can cause cynicism and despair. Pluto's eighth-house position implies a strong sexual appetite that often plays a major positive or negative role. Sexual urges can be kept secret by some of these individuals, while others may sublimate them into other activities. However they choose to apply such energy, indifference to sex is unlikely to occur. The ability to concentrate their energy and attention helps eighth-house Pluto individuals develop remarkable investigative and research skills. They are resourceful and observant, with great interest in human motivations and behavior. Pluto in the eighth house

suggests the possibility of secrecy and hidden control or manipulation related to legacies, debts, joint income, and other resources.

PLUTO IN THE NINTH HOUSE

Those who seek advanced degrees or specialized training in the belief it will give them more control or power are likely to have Pluto in the ninth house. They want to separate what is relevant from what is not. These individuals may focus such intense energy acquiring advanced knowledge or particular skills that they develop little understanding of how to handle simpler circumstances and problems. If their interest turns to philosophy or religion, they can become formidable proselytizers. Ninth-house Pluto people frequently have particular fondness for solving mysteries, puzzles, and other challenging mind games. There may be secrecy and hidden control or manipulation related to in-laws, a second marriage, court decisions, higher education, publishing, religion, politics, or cultural pursuits.

PLUTO IN THE TENTH HOUSE

Tenth-house Pluto people are those who seek to control their own destiny, and as a result are reluctant to allow anyone to assume power or influence over their decisions or the directions they take. It must be added, however, that they may not develop this desire until later in life. If, for one reason or another, they are unwilling or unable to take control over their own life, their ultimate growth and maturity is likely to be significantly impeded. Another Pluto potential includes those who focus intense energy in pursuing a career or other long-range goals. Whether or not tenth-house Pluto people gain power and status themselves, they seem able to attract the attention and association of those who do. By choice or circumstance, there may be secrecy and hidden control or manipulation related to their career, the public influence they possess, or a parent (usually the father).

PLUTO IN THE ELEVENTH HOUSE

Pluto in the eleventh house indicates those whose central theme in life is analyzing what makes them happy. To accommodate what may be an intense desire to find true happiness, these individuals make a completely new beginning with new friends and, if possible, in a new environment. The fresh start they attempt may be successful, but if it merely represents a desire to run away from unresolved problems or unsatisfactory relationships, they are certain to fail. Pluto's association with the eleventh house implies the potential of secrecy and hidden control or manipulation related to the role these individuals play in the lives of others. Understanding the necessity of directing energy away from themselves and outward into a relationship or group effort, being able to work as part of a group instead of dominating it, and focusing on common goals rather than emphasizing personal ambitions are some of the things that give ultimate influence and power to those with an eleventh-house Pluto.

PLUTO IN THE TWELFTH HOUSE

Intense interest in dreams, the subconscious mind, and psychic energy are characteristic of those who are born with Pluto in the twelfth house. Many of these individuals pursue their understanding in these areas in order to gain the hidden strength and power that come from such awareness. Other potentials for Pluto's twelfth-house position include those who are involved in secret activities and those who learn to sublimate physical desires into mystical experiences. Whether or not they get involved in the occult or subconscious mind, most of these individuals are intensely private, and may seek a solitary existence. They prefer to exercise their influence behind the scenes, and they may deliberately hide monetary assets and other resources. Pluto also indicates those whose marriage partner may work in research and development, the funeral business, or areas that involve secrecy or managing public resources.

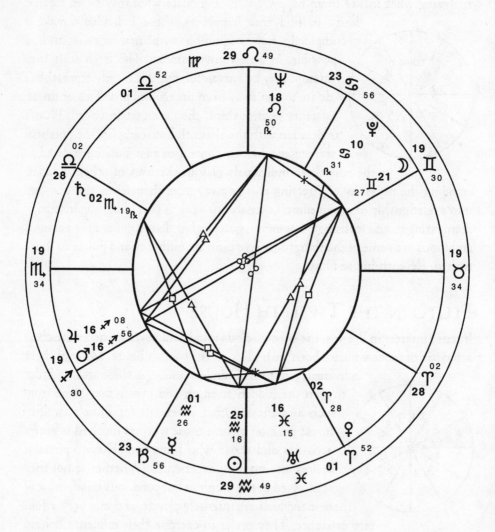

Figure 11: A Chart Depicting Some of the Aspects Discussed in Chapter Nine

216

Chapter Nine

Defining Planetary Aspects

P revious chapters discussed the three main parts of astrology: the zodiac, the horoscope, and the planets. The zodiac is a map of the sky outlined by the twelve astrological signs, each sign representing a different kind of *energy that animates the life force*. The horoscope is a specific map of the sky calculated for the time of an individual's birth or other important event. Each of the twelve houses in the horoscope represents specific *areas in which the energy of the life force is directed*. The planets as a whole represent *the life force itself*, each planet signifying different human characteristics and experiences. But we are still missing an essential fourth part. We need to set up the dynamics of integration, a way to connect the three parts. This is the purpose of planetary aspects.

What are planetary aspects?
The aspects represent the positive and negative inner dynamics that develop and motivate an individual. The planetary aspects also represent the positive and negative outer dynamics that characterize the types of actions and situations an individual initiates as well as experiences.

Understanding how the aspects are derived is simple. It involves the circle. The zodiac is a circle divided into twelve signs, the horoscope is a circle divided into twelve houses, and the aspects are also based on dividing the circle.

The circle divided by two gives the *opposition* which occurs when two planets are located 180° apart. The circle divided by three is the *trine* which occurs when two planets are located 120° apart. The circle divided by four is the *square* which occurs when two planets are located 90° apart. The circle divided by six is the *sextile* which occurs when two planets are located 60° apart. The *conjunction* occurs when two planets are located in the same degree of the same sign. Table 10 lists the aspects and their shorthand symbols.

Opposition	☍	180 °
Trine	△	120 °
Square	□	90 °
Sextile	✳	60 °
Conjunction	☌	0 °

Table 10: Planetary Aspects and their Symbols

THE OPPOSITION

Looking at the natural wheel below, you can see which signs oppose each other.

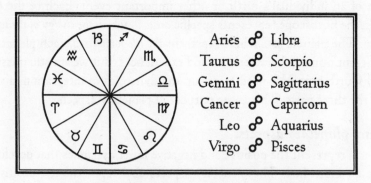

Aries	☍	Libra
Taurus	☍	Scorpio
Gemini	☍	Sagittarius
Cancer	☍	Capricorn
Leo	☍	Aquarius
Virgo	☍	Pisces

Table 11: Oppositions in the Natural Chart

A planet located in Aries is in opposition to any planet located in Libra. A planet located in Taurus is in opposition to any planet located in Scorpio, and so on.

Opposing signs divide the circle by two. A planet in one sign is 180° from any planet located in the opposite sign.

What does the opposition mean?

The opposition represents antipodal forces that cannot be resolved. There is only one solution to an opposition and that is compromise. Since the particular conditions represented by an opposition cannot be changed, they must be dealt with as they are. Life and death are the ultimate opposition. People cannot change the fact that their life will end; they can only do the best that is possible with whatever time is given to them. A blind man may not change the fact that he is sightless, but he can rise to the challenge by improving and employing his other senses to work around his disability. Not all oppositions in a horoscope represent such drastic conditions. Of all the aspects, the opposition presents us with the greatest opportunity for learning and personal growth because it presents the greatest challenges.

THE TRINE

Looking at the natural wheels below, you can see which signs trine each other.

Aries is △ Leo and Sagittarius

Taurus is △ Virgo and Capricorn

Gemini is △ Libra and Aquarius

Cancer is △ Scorpio and Pisces

Leo is △ Aries and Sagittarius

Virgo is △ Taurus and Capricorn

Libra is △ Gemini and Aquarius

Scorpio is △ Cancer and Pisces

Sagittarius is △ Aries and Leo

Capricorn is △ Taurus and Virgo

Aquarius is △ Gemini and Libra

Pisces is △ Cancer and Scorpio

Table 12: Trines in the Natural Chart

Signs that trine each other divide the circle into three parts. A planet located in Aries is 120° or trine any planet located in Leo and Sagittarius. A planet located in Taurus is 120° or trine any planet located in Virgo and Capricorn, and so on.

What does the trine mean?

In Chapter One, you learned that the twelve astrological signs are divided into four groups called elements: fire, earth, air, and water. Aries, Leo, and Sagittarius are the three fire signs; Taurus, Virgo, and Capricorn are the three earth signs; Gemini, Libra, and Aquarius are the three air signs; and Cancer, Scorpio, and Pisces are the three water signs. Notice in the wheels above that a trine occurs naturally between signs of the same element. The trine is considered to be the most fortunate of all the aspects. The dynamics of the triangle allow the energy of a situation to flow uninterrupted from one sign to another sign of the same element. The trine represents harmony, cooperation, creativity, inspiration, and generosity. It is the dynamics that bring good luck and easy attainment. Human nature being what it is, however, there are some disadvantages to the otherwise fortunate prospects that are promised by the trine. The problem is that situations that involve a trine offer very little or no challenge to the individual. A comfortable life of ease and good fortune are not factors calculated to engender any great desire in individuals for achievement. It does not encourage the perception of need or the willingness to conserve or develop assets. There is little inclination to fulfill potential or to overcome obstacles that appear. There is an almost total lack of competitiveness. A trine may, for example, signify those born into wealth. Important family connections may offer them opportunity to succeed in their chosen professions with no period of apprenticeship or initiation. They merely step out into the street and the taxi is there, they raise their hand and the silver platter appears. In love and war, these individuals emerge the winner. Sometimes these individuals do come to know that what they have attained is sadly without meaning or purpose, but, for many, the realization comes too late that what has been too easily gained has been too easily lost and nothing was gained in the bargain. No lessons to reflect upon, no job well done, no achievements to leave behind.

THE SQUARE

Looking at the natural wheels below, you can see which signs square each other.

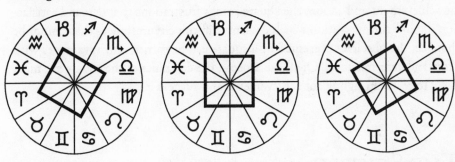

Aries is ☐ Cancer and Capricorn

Taurus is ☐ Leo and Aquarius

Gemini is ☐ Virgo and Pisces

Cancer is ☐ Aries and Libra

Leo is ☐ Taurus and Scorpio

Virgo is ☐ Gemini and Sagittarius

Libra is ☐ Cancer and Capricorn

Scorpio is ☐ Leo and Aquarius

Sagittarius is ☐ Virgo and Pisces

Capricorn is ☐ Aries and Libra

Aquarius is ☐ Taurus and Scorpio

Pisces is ☐ Gemini and Sagittarius

Table 13: Squares in the Natural Chart

Signs that square each other divide the circle into four parts. A planet located in Aries is 90° or square any planet located in Cancer and Capricorn. A planet located in Taurus is 90° or square any planet located in Leo and Aquarius, and so on.

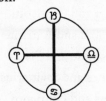

What does the square mean?

In Chapter One, you learned that the twelve signs are divided into qualities. Aries, Cancer, Libra, and Capricorn are the four cardinal signs; Taurus, Leo,

Scorpio, and Aquarius are the four fixed signs; Gemini, Virgo, Sagittarius, and Pisces are the four mutable signs. Notice that the square occurs naturally between signs of the same quality. Unlike the trine, which engenders little need for achievement and action, the square brings frustrations that demand satisfaction. Unlike the opposition which presents difficult circumstances that cannot be changed, the obstacles presented by a square can be turned into advantages with effort and determination. Of all the aspects, the dynamics of the square are most likely to result in significant achievements and success.

THE SEXTILE

Looking at the natural wheels below, you can see which signs sextile each other.

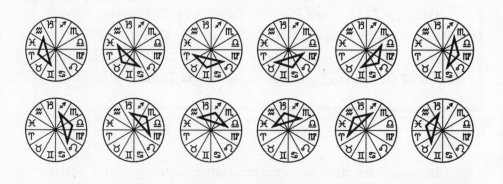

Aries is ✱ Gemini and Aquarius	Libra is ✱ Leo and Sagittarius
Taurus is ✱ Cancer and Pisces	Scorpio is ✱ Virgo and Capricorn
Gemini is ✱ Aries and Leo	Sagittarius is ✱ Libra and Aquarius
Cancer is ✱ Taurus and Virgo	Capricorn is ✱ Scorpio and Pisces
Leo is ✱ Gemini and Libra	Aquarius is ✱ Aries and Sagittarius
Virgo is ✱ Cancer and Scorpio	Pisces is ✱ Taurus and Capricorn

Table 14: Sextiles in the Natural Chart

Signs that sextile each other divide the circle into six parts. A planet located in Aries is 60° or sextile any planet located in Gemini and Aquarius. A planet located in Taurus is 60° or sextile any planet located in Cancer and Pisces, and so on.

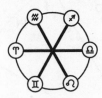 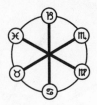

What does the sextile mean?

The sextile is associated with the trine, although it does not mean the easy fortune the trine implies. Sextiles are opportunities in life. They represent circumstances that, when taken advantage of, lead to achievement and success. They are the personification of "making one's own luck." Look at the two wheels above that are divided into six parts. They indicate the compatibility and opportunity that exists between the fire and air signs and between the earth and water signs.

THE CONJUNCTION

The conjunction is easy to picture since the circle is not divided. Two planets in the same degree of the same sign are conjunct. The conjunction is powerful. Its dynamics are interpreted according to the planets involved as well as any aspects to it from other planets. For example, if a Venus-Mars conjunction also happens to trine Jupiter, it would be considered fortunate. If, however, the Venus-Mars conjunction is opposite Saturn, it would be interpreted as negative.

STUDYING THE ASPECTS

Using the signs as guideposts, you can see at a glance what planets may aspect each other. Study the two charts in Figures 12 and 13 on the following pages. In both charts, Mercury in Taurus and Mars in Virgo are in earth signs, which automatically indicates the dynamics of a trine. In Chart One, Mercury at 6° Taurus and Mars at 6° Virgo make an exact trine of 120°. However, in Chart Two, Mercury is 29° Taurus and Mars is 10° Virgo. Here the planets are still in the same element but they are 101° apart. A 19° difference from an exact trine of

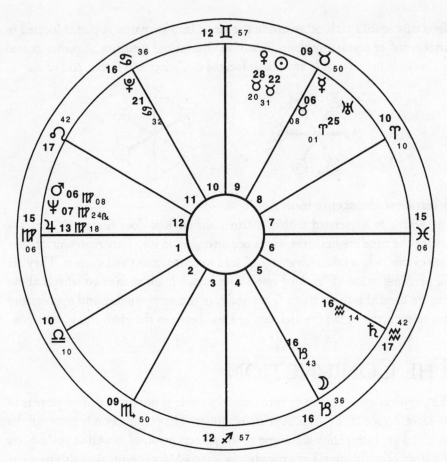

Figure 12: Chart One, May 13, 1933

120° is too wide for these planets to be considered trine. How many degrees can there be between planets in order to consider them in aspect to each other?

Astrologers are not unanimous in their choice of the number of degrees to allow between planets. Some astrologers do not use more than a 1°–2° orb while others will go as far as 12°–15°. Rarely will an aspect be considered operational if the planets are more than 15° from an exact aspect. There are different orb allowances for different aspects as well as for planets making the aspect. In general, however, the conjunction and opposition are given a 2°–5° orb, the square and trine are kept within an 8°–12° orb, while the sextile is not given more than a 1° orb. Choosing what orb to allow for the aspects eventually becomes a matter of experience on the part of individual astrologers. Remember

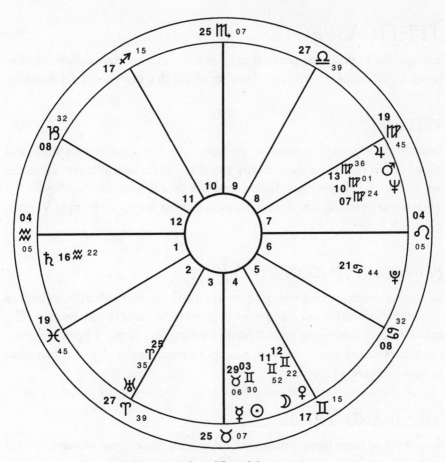

Figure 13: Chart Two, May 24, 1933

that the sextile is 60°, the square is 90°, the trine is 120°, and the opposition is 180°. Now look at some of the aspects the Sun makes in Chart One. Make any aspect valid that is not more than 15° from being exact. There are 125°47' between the Sun at 22°♉31' and Moon at 16°♑43'. This means that the Sun and Moon are 5°48' from an exact trine. The Sun at 22°♉31' and Venus at 28°♉20' are in the same sign, separated by 5°49', making them close enough to be conjunct. There are 96°16' between the Sun at 22°♉31' and Saturn at 16°♒14', which is 6°16' from an exact square. There are 59°01' between the Sun at 22°♉31' and Pluto at 21°♋32', which is less than a degree from an exact sextile. Notice that there are 175°10' between the Moon at 16°♑43' and Pluto at 21°♋32', which makes a valid opposition between them.

225

OTHER ASPECTS

Although the opposition, trine, square, sextile, and conjunction are the five primary aspects used in astrology, there are others that deserve special attention.

STELLIUM

When three or more planets are in the same sign, there is added emphasis and energy both in the house they occupy and the houses those planets rule in the chart. Chart One shows Mars, Jupiter, and Neptune as a stellium in Virgo in the twelfth house, while in Chart Two the same planets form a stellium in Virgo in the seventh house.

QUINCUNX (INCONJUNCT)

This aspect occurs when two planets are 150° apart. Essentially it implies circumstances in which one thing must be given up in order to gain another. The solution to this dynamic is an individual's willingness to pay a price for something that is gained and, even then, it is apt to mean settling for less than what may have been truly earned.

THE GRAND TRINE

When three or more planets trine each other from three signs, a Grand Trine is created. Chart One contains a Grand Trine between the Sun at 22° Taurus, Moon at 16° Capricorn, and Jupiter at 13° Virgo. The trine is a fortunate aspect to begin with, and the Grand Trine enhances this prospect. However, as in the case of all trines, there may be wasted wealth and talent because the individual fails to preserve, develop, or use what has been so easily provided.

THE GRAND CROSS

The Grand Cross is a pattern that occurs when planets form two oppositions and four squares. This aspect is well illustrated by Chart Three in Figure 14. The Sun at 18° Libra and Neptune at 25° Libra are opposite the Moon at 22° Aries. Another opposition occurs between Jupiter and Uranus at 27° Cancer and Mars at 24° Capricorn. The Sun and Neptune in Libra form two squares, one square

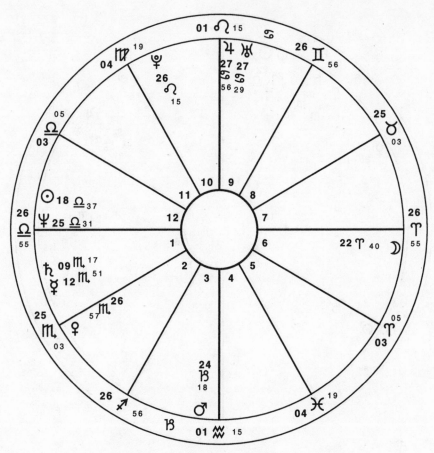

Figure 14: Chart Three, October 12, 1954

with Mars in Capricorn and the other with Jupiter and Uranus in Cancer. The Moon also forms two squares, one square with Mars in Capricorn and the other with Jupiter and Uranus in Cancer. The Grand Cross involves the most stressful aspects, so it is not surprising that those who are born with such configurations are confronted with difficult circumstances to overcome.

THE T-SQUARE

The T-square is an aspect formed by an opposition and a square. Chart Four in Figure 15 illustrates this aspect. The opposition in Chart Four occurs between Jupiter at 28° Cancer and Uranus at 27° Cancer and Mars at 26° Capricorn. In

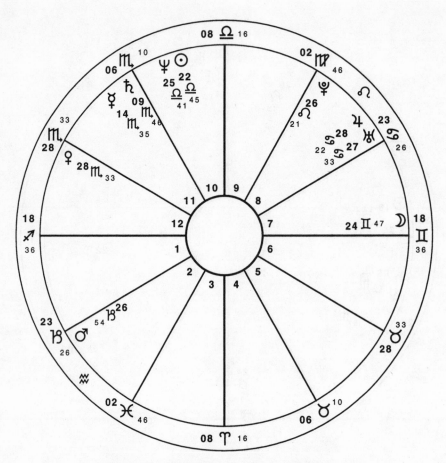

Figure 15: Chart Four, October 16, 1954

turn, the planets at each end of the opposition are square the Sun at 22° Libra and Neptune at 25° Libra. The dynamics of the T-square present circumstances in which the stress of the opposition is afforded a release. The negative energy of the opposition flows out through the square. In the case of Chart Four, the difficulty involved with Mars opposed Jupiter and Uranus can be released through the Sun and Neptune. Note here, as in all aspects, that in addition to the planets involved in the aspects, the houses in which the aspects occur are an important part of how the pattern will be interpreted in an individual's chart. In Chart Four, for example, difficult circumstances involving the second house of money and eighth house of values can be released through the tenth house of the individual's father as well as through the individual's career or long-range goals in life.

228

Chapter Ten

Planetary Aspects in the Natal Chart

SOLAR ASPECTS

As you read and think about the solar aspects, remember that these dynamics always involve the individual's ego, its development and motivation. The Sun is willpower, general vitality, and integrity. Solar aspects also include situations that involve the father or people of great influence since they are also represented by the Sun in an individual's horoscope. When studying a particular horoscope, you must also be aware of which house in the chart is ruled by Leo since the areas signified by that house are influenced by the solar aspects in the horoscope.

SOLAR CONJUNCTIONS

SUN CONJUNCT MOON

⊙ ☾ The ego, which is the unchanging core of individuality, is bound to the constantly changing emotions when the Sun and Moon are conjunct. People who are born with this aspect are apt to risk all their money on one horse, so to speak, the result of the constant struggle of deciding whether

to follow their hearts or their brains. The negative associations of this conjunction include the possibility of those who are so self-concerned that they are unable to relate to the needs of others. The positive influence signifies well-integrated personalities that may not only be opinionated and willful at times, but also dedicated and loyal.

SUN CONJUNCT MERCURY

☉ ☌ ☿ When the ego is so closely bound up with the mind, opinions and ideas are apt to be extremely subjective. Receptiveness to learning is going to stay primarily limited to self-interests, which in turn limits growth and progress. It is frequently difficult for Sun conjunct Mercury individuals to separate their own ideas from the ideas of others. Consciously or subconsciously, their egos tend to appropriate everything. If Mercury is in a different sign than the Sun, there is less ego involvement and more mental receptiveness.

SUN CONJUNCT VENUS

☉ ☌ ♀ Sun conjunct Venus suggests natural charm and social ease. On the one hand, the ego of these individuals can be the dominating influence in the attitude, behavior, and outcome of relationships and interactions with others, but should the ego be of a less determined nature, these individuals can be alternately encouraged or crushed by the positive or negative circumstances of their relationships and interactions with others. Sun conjunct Venus people want to be liked and seek a wide variety of social contacts. They are susceptible to flattery and not above using it themselves. They are attracted to art, music, and beauty in all forms. Witty and companionable, they flirt without offense. The negative side of this aspect includes those who are antisocial, rude, and hostile.

SUN CONJUNCT MARS

☉ ☌ ♂ Individuals with Sun conjunct Mars are apt to be restless. Their egos seek an outlet on some physical level. Some of these people find ego satisfaction in the development and use of physical skills; in some it becomes fierce competitiveness in sports or other physical activities; in others it results in defending themselves or their ideals at the slightest real or imagined provocation; some find it impossible to settle down; and still others are driven to practically kill themselves with overwork. There is a good bit of self-absorption when it comes to doing what they want to do, rather than what they should.

They are often guilty of possessiveness, jealousy, and quick anger. These feelings may not last too long, however, and they forget the grievance and quickly get on with other things.

SUN CONJUNCT JUPITER

⊙ ☌ ♃ The Sun conjunct Jupiter indicates generosity and enormous capacity for enjoyment. The ego satisfaction in these individuals compels them to attain or at least be closely associated with the best of everything in life on one or more levels: material prosperity, social status, intellectual and physical accomplishments, and spirituality. Whether or not these individuals pursue a formal education, their intellectual curiosity compels them to want to know everything and gives them a healthy respect for knowledge. Negative associations of this conjunction lead in opposite directions. Either these individuals ruin their health and finances by constant overestimation and indulgence, or, inspired by exaggerated self-denial, they become miserly. On the positive side, these individuals are true spiritual leaders, gifted actors, talented mimics, inspired teachers, writers, and artists.

SUN CONJUNCT SATURN

⊙ ☌ ♄ Inhibitions that these individuals exhibit as adults are likely to have been caused by an austere or restricted childhood that discouraged development of a healthy self-image. They do not want to risk anything that threatens to bruise their already damaged ego. Sun conjunct Saturn individuals are required to follow tradition and accept structure and restrictions. Most of them are very ambitious and strive for positions of authority. There is too much worry, and they tend to be sober and inflexible, always sticking rigorously to the rules. It is easier for them to accept the difficulties in life than to just relax and enjoy things without constantly looking over their shoulders for trouble. On the positive side, this aspect signifies those with great strength of character and purpose.

SUN CONJUNCT URANUS

⊙ ☌ ♅ A restless, nervous, or impatient disposition makes it hard for Sun conjunct Uranus people to relax completely. They are also apt to be rebellious, disliking conformity and confinement in any form. It is hard to accept a routine existence, and they must make their own way in life if they are to satisfy their ego's demands. No one is ever quite sure when and where these

eccentric and unpredictable individuals will pop up. Many people born with this aspect are remarkably original and ingenious. They are not often surprised or put off by things that other people would regard as outrageous, strange, or impossible. As far as Sun conjunct Uranus individuals are concerned, anything is possible.

Sun Conjunct Neptune

⊙ ☌ ♆ Sun conjunct Neptune does not inspire competitiveness or fierce ambition. When these individuals succeed, it is often a fortunate result of being in the right place at the right time. However, they are sensitive, intuitive, and spiritual. They are also deceptively strong and a master of disguise. Negative associations with this conjunction include those whose ego is so discouraged that it makes them an easy victim or disillusioned victimizer and prone to hysterics, self-delusion, and addiction. On the positive side, they may be interested and possibly gifted in art, theater, and dance. They are also apt to end up with a career in medicine, counseling, or working with the underprivileged, handicapped, or minorities. Water is the natural environment of Sun conjunct Neptune individuals.

Sun Conjunct Pluto

⊙ ☌ ♇ Sun conjunct Pluto is associated with strong self-promoters. No matter how pleasant or easygoing their outer personalities may appear, they have strong wills and very competitive dispositions. Sun conjunct Pluto individuals seek power or control. There is underlying ego involvement in everything they do. There is always danger of jealousy, possessiveness, and vengefulness. The degree to which they give in to such tendencies depends on other factors in their individual personality and background.

Solar Sextiles

Sun Sextile Moon

⊙ ⚹ ☽ Individuals with Sun sextile Moon have a fairly easy time relating to others, quickly finding ways to identify with them on one level or another. They can communicate opinions and ideas effectively and spontaneously. As a rule, these individuals do not have to go too far afield to meet others, since most of the time opportunities to do this are right at hand.

SUN SEXTILE MARS

⊙ ✱ ♂ Sun sextile Mars people are quick to take advantage of opportunities that come their way, and they are not so narrow as to limit themselves to taking only opportunities that seem to promise some obvious advantage. Their energetic response is to eagerly grab all opportunities that arouse them emotionally, mentally, or physically.

SUN SEXTILE JUPITER

⊙ ✱ ♃ People with Sun sextile Jupiter rarely have to search for opportunities to meet others who will help them. They seem to have an uncanny ability to wander into the right situation with the right people at the right time. The opportunities these individuals encounter are usually learning situations, which means either a chance for them to expand their intellectual horizons or a chance to promote their thoughts and ideas.

SUN SEXTILE SATURN

⊙ ✱ ♄ They may have to work a little harder to meet people who can help them or search a little longer to find situations that can help them get ahead, but with perseverance Sun sextile Saturn individuals nearly always succeed. Opportunities they get in life are apt to be long-lasting and solid. It also may take a little more time before they either develop their goals or can actively pursue them, but this, too, merely takes patience and preparation.

SUN SEXTILE URANUS

⊙ ✱ ♅ It is difficult for Sun sextile Uranus individuals to create or to maneuver their own opportunities to get ahead. They must learn instead to remain constantly alert and ready to take advantage of whatever comes their way since these occurrences are unpredictable, appearing suddenly and often from totally unexpected sources.

SUN SEXTILE NEPTUNE

⊙ ✱ ♆ People with highly developed intuition when it comes to recognizing opportunities are described by Sun sextile Neptune. However, lack of ambition or laziness sometimes prevents them from exploiting the advantageous situations they come across. Many opportunities they get represent the chance to gain spiritual or artistic growth.

SUN SEXTILE PLUTO

⊙ ✳ ♇ Sun sextile Pluto is usually an indication of individuals who are given opportunities to interact with those more powerful than themselves. These opportunities also represent a chance to learn the value of control and power and what happens when such privileges are abused. Not everyone they meet gives tangible assistance in the way of money or obvious favors, but they help in other ways.

SOLAR SQUARES

SUN SQUARE MOON

⊙ □ ☽ Sun square Moon indicates those more capable than most of finding situations and relationships in which they are egotistically satisfied as well as emotionally fulfilled. However, for such relationships to be successful, they will have to make some inner adjustments of one kind or another. These individuals nearly always succeed once they have learned that the key to most things they want lies in their willingness to give up one thing in order to get another.

SUN SQUARE MARS

⊙ □ ♂ The tendency to be confrontational and aggressive is one of the patterns associated with Sun square Mars. Unnecessary competitiveness and impatience are often the reasons for the personal disasters that these individuals experience. Their egos are too easily affronted and this can be their undoing. However, turning the energy of frustration into constructive action gives many of them the necessary drive to accomplish the things that, in the end, make them highly successful.

SUN SQUARE JUPITER

⊙ □ ♃ Individuals born with Sun square Jupiter are apt to deprive themselves of success through misuse of their energy and resources, being too extravagant when prudence is required and too prudent when generosity is needed. Restlessness and impatience work against their best efforts unless these tendencies are curbed. Yet, the faith and optimism these individuals inspire are the keys to their success.

SUN SQUARE SATURN

☉ □ ♄ Sun square Saturn individuals are likely to be quite successful in life, if only because they have learned how to handle the obstacles in their path. Overnight success is not the rule here, but eventual success usually is. These individuals have great expectations of themselves and confidence in what they can do, but disappointments can cause them to develop low expectations of others. They are ambitious and ready to try anything to obtain their goals.

SUN SQUARE URANUS

☉ □ ♅ Sun square Uranus indicates those who tend to be highly eccentric or possess unexpected traits hidden in their otherwise fairly straight personalities or demeanors. They may surprise themselves by their own behavior and reactions—which are by no means apt to be predictable or consistent from one time to the next. Obstacles they encounter in life are often unexpected and may at times be unusual. An orderly schedule may be too boring or even downright impossible for most of these individuals to follow.

SUN SQUARE NEPTUNE

☉ □ ♆ Those who are often at a loss to explain how and why their problems occur are apt to have Sun square Neptune. Just when these individuals think that something is resolved, it turns out there are facts they didn't know or loose ends that still require attention. Getting to the bottom of things and taking care of details is not impossible but is bound to be difficult for them. The best way for them to succeed is to handle the here and now and stick to the facts and what they actually know.

SUN SQUARE PLUTO

☉ □ ♇ Manipulating situations to one's own advantage may not be an admirable trait or even a convenient way to do things, but like it or not, this is often what Sun square Pluto people are forced to do in order to overcome obstacles that would otherwise prevent them from achieving even their unselfish goals. They constantly run into situations which require them to use all their resources. They often are unwilling to give up one thing to gain another and the result may be that, in these situations, they lose more often than they win.

Solar Trines

Sun Trine Moon

⊙△☽ Sun trine Moon indicates individuals apt to be pretty well satisfied with themselves. This aspect is not a certain indication of self-promotion and inspiring leadership, although others may thrust these things upon them. For most of these individuals, Sun trine Moon more often describes an inner contentment that enables them to stand up to the trials of rejection and other personal disappointments in life. They have a strong (or perhaps just lucky) life force and energy when survival becomes the issue.

Sun Trine Mars

⊙△♂ Self-confidence, even when it is not justified, is associated with Sun trine Mars. For those who are born with this aspect, it can mean rash behavior as well as great courage. They approach situations without bothering to get or consider all the facts, but their physical energy is apt to be so well integrated into their ego drives that they are always sure they are on the right track. Overriding any mistakes that are made along the way, they just keep going until success is won. Their efforts and actions are usually successful, although they tend to take too much for granted.

Sun Trine Jupiter

⊙△♃ Those who are honest, open, optimistic, and with a great deal of creative energy are described by Sun trine Jupiter. These individuals may be very spiritually oriented and they can also be inspiring leaders. Sometimes they are guilty of overestimation and hyperbole, and they can be very lazy and waste their talent or resources by taking too much for granted. Being put at some disadvantage is not a bad thing since, in their case, it can be the catalyst they need to accomplish real progress on their own.

Sun Trine Saturn

⊙△♄ Individuals with Sun trine Saturn have a certain type of good fortune. It is not a throw of the dice they can count on but luck they make for themselves. They may not win at horse races, but they invariably come out ahead in situations where they have worked hard and for which they have prepared well. Assistance and favors they receive are frequently from elderly friends

or relatives. They impress the right people with their prudence and hard work, which perhaps is the luckiest factor going for them since it provides the additional help they need to gain recognition for their efforts and produce lasting success.

SUN TRINE URANUS

⊙△♅ Sun trine Uranus indicates those likely to be flexible or at least able to adopt a different point of view just to see if ideas other than their own will work. Although their reactions can sometimes be unpredictable, they rarely adopt totally negative attitudes and are willing to accept almost any possibility. They are interested in and accepting of people of any background, race, and culture. There may be truly fortunate incidents that change the direction of their lives, but these are rarely situations over which they have any control or for which they are responsible.

SUN TRINE NEPTUNE

⊙△♆ Although there is a certain amount of good fortune indicated with Sun trine Neptune, it is elusive and not to be counted on. For those born with this aspect, it can mean fortunate circumstances that occur as the result of lucky hunches on their part or simply as a result of being in the right place at the right time. This aspect indicates artistic talent and sensitivity, and, fortunately or unfortunately, it also implies the ability to get away with deception and disguise.

SUN TRINE PLUTO

⊙△♇ The good fortune of those born with Sun trine Pluto may be in possessing just the right resource or talent that is needed or in knowing the right people with influential connections. Whatever assets and resources are at their disposal, these individuals use them to great advantage. They have little trouble attracting the help of powerful people or gaining positions of power or control for themselves.

SOLAR OPPOSITIONS

SUN OPPOSITE MOON

⊙☍☽ Sun opposite Moon indicates difficulty in separating ego from emotions. Those born with this aspect often fail to recognize

that something or someone they want may simply represent ego involvement instead of emotional commitment. What they are called upon (or driven) to do may often interfere with what gives them emotional satisfaction, or else it is the reverse and they chase after their desires while their talents and ambitions are wasted or remain undeveloped. Feelings of frustration ensue; then they become despondent and think the whole world is against them. This is unfortunate, for they could accomplish a great deal if they maintain a positive attitude.

SUN OPPOSITE MARS

☉ ⚭ ♂ People with Sun opposite Mars always seem to be on the edge of direct confrontations. Their egos are too easily bruised, making it impossible for them to pass up any challenges, especially physical ones, and they consequently find it necessary to prove themselves at every turn. Although they frequently possess admirable spirit and courage, these individuals can also be resentful of confinement and restrictions, which makes it hard for them to accept even the mildest form of authority.

SUN OPPOSITE JUPITER

☉ ⚭ ♃ Overestimation, indulgence, and exaggeration are some of the patterns associated with Sun opposite Jupiter. Driven by false pride or ego involvement, these individuals are prone either to promise more than is possible to deliver or to become victims of others who do this to them. In either case, these situations lead to disappointment and failed relationships until sufficient maturity and experience are attained to help lessen the potential for such difficulties to occur. If they cannot or will not curb the tendency to set unattainable goals, they risk accomplishing nothing.

SUN OPPOSITE SATURN

☉ ⚭ ♄ There are few instances when Sun opposite Saturn does not indicate severe tests of integrity and determination. There is danger that those who inherit this aspect will ultimately be provoked by their constant struggles to adopt the philosophy that the end justifies the means. An unhappy childhood, poor health, or other deprivation can cause some of them to give up altogether. Others may decide that their suffering entitles them to whatever they can get, even that which they have not earned. The individuals who deal directly and courageously with whatever they encounter achieve incredible strength and understanding that few others can match.

SUN OPPOSITE URANUS

Sun opposite Uranus indicates individuals that, by choice or by circumstances or both, are likely to be out of the main stream of society in one way or another. They frequently follow unorthodox or unusual behavior and attitudes in their personal habits and life-styles. They may suddenly shift gears for reasons apparent to no one but themselves. Many of them adopt an unpopular point of view just for the sake of being opposed. Being confined or pigeon-holed is unacceptable to them. They need to go their own way and keep their own schedule.

SUN OPPOSITE NEPTUNE

No matter how successful Sun opposite Neptune individuals are in some areas of life, accomplishing their true goals is very difficult. They may be able to capture public attention, but it may be for the wrong reason. Their message may be heard but misinterpreted. If they gain wealth and status, they find these things do not truly satisfy them. No matter what success they make of themselves in the eyes of the rest of the world, they are nevertheless attracted by goals that are illusive or unattainable.

SUN OPPOSITE PLUTO

In order to achieve their goals, Sun opposite Pluto individuals must struggle with power plays. Their attempts are frustrated at every turn by this sort of situation. Like it or not, their success is apt to be in the hands of those who have more control or more resources than they do. Understanding those who oppose them and abiding by their rules is the only way around this dilemma.

LUNAR ASPECTS

The dynamics of lunar aspects in the horoscope always involve the individual's feelings, the development of the emotional life, desires, and needs. Lunar dynamics also include situations that involve the mother, the physical residence, domestic environment, family relationships, and the individual's own offspring and creative output. These aspects describe nurture that is received as well as nurture that is given, the manner of personal expression, and the sensitivity and awareness of an individual.

LUNAR CONJUNCTIONS

MOON CONJUNCT MERCURY

☽ ☌ ☿ Moon conjunct Mercury indicates communication of feelings. People with this aspect are usually quite talkative and readily relate how they feel about everything. If there is anything to inhibit discussing their feelings directly, these individuals turn to writing or some artistic means of emotional self-expression. This aspect suggests great inquisitiveness and remarkable ability for tuning in to the thoughts and ideas of others. The problems these individuals usually encounter are a result of too much flexibility and restlessness.

MOON CONJUNCT VENUS

☽ ☌ ♀ Sensitive to others (particularly to those within their family circle), highly sociable, and incurably romantic describe individuals with Moon conjunct Venus. They are bound to be stimulated by beauty, art, music, and the luxuries and pleasures of life. Much of their inspiration and motivation comes from interacting with others, and these individuals may become emotionally crippled if such interactions are denied. They can become upset and sometimes physically ill by disharmony in their relationships and in their environment, especially their domestic environment.

MOON CONJUNCT MARS

☽ ☌ ♂ Those given to quick, impulsive actions is one way to describe those with Moon conjunct Mars. There is not apt to be much subtlety in the expression of their emotional needs. Lack of hesitancy usually leaves them no time to consider the possibility of encountering rejection or hostile reactions in others. Jealousy, impatience, and irritability are quickly induced in these individuals, but these feelings can quickly disappear as they move on to other things.

MOON CONJUNCT JUPITER

☽ ☌ ♃ Enhanced, and in some cases excessive, emotions and desires are associated with Moon conjunct Jupiter. Dramatic exhibitions of feelings is one pattern, and restlessness and compulsive acquisitions of material possessions are other potentials. Sometimes a too-high opinion of themselves can spoil their wonderful sense of humor and compassionate nature, but, as a rule,

Moon conjunct Jupiter people are very generous. They are attracted to knowledge. Many of these individuals develop into serious scholars while others have a tendency to be pseudointellectuals.

MOON CONJUNCT SATURN

☽ ☌ ♄ Emotional deprivation or restriction of one kind or another is the potential of Moon conjunct Saturn. Even when it is not the reality of their circumstances, individuals with this aspect often labor under a sense of loss or deprivation in some vital area. They may be too severe and inflexible toward everything and everyone, including themselves, tending to look at things negatively, picturing the worst case scenarios. They may be admirably ambitious but also manipulative. In relationships, they are insecure unless they know exactly where they stand. On the positive side, their emotional commitments are stable and dependable. Their strongest emotional relationships may be with those much older than themselves.

MOON CONJUNCT URANUS

☽ ☌ ♅ Restless and nervous, it is difficult for Moon conjunct Uranus people to truly relax. Their emotions are changeable, which makes it hard to predict how they will feel about situations from one time to another. The tendency associated with this aspect is to develop unusual emotional attachments or relationships. These individuals will not tolerate having their feelings dictated to them, even by those they love. Many of them are ingenious and imaginative. Those who are artistic are not apt to express their talent along conventional lines or methods. This is often a difficult aspect with respect to the conception and bearing of children.

MOON CONJUNCT NEPTUNE

☽ ☌ ♆ Individuals with Moon conjunct Neptune can become victims of their own emotions. Their imaginations are the source of remarkable creativity or the means of irrational fears that cripple their actions. Idealistic and intuitive, they are often psychic about people as well as situations other than their own. They can be insecure and dependent in relationships and oblivious to emotional as well as physical danger. Discouragement or self-pity can impede their personal growth and progress. Much depends on the strength and maturity they develop as individuals.

MOON CONJUNCT PLUTO

☽ ☌ ♇ Moon conjunct Pluto indicates those with definite likes and dislikes. They have no trouble expressing their desires and going after what they want. They do not accept rejection easily, which, in any case, may not occur too often since many of them develop formidable personal magnetism that few can resist. Power and control color all that they desire. Subconsciously or consciously, they seek to control relationships and, if there are negative factors in their personalities to support it, they can become jealous and possessive. They are excellent psychologists, researchers, and investigators.

LUNAR SEXTILES

MOON SEXTILE MERCURY

☽ ✶ ☿ Moon sextile Mercury describes individuals who seek to make use not only of their own thoughts and ideas but also those of others. They want to turn theories into some practical and personally advantageous application. Communication and contacts they have with siblings and neighbors, as well as participation in their community, are not merely pastimes for these individuals. These activities represent valuable opportunities through which they achieve personal progress and emotional growth.

MOON SEXTILE VENUS

☽ ✶ ♀ An opportunist approach to interactions with others best describes the pattern associated with Moon sextile Venus. Individuals with this aspect do not necessarily establish relationships and social contacts with the sole intention of gaining advantages, but as things usually turn out, they end up being able to make use of the connections they make. However, there is frequently enough generosity, wit, and charm in their personalities that others don't seem to mind helping or being used by them no matter what their motives may be.

MOON SEXTILE MARS

☽ ✶ ♂ All the wit and verbal expressions in the world are meaningless to individuals with Moon sextile Mars unless these intangible things are also accompanied by physical demonstrations. They seek to carry out their plans, ideas, thoughts, and desires, and they expect others to do the same.

Although they are likely to encounter many situations that allow them to take action, they are not ones to sit around waiting for such opportunities to come along. Many of them simply go out and create their own opportunities.

MOON SEXTILE JUPITER

☽ ✶ ♃ One description associated with Moon sextile Jupiter is those who develop (and are given) a number of valuable sources from which they obtain information, news, or whatever else they need in a particular situation. These individuals may not be wealthy or lucky until they absolutely need help; then, from out of the blue, they are saved at least temporarily from whatever disaster threatens.

MOON SEXTILE SATURN

☽ ✶ ♄ As a rule, Moon sextile Saturn indicates those who are able to take full advantage of opportunities because when such situations occur, the actions these individuals take are the result of their maturity and experience. By the same token, they can also lose valuable chances because they failed to develop the organization and planning skills which would have enabled them to exploit advantageous situations. Assistance often comes to them through older people or those in authority.

MOON SEXTILE URANUS

☽ ✶ ♅ Moon sextile Uranus is often an indication of remarkable instincts and great cleverness. Individuals with this aspect may never be truly prepared to take advantage of relationships or opportunities because their occurrence is unpredictable. But whether or not they are prepared, their cleverness and instincts are more than adequate to help them take advantage of opportunities when they come along.

MOON SEXTILE NEPTUNE

☽ ✶ ♆ People with Moon sextile Neptune have a remarkable sense of timing, yet they are not always sure just how they manage to turn up in the right place at the right time. These individuals are usually able to take advantage of opportunities because their innate awareness and instincts lead them in the right direction or, in some cases, stop them from being misled by false situations that appear to others as valuable opportunities.

MOON SEXTILE PLUTO

☽ ✳ ♇ Individuals with uncanny perception, the remarkable skill of being able to separate what is important and should be considered and analyzed from what is not relevant and should be discarded, are described by Moon sextile Pluto. These people are detailed, organized, and willing to put forth total concentration when their interest is aroused. Their objective assessment of exactly what an opportunity represents is not often derailed by sentimentality or personal desire.

LUNAR SQUARES

MOON SQUARE MERCURY

☽ □ ☿ Moon square Mercury does not indicate lack of intelligence, but it implies obstacles thrown in the path of attempts to learn or to communicate. Obstacles may be impatience, poor memory, lack of organization, learning disability, or physical impediments. Whatever problems they face, people with this aspect use the energy of their frustrations to succeed in overcoming them and a great many other things as well. Travel or just general mobility in getting from one place to another for them may be constantly plagued with minor difficulties.

MOON SQUARE VENUS

☽ □ ♀ Difficulty in gaining the cooperation of others is associated with Moon square Venus. People with this aspect in their natal chart have to prove themselves in some way before they are accepted or helped, and, even at that, their success is more often a result of their own efforts than because others went out of their way to assist them. Sometimes these individuals are discouraged in reaching their personal goals because of financial and family burdens that slow them down. However, the energy of frustrations in this respect is often turned into constructive channels that lead to their ultimate success.

MOON SQUARE MARS

☽ □ ♂ Those born with Moon square Mars usually succeed because of their energetic and tireless perseverance. If they try ten things, maybe only one will work, but in the end that one thing will be what matters. They are inclined to aggressiveness and even rudeness, quick temper, and the inclination to be too hasty in judgments, allowing their emotions to overrule

logical thought. Once these individuals control haste, anger, and impatience, their physical and emotional energy begins to work for them and not against them and they accomplish everything they set out to do.

MOON SQUARE JUPITER

☽ □ ♃ Moon square Jupiter indicates those who tend to become too emotionally involved in situations they should leave entirely alone. Their curiosity aroused, they wander into these traps at every turn. A poor memory does little to remind them of the last time they committed the same error in judgment. These individuals are apt to have great communicative skills in one form or another, and their ultimate success comes through developing them.

MOON SQUARE SATURN

☽ □ ♄ Outward success is nearly always possible for those with Moon square Saturn, but it isn't easy; more often than not, they are dissatisfied even after they succeed. Lack of emotional flexibility and emotional deprivation are the impediments that prevent these individuals from being truly happy. They may be guilty of always trying to get around rules and regulations, and yet they are not above imposing them on others. Reticence or awkwardness interferes with the expression of feelings. These individuals learn from mistakes and develop organization and patience which are the keys to phenomenal success.

MOON SQUARE URANUS

☽ □ ♅ The greatest hindrance that individuals with Moon square Uranus often encounter is trying to deal with unexpected and unpredictable situations for which they are almost always unprepared. Such dilemmas are often overcome by the keen instincts which most of them possess. However, there is also a great deal of nervous energy that must be controlled. Many of these individuals develop unusual emotional attachments or experience unorthodox family situations.

MOON SQUARE NEPTUNE

☽ □ ♆ Achieving desires is possible with Moon square Neptune but perhaps only after many emotionally discouraging false starts. Some of the individuals with this aspect may quit just at the edge of success, never realizing how close they were. Others develop the maturity to hang in until they succeed. Valuable time can be lost chasing unrealistic goals, useless people,

and trivial situations. Disorganization and inattention to detail can also impede their progress, but such faults can be and often are overcome.

MOON SQUARE PLUTO

☽ □ ♇ Moon square Pluto individuals have the unfortunate habit of outsmarting themselves. They are apt to have analytical ability and keen perceptiveness but such traits can sometimes get in the way. Looking for hidden motives or continually thinking there may be something beyond the obvious may simply be a waste of their time. Revenge and possessiveness can threaten the happiness of relationships. Many of them have an instinctive understanding of power, where it is, and who has it. If they overcome the need to possess power for themselves, they can then let it work for them indirectly.

LUNAR TRINES

MOON TRINE MERCURY

☽ △ ☿ It is rarely a question of whether to follow one's head or one's heart when Moon trines Mercury. Individuals with this aspect possess minds that are well integrated with their emotions. They develop organizational techniques and the ability to ascertain and analyze details even if they make no attempt to keep track of these details. Although it may not be deliberate manipulation on their part, they usually know just what to say and when to say it. The instinct to know what others want to hear and clever communication skills are what helps them get what they want in life.

MOON TRINE VENUS

☽ △ ♀ Getting others to cooperate is almost always an easy matter for individuals with Moon trine Venus, often requiring little or no real effort on their part. This aspect is associated with easy charm, gracious manners, and the potential for artistic talent. These individuals have keen instincts and highly developed social and diplomatic skills, although how they apply these abilities depends on other factors in their individual personalities.

MOON TRINE MARS

☽ △ ♂ Exceptionally strong vitality is associated with Moon trine Mars. These individuals are noncompetitive, possessed of an inner

satisfaction that frequently precludes any burning need or desire to prove themselves or their abilities to others. Their calm, easygoing temperaments can mean laziness, though when motivated, they can become passionately enthusiastic. They are often very mechanically or artistically skilled. Unfortunately, they may take such skills for granted or remain content to develop them to a minimal extent.

MOON TRINE JUPITER

☽ △ ♃ Moon trine Jupiter indicates those who can and do get away with many things in life. These individuals can talk themselves into or out of almost any situation. Surrounded by and perhaps even responsible for scandal or criminal activities, they may be the only ones to escape the consequences. Wastefulness, laziness, and taking too much for granted are all potentials accorded this aspect, but so also are great talent, genius, spirituality, and a life of generally fortunate circumstances.

MOON TRINE SATURN

☽ △ ♄ An altogether agreeable aspect for most of the individuals who inherit it, Moon trine Saturn implies recognition of talents and achievements and the reaping of rewards for hard work and dedication. The emotional lives of these individuals are usually fortunate since they generate stable, lasting relationships. When help and guidance are needed, they get it and in return they are willing to help others.

MOON TRINE URANUS

☽ △ ♅ Those with remarkable poise and the ability to handle many difficult or unusual situations with understanding and aplomb are described by Moon trine Uranus. Intellectually curious and keenly instinctive, these egalitarian individuals can emotionally identify with people everywhere and from all levels of society. Emotional attachments may be unpredictable and erratic but they are often rewarding and a unique source for personal growth.

MOON TRINE NEPTUNE

☽ △ ♆ The associations made with Moon trine Neptune are difficult to predict for each individual who inherits it. It implies good fortune, keen intuition, remarkable artistic talent, and the ability to capture the imagination of others. It can also mean addiction, laziness, and wastefulness. Developing

a strong character and clear sense of reality from youth is the key to making this aspect work for these individuals rather than against them.

MOON TRINE PLUTO

☽△♇ Moon trine Pluto implies ability to strongly focus energy and attention. Individuals with this aspect have clear, analytical desires unimpeded for the most part by undue sentimentality. Many of these individuals develop such personal magnetism that they effortlessly attract the attention and affection of others, especially those in positions of power and status.

LUNAR OPPOSITIONS

MOON OPPOSITE MERCURY

☽♂☿ Moon opposite Mercury indicates those who often find themselves in situations where their knowledge or skills are inadequate. Their first inclinations are to scramble to keep up, stall, or even misrepresent facts until they are able to find out what they need to know. These individuals may be very organized but are nevertheless always losing papers or missing details. Maturity and other factors in their personalities can reduce the worst influence of this aspect, especially since it does not imply lack of intelligence, which, in many of these individuals, is apt to be high. Nervous energy keeps them on the go, and their health can suffer from lack of proper rest.

MOON OPPOSITE VENUS

☽♂♀ Moon opposite Venus describes those who are disappointed in their relationships. Although they are not antisocial by nature, people with this aspect may by choice or circumstance lead a solitary existence. Direct negotiations break down and strategy often goes awry. Dealing with things is easier for these individuals than dealing with people. Potentials of this aspect include rudeness and careless disregard for the rights of others. Positive influences in their backgrounds can soften or mitigate the negative traits implied.

MOON OPPOSITE MARS

☽♂♂ Tendency to harbor anger and frustration is one of the patterns associated with Moon opposite Mars. Individuals who inherit this aspect are forever running into situations in which no compromise is possible and thus no solution. The emotional tension they encounter

results in unnecessary accidents and physical confrontations. Insensitivity and aggression creep into relationships, and it usually becomes a matter of too little too late when they try to patch things up. Strong positive elements in their personalities and backgrounds can help overcome some of the negative potential of this aspect. There is a possibility of injury to the head. At no time should risky water sports or other activities be attempted.

MOON OPPOSITE JUPITER

The material abundance promised by the Moon's association with Jupiter may never appear or may be wasted when Moon is opposite Jupiter, but individuals with this aspect are not usually deprived of the jolly sense of humor and great intelligence which are also implied. To be successful they are certain to have to overcome some type of emotional exaggeration in their lives, either gross indulgence or its opposite extreme.

MOON OPPOSITE SATURN

Moon opposite Saturn indicates people who have difficulty being happy or content. Everything is either black or white without any middle ground. Disappointments and problems tend to scar their emotional lives. Indulging in hedonistic activity ends badly, as does the opposite extreme of self-denial. Success for these individuals is not impossible but it comes at a high price. Authority figures are feared or avoided, and either attitude on the part of these individuals proves detrimental.

MOON OPPOSITE URANUS

Independence and even a certain perverseness characterize Moon opposite Uranus, although these inclinations may be masked in an altogether pleasant and seemingly easygoing outer personality. Individuals with this aspect are either naturally inclined to personal independence or circumstances force them to become that way. Unexpected dilemmas occur, necessitating a major change in their domestic environment or their relationships, or they may be inspired on their own to go off in a totally new direction.

MOON OPPOSITE NEPTUNE

Whatever success Moon opposite Neptune individuals achieve in other areas, their emotional lives frequently end up in quicksand; no matter how intelligent they are otherwise, they may never quite under-

stand how they got in such situations. Compassionate and too easily influenced by others for their own good, Moon opposite Neptune people never seem to get themselves on solid emotional footing. Strength of character and other factors in their personality mitigate some of the negativity connected with this aspect.

MOON OPPOSITE PLUTO

☽ ☌ ♇ Those who are compelled to go after their desires are described by Moon opposite Pluto. Individuals with this aspect are shrewd in understanding people and situations. Their keen perception makes them feel powerful in their quests, but it is not enough to help them get what they want, since others with more resources may come along to rob them of their prize. Relationships become intense and too focused to be satisfactory or successful. They are often the victim of power plays, even when they are the victors.

MERCURY ASPECTS

The dynamics of Mercury aspects in the horoscope always involve the individual's mental state, the learning process, and the manner and expression of ideas, opinions, and information. Mercury aspects also include situations that involve the individual's siblings, neighbors, community affairs, communication and contacts with others, transportation, and travel.

MERCURY CONJUNCTIONS

MERCURY CONJUNCT VENUS

☿ ☌ ♀ There is no certain indication of the depth of intellect in individuals with Mercury conjunct Venus, but these individuals are sure to have humor and charm. They are talkers—apt to possess remarkable communicative and artistic talents. Pleasure in learning can mean research and serious scholarship in some of them and fondness for gossip in others. Mercury conjunct Venus people are always busy—contacting others, traveling, running errands, conducting business matters, and attending meetings and social functions.

MERCURY CONJUNCT MARS

☿ ☌ ♂ When projects must be accomplished, those with Mercury conjunct Mars would be described as "hands on" people. These individuals want to put ideas into action and have little patience if they have to

deal too much with mere theory. Likely to possess above average mechanical or technical skills, they are also strong and active when it comes to expressing their ideas and opinions. Most of them are physically active as well as mentally alert, though they are also restless and impatient.

MERCURY CONJUNCT JUPITER

☿ ☌ ♃ They may or may not seek advanced degrees but, sooner or later, Mercury conjunct Jupiter individuals get caught up in expanding their consciousness and improving their intellectual horizons on some level. Amassing great quantities of trivia as well as real knowledge, these individuals may also possess impressive language skills. They are constant talkers as well as travelers. They are happy to share ideas and information, which is why so many of them become journalists, writers, teachers, and salespeople. Problems arise as a result of their tendency to focus on the big picture at the expense of details or fail to see the big picture because they get hopelessly bogged down with too many details. Mercury conjunct Jupiter people attach too great an importance to their own thoughts and opinions at times, and it should not be surprising that they are often guilty of exaggerating the facts.

MERCURY CONJUNCT SATURN

☿ ☌ ♄ Mercury conjunct Saturn indicates those who may be too formal and structured in their thinking to give credence to possibilities that don't fit their preconceived ideas or plans. They are ambitious and want their ideas to be looked upon as authoritative. Most of these people have little disposition for unnecessary tact or idle flattery. Some of them lack personal and seductive ways of communicating. These individuals may encounter restrictions in their learning process, but whether they are deprived of inclination or opportunity or suffer from disability cannot be predicted from the conjunction alone. On the positive side, Mercury conjunct Saturn people are highly organized, practical, and adept at managing information, ideas, and traffic.

MERCURY CONJUNCT URANUS

☿ ☌ ♅ Marked intellectual curiosity, and original, though often unorthodox or nontraditional ideas and opinions are associated with Mercury conjunct Uranus. Individuals with this aspect have unpredictable inclinations. It is not an aspect in which to expect much elegance of physical

movement except by concentrated efforts. Most of these individuals are forever bumping into things. Although in many respects they can be traditional and follow ordinary, even boring, routines, these people are apt to have keen interest in studying the occult and other unusual subjects, traveling to unique and different places, and communicating with strange and unusual people.

MERCURY CONJUNCT NEPTUNE

☿ ☌ ♆ Those who often fail to see the reality of situations, even to the point of completely exhausting the patience of others who must deal with them on this basis, are described by Mercury conjunct Neptune. However, these individuals also have remarkable farsightedness and instinctual understanding of some things that less sensitive intellects are unable to grasp. They have talent for, or at least know, a great deal about art, design, music, and the spiritual nature of things.

MERCURY CONJUNCT PLUTO

☿ ☌ ♇ Mercury conjunct Pluto indicates those who endlessly analyze ideas, relationships, and situations, wanting to get down to the basic structure of these things. Sometimes this is done to afford a better sense of themselves and sometimes it is done as a means of gaining power. Their manner of communicating and of expressing their ideas and opinions tends to be quite intense, incisive, and, in some of them, often sarcastic. Once their attention is engaged, it is totally focused, which is why many of these individuals are excellent researchers and investigators.

MERCURY SEXTILES

MERCURY SEXTILE VENUS

☿ ✶ ♀ Mercury sextile Venus indicates those apt to be mentally alert and highly sociable. Their sense of humor and intellectual curiosity afford the motivation to attain adequate education for whatever they set out to accomplish. Their engaging and interesting dispositions enable these individuals to attract opportunities for making use of their communicative or technical skills.

MERCURY SEXTILE MARS

☿ ✶ ♂ Those who get around a lot, and, though not overly aggressive, are not reticent about expressing their thoughts and ideas are the type

of people associated with Mercury sextile Mars. These individuals usually find that actual physical demonstrations they are given and their physical participation in certain activities are what afford them the best opportunities to learn. When opportunity does not come along, they are willing to go out and create whatever situations are necessary in order to turn their thoughts and ideas into action.

MERCURY SEXTILE JUPITER

☿ ✱ ♃ Opportunities that involve intellectual, communicative, or artistic skills are associated with Mercury sextile Jupiter. People with this aspect encounter fortunate circumstances in which they are able to acquire knowledge and education or develop their talents and skills. For some, this aspect includes the chance to turn knowledge or skills into monetary success, public recognition, or other tangible benefits.

MERCURY SEXTILE SATURN

☿ ✱ ♄ Opportunities that allow individuals with Mercury sextile Saturn to demonstrate or make use of intellectual or technical skills usually occur as a result of their meticulous planning or from the contacts they make with older, established, or more experienced individuals. This aspect indicates that diligence in developing intelligence and skills is what makes them highly deserving of the attention, help, and sound advice they are able to attract.

MERCURY SEXTILE URANUS

☿ ✱ ♅ Mercury sextile Uranus indicates those apt to be given a chance for intellectual growth as well as the development of their technical or mechanical skills through friends and through organizations to which they belong. They should expect the unexpected because for them opportunities often pop up without warning. However, trying to maneuver or manipulate an opportunity is rarely successful.

MERCURY SEXTILE NEPTUNE

☿ ✱ ♆ Intellectual growth is often the motivation for individuals with Mercury sextile Neptune to also attain spiritual and psychological growth. Many of them possess precognitive abilities that can be developed into remarkable powers. Learning to help themselves is often the way in which they end up helping others. Their jobs are apt to involve working with those who are handicapped, underprivileged, or institutionalized.

MERCURY SEXTILE PLUTO

☿ ✳ ♇ If there are no emotional afflictions in their personalities or backgrounds, individuals with Mercury sextile Pluto are apt to have keen perceptions and analytical abilities. There is no guarantee their endeavors will always turn out well, but there is promise that if they take advantage of every opportunity to expand their intellectual capacities, success is attained.

MERCURY SQUARES

MERCURY SQUARE MARS

☿ □ ♂ Mercury square Mars indicates individuals who allow ideas and thoughts to race too far ahead of the logic, facts, and information at hand. They have active, alert, and intelligent minds but need to develop more careful attitudes, better organization, or solid evidence and understanding before they attempt serious projects. Quick temper and accident-proneness are associated with this aspect.

MERCURY SQUARE JUPITER

☿ □ ♃ Highly intelligent but apt to get bogged down in meaningless details, Mercury square Jupiter individuals must depend on organization and structure if they want to get things done. Poor memories or attitudes result in being plagued with a lot of unnecessary work. Intellectual curiosity can mean research and scholarship or fondness for gossip and rumor.

MERCURY SQUARE SATURN

☿ □ ♄ There is no lack of intelligence in people with Mercury square Saturn, but there may be some restriction or inhibition concerning the expression of their ideas and opinions or in the learning process. These individuals may cling to outmoded principles or be dictatorial in communicating thoughts and ideas. They may suffer from lack of imagination or the means to express it. Sight, hearing, or speech impediments are possible. Mechanical skills can desert them and care should be taken when operating machinery. Travel, especially in their own neighborhoods, may be difficult for one reason or another.

MERCURY SQUARE URANUS

☿ □ ♅ The ideas and concepts generated by those with Mercury square Uranus are either futuristic or centered in the past. This does

not leave the success of their endeavors in jeopardy, but it can cause confusion in trying to get projects off the ground because others believe their ideas are either too far ahead or too far behind the times. They are often clever and original thinkers. One of their complaints is having to look after boring details, and no matter how organized they are, one of their problems is keeping track of papers and information. These individuals are apt to be clumsy, which may result in their being accident-prone.

MERCURY SQUARE NEPTUNE

☿ □ ♆ Artistic talent and a sensitive intellect are some of the characteristics associated with Mercury square Neptune. However, in trying to implement projects and schemes, these individuals may have trouble gaining recognition for their contributions and ideas or they continually run into difficulty due to lack of organization. Many of them adopt such an unrealistic approach that it is difficult to implement their ideas on a practical level.

MERCURY SQUARE PLUTO

☿ □ ♇ Those who succeed as a result of manipulation and control are described by Mercury square Pluto. The intellectual perceptions of these individuals are keenly analytical. They know how to go about doing things, and if laziness or some other factor does not interfere, they usually get what they want. They seek to know the how and why of life, especially the psychology of human motivation and behavior.

MERCURY TRINES

MERCURY TRINE MARS

☿ △ ♂ Mercury trine Mars indicates creative energy and physical enthusiasm for intellectual and communicative efforts. Individuals with this aspect attract the most fortunate prospects from everything that happens around them. They are successful when they seek new experiences and wish to improve their intellectual capabilities. They are rarely burdened with routine or repetitive situations. Most of these individuals possess mechanical skills, enjoy traveling, and keep up a constant pace of running here and there, especially within their communities. Mercury trine Mars people are apt to be fortunate in business as well as in the development, use, and recognition of their skills and talent.

MERCURY TRINE JUPITER

☿ △ ♃ Unless other factors in their personality inhibit them, people with Mercury trine Jupiter are gifted raconteurs. Whether they have anything worthy to say is beside the point; they not only say it anyway but their good fortune is such that other people pay attention. These individuals may rely too heavily at times on the intellectual efforts of others and, even worse, may appropriate the material as their own and get away with it. They think they can talk their way into or out of any situation, and much of the time they have the intelligence and communicative skills to do so. Fortunate circumstances surround them in areas that involve education, writing, publishing, communication, investments, business, travel, religious or political interests, legal matters, artistic talent, and athletic skills.

MERCURY TRINE SATURN

☿ △ ♄ Mental stability, common sense, and a correct and accurate sense of timing are characterized by Mercury trine Saturn. Individuals who inherit this aspect have organizational and administrative abilities. They are apt to wander effortlessly into many situations in life in which they are able to use their intellectual and communicative skills to great advantage. Understanding structure and purpose is one of their most valuable intellectual assets.

MERCURY TRINE URANUS

☿ △ ♅ Mercury trine Uranus is associated with intellectual curiosity and belief in the possibility of almost anything. People with this aspect frequently develop interest in unusual subjects as well as psychology, social sciences, technology, and medicine. These individuals are sociable and love to travel and meet people from many different places and backgrounds. There is little chance they will ever tolerate intellectual prudery or a snobbish attitude, either in themselves or in others.

MERCURY TRINE NEPTUNE

☿ △ ♆ Individuals with Mercury trine Neptune are apt to possess an outstanding intuition, vivid imagination, and keen intellect. However, they must be careful not to take these assets for granted or their intellectual and artistic gifts are wasted, their spirituality becomes nothing more than hollow tradition, and their psychic sensitivities are never realized or developed. Many of them have the faith healer's gift though they may not choose to call it that.

Mercury Trine Pluto

☿ △ ♇ The usual implication of Mercury trine Pluto is intellectual and communicative abilities. Whether these individuals are outgoing or prefer to remain quietly in the background, their success is a result of ability to observe and analyze human attitudes and behavior. They believe knowledge is power and, for them, it is apt to be true.

Mercury Oppositions

Mercury Opposite Mars

☿ ☍ ♂ Mercury opposite Mars implies an impatient nature that is quickly frustrated. Individuals who struggle with this aspect immediately communicate their frustration without a second thought, and thus have always to regret what they have said in anger and haste. Impatience results in physical confrontations or be restricted to verbal assaults, but clues to that inclination lie elsewhere in their background and personality. Although they may not develop the patience for it, great caution must nevertheless be exercised when they operate machinery, handle dangerous materials, and travel.

Mercury Opposite Jupiter

☿ ☍ ♃ Individuals with Mercury opposite Jupiter are apt to be exceptionally bright, but with a tendency to collect knowledge to the point of dilettantism. The practical side of things is often left out of their plans and ideas. Intellectual snobbery is a temptation these individuals can hardly resist, but they have an otherwise generous nature when it comes to sharing information and ideas. One of their biggest problems is verbalizing their thoughts. They recognize and understand the big picture which is their strength. This is just as well, since most of them have no inclination to pay attention to details.

Mercury Opposite Saturn

☿ ☍ ♄ One pattern associated with Mercury opposite Saturn is getting bogged down in endless details, rules, and regulations. People who inherit this aspect have to develop patience and ability to handle restrictive situations. Constant struggle with one impediment or another can discourage cultivation of a lively imagination and stymie motivation to venture too far in any scholarly pursuit unless it is of a strictly practical nature. Obstacles frequently

encountered with this aspect include learning disability, hearing impairment, and lack of inclination or ability to express ideas and communicate information. Travel and transportation are usually plagued with frustrating delays and other hindrances. Here again, these individuals eventually have to accept the necessity for careful planning and cautious movements.

MERCURY OPPOSITE URANUS

☿ ☌ ♅ Although instability is associated with Mercury opposite Uranus, so also are remarkable intelligence and unusual perception. Individuals with this aspect do not suffer from mental confusion or lack of ideas; their difficulty involves communication. Avoiding mental distraction is a full-time job, otherwise it is impossible to coordinate and communicate thoughts and ideas clearly. These individuals are able to learn quickly on their own or when their interest is aroused, but learning by rote is difficult. Their awareness and understanding can be astounding, but their grasp of information is highly unstable. Just when they need to relay information, it slips from memory. They may be outwardly poised and calm, but Mercury opposed Uranus individuals are apt to be inwardly nervous. A quiet environment is needed since they find it very hard to relax. Developing controlled, consistent physical movements is also a problem for them. They are often uncoordinated and constantly bump into or trip over things.

MERCURY OPPOSITE NEPTUNE

☿ ☌ ♆ Mercury opposite Neptune individuals may be expert in some special field of endeavor and they are apt to be quite clever with mechanical devices and abstract theories. When it comes to dealing with other people, however, their judgments and perceptions are frequently out of touch with reality. Their thoughts and ideas rarely depend on logic or attempts to understand the facts. Assumptions are drawn from past experiences and on their vivid, but sometimes faulty imaginations. This aspect indicates great sensitivity and spirituality. These individuals may prefer solitude, or this condition may be imposed on them for one reason or another.

MERCURY OPPOSITE PLUTO

☿ ☌ ♇ Sharing information is not always to the liking of those with Mercury opposite Pluto unless they get something useful in return. Control of information and ideas is a factor behind their motivations and

behavior. There is usually a power struggle or impediment that blocks the free flow of information or knowledge. Some of them behave mysteriously or attempt to disguise their knowledge or true motives. Consciously or subconsciously, these individuals seek knowledge in order to gain control of situations rather than to improve themselves.

VENUS ASPECTS

As you read the descriptions for Venus aspects, remember that the dynamics of this planet are going to involve romance, artistic talents and tastes, friendships (especially female relationships), social attitudes and behavior, marriage and other partnerships and alliances, pursuit of pleasure and luxury, sense of humor and fun, and values.

VENUS CONJUNCTIONS

VENUS CONJUNCT MARS

♀ ☌ ♂ When Venus combines with Mars, social inclinations are given energy and enthusiasm and an aura of warmth and vitality lies close to the surface. Individuals with this aspect are not totally dedicated to their social lives; in fact, most of them aggressively pursue other personal goals—self-improvement, development of artistic talent and interests, a career, or wealth. Venus conjunct Mars people are highly responsive to sexual encounters. If nothing in their individual personality or background discourages them, they are excellent partners in marriage, business, or any cooperative effort.

VENUS CONJUNCT JUPITER

♀ ☌ ♃ People with a generous, philanthropic nature are described by Venus conjunct Jupiter. Cultural pursuits and appreciation of knowledge are likely, but these individuals may not be patient enough, or perhaps too lazy, for great scholarship unless other factors in their background and personality give them a motivational push. At times they are guilty of making friends strictly for the purpose of furthering their own social status or gaining other personal advantages. Possessed of a keen and ready wit, Venus conjunct Jupiter people love adventure, drama, and every kind of social intercourse.

VENUS CONJUNCT SATURN

♀ ☌ ♄ Venus conjunct Saturn indicates diminished capacity for enjoyment. It doesn't mean that people with this aspect never have a fun day. However, enjoying pleasures and luxuries they possess or pursue is often restricted by poor health, debt, loneliness, or too many responsibilities. Romantic encounters are apt to be with older people or with those who represent an authority figure. In the worst cases, romantic relationships are with people of negative or repressive character or with those who become a burden. In the best cases, romantic relationships are solid and enduring. Common sense and practicality dominate the imagination and sense of humor, making it hard for Venus conjunct Saturn individuals to indulge in whimsy. On the positive side, however, they bring structure and purpose to artistic endeavors, which is often the key to making such projects important and successful rather than merely frivolous or fanciful.

VENUS CONJUNCT URANUS

♀ ☌ ♅ People with Venus conjunct Uranus should not be expected to travel the usual path when it comes to romance and other alliances. Traditional relationships and practices are possible of course, but these individuals are more than receptive to other scenarios. There is instability which means they may suddenly or unexpectedly begin or end a romance, marriage, or other partnership. Sociable in the sense of relating to large groups of people, these individuals have no trouble making a wide variety of friends and acquaintances. Involved in all types of organizations, they are popular and often hold positions of leadership. Many of them are excellent organizers and successful fund-raisers. Artistic expression and taste in individuals are likely to tend toward the very old, the ultramodern, or the highly unusual.

VENUS CONJUNCT NEPTUNE

♀ ☌ ♆ Individuals with Venus conjunct Neptune often possess a highly sensitive and refined aesthetic sense. Many of them become expert appraisers of wine or perfume. There is potential for deception and abandonment in romance, marriage, or other partnerships. Although infidelity is one possibility, deception can also occur through misplaced idealism. Many of these individuals have romantic attachments with someone from a minority group or someone involved with the navy or maritime industry, dance, photography, entertainment, or health care.

VENUS CONJUNCT PLUTO

♀ ☌ ♇ Strong desire is not to be denied when Venus is conjunct Pluto. The passionate attention of individuals with this aspect can sometimes be too intense for those on whom it is focused. Consciously or subconsciously, these individuals seek to control romantic relationships, marriage and other alliances, and cooperative efforts. In turn, power struggles allow jealousy and possessiveness to creep into relationships. However, many of these individuals learn to avoid such problems by sublimating their energy into creative projects or other worthy endeavors.

VENUS SEXTILES

VENUS SEXTILE MARS

♀ ⚹ ♂ Venus sextile Mars is associated with opportunities to establish social contacts and to interact with people in general. If individuals with this aspect are not given such opportunities, they can be just as successful in going out and creating them. This aspect is an indication of career possibilities or a chance to develop artistic skills. There may also be many opportunities for engaging in romance, whether or not they seek such situations or are in a position to take advantage of them.

VENUS SEXTILE JUPITER

♀ ⚹ ♃ People with Venus sextile Jupiter not only possess artistic, promotional or journalistic talent, but they are also given opportunities to get ahead by applying these talents in advertising, promotion, broadcasting, or teaching. They often develop a number of intelligence sources to keep informed of the news and issues they need to know. They successfully create opportunities for others as well as themselves.

VENUS SEXTILE SATURN

♀ ⚹ ♄ Assistance provided by people who are older or in positions of authority is one pattern associated with Venus sextile Saturn. Opportunities for these individuals usually represent a chance to develop artistic abilities and to improve social status. Their unselfish sacrifices for others also provide opportunities for themselves. This aspect indicates musical talent or skills in architecture and design.

VENUS SEXTILE URANUS

♀ ⚹ ♅ Individuals who approach social relationships with enthusiasm, intellectual curiosity, and egalitarian attitudes are described by Venus sextile Uranus. They are presented with opportunity to make friends and acquaintances wherever they go. Many of them experience unexpected or unusual romantic encounters or partnership arrangements. Other situations provide these individuals with a chance to work in economics, technology, finance, or the social sciences.

VENUS SEXTILE NEPTUNE

♀ ⚹ ♆ The social conscience of individuals with Venus sextile Neptune is very sensitive, involving them with others who are handicapped, confined, or members of a minority. They are highly responsive and in some cases, psychic and intuitive, in their interactions with people. They may have opportunity to engage in secret romances or in relationships with those who are mysterious or glamorous. Other situations offer opportunities to increase their spirituality and awareness. Many of these individuals possess mathematical ability, mechanical or technical skills, and artistic talent.

VENUS SEXTILE PLUTO

♀ ⚹ ♇ Venus sextile Pluto individuals have analytical ability, potential for enhanced intuitive power, and the tendency to get involved with secret schemes. They can be very discreet when necessary. Shrewd observers of human behavior, they use this understanding to gain control of situations in which, more often than not, they emerge the winner.

VENUS SQUARES

VENUS SQUARE MARS

♀ □ ♂ Venus square Mars indicates people who are apt to exhibit a certain social awkwardness. These individuals are what is often referred to as a "diamond in the rough." Quick temper and an aggressive approach in dealing with others are also present unless these traits are softened by other factors in their personality and background. Romance is frequently a matter of competition or expedience rather than passion and courtship either on their part or that of their partners. Their instincts and talent in art or music tend more toward the bold and blunt than the subdued and elegant.

VENUS SQUARE JUPITER

♀ □ ♃ People who spend half their time overindulging themselves and the other half paying for it are described by Venus square Jupiter. Their tendency to go overboard toward extravagance can also go in the reverse direction and they become abstemious and miserly. In many of these individuals, the aspect amounts to a poor sense of timing. They are overly generous in some matters or with people who don't deserve their largess, and then behave selfishly or become petty when they should have been generous. Venus square Jupiter implies problems, but it also implies that personal growth is also possible for the individuals who eventually learn to balance generosity with prudence.

VENUS SQUARE SATURN

♀ □ ♄ Venus square Saturn doesn't indicate lack of generosity in those born with this aspect, although others may not be generous toward them. Social attitudes and behavior include abruptness, even rudeness at times. Charm and grace are not apt to be natural attributes, although such qualities can be acquired. There is potential for social isolation, whether it occurs as their tendency to be a "loner" or it is imposed on them by others. Unfortunate prospects of Venus square Saturn are debts as a result of extravagance, inability to manage income, and responsibility for debts incurred by others. Social activities, relationships with women, partnership, and gaining the cooperation of others are often beset by fear and other obstacles, but, in the end, those who persevere manage to get what they want.

VENUS SQUARE URANUS

♀ □ ♅ Unusual or nontraditional are appropriate terms for some of the social inclinations of people with Venus square Uranus. Their marriage and other partnerships, as well as the romantic situations they encounter, are sure to be stimulating and may also fall into the category of unexpected or unusual. These individuals can be stubbornly addicted to their own opinions, feisty, defensive, and argumentative.

VENUS SQUARE NEPTUNE

♀ □ ♆ Deception in romance is a strong possibility for those with Venus square Neptune, although it is not certain whether these individuals will be guilty of infidelity or whether they will encounter it in their romantic

partners. They may also be deceived simply by their own unrealistic illusions and expectations concerning romantic partners, and thus doomed to disappointment when such ideals are inevitably shattered. Maturity and a more objective approach help overcome the negative potential of this aspect and may contribute to developing the sensitivity and creative talents that are its positive potentials.

VENUS SQUARE PLUTO

♀ □ ♇ Those with Venus square Pluto often find that there is a price to pay with regard to their relationships. No matter how easy or exciting relationships are at the beginning, manipulation or power struggles result in the end. Unless these individuals submit to the manipulations of others or else seek to gain control themselves, the only other alternative they may have is utter loneliness. Much, however, will be gained if they learn to minimize their own need for power and tactfully sidestep others who try to exert control.

VENUS TRINES

VENUS TRINE MARS

♀ △ ♂ Natural enthusiasm and sociability are traits associated with Venus trine Mars. Unless discouraged by more somber factors in their personality or background, these individuals easily attract the good feelings and attention of others. They usually do not bother to hide their flaws, since it is often their good fortune that others overlook their imperfections. Venus trine Mars people demonstrate their affection and companionship in a physical manner. Most of these individuals get along equally well with both sexes. They enjoy participating in sports and physical activities as a form of socializing.

VENUS TRINE JUPITER

♀ △ ♃ Wealth and worldly success are not guaranteed to those who are born with Venus trine Jupiter. The aspect does imply, however, that these individuals are naturally attracted to the good things in life, and more than likely will effortlessly be able to attain them. There is also the potential of intellectual success and talent for art, music, or drama. Sometimes the good fortune they encounter is astounding, but sometimes their wealth, in whatever form it appears, is wasted. Even if these individuals are moderate in some things, there is always some area of great lavishness, self-indulgence, or extravagance.

VENUS TRINE SATURN

♀ △ ♄ Devoted, responsible, and stable in their relationships are charac-teristic descriptions of those born with Venus trine Saturn. There is potential for longevity in friendship, marriage, and partnership, and marriage or partnership may be with someone older. Relations and interactions that these individuals have with others are usually conducted along traditional lines and established rules of legitimacy and fairness.

VENUS TRINE URANUS

♀ △ ♅ Meeting people and making friends wherever they go is rarely a problem for those with Venus trine Uranus. Their amiable and personal approach that makes even strangers feel they have known these people a long time is part of the reason these individuals succeed in life. Venus trine Uranus people are egalitarian and do not fear crossing or defying social barriers. There are no hidden meanings in their actions or conversation and no compli-cated strings attached to their social relationships.

VENUS TRINE NEPTUNE

♀ △ ♆ Musical talent or artistic and design skills are frequently described for those born with Venus trine Neptune. They may also be very fortunate in their social contacts; it sometimes is a case of being in the right place at the right time and sometimes because they have just the right looks or person-ality to attract the right people. These individuals can form relationships that become so close as to be almost psychic. If other factors in their personality or background do not interfere, they are caring and compassionate and highly successful at amusing and inspiring others.

VENUS TRINE PLUTO

♀ △ ♇ Attracting the attention and the affection of those in power as well as attaining high-ranking social positions for themselves is not often difficult for those born with Venus trine Pluto. This aspect also implies a strong sexual drive that may cause problems in youth but can bring wisdom and control when these individuals are mature enough to handle it. Pleasures they have may be many or few, but their enjoyment is intense. Their close relation-ships often become valuable psychological resources. These individuals have special talent for or success in handling resources or discovering hidden treasure.

VENUS OPPOSITIONS

VENUS OPPOSITE MARS

♀ ☍ ♂ Polite manners and elegance do not have any kind of a natural berth in the nature of those with Venus opposite Mars. It is not certain that these individuals should never aspire to attain these characteristics; it is only that such things must be assiduously acquired and once attained must be rigorously maintained. Venus opposite Mars people are passionate and/or invariably attract others so inclined. Unless their maturity and patience are enough to ensure fairness and consideration, relationships can degenerate into hostility, jealousy, possessiveness, or physical abuse. Women with this aspect may resent men or be abused by them, and men with this aspect view women the same way. Working and cooperating with others are difficult at best. There is no middle ground for compromise or peaceful coexistence. Definite terms for agreeing to disagree have to be worked out in all aspects of friendships and other close relationships.

VENUS OPPOSITE JUPITER

♀ ☍ ♃ Venus opposite Jupiter indicates those who want life to run according to their desires, which makes it difficult for others to present them with bad news or unpleasant situations. They are unwilling to handle difficulties, especially in instances when more promising situations are waiting. They may have great success in some areas but fail to grow as individuals, especially those who refuse to learn to deal with the negative side of life. Unless their background training or other characteristics in their personality modify the inclination, they completely lack discretion, and desires and social inclinations are likely to get out of control.

VENUS OPPOSITE SATURN

♀ ☍ ♄ The burden of responsibilities may interfere with the development of friendships, social activities, a sense of humor, and an easy, lighthearted approach to life when Venus is opposite Saturn. Fear of rejection may be responsible for making these individuals reluctant to engage in romantic encounters or, in some cases, even simple social encounters. The course of romance is often plagued by inhibitions or other impediments. These individuals find it difficult to achieve recognition for their creative talents, or they may

develop such talents later in life. Unwavering perseverance and a philosophical attitude in every situation are effective weapons that may help to alleviate some of the negative potential.

VENUS OPPOSITE URANUS

♀ ☍ ♅ Those with Venus opposite Uranus can never be quite sure how they will be accepted by other people. On the other hand, their own social inclinations and approach to relationships may be just as unpredictable. Unstable relationships or enforced separation from others by circumstances over which they have no control prevents them from getting too close to others for too long. Conventional society or the same old faces may become boring to them, and, as a result, they seek the more interesting company of unusual people or at least a wide assortment of people. These individuals will frequently encounter or engage in unorthodox or nontraditional social situations.

VENUS OPPOSITE NEPTUNE

♀ ☍ ♆ The charm, artistic talent, and sensitivity associated with Venus are not necessarily lacking in those with Venus opposite Neptune. However, the manner in which these traits are developed or applied is the problem. There is increased potential for disintegration of their social attitudes and behavior and for other factors that undermine their friendships as well as romantic relationships. These individuals often develop distorted or unrealistic ideas about people and must be careful in voicing their opinions. They attract others who are addicted to drugs or alcohol or those who intentionally deceive them. These individuals are easily victimized, and in turn may as easily become the victimizers. Sensitivity, clear thinking, and maturity are needed at all times.

VENUS OPPOSITE PLUTO

♀ ☍ ♇ Venus opposite Pluto indicates those fascinated by human behavior and psychology. Some of these individuals tend to manipulate social contacts but won't tolerate being controlled themselves. Some of them, however, experience the reverse and are themselves the victims of manipulation. They may associate with others who physically attract them, but they prefer being with those more powerful or socially advanced than themselves. Such inclinations may be intentional and focused or only their subconscious desire but, in the end, always trap them one way or another.

MARS ASPECTS

Physical energy and efforts describe the role of Mars in planetary aspects. As you read this planet's dynamics in each of the aspects, think of each description in terms of how an individual physically operates, the type of physical situations likely to be encountered, and the nature of male relationships as well as interactions with men in general.

MARS CONJUNCTIONS

MARS CONJUNCT JUPITER

♂ ☌ ♃ Energy and enthusiasm mark the physical pursuits and efforts of those with Mars conjunct Jupiter. They are willing to risk everything on one roll of the dice. The grand as well as the grandiose gesture is characteristic of their style and approach to life. The enthusiasm of their actions may be solely directed to increase their own importance or turned to philanthropic endeavors—in many cases, it is both. At times, the overestimation and impatience in which these individuals constantly engage are no doubt problematical for them as well as for those around them, but their keen intelligence and the greatness of their spirit are so inspiring as to minimize some of the difficulty. It is not surprising to find Mars conjunct Jupiter people putting their physical endeavors into such enterprises as publishing, promotion, cultural pursuits, linguistics, and sports.

MARS CONJUNCT SATURN

♂ ☌ ♄ For those born with Mars conjunct Saturn, there is a major conflict between what they want to do and what they may be forced to do. Acceptance of responsibility, learning from experience, and developing maturity must be achieved or they will be held back at every turn. In youth, these individuals are apt to have serious confrontations with authority, even though they require order and structure in their lives. They are apt to hold in anger or frustration until it surfaces in explosive outbursts and acts that cause accidents or other regrettable situations. On the positive side, these individuals have organizational ability and a sense of structure and purpose. Administrative skills ultimately place them in positions of authority. What they accomplish may not be easy, but results of their efforts are apt to endure.

Mars Conjunct Uranus

♂ ☌ ♅ Unpredictable, rash, and contrary describe some of the patterns associated with Mars conjunct Uranus. Individuals with this aspect tend to think of themselves as different, and in many ways they are. With a strong sense of personal independence, sometimes just stubborn contrariness, they insist on going their own way and doing things their own way. Their restless, daring spirit takes them in many different directions, and they often end up far from where they started. Care must always be taken with machinery, even though they may be thoroughly familiar with its operation.

Mars Conjunct Neptune

♂ ☌ ♆ Mars conjunct Neptune indicates those with a tendency to harbor delusions about their actions and have unrealistic notions of their physical ability. Decisions must be made carefully since there is potential for unwise action and erroneous judgment. These individuals are likely to be more than a little fond of music or art and may have talent in one of these areas. The understanding that some of these people have of machinery and physical processes in general borders on the uncanny. Their work or other activities may lead to involvement with photography, medicine, the arts, and handicapped or minority groups.

Mars Conjunct Pluto

♂ ☌ ♇ Control is the operative term for the physical efforts and energy of those born with Mars conjunct Pluto. In most cases, remarkable physical strength may be expected to give these individuals an endless capacity to work hard and play hard. They can be too intense or aggressive at times which makes others ill at ease. Weaponry, psychology, counseling, raw materials, surgery, cooking, mines and caves, secret activities and groups, or renovations are particular areas where these individuals direct their physical efforts.

Mars Sextiles

Mars sextile Jupiter

♂ ✶ ♃ Mars sextile Jupiter indicates those who receive opportunities in life to make use of whatever talent or interest they have in politics, art, music, foreign cultures or international diplomacy, promotion and advertising, law and the justice system, writing, religion, or higher education.

These individuals are fortunate because many of these valuable opportunities come along without too much effort on their part.

MARS SEXTILE SATURN

♂ ✶ ♄ Good timing is one of the hallmarks associated with Mars sextile Saturn. Individuals with this aspect often know exactly when to act or, in some cases, when not to act. They are apt to receive opportunities at just the right time to get ahead in business, construction, real estate, management, banking, or property management and development. Those with organizational skills are excellent administrators, instructors, and trainers. Mars sextile Saturn people are good at planning and aggressively promoting their own interests as well as those of others.

MARS SEXTILE URANUS

♂ ✶ ♅ Opportunities to develop and use any interest or talent in such areas as technology, institutional management and development, and in unusual subjects such as magic or astrology are indicated with Mars sextile Uranus. These individuals often have the talent (and the chance to use it) for coming up with clever and ingenious solutions to problems, especially in psychology, law, and finance.

MARS SEXTILE NEPTUNE

♂ ✶ ♆ Those with Mars sextile Neptune are not always lucky, but they often benefit from a lucky hunch. Opportunities come to them not so much through any care or planning on their part but usually because they happen to be in the right place at the right time. Areas that may give these individuals the chance to succeed include religion, art, the occult, photography, and mathematics.

MARS SEXTILE PLUTO

♂ ✶ ♇ The nature of opportunity associated with Mars sextile Pluto involves gaining some sort of power or control in either a physical or financial sense. These individuals often get a chance to advance through inheritance or handling personal assets of others. Other areas that hold the promise of opportunity for these individuals include metaphysics, psychology, taxes, insurance, renovations, raw materials or minerals, holistic medicine, and physical fitness.

MARS SQUARES

MARS SQUARE JUPITER

♂ □ ♃ Those with Mars square Jupiter can often be their own worst enemies through carelessness, laziness, and bad timing. They tend to act imprudently when they should keep a low profile, and when their knowledge or actions can really make a positive difference, they may fail to act out of laziness or disinterest. There are tendencies here for procrastination and misrepresentation. However, there is also energy enough to overcome the difficulties indicated, enabling these individuals to succeed in their goals *because* of the obstacles in their path rather than in spite of them. One potential in which these individuals may find themselves is in competition with their father or father figure.

MARS SQUARE SATURN

♂ □ ♄ Impatience and inner negativity is associated with Mars square Saturn, but these traits may not necessarily be reflected in the outer personality of individuals born with this aspect. They may have a sense of humor but are, nevertheless, what others consider a "straight arrow." They are ambitious, but the price of any success they merit will invariably require personal sacrifice. Their physical energy and health may falter or other inhibitory factors may come along in the middle of a project, forcing them to leave the task of finishing to others. Sometimes it is a case of those who refuse to give up, taking on all the responsibilities themselves or being forced to assume them in order to see something through to completion. Odds favor them if they persevere.

MARS SQUARE URANUS

♂ □ ♅ Individuals with Mars square Uranus are bound to have a quirk or two. They veer from the traditional path from time to time or perhaps make a lifetime project of seeking an unusual or alternative life-style. They are willful and independent, and even those who settle down to marriage and regular jobs may grow restless and unhappy if too much confinement or control is imposed. They can also get stuck in a rut, unwilling to help themselves, preferring to blame the world for their lack of stimulation and success. There is, however, enough unpredictability in their lives and attached to their actions that it serves to keep them on their toes and interested. Ability to direct the stimulating energy of uncertainty into productive channels is frequently their secret of success.

MARS SQUARE NEPTUNE

♂ □ ♆ One of the biggest frustrations for individuals with Mars square Neptune is having their efforts go unrewarded or, worse, their efforts produce no effect at all. Disorganization, disorderliness, and lack of motivation needlessly complicate their lives. Getting things done often seems overwhelming. In many situations they delude themselves into thinking everything will turn out all right, and this is just as well since they save themselves aggravation. Once inertia, unrealistic expectations, and vague methods or plans are overcome to the point that allows some true efforts to take place, these individuals can and do achieve their goals.

MARS SQUARE PLUTO

♂ □ ♇ The strong will, emotional intensity, and physical stamina of those with Mars square Pluto are usually enough to get them out in front. What may cause them to fall behind again, however, is being too aggressive or threatening. They have incisive minds and know exactly what they want and how to get it. Their own growth as individuals involves learning how to avoid revenge, jealousy, and possessiveness.

MARS TRINES

MARS TRINE JUPITER

♂ △ ♃ Mars trine Jupiter indicates those with the capacity to enjoy the good life. Whether or not they deserve it, they are lucky, enjoying what some refer to as blind luck. Optimistic risk takers, these individuals are ready for any adventure. They may not be physically lazy but are often given an easy way out of things. If they are not wealthy, they often manage to be taken care of by those with more means. Having a sharp wit and being around when good things happen are how these individuals progress in status or career.

MARS TRINE SATURN

♂ △ ♄ The good fortune of individuals with Mars trine Saturn often involves being taken care of or given valuable assistance by older people or those in authority. Their ambition is rarely subtle and attempts at self-promotion are transparent, but the implication of luck here is that their ploys are tolerated. Mars trine Saturn is a survival aspect. No matter what hardships are imposed, these individuals usually manage to cope better than most.

MARS TRINE URANUS

♂ △ ♅ A bold and forward nature is associated with Mars trine Uranus. These individuals are always ready for action. They see nothing wrong in speaking their mind and behaving exactly as they please without reservation. And, what is more, they usually get away with such free-wheeling actions even as others are criticized or ostracized by society for doing the very same thing. They are willing to consider the possibility of any action or situation, no matter how unusual or unconventional it may seem to others.

MARS TRINE NEPTUNE

♂ △ ♆ Even if they possess a harder side more in tune with reality, there is also a certain mellow, philosophical or spiritual sense in how individuals with Mars trine Neptune think and conduct themselves. They are attracted to people and situations that appear glamorous, sensuous, or uplifting in one way or another. Artistically talented with astute intuition, they often have the good fortune to be in the right place at the right time and know exactly what to do or, as the case may be, what not to do.

MARS TRINE PLUTO

♂ △ ♇ Mars trine Pluto indicates people with a strong sense of what they like and dislike, and just as strong an inclination to get what they want. Their passions are notably strong as is an ability to separate what is relevant and important from that which is irrelevant and unimportant. These individuals are fortunate not only to possess valuable material and nonmaterial resources, but also to know how to make use of them.

MARS OPPOSITIONS

MARS OPPOSITE JUPITER

♂ ☍ ♃ A characteristic pattern of Mars opposite Jupiter is people who want things to go their way and who will either aggressively seek to run everything or avoid handling anything, leaving such tasks to be handled by those around them. They have a well-developed appetite for pleasure. Any form of moderation, especially physical moderation, is not easily accomplished. They have a low or nonexistent tolerance for unenjoyable or unpleasant circumstances. Soldiers of fortune is how many of them see themselves, but this is dangerous since any risky venture is a situation from which few of them can expect to emerge victorious.

MARS OPPOSITE SATURN

♂ ☍ ♄ If there is a hard way to do things, individuals with Mars oppo-site Saturn will find it. Impatient with rules and regulations, they attempt to circumvent them and only end up making things worse. They are not very tolerant of others who are overbearing or authoritative, even though they may be guilty of such traits themselves. They may not always show resent-ment outwardly but seek to extricate themselves from this type of domination in one way or another, often with little success. There may be loss of parents, or parents exhibit a domineering influence these individuals find difficult to handle. For them, the key to success is in learning to deal with structure and authority in a more positive way.

MARS OPPOSITE URANUS

♂ ☍ ♅ Those with Mars opposite Uranus are unpredictable. They start out to go one way and end up headed in the opposite direction. Difficult for others to control, they find it hard to control themselves or their shifting attitudes for any length of time. Separations from friends are to be expected. There may be one or more complete changes in life, and their life-style is not likely to be conventional. Already prone to accident or violence, the worst thing these individuals can do is give in to their impatience, haste, or anger. Care must always be taken around machinery and electrical equipment.

MARS OPPOSITE NEPTUNE

♂ ☍ ♆ Actions are vague and motivated by illusions or delusions when Mars is opposite Neptune. For individuals with this aspect, it raises the potential for being either a victim or a victimizer. They may always find themselves working in the dark, either literally or figuratively. It may simply be that they enjoy creating an aura of mystery around themselves, or they actually act in secrecy, either legally or illegally. These individuals are often confused, never quite knowing if their efforts have any effect or what that effect might be.

MARS OPPOSITE PLUTO

♂ ☍ ♇ Mars opposite Pluto indicates those who are often confronted with situations that involve physical renewal or renovation in some form. Either literally or figuratively, they have to develop inner resourceful-ness and whatever intellectual or physical skills they possess in order to meet the

challenges in life. One of their biggest frustrations is having to constantly deal with what is irrelevant in order to be allowed to deal with what is relevant. They invariably run up against the futility of confronting those with more power.

SPECIAL NOTE

As we proceed to the aspects made between the outer planets, Jupiter through Pluto, it is necessary to realize that these dynamics are more apt to describe a generation rather than a single individual.

JUPITER ASPECTS

When Jupiter is involved in a planetary aspect, it reflects the dynamics of growth and expansion in an individual or in a situation. Jupiter represents the potential for generosity and optimism that in turn encourages creativity and knowledge as well as increased prosperity. It is the capacity for enjoyment and humor.

JUPITER CONJUNCTIONS

JUPITER CONJUNCT SATURN

Jupiter conjunct Saturn is associated with being offered a little of everything in life. However, those born when this conjunction occurs will rarely, if ever, get something for nothing. When something is gained, something else is lost in the bargain. Success is not denied, but they must work to get it, work to hold on to it, and take nothing for granted. Prudence is their best policy, although occasional extravagance is not only possible but also enjoyed more because it is rationed.

JUPITER CONJUNCT URANUS

A society that is in one stage of rebellion or another—in fashion, art, religion, politics, education, and philosophy—is the best way to describe the pattern associated with Jupiter conjunct Uranus. The lives of individuals born with this aspect may, for example, be heavily influenced by war. They witness the status quo turned upside down and the introduction of a new order and logic in established institutions and traditions.

JUPITER CONJUNCT NEPTUNE

♃ ☌ ♆ There is public receptiveness to spirituality in the religious sense and spiritualism in the occult sense when Jupiter is conjunct Neptune. People born in this generation reject realism, substituting it with idealism, abstraction, and impressionism, especially in art and literature. This generational flow of sentiments may or may not affect their private life, but these individuals are bound to have to deal with it on some level.

JUPITER CONJUNCT PLUTO

♃ ☌ ♇ Jupiter conjunct Pluto signifies a generation of people with an urge to explore the mysteries of nature and the universe. Their thinking and attitudes are analytical and investigative. Transforming fundamental ideas about physical, psychological, and mental conditions is their societal directive, and individuals born with this aspect will be involved with or influenced by what happens in this area, either in their professions or other activities.

JUPITER SEXTILES

JUPITER SEXTILE SATURN

♃ ✶ ♄ Individuals born with Jupiter sextile Saturn have the motivation and opportunity to promote traditional values, solid societal institutions, and strong emotional commitment to improving the world. Jupiter implies the chance, but Saturn demands that the opportunity be deserved by the generation as well as the individuals to whom it is given.

JUPITER SEXTILE URANUS

♃ ✶ ♅ Given the opportunity to change the status quo in society, individuals born with Jupiter sextile Uranus introduce innovations and viewpoints that will broaden intellectual horizons, expand technology, and promote cultural development.

JUPITER SEXTILE NEPTUNE

♃ ✶ ♆ Jupiter sextile Neptune is associated with individuals who have an opportunity to expand spiritual growth, increase understanding of spiritualism or the occult, and improve conditions in mental hospitals and prisons and among minority groups.

JUPITER SEXTILE PLUTO

♃ ⚹ ♇ Jupiter sextile Pluto implies a generation of individuals with motivation and opportunity to put scientific theory into practice. Their approach to societal structures may be more organized, detailed, and number-oriented than humanitarian in character. For example, in a society that is under the influence of the generation born with this aspect, population control may be a more important issue than discovering how to reduce the number of birth defects.

JUPITER SQUARES

JUPITER SQUARE SATURN

♃ □ ♄ Devotion to forcing thoughts and ideas on the rest of society describes the pattern of Jupiter square Saturn. Most of their ideas are accepted simply because many of the individuals born with this aspect have the energy and perseverance to mount ideological campaigns. They do not accept foolish or faddish thinking and behavior. They want to make substantial contributions to the world community.

JUPITER SQUARE URANUS

♃ □ ♅ Whether or not individuals born with Jupiter square Uranus personally agree, their generation opposes traditional ideology and social structures. Deliberately confrontational, they are stubbornly entrenched in antagonistic modes. The direction of fashion, politics, religion, philosophy, and every societal institution that they can influence is reversed.

JUPITER SQUARE NEPTUNE

♃ □ ♆ Jupiter square Neptune implies misplaced idealism, counterproductive sentimentality, and out-and-out fraud. It is imagination no one quite knows how to handle. Erosion of traditional ideals tends to make these individuals unaware of what should be valued and what should be rejected. They believe something is missing, but they are not quite sure what it is.

JUPITER SQUARE PLUTO

♃ □ ♇ Societal issues which confront Jupiter square Pluto individuals involve power and who should have it. They are forced to analyze and understand human psychological motivations and behavioral patterns in

order to resolve the problem of controlling basic resources. How much of this spills into their private affairs is a matter of other factors in their background.

JUPITER TRINES

JUPITER TRINE SATURN

♃ △ ♄ Jupiter trine Saturn implies that conditions in society are favorable for individuals born with this aspect. Many of them may be at least moderately successful, while others without this aspect may, for example, be unemployed or unsuitable in some way for the demands of current conditions.

JUPITER TRINE URANUS

♃ △ ♅ Societal conditions inspire technology to make life easier for individuals born with Jupiter trine Uranus. A new order of thinking destroys societal prejudice and institutional structures that might in the past have hindered their progress, not only as a generation but also as individuals.

JUPITER TRINE NEPTUNE

♃ △ ♆ Inspirational influences abound when Jupiter trines Neptune. Individuals with this aspect become more interested in religion. They tolerate and encourage the type of fantasy and imagination that may once have been ridiculed. However, this so-called fortunate aspect can also mean significant waste and liberalism that goes so far as to produce a society unwilling to work for a living.

JUPITER TRINE PLUTO

♃ △ ♇ Jupiter trine Pluto implies individuals who can adequately integrate power with sensitivity in societal and political structures. This does not occur automatically, but the pattern suggests that the right people will be in power in the right place at the right time.

JUPITER OPPOSITIONS

JUPITER OPPOSITE SATURN

♃ ☍ ♄ Jupiter opposite Saturn implies difficult times. These individuals are always presented with alternate situations in which

there is either too much or too little. There is no middle ground and no way to escape this influence other than to deal with it in the best way possible.

JUPITER OPPOSITE URANUS

♃ ☍ ♅ Unstable conditions and a general confusion may lead to complete chaos, the result of a complete reversal of existing conditions when Jupiter is opposite Uranus. It is an aspect of rebellion against the status quo. Unless other factors in their personality and background soften the impact, individuals born with this aspect may have to continually adjust their life and life-style as a result of the battle between ideologies.

JUPITER OPPOSITE NEPTUNE

♃ ☍ ♆ Disintegration of social, political, or religious institutions is the common pattern described for Jupiter opposite Neptune. The spread of fanatic ideals breeds hate and intolerance. Disillusionment and sorrow rule the day. Individuals with this aspect may or may not experience such negative sentiments personally, but they may suffer from its general effect on society.

JUPITER OPPOSITE PLUTO

♃ ☍ ♇ Power struggles become the order of the day with Jupiter opposite Pluto. Society is rampant with plots and counterplots, intrigue within intrigue. Suspicion, abuse of power, and secrecy may not actually describe the particular character or touch the personal affairs of individuals born with this aspect, but their lives may nevertheless be influenced in some way by the effect this atmosphere has on society in general.

SATURN ASPECTS

Saturn's aspects indicate the conditions of limitation and restriction. They also describe the qualities of endurance, maturity, and structure.

SATURN CONJUNCTIONS

SATURN CONJUNCT URANUS

♄ ☌ ♅ The generational pattern associated with Saturn conjunct Uranus is one that is concerned with the structure of societal

institutions. Religion, government, business, and other social groups become more formal and organized. Among individuals born with this aspect, there is less of a fraternal attitude and more of an emphasis on practical concerns as a whole.

SATURN CONJUNCT NEPTUNE

♄ ☌ ♆ Saturn conjunct Neptune implies bankruptcy unless other planetary aspects soften the blow. Debts of all kinds must be paid. Societal institutions that are without substance will crumble. Individuals born with this aspect may or may not have personal financial difficulties, but they are likely to have to deal on some level with such conditions in society.

SATURN CONJUNCT PLUTO

♄ ☌ ♇ Desire to find solutions is one of the hallmarks of Saturn conjunct Pluto. These individuals promote and produce important medical and scientific research. There is great concern with conservation and use of the Earth's elementary resources. These individuals may also be the ones to make significant progress in social issues that deal with the elderly and with death and dying. Another important consideration is sure to be the use, as well as abuse, of power and authority. Because Saturn is associated with responsibility and taking correct action and Pluto is associated with the deepest, most elemental forces, the conjunction of these two planets can be viewed as a link with or at least awareness of karma in an individual as well as a nation or other group of individuals.

SATURN SEXTILES

SATURN SEXTILE URANUS

♄ ✶ ♅ Conditions in society that provide opportunities to expand technological research and development, international economic institutions and trade, and societal structures are associated with Saturn sextile Uranus. Individuals born with this aspect may or may not personally participate in activities that broaden societal awareness or enhance technological research, but they will benefit from them in one way or another.

SATURN SEXTILE NEPTUNE

♄ ✶ ♆ Individuals born with Saturn sextile Neptune are involved with introducing a new stage of religious thinking, a willingness to

investigate the occult and other supernatural phenomena from a scientific point of view, or finding new uses for drugs and medicines already on the market.

SATURN SEXTILE PLUTO

♄ ✳ ♇ Opportunity to make more efficient use of natural resources comes to those who are born with Saturn sextile Pluto, although it does not indicate with certainty that their efforts will work. However, their attempts to arouse public concern in such matters are usually successful.

SATURN SQUARES

SATURN SQUARE URANUS

♄ □ ♅ When Saturn squares Uranus, it is not usually a favorable time for the stock market and there are unexpected upsets in political, economic, and societal institutions. Changes in society that accompany this aspect are troubling when they occur, but the events or the reactions to them may turn out to be providential in the future. Individuals born with this aspect are confronted with the task of finding ways to assimilate traditional ideas and methods within new and emerging trends.

SATURN SQUARE NEPTUNE

♄ □ ♆ General laxity toward structure and organization is associated with Saturn square Neptune. Noncommittal attitudes prevail just when strong commitments are necessary. Bad timing and a tendency to focus on the wrong issues result in lack of accomplishment and a feeling that something is wrong, but it leaves individuals born with this aspect no idea of how to correct the situation. They may not have a tough time with rules and regulations, but they have to deal with those who do.

SATURN SQUARE PLUTO

♄ □ ♇ Saturn square Pluto implies anger in a society that believes it was deceived by those in power. Getting back to basics seems an overriding concern, but the intensity is sometimes so great that innocent and valuable people as well as ideologies and institutions are destroyed in the process. Many individuals born with this aspect are not particularly willing to give their respect or cooperation to others unless they feel it has been earned. Then they will bend over backward to be helpful.

SATURN TRINES

SATURN TRINE URANUS

♄ △ ♅ Society enjoys a healthy economy, a bullish stock market, and relatively low unemployment when Saturn trines Uranus. Even underdeveloped nations often benefit from this aspect. The personal lives of Saturn trine Uranus individuals may also prosper on some level merely because of the generally positive conditions in society.

SATURN TRINE NEPTUNE

♄ △ ♆ Widespread and generous public support for cultural establishments, religious groups, and artistic organizations is indicated by Saturn trine Neptune. Individuals born with this aspect benefit from increased tolerance for minority groups and renewed interest and support for handicapped, underprivileged, and institutionalized people.

SATURN TRINE PLUTO

♄ △ ♇ A more equitable distribution of power, resources, and monetary assets among members of society and even among nations is characteristic of Saturn trine Pluto. Individuals with this aspect may or may not personally participate in the larger societal issues of redistribution, but many of them are well endowed with personal resources of all kinds.

SATURN OPPOSITIONS

SATURN OPPOSITE URANUS

♄ ☍ ♅ Fierce opposition between the old and the new, and the liberal and the conservative elements of society is apt to occur when Saturn is opposite Uranus. Compromise is rarely possible. When a winner is declared, there is usually no trace left of the losers or that which they represented. On one level or another, these troubled situations diminish the lives of individuals born with this aspect.

SATURN OPPOSITE NEPTUNE

♄ ☍ ♆ Saturn opposite Neptune is indicative of dangerously flawed thinking and societal attitudes. Deception, paranoia, and disil-

lusionment are prevalent, and it is to be hoped that those with clear minds and courageous hearts have some influence. Abuse of the weak and underprivileged is likely, and individuals born with this aspect may be the victims or the victimizers in such situations or they may have to deal with these situations in their professions or other activities.

SATURN OPPOSITE PLUTO

♄☍♇ The powerful seek more and more control and tend to abuse their positions of authority when Saturn is opposite Pluto. Individuals born with this aspect are confronted with a societal philosophy that is extremely inflexible in nature and fosters the Machiavellian philosophy that the end justifies the means.

URANUS ASPECTS

The dynamics of change, often rebellious and unpredictable change, are usually instigated by the aspects of Uranus.

URANUS CONJUNCTIONS

URANUS CONJUNCT NEPTUNE

♅☌♆ The conjunction of Uranus and Neptune takes place approximately every 171 years, the last occurrences being in 1821 and 1993. Although the conjunction is made within a twelve-month period, the two planets stay within the orb of a conjunction for many years. Therefore, the influences we associate with the aspect may occur prior to, on, or later than the conjunction itself. This planetary pattern is of major importance in discussing the conditions of society during the year it takes place, but by itself it has little significance in an individual's horoscope. The conjunction's significance on a personal level may be interpreted to a certain extent according to the natal house in which it is found and also if it happens to make any close aspects to other natal planets. On a societal level, the aspect is associated with turbulent change in ideals. Among other things, Uranus represents revolution and Neptune represents oppression and slavery. To further define at least the last two Neptune-Uranus conjunctions which occurred in Capricorn, one must remember that Capricorn

represents the government. In 1821, the Greek War of Independence began against the Ottoman Turks. Independence was declared by Mexico, Venezuela, Peru, Costa Rica, Guatemala, El Salvador, Honduras, and Panama. In the 1990s, under this conjunction, independence occurred again, this time in Russia. There is no doubt that countless lives are affected on a personal level by these great revolutions. Babies born during a Uranus-Neptune conjunction will live under radically different governments and societal conditions than their parents.

URANUS CONJUNCT PLUTO

♅ ☌ ♇ Uranus conjunct Pluto occurs approximately every 114 to 141 years, the last time being the mid-1960s. The revolutionary character of its influence in the United States was seen in the enormous personal and public crisis over issues like the Vietnam War and the fast-emerging drug culture. The influence may or may not affect individuals born in this generation personally, but it will have much to do with how their generation runs the world in the next century.

URANUS SEXTILES

URANUS SEXTILE NEPTUNE

♅ ✶ ♆ Uranus sextile Neptune only applies to those born from the mid- to late 1960s. Society provides opportunities for art, idealism, spirituality, and especially the advancement of minority classes. How such opportunity affects individuals born with this aspect depends on other factors in their personality and background, but they will be personally affected by a world more sensitive to civil rights, the handicapped, and other underprivileged members of society.

URANUS SEXTILE PLUTO

♅ ✶ ♇ Uranus sextile Pluto only applies to those born in the mid-1940s. The aspect is generational and implies motivation and opportunities in science (especially atomic energy), technology, and medicine. Born into a generation that had just exploded the first atomic bomb, the lives of these individuals are affected by the problems connected with atomic energy, but positively influenced by advancement in medicine, computers, and other technological inventions and innovations.

URANUS SQUARES

URANUS SQUARE NEPTUNE

♅ □ ♆ Those born during the first half of the 1950s are the Uranus square Neptune people of this century. Their generation was born into a world where popular opinion quickly gets out of control as it did, for example, during the McCarthy hearings, when the Communist witch-hunt plagued many innocent people and threw the country into a frenzy. However, harsh aspects to Neptune often mean the influences eventually disintegrate or dissolve. As individuals, this generation's life-style or social attitudes are influenced in varying degrees by this aspect.

URANUS SQUARE PLUTO

♅ □ ♇ Individuals born in the early 1930s have Uranus square Pluto. Their lives were dramatically changed as a result of the Great Depression that preceded their births. Their early years were shaped by this transformation, a transformation that affected all levels of society at the time it occurred and one that subsequently affected the behavior of this generation as adults.

URANUS TRINES

URANUS TRINE NEPTUNE

♅ △ ♆ Uranus trine Neptune is a generational aspect that occurred in the mid-1940s. It implies a fortunate period for the advancement of the arts, religion, societal institutions, and especially for the circumstances of minorities. The generation that was born with this aspect reached maturity in the 1960s and 1970s, and they promoted such ideals and activities as civil rights, antiwar demonstrations, the feminist movement, and gay rights.

URANUS TRINE PLUTO

♅ △ ♇ Uranus upsets the status quo and Pluto transforms, but in the case of Uranus trine Pluto, the result is beneficial. Prior to the mid-1920s, which was the last time this aspect occurred, the status quo of and between the sexes was transformed. Women cut their hair and shortened their dresses, and that was only the superficial part of a transformation that would

eventually alter forever the traditional roles of men and women. In turn, the changing roles of men and women led the way to more equality, not only between the sexes but between all people. The lives of individuals born in the first half of the 1920s, as well as the influence this generation exerted on other generations, benefited to one extent or another by the extraordinary and revolutionary changes that were made when this aspect occurred. At no time previous to this did individuals express themselves so freely.

URANUS OPPOSITIONS

URANUS OPPOSITE NEPTUNE

♅ ☍ ♆ A minority group, usually dedicated to ideals and beliefs contrary to those of the majority, attempts to force changes when Uranus is opposite Neptune. The lives of individuals with this aspect born between 1905 and 1910 were affected to one degree or another by unpopular attempts to control society, one example being the ultimate failure of prohibition.

URANUS OPPOSITE PLUTO

♅ ☍ ♇ The last occurrence of Uranus opposite Pluto was 1900–02. Individuals of this generation were born into a society with a dislike for those in power or institutions with too much power. It promotes assassination and kidnapping as well as the dismantling of powerful institutions. The assassination of President McKinley catapulted the United States into a union with Teddy Roosevelt. Teddy Roosevelt then exerted his efforts to curb the growth of the powerful trusts in private business. Although this influence may or may not have affected their personality and character, the lives of many in the Uranus opposite Pluto generation were nevertheless altered on some level.

NEPTUNE ASPECTS

On the negative side, the dynamic qualities of Neptune in the aspects it forms involve undermining and disguising the reality of situations. On the positive side, Neptunian patterns inspire, heighten sensitivity, and encourage imagination and fantasy.

NEPTUNE CONJUNCT PLUTO

♆ ☌ ♇ The conjunction between Neptune and Pluto occurs about every 493 years, which makes this planetary aspect insignificant in an individual's horoscope. The last generation with this aspect was born in 1891–92 and the next generation will be born in the year 2383. The ideals and spiritual concepts of Neptune are affected deeply by the transforming intensity of Pluto. The dark side of this conjunction includes the potential that the poisonous undermining and delusional fanaticism associated with Neptune can be intensified by the ruthless search for power. History provides ample description of this in the rise of American imperialism in the late nineteenth century. The drive for colonies matured with sudden force in the 1890s as a reaction to economic depression and the rise of great monopolistic corporations seemingly immune to governmental control. Feeling trapped by these powerful forces at home, the conquest of other nations offered Americans a way to restore their nationalistic spirit by becoming a larger global force.

NEPTUNE SEXTILE PLUTO

♆ ✳ ♇ Neptune sextile Pluto is an aspect of extremely long duration. The current sextile between these two planets has been affecting generations for the last forty years. The associations made with the long-term Uranus and Neptune aspect in society represent constant opportunities to change the course of existing structures and pave the way for new ones. Those who will live under the influence of the other aspects (i.e., conjunction, square, trine, and opposition) as they occur between these planets in the future will have to deal with the ideologies and other societal institutions that current generations have had the opportunities to create.

NEPTUNE SQUARE PLUTO

♆ ☐ ♇ The square between Neptune and Pluto occurs every 246 years. With a few exceptions during the second century AD, these squares occur when Pluto is transiting Pisces and Neptune is transiting either Gemini or Sagittarius. The last generation to experience this aspect was born in 1816 when Pluto transited Pisces and Neptune transited Sagittarius. The next generation of people who will be born with this aspect will not come along until 2062. To get a description of the significance of this aspect, we need to consider the combination of the signs Gemini, Sagittarius, and Pisces with the planets

Neptune and Pluto. This aspect then may be interpreted as a strong indication of a transforming agent (Pluto), such as war or plague on the negative side and research and development on the positive side, that targets imagination, spirituality, and ideals (Neptune). The transformation takes place through the energy of new ideas and information (Gemini) and ultimately with the attainment of knowledge and education (Sagittarius).

NEPTUNE TRINE PLUTO

♆ △ ♇ Once the dynamics of a trine are formed between Neptune and Pluto, the aspect keeps occurring over and over again for a period of between five and eleven years. After this period, a trine will not be formed again for hundreds of years. The last trine began in 1776 with Neptune in Virgo and Pluto in Capricorn. The trine continued to exist between the two planets throughout the next decade, finally ending in 1786, and by this time Neptune had moved into Libra while Pluto had moved into Aquarius. The trine is a fortunate aspect. Ideals (Neptune) are enhanced in the idealistic sign Virgo, and they are favored to become powerful (Pluto) in a government (Capricorn) that is established under this aspect. The founding of the United States is the best example of how this potential can be realized.

NEPTUNE OPPOSITE PLUTO

♆ ☍ ♇ Neptune opposes Pluto approximately every 493 years, the last occurrence being 1644. It is difficult to determine exactly what the significance of this aspect may be in an individual's horoscope, but its broader associations can be fairly well described from the conditions that existed in society when it occurred. Minority groups, those who are disadvantaged and enslaved, ideals, and religious beliefs (Neptune) are pitted against the people and institutions with power and resources (Pluto). Although such conditions may not be directly interpreted in the personality or character of people who are born with Neptune opposite Pluto, what happens in society will have a great impact on the quality of their lives in general and on the individual life-style of some of them.

Chapter Eleven

Interpreting the Horoscope

No matter how long I spend or how many descriptions I present when introducing students to astrology, they never really begin to learn until they study actual horoscopes. As we discuss the charts of their friends and relatives, I expand on descriptions I have already given them and add new information as it comes up in the various charts. This chapter contains horoscopes of some famous people to show interested readers how to apply the information presented in the previous chapters.

Not surprisingly, the first horoscope most students tackle is their own. Next in line are the charts of family members, friends, and neighbors. The number of charts that students gather from their personal network of friends and acquaintances is small compared to the number they need to study. One solution is to examine the lives of famous people. Reading about people is fascinating. Individuals in whom you think you have no interest start to become very interesting when you delve into some of the personal as well as public details of their lives. As an example, I have chosen Theodore Roosevelt.

THEODORE ROOSEVELT

BRIEF BACKGROUND

On a warm September afternoon in 1901, President William McKinley attended a public reception at the Pan American Exposition in Buffalo, New York. Leaving his wife Ida to rest at the home of the exposition's president, McKinley stood in the Temple of Music shaking hands with the many people who had lined up to meet him. As the event drew to a close and the doors were about to be shut, a young man named Leon Czolgosz approached with his left hand extended. His right hand was bound in a scarf as though it had been injured. As he reached McKinley, Czolgosz raised his "injured" right hand and fired two shots that ripped through the president's stomach. For the next few days it was believed McKinley would survive the attack, but his condition suddenly grew worse, and, in the early hours of September 14, he succumbed to his injuries. Twelve hours later, forty-two-year-old vice president Theodore Roosevelt became the youngest president in American history. After serving the remainder of McKinley's term, Roosevelt became president again in 1904. Elected to the office on his own this time, he declared, "I am no longer a political accident."[1]

Third cousin twice removed to President Martin Van Buren, fifth cousin to Franklin Delano Roosevelt, uncle to Eleanor Roosevelt, and great-uncle to journalists Joseph and Stewart Alsop, Theodore Roosevelt was a very popular president. The teddy bear, a toy that still remains a favorite possession of most children, was originally named for Teddy Roosevelt. Admired by sculptor John Boglum, Roosevelt was immortalized as one of the presidential faces the artist carved on Mount Rushmore. According to *People* magazine, Teddy Roosevelt "kept an astrological chart pasted to the bottom of his chessboard for handy reference."[2] I have not tried to verify this statement, but anyone familiar with the life and times of TR (as he was popularly called) would not be surprised if it turned out to be true. He possessed a brilliant and endlessly curious intellect and one of the most colorful personalities of all our chief executives. Governor of New York; vice president and president of the United States; highly successful writer of history, biography, and adventure; war hero and Nobel prize winner, Theodore Roosevelt's accomplishments are outstanding enough for ten men.

Theodore Roosevelt also endured one of the cruelest twists of fate. In 1878, at age twenty and still a student at Harvard, Teddy fell in love with Alice Lee,

daughter of a prominent Bostonian banker. Attraction to the beautiful Alice was immediate, and he pursued a spirited and unabated courtship until they finally married on October 27, 1880. In 1884, twenty-two-year-old Alice, whom Teddy called "Sunshine," became pregnant. Prior to giving birth, Alice moved in with Teddy's mother Mittie in New York City because Teddy, by this time a New York State assemblyman, was in Albany. A telegram was sent on February 12 announcing his daughter's birth. Teddy joyfully began to arrange a leave of absence, but he received a more ominous telegram telling him to come immediately. Arriving home he found his wife gravely ill with a kidney ailment that had gone undetected during her pregnancy. At the same time in another bedroom, his mother Mittie lay dying of typhoid fever. Before dawn the next morning, Valentine's Day, Mittie died and late in the afternoon so did Alice. The baby, also named Alice, survived. Teddy remarried, but throughout his life, perhaps as a measure of the intensity of his grief, he never again publicly or privately mentioned his first wife.

WHAT CAN BE LEARNED FROM A BIRTH DATE

Complete horoscopes are not always available. Beginning students may not know how to calculate a chart, or the birth hour may be unknown. Although authors frequently include the time of birth in biographies, it is not usually given in newspaper and magazine articles about famous people. In the absence of a timed chart, studying just the birth date is very helpful, especially during the learning process. I will discuss this method first, using Theodore Roosevelt as an example.

The first step is to look up the birth date in an ephemeris. An ephemeris is a book that lists the positions of the Sun, Moon, and planets at midnight Greenwich Mean Time (some ephemerides list planetary positions at noon). Ephemerides (plural of ephemeris) can be purchased in new-age bookstores. The ephemeris in this book (see Appendix A) was calculated and formatted by Time Cycles Research. It lists the planetary positions from 1900 through 1999. Having located the birth date for the individual you want to study, write down each of the planetary positions. The Sun, Moon, Mercury, Venus, and Mars have the most to offer in describing personal traits and characteristics, so we need not concern ourselves just yet with the sign positions of Jupiter through Pluto. Since Roosevelt was born in a year not covered by our ephemeris, I have listed the relevant planetary positions for midnight GMT on October 27, 1858.

☉	☽	☿	♀	♂
03°♏17'	02°♋04'	01°♏15'	17°♐29'	17°♑18'

Theodore Roosevelt was born with Sun in Scorpio, Moon in Cancer, Mercury in Scorpio, Venus in Sagittarius, and Mars in Capricorn. The basis of astrological interpretation of his natal planets and their sign positions can be found by reviewing Chapter 6 and Chapter 7.

SUN IN SCORPIO

Scorpio individuals can and often do develop superior strength of body, mind, and will. Weak and sickly as a child, Theodore Roosevelt suffered from severe bronchial asthma and stomach upsets. William DeGregorio's book of United States presidents states Roosevelt, "through rigorous exercise and sheer force of will, matured into a brawny, robust man of action."[3]

TR's physical stamina and activities were extraordinary, one relative recalling that he played ninety games of tennis in one day. His sister Corinne provides a glimpse of how deeply a Scorpio child can be motivated. One day, after Teddy had suffered a particularly acute asthma attack, his father took him aside. Corinne recalled the exchange that took place. " 'Theodore,' said his father, 'you have the mind but not the body, and without the body the mind cannot go as far as it should. You *must* make your body. It is hard drudgery to make one's body but I know you can do it!' The little boy looked up, his sister recalled, and accepted the challenge. *'I'll make my body!'* "[4]

Encouraging him to improve, Teddy's mother took him to a gymnasium. She sat and watched as her son "relentlessly pulled the weights up, let them subside, and then pulled them up again."[5] Relentless is an excellent description of Scorpio determination. Roosevelt did not stop his physical exercises in childhood. "Throughout his life he was surrounded by the paraphernalia of bodybuilding: boxing gloves, weights, dumbbells, horizontal bars. ... Later, he deliberately sought out dangerous situations—on the battlefield, in politics, in the depths of the Brazilian jungle—to prove himself."[6]

In 1912, a remarkable instance of TR's determination and strength occurred while he was campaigning as the Bull Moose party candidate. Standing in an open car on his way to make a speech in Milwaukee, Teddy was shot by a man in the crowd who fired a pistol into his chest. Roosevelt insisted on going ahead to the

rally. Standing in front of the packed auditorium in his bloody shirt, he calmly announced, "I don't know whether you fully understand that I have just been shot; but it takes more than that to kill a Bull Moose."[7] He continued to speak for the next hour and a half before seeking medical treatment. Doctors at the hospital credited Roosevelt's excellent physical condition as part of the reason he was not more seriously hurt.

MOON IN CANCER

Men with Moon in Cancer often exhibit social awkwardness. Biographer Nathan Miller writes that girls found Teddy "clumsily appealing," and his "social graces did not always come easily."[8] Childhood friend Fanny Smith remembered one cold day when Teddy's brother Elliot paid her a visit. The two of them sat talking when she noticed Teddy, "looking blue with cold," pacing up and down outside. Elliot's explanation was that Teddy had planned to visit but suddenly overcome by bashfulness, decided to remain outside. Moon in Cancer brings potential for stomach disorders, and TR suffered from nervous diarrhea or what he called "cholera morbus."

Moon in Cancer people are strongly attached to home and family. Editor Joseph Bucklin Bishop writes in his introduction to *Theodore Roosevelt's Letters To His Children,* "it was deep and abiding love of children, of family and home, that was the dominating passion of his life."[9] A vignette from Nathan Miller's biography further illustrates the devotion of TR's Cancerian Moon. " 'Ike' Hoover, the longtime chief usher, said the Roosevelt years were the wildest scramble in the history of the White House. Visitors were sometimes startled by a loud clatter as Archie or Quentin slid down the main staircase on metal trays. Cabinet members recoiled as small boys—members of the 'White House Gang,' as Quentin's buddies were known—popped out of vases in the East Room. Quentin once took his Shetland pony, Algonquin, upstairs in the elevator to visit Archie, who was sick in bed. A family parrot screeched, 'Hurrah for Roosevelt!' at unsuspecting guests. When Speaker of the House Joe Cannon tried to discuss weighty matters with the president, a kitten leaped into his lap. The South Lawn became a baseball field for the chums Quentin brought home from public school. The president was often an interested spectator and cheered the batters. 'Hit it!' he would yell. 'Hit it!' Sometimes he joined Ethel's friends for games of hide-and-seek in the attic, usually insisting upon being 'it,' one participant recalled years later.

"It was not unusual for an important meeting to be interrupted by a tap on the door of the presidential office and the appearance of a small group of boys whose leader might shyly announce, 'It's after four.'

" 'By Jove, so it is!' the president might say, and as he adjourned the meeting, he would tell his visitor that he had promised to take the boys walking at four o'clock. 'I never keep boys waiting. It's a hard trial for a boy to wait.' " [10]

No matter how confident or aggressive their outer personality, Cancerian Moon people are emotionally vulnerable on the inside. One description of Roosevelt states, "Outwardly boisterous, he inwardly suffered from bouts of pessimism and melancholy and had feared that he would not be elected on his own."[11]

MERCURY IN SCORPIO

Mercury in Scorpio indicates investigative ability and relentless pursuit of the answers to questions and other information. One quality associated with this Mercury position is ability to separate the relevant from the trivial or unimportant. Commenting on Roosevelt's intelligence, the scholar Lord Bryce once remarked, "He had a brain that could always go straight to the pith of any matter. That is a mental power of the first rank."[12]

In its natural third-house position, Mercury in Scorpio not only suggests the enhanced mental power that Roosevelt demonstrated, it also suggests involvement with writing, speaking, and community affairs—all of which fit Theodore Roosevelt in large measure. Joining New York City's Twenty-first District Republican Association shortly after his marriage, young Roosevelt's first efforts went into putting the organization on record in favor of a bill to reform the city's street-cleaning operations. Elected state assemblyman, he quickly gained a formidable reputation as a reformer in spite of his youth and political inexperience. Moving to Washington, D.C., in 1889 as one of three United States Civil Service Commissioners, Roosevelt kept the Civil Service Commission "... in a constant state of turmoil. Swooping down without warning upon far-flung outposts of his empire, he investigated rumors of fraud, held hearings, issued reports, made speeches, and wrote magazine articles to dramatize the cause of reform." [13]

VENUS IN SAGITTARIUS

People with Venus in Sagittarius are friendly and outgoing. They seek a wide variety of acquaintances and possess an enhanced capacity for enjoyment.

Roosevelt had an irresistible laugh. "You don't smile with Mr. Roosevelt," writes one reporter, "you shout with laughter with him, and then you shout again while he tries to cork up more laugh, and sputters, 'Come gentlemen, let us be serious. This is most unbecoming.' "[14] Certainly, no president ever enjoyed his position more or attracted a wider variety of people to the White House than Theodore Roosevelt. Noting his wide variety of friends and visitors, some observers wondered, "how the 'historic old house' was bearing up under the sustained assault of the Roosevelts. Life in the White House resembled nothing so much as a three-ring circus. People were always coming and going, and guests ranged from Henry Adams, who had taken to referring to the president as 'Theodorus I, Czar Rooseveltoff,' to John L. Sullivan, the prizefighter, and Bat Masterson, the frontier marshal. 'Distinguished civilized men and charming civilized women came as a habit to the White House while Roosevelt was there,' noted Owen Wister. 'For once in our history we had an American salon.' "[15]

Roosevelt was not inclined to mince words or be anyone other than himself. Venus in Sagittarius individuals are often given to bluntness or plainness of speech that others tend to view either as tactless or regard as total honesty. "Roosevelt's arrival in the White House ... was like a blast of fresh and bracing air in the fetid atmosphere of Washington. Informal, energetic, and—to the delight of reporters—as outspoken as ever, he saw dozens of people every day, listened attentively to what they had to say, and sent them on their way with machine-gun rapidity. His exuberance was infectious. 'You go into Roosevelt's presence, you feel his eyes upon you, you listen to him, and you go home and wring the personality out of your clothes,' said one visitor."[16]

In Sagittarius, Venus (as the ruler of Libra) is in its natural third-house position, which is why one potential for those with Sagittarian Venus is marriage to a person from their own community or to a grammar school classmate. TR's second wife Edith was a childhood friend.

MARS IN CAPRICORN

Mars in Capricorn signifies aggressive ambition, active individuals who do not hesitate to do as they please. These people are not totally dedicated to personal whims, however. Many of their actions result in changes that also benefit others. It would be hard to find a better example than Theodore Roosevelt. Although a member of New York's Police Board for only two years, he established "a sense of professionalism heretofore unknown to the department and made a sweeping

series of changes, reforms, and innovations that outlasted his tenure."[17] Zeal and determination also marked TR's actions as a United States civil service commis-sioner, "his boundless energy gave the commission influence it had never had before. A total of 26,000 jobs were removed from the category of political plum and placed under the merit system, and new tests for applicants were devised. For the first time, women were put on the same competitive level with men, which increased their numbers in government jobs."[18]

People with Mars in Capricorn do not accept rejection. Before he met and fell in love with his first wife Alice, Theodore was involved briefly with childhood friend Edith Carow (who became his second wife). During one summer, TR recorded in his diary that he and Edith had gone boating, picked water lilies, and taken tea together. At a certain point in the diary, he abruptly stops mentioning Edith. For the next several weeks TR appeared to be "consumed with rage." He rode his horse unusually hard, shot a neighborhood dog that ran after him, and recklessly shot off his rifle while sailing with some cousins. Comments made years later suggested the reason for Teddy's aggressive behavior was that he had asked Edith to marry him and she had refused. Not long afterwards Teddy met and fell in love with Alice Lee, who was not, at least in the beginning of their rela-tionship, any more receptive to TR than Edith had been. " 'See that girl? I am going to marry her. She won't have me, but I am going to have her!' So said Theodore Roosevelt to a friend, his teeth flashing a determined grin ..."[19] Undaunted by the coquettish Alice's disinterest, TR continued his pursuit of her heart until she became his wife two years later.

MAKING A NOTEBOOK OF BIOGRAPHICAL OBSERVATIONS

Keeping a file of birth dates and maintaining a notebook of your observations are indispensable methods in learning astrology. When reading a biography or biographical article, record the person's birth date along with the planetary sign positions for that date in your notebook.

One of the best sources of birth dates is *Encyclopaedia Britannica*. Your local library has encyclopedias in addition to *Current Biography* and other biographical dictionaries. Use the ephemeris in Appendix A to look up planetary positions for births after 1900. When you find a description in a biography that fits your idea of a certain planetary sign position, write it in your notebook. As you can see in

the preceding paragraphs about Teddy Roosevelt, a wealth of information can be extracted from the sign positions of the Sun, Moon, Mercury, Venus, and Mars on the day of birth. If the Sun, Moon, or planets happen to change signs on the day in question, write down both signs. Reading more about the person may help you decide which sign seems more appropriate. Record your observations of the traits and characteristics of friends and relatives that you think fit their charts. As you continue to read biographies and your knowledge of astrology increases, your growing collection of notes and observations becomes a valuable data bank. Say, for example, you are reading about or observing a Capricorn individual. Review previous notes you made about Capricorns. Compare the traits of people with the same Sun sign. Use this method to note similarities between people who share the same Moon sign, Mercury sign, and so on.

THE TIMED CHART

Information provided by the birth date is valuable, but it cannot provide the complex personality profile that is derived from a chart cast for the time of birth. Obtaining and verifying accurate birth records is one of the astrologer's primary goals. It is also one of the thorniest issues in today's astrological community. Readers who plan to take their studies beyond the scope of this book would do well to understand that a birth chart should always be accompanied by the source of the data for which the chart was cast. Was the source an actual birth record? Was it found in a newspaper or magazine article? A biography? Listing the source does not always guarantee accuracy, but it can correct or eliminate charts that contain errors and controversial data.

Before taking up the business of chart interpretation, students must decide how they want to calculate charts. The basics of chart calculation can be found in books listed for that purpose in the bibliography. Although it is important to master the techniques of chart calculation, most students eventually prefer to let a computer do the mathematical drudgery. Some of the best computer software is available from Time Cycles Research (see Appendix B for address). Another choice, especially for the beginning student, is to have horoscopes calculated by a chart service. New-age book stores and local astrological groups frequently offer such services for a nominal fee. Chart services are also available by mail (Appendix B, and Llewellyn's chart services on pages 438–39.)

Birth charts provide many categories to compare and study in your astrological notebook. From a calculated chart, you can note the Rising Sign (Ascendant)

as well as the signs on each of the house cusps, the house positions of natal planets, and aspects between the natal planets. I offer four charts with which you can begin an astrological notebook: Theodore Roosevelt, Grace Kelly, Ted Bundy, and Mata Hari (Figure 16 on page 299). The sources of birth data for each chart are found in Appendix C. The readers will find it helpful to redraw these four charts on a separate piece of paper to give themselves practice and to study these charts more closely as I discuss each one.

THEODORE ROOSEVELT'S HOROSCOPE

In the preceding paragraphs, I discussed Roosevelt's natal Sun through natal Mars in their respective signs to illustrate what can be learned from the birth date alone. In the following analysis, you will see how much additional information can be derived from a timed chart. According to most biographical sources, Roosevelt's birth data is October 27, 1858 at 7:45 PM in New York City. His calculated horoscope appears on page 299 in Figure 16. I will mention only a few of the features in Roosevelt's natal chart since a complete analysis and interpretation of this or any other horoscope would require a great deal more space than is available for this discussion.

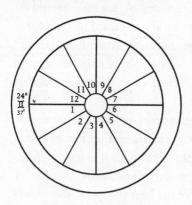

Theodore Roosevelt

The Ascendant, or Rising Sign, one of the most significant points in a horoscope, is Gemini. The description of Gemini in Chapter 3 profiles the kind of energy that astrologically characterizes Teddy Roosevelt's personality, habits, and physical fitness. Compare the astrological explanation with the following biographical accounts of Roosevelt. They contain similar descriptions of duality, constant and varied activities, and intellectual curiosity. Nathan Miller writes that in addition to reading a book a day, TR was a "Western rancher and society clubman, writer and soldier, conservationist and big-game hunter, he was, as Lord Morley said, 'a cross between Saint Vitus and Saint Paul.' "[20] George Mowry also gives an accurate appraisal of a Gemini Ascendant, stating Roosevelt was "many things to many people because he was such a bewildering array of things to himself."[21]

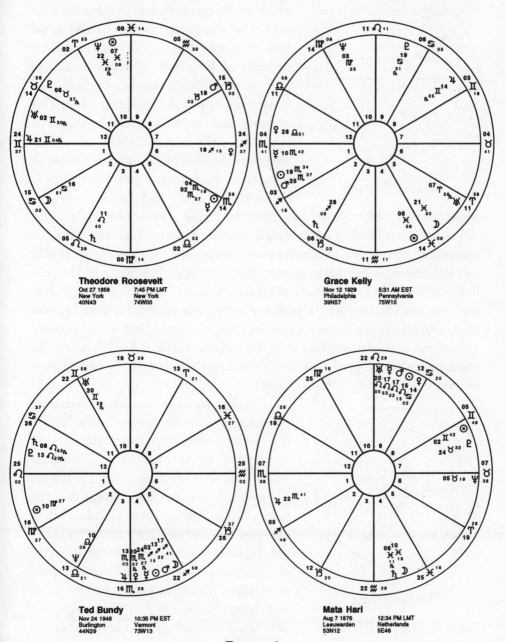

Figure 16

299

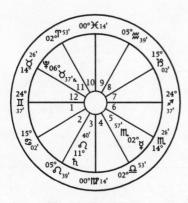

Theodore Roosevelt

The planet that rules the Rising Sign, which in this case is Gemini, is considered the ruler of the chart. Mercury rules Gemini, so we look at natal Mercury for further understanding of Roosevelt. Mercury, associated with speech, communication, learning, and transportation, played a significant role in TR's interests and activities. His classmates at Harvard describe him as having "such a startling array of deeply rooted interests that we all thought he would make a great journalist." 22

In matters of health and physical anatomy, Mercury rules the hands, the lungs, and the organs of speech and sight. With this in mind, let's look at some of natal Mercury's aspects. Mercury in Scorpio squares Saturn in Leo. Saturn indicates restrictions and the square presents difficult circumstances. Further suggesting that some of the difficulty could be poor health is Mercury opposite Pluto, the planetary ruler of the sixth house (Scorpio is on the sixth house cusp). Health is a sixth-house matter. Mercury opposite Pluto suggests health problems that, in TR's case, turned out to be bronchial asthma and poor eyesight. As a child, his asthma made it so hard to breathe he could only sleep propped up in bed or in a chair, and severe myopia made it necessary for him to wear thick glasses.

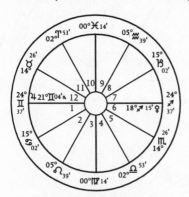

Theodore Roosevelt

Another aspect in the chart is Venus in Sagittarius opposite Jupiter in Gemini. Review the dynamics of this aspect in Chapter 10 and compare it to the following biographical description of an incident when TR left his pregnant wife, who was due to give birth at any time, to go to Albany. Author Nathan Miller offers an explanation. "Some observers see in this [behavior] another manifestation of the avoidance syndrome that appeared in critical moments of his life. In 1878, when his father was dying, he remained at Cambridge; and again, in 1898, he left his second wife barely recovering from a near-fatal illness to go off to war in Cuba." 23

The difficult dynamics of Venus (values, principles, and conduct) in Sagittarius (independent action) opposite Jupiter (ideals and personal status) lead us to suspect Roosevelt's unwillingness to compromise and lack of firm principles if they were not advantageous to his winning a situation. TR wanted a position in the new administration when William Henry Harrison was elected. Henry Cabot Lodge discussed the possibility of a post for Roosevelt with the president. Harrison replied that he was concerned about Roosevelt's "willful, impulsive, and somewhat erratic independence." [24] Similar behavior harmed Roosevelt as president when he ordered direct intervention against a friendly government in order to build the Panama Canal. "No action during Roosevelt's presidency aroused greater controversy among his contemporaries and later generations than the methods used to 'take' Panama." [25]

Speaker of the House Joseph Cannon was quoted as saying to a friend, "Roosevelt's all right, but he's got no more use for the Constitution than a tomcat has for a marriage license." [26] Another criticism was Roosevelt's "insistence on being both a political and moral leader. When he tried to justify political acts in moral terms, he sometimes cast himself in the role of insufferable hypocrite." [27] Bluntness of expression, already suggested by Venus in Sagittarius, is further emphasized here by this planet's opposition to Jupiter. TR, diplomatic and charming in many situations to be sure, was also described by fellow state legislator Isaac Hunt as "the most indiscreet guy I ever met." [28]

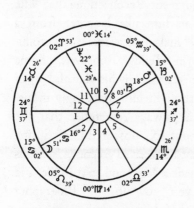

Theodore Roosevelt

Biographers portray Theodore Roosevelt's restlessness, aggressive behavior, ambition, and relentless physical drive. Though they are suggested by other factors in the natal chart, one of the strongest indicators of such characteristics is Moon opposite Mars. This aspect also indicates the possibility of accidents, especially injuries to the head (Mars). In his youth, TR took boxing lessons, a sport in which he continued to engage even as president. While in the White House, Roosevelt lost the sight in his left eye as a result of a sparring match with a military aide. TR's aggressive nature is well documented. "Despite Roosevelt's high moral tone, he possessed a streak of ruthlessness and at times broke his own rules for fairness and justice." [29] In TR's

chart, the opposition occurs between the second and eighth houses, emphasizing monetary difficulties. From an astrological point of view, it is not surprising that in his personal life "financial caution was not one of Theodore Roosevelt's trademarks," [30] and, as president, "Economics and fiscal policy were never Roosevelt's strong points." [31]

Another aspect of the Moon is a trine with Neptune in the tenth house of public career and popularity. One association with this fortunate aspect involves the great success of his historical book, *The Naval War of 1812,* and the great enthusiasm he exhibited as Assistant Secretary of the Navy. The navy is a Neptune-ruled subject. The trine indicates success. "If any job had been made to order for Theodore," writes Nathan Miller, "it was Assistant Secretary of the Navy." Roosevelt "made whirlwind inspections of the navy yards and took great delight in reviewing the navy's new battleships at sea." [32] Another demonstration of the fortunate Moon trine Neptune was Roosevelt's ability to inspire large numbers of people, and as Miller states, "probably no president has more successfully captured the imagination of the American people." [33]

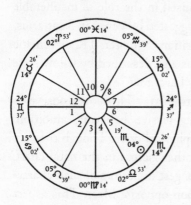

Theodore Roosevelt

Before ending the analysis of Roosevelt's chart, note the fifth-house Sun. House positions of the Sun, Moon, and other planets are described in Chapter 8. As adults, fifth-house Sun individuals retain a distinct child-like playfulness and enjoyment. Recollections that "Life bubbled over in him like laughter from a healthy child" [34] make it clear this was a prominent quality in Teddy Roosevelt. Some observers were "charmed by his youthful joy in living; others thought him irritatingly immature. 'You must always remember that the President is about six,' observed Cecil Spring Rice, an old friend. And on his forty-sixth birthday, he received greetings from his friend Secretary of War Elihu Root: 'You have made a very good start in life, and your friends have great hopes for you when you grow up.' " [35] Biographer Edmund Morris describes antics that were typical of the hyperactive, exuberant Roosevelt. "Senator Henry Cabot Lodge has been heard yelling irritably at a portly object swaying in the sky, 'Theodore! If you knew how ridiculous you look up in that tree you'd come down at once!' On winter evenings in Rock Creek

Park, strollers may observe the President of the United States wading pale and naked into the icy Potomac, followed by shivering members of the cabinet. Thumping noises in the White House library indicate that Roosevelt is being thrown around the room by a Japanese wrestler; a particularly seismographic crash, which makes the entire mansion tremble, signifies that Secretary Taft has been forced to join in the fun." [36] Perhaps the best proof of the irrepressible child comes from TR himself. In 1913, after he had left the White House and was about to go on another wilderness expedition, he declared "I have to go. It's my last chance to be a boy!" [37]

The previous paragraphs on Roosevelt's horoscope are a small sample of the in-depth information that can be interpreted from a timed chart. I suggest that the reader continue to review previous chapters for relevant information concerning the various features that I cover in the following three charts.

GRACE KELLY

BRIEF BACKGROUND

Daughter of Margaret and John B. Kelly, Grace was born November 12, 1929, at 5:31 AM in Philadelphia, Pennsylvania (Figure 16). A successful Hollywood actress in the early 1950s, Grace Kelly is remembered in various film roles, especially her outstanding performance in *The Country Girl*, for which she received an Academy Award. Worldwide media coverage that was generated when she married Prince Rainier of Monaco in 1956 was not eclipsed until the wedding of Princess Diana and Prince Charles two decades later. From her marriage until her untimely death in 1982, the world continued to think of Grace Kelly as a woman who lived a fairy-tale existence.

Commemorating Princess Grace in *The Grimaldis of Monaco*, Anne Edwards writes, "Upon her death it was plain to see that the people had held her in very special regard. She was mourned as no reigning monarch in Monaco's recent history had been. ... The years of Grace's reign as Princesse de Monaco had brought pride to the average Monegasque for her elegance, beauty, and charm, and they had loved her because of her compassion for the elderly, the young and the ill. She had helped set up senior-citizen groups, convalescent homes and a ballet school for children." [38] Notable as her public record and reputation are, they only present a one-dimensional portrait. The interpretation of her natal

chart, verified in detailed biographical descriptions of people who knew Grace intimately, reveals a much different woman whose private struggles and personality make her far more interesting and human than a fairy-tale princess.

GRACE KELLY'S HOROSCOPE

Scorpio figures prominently in descriptions of Grace Kelly. A glance at her natal chart shows why. She was born with Ascendant, Sun, Mercury, and Mars in Scorpio. Pages could be filled with biographical quotations indicating how strongly she connected with the mysterious image of Scorpio. Biographer James Spada writes not only about his own confusion but also that of other journalists faced with the task of defining Grace Kelly. "Grace became the subject of intense journalistic interest, most of it puzzled. One article after another described Grace as an enigmatic figure, a paradox even to those who knew her. Titles such as 'Who Is Grace Kelly?' 'What Makes Grace Kelly Different?' abounded, and the astute and incisive *Saturday Evening Post* reporter Pete Martin found himself no closer to understanding Grace after researching his profile of her than he was before. 'The tough thing about the Kelly story,' he wrote, is this: 'You run yourself black in the face tracking down everyone—including Grace herself—who can give you an angle on her. You talk to those who've worked with her, those who are related to her and those who are her friends. And when you have finished all this, she is still such an elusive subject that writing about her is like trying to wrap up 115 pounds of smoke.'" [39]

Grace Kelly

A passion for flowers inspired Grace to collect and press them into delicate dried floral collages. Her artful creations became so admired that a professional slide show was produced which Grace narrated. Mara Wolynski, reviewing the show in *The Village Voice*, writes a strange but accurate description of Scorpio's association with death and transformation. "Flower pressing is, perhaps, the most depressing art form known to man ... But that is what Princess Grace does ... we saw Grace Kelly wandering through the mountains with a basket in her hand like a demented Heidi, Grace Kelly squatting over a half-dead flower soon to be plucked for one of her collages,

Grace Kelly curling her lips around a pencil as she adds another fern to her fram-able morgue—'I guess I'm just a scavenger at heart,' she says."[40]

Natal Venus in the twelfth house is associated with secret fantasies, secret romances, and those who are socially so shy they are grateful to anyone who pays them the slightest attention—romantically or otherwise. Close friend Judith Kanter Quine recalls when she and Grace were first getting to know each other. Grace presents a striking image of someone with Venus in the twelfth house. " 'Oh I'm so glad you like me,' she [Grace] replied. 'I was worried that because I'm so shy you'd think I was dull when you're so gregarious and full of personality. People are always criticizing me for sitting like a board, alone in a corner of the room at a party, not joining in the way you do, and I'm aware of that, too, and wish I could stop doing it.' "[41]

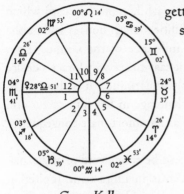

Grace Kelly

Grace had secret romances, as Don Richardson, one of her early liaisons, candidly admits. "I didn't find out about Gene Lyons [Grace's fellow actor in a Denver stock company] until years later," he says. "Apparently Grace had several other lives she kept completely secret from me."[42]

Scorpio is the Rising Sign, so its planetary ruler Pluto becomes the ruler, not only of the first house but also of the entire chart, and thus of Grace herself. Natal Pluto in Cancer is part of a Grand Trine that includes Moon in Pisces and Sun/Mars conjunction in Scorpio. A biographical encap-sulation of how this Grand Trine worked for Grace Kelly states "her entire life exemplified the triumph of appearance over reality."[43] In addi-tion to the trine between Sun/Mars, Moon, and Pluto, we must also consider the houses in which these planets are found as well as the house each planet rules.

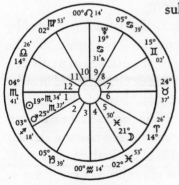

Grace Kelly

Every connection pulls the planets and the houses tighter and tighter together in the dynamics of the Grand Trine. Sun and Mars (ego drive and energy) are in the first house

305

(personality). The Moon (desires and needs) is located in the fifth house (social, creative, and romantic activities). Pluto is in the ninth house (the media, foreign countries, and people of a different race or nationality). The Moon rules the ninth house (with Cancer on the cusp) which pulls the Moon closer to Pluto in the ninth house. Scorpio rules the first house drawing its ruler Pluto closer to Sun and Mars in the first house. In turn, Mars rules the sixth house (with Aries on the cusp) and the Sun rules the tenth house (with Leo on the cusp) which brings matters related to job and daily responsibilities (sixth house) and public reputation (tenth house) under the fortunate influence of the Grand Trine. Understanding all the astrological factors makes it easy to see why Grace's desire to create a perfect public image was never seriously undermined. It is also easy to understand why she suffered from the lack of challenge in her film career and even as reigning monarch (tenth-house matters) as an unfortunate consequence of a Grand Trine.

Another aspect in Grace's natal chart must also be considered in any explanation of success in hiding her private life—Venus in Libra trine Jupiter in Gemini. Venus rules the seventh house (other people) with Taurus on the cusp, and twelfth house (that which is kept secret or hidden from others) with Libra on the cusp. Made stronger because it happens to be in Libra, a sign that it rules, Venus is related to social values and priorities, luck in general, and romance. Jupiter is in the eighth house (values imposed on her) and it rules the second house (principles and values she adopts herself). Jupiter is associated with optimism, the spirit of adventure, and daring.

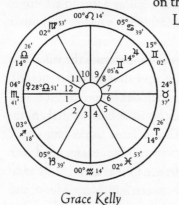

Grace Kelly

All these astrological factors, integrated by the positive dynamics of a trine, fit the following biographical situations as neatly as a jigsaw puzzle—a puzzle Grace created in order to project her public image. Her roommate recollects "despite a ban on loud music and dancing Grace would frequently perform wild dances in the hallways, dressed only in panties, and skitter back to her room whenever the elevator approached." [44] Grace's indiscretion within the walls of the Barbizon was never discovered—possibly because, as was true for most of her life, her image was so pristine that no one would have suspected her of such a flagrant flaunting of the

rules."[45] Don Richardson also talks about the big difference between the public Grace and the private Grace he knew. "Her public persona was so completely different than her private self that it was phenomenal. She was so proper, people thought of her as a nun. But when we were alone together, she used to dance naked for me to Hawaiian music. And if you don't think that was an incredible sight, you're crazy."[46]

Grace Kelly experienced inner struggles that were in great contrast to her apparent outer success. To find these troubled areas in her chart we turn to the T-square, the dynamics of which are set into motion by Saturn in Sagittarius opposite Jupiter in Gemini, and both planets square natal Moon in Pisces. The Moon (emotional life, nurturing she received as a child) acts as the conduit for the energy of the Jupiter-Saturn opposition. The Moon's fifth-house position brings into the equation her children and her romantic partners. Saturn represents authority, maturity, limitation, and restriction, while Jupiter represents ease, enjoyment, wealth, success, and the father.

Grace Kelly

The opposition between Saturn and Jupiter occurs from the second house to the eighth house. These houses are concerned with financial and emotional support. Saturn in the second house is what she worked to attain for herself, and Jupiter in the eighth house is what she was given. Biographically the opposition is summed up for us, "There was a large gap between what Grace wanted for herself and what she was forced to accept."[47] There is never a suggestion that Grace was openly rebellious. Such behavior is forestalled by Moon trine Mars, an aspect associated with those who avoid confrontation and are noncompetitive (on an emotional level). Biographical accounts agree that from an early age Grace exhibited a philosophical serenity; "What's the use of getting angry? You can't improve the situation. I can't quarrel. I'd rather give up."[48]

Her sister Lizanne's perception of Grace's "timidity" was that it did not reflect her sister's true personality. "She was very strong-willed and determined, but very mild about it."[49] In *The Bridesmaids*, Judith Quine mentions Grace's "lifelong inability to confront and her overwhelming desire to make and keep peace at all costs."[50] Quine also provides accurate descriptions in which we can

see how Grace's Moon trine Mars contrasts with the more difficult emotional situations presented by Moon square Jupiter and Saturn. "Grace became inconsistent, bouncing between a set of excessively repressive notions and dictates [Saturn] on the one hand, and a set of inordinately permissive ones [Jupiter] on the other. The most obvious example of the schism could be seen in Grace's approach to her two daughters [Moon]. Only Albert [Mars] was exempt from the inconsistencies." [51]

James Spada's biographical descriptions can be linked to Moon square Jupiter and Saturn, "... she possessed a strong rebelliousness ... and resentment against the structures of her upbringing. Most important, Grace's drives and motivations were inspired by her almost pathological need for her father's approbation. ... Her 'father complex' left her with an obsessive attraction to older, accomplished, authoritative paternal figures. She allowed this attraction to take her into imprudent liaisons that caused her great public embarrassment and no small amount of private guilt." [52] Don Richardson, who remained close to Grace throughout her life, remarked "she just had a terrible need to have someone put his arms around her. What she needed, constantly, was reassurance that she existed. She was starved for affection because of the family. She was afflicted with a great sense of emptiness, terrible loneliness." [53] Note that the third house (with Capricorn on the cusp) is ruled by Saturn. Since natal Saturn is afflicted, we would expect uneasy or distant relationships with siblings, a conclusion verified by Spada: "Children deprived of parental love and attention often forge a strong bond with their siblings, but this was not so with Grace. Her brother paid scant attention to her; her sisters didn't understand her much more than their father did, and they alternately mistreated and took advantage of her." [54]

TED BUNDY

BRIEF BACKGROUND

Ted Bundy, readers may recall, was one of the nation's most publicized serial killers. He was found guilty of brutally slaying two Florida State University coeds and attempting to murder two others in the Chi Omega sorority house in Tallahassee. Bundy was executed for the Florida murders in 1989. Evidence indicates

that, between 1973 and 1978, he was responsible for the disappearance and death of at least twenty-one young women in Washington, Oregon, Utah, Colorado, and Florida. Astrologer T. Patrick Davis is credited with obtaining Ted Bundy's birth certificate, which is the source of data used to cast his chart (Figure 16).

TED BUNDY'S HOROSCOPE

Ted Bundy was born November 24, 1946, at 10:35 PM in Burlington, Vermont. Apply what you have learned in previous chapters to Bundy's horoscope. Note the planetary signs and house positions and the aspects between the natal planets. It is important to remember as you study this chart, that other people born with the same aspect or planetary position do not possess the same orientations. Descriptions of a particular aspect or planetary position are the same for each person born with it, but the way it worked out in Ted Bundy's life, for example, is very different than the way it works in the lives of other people with the same planetary pattern.

As I discuss this chart, I will parallel astrological interpretation with biographical material and with Ted's own revelations. In what can only be described as the oddest of coincidences, crime writer Ann Rule signed a contract to write a book about a series of murders in Washington state *before* it was discovered that the killer was Ted Bundy, a man she knew well as a friend and former coworker at the Seattle Crisis Clinic. In *The Stranger Beside Me*, Rule describes Bundy's crimes, but more important for astrological analysis are the insights she presents from personal association with him.

Ted talked at length about himself in a series of interviews with writers Hugh Aynesworth and Stephen Michaud. At no time in these or any other interviews in or out of court did Ted Bundy ever confess to any of the murders with which he was charged. The things he did reveal, however, are as interesting as the things he would not or could not bring himself to discuss.

Since so many of the planetary sign positions in Ted Bundy's horoscope are either in Sagittarius or Scorpio, let's begin with these two signs. Sun, Moon, and Mars are in Sagittarius. Duality of nature and purpose characterizes the energy of Sagittarius—the kind of energy we would expect to find expressed in Ted's ego drives (Sun), in his emotional character, especially related to women (Moon), and in his physical actions (Mars). Our astrological expectations coincide with observations made by Ann Rule. "There seemed to be two Ted Bundys

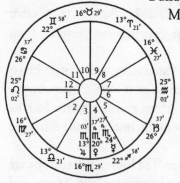

Ted Bundy

emerging. One, the perfect son, the University of Washington student who had graduated 'with distinction,' the fledgling lawyer and politician [the Sun] and the other, a charming schemer, a man who could manipulate women with ease [the Moon], whether it be sex or money he desired." On the one hand, the duality of Mars is exhibited in criminal activities inspired by a Ted Bundy "who turned cold and hostile toward women with very little provocation." [55] On the other hand, Mars is represented by participation in politics as well as his work at the Seattle Crisis Clinic and other admirable activities: "He was an ideal citizen. He even drew a commendation from the Seattle Police Department when he ran down a purse snatcher and returned the stolen bag to its owner." [56]

Mercury, Venus, and Jupiter are in Scorpio. For lack of space I'll leave Jupiter out of the discussion. Observant and detail-oriented, Mercury in Scorpio people are interested in human motivation and behavior. It is difficult to deceive them, but they are adept at deception themselves. Ted was an honors student in psychology at the University of Washington. Aside from its grisly application in Bundy's case, the following is an apt description of Mercury in Scorpio. "Ted was resourceful, intelligent, and relentless; he was always hunting, always perfecting his approach to his victims. He chose ways to dispose of their bodies with infinite care, and he assiduously studied how police investigations are conducted in order to further reduce his chances of getting caught." [57]

Venus in Scorpio people take pride in the appearance of their domestic environment and frequently demonstrate domestic interests and skills such as gardening and gourmet cooking.

Ted Bundy

Ted had a passion for plants. Recalling a nursery in Seattle, he said, "I used to go there and drool at all the plants." [58] Recycling items and using them for decorating purposes relates to Venus in Scorpio and is verified by the impressions of some Washington friends who visited Ted in Salt Lake City, Utah. "The trio from

Washington found Ted's apartment very pleasant; he'd cut pictures out of magazines and tried to duplicate the decor he favored. He had [a] bicycle tire, hung from the meat hook in his kitchen, and he used that to store knives and other kitchen utensils in a mobile effect. He had a color television set, a good stereo, and he played Mozart for them to accompany the gourmet meals he prepared." [59]

Negative facets of Venus in Scorpio include possessiveness and jealousy. Although most people were unaware of anything except his outwardly cheerful personality, Ted was very jealous. Discussing his girlfriend Meg with Ann Rule, he revealed, "We'd had a fight, and I saw some guy's car parked outside her apartment. I raced around the alley and stood up on a garbage can to look in the window. The sweat was just pouring off me and I was like a crazy man. I couldn't stand to think of Meg with another man. I couldn't believe the effect it had on me." [60] Darker instincts of manipulation, control, and possession also associated with Venus in Scorpio were more likely to emerge in Ted because of aspects that involve his natal Venus.

The fourth house in Ted's horoscope contains Sun, Moon, Mercury, Venus, and Mars. Since there is not enough space to mention all these planets, I will only discuss the Moon. Fourth-house Moon indicates that the mother is apt to be the dominant parent. For Ted this was certainly true. Bundy was his stepfather's name. Ted was an illegitimate child and never knew his real father. His mother doted on him. For his part, Ted credits his impressive academic achievements to his mother's influence, but gives no hint of deep affection for her. This could be attributed to his lack of feelings for anyone. Those with Moon in the fourth house often resemble their mother or mother's side of the family, an association clearly evidenced in this case. "Ted considered himself a Cowell. It was always the Cowell side of the family to which he gravitated. He *looked* like a Cowell. His features were a masculinized version of Louise Bundy's, his coloring just like hers. On the surface, it seemed the only genetic input he'd received from his natural father was his height." [61]

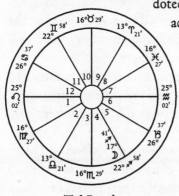

Ted Bundy

Ted Bundy's Ascendant is Leo, an indication of the attention-seeking, self-promotional nature of the energy expressed in his outer personality. He always

referred to himself as "The Golden Boy." Acting as his own attorney in many of his court appearances, Ted handled himself with arrogance, wit, and confidence. Those with Leo rising always want to be right, they want to have the last word, and they rarely admit guilt. Ted was very acquisitive and concerned with material possessions and personal status, traits that can be linked to his Leo Ascendant. "The Ted Bundy the world was allowed to see was handsome, his body honed and cultivated meticulously, a barrier of strength against eyes that might catch a glimpse of the terror inside. Ted loved *things* more than he loved people. Ted could—and did—rub elbows with the governor, travel in circles that most young men could never hope to enter. On the surface he was the very epitome of a successful man." [62]

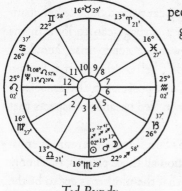

Ted Bundy

An additional note here is that his Leo Ascendant, along with Sun, Moon, and Mars in Sagittarius, puts heavy emphasis on fire signs, the attributes of which are appropriately demonstrated by his risk-taking nature and need for instant gratification. Some of the most negative traits of a fire-sign personality are found in Ted, who only experienced physical pleasure by attaining "an excitable 'high.' ... a sense of euphoria from the games he substitutes for real feelings. He knows what he wants, and because he is not hampered by guilt feelings or the needs of others, he can usually achieve instant gratification. But he can never fill up the lonesome void inside. He is insatiable, always hungry." [63]

Ted gives an accurate portrait of his fire-sign approach to life. "I've learned to live absolutely and completely and totally in the *here and now*. I don't worry, think or concern myself with the past, or, for that matter, with the future, except only to the extent necessary." [64]

Let's take a closer look at the fourth-house conjunction of Moon and Mars in Sagittarius trine the twelfth-house conjunction of Saturn and Pluto in Leo as well as his Leo Ascendant. The Moon is the emotional impact he had on others as well as his own feelings, and Mars is the direction of his physical energy and activities. The Ascendant is Ted's outer personality and self-image, Saturn represents older people, and though Pluto represents power and control, it is also associated with older women. These astrological factors, held together in the dynamics of a trine, are exhibited in the ease with which he made friends with

older women. Since Venus is not involved here, we would not necessarily asso-ciate these female relationships with any romantic inclinations. Ann Rule, who was herself an "older woman" in Ted's life, reported that one of Ted's supporters was sixty-year-old Beatrice Sloan who thought he was "a lovable rascal." He could "talk her out of almost anything." Beatrice helped Ted obtain work at the Olympic Hotel when he was a college student. She does not deny that she knew he was a schemer but felt "Ted needed her." She loaned him money as well as her car. When he needed a reference or had to fill out applications, she allowed him to use her address. [65]

Ted gained another fan when he rented a room from elderly Freda Rogers, who, according to Ann Rule, was quite taken with Ted. He lived with Rogers for five years and became "more of a son than a tenant." [66] Saturn (tradition, formality, structured situations) involved in this trine is an important factor in Ted's attitude and behavior. Pluto must be considered, along with Saturn, as part of the power and influence Ted desired. He instinctively felt he would not have to work hard to succeed (the effect of a trine) with older and more powerful men as well as women, and that part of his success required conservative and traditional behavior and attitudes on his part.

Ann Rule comments that one reason she found Ted so appealing was because he treated her with "old-world gallantry." Ted's traditionalism extended beyond gallantry, however. Saturn represents formalized situations and settings, but recall that as one of the outer planets, Saturn is also associated with society in general, and in particular with the traditional, structured institutions of society. For some people with the same aspect it might mean an active affiliation with such institutions as religion or social services, but for Ted it was politics. He was a conservative Republican. According to Ann Rule he "kept up his contacts in the Republican Party. He was a precinct committeeman and became involved in the party work as the years progressed." [67]

Ted was innately shy but he found a way to satisfy his social yearnings within the successful dynamics of his trine. "I would be characterized as shy to intro-verted. With exceptions. I spoke up in class. Believe me, if anything characterizes my classroom performance, it's being precocious. I've always been that way. In those kinds of settings. It's a formalized setting. And the ground rules are fairly strict. And your performance is measured by different rules than what happens when everybody is peeling off into little cliques." [68] Talking specifically about his political involvement, Ted related, "Politics gave me the opportunity to be close

to people. To be socially involved with them ... as a consequence of working with them. It's a sort of built-in social life which I never had." [69]

The same harsh aspects found in Ted's chart can represent an astrological catalyst for success and personal growth in the charts of other people. Within the parameters of Ted's particular karma, life experiences, and free choices, these aspects add up to a tragic history. One of the difficult aspects is the conjunction of Mercury, Venus, and Jupiter in Scorpio square Saturn and Pluto in Leo. There are endless ways to take this aspect apart. I will only focus on Venus and its square to twelfth-house Saturn and Pluto. Venus is social orientation and attitude; Saturn is authority, restriction, and fear; and Pluto is control and manipulation. The twelfth house is that which an individual deliberately hides as well as that which an individual cannot fully understand or accept.

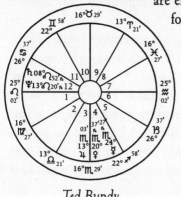

Ted Bundy

Keeping all these astrological images in mind, and knowing they are pulled together in frustrating situations signified by the square, we expect that Ted would find difficulty handling or initiating spontaneous and lighthearted social interactions. Romance, when it occurred, would be regulated by traditional responses and expectations, and identified with loss and disappointment—with no understanding on Ted's part of why any of this should be so. Ted did realize (and admitted) that he hid inadequacies to protect his ego (an ego enlarged and enhanced by his Leo Ascendant). Since he had no trouble attracting friends or lovers, it is not prudent to believe it was their rejection that made Ted socially convoluted and introspective. The reality was that, "If not among the most popular [in a high school class of 800] he at least moved near those at the top and was well liked." [70] But Ted would not or could not identify with such a description of social acceptance. Aynesworth and Michaud recorded, "As far back as he could remember of his days as a boy in Tacoma, he chose to be alone." [71]

Ted himself admitted, "A lot of my pretensions about being a scholarly type, a person interested in serious studies, was really a defense mechanism. I was accused on a couple occasions of being aloof, arrogant, and snobby. But it was just this defense mechanism to protect my somewhat introverted nature. I used that to compensate for my outright fear of socializing. Maybe also it was a way to

314

protect myself, because I couldn't achieve those kinds of social goals that I wanted."[72] His choice to be alone or to remain aloof from others was only a superficial extension of a much deeper, more sinister antisocialness. Ted was unwilling to discuss this side of his nature for very good reasons. He did not want to be connected to his crimes.

To circumspect his refusal to implicate himself, Aynesworth and Michaud proposed that Ted discuss the "killer" in the third person with the result that his descriptions often refer to "this person" or "this individual." In general conversation, Ted ventured it was his opinion that kidnapping or abduction was "the ultimate antisocial act."[73] Later, when asked if he thought the motive of the person who attacked the women was to kill them, he responded, "I believe in the beginning—the act of killing—we would *not* expect it to be the goal. It was the *possession* of this desired thing, which was, in itself—the very act of assuming possession was a very antisocial act—was giving expression to this person's need to *seize* something that was highly valued, at least on the surface, by society."[74]

Even with biographical descriptions to guide us in understanding Ted's anti-social nature, a significant potential for violence and murder is missing. For this we turn to Moon-Mars opposite Uranus. It is foolish to suggest that every indi-vidual born with Moon-Mars opposite Uranus is going to commit murder. It only indicates a potential for violent or unpredictable situations. There is, however, no better example of the worst-case scenario of this aspect than Ted Bundy. The changeable nature and unpre-dictable course that his emotions followed are attested to by the few who lived to talk about it.

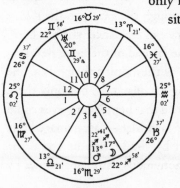

Ted Bundy

Claire Forest dated Ted one summer, and related that she only had sex with him on one occasion. Recalling that he had always been tender and affectionate with her, she said the "sex act itself had been harsh. There was no affection at all," and "afterward, it was like it had never happened." Ann Rule adds, "Claire Forest was not the only woman who would recall that Ted Bundy's manner could change suddenly from one of warmth and affection to cold fury." Lisa Temple only met him on one occasion but that was all it took to experience Ted's strange bipolar affections. He and

Lisa along with some friends went rafting and "halfway down the river, Ted's attitude changed suddenly and he seemed to delight in tormenting Lisa." Lisa recalled that later, "He drove me home … and was nice again. He said he would be back about midnight. He did come back, and we made love. I just couldn't understand the way he kept changing. One minute, he was nice, and the next he acted like he hated me." [75] In addition to its association with the act of violence, Mars anatomically relates to the head. Ted's method was to smash the skulls of his victims. At one site in Colorado where only skulls were found, "it appeared that the killer had established his own graveyard, bringing only his victims' severed heads with him." [76]

MATA HARI

BRIEF BACKGROUND

In the gloomy mist of dawn, twelve Zouave riflemen, survivors of a French regiment slaughtered at Verdun, stood in a field outside Paris. Cold and silent, they waited for the woman known as Mata Hari. Her car wound slowly through the streets, passed the Porte de Vincennes, and stopped at the castle dungeon. Two nuns, the prison chaplain, and prisoner Number 721 44625—the infamous Mata Hari—emerged from the car and passed through the gate into the *théâtre d'exécution*. The drums sounded. With the fluid grace of the dancer she had been, the prisoner walked toward a wooden stake at the far end of the field. Refusing the blindfold, she looked straight at the soldiers as they aimed their rifles. She smiled and nodded. Twelve shots rang out killing her instantly, but only three bullets struck her. Had some of the soldiers imagined that her piercing eyes could see into their hearts as they fired their weapons? Had Mata Hari managed one last time to mesmerize and fascinate? Executed by the French in 1917, the legendary Mata Hari lives on, her name made synonymous with female spies by generations who have no idea who she was.

The real Mata Hari was Margaretha Geertruida Zelle, born August 7, 1876, in Leeuwarden, an ancient Dutch city lying north of the Hook of Holland. Unfortunately, a discrepancy in the available data makes her chart controversial. American sources quote English astrologer Chryss Craswell for a birth time of 1:00 PM LMT and Douglas Lannark of Copenhagen for a birth time of 12:34 PM LMT.

Despite this difference, Mata Hari's life is worth studying. The later time puts Venus in the eighth house, otherwise all the natal planets remain in the same houses, the Rising Sign is still Scorpio, and the aspects between the planets are the same in charts cast for either birth time. I have chosen the chart cast for 12:34 PM (Figure 16).

Those who are unfamiliar with Mata Hari will find that background information is helpful before studying her horoscope. The only girl in a family of boys, Margaretha, or M'greet as she was called, was spoiled by her father. She received the education and privileges of wealth until 1889, when her life of ease and luxury suddenly vanished. Her adoring, but now bankrupt, father simply walked away, leaving his wife and family to cope as best they could. Six years later, M'greet, responding to a matrimonial ad, met and very soon wed Rudolph MacLeod, a thirty-eight-year-old army officer on home leave from the Dutch East Indies. The couple moved to Java shortly after the birth of their first child and M'greet felt she had landed in paradise. Though frequently brutalized by her husband in his drunken rages, she blossomed in her new environment.

Confined by her second pregnancy and the relentless monsoon rains, M'greet began reading books a previous occupant had left in the house. Accounts she read of Javanese history and legend and the influence of Buddhism and Hinduism captivated her imagination. She began to learn Malay, practicing the language with servants and native friends. One word that proved especially enchanting to the Leo-born M'greet was *matabari*, "eye of dawn," which meant the sun. Adopting this word as her name, she could not know how famous it would make her or how it would be identified with her for generations to come.

Sumatra was the next port of call for M'greet, Rudolph, their young son, and infant daughter. In Sumatra her paradise was shattered when a servant, seeking revenge, poisoned the children. Medical help arrived too late to save their son. The daughter recovered but Rudolph and M'greet remained desolate, beyond the reach of human comfort. The following year M'greet contracted typhoid fever and for months lay delirious and dreaming. When she recovered from the illness, her interest in the dances and rituals of India's transplanted epics and sacred texts intensified and consumed her.

Returning to Holland in 1902, M'greet separated from Rudolph. With no income, she was forced to give up her daughter and find a way to support herself. The knowledge she gained and the tragedy and illness she had experienced in the East Indies had transformed M'greet and given her fierce determination. When

she made her Paris debut in 1905, the evolution from Margaretha Geertruida Zelle MacLeod into Mata Hari, Hindu dancer, was complete.

Appearing at the *Musée Guimet* center for oriental studies, it was announced that Mata Hari had come to "perform the dances of the Devadasis and present the sacred art of expressing, by harmonious gestures, the far-off mysteries of vanished cults." [77] The assembled audience was spellbound and greeted her performance with thunderous applause. To enhance the mystery of her image it was given out that Mata Hari was born in the south of India, that she had come from a Brahmin family. Biographer Erika Ostrovsky describes M'greet's triumph as "a clever publicity stunt, the exploitation of a current fad for oriental dance." Her willingness to dance in the nude, no doubt, helped. Whatever the reasons, "with the advent of a new name, a new life had begun. Her luck appeared to have turned. In the space of one night, she had become the sensation of the season." [78]

Phenomenal success led to a second evolution that turned Mata Hari the dancer into Baroness von der Linden the courtesan, a member of what the French called *Grandes Horizontales*. With passing years, Paris, Rome, and Berlin gave their enthusiasm to new dancers and the number of her admirers waned, but when World War I began in 1914, M'greet had already established liaisons with important and influential men. These contacts led to a third evolution from Baroness von der Linden into secret agent H-21. Was it pride, arrogance, or greed that made M'greet believe she could gamble in espionage's most dangerous game and play the role of double agent? She lost the gamble, precipitating her fourth and final evolution from Germany's secret agent H-21 into the French government's prisoner Number 721 44625.

MATA HARI'S HOROSCOPE

One of the most notable features in M'greet's chart is the clustering of planets in the ninth house. Descriptions in Chapter 8 for ninth-house Sun project the image of individuals who seek to reach beyond the immediate environment for broader experiences and understanding, a tendency exhibited by M'greet's delight in traveling to the Dutch East Indies as a young bride. Ninth-house Mercury suggests those who become highly motivated to learn on their own and those who receive training or education in a foreign country as M'greet did when she became stimulated by the culture and life in Java. Ninth-house Venus implies

Mata Hari

people who think of themselves as citizens of the world and indicates the possibility of romance and other joint ventures in foreign countries, all of which can be applied to Mata Hari the international traveler, courtesan, and spy. When ninth-house Venus is knocked off balance, there is potential for unfavorable court decisions, and for Mata Hari, it was a sentence of death. Ninth-house Mars indicates the direction of her physical energy and activities. Ninth-house Uranus relates to her self-taught expertise on oriental religion and rituals, and the fact that with little or no training, she developed her talent for dancing to a high degree of competence.

The Moon-Saturn conjunction in Pisces is part of a Grand Trine involving Venus in Cancer and Jupiter as well as the Ascendant in Scorpio. Before we examine how the trine worked for Mata Hari, let's briefly note Moon conjunct Saturn. Her father deserted the family when she was thirteen and her mother died the following year. Loss of her parents and their nurturing during her childhood is an obvious demonstration of this aspect. Moon (desire) in Pisces (dancing, disguise, glamor, and mystery), Venus (beauty, charm) in Cancer (feminine image), and Jupiter (fortunate circumstances, religion, and culture) in Scorpio (sexual energy, manipulation and control, secret cults, and covert activities) are pulled together in the dynamics of a trine, an aspect associated with fortunate endeavors. That Mata Hari was wildly successful in her reincarnation as an oriental dancer, that authorities allowed her to dance nude while others who did so were jailed, and that she gained everlasting fame as a spy can all

Mata Hari

be linked with her Grand Trine. However, this also serves as an example of why one should never take the luck of a Grand Trine for granted. It was not enough to save Mata Hari from being executed, nor did it preclude her from experiencing the tragic poisoning of her children.

319

In Chapter 10, you learned that aspects between the outer planets are of such long duration that traits and characteristics associated with them are described in terms of society. How much or how little the mood and character of society associated with a particular aspect will be reflected in a single individual born with that aspect is determined by many other factors. Mata Hari was an individual whose life was beneficially as well as tragically altered in a direct way by conditions in society. This is described in her chart by the T-square involving natal Jupiter opposite natal Pluto, and both planets square natal Uranus. The opposition, occurring as it does between the first house (Mata Hari herself) and the seventh house (other people), already implies that the aspect may have personal significance for her. Jupiter opposite Pluto is associated with a society rampant with plots and counterplots, intrigue within intrigue. Jupiter square Uranus describes antagonistic modes of thinking. Uranus square Pluto relates to a society suddenly transformed by some event such as war or a great economic depression.

Mata Hari

These astrological factors emerge clearly in descriptions by Erika Ostrovsky detailing the mood of Paris society in 1916–17. "Nor was it safe in these days of strife to trust one's neighbor, mistress, barber, waiter, or shopkeeper. Hadn't they recently arrested a woman on charges of espionage for sending crates of laxatives to Brazil? And what of that waiter who drew plans of fortifications in his order book? Who knew if that harmless-looking old man in the Luxembourg, ritually surrounded by flocks of pigeons at dusk, did not wire code messages to their feet?"[79] World War I was decimating the French army with casualties and inflicting wretched deprivations in the lives of citizens. The French were xenophobic and "in no mood for clemency."[80]

This negative public morale was to have dire consequences for the prisoner Mata Hari in Saint-Lazare prison on charges of espionage. The focal point of the T-square involves more than natal Uranus in Leo. It also includes her natal Sun, Mercury, Venus, and Mars in Leo. Taking this aspect apart to analyze each planet's contributory influences is too lengthy. One example, however, is the difficult circumstances she would be expected to experience with men. Mars represents

men in general and the Sun relates to the father as well as the husband in a female's chart. These planets are square Jupiter which specifically represents the father in all charts and Pluto which implies manipulation and control. M'greet was abandoned by her father, married a much older man who no doubt was her father-substitute, and was brutalized and threatened by a husband who wanted to impose total control over her.

Another example involves Jupiter in the first house (Mata Hari herself) opposite Pluto (planetary ruler of the first house with Scorpio rising) square the conjunction of Sun (inner life), Mercury (mental processes), Mars (physical energy and activities), and Uranus (restless, unpredictable, changeable) in Leo (prideful, overestimating, self-indulgent).

Each of the astrological factors in the T-square can be found to parallel another fascinating and accurate analysis, this one provided by graphologist Edouard de Rougemont and published in 1922. "The striking thing about this handwriting is the excessive, impulsive strength of the lines and their contrasting nature. ... All these contradictory impulses reveal a tumultuous, chaotic inner life which affects the worth of all the subject's activities. ... One cannot trust such a changeable, agitated, restless nature which is always ready for extreme moves. Nothing can hold back this impetuous, fearless creature which does not measure obstacles and is overly confident of its destiny. ... One of the most marked characteristics of this personality is exaggeration: it is a dangerous tendency, for it obscures judgment, results in lack of foresight, produces blind rages, hasty resolutions, an inability to measure the consequences of actions. ... This personality is characterized by great *sang-froid* and terrifying resolve, based both on courage and blindness. ... The motives of the subject's actions are: egotism, calculation and pride." [81]

*　*　*

As I conclude this book, it is my sincerest wish that you will study each of the four charts on your own. I encourage you to obtain some of the indicated biographies and locate additional biographical material about these personalities. Compare the four charts with each other. Grace Kelly and Mata Hari, for example, have Moon in Pisces, a Scorpio Ascendant, and natal Sun conjunct Mars, all of which provide an interesting basis for comparing the two ladies. They both loved to dance, and they both possessed an uninhibited desire for the opposite sex. Mata Hari and Ted Bundy, on the other hand, have Moon in the fourth

house. What possible similarities might there be in the home life, childhood, and emotional outlook of these two very different people? There are many other points of similarity as well as differences that can be studied and compared in the four charts which I hope you will be able to discern on your own as you continue your astrological studies. I also hope you will not limit your interest in astrology to this book. Locate the astrological groups in your community and browse through the many other astrological books that are available. Most importantly, use astrology to get to know and appreciate yourself and others.

Ephemeris

HOW TO USE THE EPHEMERIS

U sing the ephemeris to look up the planetary positions for a birth date is very simple. The twenty-four hour clock is used so there are no a.m. or p.m. designations for the times given in the ephemeris. The list below will be helpful if you are not used to seeing the time designated in this way.

00:00 is 12:00 AM GMT (Midnight)	12:00 is 12:00 PM GMT (Noon)
01:00 is 01:00 AM GMT	13:00 is 01:00 PM GMT
02:00 is 02:00 AM GMT	14:00 is 02:00 PM GMT
03:00 is 03:00 AM GMT	15:00 is 03:00 PM GMT
04:00 is 04:00 AM GMT	16:00 is 04:00 PM GMT
05:00 is 05:00 AM GMT	17:00 is 05:00 PM GMT
06:00 is 06:00 AM GMT	18:00 is 06:00 PM GMT
07:00 is 07:00 AM GMT	19:00 is 07:00 PM GMT
08:00 is 08:00 AM GMT	20:00 is 08:00 PM GMT
09:00 is 09:00 AM GMT	21:00 is 09:00 PM GMT
10:00 is 10:00 AM GMT	22:00 is 10:00 PM GMT
11:00 is 11:00 PM GMT	23:00 is 11:00 PM GMT

The positions are given from the date and time a planet enters a sign until it enters the next sign. As an example, let's use a birth date of November 26, 1944. In the ephemeris turn to the year 1944 and list the positions of the Sun, Moon, and planets for November 26, 1944.

- The Sun was in Sagittarius between November 22 at 10:07 GMT and the time it entered Capricorn at 23:15 GMT on December 21.
  This tells us that on November 26 the Sun was in Sagittarius ... ☉ ♐
- The Moon was in Aries between November 25 at 8:57 GMT and the time it entered Taurus at 10:22 GMT November 27.
  This tells us that on November 26 the Moon was in Aries ... ☽ ♈
- Mercury was in Sagittarius between November 10 at 11:10 GMT and the time it entered Capricorn at 15:29 GMT December 1.
  This tells us that on November 26 Mercury was in Sagittarius ... ☿ ♐
- Venus was in Capricorn between November 16 at 07:21 GMT and the time it entered Aquarius at 04:44 GMT December 11.
  This tells us that on November 26 Venus was in Capricorn ... ♀ ♑
- Mars was in Sagittarius after November 25 at 16:15 GMT.
  This tells us that on November 26 Mars was in Sagittarius ... ♂ ♐
- Jupiter was in Virgo after July 26 at 01:33 GMT.
  This tells us that on November 26 Jupiter was in Virgo ... ♃ ♍
- Saturn was in Cancer after June 20 at 07:48 GMT.
  This tells us that on November 26 Saturn was in Cancer ... ♄ ♋
- Uranus was in Gemini the entire year.
  This tells us that on November 26 Uranus was in Gemini ... ♅ ♊
- Neptune was in Libra the entire year.
  This tells us that on November 26 Neptune was in Libra ... ♆ ♎
- Pluto was in Leo the entire year.
  This tells us that on November 26 Pluto was in Leo ... ♇ ♌

Using this method, look up planetary positions for any date. Each planetary sign position is explained in Chapter 7. If the Sun, Moon, or planets change signs and you do not know the time of birth on a given date, study characteristics of both sign positions to determine which one seems to fit best. Certain dates are marked with R or D to indicate the beginning (R) and end (D) of retrograde motion. Retrograde motion is the apparent backward movement of a planet, as viewed from Earth, due to its position in relation to the Earth. Thus a planet may appear to slow down, move backward, and perhaps even reenter a sign it had just exited. An example is found on the facing page. On March 3, 1900, Mercury entered Aries. Mercury began to retrograde (move backward) on March 15, and on March 29, returned to Pisces. Mercury began moving forward on April 7, and reentered Aries on April 17.

1900

Sun

♒ Jan 20 11:33	♈ Mar 21 01:38	♊ May 21 13:17	♌ Jul 23 08:36	♎ Sep 23 12:21	♐ Nov 22 17:47
♓ Feb 19 02:01	♉ Apr 20 13:27	♋ Jun 21 21:40	♍ Aug 23 15:20	♏ Oct 23 20:56	♑ Dec 22 06:41

Moon

Jan 1 2♑	♈ Mar 2 18:01	♋ May 2 22:23	♎ Jul 3 22:57	♑ Sep 3 22:26	♈ Nov 4 00:25
♒ Jan 2 21:25	♉ Mar 4 18:23	♌ May 5 07:00	♏ Jul 6 11:11	♒ Sep 6 02:52	♉ Nov 6 00:24
♓ Jan 4 22:08	♊ Mar 6 22:04	♍ May 7 18:35	♐ Jul 8 21:03	♓ Sep 8 03:45	♊ Nov 8 00:48
♈ Jan 6 23:44	♋ Mar 9 05:44	♎ May 10 07:08	♑ Jul 11 03:25	♈ Sep 10 03:00	♋ Nov 10 03:30
♉ Jan 9 03:25	♌ Mar 11 16:37	♏ May 12 18:40	♒ Jul 13 06:41	♉ Sep 12 02:44	♌ Nov 12 09:47
♊ Jan 11 09:36	♍ Mar 14 05:04	♐ May 15 04:07	♓ Jul 15 08:12	♊ Sep 14 04:56	♍ Nov 14 19:47
♋ Jan 13 18:05	♎ Mar 16 17:38	♑ May 17 11:18	♈ Jul 17 09:37	♋ Sep 16 10:38	♎ Nov 17 08:08
♌ Jan 16 04:30	♏ Mar 19 05:34	♒ May 19 16:30	♉ Jul 19 12:16	♌ Sep 18 19:37	♏ Nov 19 20:47
♍ Jan 18 16:26	♐ Mar 21 16:03	♓ May 21 20:00	♊ Jul 21 16:48	♍ Sep 21 06:52	♐ Nov 22 08:08
♎ Jan 21 05:07	♑ Mar 23 23:56	♈ May 23 22:21	♋ Jul 23 23:18	♎ Sep 23 19:17	♑ Nov 24 17:24
♏ Jan 23 16:53	♒ Mar 26 04:25	♉ May 26 00:20	♌ Jul 26 07:48	♏ Sep 26 08:05	♒ Nov 27 00:29
♐ Jan 26 01:50	♓ Mar 28 05:41	♊ May 28 03:04	♍ Jul 28 18:17	♐ Sep 28 20:09	♓ Nov 29 05:22
♑ Jan 28 06:46	♈ Mar 30 05:12	♋ May 30 07:53	♎ Jul 31 06:28	♑ Oct 1 05:56	♈ Dec 1 08:20
♒ Jan 30 08:12	♉ Apr 1 04:59	♌ Jun 1 15:44	♏ Aug 2 19:07	♒ Oct 3 12:02	♉ Dec 3 10:01
♓ Feb 1 07:47	♊ Apr 3 07:13	♍ Jun 4 02:33	♐ Aug 5 06:00	♓ Oct 5 14:20	♊ Dec 5 11:25
♈ Feb 3 07:37	♋ Apr 5 13:15	♎ Jun 6 14:59	♑ Aug 7 13:12	♈ Oct 7 14:05	♋ Dec 7 14:02
♉ Feb 5 09:41	♌ Apr 7 23:10	♏ Jun 9 02:44	♒ Aug 9 16:30	♉ Oct 9 13:15	♌ Dec 9 19:17
♊ Feb 7 15:06	♍ Apr 10 11:23	♐ Jun 11 12:04	♓ Aug 11 17:10	♊ Oct 11 14:00	♍ Dec 12 04:03
♋ Feb 9 23:50	♎ Apr 13 00:00	♑ Jun 13 18:30	♈ Aug 13 17:09	♋ Oct 13 18:00	♎ Dec 14 15:47
♌ Feb 12 10:49	♏ Apr 15 11:37	♒ Jun 15 22:36	♉ Aug 15 18:23	♌ Oct 16 01:52	♏ Dec 17 04:31
♍ Feb 14 22:58	♐ Apr 17 21:38	♓ Jun 18 01:27	♊ Aug 17 22:13	♍ Oct 18 12:50	♐ Dec 19 15:52
♎ Feb 17 11:36	♑ Apr 20 05:37	♈ Jun 20 03:57	♋ Aug 20 04:55	♎ Oct 21 01:24	♑ Dec 22 00:31
♏ Feb 19 23:43	♒ Apr 22 11:05	♉ Jun 22 06:52	♌ Aug 22 14:01	♏ Oct 23 14:04	♒ Dec 24 06:32
♐ Feb 22 09:52	♓ Apr 24 13:58	♊ Jun 24 10:51	♍ Aug 25 00:55	♐ Oct 26 01:49	♓ Dec 26 10:46
♑ Feb 24 16:32	♈ Apr 26 14:59	♋ Jun 26 16:27	♎ Aug 27 13:10	♑ Oct 28 11:46	♈ Dec 28 14:00
♒ Feb 26 19:14	♉ Apr 28 15:32	♌ Jun 29 00:18	♏ Aug 30 02:01	♒ Oct 30 19:01	♉ Dec 30 16:54
♓ Feb 28 19:04	♊ Apr 30 17:29	♍ Jul 1 10:42	♐ Sep 1 13:48	♓ Nov 1 23:06	

Mercury

Jan 1 24♐	♌ Jun 27 09:23
♑ Jan 9 02:05	R Jul 18 16♌
♒ Jan 28 17:09	D Aug 11 3♌
♓ Feb 15 00:01	♍ Sep 3 00:47
♈ Mar 3 21:13	♎ Sep 18 23:18
R Mar 15 9♈	♏ Oct 7 08:23
♓ Mar 29 22:43	♐ Oct 30 06:24
D Apr 7 25♓	R Nov 9 6♐
♈ Apr 17 00:57	♏ Nov 18 20:37
♉ May 11 00:08	D Nov 29 19♏
♊ May 26 10:51	♐ Dec 12 15:01
♋ Jun 9 09:20	

Venus

Jan 1 6♒	D Jul 30 7♋
♓ Jan 20 01:37	♌ Sep 8 20:50
♈ Feb 13 14:09	♍ Oct 8 13:32
♉ Mar 10 18:07	♎ Nov 3 21:30
♊ Apr 6 04:13	♏ Nov 28 21:54
♋ May 5 15:47	♐ Dec 23 07:48
R Jun 16 23♋	

Mars

Jan 1 13♑
♒ Jan 21 18:49
♓ Feb 28 22:15
♈ Apr 8 03:55
♉ May 17 09:05
♊ Jun 27 09:24
♋ Aug 10 01:28
♌ Sep 26 18:28
♍ Nov 23 08:54

Jupiter

Jan 1 1♐
R Mar 27 10♐
D Jul 29 1♐

Saturn

Jan 1 27♐
♑ Jan 21 08:12
R Apr 14 5♑
♐ Jul 18 17:37
D Sep 2 28♐
♑ Oct 17 04:59

Uranus

Jan 1 10♐
R Mar 17 12♐
D Aug 17 8♐

Neptune

Jan 1 25♊
D Mar 5 24♊
R Oct 2 29♊

Pluto

Jan 1 15♊
D Feb 27 14♊
R Sep 17 17♊

1901

Sun

♒ Jan 20 17:15	♈ Mar 21 07:22	♊ May 21 19:03	♌ Jul 23 14:20	♎ Sep 23 18:05	♐ Nov 22 23:38
♓ Feb 19 07:44	♉ Apr 20 19:11	♋ Jun 22 03:25	♍ Aug 23 21:04	♏ Oct 24 02:42	♑ Dec 22 12:35

Moon

Jan 1 18♉	♌ Mar 1 19:30	♏ May 2 16:43	♒ Jul 3 13:32	♉ Sep 2 14:15	♌ Nov 2 13:07
♊ Jan 1 19:52	♍ Mar 4 04:35	♐ May 5 05:25	♓ Jul 5 19:21	♊ Sep 4 16:31	♍ Nov 4 20:06
♋ Jan 3 23:35	♎ Mar 6 15:36	♑ May 7 16:52	♈ Jul 7 23:36	♋ Sep 6 20:10	♎ Nov 7 06:14
♌ Jan 6 04:57	♏ Mar 9 04:10	♒ May 10 01:56	♉ Jul 10 02:43	♌ Sep 9 01:26	♏ Nov 9 18:28
♍ Jan 8 13:02	♐ Mar 11 17:02	♓ May 12 07:53	♊ Jul 12 05:09	♍ Sep 11 08:32	♐ Nov 12 07:31
♎ Jan 11 00:06	♑ Mar 14 03:54	♈ May 14 10:43	♋ Jul 14 07:30	♎ Sep 13 17:51	♑ Nov 14 20:08
♏ Jan 13 12:51	♒ Mar 16 10:54	♉ May 16 11:15	♌ Jul 16 10:52	♏ Sep 16 05:30	♒ Nov 17 07:03
♐ Jan 16 00:42	♓ Mar 18 13:51	♊ May 18 11:06	♍ Jul 18 16:42	♐ Sep 18 18:31	♓ Nov 19 15:02
♑ Jan 18 09:28	♈ Mar 20 14:05	♋ May 20 12:01	♎ Jul 21 01:53	♑ Sep 21 06:43	♈ Nov 21 19:30
♒ Jan 20 14:45	♉ Mar 22 13:40	♌ May 22 15:45	♏ Jul 23 13:58	♒ Sep 23 15:44	♉ Nov 23 20:51
♓ Jan 22 17:39	♊ Mar 24 14:36	♍ May 24 23:16	♐ Jul 26 02:44	♓ Sep 25 20:41	♊ Nov 25 20:23
♈ Jan 24 19:44	♋ Mar 26 18:14	♎ May 27 10:16	♑ Jul 28 13:31	♈ Sep 27 22:28	♋ Nov 27 20:01
♉ Jan 26 22:14	♌ Mar 29 00:59	♏ May 29 23:07	♒ Jul 30 21:07	♉ Sep 29 22:47	♌ Nov 29 21:43
♊ Jan 29 01:53	♍ Mar 31 10:29	♐ Jun 1 11:42	♓ Aug 2 01:57	♊ Oct 1 23:27	♍ Dec 2 03:01
♋ Jan 31 06:48	♎ Apr 2 21:55	♑ Jun 3 22:42	♈ Aug 4 05:15	♋ Oct 4 01:52	♎ Dec 4 12:22
♌ Feb 2 13:10	♏ Apr 5 10:35	♒ Jun 6 07:29	♉ Aug 6 08:06	♌ Oct 6 06:51	♏ Dec 7 00:38
♍ Feb 4 21:31	♐ Apr 7 23:30	♓ Jun 8 13:53	♊ Aug 8 11:07	♍ Oct 8 14:27	♐ Dec 9 13:45
♎ Feb 7 08:16	♑ Apr 10 11:00	♈ Jun 10 18:00	♋ Aug 10 14:37	♎ Oct 11 00:24	♑ Dec 12 02:02
♏ Feb 9 20:56	♒ Apr 12 19:26	♉ Jun 12 20:09	♌ Aug 12 19:03	♏ Oct 13 12:19	♒ Dec 14 12:41
♐ Feb 12 09:24	♓ Apr 14 23:56	♊ Jun 14 21:08	♍ Aug 15 01:16	♐ Oct 16 01:21	♓ Dec 16 21:10
♑ Feb 14 19:08	♈ Apr 17 01:05	♋ Jun 16 22:21	♎ Aug 17 10:12	♑ Oct 18 13:59	♈ Dec 19 03:08
♒ Feb 17 00:48	♉ Apr 19 00:31	♌ Jun 19 01:22	♏ Aug 19 21:57	♒ Oct 21 00:17	♉ Dec 21 06:22
♓ Feb 19 03:04	♊ Apr 21 00:17	♍ Jun 21 07:38	♐ Aug 22 10:52	♓ Oct 23 06:45	♊ Dec 23 07:21
♈ Feb 21 03:43	♋ Apr 23 02:11	♎ Jun 23 17:40	♑ Aug 24 22:16	♈ Oct 25 09:24	♋ Dec 25 07:23
♉ Feb 23 04:39	♌ Apr 25 07:27	♏ Jun 26 06:13	♒ Aug 27 06:13	♉ Oct 27 09:34	♌ Dec 27 08:16
♊ Feb 25 07:21	♍ Apr 27 16:19	♐ Jun 28 18:49	♓ Aug 29 10:34	♊ Oct 29 09:00	♍ Dec 29 12:02
♋ Feb 27 12:20	♎ Apr 30 03:52	♑ Jul 1 05:30	♈ Aug 31 12:43	♋ Oct 31 09:41	♎ Dec 31 19:55

Mercury

Jan 1 27♐	R Jun 30 25♋
♑ Jan 2 12:26	D Jul 24 16♋
♒ Jan 21 06:28	♌ Aug 10 04:36
♓ Feb 7 10:31	♍ Aug 25 22:21
R Feb 26 21♓	♎ Sep 11 06:23
D Mar 21 8♓	♏ Oct 1 04:28
♈ Apr 15 17:05	R Oct 24 19♏
♉ May 3 13:59	D Nov 13 4♏
♊ May 17 20:06	♐ Dec 6 23:43
♋ Jun 1 23:55	♑ Dec 26 09:29

Venus

Jan 1 10♐	♌ Jul 5 05:21
♑ Jan 16 11:28	♍ Jul 29 19:11
♒ Feb 9 13:06	♎ Aug 23 12:30
♓ Mar 5 14:50	♏ Sep 17 11:25
♈ Mar 29 18:01	♐ Oct 12 19:10
♉ Apr 22 23:34	♑ Nov 7 19:23
♊ May 17 07:33	♒ Dec 5 13:33
♋ Jun 10 17:37	

Mars

Jan 1 11♍	
R Jan 13 12♍	
♌ Mar 1 19:22	
D Apr 4 23♌	
♍ May 11 06:08	
♎ Jul 13 20:07	
♏ Aug 31 18:09	
♐ Oct 14 12:46	
♑ Nov 24 04:46	

Jupiter

Jan 1 25♐	
♑ Jan 19 08:28	
R Apr 30 13♑	
D Aug 30 3♑	

Saturn

Jan 1 7♑
R Apr 26 16♑
D Sep 14 9♑

Uranus

Jan 1 14♐
R Mar 22 16♐
D Aug 22 12♐

Neptune

Jan 1 27♊
D Mar 8 26♊
♋ Jul 20 00:07
R Oct 5 1♋
♊ Dec 25 13:07

Pluto

Jan 1 16♊
D Feb 28 15♊
R Sep 19 18♊

1902

Sun

♒ Jan 20 23:12	♈ Mar 21 13:15	♊ May 22 00:53	♌ Jul 23 20:10	♎ Sep 23 23:55	♐ Nov 23 05:33
♓ Feb 19 13:39	♉ Apr 21 01:04	♋ Jun 22 09:16	♍ Aug 24 02:53	♏ Oct 24 08:34	♑ Dec 22 18:34

Moon

Jan 1 2♎	♑ Mar 4 01:02	♈ May 4 18:28	♋ Jul 4 17:06	♎ Sep 3 18:41	♑ Nov 4 17:42
♏ Jan 3 07:29	♒ Mar 6 11:20	♉ May 6 20:21	♌ Jul 6 16:53	♏ Sep 6 02:24	♒ Nov 7 06:21
♐ Jan 5 20:36	♓ Mar 8 18:15	♊ May 8 20:19	♍ Jul 8 18:42	♐ Sep 8 13:24	♓ Nov 9 17:15
♑ Jan 8 08:45	♈ Mar 10 22:20	♋ May 10 20:15	♎ Jul 11 00:16	♑ Sep 11 01:59	♈ Nov 12 00:43
♒ Jan 10 18:46	♉ Mar 13 00:54	♌ May 12 21:53	♏ Jul 13 09:54	♒ Sep 13 13:44	♉ Nov 14 04:23
♓ Jan 13 02:39	♊ Mar 15 03:13	♍ May 15 02:35	♐ Jul 15 22:15	♓ Sep 15 22:52	♊ Nov 16 05:17
♈ Jan 15 08:42	♋ Mar 17 06:02	♎ May 17 10:42	♑ Jul 18 11:02	♈ Sep 18 05:13	♋ Nov 18 05:14
♉ Jan 17 13:06	♌ Mar 19 09:53	♏ May 19 21:31	♒ Jul 20 22:36	♉ Sep 20 09:29	♌ Nov 20 06:04
♊ Jan 19 15:48	♍ Mar 21 15:10	♐ May 22 09:57	♓ Jul 23 08:22	♊ Sep 22 12:39	♍ Nov 22 09:22
♋ Jan 21 17:20	♎ Mar 23 22:30	♑ May 24 22:46	♈ Jul 25 16:14	♋ Sep 24 15:22	♎ Nov 24 15:47
♌ Jan 23 18:54	♏ Mar 26 08:18	♒ May 27 10:50	♉ Jul 27 21:55	♌ Sep 26 18:16	♏ Nov 27 01:00
♍ Jan 25 22:14	♐ Mar 28 20:23	♓ May 29 20:49	♊ Jul 30 01:14	♍ Sep 28 21:58	♐ Nov 29 12:10
♎ Jan 28 04:56	♑ Mar 31 09:10	♈ Jun 1 03:35	♋ Aug 1 02:33	♎ Oct 1 03:18	♑ Dec 2 00:31
♏ Jan 30 15:27	♒ Apr 2 20:18	♉ Jun 3 06:45	♌ Aug 3 03:05	♏ Oct 3 11:06	♒ Dec 4 13:14
♐ Feb 2 04:15	♓ Apr 5 04:02	♊ Jun 5 07:08	♍ Aug 5 04:42	♐ Oct 5 21:40	♓ Dec 7 01:01
♑ Feb 4 16:36	♈ Apr 7 08:10	♋ Jun 7 06:25	♎ Aug 7 09:14	♑ Oct 8 10:05	♈ Dec 9 10:03
♒ Feb 7 02:25	♉ Apr 9 09:48	♌ Jun 9 06:39	♏ Aug 9 17:41	♒ Oct 10 22:17	♉ Dec 11 15:10
♓ Feb 9 09:27	♊ Apr 11 10:35	♍ Jun 11 09:43	♐ Aug 12 05:24	♓ Oct 13 08:06	♊ Dec 13 16:36
♈ Feb 11 14:30	♋ Apr 13 12:02	♎ Jun 13 16:45	♑ Aug 14 18:08	♈ Oct 15 14:29	♋ Dec 15 15:53
♉ Feb 13 18:24	♌ Apr 15 15:18	♏ Jun 16 03:22	♒ Aug 17 05:37	♉ Oct 17 17:55	♌ Dec 17 15:12
♊ Feb 15 21:43	♍ Apr 17 20:56	♐ Jun 18 15:57	♓ Aug 19 14:50	♊ Oct 19 19:38	♍ Dec 19 16:38
♋ Feb 18 00:36	♎ Apr 20 05:04	♑ Jun 21 04:45	♈ Aug 21 21:55	♋ Oct 21 21:09	♎ Dec 21 21:45
♌ Feb 20 03:36	♏ Apr 22 15:26	♒ Jun 23 16:35	♉ Aug 24 03:19	♌ Oct 23 23:37	♏ Dec 24 06:38
♍ Feb 22 07:44	♐ Apr 25 03:35	♓ Jun 26 02:50	♊ Aug 26 07:12	♍ Oct 26 03:52	♐ Dec 26 18:07
♎ Feb 24 14:16	♑ Apr 27 16:25	♈ Jun 28 10:38	♋ Aug 28 09:48	♎ Oct 28 10:12	♑ Dec 29 06:43
♏ Feb 27 00:03	♒ Apr 30 04:14	♉ Jun 30 15:25	♌ Aug 30 11:44	♏ Oct 30 18:45	♒ Dec 31 19:19
♐ Mar 1 12:25	♓ May 2 13:14	♊ Jul 2 17:14	♍ Sep 1 14:12	♐ Nov 2 05:24	

Mercury

Jan 1 8♑	D Jul 5 27♊
♒ Jan 13 19:39	♋ Jul 13 09:27
♓ Feb 1 15:53	♌ Aug 2 21:21
R Feb 9 5♓	♍ Aug 17 16:34
♒ Feb 18 07:06	♎ Sep 4 02:38
D Mar 3 21♒	♏ Sep 28 06:49
♓ Mar 19 02:51	R Oct 7 3♏
♈ Apr 9 12:05	♎ Oct 16 00:00
♉ Apr 25 08:40	D Oct 28 18♎
♊ May 9 12:05	♏ Nov 10 15:05
♋ May 29 08:36	♐ Nov 30 01:30
R Jun 11 6♋	♑ Dec 19 02:59
♊ Jun 26 06:19	

Venus

Jan 1 23♒	♊ Jun 30 06:26
♓ Jan 11 17:35	♋ Jul 25 18:57
R Jan 25 3♓	♌ Aug 19 18:26
♒ Feb 6 23:18	♍ Sep 13 07:17
D Mar 7 17♒	♎ Oct 7 12:06
♓ Apr 4 19:26	♏ Oct 31 11:51
♈ May 7 07:05	♐ Nov 24 09:04
♉ Jun 4 00:00	♑ Dec 18 05:31

Mars

Jan 1 29♑
♒ Jan 1 23:56
♓ Feb 8 23:56
♈ Mar 19 04:30
♉ Apr 27 10:48
♊ Jun 7 11:16
♋ Jul 20 17:44
♌ Sep 4 14:56
♍ Oct 23 23:05
♎ Dec 20 03:44

Jupiter

Jan 1 21♑
♒ Feb 6 19:02
R Jun 6 17♒
D Oct 4 7♒

Saturn

Jan 1 17♑
R May 8 27♑
D Sep 26 21♑

Uranus

Jan 1 18♐
R Mar 27 21♐
D Aug 27 17♐

Neptune

Jan 1 29♊
D Mar 10 28♊
♋ May 21 13:39
R Oct 7 3♋

Pluto

Jan 1 17♊
D Mar 2 16♊
R Sep 20 19♊

1903

Sun

♒ Jan 21 05:13	♈ Mar 21 19:13	♊ May 22 06:45	♌ Jul 24 01:59	♎ Sep 24 05:46	♐ Nov 23 11:22
♓ Feb 19 19:39	♉ Apr 21 06:58	♋ Jun 22 15:05	♍ Aug 24 08:43	♏ Oct 24 14:25	♑ Dec 23 00:22

Moon

Jan 1 2♒	♉ Mar 3 12:00	♌ May 3 10:02	♏ Jul 3 11:57	♒ Sep 3 09:44	♉ Nov 4 08:35
♓ Jan 3 07:10	♊ Mar 5 17:15	♍ May 5 13:07	♐ Jul 5 21:29	♓ Sep 5 22:06	♊ Nov 6 13:38
♈ Jan 5 17:13	♋ Mar 7 20:34	♎ May 7 17:51	♑ Jul 8 08:56	♈ Sep 8 09:10	♋ Nov 8 16:50
♉ Jan 8 00:07	♌ Mar 9 22:22	♏ May 10 00:25	♒ Jul 10 11:20	♉ Sep 10 18:22	♌ Nov 10 19:23
♊ Jan 10 03:18	♍ Mar 11 23:46	♐ May 12 09:00	♓ Jul 13 09:58	♊ Sep 13 01:09	♍ Nov 12 22:15
♋ Jan 12 03:26	♎ Mar 14 02:17	♑ May 14 19:44	♈ Jul 15 21:35	♋ Sep 15 05:25	♎ Nov 15 01:54
♌ Jan 14 02:27	♏ Mar 16 07:25	♒ May 17 08:04	♉ Jul 18 06:26	♌ Sep 17 07:29	♏ Nov 17 06:41
♍ Jan 16 02:31	♐ Mar 18 16:00	♓ May 19 20:19	♊ Jul 20 11:24	♍ Sep 19 08:18	♐ Nov 19 13:05
♎ Jan 18 05:45	♑ Mar 21 03:31	♈ May 22 06:21	♋ Jul 22 12:45	♎ Sep 21 09:26	♑ Nov 21 21:49
♏ Jan 20 13:12	♒ Mar 23 16:05	♉ May 24 12:39	♌ Jul 24 12:04	♏ Sep 23 12:31	♒ Nov 24 09:07
♐ Jan 23 00:14	♓ Mar 26 03:22	♊ May 26 15:26	♍ Jul 26 11:32	♐ Sep 25 18:51	♓ Nov 26 21:53
♑ Jan 25 12:53	♈ Mar 28 12:12	♋ May 28 16:08	♎ Jul 28 13:11	♑ Sep 28 04:44	♈ Nov 29 09:41
♒ Jan 28 01:26	♉ Mar 30 18:27	♌ May 30 16:40	♏ Jul 30 18:25	♒ Sep 30 16:56	♉ Dec 1 18:13
♓ Jan 30 12:54	♊ Apr 1 22:49	♍ Jun 1 18:44	♐ Aug 2 03:21	♓ Oct 3 05:22	♊ Dec 3 22:55
♈ Feb 1 22:51	♋ Apr 4 01:58	♎ Jun 3 23:17	♑ Aug 4 14:47	♈ Oct 5 16:09	♋ Dec 6 00:53
♉ Feb 4 06:35	♌ Apr 6 04:37	♏ Jun 6 06:26	♒ Aug 7 03:20	♉ Oct 8 00:32	♌ Dec 8 01:57
♊ Feb 6 11:27	♍ Apr 8 07:27	♐ Jun 8 15:45	♓ Aug 9 15:49	♊ Oct 10 06:40	♍ Dec 10 03:45
♋ Feb 8 13:24	♎ Apr 10 11:11	♑ Jun 11 02:46	♈ Aug 12 03:22	♋ Oct 12 10:58	♎ Dec 12 07:21
♌ Feb 10 13:31	♏ Apr 12 16:44	♒ Jun 13 15:04	♉ Aug 14 12:50	♌ Oct 14 14:01	♏ Dec 14 12:54
♍ Feb 12 13:39	♐ Apr 15 00:54	♓ Jun 16 03:41	♊ Aug 16 19:13	♍ Oct 16 16:23	♐ Dec 16 20:17
♎ Feb 14 15:51	♑ Apr 17 11:47	♈ Jun 18 14:41	♋ Aug 18 22:11	♎ Oct 18 18:47	♑ Dec 19 05:33
♏ Feb 16 21:42	♒ Apr 20 00:14	♉ Jun 20 22:15	♌ Aug 20 22:35	♏ Oct 20 22:22	♒ Dec 21 16:47
♐ Feb 19 07:28	♓ Apr 22 11:59	♊ Jun 23 01:45	♍ Aug 22 22:11	♐ Oct 23 04:13	♓ Dec 24 05:34
♑ Feb 21 19:46	♈ Apr 24 21:05	♋ Jun 25 02:12	♎ Aug 24 22:59	♑ Oct 25 13:12	♈ Dec 26 18:06
♒ Feb 24 08:18	♉ Apr 27 02:55	♌ Jun 27 01:34	♏ Aug 27 02:45	♒ Oct 28 00:57	♉ Dec 29 03:55
♓ Feb 26 19:30	♊ Apr 29 06:05	♍ Jun 29 02:02	♐ Aug 29 10:21	♓ Oct 30 13:33	♊ Dec 31 09:32
♈ Mar 1 04:45	♋ May 1 08:00	♎ Jul 1 05:17	♑ Aug 31 21:13	♈ Nov 2 00:36	

Mercury

Jan 1 20♑	♋ Jul 10 13:07
♒ Jan 6 19:27	♌ Jul 25 12:10
R Jan 24 19♒	♍ Aug 9 17:52
D Feb 14 3♒	♎ Aug 29 05:43
♓ Mar 14 21:41	R Sep 20 17♎
♈ Apr 2 00:18	D Oct 12 2♎
♉ Apr 16 21:44	♏ Nov 4 04:53
♊ May 2 13:35	♐ Nov 22 19:21
R May 22 16♊	♑ Dec 12 00:06
D Jun 15 7♊	

Venus

Jan 1 17♑	♍ Jul 7 20:42
♒ Jan 11 02:17	♎ Aug 17 21:54
♓ Feb 4 00:45	R Aug 27 1♎
♈ Feb 28 03:00	♍ Sep 6 01:51
♉ Mar 24 11:51	D Oct 9 15♍
♊ Apr 18 06:39	♎ Nov 8 14:44
♋ May 13 16:23	♏ Dec 9 14:43
♌ Jun 9 03:09	

Mars

Jan 1 5♎	
R Feb 18 16♎	
♍ Apr 19 20:47	
D May 9 27♍	
♎ May 30 17:21	
♏ Aug 6 16:32	
♐ Sep 22 13:53	
♑ Nov 3 05:29	
♒ Dec 12 09:54	

Jupiter

Jan 1 18♒	
♓ Feb 20 07:58	
R Jul 14 23♓	
D Nov 9 13♓	

Saturn

Jan 1 27♑
♒ Jan 19 22:07
R May 20 9♒
D Oct 8 2♒

Uranus

Jan 1 22♐
R Mar 31 25♐
D Sep 1 21♐

Neptune

Jan 1 2♋
D Mar 13 0♋
R Oct 10 5♋

Pluto

Jan 1 18♊
D Mar 3 17♊
R Sep 21 20♊

1904

Sun

♒ Jan 21 10:59	♈ Mar 21 00:58	♊ May 21 12:27	♌ Jul 23 07:49	♎ Sep 23 11:40	♐ Nov 22 17:15
♓ Feb 20 01:26	♉ Apr 20 12:41	♋ Jun 21 20:50	♍ Aug 23 14:37	♏ Oct 23 20:18	♑ Dec 22 06:14

Moon

Jan 1 8♊	♍ Mar 1 09:15	♐ May 1 10:35	♓ Jul 2 06:57	♊ Sep 2 07:58	♍ Nov 2 12:39
♋ Jan 2 11:23	♎ Mar 3 08:52	♑ May 3 16:55	♈ Jul 4 19:53	♋ Sep 4 14:45	♎ Nov 4 14:25
♌ Jan 4 11:16	♏ Mar 5 10:23	♒ May 6 02:49	♉ Jul 7 07:28	♌ Sep 6 17:52	♏ Nov 6 15:20
♍ Jan 6 11:21	♐ Mar 7 15:17	♓ May 8 15:16	♊ Jul 9 15:30	♍ Sep 8 18:18	♐ Nov 8 16:52
♎ Jan 8 13:24	♑ Mar 10 00:01	♈ May 11 03:48	♋ Jul 11 19:39	♎ Sep 10 17:42	♑ Nov 10 20:55
♏ Jan 10 18:19	♒ Mar 12 11:45	♉ May 13 14:11	♌ Jul 13 21:08	♏ Sep 12 18:03	♒ Nov 13 04:46
♐ Jan 13 02:01	♓ Mar 15 00:42	♊ May 15 21:29	♍ Jul 15 21:46	♐ Sep 14 21:03	♓ Nov 15 16:12
♑ Jan 15 11:57	♈ Mar 17 13:11	♋ May 18 02:20	♎ Jul 17 23:13	♑ Sep 17 03:44	♈ Nov 18 05:13
♒ Jan 17 23:31	♉ Mar 20 00:08	♌ May 20 05:50	♏ Jul 20 02:33	♒ Sep 19 13:54	♉ Nov 20 17:05
♓ Jan 20 12:17	♊ Mar 22 08:51	♍ May 22 08:49	♐ Jul 22 08:09	♓ Sep 22 02:19	♊ Nov 23 02:23
♈ Jan 23 01:08	♋ Mar 24 14:54	♎ May 24 11:47	♑ Jul 24 16:00	♈ Sep 24 15:19	♋ Nov 25 09:16
♉ Jan 25 12:07	♌ Mar 26 18:15	♏ May 26 15:07	♒ Jul 27 01:59	♉ Sep 27 03:31	♌ Nov 27 14:24
♊ Jan 27 19:25	♍ Mar 28 19:30	♐ May 28 19:28	♓ Jul 29 13:56	♊ Sep 29 13:58	♍ Nov 29 18:25
♋ Jan 29 22:30	♎ Mar 30 19:53	♑ May 31 01:52	♈ Aug 1 02:59	♋ Oct 1 21:48	♎ Dec 1 21:32
♌ Jan 31 22:35	♏ Apr 1 21:02	♒ Jun 2 11:12	♉ Aug 3 15:12	♌ Oct 4 02:37	♏ Dec 4 00:00
♍ Feb 2 21:45	♐ Apr 4 00:40	♓ Jun 4 23:15	♊ Aug 6 00:28	♍ Oct 6 04:34	♐ Dec 6 02:37
♎ Feb 4 22:01	♑ Apr 6 07:55	♈ Jun 7 12:00	♋ Aug 8 05:43	♎ Oct 8 04:44	♑ Dec 8 06:45
♏ Feb 7 01:07	♒ Apr 8 18:47	♉ Jun 9 22:49	♌ Aug 10 07:29	♏ Oct 10 04:42	♒ Dec 10 13:52
♐ Feb 9 07:48	♓ Apr 11 07:36	♊ Jun 12 06:05	♍ Aug 12 07:24	♐ Oct 12 06:23	♓ Dec 13 00:29
♑ Feb 11 17:39	♈ Apr 13 20:02	♋ Jun 14 10:08	♎ Aug 14 07:24	♑ Oct 14 11:30	♈ Dec 15 13:17
♒ Feb 14 05:35	♉ Apr 16 06:29	♌ Jun 16 12:24	♏ Aug 16 09:10	♒ Oct 16 20:37	♉ Dec 18 01:31
♓ Feb 16 18:25	♊ Apr 18 14:31	♍ Jun 18 14:24	♐ Aug 18 13:50	♓ Oct 19 08:49	♊ Dec 20 10:56
♈ Feb 19 07:08	♋ Apr 20 20:20	♎ Jun 20 17:11	♑ Aug 20 21:36	♈ Oct 21 21:49	♋ Dec 22 17:08
♉ Feb 21 18:29	♌ Apr 23 00:25	♏ Jun 22 21:08	♒ Aug 23 08:01	♉ Oct 24 09:44	♌ Dec 24 21:02
♊ Feb 24 03:03	♍ Apr 25 03:09	♐ Jun 25 02:31	♓ Aug 25 20:15	♊ Oct 26 19:36	♍ Dec 27 00:00
♋ Feb 26 07:59	♎ Apr 27 05:04	♑ Jun 27 09:39	♈ Aug 28 09:16	♋ Oct 29 03:22	♎ Dec 29 02:55
♌ Feb 28 09:36	♏ Apr 29 07:06	♒ Jun 29 19:06	♉ Aug 30 21:43	♌ Oct 31 09:03	♏ Dec 31 06:10

Mercury

Jan 1 28♑	♋ Jul 1 22:16
♒ Jan 2 09:37	♌ Jul 16 00:19
R Jan 8 4♒	♍ Aug 1 13:25
♑ Jan 14 03:49	♎ Aug 28 07:48
D Jan 28 17♑	R Sep 2 1♎
♒ Feb 15 11:05	♍ Sep 7 20:18
♓ Mar 7 08:07	D Sep 25 16♍
♈ Mar 23 23:35	♎ Oct 9 02:07
♉ Apr 7 19:09	♏ Oct 26 20:15
R May 2 26♉	♐ Nov 14 13:47
D May 26 16♉	♑ Dec 4 14:18
♊ Jun 14 06:22	R Dec 22 17♑

Venus

Jan 1 25♏	♋ Jun 25 13:28
♐ Jan 5 03:42	♌ Jul 19 22:59
♑ Jan 30 09:26	♍ Aug 13 06:51
♒ Feb 24 03:05	♎ Sep 6 13:50
♓ Mar 19 16:01	♏ Sep 30 21:02
♈ Apr 13 03:25	♐ Oct 25 05:36
♉ May 7 14:50	♑ Nov 18 16:38
♊ Jun 1 02:25	♒ Dec 13 09:05

Mars

Jan 1 15♒
♓ Jan 19 15:48
♈ Feb 27 03:12
♉ Apr 6 18:06
♊ May 18 03:32
♋ Jun 30 14:57
♌ Aug 15 03:20
♍ Oct 1 13:52
♎ Nov 20 06:31

Jupiter

Jan 1 17♓
♈ Mar 1 02:56
♉ Aug 8 21:45
R Aug 20 0♉
♈ Aug 31 12:00
D Dec 15 20♈

Saturn

Jan 1 8♒
R May 31 21♒
D Oct 19 14♒

Uranus

Jan 1 26♐
R Apr 4 29♐
D Sep 4 25♐
♑ Dec 20 14:32

Neptune

Jan 1 4♋
D Mar 14 3♋
R Oct 11 8♋

Pluto

Jan 1 19♊
D Mar 3 18♊
R Sep 21 21♊

1905

Sun

♒ Jan 20 16:52	♈ Mar 21 06:57	♊ May 21 18:29	♌ Jul 23 13:44	♎ Sep 23 17:30	♐ Nov 22 23:04
♓ Feb 19 07:22	♉ Apr 20 18:42	♋ Jun 22 02:50	♍ Aug 23 20:28	♏ Oct 24 02:07	♑ Dec 22 12:02

Moon

Jan 1 10♏	♒ Mar 2 12:03	♉ May 3 12:50	♌ Jul 4 05:27	♏ Sep 3 04:10	♒ Nov 3 05:17
♐ Jan 2 10:07	♓ Mar 4 23:11	♊ May 6 00:21	♍ Jul 6 09:52	♐ Sep 5 06:02	♓ Nov 5 14:05
♑ Jan 4 15:19	♈ Mar 7 11:44	♋ May 8 10:01	♎ Jul 8 13:15	♑ Sep 7 10:11	♈ Nov 8 01:47
♒ Jan 6 22:42	♉ Mar 10 00:41	♌ May 10 17:33	♏ Jul 10 16:03	♒ Sep 9 17:00	♉ Nov 10 14:31
♓ Jan 9 08:56	♊ Mar 12 12:34	♍ May 12 22:38	♐ Jul 12 18:45	♓ Sep 12 02:18	♊ Nov 13 02:53
♈ Jan 11 21:27	♋ Mar 14 21:46	♎ May 15 01:10	♑ Jul 14 22:11	♈ Sep 14 13:33	♋ Nov 15 14:13
♉ Jan 14 10:09	♌ Mar 17 03:18	♏ May 17 01:49	♒ Jul 17 03:27	♉ Sep 17 02:04	♌ Nov 17 23:49
♊ Jan 16 20:23	♍ Mar 19 05:17	♐ May 19 02:04	♓ Jul 19 11:35	♊ Sep 19 14:38	♍ Nov 20 06:46
♋ Jan 19 02:55	♎ Mar 21 05:02	♑ May 21 03:54	♈ Jul 21 22:37	♋ Sep 22 01:35	♎ Nov 22 10:28
♌ Jan 21 06:12	♏ Mar 23 04:25	♒ May 23 09:10	♉ Jul 24 11:15	♌ Sep 24 09:16	♏ Nov 24 11:17
♍ Jan 23 07:45	♐ Mar 25 05:24	♓ May 25 18:32	♊ Jul 26 23:00	♍ Sep 26 13:06	♐ Nov 26 10:47
♎ Jan 25 09:08	♑ Mar 27 09:40	♈ May 28 06:51	♋ Jul 29 07:59	♎ Sep 28 13:52	♑ Nov 28 11:01
♏ Jan 27 11:35	♒ Mar 29 17:45	♉ May 30 19:39	♌ Jul 31 13:46	♏ Sep 30 13:22	♒ Nov 30 14:10
♐ Jan 29 15:43	♓ Apr 1 05:01	♊ Jun 2 06:54	♍ Aug 2 17:08	♐ Oct 2 13:33	♓ Dec 2 21:24
♑ Jan 31 21:49	♈ Apr 3 17:52	♋ Jun 4 15:57	♎ Aug 4 19:19	♑ Oct 4 16:19	♈ Dec 5 08:22
♒ Feb 3 06:06	♉ Apr 6 06:43	♌ Jun 6 22:58	♏ Aug 6 21:26	♒ Oct 6 22:34	♉ Dec 7 21:04
♓ Feb 5 16:37	♊ Apr 8 18:34	♍ Jun 9 04:16	♐ Aug 9 00:23	♓ Oct 9 08:08	♊ Dec 10 09:23
♈ Feb 8 05:01	♋ Apr 11 04:27	♎ Jun 11 07:52	♑ Aug 11 04:44	♈ Oct 11 19:48	♋ Dec 12 20:13
♉ Feb 10 17:59	♌ Apr 13 11:29	♏ Jun 13 10:00	♒ Aug 13 10:59	♉ Oct 14 08:23	♌ Dec 15 05:18
♊ Feb 13 05:16	♍ Apr 15 15:12	♐ Jun 15 11:28	♓ Aug 15 19:32	♊ Oct 16 20:58	♍ Dec 17 12:28
♋ Feb 15 13:04	♎ Apr 17 16:04	♑ Jun 17 13:46	♈ Aug 18 06:29	♋ Oct 19 08:28	♎ Dec 19 17:24
♌ Feb 17 16:59	♏ Apr 19 15:28	♒ Jun 19 18:32	♉ Aug 20 19:01	♌ Oct 21 17:32	♏ Dec 21 19:59
♍ Feb 19 18:03	♐ Apr 21 15:27	♓ Jun 22 02:56	♊ Aug 23 07:16	♍ Oct 23 23:01	♐ Dec 23 20:59
♎ Feb 21 18:02	♑ Apr 23 18:02	♈ Jun 24 14:32	♋ Aug 25 17:11	♎ Oct 26 00:53	♑ Dec 25 21:51
♏ Feb 23 18:42	♒ Apr 26 00:40	♉ Jun 27 03:15	♌ Aug 27 23:30	♏ Oct 28 00:22	♒ Dec 28 00:30
♐ Feb 25 21:29	♓ Apr 28 11:14	♊ Jun 29 14:36	♍ Aug 30 02:32	♐ Oct 29 23:33	♓ Dec 30 06:28
♑ Feb 28 03:18	♈ May 1 00:01	♋ Jul 1 23:15	♎ Sep 1 03:31	♑ Nov 1 00:36	

Mercury

Jan 1 9♑	♌ Jul 7 22:15
D Jan 11 1♑	♍ Jul 27 06:58
♒ Feb 9 05:32	R Aug 16 13♍
♓ Feb 27 22:05	D Sep 8 0♍
♈ Mar 15 19:28	♎ Oct 1 23:11
♉ Apr 1 18:50	♏ Oct 19 07:49
R Apr 13 6♉	♐ Nov 7 16:27
♈ Apr 28 12:45	♑ Dec 2 05:41
D May 7 27♈	R Dec 6 0♑
♉ May 15 19:22	♐ Dec 10 00:03
♊ Jun 8 18:03	D Dec 26 15♐
♋ Jun 23 09:52	

Venus

Jan 1 22♒	♊ Jul 8 11:57
♓ Jan 7 14:37	♋ Aug 6 08:14
♈ Feb 3 04:48	♌ Sep 1 20:15
♉ Mar 6 05:18	♍ Sep 27 04:02
R Apr 6 14♉	♎ Oct 21 18:30
♈ May 9 10:50	♏ Nov 14 22:38
D May 18 28♈	♐ Dec 8 21:29
♉ May 28 11:07	

Mars

Jan 1 23♎
♏ Jan 13 19:35
R Apr 2 25♏
D Jun 17 7♏
♐ Aug 21 19:33
♑ Oct 8 00:21
♒ Nov 18 04:26
♓ Dec 27 13:53

Jupiter

Jan 1 20♈
♉ Mar 7 18:35
♊ Jul 21 01:08
R Sep 25 6♊
♉ Dec 4 20:53

Saturn

Jan 1 18♒
♓ Apr 13 07:57
R Jun 13 2♓
♒ Aug 17 00:48
D Oct 31 26♒

Uranus

Jan 1 0♑
R Apr 8 4♑
D Sep 9 0♑

Neptune

Jan 1 6♋
D Mar 17 5♋
R Oct 14 10♋

Pluto

Jan 1 20♊
D Mar 4 19♊
R Sep 23 22♊

1906

Sun

♒ Jan 20 22:44	♈ Mar 21 12:52	♊ May 22 00:22	♌ Jul 23 19:30	♎ Sep 23 23:15	♐ Nov 23 04:54
♓ Feb 19 13:14	♉ Apr 21 00:38	♋ Jun 22 08:38	♍ Aug 24 02:12	♏ Oct 24 07:55	♑ Dec 22 17:55

Moon

Jan 1 21 ♓	♊ Mar 2 09:29	♍ May 3 07:02
♈ Jan 1 16:15	♋ Mar 4 21:18	♎ May 5 10:52
♉ Jan 4 04:31	♌ Mar 7 06:15	♏ May 7 11:21
♊ Jan 6 16:56	♍ Mar 9 11:33	♐ May 9 10:24
♋ Jan 9 03:37	♎ Mar 11 13:52	♑ May 11 10:11
♌ Jan 11 11:56	♏ Mar 13 14:46	♒ May 13 12:45
♍ Jan 13 18:10	♐ Mar 15 16:00	♓ May 15 19:06
♎ Jan 15 22:47	♑ Mar 17 18:42	♈ May 18 04:53
♏ Jan 18 02:07	♒ Mar 20 00:05	♉ May 20 16:48
♐ Jan 20 04:34	♓ Mar 22 07:36	♊ May 23 05:25
♑ Jan 22 06:59	♈ Mar 24 17:09	♋ May 25 17:53
♒ Jan 24 10:26	♉ Mar 27 04:27	♌ May 28 05:14
♓ Jan 26 16:11	♋ Apr 1 05:19	♍ May 30 14:10
♈ Jan 29 01:05	♌ Apr 3 15:29	♎ Jun 1 19:37
♉ Jan 31 12:44	♍ Apr 5 21:52	♏ Jun 3 21:34
♊ Feb 3 01:15	♎ Apr 8 00:24	♐ Jun 5 21:15
♋ Feb 5 12:20	♏ Apr 10 00:28	♑ Jun 7 20:38
♌ Feb 7 20:31	♐ Apr 12 00:07	♒ Jun 9 21:54
♍ Feb 10 01:49	♑ Apr 14 01:23	♓ Jun 12 02:39
♎ Feb 12 05:07	♒ Apr 16 05:03	♈ Jun 14 11:19
♏ Feb 14 07:32	♓ Apr 18 13:08	♉ Jun 16 22:53
♐ Feb 16 10:07	♈ Apr 20 23:14	♊ Jun 19 11:35
♑ Feb 18 13:30	♉ Apr 23 10:54	♋ Jun 21 23:50
♒ Feb 20 18:16	♊ Apr 25 23:27	♌ Jun 24 10:49
♓ Feb 23 00:50	♋ Apr 28 12:01	♍ Jun 26 19:50
♈ Feb 25 09:44	♌ Apr 30 23:08	♎ Jun 29 02:13
♉ Feb 27 20:57		♏ Jul 1 05:41

♐ Jul 3 06:51	♓ Sep 2 06:27	♊ Nov 3 00:54
♑ Jul 5 07:06	♈ Sep 4 13:03	♋ Nov 5 13:43
♒ Jul 7 08:11	♉ Sep 6 22:20	♌ Nov 8 02:12
♓ Jul 9 11:52	♊ Sep 9 10:04	♍ Nov 10 12:09
♈ Jul 11 19:10	♋ Sep 11 22:38	♎ Nov 12 18:00
♉ Jul 14 05:54	♌ Sep 14 09:36	♏ Nov 14 19:52
♊ Jul 16 18:23	♍ Sep 16 17:17	♐ Nov 16 19:28
♋ Jul 19 06:37	♎ Sep 18 21:38	♑ Nov 18 18:58
♌ Jul 21 17:09	♏ Sep 20 23:53	♒ Nov 20 20:21
♍ Jul 24 01:29	♐ Sep 23 01:33	♓ Nov 23 00:58
♎ Jul 26 07:37	♑ Sep 25 04:01	♈ Nov 25 08:52
♏ Jul 28 11:45	♒ Sep 27 07:57	♉ Nov 30 07:14
♐ Jul 30 14:16	♓ Sep 29 13:32	♋ Dec 2 19:59
♑ Aug 1 15:58	♈ Oct 1 20:55	♌ Dec 5 08:36
♒ Aug 3 17:56	♉ Oct 4 06:20	♍ Dec 7 19:29
♓ Aug 5 21:36	♊ Oct 6 17:51	♎ Dec 10 03:00
♈ Aug 8 04:07	♋ Oct 9 06:37	♏ Dec 12 06:30
♉ Aug 10 13:53	♌ Oct 11 18:25	♐ Dec 14 06:53
♊ Aug 13 02:01	♍ Oct 14 03:01	♑ Dec 16 06:01
♋ Aug 15 14:21	♎ Oct 16 07:33	♒ Dec 18 06:00
♌ Aug 18 00:00	♏ Oct 18 09:00	♓ Dec 20 08:46
♍ Aug 20 08:30	♐ Oct 20 09:14	♈ Dec 22 15:16
♎ Aug 22 13:38	♑ Oct 22 10:12	♉ Dec 25 01:13
♏ Aug 24 17:10	♒ Oct 24 13:23	♊ Dec 27 13:22
♐ Aug 26 19:54	♓ Oct 26 19:10	♋ Dec 30 02:10
♑ Aug 28 22:37	♈ Oct 29 03:17	
♒ Aug 31 01:54	♉ Oct 31 13:16	

Mercury

Jan 1 18 ♐	R Jul 29 26 ♌
♑ Jan 12 21:04	D Aug 22 13 ♌
♒ Feb 2 12:05	♍ Sep 7 21:47
♓ Feb 20 03:27	♎ Sep 24 03:23
♈ Mar 8 02:24	♏ Oct 11 23:28
R Mar 26 19 ♈	♐ Nov 1 19:44
D Apr 18 7 ♈	R Nov 20 15 ♐
♉ May 15 03:16	♏ Dec 6 23:30
♊ May 31 22:51	D Dec 9 28 ♏
♋ Jun 14 19:27	♐ Dec 13 01:58
♌ Jun 30 21:22	

Venus

Jan 1 29 ♐	♍ Jul 16 01:15
♑ Jan 1 18:22	♎ Aug 11 03:20
♒ Jan 25 15:13	♏ Sep 7 15:32
♓ Feb 18 13:12	♐ Oct 9 10:33
♈ Mar 14 13:42	R Nov 9 14 ♐
♉ Apr 7 18:00	♏ Dec 15 11:04
♊ May 2 03:12	D Dec 20 29 ♏
♋ May 26 18:14	♐ Dec 26 00:16
♌ Jun 20 16:31	

Mars

Jan 1 3 ♓
♈ Feb 4 23:45
♉ Mar 17 11:55
♊ Apr 28 16:55
♋ Jun 11 19:36
♌ Jul 27 14:07
♍ Sep 12 12:49
♎ Oct 30 04:24
♏ Dec 17 12:08

Jupiter

Jan 1 27 ♉
D Jan 21 26 ♉
♊ Mar 9 23:14
♋ Jul 30 23:53
R Oct 30 11 ♋

Saturn

Jan 1 29 ♒
♓ Jan 8 12:13
R Jun 26 15 ♓
D Nov 12 8 ♓

Uranus

Jan 1 4 ♑
R Apr 13 8 ♑
D Sep 14 4 ♑

Neptune

Jan 1 8 ♋
D Mar 19 7 ♋
R Oct 16 12 ♋

Pluto

Jan 1 21 ♊
D Mar 5 20 ♊
R Sep 24 23 ♊

1907

Sun

♒ Jan 21 04:33	♈ Mar 21 18:37	♊ May 22 06:06	♌ Jul 24 01:16	♎ Sep 24 05:08	♐ Nov 23 10:50
♓ Feb 19 19:03	♉ Apr 21 06:21	♋ Jun 22 14:23	♍ Aug 24 08:01	♏ Oct 24 13:50	♑ Dec 22 23:50

Moon

Jan 1 22♋	♎ Mar 1 21:29	♑ May 1 20:59	♈ Jul 1 21:14	♋ Sep 1 17:20	♎ Nov 2 19:43
♌ Jan 1 14:28	♏ Mar 4 02:24	♒ May 3 23:07	♉ Jul 4 04:54	♌ Sep 4 06:20	♏ Nov 5 01:22
♍ Jan 4 01:17	♐ Mar 6 06:02	♓ May 6 03:10	♊ Jul 6 15:40	♍ Sep 6 17:55	♐ Nov 7 04:24
♎ Jan 6 09:41	♑ Mar 8 09:02	♈ May 8 09:20	♋ Jul 9 04:14	♎ Sep 9 03:05	♑ Nov 9 06:22
♏ Jan 8 14:54	♒ Mar 10 11:49	♉ May 10 17:28	♌ Jul 11 17:16	♏ Sep 11 10:01	♒ Nov 11 08:37
♐ Jan 10 17:06	♓ Mar 12 14:56	♊ May 13 03:40	♍ Jul 14 05:28	♐ Sep 13 15:06	♓ Nov 13 11:52
♑ Jan 12 17:20	♈ Mar 14 19:19	♋ May 15 15:48	♎ Jul 16 15:34	♑ Sep 15 18:45	♈ Nov 15 16:24
♒ Jan 14 17:18	♉ Mar 17 02:09	♌ May 18 04:52	♏ Jul 18 22:33	♒ Sep 17 21:12	♉ Nov 17 22:30
♓ Jan 16 18:53	♊ Mar 19 12:09	♍ May 20 16:35	♐ Jul 21 02:11	♓ Sep 19 23:01	♊ Nov 20 06:43
♈ Jan 18 23:40	♋ Mar 22 00:35	♎ May 23 00:52	♑ Jul 23 03:05	♈ Sep 22 01:25	♋ Nov 22 17:22
♉ Jan 21 08:19	♌ Mar 24 13:06	♏ May 25 05:01	♒ Jul 25 02:45	♉ Sep 24 05:54	♌ Nov 25 06:03
♊ Jan 23 20:02	♍ Mar 26 23:10	♐ May 27 06:04	♓ Jul 27 03:00	♊ Sep 26 13:48	♍ Nov 27 18:48
♋ Jan 26 08:55	♎ Mar 29 05:44	♑ May 29 05:54	♈ Jul 29 05:36	♋ Sep 29 01:08	♎ Nov 30 05:09
♌ Jan 28 20:59	♏ Mar 31 09:31	♒ May 31 06:25	♉ Jul 31 11:52	♌ Oct 1 14:04	♏ Dec 2 11:35
♍ Jan 31 07:10	♐ Apr 2 11:58	♓ Jun 2 09:08	♊ Aug 2 21:54	♍ Oct 4 01:49	♐ Dec 4 14:28
♎ Feb 2 15:09	♑ Apr 4 14:23	♈ Jun 4 14:45	♋ Aug 5 10:26	♎ Oct 6 10:38	♑ Dec 6 15:18
♏ Feb 4 20:54	♒ Apr 6 17:34	♉ Jun 6 23:11	♌ Aug 7 23:25	♏ Oct 8 16:36	♒ Dec 8 15:52
♐ Feb 7 00:34	♓ Apr 8 21:46	♊ Jun 9 09:53	♍ Aug 10 11:15	♐ Oct 10 20:46	♓ Dec 10 17:43
♑ Feb 9 02:34	♈ Apr 11 03:16	♋ Jun 11 22:14	♎ Aug 12 21:05	♑ Oct 13 00:06	♈ Dec 12 21:47
♒ Feb 11 03:49	♉ Apr 13 10:33	♌ Jun 14 11:19	♏ Aug 15 04:33	♒ Oct 15 03:12	♉ Dec 15 04:24
♓ Feb 13 05:39	♊ Apr 15 20:22	♍ Jun 16 23:34	♐ Aug 17 09:30	♓ Oct 17 06:20	♊ Dec 17 13:24
♈ Feb 15 09:38	♋ Apr 18 08:33	♎ Jun 19 09:04	♑ Aug 19 12:04	♈ Oct 19 09:55	♋ Dec 20 00:29
♉ Feb 17 16:56	♌ Apr 20 21:24	♏ Jun 21 14:41	♒ Aug 21 12:59	♉ Oct 21 14:59	♌ Dec 22 13:08
♊ Feb 20 03:45	♍ Apr 23 08:15	♐ Jun 23 16:42	♓ Aug 23 13:31	♊ Oct 23 22:37	♍ Dec 25 02:05
♋ Feb 22 16:29	♎ Apr 25 15:21	♑ Jun 25 16:29	♈ Aug 25 15:26	♋ Oct 26 09:23	♎ Dec 27 13:26
♌ Feb 25 04:39	♏ Apr 27 18:45	♒ Jun 27 16:00	♉ Aug 27 20:24	♌ Oct 28 22:12	♏ Dec 29 21:24
♍ Feb 27 14:28	♐ Apr 29 20:01	♓ Jun 29 17:06	♊ Aug 30 05:17	♍ Oct 31 10:27	

Mercury

Jan 1 21♐	♌ Jun 27 08:24
♑ Jan 7 00:50	R Jul 11 7♌
♒ Jan 26 05:06	♋ Jul 26 14:43
♓ Feb 12 08:39	D Aug 4 26♋
♈ Mar 3 21:39	♌ Aug 12 16:40
R Mar 8 2♈	♍ Aug 31 06:55
♓ Mar 14 05:05	♎ Sep 16 06:57
D Mar 31 18♓	♏ Oct 5 04:34
♈ Apr 18 10:47	R Nov 3 29♏
♉ May 8 15:27	D Nov 23 12♏
♊ May 23 10:39	♐ Dec 11 03:27
♋ Jun 6 16:49	

Venus

Jan 1 1♐	♌ Aug 4 19:07
♑ Feb 6 16:30	♍ Aug 29 02:29
♒ Mar 6 20:43	♎ Sep 22 05:51
♓ Apr 2 01:27	♏ Oct 16 06:53
♈ Apr 27 12:29	♐ Nov 9 07:05
♉ May 22 15:19	♑ Dec 3 07:23
♊ Jun 16 13:13	♒ Dec 27 08:50
♋ Jul 11 06:42	

Mars

Jan 1 8♏
♐ Feb 5 09:34
♑ Apr 1 18:42
R Jun 5 19♑
D Aug 9 7♑
♒ Oct 13 14:19
♓ Nov 29 04:51

Jupiter

Jan 1 5♋
D Feb 25 0♋
♌ Aug 18 23:28
R Dec 1 13♌

Saturn

Jan 1 10♓
R Jul 9 27♓
D Nov 25 20♓

Uranus

Jan 1 8♑
R Apr 17 12♑
D Sep 18 8♑

Neptune

Jan 1 11♋
D Mar 22 9♋
R Oct 19 14♋

Pluto

Jan 1 22♊
D Mar 7 21♊
R Sep 25 24♊

1908

Sun

♒ Jan 21 10:28	♈ Mar 21 00:28	♊ May 21 12:02	♌ Jul 23 07:16	♎ Sep 23 10:58	♐ Nov 22 16:32
♓ Feb 20 00:54	♉ Apr 20 12:14	♋ Jun 21 20:22	♍ Aug 23 13:57	♏ Oct 23 19:36	♑ Dec 22 05:32

Moon

Jan 1 29♏	♒ Feb 29 00:03	♉ Apr 29 22:15	♌ Jun 30 15:14	♏ Aug 31 15:54	♒ Oct 31 23:12
♐ Jan 1 01:27	♓ Mar 2 00:04	♊ May 2 03:43	♍ Jul 3 03:57	♐ Sep 3 00:50	♓ Nov 3 02:10
♑ Jan 3 02:24	♈ Mar 4 00:19	♋ May 4 12:22	♎ Jul 5 16:19	♑ Sep 5 06:40	♈ Nov 5 03:57
♒ Jan 5 01:57	♉ Mar 6 02:49	♌ May 7 00:00	♏ Jul 8 02:21	♒ Sep 7 09:05	♉ Nov 7 05:42
♓ Jan 8 02:02	♊ Mar 8 09:12	♍ May 9 12:45	♐ Jul 10 08:47	♓ Sep 9 09:02	♊ Nov 9 09:00
♈ Jan 9 04:23	♋ Mar 10 19:38	♎ May 11 23:59	♑ Jul 12 11:38	♈ Sep 11 08:20	♋ Nov 11 15:17
♉ Jan 11 10:04	♌ Mar 13 08:27	♏ May 14 08:11	♒ Jul 14 12:06	♉ Sep 13 09:09	♌ Nov 14 01:06
♊ Jan 13 19:08	♍ Mar 15 21:08	♐ May 16 13:26	♓ Jul 16 11:58	♊ Sep 15 13:27	♍ Nov 16 13:22
♋ Jan 16 06:44	♎ Mar 18 08:02	♑ May 18 16:43	♈ Jul 18 13:02	♋ Sep 17 21:55	♎ Nov 19 01:44
♌ Jan 18 19:31	♏ Mar 20 16:51	♒ May 20 19:13	♉ Jul 20 16:46	♌ Sep 20 09:41	♏ Nov 21 12:02
♍ Jan 21 08:21	♐ Mar 22 23:43	♓ May 22 21:48	♊ Jul 22 23:46	♍ Sep 22 22:33	♐ Nov 23 19:37
♎ Jan 23 20:02	♑ Mar 25 04:47	♈ May 25 01:03	♋ Jul 25 09:44	♎ Sep 25 10:46	♑ Nov 26 00:53
♏ Jan 26 05:16	♒ Mar 27 07:56	♉ May 27 05:29	♌ Jul 27 21:37	♏ Sep 27 21:29	♒ Nov 28 04:39
♐ Jan 28 11:08	♓ Mar 29 09:32	♊ May 29 11:46	♍ Jul 30 10:23	♐ Sep 30 06:27	♓ Nov 30 07:38
♑ Jan 30 13:32	♈ Mar 31 10:40	♋ May 31 20:36	♎ Aug 1 22:55	♑ Oct 2 13:11	♈ Dec 2 10:25
♒ Feb 1 13:30	♉ Apr 2 13:03	♌ Jun 3 07:57	♏ Aug 4 09:51	♒ Oct 4 17:15	♉ Dec 4 13:36
♓ Feb 3 12:49	♊ Apr 4 18:24	♍ Jun 5 20:41	♐ Aug 6 17:45	♓ Oct 6 18:48	♊ Dec 6 18:00
♈ Feb 5 13:30	♋ Apr 7 03:42	♎ Jun 8 08:33	♑ Aug 8 21:55	♈ Oct 8 19:01	♋ Dec 9 00:32
♉ Feb 7 17:22	♌ Apr 9 15:57	♏ Jun 10 17:29	♒ Aug 10 22:52	♉ Oct 10 19:42	♌ Dec 11 09:50
♊ Feb 10 01:22	♍ Apr 12 04:40	♐ Jun 12 22:52	♓ Aug 12 22:08	♊ Oct 12 22:53	♍ Dec 13 21:38
♋ Feb 12 12:46	♎ Apr 14 15:31	♑ Jun 15 01:25	♈ Aug 14 21:48	♋ Oct 15 06:00	♎ Dec 16 10:11
♌ Feb 15 01:46	♏ Apr 16 23:42	♒ Jun 17 02:34	♉ Aug 16 23:55	♌ Oct 17 16:50	♏ Dec 18 21:10
♍ Feb 17 14:27	♐ Apr 19 05:40	♓ Jun 19 03:50	♊ Aug 19 05:46	♍ Oct 20 05:32	♐ Dec 21 05:01
♎ Feb 20 01:48	♑ Apr 21 10:09	♈ Jun 21 06:25	♋ Aug 21 15:25	♎ Oct 22 17:41	♑ Dec 23 09:37
♏ Feb 22 11:13	♒ Apr 23 13:38	♉ Jun 23 11:09	♌ Aug 24 03:30	♏ Oct 25 03:59	♒ Dec 25 12:00
♐ Feb 24 18:15	♓ Apr 25 16:25	♊ Jun 25 18:15	♍ Aug 26 16:22	♐ Oct 27 12:10	♓ Dec 27 13:37
♑ Feb 26 22:28	♈ Apr 27 18:57	♋ Jun 28 03:43	♎ Aug 29 04:46	♑ Oct 29 18:34	♈ Dec 29 15:46
					♉ Dec 31 19:24

Mercury

Jan 1 1♑	♌ Aug 6 23:55
♒ Jan 18 17:23	♍ Aug 22 01:29
♓ Feb 5 04:38	♎ Sep 7 18:05
R Feb 20 15♓	♏ Sep 28 19:49
D Mar 13 1♓	R Oct 17 12♏
♈ Apr 12 22:25	♎ Nov 1 22:16
♉ Apr 29 19:05	D Nov 6 27♎
♊ May 13 20:56	♏ Nov 11 17:09
♋ May 30 04:26	♐ Dec 3 17:55
R Jun 21 17♋	♑ Dec 22 22:30
D Jul 16 8♋	

Venus

Jan 1 5♒	D Jul 27 5♋
♓ Jan 20 13:49	♌ Sep 8 22:25
♈ Feb 14 02:56	♍ Oct 8 06:08
♉ Mar 10 08:07	♎ Nov 3 11:28
♊ Apr 5 20:57	♏ Nov 28 10:43
♋ May 5 17:50	♐ Dec 22 20:00
R Jun 14 21♋	

Mars

Jan 1 23♓
♈ Jan 11 04:50
♉ Feb 23 03:42
♊ Apr 7 04:14
♋ May 22 14:21
♌ Jul 8 03:57
♍ Aug 24 06:42
♎ Oct 10 06:00
♏ Nov 25 14:09

Jupiter

Jan 1 12♌
D Mar 30 3♌
♍ Sep 12 10:06
R Dec 30 14♍

Saturn

Jan 1 21♓
♈ Mar 19 13:52
R Jul 22 10♈
D Dec 6 3♈

Uranus

Jan 1 12♑
R Apr 21 16♑
D Sep 22 12♑

Neptune

Jan 1 13♋
D Mar 23 12♋
R Oct 20 17♋

Pluto

Jan 1 23♊
D Mar 7 22♊
R Sep 26 25♊

1909

Sun

♒ Jan 20 16:09	♈ Mar 21 06:13	♊ May 21 17:46	♌ Jul 23 13:03	♎ Sep 23 16:45	♐ Nov 22 22:19
♓ Feb 19 06:38	♉ Apr 20 17:58	♋ Jun 22 02:08	♍ Aug 23 19:45	♏ Oct 24 01:22	♑ Dec 22 11:18

Moon

Jan 1 2♉	♌ Mar 3 06:40	♏ May 4 08:04	♒ Jul 4 21:13	♉ Sep 3 17:25	♌ Nov 3 23:10
♊ Jan 3 00:52	♍ Mar 5 18:46	♐ May 6 18:15	♓ Jul 6 23:39	♊ Sep 5 19:53	♍ Nov 6 09:03
♋ Jan 5 08:23	♎ Mar 8 07:23	♑ May 9 02:25	♈ Jul 9 01:45	♋ Sep 8 01:33	♎ Nov 8 21:18
♌ Jan 7 18:00	♏ Mar 10 19:39	♒ May 11 08:24	♉ Jul 11 04:29	♌ Sep 10 10:10	♏ Nov 11 10:04
♍ Jan 10 05:33	♐ Mar 13 06:36	♓ May 13 12:14	♊ Jul 13 08:29	♍ Sep 12 20:54	♐ Nov 13 21:57
♎ Jan 12 18:10	♑ Mar 15 14:45	♈ May 15 14:13	♋ Jul 15 14:07	♎ Sep 15 08:59	♑ Nov 16 08:09
♏ Jan 15 06:00	♒ Mar 17 19:09	♉ May 17 15:23	♌ Jul 17 21:41	♏ Sep 17 21:48	♒ Nov 18 16:04
♐ Jan 17 15:00	♓ Mar 19 20:07	♊ May 19 17:13	♍ Jul 20 07:30	♐ Sep 20 10:10	♓ Nov 20 21:20
♑ Jan 19 20:09	♈ Mar 21 19:15	♋ May 21 21:14	♎ Jul 22 19:25	♑ Sep 22 20:13	♈ Nov 23 00:00
♒ Jan 21 21:59	♉ Mar 23 18:48	♌ May 24 04:34	♏ Jul 25 08:00	♒ Sep 25 02:21	♉ Nov 25 00:55
♓ Jan 23 22:08	♊ Mar 25 20:55	♍ May 26 15:13	♐ Jul 27 19:00	♓ Sep 27 04:31	♊ Nov 27 01:30
♈ Jan 25 22:35	♋ Mar 28 02:54	♎ May 29 03:38	♑ Jul 30 02:31	♈ Sep 29 04:06	♋ Nov 29 03:25
♉ Jan 28 01:02	♌ Mar 30 12:43	♏ May 31 15:37	♒ Aug 1 06:21	♉ Oct 1 03:14	♌ Dec 1 08:15
♊ Jan 30 06:22	♍ Apr 2 00:49	♐ Jun 3 01:30	♓ Aug 3 07:42	♊ Oct 3 04:03	♍ Dec 3 16:49
♋ Feb 1 14:31	♎ Apr 4 13:30	♑ Jun 5 08:53	♈ Aug 5 08:21	♋ Oct 5 08:09	♎ Dec 6 04:29
♌ Feb 4 00:49	♏ Apr 7 01:31	♒ Jun 7 14:02	♉ Aug 7 10:04	♌ Oct 7 15:57	♏ Dec 8 17:15
♍ Feb 6 12:35	♐ Apr 9 12:16	♓ Jun 9 17:38	♊ Aug 9 13:53	♍ Oct 10 02:40	♐ Dec 11 05:00
♎ Feb 9 01:09	♑ Apr 11 20:56	♈ Jun 11 20:20	♋ Aug 11 20:08	♎ Oct 12 15:00	♑ Dec 13 14:31
♏ Feb 11 13:29	♒ Apr 14 02:43	♉ Jun 13 22:49	♌ Aug 14 04:28	♏ Oct 15 03:45	♒ Dec 15 21:38
♐ Feb 13 23:46	♓ Apr 16 05:25	♊ Jun 16 01:52	♍ Aug 16 14:41	♐ Oct 17 16:02	♓ Dec 18 02:46
♑ Feb 16 06:26	♈ Apr 18 05:50	♋ Jun 18 06:26	♎ Aug 19 02:35	♑ Oct 20 02:37	♈ Dec 20 06:23
♒ Feb 18 09:06	♉ Apr 20 05:41	♌ Jun 20 13:30	♏ Aug 21 15:22	♒ Oct 22 10:11	♉ Dec 22 08:57
♓ Feb 20 09:00	♊ Apr 22 07:02	♍ Jun 22 23:29	♐ Aug 24 03:16	♓ Oct 24 14:09	♊ Dec 24 11:04
♈ Feb 22 08:07	♋ Apr 24 11:34	♎ Jun 25 11:35	♑ Aug 26 12:00	♈ Oct 26 15:00	♋ Dec 26 13:45
♉ Feb 24 08:43	♌ Apr 26 20:00	♏ Jun 27 23:51	♒ Aug 28 16:35	♉ Oct 28 14:27	♌ Dec 28 18:17
♊ Feb 26 12:31	♍ Apr 29 07:32	♐ Jun 30 10:03	♓ Aug 30 17:43	♊ Oct 30 14:25	♍ Dec 31 01:49
♋ Feb 28 20:07	♎ May 1 20:10	♑ Jul 2 17:04	♈ Sep 1 17:17	♋ Nov 1 16:55	

Mercury

Jan 1 14♑	♋ Jul 13 05:38
♒ Jan 10 08:59	♌ Jul 30 00:42
R Feb 2 29♒	♍ Aug 13 21:35
D Feb 24 13♒	♎ Sep 1 00:19
♓ Mar 17 11:31	R Sep 30 26♎
♈ Apr 6 01:27	D Oct 21 11♎
♉ Apr 21 10:01	♏ Nov 7 18:00
♊ May 5 22:07	♐ Nov 26 14:57
R Jun 2 27♊	♑ Dec 15 16:31
D Jun 26 19♊	

Venus

Jan 1 11♐	♌ Jul 4 16:32
♑ Jan 15 23:17	♍ Jul 29 06:43
♒ Feb 9 00:39	♎ Aug 23 00:34
♓ Mar 5 02:11	♏ Sep 17 00:19
♈ Mar 29 05:12	♐ Oct 12 09:24
♉ Apr 22 10:35	♑ Nov 7 12:08
♊ May 16 18:34	♒ Dec 5 13:00
♋ Jun 10 04:38	

Mars

Jan 1 23♏
♐ Jan 10 03:46
♑ Feb 24 02:02
♒ Apr 9 20:27
♓ May 25 22:46
♈ Jul 21 08:57
R Aug 23 6♈
♓ Sep 26 22:00
D Oct 24 25♓
♈ Nov 20 20:04

Jupiter

Jan 1 14♍
D May 1 4♍
♎ Oct 11 23:34

Saturn

Jan 1 3♈
R Aug 5 23♈
D Dec 19 16♈

Uranus

Jan 1 16♑
R Apr 25 21♑
D Sep 27 17♑

Neptune

Jan 1 15♋
D Mar 26 14♋
R Oct 23 19♋

Pluto

Jan 1 24♊
D Mar 8 23♊
R Sep 27 26♊

1910

Sun

♒ Jan 20 21:59	♈ Mar 21 12:02	♊ May 21 23:32	♌ Jul 23 18:46	♎ Sep 23 22:33	♐ Nov 23 04:10
♓ Feb 19 12:27	♉ Apr 20 23:45	♋ Jun 22 07:52	♍ Aug 24 01:30	♏ Oct 24 07:12	♑ Dec 22 17:11

Moon

Jan 1 11 ♍	♐ Mar 3 06:08	♓ May 3 22:50	♊ Jul 3 20:37	♍ Sep 2 22:55	♐ Nov 3 21:04
♎ Jan 2 12:37	♑ Mar 5 17:11	♈ May 6 01:23	♋ Jul 5 22:07	♎ Sep 5 07:22	♑ Nov 6 10:01
♏ Jan 5 01:17	♒ Mar 8 00:22	♉ May 8 01:31	♌ Jul 8 00:43	♏ Sep 7 18:27	♒ Nov 8 21:18
♐ Jan 7 13:20	♓ Mar 10 03:31	♊ May 10 01:03	♍ Jul 10 05:54	♐ Sep 10 07:21	♓ Nov 11 05:24
♑ Jan 9 22:39	♈ Mar 12 04:08	♋ May 12 01:50	♎ Jul 12 14:40	♑ Sep 12 19:37	♈ Nov 13 09:42
♒ Jan 12 04:52	♉ Mar 14 04:14	♌ May 14 05:31	♏ Jul 15 02:35	♒ Sep 15 04:52	♉ Nov 15 10:46
♓ Jan 14 08:50	♊ Mar 16 05:38	♍ May 16 12:57	♐ Jul 17 15:24	♓ Sep 17 10:11	♊ Nov 17 10:10
♈ Jan 16 11:45	♋ Mar 18 09:29	♎ May 18 23:44	♑ Jul 20 02:39	♈ Sep 19 12:29	♋ Nov 19 09:52
♉ Jan 18 14:37	♌ Mar 20 16:03	♏ May 21 12:26	♒ Jul 22 11:06	♉ Sep 21 13:29	♌ Nov 21 11:43
♊ Jan 20 17:57	♍ Mar 23 00:55	♐ May 24 01:16	♓ Jul 24 16:55	♊ Sep 23 14:47	♍ Nov 23 17:07
♋ Jan 22 22:02	♎ Mar 25 11:44	♑ May 26 12:55	♈ Jul 26 21:06	♋ Sep 25 17:37	♎ Nov 26 02:16
♌ Jan 25 03:23	♏ Mar 28 00:05	♒ May 28 22:31	♉ Jul 29 00:39	♌ Sep 27 22:26	♏ Nov 28 14:12
♍ Jan 27 10:51	♐ Mar 30 13:06	♓ May 31 05:30	♊ Jul 31 03:20	♍ Sep 30 05:21	♐ Dec 1 03:14
♎ Jan 29 21:04	♑ Apr 2 00:54	♈ Jun 2 09:37	♋ Aug 2 06:09	♎ Oct 2 14:28	♑ Dec 3 15:55
♏ Feb 1 09:31	♒ Apr 4 09:31	♉ Jun 4 11:18	♌ Aug 4 09:40	♏ Oct 5 01:44	♒ Dec 6 03:16
♐ Feb 3 22:04	♓ Apr 6 14:00	♊ Jun 6 11:39	♍ Aug 6 14:57	♐ Oct 7 14:36	♓ Dec 8 12:29
♑ Feb 6 08:02	♈ Apr 8 15:03	♋ Jun 8 12:16	♎ Aug 8 23:12	♑ Oct 10 03:24	♈ Dec 10 18:21
♒ Feb 8 14:13	♉ Apr 10 14:32	♌ Jun 10 14:51	♏ Aug 11 10:33	♒ Oct 12 13:50	♉ Dec 12 21:13
♓ Feb 10 17:12	♊ Apr 12 14:25	♍ Jun 12 20:51	♐ Aug 13 23:25	♓ Oct 14 20:21	♊ Dec 14 21:38
♈ Feb 12 18:40	♋ Apr 14 16:32	♎ Jun 15 06:41	♑ Aug 16 11:04	♈ Oct 16 23:06	♋ Dec 16 21:10
♉ Feb 14 20:18	♌ Apr 16 21:54	♏ Jun 17 19:07	♒ Aug 18 19:30	♉ Oct 18 23:25	♌ Dec 18 21:47
♊ Feb 16 23:18	♍ Apr 19 06:34	♐ Jun 20 07:55	♓ Aug 21 00:40	♊ Oct 20 23:17	♍ Dec 21 01:24
♋ Feb 19 04:03	♎ Apr 21 17:43	♑ Jun 22 19:13	♈ Aug 23 03:41	♋ Oct 23 00:25	♎ Dec 23 09:09
♌ Feb 21 10:28	♏ Apr 24 06:18	♒ Jun 25 04:13	♉ Aug 25 06:01	♌ Oct 25 04:07	♏ Dec 25 20:35
♍ Feb 23 18:40	♐ Apr 26 19:12	♓ Jun 27 10:57	♊ Aug 27 08:42	♍ Oct 27 10:53	♐ Dec 28 09:41
♎ Feb 26 04:57	♑ Apr 29 07:10	♈ Jun 29 15:43	♋ Aug 29 12:13	♎ Oct 29 20:29	♑ Dec 30 22:12
♏ Feb 28 17:15	♒ May 1 16:46	♉ Jul 1 18:46	♌ Aug 31 16:48	♏ Nov 1 08:11	

Mercury

Jan 1 25 ♑	♊ Jun 12 02:27
♒ Jan 3 21:13	♋ Jul 7 03:19
R Jan 17 13 ♒	♌ Jul 21 12:39
♑ Jan 31 02:15	♍ Aug 6 04:45
D Feb 7 26 ♑	♎ Aug 27 06:42
♒ Feb 15 13:06	R Sep 13 11 ♎
♓ Mar 11 21:23	♍ Sep 28 13:21
♈ Mar 29 06:48	D Oct 5 25 ♍
♉ Apr 13 00:32	♎ Oct 12 04:58
♊ Apr 30 15:58	♏ Oct 31 18:08
R May 14 7 ♊	♐ Nov 19 08:13
♉ Jun 1 23:57	♑ Dec 8 18:27
D Jun 7 28 ♉	

Venus

Jan 1 22 ♒	♊ Jun 29 19:31
♓ Jan 15 20:06	♋ Jul 25 07:02
R Jan 22 0 ♓	♌ Aug 19 05:58
♒ Jan 29 09:57	♍ Sep 12 18:30
D Mar 5 15 ♒	♎ Oct 6 23:13
♓ Apr 5 09:47	♏ Oct 30 22:53
♈ May 7 02:27	♐ Nov 23 20:09
♉ Jun 3 14:59	♑ Dec 17 16:36

Mars

Jan 1 17 ♈
♉ Jan 23 01:48
♊ Mar 14 07:17
♋ May 1 20:57
♌ Jun 19 03:37
♍ Aug 6 01:02
♎ Sep 22 00:19
♏ Nov 6 13:37
♐ Dec 20 12:16

Jupiter

Jan 1 13 ♎
R Jan 29 14 ♎
D Jun 1 4 ♎
♏ Nov 11 16:57

Saturn

Jan 1 16 ♈
♉ May 17 06:45
R Aug 19 6 ♉
♈ Dec 15 01:07

Uranus

Jan 1 20 ♑
R Apr 30 25 ♑
D Oct 1 21 ♑

Neptune

Jan 1 18 ♋
D Mar 28 16 ♋
R Oct 25 21 ♋

Pluto

Jan 1 25 ♊
D Mar 10 24 ♊
R Sep 28 27 ♊

1911

Sun

♒ Jan 21 03:50	♈ Mar 21 17:54	♊ May 22 05:19	♌ Jul 24 00:32	♎ Sep 24 04:24	♐ Nov 23 10:00
♓ Feb 19 18:20	♉ Apr 21 05:36	♋ Jun 22 13:37	♍ Aug 24 07:17	♏ Oct 24 13:03	♑ Dec 22 22:56

Moon

Jan 1 13 ♑	♈ Mar 2 12:48	♋ May 2 11:06	♎ Jul 2 13:57	♑ Sep 2 14:36	♈ Nov 3 13:49
♒ Jan 2 09:01	♉ Mar 4 16:21	♌ May 4 13:08	♏ Jul 4 23:25	♒ Sep 5 02:35	♉ Nov 5 17:54
♓ Jan 4 17:50	♊ Mar 6 19:22	♍ May 6 17:49	♐ Jul 7 11:37	♓ Sep 7 12:17	♊ Nov 7 19:28
♈ Jan 7 00:31	♋ Mar 8 22:23	♎ May 9 01:26	♑ Jul 10 00:30	♈ Sep 9 19:30	♋ Nov 9 20:11
♉ Jan 9 05:00	♌ Mar 11 01:45	♏ May 11 11:35	♒ Jul 12 12:32	♉ Sep 12 00:48	♌ Nov 11 21:35
♊ Jan 11 07:15	♍ Mar 13 06:03	♐ May 13 23:32	♓ Jul 14 23:02	♊ Sep 14 04:46	♍ Nov 14 01:05
♋ Jan 13 08:02	♎ Mar 15 12:19	♑ May 16 12:20	♈ Jul 17 07:34	♋ Sep 16 07:47	♎ Nov 16 07:03
♌ Jan 15 08:49	♏ Mar 17 21:20	♒ May 19 00:39	♉ Jul 19 13:32	♌ Sep 18 10:16	♏ Nov 18 15:26
♍ Jan 17 11:30	♐ Mar 20 09:03	♓ May 21 10:52	♊ Jul 21 16:40	♍ Sep 20 13:05	♐ Nov 21 01:53
♎ Jan 19 17:46	♑ Mar 22 21:52	♈ May 23 17:39	♋ Jul 23 17:29	♎ Sep 22 17:20	♑ Nov 23 13:53
♏ Jan 22 04:05	♒ Mar 25 09:12	♉ May 25 20:46	♌ Jul 25 17:23	♏ Sep 25 00:16	♒ Nov 26 02:38
♐ Jan 24 16:53	♓ Mar 27 17:13	♊ May 27 21:12	♍ Jul 27 18:25	♐ Sep 27 10:21	♓ Nov 28 14:31
♑ Jan 27 05:00	♈ Mar 29 21:50	♋ May 29 20:37	♎ Jul 29 22:30	♑ Sep 29 22:37	♈ Nov 30 23:35
♒ Jan 29 15:57	♉ Apr 1 00:14	♌ May 31 21:01	♏ Aug 1 06:44	♒ Oct 2 10:55	♉ Dec 3 04:42
♓ Jan 31 23:55	♊ Apr 3 01:49	♍ Jun 3 00:13	♐ Aug 3 18:20	♓ Oct 4 20:59	♊ Dec 5 06:18
♈ Feb 3 05:57	♋ Apr 5 03:51	♎ Jun 5 07:06	♑ Aug 6 07:08	♈ Oct 7 03:54	♋ Dec 7 05:55
♉ Feb 5 10:35	♌ Apr 7 07:13	♏ Jun 7 17:19	♒ Aug 8 19:02	♉ Oct 9 08:12	♌ Dec 9 05:37
♊ Feb 7 14:01	♍ Apr 9 12:22	♐ Jun 10 05:37	♓ Aug 11 04:59	♊ Oct 11 10:54	♍ Dec 11 07:26
♋ Feb 9 16:28	♎ Apr 11 19:34	♑ Jun 12 18:26	♈ Aug 13 13:02	♋ Oct 13 13:10	♎ Dec 13 12:35
♌ Feb 11 18:32	♏ Apr 14 05:06	♒ Jun 15 06:43	♉ Aug 15 19:10	♌ Oct 15 15:53	♏ Dec 15 21:07
♍ Feb 13 21:39	♐ Apr 16 16:45	♓ Jun 17 17:25	♊ Aug 17 23:22	♍ Oct 17 19:40	♐ Dec 18 08:08
♎ Feb 16 03:21	♑ Apr 19 05:33	♈ Jun 20 01:30	♋ Aug 20 01:42	♎ Oct 20 01:05	♑ Dec 20 20:23
♏ Feb 18 12:39	♒ Apr 21 17:33	♉ Jun 22 06:14	♌ Aug 22 02:53	♏ Oct 22 08:36	♒ Dec 23 09:04
♐ Feb 21 00:52	♓ Apr 24 02:39	♊ Jun 24 07:45	♍ Aug 24 04:26	♐ Oct 24 18:34	♓ Dec 25 21:17
♑ Feb 23 13:36	♈ Apr 26 08:01	♋ Jun 26 07:20	♎ Aug 26 08:05	♑ Oct 27 06:36	♈ Dec 28 07:35
♒ Feb 26 00:17	♉ Apr 28 10:11	♌ Jun 28 06:53	♏ Aug 28 15:16	♒ Oct 29 19:12	♉ Dec 30 14:30
♓ Feb 28 07:50	♊ Apr 30 10:38	♍ Jun 30 08:34	♐ Aug 31 01:59	♓ Nov 1 06:10	

Mercury

Jan 1 27 ♑	♌ Jul 13 03:14
R Jan 1 26 ♑	♍ Jul 30 13:43
D Jan 21 11 ♑	R Aug 27 23 ♍
♒ Feb 13 03:58	D Sep 18 10 ♍
♓ Mar 4 21:05	♎ Oct 6 20:37
♈ Mar 21 03:31	♏ Oct 24 06:37
♉ Apr 5 08:59	♐ Nov 12 04:55
R Apr 24 17 ♉	♑ Dec 3 01:45
D May 18 8 ♉	R Dec 16 10 ♑
♊ Jun 13 01:15	♐ Dec 27 16:33
♋ Jun 28 23:59	

Venus

Jan 1 17 ♑	♌ Jun 8 18:54
♒ Jan 10 13:27	♍ Jul 7 19:13
♓ Feb 3 12:00	R Aug 25 29 ♍
♈ Feb 27 14:27	D Oct 6 13 ♍
♉ Mar 23 23:35	♎ Nov 9 00:54
♊ Apr 17 18:54	♏ Dec 9 09:23
♋ May 13 05:44	

Mars

Jan 1 8 ♐	
♑ Jan 31 21:25	
♒ Mar 14 00:01	
♓ Apr 23 08:10	
♈ Jun 2 21:34	
♉ Jul 15 15:55	
♊ Sep 5 14:49	
R Oct 18 10 ♊	
♉ Nov 30 04:29	
D Dec 29 24 ♉	

Jupiter

Jan 1 9 ♏
R Mar 1 14 ♏
D Jul 2 4 ♏
♐ Dec 10 11:15

Saturn

Jan 1 29 ♈
D Jan 2 29 ♈
♉ Jan 20 05:14
R Sep 2 20 ♉

Uranus

Jan 1 24 ♑
R May 4 29 ♑
D Oct 6 25 ♑

Neptune

Jan 1 20 ♋
D Mar 31 18 ♋
R Oct 28 23 ♋

Pluto

Jan 1 26 ♊
D Mar 11 25 ♊
R Sep 30 29 ♊

1912

Sun

♒ Jan 21 09:31	♈ Mar 20 23:30	♊ May 21 10:56	♌ Jul 23 06:14	♎ Sep 23 10:10	♐ Nov 22 15:48
♓ Feb 19 23:58	♉ Apr 20 11:12	♋ Jun 21 19:16	♍ Aug 23 13:03	♏ Oct 23 18:51	♑ Dec 22 04:46

Moon

Jan 1 19♉	♌ Feb 29 13:42	♏ Apr 30 14:46	♒ Jul 1 10:56	♉ Sep 1 09:19	♌ Nov 1 11:45
♊ Jan 1 17:28	♍ Mar 2 14:13	♐ May 2 22:29	♓ Jul 3 23:38	♊ Sep 3 16:44	♍ Nov 3 14:34
♋ Jan 3 17:23	♎ Mar 4 15:52	♑ May 5 08:40	♈ Jul 6 11:30	♋ Sep 5 21:04	♎ Nov 5 17:31
♌ Jan 5 16:16	♏ Mar 6 20:23	♒ May 7 20:49	♉ Jul 8 20:33	♌ Sep 7 22:42	♏ Nov 7 21:17
♍ Jan 7 16:23	♐ Mar 9 04:43	♓ May 10 09:06	♊ Jul 11 01:33	♍ Sep 9 22:51	♐ Nov 10 02:47
♎ Jan 9 19:40	♑ Mar 11 16:10	♈ May 12 19:19	♋ Jul 13 02:54	♎ Sep 11 23:17	♑ Nov 12 10:47
♏ Jan 12 03:06	♒ Mar 14 04:49	♉ May 15 02:02	♌ Jul 15 02:15	♏ Sep 14 01:53	♒ Nov 14 21:44
♐ Jan 14 13:56	♓ Mar 16 16:27	♊ May 17 05:32	♍ Jul 17 01:49	♐ Sep 16 07:57	♓ Nov 17 10:23
♑ Jan 17 02:28	♈ Mar 19 01:58	♋ May 19 07:04	♎ Jul 19 03:36	♑ Sep 18 17:41	♈ Nov 19 22:15
♒ Jan 19 15:06	♉ Mar 21 09:16	♌ May 21 08:17	♏ Jul 21 08:52	♒ Sep 21 05:51	♉ Nov 22 07:11
♓ Jan 22 03:04	♊ Mar 23 14:37	♍ May 23 10:39	♐ Jul 23 17:34	♓ Sep 23 18:23	♊ Nov 24 12:40
♈ Jan 24 13:40	♋ Mar 25 18:21	♎ May 25 14:59	♑ Jul 26 04:40	♈ Sep 26 05:43	♋ Nov 26 15:36
♉ Jan 26 21:50	♌ Mar 27 20:54	♏ May 27 21:25	♒ Jul 28 17:00	♉ Sep 28 15:03	♌ Nov 28 17:33
♊ Jan 29 02:40	♍ Mar 29 22:57	♐ May 30 05:54	♓ Jul 31 05:38	♊ Sep 30 22:10	♍ Nov 30 19:54
♋ Jan 31 04:13	♎ Apr 1 01:38	♑ Jun 1 16:15	♈ Aug 2 17:38	♋ Oct 3 03:08	♎ Dec 2 23:25
♌ Feb 2 03:45	♏ Apr 3 06:15	♒ Jun 4 04:17	♉ Aug 5 03:36	♌ Oct 5 06:10	♏ Dec 5 04:21
♍ Feb 4 03:22	♐ Apr 5 13:47	♓ Jun 6 16:53	♊ Aug 7 10:08	♍ Oct 7 07:53	♐ Dec 7 10:48
♎ Feb 6 05:12	♑ Apr 8 00:22	♈ Jun 9 04:02	♋ Aug 9 12:55	♎ Oct 9 09:23	♑ Dec 9 19:08
♏ Feb 8 10:52	♒ Apr 10 12:46	♉ Jun 11 11:45	♌ Aug 11 12:59	♏ Oct 11 12:03	♒ Dec 12 05:50
♐ Feb 10 20:35	♓ Apr 13 00:41	♊ Jun 13 15:31	♍ Aug 13 12:13	♐ Oct 13 17:17	♓ Dec 14 18:24
♑ Feb 13 08:51	♈ Apr 15 10:13	♋ Jun 15 16:24	♎ Aug 15 12:47	♑ Oct 16 01:55	♈ Dec 17 06:59
♒ Feb 15 21:32	♉ Apr 17 16:50	♌ Jun 17 16:15	♏ Aug 17 16:28	♒ Oct 18 13:30	♉ Dec 19 18:00
♓ Feb 18 09:12	♊ Apr 19 21:01	♍ Jun 19 17:09	♐ Aug 19 23:58	♓ Oct 21 02:07	♊ Dec 21 22:50
♈ Feb 20 19:15	♋ Apr 21 23:53	♎ Jun 21 20:32	♑ Aug 22 10:42	♈ Oct 23 13:29	♋ Dec 24 01:10
♉ Feb 23 03:24	♌ Apr 24 02:21	♏ Jun 24 02:56	♒ Aug 24 23:06	♉ Oct 25 22:13	♌ Dec 26 01:43
♊ Feb 25 09:14	♍ Apr 26 05:16	♐ Jun 26 11:57	♓ Aug 27 11:38	♊ Oct 28 04:22	♍ Dec 28 02:27
♋ Feb 27 12:28	♎ Apr 28 09:14	♑ Jun 28 22:49	♈ Aug 29 23:19	♋ Oct 30 08:35	♎ Dec 30 04:54

Mercury

Jan 1 25♐	♌ Jul 4 08:58
D Jan 5 24♐	♍ Jul 26 08:20
♑ Jan 15 07:09	R Aug 8 6♍
♒ Feb 7 02:24	♌ Aug 21 03:02
♓ Feb 25 06:29	D Sep 1 23♌
♈ Mar 12 01:42	♍ Sep 10 17:19
R Apr 5 29♈	♎ Sep 28 07:28
D Apr 29 18♈	♏ Oct 15 18:52
♉ May 16 19:37	♐ Nov 4 14:51
♊ Jun 5 05:02	R Nov 29 24♐
♋ Jun 19 08:58	D Dec 18 8♐

Venus

Jan 1 25♏	♋ Jun 25 00:13
♐ Jan 4 18:38	♌ Jul 19 09:45
♑ Jan 29 22:44	♍ Aug 12 17:43
♒ Feb 23 15:29	♎ Sep 6 00:53
♓ Mar 19 03:48	♏ Sep 30 08:27
♈ Apr 12 14:49	♐ Oct 24 17:24
♉ May 7 01:54	♑ Nov 18 05:02
♊ May 31 13:19	♒ Dec 12 22:23

Mars

Jan 1 24♉
♊ Jan 30 21:02
♋ Apr 5 11:27
♌ May 28 08:17
♍ Jul 17 02:44
♎ Sep 2 17:10
♏ Oct 18 02:42
♐ Nov 30 07:49

Jupiter

Jan 1 4♐
R Apr 1 15♐
D Aug 2 5♐

Saturn

Jan 1 13♉
D Jan 15 13♉
♊ Jul 7 05:24
R Sep 16 4♊
♉ Nov 30 19:34

Uranus

Jan 1 28♑
♒ Jan 30 22:58
R May 8 3♒
♑ Sep 4 15:06
D Oct 9 29♑
♒ Nov 12 10:00

Neptune

Jan 1 22♋
D Apr 1 20♋
R Oct 29 26♋

Pluto

Jan 1 27♊
D Mar 11 26♊
♋ Sep 10 14:39
R Sep 30 0♋
♊ Oct 20 10:11

1913

Sun

♒ Jan 20 15:21	♈ Mar 21 05:18	♊ May 21 16:50	♌ Jul 23 12:04
♓ Feb 19 05:45	♉ Apr 20 17:02	♋ Jun 22 01:10	♍ Aug 23 18:48

♎ Sep 23 15:53	♐ Nov 22 21:35
♏ Oct 24 00:36	♑ Dec 22 10:34

Moon

Jan 1 24♎	♑ Mar 1 13:52	♈ May 2 16:37	♋ Jul 3 09:28
♏ Jan 1 09:48	♒ Mar 4 01:21	♉ May 5 03:34	♌ Jul 5 11:38
♐ Jan 3 17:00	♓ Mar 6 14:09	♊ May 7 11:49	♍ Jul 7 13:00
♑ Jan 6 02:09	♈ Mar 9 02:56	♋ May 9 17:41	♎ Jul 9 14:59
♒ Jan 8 13:06	♉ Mar 11 14:35	♌ May 11 21:57	♏ Jul 11 18:25
♓ Jan 11 01:36	♊ Mar 13 23:59	♍ May 14 01:08	♐ Jul 13 23:37
♈ Jan 13 14:35	♋ Mar 16 06:20	♎ May 16 03:44	♑ Jul 16 06:39
♉ Jan 16 01:46	♌ Mar 18 09:24	♏ May 18 06:14	♒ Jul 18 15:47
♊ Jan 18 09:05	♍ Mar 20 10:07	♐ May 20 09:38	♓ Jul 21 03:10
♋ Jan 20 12:14	♎ Mar 22 09:53	♑ May 22 15:12	♈ Jul 23 16:06
♌ Jan 22 12:24	♏ Mar 24 10:35	♒ May 24 23:59	♉ Jul 26 04:29
♍ Jan 24 11:46	♐ Mar 26 13:58	♓ May 27 11:46	♊ Jul 28 13:56
♎ Jan 26 12:24	♑ Mar 28 21:07	♈ May 30 00:35	♋ Jul 30 19:23
♏ Jan 28 15:48	♒ Mar 31 07:52	♉ Jun 1 11:44	♌ Aug 1 21:23
♐ Jan 30 22:30	♓ Apr 2 20:38	♊ Jun 3 19:42	♍ Aug 3 21:43
♑ Feb 2 07:57	♈ Apr 5 09:21	♋ Jun 6 00:40	♎ Aug 5 22:11
♒ Feb 4 19:25	♉ Apr 7 20:31	♌ Jun 8 03:50	♏ Aug 8 00:22
♓ Feb 7 08:01	♊ Apr 10 05:30	♍ Jun 10 06:30	♐ Aug 10 05:02
♈ Feb 9 20:58	♋ Apr 12 12:08	♎ Jun 12 09:26	♑ Aug 12 12:23
♉ Feb 12 08:45	♌ Apr 14 16:30	♏ Jun 14 13:00	♒ Aug 14 22:08
♊ Feb 14 17:37	♍ Apr 16 18:51	♐ Jun 16 17:30	♓ Aug 17 09:50
♋ Feb 16 22:28	♎ Apr 18 20:01	♑ Jun 18 23:40	♈ Aug 19 22:47
♌ Feb 18 23:45	♏ Apr 20 21:14	♒ Jun 21 08:19	♉ Aug 22 11:30
♍ Feb 20 23:07	♐ Apr 23 00:01	♓ Jun 23 19:45	♊ Aug 24 22:02
♎ Feb 22 22:36	♑ Apr 25 05:55	♈ Jun 26 08:37	♋ Aug 27 04:53
♏ Feb 25 00:09	♒ Apr 27 15:31	♉ Jun 28 20:21	♌ Aug 29 07:54
♐ Feb 27 05:10	♓ Apr 30 03:52	♊ Jul 1 04:47	♍ Aug 31 08:15

♎ Sep 2 07:46	♑ Nov 2 10:07	♓ Dec 2 02:41
♏ Sep 4 08:20	♒ Nov 4 17:42	♈ Dec 4 13:00
♐ Sep 6 11:31	♓ Nov 7 05:00	♉ Dec 7 01:44
♑ Sep 8 18:06	♈ Nov 9 18:00	♊ Dec 9 14:11
♒ Sep 11 03:54	♉ Nov 12 06:16	♋ Dec 12 00:07
♓ Sep 13 15:57	♊ Nov 14 16:23	♌ Dec 14 07:10
♈ Sep 16 04:54	♋ Nov 17 00:17	♍ Dec 16 12:07
♉ Sep 18 17:33	♌ Nov 19 06:17	♎ Dec 18 16:00
♊ Sep 21 04:33	♍ Nov 21 10:39	♏ Dec 20 19:19
♋ Sep 23 12:44	♎ Nov 23 13:30	♐ Dec 22 22:21
♌ Sep 25 17:25	♏ Nov 25 15:12	♑ Dec 25 01:28
♍ Sep 27 19:01	♐ Nov 27 16:53	♒ Dec 27 05:35
♎ Sep 29 18:45	♑ Nov 29 20:11	♓ Dec 29 12:00
♏ Oct 1 18:29	♒ Dec 2 02:41	♈ Dec 31 21:37
♐ Oct 3 20:07		
♑ Oct 6 01:09		
♒ Oct 8 08:06		
♓ Oct 10 22:06		
♈ Oct 13 11:08		
♉ Oct 15 23:30		
♊ Oct 18 10:11		
♋ Oct 20 18:45		
♌ Oct 23 00:45		
♍ Oct 25 04:06		
♎ Oct 27 05:16		
♏ Oct 29 05:29		
♐ Oct 31 06:28		

Mercury

Jan 1 18♐	♌ Jun 28 05:49
♑ Jan 10 05:12	R Jul 21 19♌
♒ Jan 30 01:49	D Aug 14 6♌
♓ Feb 16 10:43	♍ Sep 4 10:56
♈ Mar 4 22:25	♎ Sep 20 10:03
R Mar 18 12♈	♏ Oct 8 14:52
♓ Apr 7 14:28	♐ Oct 30 18:20
D Apr 10 28♓	R Nov 12 9♐
♈ Apr 14 01:21	♏ Nov 23 12:26
♉ May 12 06:14	D Dec 2 21♏
♊ May 28 00:27	♐ Dec 13 08:56
♋ Jun 10 21:41	

Venus

Jan 1 22♒	♊ Jul 8 09:18
♓ Jan 7 05:29	♋ Aug 5 23:32
♈ Feb 2 23:21	♌ Sep 1 09:20
♉ Mar 6 16:59	♍ Sep 26 16:06
R Apr 3 12♉	♎ Oct 21 06:02
♈ May 2 05:20	♏ Nov 14 09:54
D May 16 26♈	♐ Dec 8 08:37
♉ May 31 09:50	

Mars

Jan 1 22♐	♉ Jun 17 00:38
♑ Jan 10 13:48	♊ Jul 29 10:25
♒ Feb 19 08:06	♋ Sep 15 17:10
♓ Mar 30 05:56	R Nov 26 24♋
♈ May 8 02:58	

Jupiter

Jan 1 29♐	
♑ Jan 2 19:02	
R May 5 17♑	
D Sep 4 8♑	

Saturn

Jan 1 27♉
D Jan 28 27♉
♊ Mar 26 12:19
R Sep 30 18♊

Uranus

Jan 1 2♒
R May 12 7♒
D Oct 13 3♒

Neptune

Jan 1 25♋
D Apr 4 23♋
R Nov 1 28♋

Pluto

Jan 1 28♊
D Mar 12 28♊
♋ Jul 9 21:29
R Oct 1 1♋
♊ Dec 28 04:20

338

1914

Sun

♒ Jan 20 21:12	♈ Mar 21 11:10	♊ May 21 22:36	♌ Jul 23 17:46	♎ Sep 23 21:37	♐ Nov 23 03:22
♓ Feb 19 11:37	♉ Apr 20 22:52	♋ Jun 22 06:54	♍ Aug 24 00:30	♏ Oct 24 06:20	♑ Dec 22 16:24

Moon

Jan 1 1♓	♊ Mar 4 02:14	♍ May 4 14:01	♐ Jul 4 10:25	♓ Sep 3 16:26	♊ Nov 4 16:43
♈ Jan 3 09:57	♋ Mar 6 11:33	♎ May 6 16:12	♑ Jul 6 12:52	♈ Sep 6 02:59	♋ Nov 7 04:31
♉ Jan 5 22:43	♌ Mar 8 17:02	♏ May 8 16:19	♒ Jul 8 17:10	♉ Sep 8 15:14	♌ Nov 9 14:36
♊ Jan 8 09:13	♍ Mar 10 19:02	♐ May 10 16:04	♓ Jul 11 00:31	♊ Sep 11 03:52	♍ Nov 11 21:41
♋ Jan 10 16:11	♎ Mar 12 18:57	♑ May 12 17:30	♈ Jul 13 11:14	♋ Sep 13 14:56	♎ Nov 14 01:09
♌ Jan 12 20:12	♏ Mar 14 18:39	♒ May 14 22:28	♉ Jul 15 23:47	♌ Sep 15 22:40	♏ Nov 16 01:35
♍ Jan 14 22:38	♐ Mar 16 19:59	♓ May 17 07:38	♊ Jul 18 11:45	♍ Sep 18 02:40	♐ Nov 18 00:42
♎ Jan 17 00:52	♑ Mar 19 00:22	♈ May 19 19:53	♋ Jul 20 21:12	♎ Sep 20 03:51	♑ Nov 20 00:42
♏ Jan 19 03:44	♒ Mar 21 08:15	♉ May 22 08:51	♌ Jul 23 03:42	♏ Sep 22 03:51	♒ Nov 22 03:42
♐ Jan 21 07:38	♓ Mar 23 19:01	♊ May 24 20:36	♍ Jul 25 07:59	♐ Sep 24 04:34	♓ Nov 24 10:52
♑ Jan 23 12:58	♈ Mar 26 07:29	♋ May 27 06:27	♎ Jul 27 11:05	♑ Sep 26 07:33	♈ Nov 26 21:43
♒ Jan 25 20:12	♉ Mar 28 20:25	♌ May 29 14:20	♏ Jul 29 13:44	♒ Sep 28 13:35	♉ Nov 29 10:21
♓ Jan 28 05:53	♊ Mar 31 08:40	♍ May 31 20:12	♐ Jul 31 16:34	♓ Sep 30 22:32	♊ Dec 1 22:52
♈ Jan 30 17:56	♋ Apr 2 18:58	♎ Jun 2 23:50	♑ Aug 2 20:14	♈ Oct 3 09:37	♋ Dec 4 10:17
♉ Feb 2 06:53	♌ Apr 5 02:05	♏ Jun 5 01:29	♒ Aug 5 01:26	♉ Oct 5 21:58	♌ Dec 6 20:13
♊ Feb 4 18:19	♍ Apr 7 05:36	♐ Jun 7 02:12	♓ Aug 7 09:02	♊ Oct 8 10:39	♍ Dec 9 04:03
♋ Feb 7 02:15	♎ Apr 9 06:10	♑ Jun 9 03:40	♈ Aug 9 19:24	♋ Oct 10 22:25	♎ Dec 11 09:07
♌ Feb 9 06:25	♏ Apr 11 05:25	♒ Jun 11 07:46	♉ Aug 12 07:45	♌ Oct 13 07:35	♏ Dec 13 11:21
♍ Feb 11 07:58	♐ Apr 13 05:21	♓ Jun 13 15:44	♊ Aug 14 20:06	♍ Oct 15 13:02	♐ Dec 15 11:38
♎ Feb 13 08:37	♑ Apr 15 07:57	♈ Jun 16 03:10	♋ Aug 17 06:10	♎ Oct 17 14:49	♑ Dec 17 11:45
♏ Feb 15 09:54	♒ Apr 17 14:31	♉ Jun 18 16:00	♌ Aug 19 12:51	♏ Oct 19 14:20	♒ Dec 19 13:47
♐ Feb 17 13:03	♓ Apr 20 00:51	♊ Jun 21 03:44	♍ Aug 21 16:30	♐ Oct 21 13:39	♓ Dec 21 19:24
♑ Feb 19 18:37	♈ Apr 22 13:29	♋ Jun 23 13:07	♎ Aug 23 18:18	♑ Oct 23 14:54	♈ Dec 24 05:01
♒ Feb 22 02:39	♉ Apr 25 02:27	♌ Jun 25 20:14	♏ Aug 25 19:43	♒ Oct 25 19:38	♉ Dec 26 17:17
♓ Feb 24 13:00	♊ Apr 27 14:28	♍ Jun 28 01:34	♐ Aug 27 21:59	♓ Oct 28 04:12	♊ Dec 29 05:52
♈ Feb 27 01:07	♋ Apr 30 00:49	♎ Jun 30 05:32	♑ Aug 30 01:56	♈ Oct 30 15:34	♋ Dec 31 17:00
♉ Mar 1 14:07	♌ May 2 08:53	♏ Jul 2 08:18	♒ Sep 1 08:02	♉ Nov 2 04:07	

Mercury

Jan 1 25♐	R Jul 3 29♋
♑ Jan 3 19:20	D Jul 27 19♋
♒ Jan 22 15:49	♌ Aug 11 06:15
♓ Feb 8 19:04	♍ Aug 27 10:45
R Mar 1 24♓	♎ Sep 12 15:45
D Mar 24 11♓	♏ Oct 2 05:51
♈ Apr 16 15:55	R Oct 27 22♏
♉ May 5 00:47	D Nov 16 6♏
♊ May 19 10:02	♐ Dec 8 04:48
♋ Jun 3 05:37	♑ Dec 27 17:41

Venus

Jan 1 29♐	♍ Jul 15 14:11
♑ Jan 1 05:25	♎ Aug 10 18:14
♒ Jan 25 02:11	♏ Sep 7 11:01
♓ Feb 18 00:04	♐ Oct 10 01:54
♈ Mar 14 00:29	R Nov 7 12♐
♉ Apr 7 04:49	♏ Dec 5 23:14
♊ May 1 14:10	D Dec 18 26♏
♋ May 26 05:31	♐ Dec 30 23:23
♌ Jun 20 04:24	

Mars

Jan 1 16♋
D Feb 12 5♋
♌ May 1 20:15
♍ Jun 26 04:34
♎ Aug 14 14:11
♏ Sep 29 10:37
♐ Nov 11 10:51
♑ Dec 22 03:49

Jupiter

Jan 1 25♑
♒ Jan 21 14:27
R Jun 11 22♒
D Oct 9 12♒

Saturn

Jan 1 12♊
D Feb 11 11♊
♋ Aug 24 17:16
R Oct 15 2♋
♊ Dec 7 06:49

Uranus

Jan 1 6♒
R May 17 11♒
D Oct 18 7♒

Neptune

Jan 1 27♋
D Apr 6 25♋
♌ Sep 23 20:53
R Nov 3 0♌
♋ Dec 14 20:06

Pluto

Jan 1 29♊
D Mar 14 29♊
♋ May 26 19:52
R Oct 3 2♋

1915

Sun

♒ Jan 21 03:01	♈ Mar 21 16:52	♊ May 22 04:11	♌ Jul 23 23:27	♎ Sep 24 03:25	♐ Nov 23 09:14
♓ Feb 19 17:25	♉ Apr 21 04:30	♋ Jun 22 12:30	♍ Aug 24 06:16	♏ Oct 24 12:10	♑ Dec 22 22:15

Moon

Jan 1 3♋	♎ Mar 3 04:13	♑ May 3 00:39	♈ Jul 3 08:22	♋ Sep 3 11:11	♎ Nov 4 07:28
♌ Jan 3 02:12	♏ Mar 5 06:03	♒ May 5 03:22	♉ Jul 5 19:00	♌ Sep 5 22:24	♏ Nov 6 09:37
♍ Jan 5 09:27	♐ Mar 7 07:57	♓ May 7 09:40	♊ Jul 8 07:30	♍ Sep 8 06:42	♐ Nov 8 09:35
♎ Jan 7 14:52	♑ Mar 9 10:57	♈ May 9 19:08	♋ Jul 10 19:55	♎ Sep 10 11:59	♑ Nov 10 09:32
♏ Jan 9 18:24	♒ Mar 11 15:40	♉ May 12 06:40	♌ Jul 13 07:06	♏ Sep 12 15:14	♒ Nov 12 11:21
♐ Jan 11 20:23	♓ Mar 13 22:15	♊ May 14 19:07	♍ Jul 15 16:22	♐ Sep 14 17:40	♓ Nov 14 16:04
♑ Jan 13 21:50	♈ Mar 16 06:53	♋ May 17 07:47	♎ Jul 17 23:20	♑ Sep 16 20:19	♈ Nov 16 23:38
♒ Jan 16 00:16	♉ Mar 18 17:37	♌ May 19 19:30	♏ Jul 20 03:49	♒ Sep 18 23:49	♉ Nov 19 09:28
♓ Jan 18 05:14	♊ Mar 21 05:57	♍ May 22 04:46	♐ Jul 22 06:05	♓ Sep 21 04:30	♊ Nov 21 20:56
♈ Jan 20 13:40	♋ Mar 23 18:21	♎ May 24 10:15	♑ Jul 24 07:03	♈ Sep 23 10:54	♋ Nov 24 09:32
♉ Jan 23 01:11	♌ Mar 26 04:36	♏ May 26 12:00	♒ Jul 26 08:10	♉ Sep 25 19:33	♌ Nov 26 22:22
♊ Jan 25 13:47	♍ Mar 28 11:12	♐ May 28 11:25	♓ Jul 28 11:02	♊ Sep 28 06:42	♍ Nov 29 09:31
♋ Jan 28 01:07	♎ Mar 30 14:09	♑ May 30 10:38	♈ Jul 30 17:05	♋ Sep 30 19:20	♎ Dec 1 17:09
♌ Jan 30 09:53	♏ Apr 1 14:47	♒ Jun 1 11:49	♉ Aug 2 02:38	♌ Oct 3 07:12	♏ Dec 3 20:33
♍ Feb 1 16:08	♐ Apr 3 15:04	♓ Jun 3 16:30	♊ Aug 4 14:41	♍ Oct 5 16:04	♐ Dec 5 20:46
♎ Feb 3 20:32	♑ Apr 5 16:46	♈ Jun 6 01:06	♋ Aug 7 03:09	♎ Oct 7 21:07	♑ Dec 7 19:52
♏ Feb 5 23:46	♒ Apr 7 21:02	♉ Jun 8 12:29	♌ Aug 9 14:07	♏ Oct 9 23:18	♒ Dec 9 19:59
♐ Feb 8 02:32	♓ Apr 10 04:07	♊ Jun 11 01:06	♍ Aug 11 22:42	♐ Oct 12 00:21	♓ Dec 11 22:56
♑ Feb 10 05:23	♈ Apr 12 13:30	♋ Jun 13 13:36	♎ Aug 14 04:54	♑ Oct 14 01:54	♈ Dec 14 05:29
♒ Feb 12 09:08	♉ Apr 15 00:37	♌ Jun 16 01:11	♏ Aug 16 09:16	♒ Oct 16 05:14	♉ Dec 16 15:14
♓ Feb 14 14:46	♊ Apr 17 12:57	♍ Jun 18 10:52	♐ Aug 18 12:18	♓ Oct 18 10:36	♊ Dec 19 03:01
♈ Feb 16 22:45	♋ Apr 20 01:35	♎ Jun 20 17:38	♑ Aug 20 14:37	♈ Oct 20 17:57	♋ Dec 21 15:44
♉ Feb 19 09:36	♌ Apr 22 12:52	♏ Jun 22 21:02	♒ Aug 22 17:01	♉ Oct 23 03:07	♌ Dec 24 04:23
♊ Feb 21 22:05	♍ Apr 24 20:52	♐ Jun 24 21:44	♓ Aug 24 20:35	♊ Oct 25 14:14	♍ Dec 26 15:50
♋ Feb 24 09:57	♎ Apr 27 00:46	♑ Jun 26 21:21	♈ Aug 27 02:20	♋ Oct 28 02:53	♎ Dec 29 00:41
♌ Feb 26 19:09	♏ Apr 29 01:23	♒ Jun 28 21:53	♉ Aug 29 11:07	♌ Oct 30 15:25	♏ Dec 31 05:55
♍ Mar 1 01:03	♐ May 1 00:36	♓ Jul 1 01:13	♊ Aug 31 22:37	♍ Nov 2 01:30	

Mercury

Jan 1 6♑
♒ Jan 15 04:26
♓ Feb 2 10:38
R Feb 12 8♓
♒ Feb 23 15:03
D Mar 6 24♒
♓ Mar 19 08:44
♈ Apr 10 19:11
♉ Apr 26 21:41
♊ May 10 23:55
♋ May 29 10:39
R Jun 14 9♋
D Jul 8 0♋
♌ Aug 4 09:00
♍ Aug 19 04:35
♎ Sep 5 09:05
♏ Sep 28 07:57
R Oct 10 6♏
♎ Oct 21 01:15
D Oct 31 20♎
♏ Nov 11 14:00
♐ Dec 1 09:19
♑ Dec 20 11:14

Venus

Jan 1 0♐	♌ Aug 4 05:46
♑ Feb 6 15:55	♍ Aug 28 13:06
♒ Mar 6 13:10	♎ Sep 21 16:31
♓ Apr 1 15:16	♏ Oct 15 17:42
♈ Apr 27 00:55	♐ Nov 8 18:05
♉ May 22 02:56	♑ Dec 2 18:36
♊ Jun 16 00:22	♒ Dec 26 20:18
♋ Jul 10 17:31	

Mars

Jan 1 7♑
♒ Jan 30 06:17
♓ Mar 9 13:00
♈ Apr 16 20:47
♉ May 26 03:20
♊ Jul 6 06:24
♋ Aug 19 09:13
♌ Oct 7 20:51
R Dec 31 29♌

Jupiter

Jan 1 22♒
♓ Feb 4 00:29
R Jul 19 28♓
D Nov 14 18♓

Saturn

Jan 1 27♊
D Feb 26 25♊
♋ May 11 21:24
R Oct 29 16♋

Uranus

Jan 1 9♒
R May 21 15♒
D Oct 22 11♒

Neptune

Jan 1 29♋
D Apr 9 27♋
♌ Jul 19 13:28
R Nov 6 2♌

Pluto

Jan 1 1♋
D Mar 15 0♋
R Oct 4 3♋

1916

Sun

♒ Jan 21 08:54	♈ Mar 20 22:47	♊ May 21 10:07	♌ Jul 23 05:21	♎ Sep 23 09:17	♐ Nov 22 14:58
♓ Feb 19 23:17	♉ Apr 20 10:24	♋ Jun 21 18:25	♍ Aug 23 12:09	♏ Oct 23 17:59	♑ Dec 22 03:59

Moon

Jan 1 10♏	♒ Mar 1 03:17	♉ May 1 07:48	♌ Jul 2 06:55	♏ Sep 2 01:24	♒ Nov 2 00:48
♐ Jan 2 07:43	♓ Mar 3 05:27	♊ May 3 17:11	♍ Jul 4 19:31	♐ Sep 4 07:05	♓ Nov 4 04:04
♑ Jan 4 07:25	♈ Mar 5 08:56	♋ May 6 04:52	♎ Jul 7 06:04	♑ Sep 6 10:43	♈ Nov 6 07:58
♒ Jan 6 06:58	♉ Mar 7 15:06	♌ May 8 17:51	♏ Jul 9 13:15	♒ Sep 8 12:38	♉ Nov 8 13:06
♓ Jan 8 08:20	♊ Mar 10 00:45	♍ May 11 05:43	♐ Jul 11 16:43	♓ Sep 10 13:40	♊ Nov 10 20:18
♈ Jan 10 13:06	♋ Mar 12 13:03	♎ May 13 14:14	♑ Jul 13 17:19	♈ Sep 12 15:17	♋ Nov 13 06:19
♉ Jan 12 21:42	♌ Mar 15 01:39	♏ May 15 18:41	♒ Jul 15 16:46	♉ Sep 14 19:08	♌ Nov 15 18:44
♊ Jan 15 09:17	♍ Mar 17 12:12	♐ May 17 20:09	♓ Jul 17 16:53	♊ Sep 17 02:37	♍ Nov 18 07:31
♋ Jan 17 22:06	♎ Mar 19 19:36	♑ May 19 20:30	♈ Jul 19 19:31	♋ Sep 19 13:44	♎ Nov 20 18:02
♌ Jan 20 10:31	♏ Mar 22 00:25	♒ May 21 21:32	♉ Jul 22 01:45	♌ Sep 22 02:39	♏ Nov 23 00:47
♍ Jan 22 21:31	♐ Mar 24 03:47	♓ May 24 00:34	♊ Jul 24 11:35	♍ Sep 24 14:45	♐ Nov 25 04:10
♎ Jan 25 06:24	♑ Mar 26 06:43	♈ May 26 06:02	♋ Jul 26 23:52	♎ Sep 27 00:21	♑ Nov 27 05:43
♏ Jan 27 12:43	♒ Mar 28 09:46	♉ May 28 13:52	♌ Jul 29 12:55	♏ Sep 29 07:21	♒ Nov 29 07:06
♐ Jan 29 16:17	♓ Mar 30 13:17	♊ May 30 23:53	♍ Aug 1 01:16	♐ Oct 1 12:26	♓ Dec 1 09:28
♑ Jan 31 17:41	♈ Apr 1 17:47	♋ Jun 2 11:44	♎ Aug 3 11:54	♑ Oct 3 16:23	♈ Dec 3 13:33
♒ Feb 2 18:07	♉ Apr 4 00:09	♌ Jun 5 00:45	♏ Aug 5 19:54	♒ Oct 5 19:28	♉ Dec 5 19:34
♓ Feb 4 19:14	♊ Apr 6 09:18	♍ Jun 7 13:14	♐ Aug 8 00:55	♓ Oct 7 22:00	♊ Dec 8 03:40
♈ Feb 6 22:45	♋ Apr 8 21:09	♎ Jun 9 22:57	♑ Aug 10 03:06	♈ Oct 10 00:40	♋ Dec 10 13:58
♉ Feb 9 05:49	♌ Apr 11 10:01	♏ Jun 12 04:39	♒ Aug 12 03:26	♉ Oct 12 04:44	♌ Dec 13 02:16
♊ Feb 11 16:29	♍ Apr 13 21:06	♐ Jun 14 06:40	♓ Aug 14 03:28	♊ Oct 14 11:37	♍ Dec 15 15:18
♋ Feb 14 05:12	♎ Apr 16 04:39	♑ Jun 16 06:31	♈ Aug 16 05:00	♋ Oct 16 21:57	♎ Dec 18 02:49
♌ Feb 16 17:37	♏ Apr 18 08:46	♒ Jun 18 06:16	♉ Aug 18 09:45	♌ Oct 19 10:38	♏ Dec 20 10:52
♍ Feb 19 04:07	♐ Apr 20 10:52	♓ Jun 20 07:38	♊ Aug 20 18:25	♍ Oct 21 23:02	♐ Dec 22 14:57
♎ Feb 21 12:13	♑ Apr 22 12:34	♈ Jun 22 11:55	♋ Aug 23 06:20	♎ Oct 24 08:44	♑ Dec 24 16:06
♏ Feb 23 18:07	♒ Apr 24 15:06	♉ Jun 24 19:25	♌ Aug 25 19:23	♏ Oct 26 15:07	♒ Dec 26 16:04
♐ Feb 25 22:20	♓ Apr 26 19:05	♊ Jun 27 05:42	♍ Aug 28 07:29	♐ Oct 28 19:07	♓ Dec 28 16:40
♑ Feb 28 01:11	♈ Apr 29 00:35	♋ Jun 29 17:54	♎ Aug 30 17:34	♑ Oct 30 22:00	♈ Dec 30 19:25

Mercury

Jan 1 18♑	♋ Jul 10 18:22
♒ Jan 8 01:23	♌ Jul 26 01:43
R Jan 27 22♒	♍ Aug 10 04:03
D Feb 17 6♒	♎ Aug 29 04:58
♓ Mar 15 00:21	R Sep 22 20♎
♈ Apr 2 10:59	D Oct 14 4♎
♉ Apr 17 11:01	♏ Nov 4 12:25
♊ May 2 16:29	♐ Nov 23 03:42
R May 25 19♊	♑ Dec 12 07:09
D Jun 18 10♊	

Venus

Jan 1 6♒	D Jul 25 3♋
♓ Jan 20 01:39	♌ Sep 8 22:22
♈ Feb 13 15:24	♍ Oct 7 22:09
♉ Mar 9 21:48	♎ Nov 3 01:00
♊ Apr 5 13:30	♏ Nov 27 23:08
♋ May 5 20:39	♐ Dec 22 07:50
R Jun 12 19♋	

Mars

Jan 1 29♌	
D Mar 21 10♌	
♍ May 28 18:32	
♎ Jul 23 05:07	
♏ Sep 8 17:34	
♐ Oct 22 02:55	
♑ Dec 1 17:04	

Jupiter

Jan 1 22♓	
♈ Feb 12 07:07	
♉ Jun 26 01:52	
R Aug 25 5♉	
♈ Oct 26 14:50	
D Dec 20 25♈	

Saturn

Jan 1 13♋
D Mar 11 9♋
♌ Oct 17 17:13
R Nov 12 0♌
♋ Dec 7 18:18

Uranus

Jan 1 13♒
R May 24 19♒
D Oct 26 15♒

Neptune

Jan 1 1♌
♋ Mar 19 14:51
D Apr 10 29♋
♌ May 2 11:07
R Nov 7 4♌

Pluto

Jan 1 2♋
D Mar 15 1♋
R Oct 5 4♋

1917

Sun

♒ Jan 20 14:37	♈ Mar 21 04:34	♊ May 21 15:55	♌ Jul 23 11:06	♎ Sep 23 14:59	♐ Nov 22 20:43
♓ Feb 19 05:04	♉ Apr 20 16:14	♋ Jun 22 00:12	♍ Aug 23 17:52	♏ Oct 23 23:42	♑ Dec 22 09:45

Moon

Jan 1 16 ♈	♋ Mar 2 08:52	♎ May 3 12:51	♑ Jul 4 01:25	♈ Sep 2 22:20	♋ Nov 3 04:07
♉ Jan 2 01:04	♌ Mar 4 21:35	♏ May 5 21:38	♒ Jul 6 02:24	♉ Sep 4 23:06	♌ Nov 5 13:42
♊ Jan 4 09:38	♍ Mar 7 10:29	♐ May 8 03:44	♓ Jul 8 02:53	♊ Sep 7 03:18	♍ Nov 8 01:55
♋ Jan 6 20:34	♎ Mar 9 22:00	♑ May 10 07:58	♈ Jul 10 04:25	♋ Sep 9 11:39	♎ Nov 10 14:25
♌ Jan 9 09:01	♏ Mar 12 07:39	♒ May 12 11:16	♉ Jul 12 08:12	♌ Sep 11 23:12	♏ Nov 13 01:11
♍ Jan 11 22:01	♐ Mar 14 15:18	♓ May 14 14:11	♊ Jul 14 14:46	♍ Sep 14 12:01	♐ Nov 15 09:36
♎ Jan 14 10:04	♑ Mar 16 20:37	♈ May 16 17:04	♋ Jul 16 23:59	♎ Sep 17 00:31	♑ Nov 17 15:53
♏ Jan 16 19:30	♒ Mar 18 23:33	♉ May 18 20:37	♌ Jul 19 11:15	♏ Sep 19 11:55	♒ Nov 19 20:37
♐ Jan 19 01:16	♓ Mar 21 00:30	♊ May 21 01:52	♍ Jul 21 23:51	♐ Sep 21 21:31	♓ Nov 22 00:03
♑ Jan 21 03:27	♈ Mar 23 00:52	♋ May 23 09:47	♎ Jul 24 12:31	♑ Sep 24 04:35	♈ Nov 24 02:03
♒ Jan 23 03:19	♉ Mar 25 02:35	♌ May 25 20:41	♏ Jul 26 23:39	♒ Sep 26 08:33	♉ Nov 26 04:54
♓ Jan 25 02:40	♊ Mar 27 07:28	♍ May 28 09:20	♐ Jul 29 07:37	♓ Sep 28 09:39	♊ Nov 28 08:13
♈ Jan 27 03:32	♋ Mar 29 16:28	♎ May 30 21:20	♑ Jul 31 11:47	♈ Sep 30 09:15	♋ Nov 30 13:47
♉ Jan 29 07:33	♌ Apr 1 04:37	♏ Jun 2 06:34	♒ Aug 2 12:48	♉ Oct 2 09:24	♌ Dec 2 22:31
♊ Jan 31 15:24	♍ Apr 3 17:32	♐ Jun 4 12:26	♓ Aug 4 12:20	♊ Oct 4 12:13	♍ Dec 5 10:06
♋ Feb 3 02:30	♎ Apr 6 04:52	♑ Jun 6 15:45	♈ Aug 6 12:18	♋ Oct 6 19:06	♎ Dec 7 22:40
♌ Feb 5 15:15	♏ Apr 8 13:53	♒ Jun 8 17:44	♉ Aug 8 14:36	♌ Oct 9 05:49	♏ Dec 10 09:51
♍ Feb 8 04:08	♐ Apr 10 20:50	♓ Jun 10 19:42	♊ Aug 10 20:22	♍ Oct 11 18:31	♐ Dec 12 18:09
♎ Feb 10 16:03	♑ Apr 13 02:07	♈ Jun 12 22:30	♋ Aug 13 05:38	♎ Oct 14 06:58	♑ Dec 14 23:34
♏ Feb 13 02:06	♒ Apr 15 05:56	♉ Jun 15 02:47	♌ Aug 15 17:18	♏ Oct 16 17:53	♒ Dec 17 02:59
♐ Feb 15 09:22	♓ Apr 17 08:24	♊ Jun 17 09:00	♍ Aug 18 06:00	♐ Oct 19 03:00	♓ Dec 19 05:31
♑ Feb 17 13:24	♈ Apr 19 10:09	♋ Jun 19 17:33	♎ Aug 20 18:41	♑ Oct 21 10:12	♈ Dec 21 08:06
♒ Feb 19 14:32	♉ Apr 21 12:30	♌ Jun 22 04:26	♏ Aug 23 06:15	♒ Oct 23 15:16	♉ Dec 23 11:25
♓ Feb 21 14:05	♊ Apr 23 17:04	♍ Jun 24 16:58	♐ Aug 25 15:26	♓ Oct 25 18:01	♊ Dec 25 16:02
♈ Feb 23 13:59	♋ Apr 26 01:07	♎ Jun 27 05:25	♑ Aug 27 21:14	♈ Oct 27 19:07	♋ Dec 27 22:29
♉ Feb 25 16:19	♌ Apr 28 12:30	♏ Jun 29 15:37	♒ Aug 29 23:27	♉ Oct 29 19:58	♌ Dec 30 07:13
♊ Feb 27 22:33	♍ May 1 01:19	♐ Jul 1 22:12	♓ Aug 31 23:11	♊ Oct 31 22:26	

Mercury

Jan 1 29 ♑	♋ Jul 3 10:23
♒ Jan 1 16:56	♌ Jul 17 13:25
R Jan 10 6 ♒	♍ Aug 2 19:20
♑ Jan 18 04:30	♎ Aug 26 23:17
D Jan 30 19 ♑	R Sep 5 4 ♎
♒ Feb 15 03:00	♍ Sep 14 12:19
♓ Mar 8 15:30	D Sep 28 18 ♍
♈ Mar 25 11:35	♎ Oct 10 05:06
♉ Apr 9 05:41	♏ Oct 28 05:21
R May 5 29 ♉	♐ Nov 15 21:28
D May 29 19 ♉	♑ Dec 5 17:00
♊ Jun 14 18:02	R Dec 25 20 ♑

Venus

Jan 1 12 ♐	♌ Jul 4 03:19
♑ Jan 15 10:45	♍ Jul 28 17:50
♒ Feb 8 11:50	♎ Aug 22 12:16
♓ Mar 4 13:08	♏ Sep 16 12:55
♈ Mar 28 16:00	♐ Oct 11 23:30
♉ Apr 21 21:16	♑ Nov 7 04:59
♊ May 16 05:09	♒ Dec 5 13:16
♋ Jun 9 15:15	

Mars

Jan 1 23 ♑	
♒ Jan 9 12:54	
♓ Feb 16 13:30	
♈ Mar 26 17:35	
♉ May 4 22:09	
♊ Jun 14 20:53	
♋ Jul 28 04:03	
♌ Sep 12 10:52	
♍ Nov 2 10:48	

Jupiter

Jan 1 25 ♈
♉ Feb 12 16:32
♊ Jun 30 00:04
R Sep 30 11 ♊

Saturn

Jan 1 28 ♋
D Mar 26 23 ♋
♌ Jun 24 14:01
R Nov 26 14 ♌

Uranus

Jan 1 17 ♒
R May 29 23 ♒
D Oct 30 19 ♒

Neptune

Jan 1 4 ♌
D Apr 13 2 ♌
R Nov 9 7 ♌

Pluto

Jan 1 3 ♋
D Mar 16 2 ♋
R Oct 6 5 ♋

1918

Sun

♒ Jan 20 20:25	♈ Mar 21 10:26	♊ May 21 21:45	♌ Jul 23 16:51	♎ Sep 23 20:45	♐ Nov 23 02:37
♓ Feb 19 10:53	♉ Apr 20 22:05	♋ Jun 22 05:59	♍ Aug 23 23:37	♏ Oct 24 05:33	♑ Dec 22 15:41

Moon

Jan 1 20 ♌	♏ Mar 2 09:31	♒ May 3 00:12	♉ Jul 2 20:43	♌ Sep 2 00:51	♏ Nov 2 23:31
♍ Jan 1 18:22	♐ Mar 4 20:46	♓ May 5 04:07	♊ Jul 5 00:02	♍ Sep 4 10:55	♐ Nov 5 11:51
♎ Jan 4 06:55	♑ Mar 7 05:04	♈ May 7 05:39	♋ Jul 7 04:40	♎ Sep 6 22:33	♑ Nov 7 22:49
♏ Jan 6 18:49	♒ Mar 9 09:22	♉ May 9 06:03	♌ Jul 9 11:19	♏ Sep 9 11:18	♒ Nov 10 07:25
♐ Jan 9 01:26	♓ Mar 11 10:11	♊ May 11 07:05	♍ Jul 11 20:32	♐ Sep 11 23:50	♓ Nov 12 12:50
♑ Jan 11 09:26	♈ Mar 13 09:15	♋ May 13 10:30	♎ Jul 14 08:08	♑ Sep 14 10:01	♈ Nov 15 15:10
♒ Jan 13 11:55	♉ Mar 15 08:47	♌ May 15 17:30	♏ Jul 16 20:40	♒ Sep 16 16:13	♉ Nov 16 15:25
♓ Jan 15 12:53	♊ Mar 17 10:56	♍ May 18 04:00	♐ Jul 19 07:49	♓ Sep 18 18:25	♊ Nov 18 15:19
♈ Jan 17 14:02	♋ Mar 19 16:56	♎ May 20 16:25	♑ Jul 21 15:45	♈ Sep 20 18:06	♋ Nov 20 16:46
♉ Jan 19 16:48	♌ Mar 22 02:37	♏ May 23 04:36	♒ Jul 23 20:18	♉ Sep 22 17:27	♌ Nov 22 21:22
♊ Jan 21 21:51	♍ Mar 24 14:30	♐ May 25 15:07	♓ Jul 25 22:31	♊ Sep 24 18:29	♍ Nov 25 05:50
♋ Jan 24 05:15	♎ Mar 27 03:06	♑ May 27 23:27	♈ Jul 27 23:59	♋ Sep 26 22:44	♎ Nov 27 17:23
♌ Jan 26 14:44	♏ Mar 29 15:27	♒ May 30 05:37	♉ Jul 30 02:06	♌ Sep 29 06:24	♏ Nov 30 06:12
♍ Jan 29 01:57	♐ Apr 1 02:46	♓ Jun 1 09:52	♊ Aug 1 05:46	♍ Oct 1 16:45	♐ Dec 2 18:20
♎ Jan 31 14:25	♑ Apr 3 11:59	♈ Jun 3 12:37	♋ Aug 3 11:20	♎ Oct 4 04:43	♑ Dec 5 04:40
♏ Feb 3 02:51	♒ Apr 5 17:56	♉ Jun 5 14:29	♌ Aug 5 18:47	♏ Oct 6 17:27	♒ Dec 7 12:51
♐ Feb 5 13:13	♓ Apr 7 20:21	♊ Jun 7 16:34	♍ Aug 8 04:16	♐ Oct 9 06:03	♓ Dec 9 18:46
♑ Feb 7 19:56	♈ Apr 9 20:17	♋ Jun 9 20:13	♎ Aug 10 15:45	♑ Oct 11 17:06	♈ Dec 11 22:32
♒ Feb 9 22:46	♉ Apr 11 19:39	♌ Jun 12 02:35	♏ Aug 13 04:26	♒ Oct 14 00:52	♉ Dec 14 00:35
♓ Feb 11 22:56	♊ Apr 13 20:37	♍ Jun 14 12:09	♐ Aug 15 16:22	♓ Oct 16 04:40	♊ Dec 16 01:49
♈ Feb 13 22:30	♋ Apr 16 00:57	♎ Jun 17 00:08	♑ Aug 18 01:16	♈ Oct 18 05:14	♋ Dec 18 03:34
♉ Feb 15 23:31	♌ Apr 18 09:18	♏ Jun 19 12:28	♒ Aug 20 06:10	♉ Oct 20 04:20	♌ Dec 20 07:24
♊ Feb 18 03:28	♍ Apr 20 20:45	♐ Jun 21 23:04	♓ Aug 22 07:48	♊ Oct 22 04:09	♍ Dec 22 14:33
♋ Feb 20 10:50	♎ Apr 23 09:24	♑ Jun 24 06:49	♈ Aug 24 07:55	♋ Oct 24 06:39	♎ Dec 25 01:08
♌ Feb 22 20:52	♏ Apr 25 21:37	♒ Jun 26 12:00	♉ Aug 26 08:34	♌ Oct 26 12:53	♏ Dec 27 13:48
♍ Feb 25 08:32	♐ Apr 28 08:30	♓ Jun 28 15:25	♊ Aug 28 11:18	♍ Oct 28 22:40	♐ Dec 30 02:02
♎ Feb 27 21:00	♑ Apr 30 17:33	♈ Jun 30 18:03	♋ Aug 30 16:50	♎ Oct 31 10:45	

Mercury

Jan 1 15 ♑	♍ Jul 28 01:56
D Jan 14 4 ♑	R Aug 19 16 ♍
♒ Feb 10 09:23	D Sep 11 3 ♍
♓ Mar 1 07:52	♎ Oct 3 09:01
♈ Mar 17 07:27	♏ Oct 20 16:43
♉ Apr 2 13:14	♐ Nov 8 22:09
R Apr 16 9 ♉	♑ Dec 1 15:57
D May 10 0 ♉	R Dec 9 3 ♑
♊ Jun 10 01:05	♐ Dec 15 13:00
♋ Jun 24 23:51	D Dec 28 18 ♐
♌ Jul 9 08:33	

Venus

Jan 1 21 ♒	♋ Jul 24 18:41
R Jan 20 28 ♒	♌ Aug 18 17:05
D Mar 2 12 ♒	♍ Sep 12 05:23
♓ Apr 5 20:07	♎ Oct 6 10:00
♈ May 6 20:57	♏ Oct 30 09:43
♉ Jun 3 05:24	♐ Nov 23 07:01
♊ Jun 29 08:09	♑ Dec 17 03:32

Mars

Jan 1 26 ♍
♎ Jan 11 08:58
R Feb 3 3 ♎
♍ Feb 25 18:32
D Apr 25 13 ♍
♎ Jun 23 19:09
♏ Aug 17 03:55
♐ Oct 1 07:32
♑ Nov 11 10:07
♒ Dec 20 09:03

Jupiter

Jan 1 2 ♊
D Jan 26 1 ♊
♋ Jul 13 06:20
R Nov 3 15 ♋

Saturn

Jan 1 13 ♌
D Apr 9 7 ♌
R Dec 9 28 ♌

Uranus

Jan 1 21 ♒
R Jun 2 27 ♒
D Nov 3 23 ♒

Neptune

Jan 1 6 ♌
D Apr 15 4 ♌
R Nov 12 9 ♌

Pluto

Jan 1 4 ♋
D Mar 18 3 ♋
R Oct 7 6 ♋

1919

Sun

♒ Jan 21 02:20	♈ Mar 21 16:19	♊ May 22 03:40	♌ Jul 23 22:46	♎ Sep 24 02:37	♐ Nov 23 08:28
♓ Feb 19 16:48	♉ Apr 21 03:59	♋ Jun 22 11:54	♍ Aug 24 05:30	♏ Oct 24 11:23	♑ Dec 22 21:28

Moon

Jan 1 23 ♐	♓ Mar 1 17:14	♊ May 1 15:00	♍ Jul 1 19:06	♐ Sep 1 19:56	♓ Nov 2 19:19
♑ Jan 1 12:00	♈ Mar 3 18:27	♋ May 3 15:49	♎ Jul 4 03:34	♑ Sep 4 08:19	♈ Nov 4 23:30
♒ Jan 3 19:14	♉ Mar 5 19:13	♌ May 5 19:36	♏ Jul 6 15:18	♒ Sep 6 17:54	♉ Nov 7 00:30
♓ Jan 6 00:18	♊ Mar 7 21:08	♍ May 8 03:00	♐ Jul 9 04:12	♓ Sep 8 23:44	♊ Nov 9 00:02
♈ Jan 8 04:01	♋ Mar 10 01:08	♎ May 10 13:31	♑ Jul 11 15:55	♈ Sep 11 02:46	♋ Nov 11 00:02
♉ Jan 10 07:01	♌ Mar 12 07:17	♏ May 13 01:56	♒ Jul 14 01:12	♉ Sep 13 04:33	♌ Nov 13 02:13
♊ Jan 12 09:48	♍ Mar 14 15:24	♐ May 15 14:53	♓ Jul 16 08:06	♊ Sep 15 06:35	♍ Nov 15 07:39
♋ Jan 14 12:54	♎ Mar 17 01:29	♑ May 18 03:05	♈ Jul 18 13:05	♋ Sep 17 09:38	♎ Nov 17 16:30
♌ Jan 16 17:15	♏ Mar 19 13:24	♒ May 20 13:23	♉ Jul 20 16:43	♌ Sep 19 14:07	♏ Nov 20 03:58
♍ Jan 18 23:56	♐ Mar 22 02:22	♓ May 22 20:43	♊ Jul 22 19:19	♍ Sep 21 20:14	♐ Nov 22 16:47
♎ Jan 21 09:42	♑ Mar 24 14:23	♈ May 25 00:45	♋ Jul 24 21:24	♎ Sep 24 04:24	♑ Nov 25 05:44
♏ Jan 23 21:59	♒ Mar 26 23:11	♉ May 27 02:01	♌ Jul 27 00:00	♏ Sep 26 14:59	♒ Nov 27 17:37
♐ Jan 26 10:33	♓ Mar 29 03:45	♊ May 29 01:52	♍ Jul 29 04:28	♐ Sep 29 03:36	♓ Nov 30 03:01
♑ Jan 28 20:53	♈ Mar 31 04:56	♋ May 31 01:50	♎ Jul 31 12:05	♑ Oct 1 16:28	♈ Dec 2 09:01
♒ Jan 31 03:43	♉ Apr 2 04:39	♌ Jun 2 04:26	♏ Aug 2 23:07	♒ Oct 4 03:02	♉ Dec 4 11:33
♓ Feb 2 07:36	♊ Apr 4 04:54	♍ Jun 4 10:17	♐ Aug 5 11:57	♓ Oct 6 09:44	♊ Dec 6 11:36
♈ Feb 4 10:02	♋ Apr 6 07:22	♎ Jun 6 19:57	♑ Aug 7 23:52	♈ Oct 8 12:44	♋ Dec 8 10:53
♉ Feb 6 12:22	♌ Apr 8 12:47	♏ Jun 9 08:15	♒ Aug 10 08:56	♉ Oct 10 13:31	♌ Dec 10 11:28
♊ Feb 8 15:30	♍ Apr 10 21:06	♐ Jun 11 21:12	♓ Aug 12 14:59	♊ Oct 12 13:58	♍ Dec 12 15:05
♋ Feb 10 19:46	♎ Apr 13 07:42	♑ Jun 14 09:03	♈ Aug 14 18:58	♋ Oct 14 15:39	♎ Dec 14 22:47
♌ Feb 13 01:16	♏ Apr 15 19:53	♒ Jun 16 18:58	♉ Aug 16 22:05	♌ Oct 16 19:31	♏ Dec 17 10:00
♍ Feb 15 08:31	♐ Apr 18 08:51	♓ Jun 19 02:31	♊ Aug 19 01:02	♍ Oct 19 01:57	♐ Dec 19 22:58
♎ Feb 17 18:05	♑ Apr 20 21:13	♈ Jun 21 07:37	♋ Aug 21 04:12	♎ Oct 21 10:50	♑ Dec 22 11:49
♏ Feb 20 06:02	♒ Apr 23 07:07	♉ Jun 23 10:29	♌ Aug 23 07:58	♏ Oct 23 21:51	♒ Dec 24 23:19
♐ Feb 22 18:55	♓ Apr 25 13:16	♊ Jun 25 11:41	♍ Aug 25 13:07	♐ Oct 26 10:30	♓ Dec 27 08:55
♑ Feb 25 06:07	♈ Apr 27 15:40	♋ Jun 27 12:27	♎ Aug 27 20:40	♑ Oct 28 23:34	♈ Dec 29 16:05
♒ Feb 27 13:35	♉ Apr 29 15:36	♌ Jun 29 14:22	♏ Aug 30 07:14	♒ Oct 31 11:07	♉ Dec 31 20:28

Mercury

Jan 1 19 ♐	♌ Jul 2 02:05
♑ Jan 13 18:23	R Aug 1 29 ♌
♒ Feb 3 19:24	D Aug 25 16 ♌
♓ Feb 21 14:10	♍ Sep 9 03:48
♈ Mar 9 10:43	♎ Sep 25 14:15
R Mar 29 22 ♈	♏ Oct 13 07:27
D Apr 21 10 ♈	♐ Nov 2 19:22
♉ May 16 02:41	R Nov 22 18 ♐
♊ Jun 2 11:06	D Dec 12 1 ♐
♋ Jun 16 08:43	

Venus

Jan 1 18 ♑	♌ Jun 8 10:40
♒ Jan 10 00:27	♍ Jul 7 18:25
♓ Feb 2 23:07	R Aug 22 27 ♍
♈ Feb 27 01:42	D Oct 4 11 ♍
♉ Mar 23 11:07	♎ Nov 9 08:05
♊ Apr 17 07:02	♏ Dec 9 03:28
♋ May 12 19:00	

Mars

Jan 1 9 ♒
♓ Jan 27 11:21
♈ Mar 6 18:48
♉ Apr 15 05:02
♊ May 26 09:35
♋ Jul 8 17:12
♌ Aug 23 06:13
♍ Oct 10 03:47
♎ Nov 30 12:14

Jupiter

Jan 1 10 ♋
D Mar 2 5 ♋
♌ Aug 2 09:21
R Dec 5 18 ♌

Saturn

Jan 1 27 ♌
D Apr 23 21 ♌
♍ Aug 12 14:22
R Dec 23 11 ♍

Uranus

Jan 1 25 ♒
♓ Apr 1 01:45
R Jun 6 1 ♓
♒ Aug 16 21:37
D Nov 8 27 ♒

Neptune

Jan 1 8 ♌
D Apr 18 6 ♌
R Nov 14 11 ♌

Pluto

Jan 1 5 ♋
D Mar 19 4 ♋
R Oct 9 7 ♋

1920

Sun

♒ Jan 21 08:07	♈ Mar 20 21:59	♊ May 21 09:21	♌ Jul 23 04:33	♎ Sep 23 08:28	♐ Nov 22 14:15
♓ Feb 19 22:30	♉ Apr 20 09:38	♋ Jun 21 17:39	♍ Aug 23 11:20	♏ Oct 23 17:13	♑ Dec 22 03:17

Moon

Jan 1 2♉	♌ Mar 1 17:21	♏ May 2 01:36	♒ Jul 3 02:30	♉ Sep 2 16:19	♌ Nov 2 13:36
♊ Jan 2 22:11	♍ Mar 3 20:39	♐ May 4 12:59	♓ Jul 5 13:36	♊ Sep 4 20:57	♍ Nov 4 17:02
♋ Jan 4 22:19	♎ Mar 6 01:52	♑ May 7 01:38	♈ Jul 7 22:37	♋ Sep 7 00:03	♎ Nov 6 22:23
♌ Jan 6 22:30	♏ Mar 8 10:08	♒ May 9 14:08	♉ Jul 10 04:45	♌ Sep 9 02:01	♏ Nov 9 05:49
♍ Jan 9 00:45	♐ Mar 10 21:35	♓ May 12 00:31	♊ Jul 12 07:39	♍ Sep 11 03:53	♐ Nov 11 15:25
♎ Jan 11 06:46	♑ Mar 13 10:25	♈ May 14 07:23	♋ Jul 14 08:02	♎ Sep 13 07:09	♑ Nov 14 03:01
♏ Jan 13 16:56	♒ Mar 15 21:57	♉ May 16 10:34	♌ Jul 16 07:31	♏ Sep 15 13:17	♒ Nov 16 15:44
♐ Jan 16 05:42	♓ Mar 18 06:23	♊ May 18 11:13	♍ Jul 18 08:12	♐ Sep 17 22:56	♓ Nov 19 03:39
♑ Jan 18 18:34	♈ Mar 20 11:42	♋ May 20 11:00	♎ Jul 20 12:01	♑ Sep 20 11:08	♈ Nov 21 12:45
♒ Jan 21 05:38	♉ Mar 22 14:58	♌ May 22 11:49	♏ Jul 22 20:01	♒ Sep 22 23:32	♉ Nov 23 18:01
♓ Jan 23 14:34	♊ Mar 24 17:24	♍ May 24 15:09	♐ Jul 25 07:30	♓ Sep 25 09:57	♊ Nov 25 19:59
♈ Jan 25 21:31	♋ Mar 26 20:00	♎ May 26 21:49	♑ Jul 27 20:21	♈ Sep 27 17:34	♋ Nov 27 20:12
♉ Jan 28 02:42	♌ Mar 28 23:19	♏ May 29 07:31	♒ Jul 30 08:36	♉ Sep 29 22:49	♌ Nov 29 20:32
♊ Jan 30 06:04	♍ Mar 31 03:47	♐ May 31 19:20	♓ Aug 1 19:17	♊ Oct 2 02:32	♍ Dec 1 22:45
♋ Feb 1 07:52	♎ Apr 2 09:59	♑ Jun 3 08:04	♈ Aug 4 04:09	♋ Oct 4 05:29	♎ Dec 4 03:49
♌ Feb 3 09:04	♏ Apr 4 18:32	♒ Jun 5 20:37	♉ Aug 6 10:54	♌ Oct 6 08:14	♏ Dec 6 11:51
♍ Feb 5 11:17	♐ Apr 7 05:40	♓ Jun 8 07:42	♊ Aug 8 15:15	♍ Oct 8 11:22	♐ Dec 8 22:08
♎ Feb 7 16:19	♑ Apr 9 18:23	♈ Jun 10 15:57	♋ Aug 10 17:11	♎ Oct 10 15:44	♑ Dec 11 09:59
♏ Feb 10 01:12	♒ Apr 12 06:30	♉ Jun 12 20:35	♌ Aug 12 17:40	♏ Oct 12 22:12	♒ Dec 13 22:37
♐ Feb 12 13:20	♓ Apr 14 15:49	♊ Jun 14 21:57	♍ Aug 14 18:26	♐ Oct 15 07:30	♓ Dec 16 11:02
♑ Feb 15 02:13	♈ Apr 16 21:28	♋ Jun 16 21:25	♎ Aug 16 21:26	♑ Oct 17 19:15	♈ Dec 18 21:28
♒ Feb 17 13:00	♉ Apr 19 00:07	♌ Jun 18 21:00	♏ Aug 19 04:11	♒ Oct 20 07:52	♉ Dec 21 04:22
♓ Feb 19 21:38	♊ Apr 21 01:13	♍ Jun 20 22:44	♐ Aug 21 14:43	♓ Oct 22 18:55	♊ Dec 23 07:13
♈ Feb 22 03:36	♋ Apr 23 02:21	♎ Jun 23 04:05	♑ Aug 24 03:21	♈ Oct 25 02:52	♋ Dec 25 07:12
♉ Feb 24 08:05	♌ Apr 25 04:48	♏ Jun 25 13:19	♒ Aug 26 15:36	♉ Oct 27 07:32	♌ Dec 27 06:16
♊ Feb 26 11:41	♍ Apr 27 09:21	♐ Jun 28 01:13	♓ Aug 29 01:53	♊ Oct 29 09:59	♍ Dec 29 06:37
♋ Feb 28 14:40	♎ Apr 29 16:17	♑ Jun 30 14:06	♈ Aug 31 10:03	♋ Oct 31 11:34	♎ Dec 31 10:06

Mercury

Jan 1 19♐	R Jul 13 11♌
♑ Jan 8 05:55	♋ Aug 2 23:22
♒ Jan 27 13:49	D Aug 6 29♋
♓ Feb 13 18:41	♌ Aug 10 08:52
♈ Mar 2 19:33	♍ Aug 31 18:22
R Mar 10 5♈	♎ Sep 16 17:13
♓ Mar 19 16:30	♏ Oct 5 09:27
D Apr 2 20♓	♐ Oct 30 12:40
♈ Apr 17 18:00	R Nov 5 2♐
♉ May 9 00:03	♏ Nov 10 20:04
♊ May 24 00:31	D Nov 25 15♏
♋ Jun 7 02:52	♐ Dec 11 04:30
♌ Jun 26 12:27	

Venus

Jan 1 26♏	♋ Jun 24 10:53
♐ Jan 4 09:19	♌ Jul 18 20:24
♑ Jan 29 11:54	♍ Aug 12 04:30
♒ Feb 23 03:46	♎ Sep 5 11:53
♓ Mar 18 15:31	♏ Sep 29 19:44
♈ Apr 12 02:06	♐ Oct 24 05:09
♉ May 6 12:53	♑ Nov 17 17:24
♊ May 31 00:04	♒ Dec 12 11:42

Mars

Jan 1 16♎	
♏ Jan 31 23:04	
R Mar 15 9♏	
♎ Apr 23 20:18	
D May 31 20♎	
♏ Jul 10 18:12	
♐ Sep 4 20:21	
♑ Oct 18 13:07	
♒ Nov 27 13:30	

Jupiter

Jan 1 16♌	
D Apr 4 8♌	
♍ Aug 27 06:01	

Saturn

Jan 1 11♍	
D May 7 4♍	

Uranus

Jan 1 28♒	
♓ Jan 22 18:31	
R Jun 10 5♓	
D Nov 11 1♓	

Neptune

Jan 1 10♌	
D Apr 19 8♌	
R Nov 16 13♌	

Pluto

Jan 1 6♋	
D Mar 20 5♋	
R Oct 9 8♋	

1921

Sun

♒ Jan 20 13:55	♈ Mar 21 03:50	♊ May 21 15:16	♌ Jul 23 10:30	♎ Sep 23 14:19	♐ Nov 22 20:04
♓ Feb 19 04:21	♉ Apr 20 15:31	♋ Jun 21 23:36	♍ Aug 23 17:15	♏ Oct 23 23:01	♑ Dec 22 09:06

Moon

Jan 1 7♎	♑ Mar 3 05:02	♈ May 4 08:13	♋ Jul 4 16:54	♎ Sep 3 13:04	♑ Nov 3 23:37
♏ Jan 2 17:27	♒ Mar 5 17:44	♉ May 6 15:30	♌ Jul 6 16:32	♏ Sep 5 15:22	♒ Nov 6 10:16
♐ Jan 5 03:57	♓ Mar 8 05:42	♊ May 8 19:51	♍ Jul 8 16:26	♐ Sep 7 21:20	♓ Nov 8 22:50
♑ Jan 7 16:08	♈ Mar 10 15:58	♋ May 10 22:19	♎ Jul 10 18:27	♑ Sep 10 06:58	♈ Nov 11 10:52
♒ Jan 10 04:49	♉ Mar 13 00:14	♌ May 13 00:16	♏ Jul 12 23:41	♒ Sep 12 19:00	♉ Nov 13 20:18
♓ Jan 12 17:10	♊ Mar 15 06:27	♍ May 15 02:51	♐ Jul 15 08:05	♓ Sep 15 07:38	♊ Nov 16 02:39
♈ Jan 15 04:13	♋ Mar 17 10:35	♎ May 17 06:45	♑ Jul 17 18:43	♈ Sep 17 19:28	♋ Nov 18 06:40
♉ Jan 17 12:40	♌ Mar 19 12:50	♏ May 19 12:21	♒ Jul 20 06:43	♉ Sep 20 05:40	♌ Nov 20 09:31
♊ Jan 19 17:22	♍ Mar 21 14:07	♐ May 21 19:52	♓ Jul 22 19:23	♊ Sep 22 13:40	♍ Nov 22 12:16
♋ Jan 21 18:35	♎ Mar 23 15:48	♑ May 24 05:34	♈ Jul 25 07:40	♋ Sep 24 19:06	♎ Nov 24 15:30
♌ Jan 23 17:44	♏ Mar 25 19:32	♒ May 26 17:16	♉ Jul 27 17:57	♌ Sep 26 21:57	♏ Nov 26 19:36
♍ Jan 25 17:04	♐ Mar 28 02:33	♓ May 29 05:50	♊ Jul 30 00:36	♍ Sep 28 23:00	♐ Nov 29 01:02
♎ Jan 27 18:45	♑ Mar 30 12:57	♈ May 31 17:04	♋ Aug 1 03:18	♎ Sep 30 23:39	♑ Dec 1 08:32
♏ Jan 30 00:23	♒ Apr 2 01:21	♉ Jun 3 01:03	♌ Aug 3 03:09	♏ Oct 3 01:35	♒ Dec 3 18:41
♐ Feb 1 10:03	♓ Apr 4 13:27	♊ Jun 5 05:16	♍ Aug 5 02:17	♐ Oct 5 06:22	♓ Dec 6 07:03
♑ Feb 3 22:13	♈ Apr 6 23:30	♋ Jun 7 06:45	♎ Aug 7 02:51	♑ Oct 7 14:44	♈ Dec 8 19:35
♒ Feb 6 10:57	♉ Apr 9 06:59	♌ Jun 9 07:17	♏ Aug 9 06:31	♒ Oct 10 02:11	♉ Dec 11 05:44
♓ Feb 8 23:02	♊ Apr 11 12:16	♍ Jun 11 08:39	♐ Aug 11 13:58	♓ Oct 12 14:50	♊ Dec 13 12:06
♈ Feb 11 09:50	♋ Apr 13 15:58	♎ Jun 13 12:08	♑ Aug 14 00:29	♈ Oct 15 02:34	♋ Dec 15 15:10
♉ Feb 13 18:44	♌ Apr 15 18:46	♏ Jun 15 18:09	♒ Aug 16 12:41	♉ Oct 17 12:06	♌ Dec 17 16:33
♊ Feb 16 00:53	♍ Apr 17 21:21	♐ Jun 18 02:28	♓ Aug 19 01:20	♊ Oct 19 19:20	♍ Dec 19 18:01
♋ Feb 18 03:57	♎ Apr 20 00:23	♑ Jun 20 12:38	♈ Aug 21 13:29	♋ Oct 22 00:30	♎ Dec 21 20:52
♌ Feb 20 04:32	♏ Apr 22 04:53	♒ Jun 23 00:22	♉ Aug 24 00:05	♌ Oct 24 04:07	♏ Dec 24 01:32
♍ Feb 22 04:20	♐ Apr 24 11:43	♓ Jun 25 13:03	♊ Aug 26 07:56	♍ Oct 26 06:40	♐ Dec 26 08:00
♎ Feb 24 05:19	♑ Apr 26 21:26	♈ Jun 28 01:02	♋ Aug 28 12:17	♎ Oct 28 08:47	♑ Dec 28 16:15
♏ Feb 26 09:27	♒ Apr 29 09:24	♉ Jun 30 10:12	♌ Aug 30 13:30	♏ Oct 30 11:33	♒ Dec 31 02:31
♐ Feb 28 17:36	♓ May 1 21:45	♊ Jul 2 15:22	♍ Sep 1 13:06	♐ Nov 1 16:07	

Mercury

Jan 1 0♑	D Jul 19 11♋
♒ Jan 19 02:27	♌ Aug 8 07:37
♓ Feb 5 10:21	♍ Aug 23 13:52
R Feb 21 17♓	♎ Sep 9 02:51
D Mar 16 4♓	♏ Sep 29 16:03
♈ Apr 14 02:31	R Oct 20 15♏
♉ May 1 06:58	D Nov 9 0♏
♊ May 15 10:07	♐ Dec 5 00:22
♋ May 31 05:04	♑ Dec 24 06:44
R Jun 25 20♋	

Venus

Jan 1 23♒	♊ Jul 8 05:59
♓ Jan 6 20:32	♋ Aug 5 14:39
♈ Feb 2 18:35	♌ Aug 31 22:23
♉ Mar 7 09:09	♍ Sep 26 04:07
R Apr 1 10♉	♎ Oct 20 17:34
♈ Apr 25 23:51	♏ Nov 13 21:09
D May 14 23♈	♐ Dec 7 19:46
♉ Jun 2 04:28	

Mars

Jan 1 26♒	
♓ Jan 5 07:35	
♈ Feb 13 05:14	
♉ Mar 25 06:25	
♊ May 6 01:40	
♋ Jun 18 20:34	
♌ Aug 3 10:56	
♍ Sep 19 11:33	
♎ Nov 6 16:07	
♏ Dec 26 11:40	

Jupiter

Jan 1 18♍
R Jan 3 18♍
D May 6 8♍
♎ Sep 25 23:19

Saturn

Jan 1 24♍
R Jan 4 24♍
D May 20 17♍
♎ Oct 7 18:08

Uranus

Jan 1 2♓
R Jun 14 9♓
D Nov 15 5♓

Neptune

Jan 1 13♌
D Apr 22 10♌
R Nov 18 15♌

Pluto

Jan 1 7♋
D Mar 21 6♋
R Oct 11 10♋

1922

Sun

♒ Jan 20 19:48	♈ Mar 21 09:47	♊ May 21 21:07	♌ Jul 23 16:17	♎ Sep 23 20:11	♐ Nov 23 01:55
♓ Feb 19 10:15	♉ Apr 20 21:26	♋ Jun 22 05:23	♍ Aug 23 23:02	♏ Oct 24 04:53	♑ Dec 22 14:59

Moon

Jan 1 10♒	♉ Mar 3 04:51	♌ May 3 14:05	♏ Jul 3 10:29	♒ Sep 2 18:12	♉ Nov 3 19:38
♓ Jan 2 14:42	♊ Mar 5 14:47	♍ May 5 17:18	♐ Jul 5 15:04	♓ Sep 5 05:40	♊ Nov 6 06:32
♈ Jan 5 03:41	♋ Mar 7 21:19	♎ May 7 19:21	♑ Jul 7 21:12	♈ Sep 7 18:27	♋ Nov 8 15:22
♉ Jan 7 14:58	♌ Mar 10 00:08	♏ May 9 21:00	♒ Jul 10 05:27	♉ Sep 10 07:24	♌ Nov 10 22:05
♊ Jan 9 22:27	♍ Mar 12 00:22	♐ May 11 23:32	♓ Jul 12 16:14	♊ Sep 12 18:49	♍ Nov 13 02:36
♋ Jan 12 01:47	♎ Mar 13 23:43	♑ May 14 04:24	♈ Jul 15 04:58	♋ Sep 15 03:13	♎ Nov 15 05:00
♌ Jan 14 02:19	♏ Mar 16 00:12	♒ May 16 12:45	♉ Jul 17 17:27	♌ Sep 17 07:48	♏ Nov 17 05:59
♍ Jan 16 02:13	♐ Mar 18 03:32	♓ May 19 00:20	♊ Jul 20 03:09	♍ Sep 19 09:07	♐ Nov 19 06:52
♎ Jan 18 03:20	♑ Mar 20 10:40	♈ May 21 13:11	♋ Jul 22 08:56	♎ Sep 21 08:42	♑ Nov 21 09:30
♏ Jan 20 07:01	♒ Mar 22 21:17	♉ May 24 00:45	♌ Jul 24 11:25	♏ Sep 23 08:27	♒ Nov 23 15:35
♐ Jan 22 13:32	♓ Mar 25 09:54	♊ May 26 09:27	♍ Jul 26 12:21	♐ Sep 25 10:10	♓ Nov 26 01:38
♑ Jan 24 22:28	♈ Mar 27 22:49	♋ May 28 15:25	♎ Jul 28 13:26	♑ Sep 27 15:15	♈ Nov 28 14:18
♒ Jan 27 09:16	♉ Mar 30 10:36	♌ May 30 19:33	♏ Jul 30 15:58	♒ Sep 30 00:01	♉ Dec 1 02:59
♓ Jan 29 21:32	♊ Apr 1 20:29	♍ Jun 1 22:48	♐ Aug 1 20:35	♓ Oct 2 11:39	♊ Dec 3 13:32
♈ Feb 1 10:34	♋ Apr 4 03:45	♎ Jun 4 01:43	♑ Aug 4 03:22	♈ Oct 5 00:35	♋ Dec 5 21:32
♉ Feb 3 22:39	♌ Apr 6 08:13	♏ Jun 6 04:42	♒ Aug 6 12:19	♉ Oct 7 13:19	♌ Dec 8 03:31
♊ Feb 6 07:40	♍ Apr 8 10:07	♐ Jun 8 08:16	♓ Aug 8 23:21	♊ Oct 10 00:44	♍ Dec 10 08:08
♋ Feb 8 12:28	♎ Apr 10 10:35	♑ Jun 10 13:30	♈ Aug 11 12:04	♋ Oct 12 09:51	♎ Dec 12 11:38
♌ Feb 10 13:38	♏ Apr 12 11:06	♒ Jun 12 21:23	♉ Aug 14 00:55	♌ Oct 14 16:01	♏ Dec 14 14:14
♍ Feb 12 12:58	♐ Apr 14 13:25	♓ Jun 15 08:23	♊ Aug 16 11:41	♍ Oct 16 19:04	♐ Dec 16 16:28
♎ Feb 14 12:34	♑ Apr 16 19:01	♈ Jun 17 21:12	♋ Aug 18 18:40	♎ Oct 18 19:43	♑ Dec 18 19:33
♏ Feb 16 14:21	♒ Apr 19 04:27	♉ Jun 20 09:08	♌ Aug 20 21:44	♏ Oct 20 19:26	♒ Dec 21 01:07
♐ Feb 18 19:30	♓ Apr 21 16:43	♊ Jun 22 18:00	♍ Aug 22 22:14	♐ Oct 22 20:05	♓ Dec 23 10:12
♑ Feb 21 04:05	♈ Apr 24 05:37	♋ Jun 24 23:27	♎ Aug 24 22:05	♑ Oct 24 23:33	♈ Dec 25 22:22
♒ Feb 23 15:12	♉ Apr 26 17:07	♌ Jun 27 02:28	♏ Aug 26 23:00	♒ Oct 27 06:59	♉ Dec 28 11:12
♓ Feb 26 03:44	♊ Apr 29 02:18	♍ Jun 29 04:35	♐ Aug 29 02:25	♓ Oct 29 18:05	♊ Dec 30 22:02
♈ Feb 28 16:40	♋ May 1 09:12	♎ Jul 1 07:04	♑ Aug 31 08:53	♈ Nov 1 07:04	

Mercury

Jan 1 12♑	D Jun 29 22♊
♒ Jan 11 17:02	♋ Jul 13 20:30
♓ Feb 1 17:23	♌ Jul 31 13:25
R Feb 5 1♓	♍ Aug 15 08:57
♒ Feb 9 04:54	♎ Sep 2 04:32
D Feb 27 16♒	♏ Oct 1 09:49
♓ Mar 18 06:28	R Oct 3 29♎
♈ Apr 7 10:20	♎ Oct 5 00:00
♉ Apr 22 23:15	D Oct 24 14♎
♊ May 7 06:54	♏ Nov 8 22:21
♋ Jun 1 03:50	♐ Nov 27 23:04
R Jun 5 0♋	♑ Dec 17 00:25
♊ Jun 10 22:54	

Venus

Jan 1 0♑	♍ Jul 15 03:22
♒ Jan 24 13:13	♎ Aug 10 09:31
♓ Feb 17 11:06	♏ Sep 7 07:19
♈ Mar 13 11:30	♐ Oct 10 22:44
♉ Apr 6 15:50	R Nov 4 9♐
♊ May 1 01:20	♏ Nov 28 21:54
♋ May 25 16:59	D Dec 15 24♏
♌ Jun 19 16:30	

Mars

Jan 1 3♏
♐ Feb 18 16:13
R May 8 25♐
D Jul 17 11♐
♑ Sep 13 13:08
♒ Oct 30 18:55
♓ Dec 11 13:09

Jupiter

Jan 1 17♎
R Feb 2 18♎
D Jun 6 8♎
♏ Oct 26 19:06

Saturn

Jan 1 7♎
R Jan 17 7♎
D Jun 3 0♎

Uranus

Jan 1 6♓
R Jun 18 13♓
D Nov 19 9♓

Neptune

Jan 1 15♌
D Apr 24 13♌
R Nov 21 18♌

Pluto

Jan 1 8♋
D Mar 22 7♋
R Oct 12 11♋

1923

Sun

♒ Jan 21 01:37	♈ Mar 21 15:31	♊ May 22 02:46	♌ Jul 23 22:00	♎ Sep 24 02:04	♐ Nov 23 07:53
♓ Feb 19 16:03	♉ Apr 21 03:07	♋ Jun 22 11:02	♍ Aug 24 04:51	♏ Oct 24 10:51	♑ Dec 22 20:54

Moon

Jan 1 13♊	♍ Mar 2 08:40	♐ May 2 05:59	♓ Jul 2 13:27	♊ Sep 2 16:50	♍ Nov 3 12:05
♋ Jan 2 05:38	♎ Mar 4 09:00	♑ May 4 07:13	♈ Jul 4 23:50	♋ Sep 5 03:58	♎ Nov 5 15:22
♌ Jan 4 10:32	♏ Mar 6 09:16	♒ May 6 12:03	♉ Jul 7 12:24	♌ Sep 7 11:54	♏ Nov 7 15:37
♍ Jan 6 13:58	♐ Mar 8 11:05	♓ May 8 21:05	♊ Jul 10 00:37	♍ Sep 9 16:15	♐ Nov 9 14:37
♎ Jan 8 16:57	♑ Mar 10 15:32	♈ May 11 09:12	♋ Jul 12 10:32	♎ Sep 11 18:02	♑ Nov 11 14:37
♏ Jan 10 20:04	♒ Mar 12 23:01	♉ May 13 22:13	♌ Jul 14 17:53	♏ Sep 13 18:46	♒ Nov 13 17:38
♐ Jan 12 23:33	♓ Mar 15 09:06	♊ May 16 10:26	♍ Jul 16 23:10	♐ Sep 15 20:05	♓ Nov 16 00:45
♑ Jan 15 03:55	♈ Mar 17 21:04	♋ May 18 21:02	♎ Jul 19 03:04	♑ Sep 17 23:14	♈ Nov 18 11:24
♒ Jan 17 10:05	♉ Mar 20 09:59	♌ May 21 05:39	♏ Jul 21 06:07	♒ Sep 20 04:52	♉ Nov 20 23:53
♓ Jan 19 18:55	♊ Mar 22 22:31	♍ May 23 11:54	♐ Jul 23 08:42	♓ Sep 22 13:02	♊ Nov 23 12:31
♈ Jan 22 06:36	♋ Mar 25 09:04	♎ May 25 15:24	♑ Jul 25 11:32	♈ Sep 24 23:22	♋ Nov 26 00:26
♉ Jan 24 19:32	♌ Mar 27 16:12	♏ May 27 16:33	♒ Jul 27 15:42	♉ Sep 27 11:21	♌ Nov 28 11:00
♊ Jan 27 07:07	♍ Mar 29 19:35	♐ May 29 16:30	♓ Jul 29 22:23	♊ Sep 30 00:04	♍ Nov 30 19:17
♋ Jan 29 15:19	♎ Mar 31 20:06	♑ May 31 17:27	♈ Aug 1 08:11	♋ Oct 2 12:00	♎ Dec 3 00:23
♌ Jan 31 19:56	♏ Apr 2 19:26	♒ Jun 2 21:02	♉ Aug 3 20:20	♌ Oct 4 21:14	♏ Dec 5 02:14
♍ Feb 2 22:10	♐ Apr 4 19:32	♓ Jun 5 04:43	♊ Aug 6 08:46	♍ Oct 7 02:39	♐ Dec 7 01:56
♎ Feb 4 23:37	♑ Apr 6 22:19	♈ Jun 7 14:02	♋ Aug 8 19:07	♎ Oct 9 04:34	♑ Dec 9 01:30
♏ Feb 7 01:36	♒ Apr 9 04:48	♉ Jun 10 04:55	♌ Aug 11 02:18	♏ Oct 11 04:25	♒ Dec 11 03:08
♐ Feb 9 04:57	♓ Apr 11 14:50	♊ Jun 12 17:02	♍ Aug 13 06:43	♐ Oct 13 04:07	♓ Dec 13 08:35
♑ Feb 11 10:07	♈ Apr 14 03:07	♋ Jun 15 03:08	♎ Aug 15 09:26	♑ Oct 15 05:41	♈ Dec 15 18:06
♒ Feb 13 17:17	♉ Apr 16 16:06	♌ Jun 17 11:11	♏ Aug 17 11:37	♒ Oct 17 10:29	♉ Dec 18 06:21
♓ Feb 16 02:42	♊ Apr 19 04:32	♍ Jun 19 17:21	♐ Aug 19 14:12	♓ Oct 19 18:42	♊ Dec 20 19:02
♈ Feb 18 14:18	♋ Apr 21 15:26	♎ Jun 21 21:44	♑ Aug 21 17:49	♈ Oct 22 05:33	♋ Dec 23 06:39
♉ Feb 21 03:14	♌ Apr 23 23:50	♏ Jun 24 00:20	♒ Aug 23 23:02	♉ Oct 24 17:46	♌ Dec 25 16:38
♊ Feb 23 15:30	♍ Apr 26 04:55	♐ Jun 26 01:46	♓ Aug 26 06:24	♊ Oct 27 06:27	♍ Dec 28 00:50
♋ Feb 26 00:57	♎ Apr 28 06:47	♑ Jun 28 03:19	♈ Aug 28 16:13	♋ Oct 29 18:39	♎ Dec 30 06:50
♌ Feb 28 06:29	♏ Apr 30 06:31	♒ Jun 30 06:43	♉ Aug 31 04:10	♌ Nov 1 04:59	

Mercury

Jan 1 23♑	♋ Jul 8 12:49
♒ Jan 4 23:27	♌ Jul 23 02:05
R Jan 20 15♒	♍ Aug 7 13:31
♑ Feb 6 15:50	♎ Aug 27 22:29
D Feb 10 29♑	R Sep 16 13♎
♒ Feb 14 00:37	♍ Oct 4 11:39
♓ Mar 13 02:55	D Oct 8 28♍
♈ Mar 30 18:14	♎ Oct 11 22:30
♉ Apr 14 12:55	♏ Nov 2 02:42
♊ May 1 04:57	♐ Nov 20 16:26
R May 17 11♊	♑ Dec 10 00:06
D Jun 10 1♊	

Venus

Jan 1 29♏	♋ Jul 10 04:35
♐ Jan 2 07:29	♌ Aug 3 16:42
♑ Feb 6 14:34	♍ Aug 27 23:59
♒ Mar 6 05:36	♎ Sep 21 03:28
♓ Apr 1 05:15	♏ Oct 15 04:48
♈ Apr 26 13:36	♐ Nov 8 05:21
♉ May 21 14:51	♑ Dec 2 06:03
♊ Jun 15 11:45	♒ Dec 26 08:00

Mars

Jan 1 14♓
♈ Jan 21 10:06
♉ Mar 4 00:47
♊ Apr 16 02:55
♋ May 30 21:21
♌ Jul 16 01:23
♍ Sep 1 00:53
♎ Oct 18 04:16
♏ Dec 4 02:04

Jupiter

Jan 1 13♏
R Mar 5 18♏
D Jul 7 9♏
♐ Nov 24 17:01

Saturn

Jan 1 19♎
R Jan 29 20♎
D Jun 16 13♎
♏ Dec 20 05:08

Uranus

Jan 1 10♓
R Jun 23 17♓
D Nov 23 13♓

Neptune

Jan 1 17♌
D Apr 27 15♌
R Nov 23 20♌

Pluto

Jan 1 10♋
D Mar 24 9♋
R Oct 13 12♋

1924

Sun

♒ Jan 21 07:30	♈ Mar 20 21:22	♊ May 21 08:42	♌ Jul 23 03:58	♎ Sep 23 07:57	♐ Nov 22 13:45
♓ Feb 19 21:53	♉ Apr 20 09:00	♋ Jun 21 17:01	♍ Aug 23 10:47	♏ Oct 23 16:44	♑ Dec 22 02:43

Moon

Jan 1 23♎	♑ Feb 29 03:12	♈ Apr 30 09:38	♋ Jul 1 09:26	♎ Sep 1 02:37	♑ Nov 1 00:39
♏ Jan 1 10:23	♒ Mar 2 07:10	♉ May 2 20:37	♌ Jul 3 21:10	♏ Sep 3 06:53	♒ Nov 3 02:53
♐ Jan 3 11:46	♓ Mar 4 12:44	♊ May 5 08:46	♍ Jul 6 07:14	♐ Sep 5 10:00	♓ Nov 5 07:33
♑ Jan 5 12:21	♈ Mar 6 20:24	♋ May 7 21:29	♎ Jul 8 14:55	♑ Sep 7 12:40	♈ Nov 7 14:38
♒ Jan 7 13:52	♉ Mar 9 06:35	♌ May 10 09:29	♏ Jul 10 19:35	♒ Sep 9 15:32	♉ Nov 9 23:42
♓ Jan 9 18:13	♊ Mar 11 18:43	♍ May 12 18:55	♐ Jul 12 21:30	♓ Sep 11 19:15	♊ Nov 12 10:33
♈ Jan 12 02:21	♋ Mar 14 07:07	♎ May 15 00:27	♑ Jul 14 21:47	♈ Sep 14 00:42	♋ Nov 14 22:55
♉ Jan 14 13:48	♌ Mar 16 17:31	♏ May 17 02:10	♒ Jul 16 22:10	♉ Sep 16 08:38	♌ Nov 17 11:50
♊ Jan 17 02:27	♍ Mar 19 00:25	♐ May 19 01:32	♓ Jul 19 00:29	♊ Sep 18 19:23	♍ Nov 19 23:10
♋ Jan 19 14:05	♎ Mar 21 04:00	♑ May 21 00:48	♈ Jul 21 06:12	♋ Sep 21 07:53	♎ Nov 22 06:50
♌ Jan 21 23:33	♏ Mar 23 05:27	♒ May 23 02:04	♉ Jul 23 15:36	♌ Sep 23 19:52	♏ Nov 24 10:16
♍ Jan 24 06:48	♐ Mar 25 06:28	♓ May 25 06:48	♊ Jul 26 03:36	♍ Sep 26 05:06	♐ Nov 26 10:27
♎ Jan 26 12:14	♑ Mar 27 08:37	♈ May 27 15:15	♋ Jul 28 16:10	♎ Sep 28 10:52	♑ Nov 28 09:57
♏ Jan 28 16:07	♒ Mar 29 12:45	♉ May 30 02:21	♌ Jul 31 03:38	♏ Sep 30 13:58	♒ Nov 30 10:25
♐ Jan 30 18:51	♓ Mar 31 19:12	♊ Jun 1 14:46	♍ Aug 2 13:05	♐ Oct 2 15:53	♓ Dec 2 13:37
♑ Feb 1 21:01	♈ Apr 3 03:45	♋ Jun 4 03:25	♎ Aug 4 20:19	♑ Oct 4 18:01	♈ Dec 4 20:10
♒ Feb 3 23:42	♉ Apr 5 14:11	♌ Jun 6 15:28	♏ Aug 7 01:24	♒ Oct 6 21:19	♉ Dec 7 05:33
♓ Feb 6 04:11	♊ Apr 8 02:13	♍ Jun 9 01:40	♐ Aug 9 04:31	♓ Oct 9 02:06	♊ Dec 9 16:52
♈ Feb 8 11:36	♋ Apr 10 14:52	♎ Jun 11 08:40	♑ Aug 11 06:20	♈ Oct 11 08:30	♋ Dec 12 05:19
♉ Feb 10 22:08	♌ Apr 13 02:15	♏ Jun 13 11:57	♒ Aug 13 07:51	♉ Oct 13 16:49	♌ Dec 14 18:12
♊ Feb 13 10:33	♍ Apr 15 10:21	♐ Jun 15 12:16	♓ Aug 15 10:28	♊ Oct 16 03:22	♍ Dec 17 06:05
♋ Feb 15 22:32	♎ Apr 17 14:25	♑ Jun 17 11:28	♈ Aug 17 15:31	♋ Oct 18 15:47	♎ Dec 19 15:15
♌ Feb 18 08:09	♏ Apr 19 15:23	♒ Jun 19 11:41	♉ Aug 19 23:54	♌ Oct 21 04:21	♏ Dec 21 20:24
♍ Feb 20 14:44	♐ Apr 21 15:03	♓ Jun 21 14:52	♊ Aug 22 11:14	♍ Oct 23 14:33	♐ Dec 23 21:54
♎ Feb 22 18:57	♑ Apr 23 15:32	♈ Jun 23 21:23	♋ Aug 24 23:46	♎ Oct 25 20:49	♑ Dec 25 21:18
♏ Feb 24 21:45	♒ Apr 25 18:29	♉ Jun 26 08:27	♌ Aug 27 11:17	♏ Oct 27 23:25	♒ Dec 27 20:40
♐ Feb 27 00:16	♓ Apr 28 00:39	♊ Jun 28 20:51	♍ Aug 29 20:18	♐ Oct 30 00:02	♓ Dec 29 22:05

Mercury

Jan 1 28♑	♋ Jun 29 13:24
R Jan 4 29♑	♌ Jul 13 15:40
D Jan 24 12♑	♍ Jul 30 16:37
♒ Feb 14 03:06	R Aug 29 27♍
♓ Mar 5 06:01	D Sep 20 11♍
♈ Mar 21 15:38	♎ Oct 7 04:29
♉ Apr 5 16:24	♏ Oct 24 15:58
R Apr 27 21♉	♐ Nov 12 12:06
D May 21 11♉	♑ Dec 2 23:49
♊ Jun 13 01:31	R Dec 18 13♑

Venus

Jan 1 7♒	D Jul 23 1♋
♓ Jan 19 13:46	♌ Sep 8 21:39
♈ Feb 13 04:10	♍ Oct 7 14:14
♉ Mar 9 11:56	♎ Nov 2 14:42
♊ Apr 5 06:45	♏ Nov 27 11:47
♋ May 6 01:52	♐ Dec 21 19:53
R Jun 10 17♋	

Mars

Jan 1 17♏	
♐ Jan 19 19:02	
♑ Mar 6 19:00	
♒ Apr 24 16:00	
♓ Jun 24 15:39	
R Jul 24 4♓	
♒ Aug 24 16:52	
D Sep 22 25♒	
♓ Oct 19 18:59	
♈ Dec 19 11:07	

Jupiter

Jan 1 8♐
R Apr 6 19♐
D Aug 7 10♐
♑ Dec 18 05:52

Saturn

Jan 1 0♏
R Feb 11 2♏
♎ Apr 6 06:32
D Jun 29 25♎
♏ Sep 13 23:18

Uranus

Jan 1 14♓
R Jun 26 21♓
D Nov 27 17♓

Neptune

Jan 1 19♌
D Apr 28 17♌
R Nov 25 22♌

Pluto

Jan 1 11♋
D Mar 24 10♋
R Oct 14 13♋

1925

Sun

♒ Jan 20 13:20	♈ Mar 21 03:12	♊ May 21 14:34	♌ Jul 23 09:45	♎ Sep 23 13:42	♐ Nov 22 19:32
♓ Feb 19 03:43	♉ Apr 20 14:51	♋ Jun 21 22:51	♍ Aug 23 16:31	♏ Oct 23 22:29	♑ Dec 22 08:36

Moon

Jan 1 28♓	♊ Mar 1 13:26	♍ May 2 18:37	♐ Jul 3 06:54	♓ Sep 2 04:02	♊ Nov 2 09:44
♈ Jan 1 02:57	♋ Mar 4 01:36	♎ May 5 03:25	♑ Jul 5 07:24	♈ Sep 4 05:01	♋ Nov 4 19:05
♉ Jan 3 11:30	♌ Mar 6 14:21	♏ May 7 08:20	♒ Jul 7 06:48	♉ Sep 6 08:27	♌ Nov 7 07:15
♊ Jan 5 22:52	♍ Mar 9 02:47	♐ May 9 10:27	♓ Jul 9 07:06	♊ Sep 8 14:16	♍ Nov 9 20:06
♋ Jan 8 11:32	♎ Mar 11 09:43	♑ May 11 11:30	♈ Jul 11 09:51	♋ Sep 11 02:34	♎ Nov 12 06:51
♌ Jan 11 00:13	♏ Mar 13 15:37	♒ May 13 13:07	♉ Jul 13 16:04	♌ Sep 13 15:28	♏ Nov 14 14:05
♍ Jan 13 11:54	♐ Mar 15 19:51	♓ May 15 16:23	♊ Jul 16 01:36	♍ Sep 16 03:55	♐ Nov 16 18:12
♎ Jan 15 21:31	♑ Mar 17 23:07	♈ May 17 21:34	♋ Jul 18 13:31	♎ Sep 18 14:16	♑ Nov 18 20:37
♏ Jan 18 04:10	♒ Mar 20 01:51	♉ May 20 04:40	♌ Jul 21 02:32	♏ Sep 20 22:17	♒ Nov 20 22:48
♐ Jan 20 07:32	♓ Mar 22 04:32	♊ May 22 13:49	♍ Jul 23 15:17	♐ Sep 23 04:16	♓ Nov 23 01:38
♑ Jan 22 08:21	♈ Mar 24 08:02	♋ May 25 01:07	♎ Jul 26 02:30	♑ Sep 25 08:37	♈ Nov 25 05:31
♒ Jan 24 08:08	♉ Mar 26 13:32	♌ May 27 13:58	♏ Jul 28 10:55	♒ Sep 27 11:29	♉ Nov 27 10:46
♓ Jan 26 08:44	♊ Mar 28 22:07	♍ May 30 02:35	♐ Jul 30 15:55	♓ Sep 29 13:19	♊ Nov 29 17:50
♈ Jan 28 11:59	♋ Mar 31 09:42	♎ Jun 1 12:29	♑ Aug 1 17:45	♈ Oct 1 15:05	♋ Dec 2 03:18
♉ Jan 30 18:57	♌ Apr 2 22:31	♏ Jun 3 18:21	♒ Aug 3 17:39	♉ Oct 3 18:19	♌ Dec 4 15:13
♊ Feb 2 05:32	♍ Apr 5 09:53	♐ Jun 5 20:33	♓ Aug 5 17:22	♊ Oct 6 00:34	♍ Dec 7 04:12
♋ Feb 4 18:09	♎ Apr 7 18:03	♑ Jun 7 20:44	♈ Aug 7 18:45	♋ Oct 8 10:31	♎ Dec 9 15:51
♌ Feb 7 06:48	♏ Apr 9 23:02	♒ Jun 9 20:54	♉ Aug 9 23:22	♌ Oct 10 23:08	♏ Dec 12 00:03
♍ Feb 9 18:00	♐ Apr 12 02:05	♓ Jun 11 22:39	♊ Aug 12 07:55	♍ Oct 13 11:42	♐ Dec 14 04:23
♎ Feb 12 03:05	♑ Apr 14 04:31	♈ Jun 14 03:02	♋ Aug 14 19:38	♎ Oct 15 21:57	♑ Dec 16 05:59
♏ Feb 14 08:09	♒ Apr 16 07:23	♉ Jun 16 10:14	♌ Aug 17 08:40	♏ Oct 18 05:12	♒ Dec 18 06:35
♐ Feb 16 14:27	♓ Apr 18 11:01	♊ Jun 18 19:55	♍ Aug 19 21:13	♐ Oct 20 10:09	♓ Dec 20 07:51
♑ Feb 18 17:01	♈ Apr 20 15:44	♋ Jun 21 07:35	♎ Aug 22 08:05	♑ Oct 22 13:56	♈ Dec 22 10:56
♒ Feb 20 18:21	♉ Apr 22 21:59	♌ Jun 23 20:30	♏ Aug 24 16:44	♒ Oct 24 17:12	♉ Dec 24 16:25
♓ Feb 22 19:35	♊ Apr 25 06:31	♍ Jun 26 09:21	♐ Aug 26 22:50	♓ Oct 26 20:14	♊ Dec 27 00:18
♈ Feb 24 22:21	♋ Apr 27 17:44	♎ Jun 28 20:14	♑ Aug 29 02:18	♈ Oct 28 23:23	♋ Dec 29 ...
♉ Feb 27 04:03	♌ Apr 30 06:37	♏ Jul 1 03:32	♒ Aug 31 03:40	♉ Oct 31 03:28	♌ Dec 31 22:26

Mercury

Jan 1 29♐	♋ Jun 20 23:10
D Jan 6 27♐	♌ Jul 5 17:54
♑ Jan 14 07:07	♍ Jul 26 11:37
♒ Feb 7 08:12	R Aug 11 9♍
♓ Feb 25 16:54	♌ Aug 27 06:25
♈ Mar 13 12:36	D Sep 4 26♌
♉ Apr 1 15:41	♍ Sep 11 04:50
R Apr 8 2♉	♎ Sep 29 18:03
♈ Apr 15 23:24	♏ Oct 17 03:57
D May 2 21♈	♐ Nov 5 18:57
♉ May 17 02:15	R Dec 1 27♐
♊ Jun 6 15:24	D Dec 21 11♐

Venus

Jan 1 12♐	♌ Jul 3 14:31
♑ Jan 14 22:26	♍ Jul 28 05:23
♒ Feb 7 23:15	♎ Aug 22 00:25
♓ Mar 4 00:22	♏ Sep 16 02:00
♈ Mar 28 03:03	♐ Oct 11 14:07
♉ Apr 21 08:15	♑ Nov 6 22:31
♊ May 15 16:06	♒ Dec 5 15:12
♋ Jun 9 02:15	

Mars

Jan 1 7♈
♉ Feb 5 10:24
♊ Mar 24 00:43
♋ May 9 22:50
♌ Jun 26 09:10
♍ Aug 12 21:14
♎ Sep 28 19:01
♏ Nov 13 13:58
♐ Dec 28 00:36

Jupiter

Jan 1 3♑
R May 10 22♑
D Sep 9 12♑

Saturn

Jan 1 12♏
R Feb 22 14♏
D Jul 11 7♏

Uranus

Jan 1 18♓
R Jun 30 25♓
D Dec 1 21♓

Neptune

Jan 1 22♌
D May 1 19♌
R Nov 27 24♌

Pluto

Jan 1 12♋
D Mar 25 11♋
R Oct 15 14♋

1926

Sun

♒ Jan 20 19:12	♈ Mar 21 09:01	♊ May 21 20:17	♌ Jul 23 15:27
♓ Feb 19 09:36	♉ Apr 20 20:38	♋ Jun 22 04:33	♍ Aug 23 22:16

♎ Sep 23 19:29	♐ Nov 23 01:26	
♏ Oct 24 04:19	♑ Dec 22 14:32	

Moon

Jan 1 0 ♌	♏ Mar 3 22:28	♒ May 4 03:30	♉ Jul 3 23:59	♌ Sep 3 13:00
♍ Jan 3 11:25	♐ Mar 6 06:40	♓ May 6 06:31	♊ Jul 6 05:56	♍ Sep 6 01:39
♎ Jan 5 23:43	♑ Mar 8 12:06	♈ May 8 08:55	♋ Jul 8 14:15	♎ Sep 8 14:22
♏ Jan 8 09:19	♒ Mar 10 14:39	♉ May 10 11:33	♌ Jul 11 00:49	♏ Sep 11 02:15
♐ Jan 10 15:01	♓ Mar 12 15:02	♊ May 12 15:45	♍ Jul 13 13:07	♐ Sep 13 12:21
♑ Jan 12 17:09	♈ Mar 14 14:52	♋ May 14 22:52	♎ Jul 16 01:51	♑ Sep 15 19:36
♒ Jan 14 17:07	♉ Mar 16 16:06	♌ May 17 09:20	♏ Jul 18 13:07	♒ Sep 17 23:22
♓ Jan 16 16:48	♊ Mar 18 20:40	♍ May 19 21:53	♐ Jul 20 21:09	♓ Sep 20 00:05
♈ Jan 18 18:02	♋ Mar 21 05:30	♎ May 22 10:04	♑ Jul 23 01:28	♈ Sep 21 23:19
♉ Jan 20 22:14	♌ Mar 23 17:35	♏ May 24 19:40	♒ Jul 25 02:47	♉ Sep 23 23:12
♊ Jan 23 05:55	♍ Mar 26 06:36	♐ May 27 02:14	♓ Jul 27 02:45	♊ Sep 26 01:50
♋ Jan 25 16:30	♎ Mar 28 18:25	♑ May 29 06:23	♈ Jul 29 03:13	♋ Sep 28 08:34
♌ Jan 28 04:52	♏ Mar 31 04:16	♒ May 31 09:18	♉ Jul 31 05:45	♌ Sep 30 19:09
♍ Jan 30 17:47	♐ Apr 2 12:07	♓ Jun 2 11:53	♊ Aug 2 11:23	♍ Oct 3 07:48
♎ Feb 2 06:10	♑ Apr 4 18:03	♈ Jun 4 14:44	♋ Aug 4 20:08	♎ Oct 5 20:28
♏ Feb 4 16:38	♒ Apr 6 22:00	♉ Jun 6 18:27	♌ Aug 7 07:11	♏ Oct 8 07:57
♐ Feb 7 00:01	♓ Apr 9 00:03	♊ Jun 8 23:41	♍ Aug 9 19:38	♐ Oct 10 17:54
♑ Feb 9 03:48	♈ Apr 11 01:02	♋ Jun 11 07:13	♎ Aug 12 08:25	♑ Oct 13 01:47
♒ Feb 11 04:36	♉ Apr 13 02:31	♌ Jun 13 17:28	♏ Aug 14 20:17	♒ Oct 15 07:02
♓ Feb 13 03:57	♊ Apr 15 06:20	♍ Jun 16 05:47	♐ Aug 17 05:38	♓ Oct 17 09:28
♈ Feb 15 03:46	♋ Apr 17 13:53	♎ Jun 18 18:18	♑ Aug 19 11:22	♈ Oct 19 09:54
♉ Feb 17 06:07	♌ Apr 20 01:07	♏ Jun 21 04:39	♒ Aug 21 13:30	♉ Oct 21 10:01
♊ Feb 19 12:21	♍ Apr 22 13:57	♐ Jun 23 11:35	♓ Aug 23 13:13	♊ Oct 23 11:49
♋ Feb 21 22:28	♎ Apr 25 01:52	♑ Jun 25 15:18	♈ Aug 25 12:29	♋ Oct 25 17:08
♌ Feb 24 10:58	♏ Apr 27 11:17	♒ Jun 27 17:00	♉ Aug 27 13:24	♌ Oct 28 02:30
♍ Feb 26 23:59	♐ Apr 29 18:19	♓ Jun 29 18:13	♊ Aug 29 17:38	♍ Oct 30 14:41
♎ Mar 1 12:02	♑ May 1 23:32	♈ Jul 1 20:14	♋ Sep 1 01:48	♎ Nov 2 03:22

♏ Nov 4 14:37	
♐ Nov 6 23:51	
♑ Nov 9 07:10	
♒ Nov 11 12:42	
♓ Nov 13 16:22	
♈ Nov 15 18:26	
♉ Nov 17 19:53	
♊ Nov 19 22:09	
♋ Nov 22 02:54	
♌ Nov 24 11:10	
♍ Nov 26 22:34	
♎ Nov 29 11:13	
♏ Dec 1 22:38	
♐ Dec 4 07:31	
♑ Dec 6 13:52	
♒ Dec 8 18:22	
♓ Dec 10 21:44	
♈ Dec 13 00:31	
♉ Dec 15 03:22	
♊ Dec 17 06:59	
♋ Dec 19 12:19	
♌ Dec 21 20:15	
♍ Dec 24 07:02	
♎ Dec 26 19:30	
♏ Dec 29 07:28	
♐ Dec 31 16:50	

Mercury

Jan 1 17 ♐	R Jul 24 21 ♌
♑ Jan 11 07:24	D Aug 17 9 ♌
♒ Jan 31 10:06	♍ Sep 5 20:25
♓ Feb 17 21:35	♎ Sep 21 21:00
♈ Mar 6 03:05	♏ Oct 9 21:50
R Mar 21 14 ♈	♐ Oct 31 11:00
D Apr 13 1 ♈	R Nov 15 11 ♐
♉ May 13 10:53	♏ Nov 28 04:59
♊ May 29 13:52	D Dec 5 24 ♏
♋ Jun 12 10:07	♐ Dec 13 20:16
♌ Jun 29 05:16	

Venus

Jan 1 20 ♒	♋ Jul 24 06:42
R Jan 17 26 ♒	♌ Aug 18 04:35
D Feb 28 10 ♒	♍ Sep 11 16:37
♓ Apr 6 03:53	♎ Oct 5 21:08
♈ May 6 15:14	♏ Oct 29 20:51
♉ Jun 2 20:00	♐ Nov 22 18:10
♊ Jun 28 21:03	♑ Dec 16 14:47

Mars

Jan 1 2 ♐	
♑ Feb 9 03:32	
♒ Mar 23 04:37	
♓ May 3 17:01	
♈ Jun 15 00:45	
♉ Aug 1 09:27	
R Sep 29 19 ♉	
D Dec 7 4 ♉	

Jupiter

Jan 1 28 ♑	
♒ Jan 6 01:01	
R Jun 16 27 ♒	
D Oct 14 17 ♒	

Saturn

Jan 1 22 ♏
R Mar 6 26 ♏
D Jul 24 19 ♏
♐ Dec 2 23:12

Uranus

Jan 1 21 ♓
R Jul 5 29 ♓
D Dec 5 25 ♓

Neptune

Jan 1 24 ♌
D May 3 21 ♌
R Nov 29 26 ♌

Pluto

Jan 1 13 ♋
D Mar 27 12 ♋
R Oct 17 15 ♋

1927

Sun

♒ Jan 21 01:10	♈ Mar 21 14:59	♊ May 22 02:10	♌ Jul 23 21:21	♎ Sep 24 01:23	♐ Nov 23 07:16
♓ Feb 19 15:34	♉ Apr 21 02:32	♋ Jun 22 10:26	♍ Aug 24 04:10	♏ Oct 24 10:10	♑ Dec 22 20:19

Moon

Jan 1 3♐	♓ Mar 3 00:05	♊ May 2 20:52	♍ Jul 3 09:25	♐ Sep 3 13:09	♓ Nov 4 03:55
♑ Jan 2 22:51	♈ Mar 4 23:18	♋ May 4 23:51	♎ Jul 5 20:46	♑ Sep 5 23:28	♈ Nov 6 05:53
♒ Jan 5 02:10	♉ Mar 6 23:07	♌ May 7 06:38	♏ Jul 8 09:17	♒ Sep 8 05:49	♉ Nov 8 05:37
♓ Jan 7 04:06	♊ Mar 9 01:29	♍ May 9 17:01	♐ Jul 10 20:37	♓ Sep 10 08:15	♊ Nov 10 05:02
♈ Jan 9 05:59	♋ Mar 11 07:29	♎ May 12 05:27	♑ Jul 13 05:06	♈ Sep 12 08:16	♋ Nov 12 06:15
♉ Jan 11 08:56	♌ Mar 13 16:51	♏ May 14 17:51	♒ Jul 15 10:30	♉ Sep 14 08:01	♌ Nov 14 10:48
♊ Jan 13 13:30	♍ Mar 16 04:22	♐ May 17 04:56	♓ Jul 17 13:42	♊ Sep 16 09:27	♍ Nov 16 19:12
♋ Jan 15 19:58	♎ Mar 18 16:48	♑ May 19 14:11	♈ Jul 19 15:57	♋ Sep 18 13:49	♎ Nov 19 06:40
♌ Jan 18 04:30	♏ Mar 21 05:20	♒ May 21 21:16	♉ Jul 21 18:23	♌ Sep 20 21:13	♏ Nov 21 19:26
♍ Jan 20 15:08	♐ Mar 23 17:06	♓ May 24 02:00	♊ Jul 23 21:45	♍ Sep 23 07:01	♐ Nov 24 07:52
♎ Jan 23 03:25	♑ Mar 26 02:38	♈ May 26 04:36	♋ Jul 26 02:30	♎ Sep 25 18:29	♑ Nov 26 19:01
♏ Jan 25 15:53	♒ Mar 28 08:39	♉ May 28 05:50	♌ Jul 28 09:00	♏ Sep 28 07:05	♒ Nov 29 04:06
♐ Jan 28 02:20	♓ Mar 30 10:52	♊ May 30 07:02	♍ Jul 30 17:40	♐ Sep 30 19:52	♓ Dec 1 10:35
♑ Jan 30 09:12	♈ Apr 1 10:30	♋ Jun 1 09:49	♎ Aug 2 04:43	♑ Oct 3 07:11	♈ Dec 3 14:19
♒ Feb 1 12:22	♉ Apr 3 09:36	♌ Jun 3 15:37	♏ Aug 4 17:15	♒ Oct 5 15:06	♉ Dec 5 15:45
♓ Feb 3 13:07	♊ Apr 5 10:25	♍ Jun 6 00:54	♐ Aug 7 05:14	♓ Oct 7 18:49	♊ Dec 7 16:09
♈ Feb 5 13:19	♋ Apr 7 14:41	♎ Jun 8 12:48	♑ Aug 9 14:22	♈ Oct 9 19:13	♋ Dec 9 17:11
♉ Feb 7 14:50	♌ Apr 9 22:59	♏ Jun 11 01:15	♒ Aug 11 19:45	♉ Oct 11 18:17	♌ Dec 11 20:31
♊ Feb 9 18:53	♍ Apr 12 10:19	♐ Jun 13 12:15	♓ Aug 13 22:04	♊ Oct 13 18:10	♍ Dec 14 03:24
♋ Feb 12 01:50	♎ Apr 14 22:52	♑ Jun 15 20:51	♈ Aug 15 22:56	♋ Oct 15 20:49	♎ Dec 16 13:53
♌ Feb 14 11:11	♏ Apr 17 11:19	♒ Jun 18 03:04	♉ Aug 18 00:12	♌ Oct 18 03:06	♏ Dec 19 02:31
♍ Feb 16 22:14	♐ Apr 19 22:49	♓ Jun 20 07:25	♊ Aug 20 03:07	♍ Oct 20 12:43	♐ Dec 21 14:59
♎ Feb 19 10:30	♑ Apr 22 08:35	♈ Jun 22 10:29	♋ Aug 22 08:18	♎ Oct 23 00:26	♑ Dec 24 01:37
♏ Feb 21 23:08	♒ Apr 24 15:43	♉ Jun 24 12:53	♌ Aug 24 15:38	♏ Oct 25 13:07	♒ Dec 26 09:53
♐ Feb 24 10:33	♓ Apr 26 19:37	♊ Jun 26 15:25	♍ Aug 27 00:54	♐ Oct 28 01:48	♓ Dec 28 16:00
♑ Feb 26 18:54	♈ Apr 28 20:42	♋ Jun 28 19:03	♎ Aug 29 12:01	♑ Oct 30 13:22	♈ Dec 30 20:17
♒ Feb 28 23:14	♉ Apr 30 20:28	♌ Jul 1 00:47	♏ Sep 1 00:35	♒ Nov 1 22:26	

Mercury

Jan 1 23♐	R Jul 6 2♌
♑ Jan 5 01:55	♋ Jul 14 04:33
♒ Jan 24 01:14	D Jul 30 22♋
♓ Feb 10 04:36	♌ Aug 12 03:22
R Mar 4 27♓	♍ Aug 28 23:02
D Mar 27 14♓	♎ Sep 14 01:46
♈ Apr 17 12:28	♏ Oct 3 08:40
♉ May 6 11:31	R Oct 30 24♏
♊ May 21 00:03	D Nov 19 9♏
♋ Jun 4 13:44	♐ Dec 9 09:24
♌ Jun 28 18:49	♑ Dec 29 01:48

Venus

Jan 1 19♑	♌ Jun 8 02:57
♒ Jan 9 11:46	♍ Jul 7 19:04
♓ Feb 2 10:31	R Aug 20 24♍
♈ Feb 26 13:14	D Oct 2 8♍
♉ Mar 22 22:55	♎ Nov 9 13:28
♊ Apr 16 19:26	♏ Dec 8 21:26
♋ May 12 08:35	

Mars

Jan 1 7♉
♊ Feb 22 00:54
♋ Apr 17 01:39
♌ Jun 6 11:40
♍ Jul 25 07:51
♎ Sep 10 14:25
♏ Oct 26 00:20
♐ Dec 8 11:04

Jupiter

Jan 1 26♒
♓ Jan 18 11:14
♈ Jun 6 09:38
R Jul 24 3♈
♓ Sep 11 04:28
D Nov 19 23♓

Saturn

Jan 1 3♐
R Mar 18 7♐
D Aug 5 1♐

Uranus

Jan 1 25♓
♈ Mar 31 17:24
R Jul 9 3♈
♓ Nov 4 10:34
D Dec 9 29♓

Neptune

Jan 1 26♌
D May 6 24♌
R Dec 2 29♌

Pluto

Jan 1 14♋
D Mar 28 13♋
R Oct 18 17♋

1928

Sun

♒ Jan 21 06:58	♈ Mar 20 20:42	♊ May 21 07:52	♌ Jul 23 03:03	♎ Sep 23 07:08	♐ Nov 22 13:02
♓ Feb 19 21:20	♉ Apr 20 08:15	♋ Jun 21 16:07	♍ Aug 23 09:55	♏ Oct 23 15:57	♑ Dec 22 02:05

Moon

Jan 1 16 ♈	♋ Feb 29 17:04	♎ May 1 03:36	♑ Jul 2 05:22	♈ Sep 1 17:25	♋ Nov 1 14:39
♉ Jan 1 23:14	♌ Mar 2 22:37	♏ May 3 15:38	♒ Jul 4 15:31	♉ Sep 3 20:07	♌ Nov 3 17:14
♊ Jan 4 01:20	♍ Mar 5 05:51	♐ May 6 04:31	♓ Jul 6 23:21	♊ Sep 5 22:43	♍ Nov 5 22:40
♋ Jan 6 03:27	♎ Mar 7 15:03	♑ May 8 17:08	♈ Jul 9 05:02	♋ Sep 8 01:15	♎ Nov 8 07:04
♌ Jan 8 06:51	♏ Mar 10 02:31	♒ May 11 03:57	♉ Jul 11 08:49	♌ Sep 10 05:49	♏ Nov 10 17:53
♍ Jan 10 12:52	♐ Mar 12 15:23	♓ May 13 11:35	♊ Jul 13 10:58	♍ Sep 12 11:00	♐ Nov 13 06:20
♎ Jan 12 22:16	♑ Mar 15 03:32	♈ May 15 15:29	♋ Jul 15 12:19	♎ Sep 14 18:12	♑ Nov 15 19:25
♏ Jan 15 10:26	♒ Mar 17 22:30	♉ May 17 16:25	♌ Jul 17 14:05	♏ Sep 17 04:04	♒ Nov 18 07:38
♐ Jan 17 23:06	♓ Mar 19 17:19	♊ May 19 15:55	♍ Jul 19 17:52	♐ Sep 19 16:23	♓ Nov 20 17:18
♑ Jan 20 09:48	♈ Mar 21 18:53	♋ May 21 15:57	♎ Jul 22 01:02	♑ Sep 22 05:15	♈ Nov 22 23:14
♒ Jan 22 17:27	♉ Mar 23 19:06	♌ May 23 18:16	♏ Jul 24 11:46	♒ Sep 24 16:01	♉ Nov 25 01:30
♓ Jan 24 22:24	♊ Mar 25 19:52	♍ May 26 00:06	♐ Jul 27 00:34	♓ Sep 26 23:00	♊ Nov 27 01:24
♈ Jan 27 01:48	♋ Mar 27 22:40	♎ May 28 09:36	♑ Jul 29 12:46	♈ Sep 29 02:31	♋ Nov 29 00:44
♉ Jan 29 04:42	♌ Mar 30 04:04	♏ May 30 21:40	♒ Jul 31 22:32	♉ Oct 1 03:59	♌ Dec 1 01:28
♊ Jan 31 07:47	♍ Apr 1 11:53	♐ Jun 2 10:37	♓ Aug 3 05:34	♊ Oct 3 05:09	♍ Dec 3 05:15
♋ Feb 2 11:20	♎ Apr 3 21:46	♑ Jun 4 22:58	♈ Aug 5 10:32	♋ Oct 5 07:21	♎ Dec 5 12:51
♌ Feb 4 15:52	♏ Apr 6 09:26	♒ Jun 7 09:41	♉ Aug 7 14:17	♌ Oct 7 11:17	♏ Dec 7 23:44
♍ Feb 6 22:08	♐ Apr 8 22:20	♓ Jun 9 17:54	♊ Aug 9 17:21	♍ Oct 9 17:13	♐ Dec 10 12:28
♎ Feb 9 07:03	♑ Apr 11 10:55	♈ Jun 11 23:13	♋ Aug 11 20:02	♎ Oct 12 01:13	♑ Dec 13 01:29
♏ Feb 11 18:41	♒ Apr 13 21:05	♉ Jun 14 01:46	♌ Aug 13 22:56	♏ Oct 14 11:28	♒ Dec 15 13:34
♐ Feb 14 07:31	♓ Apr 16 03:19	♊ Jun 16 02:23	♍ Aug 16 02:23	♐ Oct 16 23:43	♓ Dec 17 23:49
♑ Feb 16 18:52	♈ Apr 18 05:38	♋ Jun 18 02:34	♎ Aug 18 09:51	♑ Oct 19 12:49	♈ Dec 20 07:14
♒ Feb 19 02:46	♉ Apr 20 05:36	♌ Jun 20 04:02	♏ Aug 20 19:56	♒ Oct 22 00:32	♉ Dec 22 11:24
♓ Feb 21 07:05	♊ Apr 22 05:09	♍ Jun 22 08:25	♐ Aug 23 08:28	♓ Oct 24 08:50	♊ Dec 24 12:40
♈ Feb 23 09:08	♋ Apr 24 06:14	♎ Jun 24 16:42	♑ Aug 25 20:59	♈ Oct 26 13:04	♋ Dec 26 12:17
♉ Feb 25 10:42	♌ Apr 26 10:10	♏ Jun 27 04:15	♒ Aug 28 06:57	♉ Oct 28 14:15	♌ Dec 28 12:05
♊ Feb 27 13:07	♍ Apr 28 17:28	♐ Jun 29 17:13	♓ Aug 30 13:30	♊ Oct 30 14:11	♍ Dec 30 14:12

Mercury

Jan 1 4 ♑	D Jul 10 3 ♋
♒ Jan 16 13:35	♌ Aug 4 20:01
♓ Feb 3 10:34	♍ Aug 19 17:00
R Feb 15 10 ♓	♎ Sep 5 16:09
♒ Feb 29 05:46	♏ Sep 27 18:22
D Mar 8 26 ♒	R Oct 12 8 ♏
♓ Mar 18 01:56	♎ Oct 24 21:23
♈ Apr 11 02:05	D Nov 2 23 ♎
♉ Apr 27 10:34	♏ Nov 11 09:22
♊ May 11 12:05	♐ Dec 1 16:55
♋ May 28 23:06	♑ Dec 20 19:36
R Jun 16 12 ♋	

Venus

Jan 1 26 ♏	♋ Jun 23 21:43
♐ Jan 4 00:05	♌ Jul 18 07:15
♑ Jan 29 01:12	♍ Aug 11 15:28
♒ Feb 22 16:14	♎ Sep 4 23:06
♓ Mar 18 03:24	♏ Sep 29 07:17
♈ Apr 11 13:33	♐ Oct 23 17:12
♉ May 6 00:00	♑ Nov 17 06:05
♊ May 30 10:59	♒ Dec 12 01:23

Mars

Jan 1 16 ♐
♑ Jan 19 02:01
♒ Feb 28 06:28
♓ Apr 7 14:15
♈ May 16 21:29
♉ Jun 26 09:03
♊ Aug 9 04:01
♋ Oct 3 03:53
R Nov 12 9 ♋
♊ Dec 20 05:15

Jupiter

Jan 1 26 ♓
♈ Jan 23 02:43
♉ Jun 4 04:50
R Aug 30 10 ♉
D Dec 25 0 ♉

Saturn

Jan 1 13 ♐
R Mar 28 19 ♐
D Aug 17 12 ♐

Uranus

Jan 1 29 ♓
♈ Jan 13 08:55
R Jul 12 7 ♈
D Dec 12 3 ♈

Neptune

Jan 1 28 ♌
D May 7 26 ♌
♍ Sep 21 12:21
R Dec 3 1 ♍

Pluto

Jan 1 16 ♋
D Mar 28 14 ♋
R Oct 19 18 ♋

1929

Sun

♒ Jan 20 12:44	♈ Mar 21 02:35	♊ May 21 13:47	♌ Jul 23 08:55	♎ Sep 23 12:54	♐ Nov 22 18:48
♓ Feb 19 03:07	♉ Apr 20 14:10	♋ Jun 21 22:01	♍ Aug 23 15:43	♏ Oct 23 21:43	♑ Dec 22 07:53

Moon

Jan 1 19 ♍	♐ Mar 2 10:03	♓ May 3 13:51	♊ Jul 3 22:12	♍ Sep 2 18:25	♐ Nov 3 04:47
♎ Jan 1 20:08	♑ Mar 4 22:54	♈ May 5 20:50	♋ Jul 5 22:20	♎ Sep 4 20:50	♑ Nov 5 15:57
♏ Jan 4 06:09	♒ Mar 7 10:44	♉ May 8 00:17	♌ Jul 7 21:36	♏ Sep 7 02:19	♒ Nov 8 04:31
♐ Jan 6 18:49	♓ Mar 9 19:43	♊ May 10 01:22	♍ Jul 9 22:08	♐ Sep 9 11:37	♓ Nov 10 16:30
♑ Jan 9 07:51	♈ Mar 12 01:51	♋ May 12 01:44	♎ Jul 12 01:53	♑ Sep 11 23:43	♈ Nov 13 01:43
♒ Jan 11 19:32	♉ Mar 14 06:03	♌ May 14 03:02	♏ Jul 14 09:44	♒ Sep 14 12:16	♉ Nov 15 07:17
♓ Jan 14 05:20	♊ Mar 16 09:22	♍ May 16 06:32	♐ Jul 16 21:00	♓ Sep 16 23:07	♊ Nov 17 09:52
♈ Jan 16 13:06	♋ Mar 18 12:22	♎ May 18 12:51	♑ Jul 19 09:46	♈ Sep 19 07:30	♋ Nov 19 10:52
♉ Jan 18 18:37	♌ Mar 20 15:26	♏ May 20 21:52	♒ Jul 21 22:19	♉ Sep 21 13:45	♌ Nov 21 11:57
♊ Jan 20 21:43	♍ Mar 22 19:05	♐ May 23 09:02	♓ Jul 24 09:39	♊ Sep 23 18:23	♍ Nov 23 14:31
♋ Jan 22 22:52	♎ Mar 25 00:10	♑ May 25 21:34	♈ Jul 26 19:12	♋ Sep 25 21:51	♎ Nov 25 19:22
♌ Jan 24 23:15	♏ Mar 27 07:49	♒ May 28 10:16	♉ Jul 29 02:24	♌ Sep 28 00:27	♏ Nov 28 02:39
♍ Jan 27 00:46	♐ Mar 29 18:25	♓ May 30 21:37	♊ Jul 31 06:43	♍ Sep 30 02:51	♐ Nov 30 12:06
♎ Jan 29 05:18	♑ Apr 1 07:03	♈ Jun 2 05:58	♋ Aug 2 08:15	♎ Oct 2 06:08	♑ Dec 2 23:24
♏ Jan 31 13:56	♒ Apr 3 19:16	♉ Jun 4 10:33	♌ Aug 4 08:10	♏ Oct 4 11:39	♒ Dec 5 11:57
♐ Feb 3 01:58	♓ Apr 6 04:52	♊ Jun 6 11:57	♍ Aug 6 08:21	♐ Oct 6 20:17	♓ Dec 8 00:26
♑ Feb 5 15:00	♈ Apr 8 10:56	♋ Jun 8 11:35	♎ Aug 8 10:54	♑ Oct 9 07:49	♈ Dec 10 10:56
♒ Feb 8 02:34	♉ Apr 10 14:16	♌ Jun 10 11:24	♏ Aug 10 17:21	♒ Oct 11 20:24	♉ Dec 12 17:49
♓ Feb 10 11:41	♊ Apr 12 16:11	♍ Jun 12 13:20	♐ Aug 13 03:44	♓ Oct 14 07:39	♊ Dec 14 20:47
♈ Feb 12 18:40	♋ Apr 14 18:03	♎ Jun 14 18:38	♑ Aug 15 16:20	♈ Oct 16 16:02	♋ Dec 16 21:03
♉ Feb 15 00:01	♌ Apr 16 20:05	♏ Jun 17 03:31	♒ Aug 18 04:50	♉ Oct 18 21:27	♌ Dec 18 20:34
♊ Feb 17 04:01	♍ Apr 19 01:05	♐ Jun 19 15:02	♓ Aug 20 15:45	♊ Oct 21 00:53	♍ Dec 20 21:21
♋ Feb 19 06:45	♎ Apr 21 07:12	♑ Jun 22 03:44	♈ Aug 23 00:46	♋ Oct 23 03:23	♎ Dec 23 01:03
♌ Feb 21 08:40	♏ Apr 23 15:34	♒ Jun 24 16:23	♉ Aug 25 07:54	♌ Oct 25 05:55	♏ Dec 25 08:11
♍ Feb 23 10:58	♐ Apr 26 02:15	♓ Jun 27 03:58	♊ Aug 27 13:03	♍ Oct 27 09:07	♐ Dec 27 18:10
♎ Feb 25 15:15	♑ Apr 28 14:42	♈ Jun 29 13:21	♋ Aug 29 16:04	♎ Oct 29 13:38	♑ Dec 30 05:56
♏ Feb 27 22:53	♒ May 1 03:18	♉ Jul 1 19:30	♌ Aug 31 17:25	♏ Oct 31 20:00	

Mercury

Jan 1 17 ♑	♋ Jul 11 21:30
♒ Jan 8 08:07	♌ Jul 27 15:10
R Jan 29 24 ♒	♍ Aug 11 14:49
D Feb 19 9 ♒	♎ Aug 30 06:09
♓ Mar 16 01:14	R Sep 25 22 ♎
♈ Apr 3 21:22	D Oct 17 7 ♎
♉ Apr 19 00:27	♏ Nov 5 19:30
♊ May 3 21:52	♐ Nov 24 12:04
R May 28 22 ♊	♑ Dec 13 14:42
D Jun 21 13 ♊	

Venus

Jan 1 23 ♒	♊ Jul 8 01:59
♓ Jan 6 12:00	♋ Aug 5 05:37
♈ Feb 2 14:34	♌ Aug 31 11:23
♉ Mar 8 07:22	♍ Sep 25 16:13
R Mar 30 8 ♉	♎ Oct 20 05:12
♈ Apr 20 02:09	♏ Nov 13 08:34
D May 11 21 ♈	♐ Dec 7 07:03
♉ Jun 3 09:45	

Mars

Jan 1 25 ♊
D Jan 27 21 ♊
♋ Mar 10 23:02
♌ May 13 02:38
♍ Jul 4 10:04
♎ Aug 21 21:58
♏ Oct 6 12:25
♐ Nov 18 13:31
♑ Dec 29 10:47

Jupiter

Jan 1 0 ♉
♊ Jun 12 12:51
R Oct 5 16 ♊

Saturn

Jan 1 23 ♐
♑ Mar 15 14:29
R Apr 9 0 ♑
♐ May 5 03:48
D Aug 29 23 ♐
♑ Nov 30 04:22

Uranus

Jan 1 3 ♈
R Jul 17 11 ♈
D Dec 17 7 ♈

Neptune

Jan 1 1 ♍
♌ Feb 19 11:09
D May 9 28 ♌
♍ Jul 24 15:00
R Dec 6 3 ♍

Pluto

Jan 1 17 ♋
D Mar 30 16 ♋
R Oct 21 19 ♋

1930

Sun

♒ Jan 20 18:34	♈ Mar 21 08:29	♊ May 21 19:40	♌ Jul 23 14:40	♎ Sep 23 18:39	♐ Nov 23 00:38
♓ Feb 19 09:00	♉ Apr 20 20:05	♋ Jun 22 03:50	♍ Aug 23 21:26	♏ Oct 24 03:29	♑ Dec 22 13:43

Moon

Jan 1 20 ♑	♈ Mar 2 06:07	♋ May 2 13:53	♎ Jul 2 09:46	♑ Sep 1 20:35	♈ Nov 2 23:34
♒ Jan 1 18:28	♉ Mar 4 15:18	♌ May 4 16:30	♏ Jul 4 14:55	♒ Sep 4 08:27	♉ Nov 5 09:37
♓ Jan 4 07:04	♊ Mar 6 22:15	♍ May 6 19:09	♐ Jul 6 22:49	♓ Sep 6 21:05	♊ Nov 7 16:57
♈ Jan 6 18:26	♋ Mar 9 02:34	♎ May 8 22:30	♑ Jul 9 08:49	♈ Sep 9 09:21	♋ Nov 9 22:05
♉ Jan 9 02:59	♌ Mar 11 04:25	♏ May 11 03:05	♒ Jul 11 20:21	♉ Sep 11 20:17	♌ Nov 12 01:45
♊ Jan 11 07:34	♍ Mar 13 04:52	♐ May 13 09:38	♓ Jul 14 08:57	♊ Sep 14 05:00	♍ Nov 14 04:42
♋ Jan 13 08:34	♎ Mar 15 05:42	♑ May 15 18:39	♈ Jul 16 21:24	♋ Sep 16 10:42	♎ Nov 16 07:27
♌ Jan 15 07:36	♏ Mar 17 08:45	♒ May 18 06:02	♉ Jul 19 07:53	♌ Sep 18 13:17	♏ Nov 18 10:35
♍ Jan 17 06:57	♐ Mar 19 15:22	♓ May 20 18:34	♊ Jul 21 14:38	♍ Sep 20 13:45	♐ Nov 20 15:00
♎ Jan 19 08:43	♑ Mar 22 01:39	♈ May 23 05:55	♋ Jul 23 17:21	♎ Sep 22 13:43	♑ Nov 22 21:41
♏ Jan 21 14:24	♒ Mar 24 14:05	♉ May 25 14:15	♌ Jul 25 17:18	♏ Sep 24 15:06	♒ Nov 25 07:22
♐ Jan 23 23:56	♓ Mar 27 02:22	♊ May 27 19:07	♍ Jul 27 16:33	♐ Sep 26 19:33	♓ Nov 27 19:31
♑ Jan 26 11:53	♈ Mar 29 12:59	♋ May 29 21:25	♎ Jul 29 17:17	♑ Sep 29 03:47	♈ Nov 30 08:06
♒ Jan 29 00:35	♉ Mar 31 21:22	♌ May 31 22:45	♏ Jul 31 21:04	♒ Oct 1 15:08	♉ Dec 2 18:31
♓ Jan 31 12:58	♊ Apr 3 03:42	♍ Jun 3 00:37	♐ Aug 3 04:24	♓ Oct 4 03:46	♊ Dec 5 01:31
♈ Feb 3 00:22	♋ Apr 5 08:11	♎ Jun 5 04:04	♑ Aug 5 14:34	♈ Oct 6 15:51	♋ Dec 7 05:31
♉ Feb 5 09:47	♌ Apr 7 11:09	♏ Jun 7 09:29	♒ Aug 8 02:25	♉ Oct 9 02:14	♌ Dec 9 07:52
♊ Feb 7 16:07	♍ Apr 9 13:10	♐ Jun 9 16:55	♓ Aug 10 15:01	♊ Oct 11 10:29	♍ Dec 11 10:04
♋ Feb 9 18:54	♎ Apr 11 15:17	♑ Jun 12 02:19	♈ Aug 13 03:31	♋ Oct 13 16:29	♎ Dec 13 13:05
♌ Feb 11 19:00	♏ Apr 13 18:44	♒ Jun 14 13:37	♉ Aug 15 14:37	♌ Oct 15 20:18	♏ Dec 15 17:18
♍ Feb 13 18:14	♐ Apr 16 00:48	♓ Jun 17 02:12	♊ Aug 17 22:45	♍ Oct 17 22:25	♐ Dec 17 22:53
♎ Feb 15 18:49	♑ Apr 18 10:07	♈ Jun 19 14:15	♋ Aug 20 03:01	♏ Oct 22 01:31	♑ Dec 20 06:10
♏ Feb 17 22:44	♒ Apr 20 21:58	♉ Jun 21 23:35	♌ Aug 22 03:57	♐ Oct 24 05:22	♒ Dec 22 15:43
♐ Feb 20 06:47	♓ Apr 23 10:23	♊ Jun 24 04:59	♍ Aug 24 03:13	♑ Oct 26 12:26	♓ Dec 25 03:35
♑ Feb 22 18:12	♈ Apr 25 21:08	♋ Jun 26 06:57	♎ Aug 26 02:58	♒ Oct 28 22:52	♈ Dec 27 16:29
♒ Feb 25 06:57	♉ Apr 28 05:08	♌ Jun 28 07:06	♏ Aug 28 05:10	♓ Oct 31 11:21	♉ Dec 30 03:50
♓ Feb 27 19:12	♊ Apr 30 10:26	♍ Jun 30 07:28	♐ Aug 30 11:04		

Mercury

Jan 1 27 ♑	♊ Jun 14 19:31
♒ Jan 2 10:27	♋ Jul 4 22:17
R Jan 13 9 ♒	♌ Jul 19 02:40
♑ Jan 23 00:19	♍ Aug 4 02:51
D Feb 2 22 ♑	♎ Aug 26 18:16
♒ Feb 15 15:24	R Sep 8 6 ♎
♓ Mar 9 22:25	♍ Sep 20 02:01
♈ Mar 26 23:40	D Sep 30 21 ♍
♉ Apr 10 17:00	♎ Oct 11 04:58
♊ May 1 05:18	♏ Oct 29 14:36
R May 8 2 ♊	♐ Nov 17 05:31
♉ May 17 11:15	♑ Dec 6 21:13
D Jun 1 23 ♉	R Dec 27 23 ♑

Venus

Jan 1 1 ♑	♍ Jul 14 16:35
♒ Jan 24 00:22	♎ Aug 10 00:57
♓ Feb 16 22:11	♏ Sep 7 04:08
♈ Mar 12 22:33	♐ Oct 12 02:57
♉ Apr 6 02:57	R Nov 2 7 ♐
♊ Apr 30 12:35	♏ Nov 22 07:27
♋ May 25 04:33	D Dec 13 22 ♏
♌ Jun 19 04:37	

Mars

Jan 1 1 ♑
♒ Feb 6 18:26
♓ Mar 17 05:59
♈ Apr 24 17:31
♉ Jun 3 03:18
♊ Jul 14 12:38
♋ Aug 28 11:22
♌ Oct 20 14:40
R Dec 18 16 ♌

Jupiter

Jan 1 7 ♊
D Jan 31 6 ♊
♋ Jun 26 23:28
R Nov 8 20 ♋

Saturn

Jan 1 3 ♑
R Apr 21 11 ♑
D Sep 9 5 ♑

Uranus

Jan 1 7 ♈
R Jul 21 15 ♈
D Dec 21 11 ♈

Neptune

Jan 1 3 ♍
D May 12 0 ♍
R Dec 8 5 ♍

Pluto

Jan 1 18 ♋
D Mar 31 17 ♋
R Oct 22 20 ♋

1931

Sun

♒ Jan 21 00:21	♈ Mar 21 14:10	♊ May 22 01:17	♌ Jul 23 20:20	♎ Sep 24 00:24	♐ Nov 23 06:25
♓ Feb 19 14:43	♉ Apr 21 01:43	♋ Jun 22 09:28	♍ Aug 24 03:10	♏ Oct 24 09:17	♑ Dec 22 19:30

Moon

Jan 1 23♉	♌ Mar 1 14:24	♏ May 1 11:24	♒ Jul 1 18:55	♉ Sep 1 20:58	♌ Nov 2 13:38
♊ Jan 1 11:34	♍ Mar 3 14:19	♐ May 3 13:12	♓ Jul 4 05:09	♊ Sep 4 08:42	♍ Nov 4 18:06
♋ Jan 3 15:21	♎ Mar 5 13:31	♑ May 5 17:35	♈ Jul 6 17:39	♋ Sep 6 17:14	♎ Nov 6 20:01
♌ Jan 5 16:31	♏ Mar 7 14:01	♒ May 8 01:35	♉ Jul 9 06:13	♌ Sep 8 21:46	♏ Nov 8 20:20
♍ Jan 7 17:06	♐ Mar 9 17:30	♓ May 10 13:01	♊ Jul 11 16:13	♍ Sep 10 23:02	♐ Nov 10 20:37
♎ Jan 9 18:47	♑ Mar 12 00:39	♈ May 13 01:55	♋ Jul 13 22:30	♎ Sep 12 22:43	♑ Nov 12 22:51
♏ Jan 11 22:39	♒ Mar 14 11:02	♉ May 15 13:53	♌ Jul 16 01:40	♏ Sep 14 22:39	♒ Nov 15 04:39
♐ Jan 14 04:50	♓ Mar 16 23:25	♊ May 17 23:25	♍ Jul 18 03:22	♐ Sep 17 00:39	♓ Nov 17 14:32
♑ Jan 16 13:01	♈ Mar 19 12:22	♋ May 20 06:25	♎ Jul 20 05:05	♑ Sep 19 05:47	♈ Nov 20 03:07
♒ Jan 18 23:02	♉ Mar 22 00:44	♌ May 22 11:27	♏ Jul 22 07:55	♒ Sep 21 14:17	♉ Nov 22 16:00
♓ Jan 21 10:53	♊ Mar 24 11:18	♍ May 24 15:06	♐ Jul 24 12:18	♓ Sep 24 01:28	♊ Nov 25 03:10
♈ Jan 23 23:54	♋ Mar 26 19:04	♎ May 26 17:51	♑ Jul 26 18:22	♈ Sep 26 14:09	♋ Nov 27 12:08
♉ Jan 26 12:08	♌ Mar 28 23:29	♏ May 28 20:07	♒ Jul 29 02:23	♉ Sep 29 03:05	♌ Nov 29 19:06
♊ Jan 28 21:18	♍ Mar 31 00:57	♐ May 30 22:47	♓ Jul 31 12:45	♊ Oct 1 15:02	♍ Dec 2 00:16
♋ Jan 31 02:09	♎ Apr 2 00:48	♑ Jun 2 03:06	♈ Aug 3 01:09	♋ Oct 4 00:38	♎ Dec 4 03:44
♌ Feb 2 03:23	♏ Apr 4 00:49	♒ Jun 4 10:22	♉ Aug 5 14:04	♌ Oct 6 06:48	♏ Dec 6 05:42
♍ Feb 4 02:57	♐ Apr 6 02:52	♓ Jun 6 21:00	♊ Aug 8 01:01	♍ Oct 8 09:34	♐ Dec 8 07:04
♎ Feb 6 02:54	♑ Apr 8 08:19	♈ Jun 9 09:44	♋ Aug 10 08:10	♎ Oct 10 09:49	♑ Dec 10 09:17
♏ Feb 8 05:04	♒ Apr 10 17:39	♉ Jun 11 21:53	♌ Aug 12 11:31	♏ Oct 12 09:17	♒ Dec 12 14:09
♐ Feb 10 10:21	♓ Apr 13 05:47	♊ Jun 14 07:22	♍ Aug 14 12:24	♐ Oct 14 09:49	♓ Dec 14 22:50
♑ Feb 12 18:39	♈ Apr 15 18:46	♋ Jun 16 13:36	♎ Aug 16 12:44	♑ Oct 16 13:17	♈ Dec 17 10:49
♒ Feb 15 05:14	♉ Apr 18 06:49	♌ Jun 18 17:36	♏ Aug 18 14:10	♒ Oct 18 20:38	♉ Dec 19 23:44
♓ Feb 17 17:22	♊ Apr 20 16:55	♍ Jun 20 20:32	♐ Aug 20 17:46	♓ Oct 21 07:31	♊ Dec 22 10:58
♈ Feb 20 06:20	♋ Apr 23 00:42	♎ Jun 22 23:21	♑ Aug 22 23:58	♈ Oct 23 20:20	♋ Dec 24 19:21
♉ Feb 22 18:52	♌ Apr 25 06:02	♏ Jun 25 02:34	♒ Aug 25 08:37	♉ Oct 26 09:12	♌ Dec 27 01:15
♊ Feb 25 05:13	♍ Apr 27 09:08	♐ Jun 27 06:25	♓ Aug 27 19:27	♊ Oct 28 20:46	♍ Dec 29 05:39
♋ Feb 27 11:46	♎ Apr 29 10:33	♑ Jun 29 11:35	♈ Aug 30 07:55	♊ Oct 31 06:25	♎ Dec 31 09:17

Mercury

Jan 1 21♑	♍ Jul 28 22:57
D Jan 17 7♑	R Aug 22 18 ♍
♒ Feb 11 12:26	D Sep 14 6 ♍
♓ Mar 2 17:24	♎ Oct 4 18:19
♈ Mar 18 19:29	♏ Oct 22 02:15
♉ Apr 3 13:45	♐ Nov 10 04:22
R Apr 19 12♉	♑ Dec 2 00:18
D May 13 3♉	R Dec 11 6♑
♊ Jun 11 07:16	♐ Dec 20 07:55
♋ Jun 26 13:50	D Dec 31 20♐
♌ Jul 10 20:05	

Venus

Jan 1 28♏	♋ Jul 9 15:34
♐ Jan 3 20:12	♌ Aug 3 03:27
♑ Feb 6 12:24	♍ Aug 27 10:40
♒ Mar 5 21:44	♎ Sep 20 14:15
♓ Mar 31 19:04	♏ Oct 14 15:44
♈ Apr 26 02:11	♐ Nov 7 16:30
♉ May 21 02:38	♑ Dec 1 17:27
♊ Jun 14 23:04	♒ Dec 25 19:42

Mars

Jan 1 15♌	
♋ Feb 16 15:13	
D Mar 8 27♋	
♌ Mar 30 04:19	
♍ Jun 10 15:02	
♎ Aug 1 16:45	
♏ Sep 17 08:37	
♐ Oct 30 12:44	
♑ Dec 10 03:06	

Jupiter

Jan 1 16♋
D Mar 7 10♋
♌ Jul 17 08:25
R Dec 9 22♌

Saturn

Jan 1 13♑
R May 3 23♑
D Sep 21 16♑

Uranus

Jan 1 11♈
R Jul 26 19♈
D Dec 25 15♈

Neptune

Jan 1 5♍
D May 15 2♍
R Dec 11 7♍

Pluto

Jan 1 20♋
D Apr 2 18♋
R Oct 24 22♋

356

1932

Sun

♒ Jan 21 06:07	♈ Mar 20 19:54	♊ May 21 07:08	♌ Jul 23 02:18	♎ Sep 23 06:17	♐ Nov 22 12:09
♓ Feb 19 20:30	♉ Apr 20 07:30	♋ Jun 21 15:24	♍ Aug 23 09:06	♏ Oct 23 15:03	♑ Dec 22 01:13

Moon

Jan 1   8♎
♏ Jan 2 12:23
♐ Jan 4 15:15
♑ Jan 6 18:37
♒ Jan 8 23:42
♓ Jan 11 07:49
♈ Jan 13 19:07
♉ Jan 16 08:01
♊ Jan 18 19:47
♋ Jan 21 04:22
♌ Jan 23 09:39
♍ Jan 25 12:45
♎ Jan 27 15:06
♏ Jan 29 17:42
♐ Jan 31 21:06
♑ Feb 3 01:37
♒ Feb 5 07:48
♓ Feb 7 16:13
♈ Feb 10 03:17
♉ Feb 12 16:05
♊ Feb 15 04:27
♋ Feb 17 14:01
♌ Feb 19 19:48
♍ Feb 21 22:25
♎ Feb 23 23:21
♏ Feb 26 00:20
♐ Feb 28 02:37
♑ Mar 1 07:06
♒ Mar 3 13:59
♓ Mar 5 23:15
♈ Mar 8 10:34
♉ Mar 10 23:18
♊ Mar 13 12:01
♋ Mar 15 22:45
♌ Mar 18 05:55
♍ Mar 20 09:18
♎ Mar 22 09:55
♏ Mar 24 09:35
♐ Mar 26 10:07
♑ Mar 28 13:07
♒ Mar 30 19:30
♓ Apr 2 05:04
♈ Apr 4 16:52
♉ Apr 7 05:42
♊ Apr 9 18:26
♋ Apr 12 05:45
♌ Apr 14 14:20
♎ Apr 18 21:00
♏ Apr 20 20:33
♐ Apr 22 19:56
♑ Apr 24 21:14
♒ Apr 27 02:04
♓ Apr 29 10:54
♈ May 1 22:46
♉ May 4 11:45
♊ May 7 00:20
♋ May 9 11:34
♌ May 11 20:45
♍ May 14 03:13
♎ May 16 06:31
♏ May 18 07:13
♐ May 20 06:46
♑ May 22 07:11
♒ May 24 10:30
♓ May 26 17:57
♈ May 29 05:09
♉ May 31 18:03
♊ Jun 3 06:31
♋ Jun 5 17:20
♌ Jun 8 02:14
♍ Jun 10 09:05
♎ Jun 12 13:40
♏ Jun 14 15:59
♐ Jun 16 16:45
♑ Jun 18 17:31
♒ Jun 20 20:12
♓ Jun 23 02:24
♈ Jun 25 12:34
♉ Jun 28 01:07
♊ Jun 30 13:34
♋ Jul 3 00:05
♌ Jul 5 08:17
♍ Jul 7 14:33
♎ Jul 9 19:11
♏ Jul 11 22:27
♐ Jul 14 00:38
♑ Jul 16 02:35
♒ Jul 18 05:43
♓ Jul 20 11:34
♈ Jul 22 20:51
♉ Jul 25 08:54
♊ Jul 27 21:25
♋ Jul 30 08:07
♌ Aug 1 15:57
♍ Aug 3 21:15
♎ Aug 6 00:55
♏ Aug 8 03:48
♐ Aug 10 06:31
♑ Aug 12 09:38
♒ Aug 14 13:53
♓ Aug 16 20:13
♈ Aug 19 05:17
♉ Aug 21 16:54
♊ Aug 24 05:33
♋ Aug 26 16:50
♌ Aug 29 01:03
♍ Aug 31 05:58
♎ Sep 2 08:31
♏ Sep 4 10:05
♐ Sep 6 11:59
♑ Sep 8 15:10
♒ Sep 10 20:15
♓ Sep 13 03:29
♈ Sep 15 13:01
♉ Sep 18 00:32
♊ Sep 20 13:12
♋ Sep 23 01:12
♌ Sep 25 10:31
♍ Sep 27 16:06
♎ Sep 29 18:22
♏ Oct 1 18:44
♐ Oct 3 19:02
♑ Oct 5 21:00
♒ Oct 8 01:43
♓ Oct 10 09:25
♈ Oct 12 19:34
♉ Oct 15 07:23
♊ Oct 17 20:01
♋ Oct 20 08:25
♌ Oct 22 18:57
♍ Oct 25 02:02
♎ Oct 27 05:30
♏ Oct 29 05:30
♐ Oct 31 04:39
♑ Nov 2 04:53
♒ Nov 4 08:05
♓ Nov 6 15:05
♈ Nov 9 01:24
♉ Nov 11 13:32
♊ Nov 14 02:13
♋ Nov 16 14:31
♌ Nov 19 01:34
♍ Nov 21 10:07
♎ Nov 23 15:07
♏ Nov 25 16:37
♐ Nov 27 15:58
♑ Nov 29 15:16
♒ Dec 1 16:46
♓ Dec 3 22:07
♈ Dec 6 07:34
♉ Dec 8 19:25
♊ Dec 11 08:25
♋ Dec 13 20:27
♌ Dec 16 07:11
♍ Dec 18 16:08
♎ Dec 20 22:30
♏ Dec 23 01:52
♐ Dec 25 02:41
♑ Dec 27 02:31
♒ Dec 29 03:22
♓ Dec 31 07:15

Mercury

Jan 1 20 ♐
♑ Jan 14 12:43
♒ Feb 5 02:40
♓ Feb 23 00:45
♈ Mar 9 20:12
R Mar 31 24 ♈
D Apr 24 13 ♈
♉ May 15 22:25
♊ Jun 2 23:12
♋ Jun 16 22:34
♌ Jul 2 08:15
♍ Jul 27 20:46
R Aug 3 2 ♍
♌ Aug 10 07:46
D Aug 27 19 ♌
♍ Sep 9 07:24
♎ Sep 26 01:12
♏ Oct 13 15:38
♐ Nov 2 20:37
R Nov 24 20 ♐
D Dec 14 4 ♐

Venus

Jan 1 7 ♒
♓ Jan 19 01:51
♈ Feb 12 16:58
♉ Mar 9 02:06
♊ Apr 5 00:18
♋ May 6 09:06
R Jun 7 15 ♋
♊ Jul 13 10:08
D Jul 20 28 ♊
♋ Jul 28 12:59
♌ Sep 8 19:38
♍ Oct 7 05:42
♎ Nov 2 04:02
♏ Nov 27 00:06
♐ Dec 21 07:42

Mars

Jan 1 16 ♑
♒ Jan 18 00:34
♓ Feb 25 02:37
♈ Apr 3 07:05
♉ May 12 10:59
♊ Jun 22 09:22
♋ Aug 4 19:52
♌ Sep 20 19:40
♍ Nov 13 21:21

Jupiter

Jan 1 21 ♌
D Apr 8 12 ♌
♍ Aug 11 07:33

Saturn

Jan 1 23 ♑
♒ Feb 24 02:18
R May 14 4 ♒
♑ Aug 13 12:10
D Oct 2 28 ♑
♒ Nov 20 01:34

Uranus

Jan 1 15 ♈
R Jul 29 23 ♈
D Dec 28 19 ♈

Neptune

Jan 1 7 ♍
D May 16 5 ♍
R Dec 12 10 ♍

Pluto

Jan 1 21 ♋
D Apr 2 19 ♋
R Oct 24 23 ♋

1933

Sun

♒ Jan 20 11:52	♈ Mar 21 01:40	♊ May 21 12:55	♌ Jul 23 08:04	♎ Sep 23 12:00	♐ Nov 22 17:52
♓ Feb 19 02:15	♉ Apr 20 13:16	♋ Jun 21 21:10	♍ Aug 23 14:51	♏ Oct 23 20:46	♑ Dec 22 06:58

Moon

Jan 1 9♓	♊ Mar 3 07:16	♍ May 4 08:39	♐ Jul 4 12:30	♓ Sep 3 09:43	♊ Nov 4 00:00
♈ Jan 2 15:13	♋ Mar 5 19:43	♎ May 6 14:16	♑ Jul 6 12:15	♈ Sep 5 14:14	♋ Nov 6 12:04
♉ Jan 5 02:36	♌ Mar 8 06:17	♏ May 8 16:06	♒ Jul 8 12:04	♉ Sep 7 21:34	♌ Nov 9 00:58
♊ Jan 7 15:19	♍ Mar 10 13:40	♐ May 10 15:43	♓ Jul 10 14:00	♊ Sep 10 07:59	♍ Nov 11 12:23
♋ Jan 10 03:16	♎ Mar 12 18:02	♑ May 12 15:15	♈ Jul 12 19:30	♋ Sep 12 20:23	♎ Nov 13 20:12
♌ Jan 12 13:26	♏ Mar 14 20:27	♒ May 14 16:45	♉ Jul 15 04:48	♌ Sep 15 08:30	♏ Nov 15 23:51
♍ Jan 14 21:41	♐ Mar 16 22:17	♓ May 16 21:32	♊ Jul 17 16:44	♍ Sep 17 18:13	♐ Nov 18 00:35
♎ Jan 17 04:02	♑ Mar 19 00:46	♈ May 19 05:44	♋ Jul 20 05:24	♎ Sep 20 00:50	♑ Nov 20 00:22
♏ Jan 19 08:23	♒ Mar 21 04:37	♉ May 21 16:26	♌ Jul 22 17:17	♏ Sep 22 04:59	♒ Nov 22 01:21
♐ Jan 21 10:53	♓ Mar 23 10:14	♊ May 24 04:31	♍ Jul 25 03:36	♐ Sep 24 07:48	♓ Nov 24 04:49
♑ Jan 23 12:17	♈ Mar 25 17:49	♋ May 26 17:11	♎ Jul 27 11:43	♑ Sep 26 10:22	♈ Nov 26 11:12
♒ Jan 25 13:55	♉ Mar 28 03:30	♌ May 29 05:33	♏ Jul 29 17:20	♒ Sep 28 13:27	♉ Nov 28 20:02
♓ Jan 27 17:31	♊ Mar 30 15:13	♍ May 31 16:06	♐ Jul 31 20:25	♓ Sep 30 17:25	♊ Dec 1 06:44
♈ Jan 30 00:21	♋ Apr 2 03:49	♎ Jun 2 23:15	♑ Aug 2 21:40	♈ Oct 2 22:51	♋ Dec 3 18:51
♉ Feb 1 10:39	♌ Apr 4 15:16	♏ Jun 5 02:24	♒ Aug 4 22:22	♉ Oct 5 06:18	♌ Dec 6 07:48
♊ Feb 3 23:04	♍ Apr 6 23:33	♐ Jun 7 02:32	♓ Aug 7 00:09	♊ Oct 7 16:17	♍ Dec 8 19:58
♋ Feb 6 11:13	♎ Apr 9 04:00	♑ Jun 9 01:32	♈ Aug 9 04:39	♋ Oct 10 04:29	♎ Dec 11 05:17
♌ Feb 8 21:16	♏ Apr 11 05:31	♒ Jun 11 01:40	♉ Aug 11 12:44	♌ Oct 12 17:00	♏ Dec 13 10:26
♍ Feb 11 04:43	♐ Apr 13 05:52	♓ Jun 13 04:49	♊ Aug 13 23:57	♍ Oct 15 03:23	♐ Dec 15 11:47
♎ Feb 13 09:59	♑ Apr 15 06:52	♈ Jun 15 11:51	♋ Aug 16 12:31	♎ Oct 17 10:07	♑ Dec 17 11:08
♏ Feb 15 13:46	♒ Apr 17 10:02	♉ Jun 17 22:11	♌ Aug 19 00:22	♏ Oct 19 13:27	♒ Dec 19 10:36
♐ Feb 17 16:42	♓ Apr 19 15:53	♊ Jun 20 10:25	♍ Aug 21 10:07	♐ Oct 21 14:54	♓ Dec 21 12:15
♑ Feb 19 19:22	♈ Apr 22 00:14	♋ Jun 22 23:06	♎ Aug 23 17:29	♑ Oct 23 16:12	♈ Dec 23 17:15
♒ Feb 21 22:28	♉ Apr 24 10:30	♌ Jun 25 11:16	♏ Aug 25 22:44	♒ Oct 25 18:47	♉ Dec 26 01:42
♓ Feb 24 02:56	♊ Apr 26 22:17	♍ Jun 27 22:01	♐ Aug 28 02:20	♓ Oct 27 23:16	♊ Dec 28 12:42
♈ Feb 26 09:42	♋ Apr 29 10:57	♎ Jun 30 06:10	♑ Aug 30 04:52	♈ Oct 30 05:39	♋ Dec 31 01:06
♉ Feb 28 19:20	♌ May 1 23:06	♏ Jul 2 10:56	♒ Sep 1 06:59	♉ Nov 1 13:52	

Mercury

Jan 1 24♐	♌ Jun 27 01:46
♑ Jan 8 10:25	R Jul 16 14♌
♒ Jan 27 22:34	D Aug 9 2♌
♓ Feb 14 05:05	♍ Sep 2 05:49
♈ Mar 3 10:44	♎ Sep 18 03:46
R Mar 13 7♈	♏ Oct 6 15:03
♓ Mar 25 21:52	♐ Oct 30 04:17
D Apr 5 23♓	R Nov 8 5♐
♈ Apr 17 15:21	♏ Nov 16 02:01
♉ May 10 07:39	D Nov 28 17♏
♊ May 25 14:24	♐ Dec 12 03:42
♋ Jun 8 14:14	

Venus

Jan 1 13♐	♌ Jul 3 01:29
♑ Jan 14 09:54	♍ Jul 27 16:44
♒ Feb 7 10:29	♎ Aug 21 12:21
♓ Mar 3 11:24	♏ Sep 15 14:52
♈ Mar 27 13:56	♐ Oct 11 04:30
♉ Apr 20 19:01	♑ Nov 6 16:03
♊ May 15 02:47	♒ Dec 5 18:02
♋ Jun 8 13:02	

Mars

Jan 1 15♍
R Jan 21 20♍
D Apr 12 0♍
♎ Jul 6 22:11
♏ Aug 26 06:34
♐ Oct 9 11:37
♑ Nov 19 07:14
♒ Dec 28 03:41

Jupiter

Jan 1 23♍
R Jan 8 23♍
D May 10 13♍
♎ Sep 10 05:14

Saturn

Jan 1 4♒
R May 27 16♒
D Oct 14 9♒

Uranus

Jan 1 19♈
R Aug 2 27♈

Neptune

Jan 1 10♍
D May 19 7♍
R Dec 15 12♍

Pluto

Jan 1 22♋
D Apr 4 21♋
R Oct 26 24♋

1934

Sun

♒ Jan 20 17:37	♈ Mar 21 07:28	♊ May 21 18:35	♌ Jul 23 13:42	♎ Sep 23 17:45	♐ Nov 22 23:43
♓ Feb 19 08:01	♉ Apr 20 19:00	♋ Jun 22 02:47	♍ Aug 23 20:32	♏ Oct 24 02:36	♑ Dec 22 12:48

Moon

Jan 1 11 ♋	♎ Mar 3 00:01	♑ May 3 02:53	♈ Jul 3 00:38	♋ Sep 2 15:40	♎ Nov 3 19:40
♌ Jan 2 13:54	♏ Mar 5 06:59	♒ May 5 05:06	♉ Jul 5 06:46	♌ Sep 5 04:31	♏ Nov 6 03:31
♍ Jan 5 02:09	♐ Mar 7 11:58	♓ May 7 08:25	♊ Jul 7 15:54	♍ Sep 7 17:15	♐ Nov 8 08:32
♎ Jan 7 12:20	♑ Mar 9 15:21	♈ May 9 13:07	♋ Jul 10 03:20	♎ Sep 10 04:23	♑ Nov 10 11:56
♏ Jan 9 19:10	♒ Mar 11 17:36	♉ May 11 19:23	♌ Jul 12 16:07	♏ Sep 12 13:19	♒ Nov 12 14:51
♐ Jan 11 22:16	♓ Mar 13 19:25	♊ May 14 03:38	♍ Jul 15 05:07	♐ Sep 14 20:02	♓ Nov 14 17:56
♑ Jan 13 22:36	♈ Mar 15 22:00	♋ May 16 14:16	♎ Jul 17 16:47	♑ Sep 17 00:35	♈ Nov 16 21:25
♒ Jan 15 21:55	♉ Mar 18 02:44	♌ May 19 02:55	♏ Jul 20 01:30	♒ Sep 19 03:05	♉ Nov 19 01:46
♓ Jan 17 22:16	♊ Mar 20 10:51	♍ May 21 15:35	♐ Jul 22 06:26	♓ Sep 21 04:13	♊ Nov 21 07:47
♈ Jan 20 01:27	♋ Mar 22 22:11	♎ May 24 01:43	♑ Jul 24 08:02	♈ Sep 23 05:13	♋ Nov 23 16:25
♉ Jan 22 08:25	♌ Mar 25 11:01	♏ May 26 07:51	♒ Jul 26 07:43	♉ Sep 25 07:46	♌ Nov 26 03:53
♊ Jan 24 18:52	♍ Mar 27 22:44	♐ May 28 10:28	♓ Jul 28 07:20	♊ Sep 27 13:32	♍ Nov 28 16:52
♋ Jan 27 07:24	♎ Mar 30 07:35	♑ May 30 11:12	♈ Jul 30 08:44	♋ Sep 29 23:14	♎ Dec 1 04:37
♌ Jan 29 20:11	♏ Apr 1 13:34	♒ Jun 1 11:55	♉ Aug 1 13:25	♌ Oct 2 11:43	♏ Dec 3 13:06
♍ Feb 1 07:59	♐ Apr 3 17:36	♓ Jun 3 14:06	♊ Aug 3 21:47	♍ Oct 5 00:29	♐ Dec 5 17:52
♎ Feb 3 17:59	♑ Apr 5 20:44	♈ Jun 5 18:30	♋ Aug 6 09:12	♎ Oct 7 11:19	♑ Dec 7 20:09
♏ Feb 6 01:30	♒ Apr 7 23:42	♉ Jun 8 01:16	♌ Aug 8 22:07	♏ Oct 9 19:30	♒ Dec 9 21:32
♐ Feb 8 06:14	♓ Apr 10 02:52	♊ Jun 10 10:12	♍ Aug 11 10:57	♐ Oct 12 01:31	♓ Dec 11 23:30
♑ Feb 10 08:22	♈ Apr 12 06:40	♋ Jun 12 21:14	♎ Aug 13 22:32	♑ Oct 14 06:03	♈ Dec 14 02:51
♒ Feb 12 08:57	♉ Apr 14 11:55	♌ Jun 15 09:51	♏ Aug 16 07:50	♒ Oct 16 09:31	♉ Dec 16 07:55
♓ Feb 14 09:26	♊ Apr 16 19:40	♍ Jun 17 22:51	♐ Aug 18 14:11	♓ Oct 18 12:08	♊ Dec 18 14:58
♈ Feb 16 11:38	♋ Apr 19 06:25	♎ Jun 20 09:59	♑ Aug 20 17:27	♈ Oct 20 14:28	♋ Dec 21 00:09
♉ Feb 18 17:02	♌ Apr 21 19:09	♏ Jun 22 17:23	♒ Aug 22 18:18	♉ Oct 22 17:34	♌ Dec 23 11:37
♊ Feb 21 02:15	♍ Apr 24 07:19	♐ Jun 24 20:49	♓ Aug 24 18:06	♊ Oct 24 22:56	♍ Dec 26 00:31
♋ Feb 23 14:21	♎ Apr 26 16:31	♑ Jun 26 21:23	♈ Aug 26 18:43	♋ Oct 27 07:46	♎ Dec 28 12:59
♌ Feb 26 03:13	♏ Apr 28 22:07	♒ Jun 28 21:01	♉ Aug 28 21:53	♌ Oct 29 19:42	♏ Dec 30 22:40
♍ Feb 28 14:45	♐ May 1 01:01	♓ Jun 30 21:38	♊ Aug 31 04:54	♍ Nov 1 08:36	

Mercury

Jan 1 28 ♐	R Jun 28 23 ♋
♑ Jan 1 18:42	D Jul 22 14 ♋
♒ Jan 20 11:43	♌ Aug 9 13:54
♓ Feb 6 17:13	♍ Aug 25 02:18
R Feb 24 20 ♓	♎ Sep 10 11:30
D Mar 19 7 ♓	♏ Sep 30 14:49
♈ Apr 15 04:36	R Oct 22 18 ♏
♉ May 2 18:49	D Nov 12 2 ♏
♊ May 16 23:42	♐ Dec 6 06:39
♋ Jun 1 08:14	♑ Dec 25 14:59

Venus

Jan 1 19 ♒	♋ Jul 23 18:20
R Jan 15 23 ♒	♌ Aug 17 15:45
D Feb 25 7 ♒	♍ Sep 11 03:32
♓ Apr 6 09:17	♎ Oct 5 07:56
♈ May 6 08:52	♏ Oct 29 07:36
♉ Jun 2 10:09	♐ Nov 22 04:57
♊ Jun 28 09:36	♑ Dec 16 01:37

Mars

Jan 1 3 ♒
♓ Feb 4 04:12
♈ Mar 14 09:07
♉ Apr 22 15:45
♊ Jun 2 16:23
♋ Jul 15 21:39
♌ Aug 30 13:43
♍ Oct 18 04:59
♎ Dec 11 09:39

Jupiter

Jan 1 21 ♎
R Feb 7 23 ♎
D Jun 10 13 ♎
♏ Oct 11 04:56

Saturn

Jan 1 14 ♒
R Jun 8 28 ♒
D Oct 26 21 ♒

Uranus

Jan 1 23 ♈
D Jan 2 23 ♈
♉ Jun 6 14:57
R Aug 7 1 ♉
♈ Oct 10 01:14

Neptune

Jan 1 12 ♍
D May 21 9 ♍
R Dec 17 14 ♍

Pluto

Jan 1 23 ♋
D Apr 5 22 ♋
R Oct 28 26 ♋

1935

Sun

♒ Jan 20 23:29	♈ Mar 21 13:16	♊ May 22 00:24	♌ Jul 23 19:33	♎ Sep 23 23:40	♐ Nov 23 05:37
♓ Feb 19 13:52	♉ Apr 21 00:48	♋ Jun 22 08:37	♍ Aug 24 02:24	♏ Oct 24 08:32	♑ Dec 22 18:39

Moon

Jan 1 13 ♍	♒ Mar 2 05:15	♉ May 2 02:09	♌ Jul 2 14:12	♏ Sep 2 16:22	♒ Nov 3 04:37
♐ Jan 2 04:27	♓ Mar 4 05:13	♊ May 4 05:25	♍ Jul 5 02:08	♐ Sep 5 02:47	♓ Nov 5 08:19
♑ Jan 4 06:43	♈ Mar 6 04:39	♋ May 6 11:50	♎ Jul 7 14:52	♑ Sep 7 10:07	♈ Nov 7 09:53
♒ Jan 6 07:04	♉ Mar 8 05:42	♌ May 8 21:54	♏ Jul 10 02:15	♒ Sep 9 13:44	♉ Nov 9 10:29
♓ Jan 8 07:16	♊ Mar 10 10:10	♍ May 11 10:25	♐ Jul 12 10:27	♓ Sep 11 14:14	♊ Nov 11 11:52
♈ Jan 10 09:01	♋ Mar 12 18:50	♎ May 13 22:48	♑ Jul 14 15:02	♈ Sep 13 13:20	♋ Nov 13 15:55
♉ Jan 12 13:24	♌ Mar 15 06:46	♏ May 16 08:54	♒ Jul 16 16:52	♉ Sep 15 13:09	♌ Nov 15 23:50
♊ Jan 14 20:41	♍ Mar 17 19:51	♐ May 18 16:11	♓ Jul 18 17:31	♊ Sep 17 15:47	♍ Nov 18 11:10
♋ Jan 17 06:37	♎ Mar 20 08:08	♑ May 20 21:20	♈ Jul 20 18:32	♋ Sep 19 22:27	♎ Nov 20 23:52
♌ Jan 19 18:26	♏ Mar 22 18:44	♒ May 23 01:07	♉ Jul 22 21:20	♌ Sep 22 08:50	♏ Nov 23 11:36
♍ Jan 22 07:19	♐ Mar 25 03:22	♓ May 25 04:12	♊ Jul 25 02:40	♍ Sep 24 21:18	♐ Nov 25 21:07
♎ Jan 24 19:58	♑ Mar 27 09:47	♈ May 27 06:59	♋ Jul 27 10:43	♎ Sep 27 10:05	♑ Nov 28 04:28
♏ Jan 27 06:45	♒ Mar 29 13:42	♉ May 29 09:59	♌ Jul 29 21:02	♏ Sep 29 22:05	♒ Nov 30 10:00
♐ Jan 29 14:11	♓ Mar 31 15:15	♊ May 31 14:11	♍ Aug 1 09:05	♐ Oct 2 08:40	♓ Dec 2 14:01
♑ Jan 31 17:46	♈ Apr 2 15:30	♋ Jun 2 20:42	♎ Aug 3 21:53	♑ Oct 4 17:01	♈ Dec 4 16:52
♒ Feb 2 18:24	♉ Apr 4 16:17	♌ Jun 5 06:19	♏ Aug 6 09:55	♒ Oct 6 22:20	♉ Dec 6 19:03
♓ Feb 4 17:45	♊ Apr 6 19:34	♍ Jun 7 18:24	♐ Aug 8 19:24	♓ Oct 9 00:25	♊ Dec 8 21:36
♈ Feb 6 17:49	♋ Apr 9 02:49	♎ Jun 10 06:59	♑ Aug 11 01:08	♈ Oct 11 00:20	♋ Dec 11 01:52
♉ Feb 8 20:21	♌ Apr 11 13:52	♏ Jun 12 17:35	♒ Aug 13 03:21	♉ Oct 12 23:54	♌ Dec 13 09:05
♊ Feb 11 02:35	♍ Apr 14 02:45	♐ Jun 15 00:57	♓ Aug 15 03:19	♊ Oct 15 01:16	♍ Dec 15 19:31
♋ Feb 13 12:23	♎ Apr 16 15:00	♑ Jun 17 05:20	♈ Aug 17 02:55	♋ Oct 17 06:21	♎ Dec 18 07:57
♌ Feb 16 00:35	♏ Apr 19 01:08	♒ Jun 19 07:55	♉ Aug 19 04:07	♌ Oct 19 15:35	♏ Dec 20 20:01
♍ Feb 18 13:32	♐ Apr 21 09:05	♓ Jun 21 09:55	♊ Aug 21 08:24	♍ Oct 22 03:44	♐ Dec 23 05:43
♎ Feb 21 02:01	♑ Apr 23 15:13	♈ Jun 23 12:21	♋ Aug 23 16:16	♎ Oct 24 16:30	♑ Dec 25 12:26
♏ Feb 23 13:04	♒ Apr 25 19:43	♉ Jun 25 15:53	♌ Aug 26 03:00	♏ Oct 27 04:13	♒ Dec 27 16:45
♐ Feb 25 21:40	♓ Apr 27 22:39	♊ Jun 27 21:05	♍ Aug 28 15:20	♐ Oct 29 14:16	♓ Dec 29 19:42
♑ Feb 28 03:04	♈ Apr 30 00:25	♋ Jun 30 04:26	♎ Aug 31 04:07	♑ Oct 31 22:30	♈ Dec 31 22:14

Mercury

Jan 1 10 ♑	D Jul 3 25 ♊
♒ Jan 13 01:11	♋ Jul 13 22:40
♓ Feb 1 11:22	♌ Aug 2 01:50
R Feb 8 4 ♓	♍ Aug 16 20:41
♒ Feb 15 03:14	♎ Sep 3 09:32
D Mar 2 19 ♒	♏ Sep 28 16:07
♓ Mar 18 21:58	R Oct 6 2 ♏
♈ Apr 8 18:35	♎ Oct 12 18:17
♉ Apr 24 12:27	D Oct 27 16 ♎
♊ May 8 17:29	♏ Nov 10 01:46
♋ May 29 19:01	♐ Nov 29 07:07
R Jun 9 4 ♋	♑ Dec 18 08:28
♊ Jun 20 17:58	

Venus

Jan 1 20 ♑	♌ Jun 7 19:14
♒ Jan 8 22:42	♍ Jul 7 20:37
♓ Feb 1 21:34	R Aug 18 22 ♍
♈ Feb 26 00:27	D Sep 29 6 ♍
♉ Mar 22 10:29	♎ Nov 9 16:30
♊ Apr 16 07:36	♏ Dec 8 14:34
♋ May 11 22:02	

Mars

Jan 1 9 ♎
R Feb 27 24 ♎
D May 17 5 ♎
♏ Jul 29 17:20
♐ Sep 16 13:10
♑ Oct 28 18:20
♒ Dec 7 04:33

Jupiter

Jan 1 16 ♏
R Mar 10 23 ♏
D Jul 11 13 ♏
♐ Nov 9 02:47

Saturn

Jan 1 24 ♒
♓ Feb 14 13:24
R Jun 21 10 ♓
D Nov 7 3 ♓

Uranus

Jan 1 27 ♈
D Jan 6 27 ♈
♉ Mar 28 02:27
R Aug 11 5 ♉

Neptune

Jan 1 14 ♍
D May 24 11 ♍
R Dec 19 16 ♍

Pluto

Jan 1 25 ♋
D Apr 7 23 ♋
R Oct 29 27 ♋

1936

Sun

♒ Jan 21 05:15	♈ Mar 20 18:58	♊ May 21 06:05	♌ Jul 23 01:15	♎ Sep 23 05:24	♐ Nov 22 11:23
♓ Feb 19 19:34	♉ Apr 20 06:29	♋ Jun 21 14:20	♍ Aug 23 08:09	♏ Oct 23 14:17	♑ Dec 22 00:26

Moon

Jan 1 1 ♈	♋ Mar 1 22:25	♎ May 2 18:42	♑ Jul 3 18:34	♈ Sep 2 22:43	♋ Nov 2 19:59
♉ Jan 3 01:10	♌ Mar 4 07:20	♏ May 5 07:15	♒ Jul 6 00:55	♉ Sep 4 23:04	♌ Nov 5 00:37
♊ Jan 5 05:04	♍ Mar 6 18:18	♐ May 7 18:53	♓ Jul 8 05:10	♊ Sep 7 00:53	♍ Nov 7 08:59
♋ Jan 7 10:29	♎ Mar 9 06:25	♑ May 10 04:56	♈ Jul 10 08:10	♋ Sep 9 05:15	♎ Nov 9 20:14
♌ Jan 9 18:01	♏ Mar 11 19:03	♒ May 12 12:46	♉ Jul 12 10:45	♌ Sep 11 12:13	♏ Nov 12 08:52
♍ Jan 12 04:04	♐ Mar 14 07:05	♓ May 14 17:52	♊ Jul 14 13:37	♍ Sep 13 21:19	♐ Nov 14 21:32
♎ Jan 14 16:09	♑ Mar 16 16:51	♈ May 16 20:14	♋ Jul 16 17:27	♎ Sep 16 08:12	♑ Nov 17 09:20
♏ Jan 17 04:37	♒ Mar 18 22:52	♉ May 18 20:46	♌ Jul 18 22:56	♏ Sep 18 20:32	♒ Nov 19 19:09
♐ Jan 19 15:10	♓ Mar 21 00:59	♊ May 20 21:12	♍ Jul 21 06:52	♐ Sep 21 09:23	♓ Nov 22 02:04
♑ Jan 21 22:17	♈ Mar 23 00:30	♋ May 22 23:18	♎ Jul 23 17:30	♑ Sep 23 20:53	♈ Nov 24 05:37
♒ Jan 24 02:01	♉ Mar 24 23:37	♌ May 25 04:40	♏ Jul 26 05:54	♒ Sep 26 04:52	♉ Nov 26 06:27
♓ Jan 26 03:35	♊ Mar 27 00:30	♍ May 27 13:47	♐ Jul 28 17:56	♓ Sep 28 08:38	♊ Nov 28 06:12
♈ Jan 28 04:35	♋ Mar 29 04:52	♎ May 30 01:37	♑ Jul 31 03:23	♈ Sep 30 09:08	♋ Nov 30 06:40
♉ Jan 30 06:37	♌ Mar 31 13:03	♏ Jun 1 14:11	♒ Aug 2 09:24	♉ Oct 2 08:24	♌ Dec 2 09:43
♊ Feb 1 10:37	♍ Apr 3 00:06	♐ Jun 4 01:36	♓ Aug 4 12:36	♊ Oct 4 08:37	♍ Dec 4 16:30
♋ Feb 3 16:56	♎ Apr 5 12:30	♑ Jun 6 11:02	♈ Aug 6 14:20	♋ Oct 6 11:28	♎ Dec 7 02:55
♌ Feb 5 01:26	♏ Apr 8 01:05	♒ Jun 8 18:17	♉ Aug 8 16:10	♌ Oct 8 17:44	♏ Dec 9 15:15
♍ Feb 8 11:47	♐ Apr 10 13:02	♓ Jun 10 23:27	♊ Aug 10 19:10	♍ Oct 11 03:00	♐ Dec 12 04:07
♎ Feb 10 23:44	♑ Apr 12 23:22	♈ Jun 13 02:45	♋ Aug 12 23:51	♎ Oct 13 14:18	♑ Dec 14 15:24
♏ Feb 13 12:23	♒ Apr 15 06:48	♉ Jun 15 04:48	♌ Aug 15 06:19	♏ Oct 16 02:45	♒ Dec 17 00:42
♐ Feb 15 23:56	♓ Apr 17 10:37	♊ Jun 17 06:28	♍ Aug 17 14:43	♐ Oct 18 15:37	♓ Dec 19 07:43
♑ Feb 18 08:20	♈ Apr 19 11:19	♋ Jun 19 09:07	♎ Aug 20 01:16	♑ Oct 21 03:37	♈ Dec 21 12:25
♒ Feb 20 12:45	♉ Apr 21 10:36	♌ Jun 21 14:06	♏ Aug 22 13:35	♒ Oct 23 12:59	♉ Dec 23 15:04
♓ Feb 22 13:54	♊ Apr 23 10:36	♍ Jun 23 22:14	♐ Aug 25 02:09	♓ Oct 25 18:27	♊ Dec 25 16:24
♈ Feb 24 13:34	♋ Apr 25 13:22	♎ Jun 26 09:22	♑ Aug 27 12:35	♈ Oct 27 20:09	♋ Dec 27 17:36
♉ Feb 26 13:50	♌ Apr 27 20:02	♏ Jun 28 21:51	♒ Aug 29 19:11	♉ Oct 29 19:33	♌ Dec 29 20:13
♊ Feb 28 16:30	♍ Apr 30 06:22	♐ Jul 1 09:26	♓ Aug 31 22:05	♊ Oct 31 18:48	

Mercury

Jan 1 21 ♑	♋ Jul 8 20:59
♒ Jan 6 03:38	♌ Jul 23 15:38
R Jan 23 18 ♒	♍ Aug 7 22:57
D Feb 13 2 ♒	♎ Aug 27 17:37
♓ Mar 13 06:46	R Sep 18 16 ♎
♈ Mar 31 05:04	D Oct 10 0 ♎
♉ Apr 15 01:51	♏ Nov 2 10:57
♊ May 1 00:47	♐ Nov 21 00:40
R May 19 14 ♊	♑ Dec 10 06:35
D Jun 12 5 ♊	

Venus

Jan 1 26 ♏	♋ Jun 23 08:16
♐ Jan 3 14:15	♌ Jul 17 17:51
♑ Jan 28 13:59	♍ Aug 11 02:11
♒ Feb 22 04:14	♎ Sep 4 10:02
♓ Mar 17 14:54	♏ Sep 28 18:35
♈ Apr 11 00:40	♐ Oct 23 04:57
♉ May 5 10:51	♑ Nov 16 18:31
♊ May 29 21:39	♒ Dec 11 14:49

Mars

Jan 1 19 ♒
♓ Jan 14 13:59
♈ Feb 22 04:07
♉ Apr 1 21:30
♊ May 13 09:18
♋ Jun 25 21:58
♌ Aug 10 09:45
♍ Sep 26 14:51
♎ Nov 14 14:59

Jupiter

Jan 1 11 ♐
R Apr 10 24 ♐
D Aug 11 14 ♐
♑ Dec 2 08:08

Saturn

Jan 1 5 ♓
R Jul 3 22 ♓
D Nov 19 15 ♓

Uranus

Jan 1 1 ♉
D Jan 10 1 ♉
R Aug 15 9 ♉

Neptune

Jan 1 16 ♍
D May 25 13 ♍
R Dec 21 18 ♍

Pluto

Jan 1 26 ♋
D Apr 7 25 ♋
R Oct 30 28 ♋

1937

Sun

♒ Jan 20 11:01	♈ Mar 21 00:45	♊ May 21 11:57	♌ Jul 23 07:06	♎ Sep 23 11:12	♐ Nov 22 17:14
♓ Feb 19 01:22	♉ Apr 20 12:19	♋ Jun 21 20:12	♍ Aug 23 13:56	♏ Oct 23 20:04	♑ Dec 22 06:20

Moon

Jan 1 29♌	♏ Mar 1 15:22	♒ May 2 18:07	♉ Jul 3 00:34	♌ Sep 1 21:21	♏ Nov 2 07:48
♍ Jan 1 01:45	♐ Mar 4 04:07	♓ May 5 01:56	♊ Jul 5 02:15	♍ Sep 4 01:33	♐ Nov 4 19:46
♎ Jan 3 10:54	♑ Mar 6 16:22	♈ May 7 05:46	♋ Jul 7 02:53	♎ Sep 6 07:48	♑ Nov 7 08:50
♏ Jan 5 22:57	♒ Mar 9 01:34	♉ May 9 06:31	♌ Jul 9 03:59	♏ Sep 8 16:58	♒ Nov 9 21:18
♐ Jan 8 11:41	♓ Mar 11 06:49	♊ May 11 05:56	♍ Jul 11 07:14	♐ Sep 11 04:58	♓ Nov 12 07:07
♑ Jan 10 22:52	♈ Mar 13 08:59	♋ May 13 06:00	♎ Jul 13 14:04	♑ Sep 13 17:51	♈ Nov 14 12:59
♒ Jan 13 07:25	♉ Mar 15 09:53	♌ May 15 08:27	♏ Jul 16 00:36	♒ Sep 16 04:51	♉ Nov 16 15:12
♓ Jan 15 13:28	♊ Mar 17 11:17	♍ May 17 14:17	♐ Jul 18 13:20	♓ Sep 18 12:19	♊ Nov 18 15:08
♈ Jan 17 17:47	♋ Mar 19 14:24	♎ May 19 23:34	♑ Jul 21 01:50	♈ Sep 20 16:30	♋ Nov 20 14:46
♉ Jan 19 21:06	♌ Mar 21 19:34	♏ May 22 11:17	♒ Jul 23 12:19	♉ Sep 22 18:48	♌ Nov 22 15:54
♊ Jan 21 23:54	♍ Mar 24 02:42	♐ May 25 00:09	♓ Jul 25 20:20	♊ Sep 24 20:44	♍ Nov 24 19:54
♋ Jan 24 02:37	♎ Mar 26 11:46	♑ May 27 12:52	♈ Jul 28 02:15	♋ Sep 26 23:23	♎ Nov 27 03:22
♌ Jan 26 06:06	♏ Mar 28 22:51	♒ May 30 00:13	♉ Jul 30 06:30	♌ Sep 29 03:14	♏ Nov 29 13:46
♍ Jan 28 11:30	♐ Mar 31 11:32	♓ Jun 1 08:57	♊ Aug 1 09:28	♍ Oct 1 08:28	♐ Dec 2 02:05
♎ Jan 30 19:48	♑ Apr 3 00:16	♈ Jun 3 14:21	♋ Aug 3 11:34	♎ Oct 3 15:30	♑ Dec 4 15:06
♏ Feb 2 07:09	♒ Apr 5 10:37	♉ Jun 5 16:35	♌ Aug 5 13:34	♏ Oct 6 00:54	♒ Dec 7 03:40
♐ Feb 4 19:57	♓ Apr 7 16:58	♊ Jun 7 16:45	♍ Aug 7 16:53	♐ Oct 8 12:43	♓ Dec 9 14:20
♑ Feb 7 07:33	♈ Apr 9 19:28	♋ Jun 9 16:30	♎ Aug 9 22:57	♑ Oct 11 01:46	♈ Dec 11 21:53
♒ Feb 9 16:00	♉ Apr 11 19:38	♌ Jun 11 17:43	♏ Aug 12 08:37	♒ Oct 13 13:36	♉ Dec 14 01:49
♓ Feb 11 21:09	♊ Apr 13 19:33	♍ Jun 13 22:01	♐ Aug 14 20:50	♓ Oct 15 22:03	♊ Dec 16 02:40
♈ Feb 14 00:12	♋ Apr 15 21:01	♎ Jun 16 06:07	♑ Aug 17 09:37	♈ Oct 18 02:32	♋ Dec 18 02:01
♉ Feb 16 02:35	♌ Apr 18 01:10	♏ Jun 18 17:30	♒ Aug 19 20:05	♉ Oct 20 04:08	♌ Dec 20 01:48
♊ Feb 18 05:21	♍ Apr 20 08:15	♐ Jun 21 06:24	♓ Aug 22 03:27	♊ Oct 22 04:39	♍ Dec 22 03:55
♋ Feb 20 09:03	♎ Apr 22 17:51	♑ Jun 23 18:58	♈ Aug 24 08:22	♋ Oct 24 05:45	♎ Dec 24 09:52
♌ Feb 22 13:51	♏ Apr 25 05:19	♒ Jun 26 05:54	♉ Aug 26 11:56	♌ Oct 26 08:41	♏ Dec 26 19:44
♍ Feb 24 20:04	♐ Apr 27 18:03	♓ Jun 28 14:36	♊ Aug 28 15:00	♍ Oct 28 14:00	♐ Dec 29 08:12
♎ Feb 27 04:26	♑ Apr 30 06:55	♈ Jun 30 20:50	♋ Aug 30 18:02	♎ Oct 30 21:46	♑ Dec 31 21:17

Mercury

Jan 1 29♑	♊ Jun 13 22:30
♒ Jan 1 16:11	♋ Jul 1 02:17
R Jan 5 2♒	♌ Jul 15 04:06
♑ Jan 9 21:32	♍ Jul 31 20:56
D Jan 26 15♑	R Sep 1 29♍
♒ Feb 14 00:13	D Sep 23 14♍
♓ Mar 6 14:04	♎ Oct 8 10:11
♈ Mar 23 03:40	♏ Oct 26 01:13
♉ Apr 7 01:05	♐ Nov 13 19:27
R Apr 30 24♉	♑ Dec 4 00:04
D May 24 14♉	R Dec 20 16♑

Venus

Jan 1 24♒	♊ Jul 7 21:13
♓ Jan 6 03:20	♋ Aug 4 20:11
♈ Feb 2 10:42	♌ Aug 31 00:05
♉ Mar 9 13:07	♍ Sep 25 04:02
R Mar 27 5♉	♎ Oct 19 16:32
♈ Apr 14 04:38	♏ Nov 12 19:43
D May 9 19♈	♐ Dec 6 18:04
♉ Jun 4 06:43	♑ Dec 30 14:41

Mars

Jan 1 27♎
♏ Jan 5 20:38
♐ Mar 13 03:45
R Apr 14 5♐
♏ May 14 21:22
D Jun 27 19♏
♐ Aug 8 22:02
♑ Sep 30 09:06
♒ Nov 11 18:39
♓ Dec 21 17:58

Jupiter

Jan 1 6♑
R May 15 27♑
D Sep 13 17♑
♒ Dec 20 03:12

Saturn

Jan 1 17♓
♈ Apr 25 05:24
R Jul 17 5♈
♓ Oct 18 06:09
D Dec 1 28♓

Uranus

Jan 1 5♉
D Jan 13 5♉
R Aug 19 13♉

Neptune

Jan 1 18♍
D May 27 16♍
R Dec 23 21♍

Pluto

Jan 1 28♋
D Apr 9 26♋
♌ Oct 7 11:01
R Oct 31 0♌
♋ Nov 25 12:00

1938

Sun

♒ Jan 20 16:57	♈ Mar 21 06:43	♊ May 21 17:50	♌ Jul 23 12:55	♎ Sep 23 17:00	♐ Nov 22 23:07
♓ Feb 19 07:20	♉ Apr 20 18:14	♋ Jun 22 02:02	♍ Aug 23 19:46	♏ Oct 24 01:54	♑ Dec 22 12:14

Moon

Jan 1 1 ♑	♈ Mar 3 16:15	♋ May 3 16:50	♎ Jul 3 16:07	♑ Sep 3 12:28	♈ Nov 4 14:34
♒ Jan 3 09:30	♉ Mar 5 21:28	♌ May 5 18:42	♏ Jul 5 23:47	♒ Sep 6 01:09	♉ Nov 6 20:39
♓ Jan 5 20:06	♊ Mar 8 01:32	♍ May 7 22:16	♐ Jul 8 10:45	♓ Sep 8 12:27	♊ Nov 9 00:02
♈ Jan 8 04:28	♋ Mar 10 04:46	♎ May 10 04:05	♑ Jul 10 23:21	♈ Sep 10 21:40	♋ Nov 11 01:58
♉ Jan 10 10:06	♌ Mar 12 07:23	♏ May 12 12:16	♒ Jul 13 12:04	♉ Sep 13 04:53	♌ Nov 13 03:48
♊ Jan 12 12:49	♍ Mar 14 10:05	♐ May 14 22:39	♓ Jul 15 23:55	♊ Sep 15 10:22	♍ Nov 15 06:38
♋ Jan 14 13:21	♎ Mar 16 14:08	♑ May 17 10:50	♈ Jul 18 10:02	♋ Sep 17 14:09	♎ Nov 17 11:02
♌ Jan 16 13:08	♏ Mar 18 20:53	♒ May 19 23:37	♉ Jul 20 17:31	♌ Sep 19 16:26	♏ Nov 19 17:24
♍ Jan 18 14:12	♐ Mar 21 07:01	♓ May 22 11:08	♊ Jul 22 21:43	♍ Sep 21 18:00	♐ Nov 22 01:55
♎ Jan 20 18:26	♑ Mar 23 19:31	♈ May 24 19:34	♋ Jul 24 22:53	♎ Sep 23 20:18	♑ Nov 24 12:37
♏ Jan 23 02:55	♒ Mar 26 07:54	♉ May 27 00:17	♌ Jul 26 22:25	♏ Sep 26 00:55	♒ Nov 27 00:58
♐ Jan 25 14:51	♓ Mar 28 17:52	♊ May 29 01:52	♍ Jul 28 22:15	♐ Sep 28 09:01	♓ Nov 29 13:30
♑ Jan 28 03:58	♈ Mar 31 00:32	♋ May 31 01:52	♎ Jul 31 00:35	♑ Sep 30 20:19	♈ Dec 2 00:01
♒ Jan 30 16:00	♉ Apr 2 04:43	♌ Jun 2 02:08	♏ Aug 2 06:48	♒ Oct 3 08:57	♉ Dec 4 07:01
♓ Feb 2 01:57	♊ Apr 4 07:32	♍ Jun 4 04:21	♐ Aug 4 17:00	♓ Oct 5 20:27	♊ Dec 6 10:17
♈ Feb 4 09:53	♋ Apr 6 10:07	♎ Jun 6 09:35	♑ Aug 7 05:33	♈ Oct 8 05:21	♋ Dec 8 11:08
♉ Feb 6 15:58	♌ Apr 8 13:04	♏ Jun 8 18:00	♒ Aug 9 18:15	♉ Oct 10 11:41	♌ Dec 10 11:16
♊ Feb 8 20:08	♍ Apr 10 16:51	♐ Jun 11 04:56	♓ Aug 12 05:43	♊ Oct 12 16:09	♍ Dec 12 12:37
♋ Feb 10 22:26	♎ Apr 12 22:02	♑ Jun 13 17:20	♈ Aug 14 15:34	♋ Oct 14 19:30	♎ Dec 14 16:27
♌ Feb 12 23:33	♏ Apr 15 05:20	♒ Jun 16 06:06	♉ Aug 16 23:24	♌ Oct 16 22:19	♏ Dec 16 23:13
♍ Feb 15 00:57	♐ Apr 17 17:00	♓ Jun 18 18:01	♊ Aug 19 04:51	♍ Oct 19 01:08	♐ Dec 19 08:30
♎ Feb 17 04:27	♑ Apr 20 03:30	♈ Jun 21 03:39	♋ Aug 21 07:38	♎ Oct 21 04:43	♑ Dec 21 19:37
♏ Feb 19 11:37	♒ Apr 22 16:09	♉ Jun 23 09:48	♌ Aug 23 08:25	♏ Oct 23 10:00	♒ Dec 24 07:57
♐ Feb 21 22:32	♓ Apr 25 02:53	♊ Jun 25 12:24	♍ Aug 25 08:41	♐ Oct 25 17:54	♓ Dec 26 20:40
♑ Feb 24 11:28	♈ Apr 27 10:07	♋ Jun 27 12:26	♎ Aug 27 10:26	♑ Oct 28 04:38	♈ Dec 29 08:14
♒ Feb 26 23:35	♉ Apr 29 14:00	♌ Jun 29 11:44	♏ Aug 29 15:25	♒ Oct 30 17:08	♉ Dec 31 16:47
♓ Mar 1 09:13	♊ May 1 15:45	♍ Jul 1 12:22	♐ Sep 1 00:27	♓ Nov 2 05:09	

Mercury

Jan 1 5 ♑	♋ Jun 22 13:07
♐ Jan 7 00:20	♌ Jul 7 03:13
D Jan 9 29 ♐	♍ Jul 26 22:25
♑ Jan 12 21:45	R Aug 14 12 ♍
♒ Feb 8 13:17	♌ Sep 3 04:08
♓ Feb 27 03:00	D Sep 6 29 ♌
♈ Mar 15 00:18	♍ Sep 10 16:16
♉ Apr 1 13:37	♎ Oct 1 04:22
R Apr 11 5 ♉	♏ Oct 18 12:45
♈ Apr 23 13:49	♐ Nov 6 23:42
D May 5 24 ♈	R Dec 4 29 ♐
♉ May 16 17:15	D Dec 24 13 ♐
♊ Jun 8 00:18	

Venus

Jan 1 1 ♑	♍ Jul 14 05:46
♒ Jan 23 11:15	♎ Aug 9 16:30
♓ Feb 16 09:00	♏ Sep 7 01:38
♈ Mar 12 09:20	♐ Oct 13 18:55
♉ Apr 5 13:46	R Oct 30 4 ♐
♊ Apr 29 23:34	♏ Nov 15 16:06
♋ May 24 15:52	D Dec 10 19 ♏
♌ Jun 18 16:36	

Mars

Jan 1 7 ♓
♈ Jan 30 12:45
♉ Mar 12 07:52
♊ Apr 23 18:38
♋ Jun 7 01:30
♌ Jul 22 22:24
♍ Sep 7 20:19
♎ Oct 25 06:22
♏ Dec 11 23:15

Jupiter

Jan 1 2 ♒
♓ May 14 06:01
R Jun 21 2 ♓
♒ Jul 30 04:57
D Oct 19 22 ♒
♓ Dec 29 17:58

Saturn

Jan 1 29 ♓
♈ Jan 14 10:10
R Jul 30 18 ♈
D Dec 14 11 ♈

Uranus

Jan 1 9 ♉
D Jan 18 9 ♉
R Aug 24 17 ♉

Neptune

Jan 1 21 ♍
D May 30 18 ♍
R Dec 26 23 ♍

Pluto

Jan 1 29 ♋
D Apr 11 27 ♋
♌ Aug 3 17:29
R Nov 2 1 ♌

1939

Sun

♒ Jan 20 22:52	♈ Mar 21 12:30	♊ May 21 23:29	♌ Jul 23 18:37	♎ Sep 23 22:50	♐ Nov 23 04:57
♓ Feb 19 13:11	♉ Apr 20 23:58	♋ Jun 22 07:40	♍ Aug 24 01:31	♏ Oct 24 07:46	♑ Dec 22 18:04

Moon

Jan 1 3 ♉	♌ Mar 2 19:30	♏ May 2 17:36	♒ Jul 3 09:53	♉ Sep 3 10:47	♌ Nov 3 18:00
♊ Jan 2 21:19	♍ Mar 4 19:15	♐ May 4 23:10	♓ Jul 5 22:16	♊ Sep 5 20:00	♍ Nov 5 20:56
♋ Jan 4 22:20	♎ Mar 6 19:25	♑ May 7 07:32	♈ Jul 8 10:49	♋ Sep 8 01:52	♎ Nov 7 23:02
♌ Jan 6 21:31	♏ Mar 8 21:59	♒ May 9 18:40	♉ Jul 10 21:25	♌ Sep 10 04:10	♏ Nov 10 01:13
♍ Jan 8 21:07	♐ Mar 11 04:23	♓ May 12 07:08	♊ Jul 13 04:20	♍ Sep 12 04:08	♐ Nov 12 04:40
♎ Jan 10 23:10	♑ Mar 13 14:35	♈ May 14 18:40	♋ Jul 15 07:15	♎ Sep 14 03:38	♑ Nov 14 10:42
♏ Jan 13 04:53	♒ Mar 16 03:00	♉ May 17 03:27	♌ Jul 17 07:30	♏ Sep 16 04:43	♒ Nov 16 19:59
♐ Jan 15 14:09	♓ Mar 18 15:30	♊ May 19 09:05	♍ Jul 19 07:07	♐ Sep 18 09:00	♓ Nov 19 07:58
♑ Jan 18 01:43	♈ Mar 21 02:39	♋ May 21 12:22	♎ Jul 21 08:10	♑ Sep 20 17:10	♈ Nov 21 20:35
♒ Jan 20 14:15	♉ Mar 23 11:58	♌ May 23 14:33	♏ Jul 23 12:02	♒ Sep 23 04:23	♉ Nov 24 07:22
♓ Jan 23 02:50	♊ Mar 25 19:13	♍ May 25 16:50	♐ Jul 25 19:08	♓ Sep 25 16:58	♊ Nov 26 15:08
♈ Jan 25 14:41	♋ Mar 28 00:19	♎ May 27 20:06	♑ Jul 28 04:50	♈ Sep 28 05:21	♋ Nov 28 20:11
♉ Jan 28 00:27	♌ Mar 30 03:14	♏ May 30 00:46	♒ Jul 30 16:14	♉ Sep 30 16:28	♌ Nov 30 23:33
♊ Jan 30 06:49	♍ Apr 1 04:37	♐ Jun 1 07:14	♓ Aug 2 04:40	♊ Oct 3 01:37	♍ Dec 3 02:21
♋ Feb 1 09:21	♎ Apr 3 05:47	♑ Jun 3 15:48	♈ Aug 4 17:20	♋ Oct 5 08:15	♎ Dec 5 05:21
♌ Feb 3 09:04	♏ Apr 5 08:20	♒ Jun 6 02:39	♉ Aug 7 04:47	♌ Oct 7 12:09	♏ Dec 7 08:57
♍ Feb 5 08:01	♐ Apr 7 13:47	♓ Jun 8 15:03	♊ Aug 9 13:06	♍ Oct 9 13:45	♐ Dec 9 13:31
♎ Feb 7 08:29	♑ Apr 9 22:46	♈ Jun 11 03:09	♋ Aug 11 17:20	♎ Oct 11 14:15	♑ Dec 11 19:51
♏ Feb 9 12:22	♒ Apr 12 10:32	♉ Jun 13 12:42	♌ Aug 13 18:08	♏ Oct 13 15:18	♓ Dec 16 16:13
♐ Feb 11 20:23	♓ Apr 14 23:04	♊ Jun 15 18:31	♍ Aug 15 17:18	♐ Oct 15 18:36	♈ Dec 19 05:01
♑ Feb 14 07:40	♈ Apr 17 10:11	♋ Jun 17 21:05	♎ Aug 17 17:02	♑ Oct 18 01:22	♉ Dec 21 16:31
♒ Feb 16 20:21	♉ Apr 19 18:55	♌ Jun 19 21:58	♏ Aug 19 19:20	♒ Oct 20 11:38	♊ Dec 24 00:37
♓ Feb 19 08:51	♊ Apr 22 01:15	♍ Jun 21 22:55	♐ Aug 22 01:12	♓ Oct 23 00:03	♋ Dec 26 05:02
♈ Feb 21 20:22	♋ Apr 24 05:42	♎ Jun 24 01:30	♑ Aug 24 10:32	♈ Oct 25 12:27	♌ Dec 28 07:05
♉ Feb 24 06:19	♌ Apr 26 08:54	♏ Jun 26 06:23	♒ Aug 26 22:08	♉ Oct 27 23:09	♍ Dec 30 08:28
♊ Feb 26 13:47	♍ Apr 28 11:25	♐ Jun 28 13:37	♓ Aug 29 10:42	♊ Oct 30 07:30	
♋ Feb 28 18:05	♎ Apr 30 14:01	♑ Jun 30 22:52	♈ Aug 31 23:14	♋ Nov 1 13:40	

Mercury

Jan 1 17 ♐	R Jul 27 24 ♌
♑ Jan 12 07:48	D Aug 20 12 ♌
♒ Feb 1 17:55	♍ Sep 7 05:08
♓ Feb 19 08:10	♎ Sep 23 07:46
♈ Mar 7 09:21	♏ Oct 11 05:24
R Mar 24 17 ♈	♐ Nov 1 06:47
D Apr 16 5 ♈	R Nov 18 14 ♐
♉ May 14 13:42	♏ Dec 3 07:01
♊ May 31 02:42	D Dec 8 27 ♏
♋ Jun 13 23:09	♐ Dec 13 18:54
♌ Jun 30 06:46	

Venus

Jan 1 27 ♏	♋ Jul 9 02:24
♐ Jan 4 21:50	♌ Aug 2 14:11
♑ Feb 6 09:17	♍ Aug 26 21:23
♒ Mar 5 13:25	♎ Sep 20 01:03
♓ Mar 31 08:33	♏ Oct 14 02:40
♈ Apr 25 14:30	♐ Nov 7 03:39
♉ May 20 14:14	♑ Dec 1 04:50
♊ Jun 14 10:10	♒ Dec 25 07:23

Mars

Jan 1 12 ♏	R Jun 22 5 ♒
♐ Jan 29 09:43	♑ Jul 21 19:01
♑ Mar 21 07:15	D Aug 24 24 ♑
♒ May 24 23:53	♒ Sep 24 00:24
	♓ Nov 19 16:00

Jupiter

Jan 1 0 ♓
♈ May 11 13:57
R Jul 29 8 ♈
♓ Oct 30 00:58
D Nov 24 28 ♓
♈ Dec 20 16:38

Saturn

Jan 1 11 ♈
♉ Jul 6 03:45
R Aug 14 1 ♉
♈ Sep 22 06:55
D Dec 28 24 ♈

Uranus

Jan 1 14 ♉
D Jan 22 13 ♉
R Aug 28 21 ♉

Neptune

Jan 1 23 ♍
D Jun 1 20 ♍
R Dec 28 25 ♍

Pluto

Jan 1 0 ♌
♋ Feb 7 14:37
D Apr 12 29 ♋
♌ Jun 14 03:59
R Nov 4 2 ♌

1940

Sun

♒ Jan 21 04:44	♈ Mar 20 18:23	♊ May 21 05:24	♌ Jul 23 00:36	♎ Sep 23 04:47	♐ Nov 22 10:49
♓ Feb 19 19:04	♉ Apr 20 05:52	♋ Jun 21 13:38	♍ Aug 23 07:30	♏ Oct 23 13:39	♑ Dec 21 23:54

Moon

Jan 1 23 ♍	♐ Feb 29 07:53	♓ May 1 01:54	♊ Jul 2 05:15	♍ Sep 1 12:55	♐ Nov 1 10:21
♎ Jan 1 10:43	♑ Mar 2 15:01	♈ May 3 14:51	♋ Jul 4 12:09	♎ Sep 3 12:53	♑ Nov 3 12:22
♏ Jan 3 14:35	♒ Mar 5 01:07	♉ May 6 03:12	♌ Jul 6 16:11	♏ Sep 5 13:15	♒ Nov 5 18:02
♐ Jan 5 20:12	♓ Mar 7 13:07	♊ May 8 13:32	♍ Jul 8 18:44	♐ Sep 7 15:36	♓ Nov 8 03:45
♑ Jan 8 03:28	♈ Mar 10 01:59	♋ May 10 21:32	♎ Jul 10 21:05	♑ Sep 9 20:44	♈ Nov 10 16:11
♒ Jan 10 12:41	♉ Mar 12 14:43	♌ May 13 03:22	♏ Jul 13 00:06	♒ Sep 12 04:51	♉ Nov 13 05:13
♓ Jan 13 00:02	♊ Mar 15 01:52	♍ May 15 07:16	♐ Jul 15 04:04	♓ Sep 14 15:24	♊ Nov 15 16:59
♈ Jan 15 12:54	♋ Mar 17 09:57	♎ May 17 09:40	♑ Jul 17 09:17	♈ Sep 17 03:43	♋ Nov 18 02:52
♉ Jan 18 01:14	♌ Mar 19 14:15	♏ May 19 11:12	♒ Jul 19 16:22	♉ Sep 19 16:45	♌ Nov 20 10:37
♊ Jan 20 10:31	♍ Mar 21 15:20	♐ May 21 13:00	♓ Jul 22 01:57	♊ Sep 22 05:05	♍ Nov 22 16:09
♋ Jan 22 15:35	♎ Mar 23 14:46	♑ May 23 16:33	♈ Jul 24 14:00	♋ Sep 24 14:57	♎ Nov 24 19:25
♌ Jan 24 17:10	♏ Mar 25 14:33	♒ May 25 23:17	♉ Jul 27 02:56	♌ Sep 26 21:08	♏ Nov 26 20:43
♍ Jan 26 17:12	♐ Mar 27 16:30	♓ May 28 09:39	♊ Jul 29 14:04	♍ Sep 28 23:40	♐ Nov 28 21:18
♎ Jan 28 17:42	♑ Mar 29 22:00	♈ May 30 22:19	♋ Jul 31 21:31	♎ Sep 30 23:45	♑ Nov 30 22:50
♏ Jan 30 20:16	♒ Apr 1 07:12	♉ Jun 2 10:43	♌ Aug 3 01:20	♏ Oct 2 23:12	♒ Dec 3 03:12
♐ Feb 2 01:35	♓ Apr 3 19:10	♊ Jun 4 20:49	♍ Aug 5 02:50	♐ Oct 4 23:53	♓ Dec 5 11:35
♑ Feb 4 09:25	♈ Apr 6 08:10	♋ Jun 7 04:02	♎ Aug 7 03:48	♑ Oct 7 03:27	♈ Dec 7 23:24
♒ Feb 6 19:21	♉ Apr 8 20:37	♌ Jun 9 09:00	♏ Aug 9 05:44	♒ Oct 9 10:44	♉ Dec 10 12:26
♓ Feb 9 06:58	♊ Apr 11 07:31	♍ Jun 11 12:41	♐ Aug 11 09:28	♓ Oct 11 21:17	♊ Dec 13 00:06
♈ Feb 11 19:49	♋ Apr 13 16:04	♎ Jun 13 15:43	♑ Aug 13 15:15	♈ Oct 14 09:49	♋ Dec 15 09:19
♉ Feb 14 08:36	♌ Apr 15 21:44	♏ Jun 15 18:30	♒ Aug 15 23:07	♉ Oct 16 22:49	♌ Dec 17 16:15
♊ Feb 16 19:08	♍ Apr 18 00:34	♐ Jun 17 21:32	♓ Aug 18 09:09	♊ Oct 19 10:58	♍ Dec 19 21:34
♋ Feb 19 01:46	♎ Apr 20 01:22	♑ Jun 20 01:44	♈ Aug 20 21:13	♋ Oct 21 21:18	♎ Dec 22 01:36
♌ Feb 21 04:19	♏ Apr 22 01:32	♒ Jun 22 08:15	♉ Aug 23 10:15	♌ Oct 24 04:50	♏ Dec 24 04:30
♍ Feb 23 04:10	♐ Apr 24 02:47	♓ Jun 24 17:55	♊ Aug 25 22:11	♍ Oct 26 09:09	♐ Dec 26 06:36
♎ Feb 25 03:28	♑ Apr 26 06:48	♈ Jun 27 06:13	♋ Aug 28 06:52	♎ Oct 28 10:36	♑ Dec 28 08:58
♏ Feb 27 04:12	♒ Apr 28 14:38	♉ Jun 29 18:51	♌ Aug 30 11:31	♏ Oct 30 10:24	♒ Dec 30 13:07

Mercury

Jan 1 22 ♐	♌ Jun 26 14:30
♑ Jan 6 07:53	R Jul 8 5 ♌
♒ Jan 25 10:16	♋ Jul 21 01:43
♓ Feb 11 13:58	D Aug 1 25 ♋
♈ Mar 4 09:54	♌ Aug 11 17:24
R Mar 6 0 ♈	♍ Aug 29 11:14
♓ Mar 8 02:52	♎ Sep 14 11:35
D Mar 29 17 ♓	♏ Oct 3 12:15
♈ Apr 17 05:12	R Nov 1 27 ♏
♉ May 6 21:22	D Nov 21 12 ♏
♊ May 21 13:58	♐ Dec 9 12:42
♋ Jun 4 22:45	♑ Dec 29 09:34

Venus

Jan 1 8 ♒	D Jul 18 26 ♊
♓ Jan 18 13:57	♋ Aug 1 02:39
♈ Feb 12 05:50	♌ Sep 8 16:57
♉ Mar 8 16:25	♍ Oct 6 21:08
♊ Apr 4 18:10	♎ Nov 1 17:23
♋ May 6 18:51	♏ Nov 26 12:31
R Jun 5 13 ♋	♐ Dec 20 19:35
♊ Jul 5 16:03	

Mars

Jan 1 27 ♓
♈ Jan 4 00:03
♉ Feb 17 02:06
♊ Apr 1 18:48
♋ May 17 14:56
♌ Jul 3 10:37
♍ Aug 19 16:04
♎ Oct 5 14:23
♏ Nov 20 17:12

Jupiter

Jan 1 1 ♈
♉ May 16 08:09
R Sep 4 15 ♉
D Dec 31 5 ♉

Saturn

Jan 1 24 ♈
♉ Mar 20 09:26
R Aug 27 14 ♉

Uranus

Jan 1 18 ♉
D Jan 26 17 ♉
R Sep 1 26 ♉

Neptune

Jan 1 25 ♍
D Jun 3 22 ♍
R Dec 29 27 ♍

Pluto

Jan 1 2 ♌
D Apr 13 0 ♌
R Nov 5 4 ♌

1941

Sun

♒ Jan 20 10:32	♈ Mar 21 00:20	♊ May 21 11:22	♌ Jul 23 06:25	♎ Sep 23 10:32	♐ Nov 22 16:36
♓ Feb 19 00:55	♉ Apr 20 11:50	♋ Jun 21 19:33	♍ Aug 23 13:16	♏ Oct 23 19:27	♑ Dec 22 05:43

Moon

Jan 1 19♒	♉ Mar 2 12:22	♌ May 3 11:33	♏ Jul 3 14:34	♒ Sep 2 11:37	♉ Nov 3 03:19
♓ Jan 1 20:34	♊ Mar 5 01:11	♍ May 5 18:05	♐ Jul 5 16:12	♓ Sep 4 17:52	♊ Nov 5 15:51
♈ Jan 4 07:33	♋ Mar 7 12:02	♎ May 7 21:10	♑ Jul 7 17:20	♈ Sep 7 02:28	♋ Nov 8 04:25
♉ Jan 6 20:28	♌ Mar 9 19:19	♏ May 9 21:32	♒ Jul 9 19:35	♉ Sep 9 13:31	♌ Nov 10 15:48
♊ Jan 9 08:27	♍ Mar 11 22:51	♐ May 11 20:49	♓ Jul 12 00:41	♊ Sep 12 02:05	♍ Nov 13 00:28
♋ Jan 11 17:33	♎ Mar 13 23:51	♑ May 13 21:02	♈ Jul 14 09:34	♋ Sep 14 14:09	♎ Nov 15 05:20
♌ Jan 13 23:38	♏ Mar 16 00:02	♒ May 16 00:15	♉ Jul 16 21:28	♌ Sep 16 23:36	♏ Nov 17 06:40
♍ Jan 16 03:45	♐ Mar 18 01:07	♓ May 18 07:33	♊ Jul 19 10:08	♍ Sep 19 05:29	♐ Nov 19 05:53
♎ Jan 18 06:59	♑ Mar 20 04:25	♈ May 20 18:34	♋ Jul 21 21:15	♎ Sep 21 08:16	♑ Nov 21 05:11
♏ Jan 20 10:04	♒ Mar 22 10:33	♉ May 23 07:26	♌ Jul 24 05:47	♏ Sep 23 09:23	♒ Nov 23 06:45
♐ Jan 22 13:15	♓ Mar 24 19:29	♊ May 25 20:10	♍ Jul 26 12:02	♐ Sep 25 10:24	♓ Nov 25 12:07
♑ Jan 24 16:59	♈ Mar 27 06:39	♋ May 28 07:36	♎ Jul 28 16:40	♑ Sep 27 12:44	♈ Nov 27 21:25
♒ Jan 26 22:05	♉ Mar 29 19:12	♌ May 30 17:15	♏ Jul 30 20:09	♒ Sep 29 17:16	♉ Nov 30 09:18
♓ Jan 29 05:33	♊ Apr 1 08:06	♍ Jun 2 00:38	♐ Aug 1 22:49	♓ Oct 2 00:17	♊ Dec 2 22:00
♈ Jan 31 16:01	♋ Apr 3 19:43	♎ Jun 4 05:16	♑ Aug 4 01:16	♈ Oct 4 09:37	♋ Dec 5 10:21
♉ Feb 3 04:40	♌ Apr 6 04:25	♏ Jun 6 07:12	♒ Aug 6 04:31	♉ Oct 6 20:51	♌ Dec 7 21:43
♊ Feb 5 17:09	♍ Apr 8 09:21	♐ Jun 8 07:23	♓ Aug 8 09:50	♊ Oct 9 09:22	♍ Dec 10 07:11
♋ Feb 8 02:57	♎ Apr 10 10:53	♑ Jun 10 07:30	♈ Aug 10 18:13	♋ Oct 11 21:52	♎ Dec 12 13:46
♌ Feb 10 09:06	♏ Apr 12 10:30	♒ Jun 12 09:41	♉ Aug 13 05:32	♌ Oct 14 08:29	♏ Dec 14 16:52
♍ Feb 12 12:21	♐ Apr 14 10:07	♓ Jun 14 15:32	♊ Aug 15 18:08	♍ Oct 16 15:36	♐ Dec 16 17:10
♎ Feb 14 14:07	♑ Apr 16 11:37	♈ Jun 17 01:30	♋ Aug 18 05:37	♎ Oct 18 18:53	♑ Dec 18 16:26
♏ Feb 16 15:51	♒ Apr 18 16:30	♉ Jun 19 14:01	♌ Aug 20 14:15	♏ Oct 20 19:25	♒ Dec 20 16:52
♐ Feb 18 18:37	♓ Apr 21 01:07	♊ Jun 22 02:43	♍ Aug 22 19:52	♐ Oct 22 19:00	♓ Dec 22 20:32
♑ Feb 20 22:52	♈ Apr 23 12:34	♋ Jun 24 13:51	♎ Aug 24 23:20	♑ Oct 24 19:39	♈ Dec 25 04:24
♒ Feb 23 05:00	♉ Apr 26 01:22	♌ Jun 26 22:54	♏ Aug 27 01:49	♒ Oct 26 23:01	♉ Dec 27 15:42
♓ Feb 25 13:17	♊ Apr 28 14:10	♍ Jun 29 06:02	♐ Aug 29 04:12	♓ Oct 29 05:50	♊ Dec 30 04:27
♈ Feb 27 23:54	♋ May 1 01:55	♎ Jul 1 11:16	♑ Aug 31 07:17	♈ Oct 31 15:38	

Mercury

Jan 1 4♑	D Jul 14 6♋
♒ Jan 16 22:40	♌ Aug 6 05:57
♓ Feb 3 13:05	♍ Aug 21 05:16
R Feb 17 13♓	♎ Sep 6 23:41
♒ Mar 7 02:46	♏ Sep 28 09:12
D Mar 11 29♒	R Oct 15 11♏
♓ Mar 16 12:24	♎ Oct 29 20:17
♈ Apr 12 07:21	D Nov 5 26♎
♉ Apr 28 23:13	♏ Nov 11 19:28
♊ May 13 00:45	♐ Dec 3 00:08
♋ May 29 17:35	♑ Dec 22 03:52
R Jun 19 15♋	

Venus

Jan 1 13♐	♌ Jul 2 12:32
♑ Jan 13 21:28	♍ Jul 27 04:10
♒ Feb 6 21:49	♎ Aug 21 00:26
♓ Mar 2 22:33	♏ Sep 15 03:59
♈ Mar 27 00:58	♐ Oct 10 19:20
♉ Apr 20 05:54	♑ Nov 6 10:16
♊ May 14 13:37	♒ Dec 5 23:08
♋ Jun 7 23:54	

Mars

Jan 1 27♏
♐ Jan 4 19:43
♑ Feb 17 23:29
♒ Apr 2 11:47
♓ May 16 04:49
♈ Jul 2 04:49
R Sep 6 23♈
D Nov 10 10♈

Jupiter

Jan 1 5♉
♊ May 26 13:19
R Oct 10 21♊

Saturn

Jan 1 7♉
D Jan 9 7♉
R Sep 10 28♉

Uranus

Jan 1 22♉
D Jan 30 22♉
♊ Aug 7 13:04
R Sep 5 0♊
♉ Oct 5 04:09

Neptune

Jan 1 27♍
D Jun 5 24♍

Pluto

Jan 1 3♌
D Apr 14 2♌
R Nov 6 5♌

1942

Sun

♒ Jan 20 16:25	♈ Mar 21 06:10	♊ May 21 17:11	♌ Jul 23 12:08	♎ Sep 23 16:19	♐ Nov 22 22:30
♓ Feb 19 06:47	♉ Apr 20 17:40	♋ Jun 22 01:19	♍ Aug 23 19:00	♏ Oct 24 01:15	♑ Dec 22 11:38

Moon

Jan 1 21 ♊	♍ Mar 2 03:04	♐ May 2 06:02	♓ Jul 2 03:45	♊ Sep 1 20:39	♍ Nov 3 01:19
♋ Jan 1 16:40	♎ Mar 4 08:22	♑ May 4 06:04	♈ Jul 4 09:09	♋ Sep 4 08:59	♎ Nov 5 09:21
♌ Jan 4 03:31	♏ Mar 6 11:50	♒ May 6 07:54	♉ Jul 6 18:22	♌ Sep 6 21:15	♏ Nov 7 13:27
♍ Jan 6 12:42	♐ Mar 8 14:28	♓ May 8 12:43	♊ Jul 9 06:09	♍ Sep 9 07:30	♐ Nov 9 14:46
♎ Jan 8 19:48	♑ Mar 10 17:08	♈ May 10 20:31	♋ Jul 11 18:50	♎ Sep 11 15:04	♑ Nov 11 15:18
♏ Jan 11 00:23	♒ Mar 12 20:30	♉ May 13 06:36	♌ Jul 14 07:07	♏ Sep 13 20:17	♒ Nov 13 16:48
♐ Jan 13 02:31	♓ Mar 15 01:07	♊ May 15 18:15	♍ Jul 16 18:07	♐ Sep 15 23:58	♓ Nov 15 20:28
♑ Jan 15 03:06	♈ Mar 17 07:39	♋ May 18 06:47	♎ Jul 19 03:01	♑ Sep 18 02:47	♈ Nov 18 02:30
♒ Jan 17 03:51	♉ Mar 19 16:37	♌ May 20 19:21	♏ Jul 21 09:01	♒ Sep 20 05:27	♉ Nov 20 10:36
♓ Jan 19 06:43	♊ Mar 22 04:00	♍ May 23 06:06	♐ Jul 23 11:58	♓ Sep 22 08:33	♊ Nov 22 20:34
♈ Jan 21 13:07	♋ Mar 24 16:32	♎ May 25 13:22	♑ Jul 25 12:38	♈ Sep 24 12:57	♋ Nov 25 08:15
♉ Jan 23 23:17	♌ Mar 27 04:04	♏ May 27 16:30	♒ Jul 27 12:37	♉ Sep 26 19:33	♌ Nov 27 21:08
♊ Jan 26 11:42	♍ Mar 29 12:36	♐ May 29 16:37	♓ Jul 29 13:48	♊ Sep 29 05:04	♍ Nov 30 09:28
♋ Jan 29 00:02	♎ Mar 31 17:36	♑ May 31 15:43	♈ Jul 31 17:55	♋ Oct 1 17:02	♎ Dec 2 18:54
♌ Jan 31 10:36	♏ Apr 2 19:53	♒ Jun 2 15:59	♉ Aug 3 01:47	♌ Oct 4 05:35	♏ Dec 5 00:05
♍ Feb 2 18:57	♐ Apr 4 21:03	♓ Jun 4 19:13	♊ Aug 5 12:53	♍ Oct 6 16:12	♐ Dec 7 01:32
♎ Feb 5 01:17	♑ Apr 6 22:40	♈ Jun 7 02:11	♋ Aug 8 01:30	♎ Oct 8 23:32	♑ Dec 9 01:07
♏ Feb 7 05:56	♒ Apr 9 01:55	♉ Jun 9 12:16	♌ Aug 10 13:38	♏ Oct 11 03:45	♒ Dec 11 00:55
♐ Feb 9 09:05	♓ Apr 11 07:19	♊ Jun 12 00:10	♍ Aug 13 00:08	♐ Oct 13 06:09	♓ Dec 13 02:55
♑ Feb 11 11:17	♈ Apr 13 14:49	♋ Jun 14 12:48	♎ Aug 15 08:31	♑ Oct 15 08:13	♈ Dec 15 08:04
♒ Feb 13 13:27	♉ Apr 16 00:17	♌ Jun 17 01:19	♏ Aug 17 14:37	♒ Oct 17 11:00	♉ Dec 17 16:15
♓ Feb 15 16:50	♊ Apr 18 11:36	♍ Jun 19 12:32	♐ Aug 19 18:35	♓ Oct 19 15:04	♊ Dec 20 02:45
♈ Feb 17 22:46	♋ Apr 21 00:08	♎ Jun 21 21:03	♑ Aug 21 20:45	♈ Oct 21 20:36	♋ Dec 22 14:44
♉ Feb 20 07:56	♌ Apr 23 12:21	♏ Jun 24 01:50	♒ Aug 23 22:07	♉ Oct 24 03:51	♌ Dec 25 03:35
♊ Feb 22 19:47	♍ Apr 25 22:02	♐ Jun 26 03:07	♓ Aug 25 23:55	♊ Oct 26 13:17	♍ Dec 27 16:09
♋ Feb 25 08:15	♎ Apr 28 03:49	♑ Jun 28 02:29	♈ Aug 28 03:39	♋ Oct 29 01:00	♎ Dec 30 02:43
♌ Feb 27 19:06	♏ Apr 30 05:59	♒ Jun 30 01:59	♉ Aug 30 10:29	♌ Oct 31 13:48	

Mercury

Jan 1 15 ♑	♋ Jul 12 20:40
♒ Jan 9 15:24	♌ Jul 29 04:26
R Feb 1 27 ♒	♍ Aug 13 01:45
D Feb 22 12 ♒	♎ Aug 31 08:31
♓ Mar 17 00:17	R Sep 28 25 ♎
♈ Apr 5 07:05	D Oct 20 10 ♎
♉ Apr 20 13:43	♏ Nov 7 01:49
♊ May 5 04:28	♐ Nov 25 20:22
R May 31 25 ♊	♑ Dec 14 22:23
D Jun 24 17 ♊	

Venus

Jan 1 18 ♒	♋ Jul 23 06:08
R Jan 13 21 ♒	♌ Aug 17 03:04
D Feb 23 5 ♒	♍ Sep 10 14:38
♓ Apr 6 13:09	♎ Oct 4 18:59
♈ May 6 02:24	♏ Oct 28 18:41
♉ Jun 2 00:24	♐ Nov 21 16:06
♊ Jun 27 22:15	♑ Dec 15 12:51

Mars

Jan 1 24 ♈
♉ Jan 11 22:03
♊ Mar 7 08:07
♋ Apr 26 06:28
♌ Jun 14 04:03
♍ Aug 1 08:35
♎ Sep 17 10:17
♏ Nov 1 22:38
♐ Dec 15 16:56

Jupiter

Jan 1 13 ♊
D Feb 5 11 ♊
♋ Jun 10 10:40
R Nov 12 25 ♋

Saturn

Jan 1 22 ♉
D Jan 23 21 ♉
♊ May 8 19:19
R Sep 25 12 ♊

Uranus

Jan 1 26 ♉
D Feb 3 26 ♉
♊ May 15 03:14
R Sep 10 4 ♊

Neptune

Jan 1 29 ♍
R Jan 1 29 ♍
D Jun 8 27 ♍
♎ Oct 3 16:43

Pluto

Jan 1 5 ♌
D Apr 16 3 ♌
R Nov 8 7 ♌

1943

Sun

♒ Jan 20 22:19	♈ Mar 21 12:02	♊ May 21 23:06	♌ Jul 23 18:08	♎ Sep 23 22:15	♐ Nov 23 04:24
♓ Feb 19 12:41	♉ Apr 20 23:33	♋ Jun 22 07:16	♍ Aug 24 00:59	♏ Oct 24 07:11	♑ Dec 22 17:31

Moon

Jan 1 24 ♎	♑ Mar 1 07:19	♈ May 1 04:38	♋ Jul 1 17:13	♎ Sep 1 18:32	♑ Nov 2 03:37
♏ Jan 1 09:40	♒ Mar 3 08:56	♉ May 3 09:57	♌ Jul 4 05:38	♏ Sep 4 04:20	♒ Nov 4 07:08
♐ Jan 3 12:32	♓ Mar 5 09:53	♊ May 5 17:15	♍ Jul 6 18:44	♐ Sep 6 11:37	♓ Nov 6 10:15
♑ Jan 5 12:34	♈ Mar 7 11:40	♋ May 8 03:16	♎ Jul 9 06:44	♑ Sep 8 16:12	♈ Nov 8 13:09
♒ Jan 7 11:40	♉ Mar 9 15:52	♌ May 10 15:39	♏ Jul 11 15:40	♒ Sep 10 18:18	♉ Nov 10 16:31
♓ Jan 9 12:01	♊ Mar 11 23:38	♍ May 13 04:22	♐ Jul 13 20:37	♓ Sep 12 18:45	♊ Nov 12 21:30
♈ Jan 11 15:20	♋ Mar 14 10:50	♎ May 15 14:43	♑ Jul 15 22:06	♈ Sep 14 19:07	♋ Nov 15 05:21
♉ Jan 13 22:21	♌ Mar 16 23:40	♏ May 17 21:19	♒ Jul 17 21:45	♉ Sep 16 21:14	♌ Nov 17 16:27
♊ Jan 16 08:37	♍ Mar 19 11:42	♐ May 20 00:32	♓ Jul 19 21:29	♊ Sep 19 02:41	♍ Nov 20 05:20
♋ Jan 18 20:53	♎ Mar 21 21:21	♑ May 22 01:59	♈ Jul 21 23:08	♋ Sep 21 12:09	♎ Nov 22 17:17
♌ Jan 21 09:43	♏ Mar 24 04:23	♒ May 24 03:22	♉ Jul 24 03:52	♌ Sep 24 00:32	♏ Nov 25 02:09
♍ Jan 23 22:03	♐ Mar 26 09:22	♓ May 26 05:58	♊ Jul 26 12:02	♍ Sep 26 13:30	♐ Nov 27 07:33
♎ Jan 26 08:46	♑ Mar 28 13:05	♈ May 28 10:15	♋ Jul 28 23:40	♎ Sep 29 00:55	♑ Nov 29 10:42
♏ Jan 28 16:50	♒ Mar 30 15:57	♉ May 30 16:24	♌ Jul 31 11:41	♏ Oct 1 10:04	♒ Dec 1 13:01
♐ Jan 30 21:34	♓ Apr 1 18:26	♊ Jun 2 00:28	♍ Aug 3 00:45	♐ Oct 3 17:02	♓ Dec 3 15:36
♑ Feb 1 23:15	♈ Apr 3 21:18	♋ Jun 4 10:45	♎ Aug 5 12:50	♑ Oct 5 22:10	♈ Dec 5 19:00
♒ Feb 3 23:10	♉ Apr 6 01:36	♌ Jun 6 23:02	♏ Aug 7 22:38	♒ Oct 8 01:38	♉ Dec 7 23:30
♓ Feb 5 23:07	♊ Apr 8 08:40	♍ Jun 9 12:02	♐ Aug 10 05:08	♓ Oct 10 03:44	♊ Dec 10 05:32
♈ Feb 8 01:00	♋ Apr 10 19:03	♎ Jun 11 23:21	♑ Aug 12 08:09	♈ Oct 12 05:12	♋ Dec 12 13:46
♉ Feb 10 06:17	♌ Apr 13 07:38	♏ Jun 14 06:59	♒ Aug 14 08:36	♉ Oct 14 07:26	♌ Dec 15 00:36
♊ Feb 12 15:24	♍ Apr 15 19:58	♐ Jun 16 10:35	♓ Aug 16 08:06	♊ Oct 16 12:06	♍ Dec 17 13:22
♋ Feb 15 03:23	♎ Apr 18 05:40	♑ Jun 18 11:30	♈ Aug 18 08:32	♋ Oct 18 20:27	♎ Dec 20 01:54
♌ Feb 17 16:17	♏ Apr 20 12:02	♒ Jun 20 11:34	♉ Aug 20 11:38	♌ Oct 21 08:12	♏ Dec 22 11:45
♍ Feb 20 04:20	♐ Apr 22 15:55	♓ Jun 22 12:36	♊ Aug 22 18:34	♍ Oct 23 21:08	♐ Dec 24 17:43
♎ Feb 22 14:30	♑ Apr 24 18:39	♈ Jun 24 15:51	♋ Aug 25 05:06	♎ Oct 26 08:37	♑ Dec 26 20:23
♏ Feb 24 22:25	♒ Apr 26 21:21	♉ Jun 26 21:51	♌ Aug 27 17:45	♏ Oct 28 17:14	♒ Dec 28 21:21
♐ Feb 27 03:59	♓ Apr 29 00:36	♊ Jun 29 06:25	♍ Aug 30 06:46	♐ Oct 30 23:14	♓ Dec 30 22:16

Mercury

Jan 1 26 ♑	♊ Jun 14 01:56
♒ Jan 3 08:37	♋ Jul 6 09:00
R Jan 15 11 ♒	♌ Jul 20 16:09
♑ Jan 28 00:07	♍ Aug 5 10:35
D Feb 5 25 ♑	♎ Aug 27 00:34
♒ Feb 15 19:19	R Sep 11 9 ♎
♓ Mar 11 05:12	♍ Sep 25 09:51
♈ Mar 28 11:20	D Oct 3 23 ♍
♉ Apr 12 04:59	♎ Oct 11 23:11
♊ Apr 30 16:16	♏ Oct 30 23:42
R May 12 5 ♊	♐ Nov 18 13:40
♉ May 26 10:00	♑ Dec 8 01:37
D Jun 5 26 ♉	R Dec 30 25 ♑

Venus

Jan 1 20 ♑	♌ Jun 7 12:16
♒ Jan 8 10:02	♍ Jul 8 00:07
♓ Feb 1 09:00	R Aug 15 20 ♍
♈ Feb 25 12:03	D Sep 27 4 ♍
♉ Mar 21 22:25	♎ Nov 9 18:26
♊ Apr 15 20:13	♏ Dec 8 07:46
♋ May 11 12:00	

Mars

Jan 1 11 ♐
♑ Jan 26 19:11
♒ Mar 8 12:50
♓ Apr 17 10:31
♈ May 27 09:36
♉ Jul 7 23:20
♊ Aug 24 00:05
R Oct 28 22 ♊

Jupiter

Jan 1 21 ♋
D Mar 12 15 ♋
♌ Jun 30 22:20
R Dec 13 27 ♌

Saturn

Jan 1 6 ♊
D Feb 6 5 ♊
R Oct 9 26 ♊

Uranus

Jan 1 1 ♊
D Feb 8 0 ♊
R Sep 14 8 ♊

Neptune

Jan 1 2 ♎
R Jan 3 2 ♎
♍ Apr 17 11:09
D Jun 10 29 ♍
♎ Aug 2 19:08

Pluto

Jan 1 6 ♌
D Apr 18 4 ♌
R Nov 10 8 ♌

1944

Sun

♒ Jan 21 04:08	♈ Mar 20 17:47	♊ May 21 04:52	♌ Jul 22 23:58	♎ Sep 23 04:04	♐ Nov 22 10:07
♓ Feb 19 18:27	♉ Apr 20 05:16	♋ Jun 21 13:04	♍ Aug 23 06:48	♏ Oct 23 12:58	♑ Dec 21 23:15

Moon

Jan 1 15♓	♊ Mar 1 00:04	♍ May 1 23:04	♐ Jul 2 23:37	♓ Sep 2 04:13	♊ Nov 2 01:28
♈ Jan 2 00:34	♋ Mar 3 08:37	♎ May 4 11:38	♑ Jul 5 04:42	♈ Sep 4 03:26	♋ Nov 4 05:04
♉ Jan 4 04:57	♌ Mar 5 20:18	♏ May 6 22:17	♒ Jul 7 07:13	♉ Sep 6 03:27	♌ Nov 6 12:44
♊ Jan 6 11:43	♍ Mar 8 09:18	♐ May 9 06:26	♓ Jul 9 08:38	♊ Sep 8 06:13	♍ Nov 8 23:59
♋ Jan 8 20:47	♎ Mar 10 21:54	♑ May 11 12:32	♈ Jul 11 10:17	♋ Sep 10 12:46	♎ Nov 11 12:44
♌ Jan 11 07:56	♏ Mar 13 09:12	♒ May 13 17:10	♉ Jul 13 13:15	♌ Sep 12 22:50	♏ Nov 14 00:46
♍ Jan 13 20:37	♐ Mar 15 18:30	♓ May 15 20:35	♊ Jul 15 18:10	♍ Sep 15 10:59	♐ Nov 16 11:01
♎ Jan 16 09:28	♑ Mar 18 01:12	♈ May 17 23:02	♋ Jul 18 01:21	♎ Sep 17 23:47	♑ Nov 18 19:20
♏ Jan 18 20:27	♒ Mar 20 04:54	♉ May 20 01:15	♌ Jul 20 10:50	♏ Sep 20 12:10	♒ Nov 21 01:47
♐ Jan 21 03:52	♓ Mar 22 05:59	♊ May 22 04:26	♍ Jul 22 22:24	♐ Sep 22 23:15	♓ Nov 23 06:18
♑ Jan 23 07:27	♈ Mar 24 05:41	♋ May 24 10:04	♎ Jul 25 11:07	♑ Sep 25 07:54	♈ Nov 25 08:57
♒ Jan 25 08:10	♉ Mar 26 06:00	♌ May 26 19:04	♏ Jul 27 23:15	♒ Sep 27 13:09	♉ Nov 27 10:22
♓ Jan 27 07:48	♊ Mar 28 08:58	♍ May 29 06:58	♐ Jul 30 08:50	♓ Sep 29 14:57	♊ Nov 29 11:55
♈ Jan 29 08:14	♋ Mar 30 15:59	♎ May 31 19:36	♑ Aug 1 14:41	♈ Oct 1 14:30	♋ Dec 1 15:16
♉ Jan 31 11:06	♌ Apr 2 02:54	♏ Jun 3 06:31	♒ Aug 3 17:10	♉ Oct 3 13:46	♌ Dec 3 21:52
♊ Feb 2 17:16	♍ Apr 4 15:48	♐ Jun 5 14:27	♓ Aug 5 17:35	♊ Oct 5 14:59	♍ Dec 6 08:02
♋ Feb 5 02:38	♎ Apr 7 04:22	♑ Jun 7 19:40	♈ Aug 7 17:42	♋ Oct 7 19:55	♎ Dec 8 20:28
♌ Feb 7 14:18	♏ Apr 9 15:10	♒ Jun 9 23:12	♉ Aug 9 19:19	♌ Oct 10 05:02	♏ Dec 11 08:41
♍ Feb 10 03:06	♐ Apr 12 00:01	♓ Jun 12 01:57	♊ Aug 11 23:37	♍ Oct 12 17:04	♐ Dec 13 18:49
♎ Feb 12 15:53	♑ Apr 14 06:55	♈ Jun 14 04:40	♋ Aug 14 07:03	♎ Oct 15 05:55	♑ Dec 16 02:21
♏ Feb 15 03:23	♒ Apr 16 11:45	♉ Jun 16 07:52	♌ Aug 16 17:52	♏ Oct 17 18:02	♒ Dec 18 07:44
♐ Feb 17 12:15	♓ Apr 18 14:28	♊ Jun 18 12:10	♍ Aug 19 04:59	♐ Oct 20 04:50	♓ Dec 20 11:39
♑ Feb 19 17:33	♈ Apr 20 15:35	♋ Jun 20 18:27	♎ Aug 21 17:44	♑ Oct 22 13:48	♈ Dec 22 14:41
♒ Feb 21 19:27	♉ Apr 22 16:29	♌ Jun 23 03:24	♏ Aug 24 06:13	♒ Oct 24 20:18	♉ Dec 24 17:23
♓ Feb 23 19:08	♊ Apr 24 18:59	♍ Jun 25 14:57	♐ Aug 26 16:51	♓ Oct 26 23:53	♊ Dec 26 20:25
♈ Feb 25 18:30	♋ Apr 27 00:47	♎ Jun 28 03:39	♑ Aug 29 00:12	♈ Oct 29 00:53	♋ Dec 29 00:43
♉ Feb 27 19:35	♌ Apr 29 10:35	♏ Jun 30 15:09	♒ Aug 31 03:44	♉ Oct 31 00:45	♌ Dec 31 07:19

Mercury

Jan 1 25♑	♌ Jul 11 07:36
D Jan 19 9♑	♍ Jul 28 23:13
♒ Feb 12 14:20	R Aug 24 21♍
♓ Mar 3 02:51	D Sep 16 8♍
♈ Mar 19 07:43	♎ Oct 5 03:27
♉ Apr 3 17:32	♏ Oct 22 11:33
R Apr 22 15♉	♐ Nov 10 11:10
D May 15 6♉	♑ Dec 1 15:29
♊ Jun 11 11:49	R Dec 13 8♑
♋ Jun 27 03:39	♐ Dec 23 23:31

Venus

Jan 1 27♏	♋ Jun 22 19:13
♐ Jan 3 04:44	♌ Jul 17 04:48
♑ Jan 28 03:12	♍ Aug 10 13:14
♒ Feb 21 16:39	♎ Sep 3 21:18
♓ Mar 17 02:45	♏ Sep 28 06:12
♈ Apr 10 12:08	♐ Oct 22 17:05
♉ May 4 22:04	♑ Nov 16 07:21
♊ May 29 08:40	♒ Dec 11 04:44

Mars

Jan 1 5♊
D Jan 10 5♊
♋ Mar 28 10:00
♌ May 22 14:15
♍ Jul 12 02:59
♎ Aug 29 00:30
♏ Oct 13 12:12
♐ Nov 25 16:15

Jupiter

Jan 1 26♌
D Apr 13 17♌
♍ Jul 26 01:33

Saturn

Jan 1 21♊
D Feb 20 19♊
♋ Jun 20 07:48
R Oct 23 10♋

Uranus

Jan 1 5♊
D Feb 12 4♊
R Sep 18 13♊

Neptune

Jan 1 4♎
R Jan 6 4♎
D Jun 12 1♎

Pluto

Jan 1 8♌
D Apr 18 6♌
R Nov 11 10♌

1945

Sun

♒ Jan 20 09:53	♈ Mar 20 23:37	♊ May 21 10:39	♌ Jul 23 05:47	♎ Sep 23 09:52	♐ Nov 22 15:55
♓ Feb 19 00:15	♉ Apr 20 11:06	♋ Jun 21 18:52	♍ Aug 23 12:38	♏ Oct 23 18:45	♑ Dec 22 05:04

Moon

Jan 1 8♌	♏ Mar 3 08:32	♒ May 4 04:06	♉ Jul 4 03:03	♌ Sep 3 03:19	♏ Nov 3 22:29
♍ Jan 2 16:49	♐ Mar 5 20:43	♓ May 6 09:21	♊ Jul 6 05:18	♍ Sep 5 11:36	♐ Nov 6 11:16
♎ Jan 5 04:44	♑ Mar 8 06:37	♈ May 8 11:24	♋ Jul 8 08:10	♎ Sep 7 21:47	♑ Nov 8 23:35
♏ Jan 7 17:13	♒ Mar 10 12:40	♉ May 10 11:23	♌ Jul 10 12:43	♏ Sep 10 09:46	♒ Nov 11 09:58
♐ Jan 10 03:54	♓ Mar 12 14:50	♊ May 12 11:12	♍ Jul 12 19:57	♐ Sep 12 22:36	♓ Nov 13 17:05
♑ Jan 12 11:28	♈ Mar 14 14:32	♋ May 14 12:50	♎ Jul 15 06:12	♑ Sep 15 10:10	♈ Nov 15 20:23
♒ Jan 14 15:57	♉ Mar 16 13:53	♌ May 16 17:57	♏ Jul 17 18:27	♒ Sep 17 18:19	♉ Nov 17 20:46
♓ Jan 16 18:26	♊ Mar 18 15:03	♍ May 19 02:56	♐ Jul 20 06:36	♓ Sep 19 22:19	♊ Nov 19 20:01
♈ Jan 18 20:20	♋ Mar 20 19:30	♎ May 21 14:42	♑ Jul 22 16:29	♈ Sep 21 23:10	♋ Nov 21 20:13
♉ Jan 20 22:48	♌ Mar 23 03:30	♏ May 24 03:20	♒ Jul 24 23:15	♉ Sep 23 22:52	♌ Nov 23 23:12
♊ Jan 23 02:34	♍ Mar 25 14:11	♐ May 26 15:10	♓ Jul 27 03:25	♊ Sep 25 23:31	♍ Nov 26 05:59
♋ Jan 25 08:05	♎ Mar 28 02:15	♑ May 29 01:24	♈ Jul 29 06:06	♋ Sep 28 02:37	♎ Nov 28 16:17
♌ Jan 27 15:31	♏ Mar 30 14:50	♒ May 31 09:36	♉ Jul 31 08:29	♌ Sep 30 08:46	♏ Dec 1 04:43
♍ Jan 30 01:08	♐ Apr 2 03:06	♓ Jun 2 15:24	♊ Aug 2 11:22	♍ Oct 2 17:33	♐ Dec 3 17:30
♎ Feb 1 12:45	♑ Apr 4 13:51	♈ Jun 4 18:50	♋ Aug 4 15:22	♎ Oct 5 04:15	♑ Dec 6 05:22
♏ Feb 4 01:22	♒ Apr 6 21:27	♉ Jun 6 20:22	♌ Aug 6 20:52	♏ Oct 7 16:23	♒ Dec 8 15:34
♐ Feb 6 12:57	♓ Apr 9 01:09	♊ Jun 8 21:14	♍ Aug 9 04:23	♐ Oct 10 05:16	♓ Dec 10 23:08
♑ Feb 8 21:28	♈ Apr 11 01:37	♋ Jun 10 23:01	♎ Aug 11 14:20	♑ Oct 12 17:32	♈ Dec 13 04:14
♒ Feb 11 02:12	♉ Apr 13 00:40	♌ Jun 13 03:20	♏ Aug 14 02:23	♒ Oct 15 03:05	♉ Dec 15 06:28
♓ Feb 13 03:52	♊ Apr 15 00:30	♍ Jun 15 11:07	♐ Aug 16 14:56	♓ Oct 17 08:34	♊ Dec 17 07:03
♈ Feb 15 04:11	♋ Apr 17 03:14	♎ Jun 17 22:06	♑ Aug 19 01:30	♈ Oct 19 10:08	♋ Dec 19 07:27
♉ Feb 17 05:05	♌ Apr 19 09:51	♏ Jun 20 10:35	♒ Aug 21 08:32	♉ Oct 21 09:29	♌ Dec 21 09:29
♊ Feb 19 08:00	♍ Apr 21 20:02	♐ Jun 22 22:27	♓ Aug 23 12:04	♊ Oct 23 08:49	♍ Dec 23 14:42
♋ Feb 21 13:42	♎ Apr 24 08:15	♑ Jun 25 08:14	♈ Aug 25 13:30	♋ Oct 25 10:09	♎ Dec 25 23:44
♌ Feb 23 21:58	♏ Apr 26 20:52	♒ Jun 27 15:36	♉ Aug 27 14:34	♌ Oct 27 14:55	♏ Dec 28 11:41
♍ Feb 26 08:13	♐ Apr 29 08:56	♓ Jun 29 20:51	♊ Aug 29 16:46	♍ Oct 29 23:12	♐ Dec 31 00:31
♎ Feb 28 19:56	♑ May 1 19:39	♈ Jul 2 00:28	♋ Aug 31 20:59	♎ Nov 1 10:07	

Mercury

Jan 1 22♐	♌ Jul 3 15:40
D Jan 2 23♐	♍ Jul 26 14:54
♑ Jan 14 02:47	R Aug 6 4♍
♒ Feb 5 09:21	♌ Aug 17 08:37
♓ Feb 23 11:24	D Aug 30 22♌
♈ Mar 11 06:49	♍ Sep 10 07:25
R Apr 3 27♈	♎ Sep 27 12:08
D Apr 27 16♈	♏ Oct 15 00:22
♉ May 16 15:03	♐ Nov 3 23:19
♊ Jun 4 10:28	R Nov 27 23♐
♋ Jun 18 12:27	D Dec 17 6♐

Venus

Jan 1 24♒	♊ Jul 7 16:22
♓ Jan 5 19:19	♋ Aug 4 10:57
♈ Feb 2 08:08	♌ Aug 30 13:04
♉ Mar 11 10:56	♍ Sep 24 16:06
R Mar 25 3♉	♎ Oct 19 04:09
♈ Apr 7 19:42	♏ Nov 12 07:06
D May 6 17♈	♐ Dec 6 05:22
♉ Jun 4 22:59	♑ Dec 30 01:55

Mars

Jan 1 26♐
♑ Jan 5 19:31
♒ Feb 14 10:03
♓ Mar 25 03:47
♈ May 2 20:37
♉ Jun 11 12:09
♊ Jul 23 09:03
♋ Sep 7 21:01
♌ Nov 11 21:28
R Dec 4 3♌
♋ Dec 26 14:53

Jupiter

Jan 1 27♍
R Jan 12 27♍
D May 14 17♍
♎ Aug 25 06:18

Saturn

Jan 1 7♋
D Mar 5 3♋
R Nov 6 24♋

Uranus

Jan 1 9♊
D Feb 15 9♊
R Sep 23 17♊

Neptune

Jan 1 6♎
R Jan 7 6♎
D Jun 14 3♎

Pluto

Jan 1 9♌
D Apr 20 7♌
R Nov 13 11♌

1946

Sun

♒ Jan 20 15:45	♈ Mar 21 05:31	♊ May 21 16:31
♓ Feb 19 06:07	♉ Apr 20 16:59	♋ Jun 22 00:43

♌ Jul 23 11:37	♎ Sep 23 15:45	♐ Nov 22 21:49
♍ Aug 23 18:27	♏ Oct 24 00:39	♑ Dec 22 10:55

Moon

Jan 1 11 ♐	♓ Mar 2 20:24	♊ May 2 20:02	♍ Jul 2 20:44	♐ Sep 2 17:31	♓ Nov 3 20:32
♑ Jan 2 12:10	♈ Mar 4 23:22	♋ May 4 20:22	♎ Jul 5 03:21	♑ Sep 5 06:22	♈ Nov 6 02:28
♒ Jan 4 21:38	♉ Mar 7 01:07	♌ May 6 23:04	♏ Jul 7 13:40	♒ Sep 7 17:40	♉ Nov 8 04:49
♓ Jan 7 04:47	♊ Mar 9 03:10	♍ May 9 04:56	♐ Jul 10 02:19	♓ Sep 10 01:46	♊ Nov 10 05:07
♈ Jan 9 09:55	♋ Mar 11 06:27	♎ May 11 13:53	♑ Jul 12 15:04	♈ Sep 12 06:48	♋ Nov 12 05:15
♉ Jan 11 13:25	♌ Mar 13 11:14	♏ May 14 01:07	♒ Jul 15 02:15	♉ Sep 14 10:03	♌ Nov 14 06:52
♊ Jan 13 15:42	♍ Mar 15 17:32	♐ May 16 13:46	♓ Jul 17 11:15	♊ Sep 16 12:45	♍ Nov 16 11:04
♋ Jan 15 17:32	♎ Mar 18 01:39	♑ May 19 02:41	♈ Jul 19 17:58	♋ Sep 18 15:42	♎ Nov 18 18:12
♌ Jan 17 20:02	♏ Mar 20 12:03	♒ May 21 14:31	♉ Jul 21 22:34	♌ Sep 20 19:11	♏ Nov 21 03:58
♍ Jan 20 00:40	♐ Mar 23 00:29	♓ May 23 23:38	♊ Jul 24 01:17	♍ Sep 22 23:37	♐ Nov 23 15:43
♎ Jan 22 08:31	♑ Mar 25 13:16	♈ May 26 05:05	♋ Jul 26 02:42	♎ Sep 25 05:39	♑ Nov 26 04:38
♏ Jan 24 19:39	♒ Mar 27 23:51	♉ May 28 07:04	♌ Jul 28 03:57	♏ Sep 27 14:12	♒ Nov 28 17:29
♐ Jan 27 08:27	♓ Mar 30 06:25	♊ May 30 06:53	♍ Jul 30 06:31	♐ Sep 30 01:31	♓ Dec 1 04:29
♑ Jan 29 20:17	♈ Apr 1 09:16	♋ Jun 1 06:28	♎ Aug 1 12:03	♑ Oct 2 14:29	♈ Dec 3 12:04
♒ Feb 1 05:22	♉ Apr 3 09:55	♌ Jun 3 07:38	♏ Aug 3 21:22	♒ Oct 5 02:27	♉ Dec 5 15:47
♓ Feb 3 11:32	♊ Apr 5 10:25	♍ Jun 5 11:56	♐ Aug 6 09:36	♓ Oct 7 11:09	♊ Dec 7 16:30
♈ Feb 5 15:38	♋ Apr 7 12:21	♎ Jun 7 19:56	♑ Aug 8 22:23	♈ Oct 9 16:05	♋ Dec 9 15:49
♉ Feb 7 18:45	♌ Apr 9 16:36	♏ Jun 10 07:04	♒ Aug 11 09:23	♉ Oct 11 18:20	♌ Dec 11 15:46
♊ Feb 9 21:45	♍ Apr 11 23:19	♐ Jun 12 19:50	♓ Aug 13 17:39	♊ Oct 13 19:35	♍ Dec 13 18:08
♋ Feb 12 00:59	♎ Apr 14 08:13	♑ Jun 15 08:38	♈ Aug 15 23:37	♋ Oct 15 21:22	♎ Dec 16 00:06
♌ Feb 14 04:50	♏ Apr 16 19:03	♒ Jun 17 20:15	♉ Aug 18 03:59	♌ Oct 18 00:35	♏ Dec 18 09:43
♍ Feb 16 10:03	♐ Apr 19 07:30	♓ Jun 20 05:42	♊ Aug 20 07:22	♍ Oct 20 05:35	♐ Dec 20 21:47
♎ Feb 18 17:36	♑ Apr 21 20:28	♈ Jun 22 12:19	♋ Aug 22 10:06	♎ Oct 22 12:32	♑ Dec 23 10:50
♏ Feb 21 04:04	♒ Apr 24 07:55	♉ Jun 24 15:55	♌ Aug 24 12:38	♏ Oct 24 21:40	♒ Dec 25 23:23
♐ Feb 23 16:40	♓ Apr 26 15:54	♊ Jun 26 17:07	♍ Aug 26 15:53	♐ Oct 27 09:02	♓ Dec 28 10:43
♑ Feb 26 05:00	♈ Apr 28 19:46	♋ Jun 28 17:10	♎ Aug 28 21:15	♑ Oct 29 21:59	♈ Dec 30 19:30
♒ Feb 28 14:34	♉ Apr 30 20:31	♌ Jun 30 17:46	♏ Aug 31 05:49	♒ Nov 1 10:35	

Mercury

Jan 1 18 ♐	♌ Jun 27 18:55
♑ Jan 9 14:15	R Jul 19 17 ♌
♒ Jan 29 07:25	D Aug 12 4 ♌
♓ Feb 15 15:44	♍ Sep 3 16:24
♈ Mar 4 09:22	♎ Sep 19 14:35
R Mar 16 10 ♈	♏ Oct 7 21:17
♓ Apr 1 17:56	♐ Oct 30 11:22
D Apr 9 26 ♓	R Nov 11 7 ♐
♈ Apr 16 14:53	♏ Nov 20 20:08
♉ May 11 14:28	D Dec 1 20 ♏
♊ May 27 04:11	♐ Dec 13 00:10
♋ Jun 10 01:51	

Venus

Jan 1 2 ♑	♍ Jul 13 19:25
♒ Jan 22 22:28	♎ Aug 9 08:38
♓ Feb 15 20:11	♏ Sep 7 00:22
♈ Mar 11 20:31	♐ Oct 16 11:15
♉ Apr 5 01:00	R Oct 28 2 ♐
♊ Apr 29 10:57	♏ Nov 8 08:25
♋ May 24 03:38	D Dec 8 17 ♏
♌ Jun 18 05:00	

Mars

Jan 1 28 ♋
D Feb 21 14 ♋
♌ Apr 22 19:35
♍ Jun 20 08:33
♎ Aug 9 13:22
♏ Sep 24 16:29
♐ Nov 6 18:23
♑ Dec 17 10:53

Jupiter

Jan 1 24 ♎
R Feb 11 27 ♎
D Jun 14 17 ♎
♏ Sep 25 10:07

Saturn

Jan 1 22 ♋
D Mar 20 17 ♋
♌ Aug 2 15:19
R Nov 20 8 ♌

Uranus

Jan 1 14 ♊
D Feb 20 13 ♊
R Sep 27 21 ♊

Neptune

Jan 1 8 ♎
R Jan 10 8 ♎
D Jun 17 5 ♎

Pluto

Jan 1 11 ♌
D Apr 22 9 ♌
R Nov 15 13 ♌

1947

Sun

♒ Jan 20 21:35	♈ Mar 21 11:15	♊ May 21 22:08	♌ Jul 23 17:13	♎ Sep 23 21:29	♐ Nov 23 03:39
♓ Feb 19 11:55	♉ Apr 20 22:39	♋ Jun 22 06:19	♍ Aug 24 00:08	♏ Oct 24 06:27	♑ Dec 22 16:44

Moon

Jan 1 15♈	♋ Mar 1 20:58	♎ May 1 19:23	♑ Jul 2 13:02	♈ Sep 2 12:01	♋ Nov 2 17:31
♉ Jan 2 01:06	♌ Mar 3 22:59	♏ May 4 02:35	♒ Jul 5 01:49	♉ Sep 4 20:10	♌ Nov 4 20:02
♊ Jan 4 03:25	♍ Mar 6 00:45	♐ May 6 12:08	♓ Jul 7 14:02	♊ Sep 7 02:17	♍ Nov 6 22:54
♋ Jan 6 03:27	♎ Mar 8 03:50	♑ May 8 23:55	♈ Jul 10 00:34	♋ Sep 9 06:12	♎ Nov 9 02:41
♌ Jan 8 02:53	♏ Mar 10 09:49	♒ May 11 12:41	♉ Jul 12 08:12	♌ Sep 11 08:02	♏ Nov 11 08:01
♍ Jan 10 03:44	♐ Mar 12 19:33	♓ May 14 00:20	♊ Jul 14 12:17	♍ Sep 13 08:50	♐ Nov 13 15:32
♎ Jan 12 07:53	♑ Mar 15 07:59	♈ May 16 08:56	♋ Jul 16 13:13	♎ Sep 15 10:15	♑ Nov 16 01:36
♏ Jan 14 16:14	♒ Mar 17 20:35	♉ May 18 13:51	♌ Jul 18 12:34	♏ Sep 17 14:10	♒ Nov 18 13:45
♐ Jan 17 04:03	♓ Mar 20 06:57	♊ May 20 15:50	♍ Jul 20 12:19	♐ Sep 19 21:48	♓ Nov 21 02:15
♑ Jan 19 17:11	♈ Mar 22 14:22	♋ May 22 16:27	♎ Jul 22 14:33	♑ Sep 22 08:58	♈ Nov 23 12:52
♒ Jan 22 05:37	♉ Mar 24 19:29	♌ May 24 17:17	♏ Jul 24 20:40	♒ Sep 24 21:37	♉ Nov 25 20:06
♓ Jan 24 16:23	♊ Mar 26 23:15	♍ May 26 19:50	♐ Jul 27 06:40	♓ Sep 27 09:23	♊ Nov 27 23:55
♈ Jan 27 01:09	♋ Mar 29 02:25	♎ May 29 00:53	♑ Jul 29 19:01	♈ Sep 29 18:58	♋ Nov 30 01:30
♉ Jan 29 07:45	♌ Mar 31 05:21	♏ May 31 08:41	♒ Aug 1 07:49	♉ Oct 2 02:15	♌ Dec 2 02:30
♊ Jan 31 11:52	♍ Apr 2 08:30	♐ Jun 2 18:53	♓ Aug 3 19:49	♊ Oct 4 07:44	♍ Dec 4 04:24
♋ Feb 2 13:37	♎ Apr 4 12:39	♑ Jun 5 06:50	♈ Aug 6 06:19	♋ Oct 6 11:46	♎ Dec 6 08:13
♌ Feb 4 14:00	♏ Apr 6 18:55	♒ Jun 7 19:37	♉ Aug 8 14:42	♌ Oct 8 14:44	♏ Dec 8 14:23
♍ Feb 6 14:40	♐ Apr 9 04:11	♓ Jun 10 07:47	♊ Aug 10 20:16	♍ Oct 10 16:56	♐ Dec 10 22:49
♎ Feb 8 17:38	♑ Apr 11 16:07	♈ Jun 12 17:34	♋ Aug 12 22:49	♎ Oct 12 19:30	♑ Dec 13 09:14
♏ Feb 11 00:27	♒ Apr 14 04:51	♉ Jun 14 23:44	♌ Aug 14 23:06	♏ Oct 14 23:44	♒ Dec 15 21:15
♐ Feb 13 11:15	♓ Apr 16 15:46	♊ Jun 17 02:20	♍ Aug 16 22:48	♐ Oct 17 06:52	♓ Dec 18 09:59
♑ Feb 16 00:12	♈ Apr 18 23:24	♋ Jun 19 02:34	♎ Aug 19 00:03	♑ Oct 19 17:14	♈ Dec 20 21:37
♒ Feb 18 12:38	♉ Apr 21 03:54	♌ Jun 21 02:07	♏ Aug 21 04:44	♒ Oct 22 05:38	♉ Dec 23 06:10
♓ Feb 20 22:56	♊ Apr 23 06:26	♍ Jun 23 03:00	♐ Aug 23 13:33	♓ Oct 24 17:45	♊ Dec 25 10:47
♈ Feb 23 06:57	♋ Apr 25 08:21	♎ Jun 25 06:50	♑ Aug 26 01:30	♈ Oct 27 03:30	♋ Dec 27 12:02
♉ Feb 25 13:07	♌ Apr 27 10:44	♏ Jun 27 14:16	♒ Aug 28 14:17	♉ Oct 29 10:15	♌ Dec 29 11:41
♊ Feb 27 17:46	♍ Apr 29 14:15	♐ Jun 30 00:45	♓ Aug 31 02:02	♊ Oct 31 14:35	♍ Dec 31 11:46

Mercury

Jan 1 26♐	R Jul 1 27♋
♑ Jan 3 01:43	D Jul 25 17♋
♒ Jan 21 21:05	♌ Aug 10 17:47
♓ Feb 8 01:48	♍ Aug 26 14:49
R Feb 27 23♓	♎ Sep 11 20:49
D Mar 22 9♓	♏ Oct 1 15:27
♈ Apr 16 04:50	R Oct 25 20♏
♉ May 4 05:57	D Nov 15 5♏
♊ May 18 13:32	♐ Dec 7 12:30
♋ Jun 2 13:48	♑ Dec 26 23:17

Venus

Jan 1 26♏	♋ Jul 8 13:29
♐ Jan 5 16:49	♌ Aug 2 01:06
♑ Feb 6 05:40	♍ Aug 26 08:17
♒ Mar 5 05:08	♎ Sep 19 12:01
♓ Mar 30 22:14	♏ Oct 13 13:49
♈ Apr 25 03:03	♐ Nov 6 14:58
♉ May 20 02:06	♑ Nov 30 16:22
♊ Jun 13 21:34	♒ Dec 24 19:10

Mars

Jan 1 11♑
♒ Jan 25 11:44
♓ Mar 4 16:46
♈ Apr 11 23:02
♉ May 21 03:46
♊ Jul 1 03:37
♋ Aug 13 21:41
♌ Oct 1 02:45
♍ Dec 1 12:06

Jupiter

Jan 1 20♏
R Mar 14 27♏
D Jul 15 17♏
♐ Oct 24 02:22

Saturn

Jan 1 7♌
D Apr 3 1♌
R Dec 4 22♌

Uranus

Jan 1 18♊
D Feb 25 17♊
R Oct 2 26♊

Neptune

Jan 1 10♎
R Jan 12 10♎
D Jun 19 8♎

Pluto

Jan 1 12♌
D Apr 23 10♌
R Nov 16 14♌

1948

Sun

≈ Jan 21 03:20	♈ Mar 20 16:57	♊ May 21 03:58	♌ Jul 22 23:07	♎ Sep 23 03:22	♐ Nov 22 09:28
♓ Feb 19 17:37	♉ Apr 20 04:26	♋ Jun 21 12:10	♍ Aug 23 06:01	♏ Oct 23 12:18	♑ Dec 21 22:32

Moon

Jan 1 7 ♍	♐ Mar 1 17:40	♓ May 2 19:43	♊ Jul 3 17:47	♍ Sep 2 18:20	♐ Nov 2 18:09
♎ Jan 2 14:10	♑ Mar 4 03:49	♈ May 5 07:27	♋ Jul 5 21:05	♎ Sep 4 17:35	♑ Nov 4 23:38
♏ Jan 4 19:51	≈ Mar 6 16:13	♉ May 7 16:48	♌ Jul 7 21:52	♏ Sep 6 18:34	≈ Nov 7 08:40
♐ Jan 7 04:39	♓ Mar 9 04:52	♊ May 9 23:19	♍ Jul 9 22:03	♐ Sep 8 22:51	♓ Nov 9 20:33
♑ Jan 9 15:41	♈ Mar 11 16:32	♋ May 12 03:38	♎ Jul 11 23:30	♑ Sep 11 06:55	♈ Nov 12 09:12
≈ Jan 12 03:53	♉ Mar 14 02:39	♌ May 14 06:39	♏ Jul 14 03:27	≈ Sep 13 17:58	♉ Nov 14 20:23
♓ Jan 14 16:34	♊ Mar 16 10:45	♍ May 16 09:14	♐ Jul 16 10:09	♓ Sep 16 06:25	♊ Nov 17 05:01
♈ Jan 17 04:44	♋ Mar 18 16:13	♎ May 18 12:06	♑ Jul 18 19:12	♈ Sep 18 19:01	♋ Nov 19 11:11
♉ Jan 19 14:41	♌ Mar 20 18:58	♏ May 20 15:54	≈ Jul 21 06:01	♉ Sep 21 06:45	♌ Nov 21 15:31
♊ Jan 21 21:01	♍ Mar 22 19:42	♐ May 22 21:22	♓ Jul 23 18:12	♊ Sep 23 16:39	♍ Nov 23 18:47
♋ Jan 23 23:22	♎ Mar 24 20:00	♑ May 25 05:07	♈ Jul 26 06:57	♋ Sep 25 23:45	♎ Nov 25 21:32
♌ Jan 25 22:58	♏ Mar 26 21:48	≈ May 27 15:29	♉ Jul 28 18:34	♌ Sep 28 03:35	♏ Nov 28 00:18
♍ Jan 27 21:55	♐ Mar 29 02:45	♓ May 30 03:45	♊ Jul 31 03:00	♍ Sep 30 04:39	♐ Nov 30 03:51
♎ Jan 29 22:29	♑ Mar 31 11:34	♈ Jun 1 15:53	♋ Aug 2 07:20	♎ Oct 2 04:29	♑ Dec 2 09:16
♏ Feb 1 02:27	≈ Apr 2 23:17	♉ Jun 4 01:43	♌ Aug 4 08:13	♏ Oct 4 04:57	≈ Dec 4 17:32
♐ Feb 3 10:26	♓ Apr 5 11:56	♊ Jun 6 08:06	♍ Aug 6 07:31	♐ Oct 6 07:53	♓ Dec 7 04:45
♑ Feb 5 21:29	♈ Apr 7 23:28	♋ Jun 8 11:28	♎ Aug 8 07:29	♑ Oct 8 14:31	♈ Dec 9 17:29
≈ Feb 8 09:59	♉ Apr 10 08:58	♌ Jun 10 13:10	♏ Aug 10 09:55	≈ Oct 11 00:42	♉ Dec 12 05:08
♓ Feb 10 22:35	♊ Apr 12 16:20	♍ Jun 12 14:47	♐ Aug 12 15:48	♓ Oct 13 13:03	♊ Dec 14 13:44
♈ Feb 13 10:36	♋ Apr 14 21:41	♎ Jun 14 17:33	♑ Aug 15 00:50	♈ Oct 16 01:35	♋ Dec 16 19:01
♉ Feb 15 21:07	♌ Apr 17 01:15	♏ Jun 16 22:03	≈ Aug 17 12:01	♉ Oct 18 12:53	♌ Dec 18 22:03
♊ Feb 18 04:55	♍ Apr 19 03:29	♐ Jun 19 04:28	♓ Aug 20 00:22	♊ Oct 20 22:13	♍ Dec 21 00:19
♋ Feb 20 09:08	♎ Apr 21 05:15	♑ Jun 21 12:50	♈ Aug 22 13:05	♋ Oct 23 05:20	♎ Dec 23 02:59
♌ Feb 22 10:26	♏ Apr 23 07:49	≈ Jun 23 23:15	♉ Aug 25 01:03	♌ Oct 25 10:08	♏ Dec 25 06:38
♍ Feb 24 09:22	♐ Apr 25 12:30	♓ Jun 26 11:22	♊ Aug 27 10:39	♍ Oct 27 12:52	♐ Dec 27 11:29
♎ Feb 26 09:04	♑ Apr 27 20:20	♈ Jun 28 23:55	♋ Aug 29 16:33	♎ Oct 29 14:15	♑ Dec 29 17:45
♏ Feb 28 11:22	≈ Apr 30 07:15	♉ Jul 1 10:39	♌ Aug 31 18:41	♏ Oct 31 15:30	

Mercury

Jan 1 7 ♑	D Jul 5 28 ♊
≈ Jan 14 10:07	♋ Jul 11 20:40
♓ Feb 2 01:17	♌ Aug 2 13:54
R Feb 11 6 ♓	♍ Aug 17 08:41
≈ Feb 20 11:06	♎ Sep 3 15:41
D Mar 4 22 ≈	♏ Sep 27 06:58
♓ Mar 18 08:10	R Oct 8 4 ♏
♈ Apr 9 02:31	♎ Oct 17 03:23
♉ Apr 25 01:37	D Oct 28 19 ♎
♊ May 9 04:30	♏ Nov 10 02:37
♋ May 28 11:00	♐ Nov 29 15:08
R Jun 11 7 ♋	♑ Dec 18 16:47
♊ Jun 28 18:03	

Venus

Jan 1 8 ≈	D Jul 16 24 ♊
♓ Jan 18 02:13	♋ Aug 3 02:22
♈ Feb 11 18:49	♌ Sep 8 13:37
♉ Mar 8 06:58	♍ Oct 6 12:24
♊ Apr 4 12:39	♎ Nov 1 06:43
♋ May 7 08:27	♏ Nov 26 00:54
R Jun 3 11 ♋	♐ Dec 20 07:27
♊ Jun 29 08:00	

Mars

Jan 1 7 ♍
R Jan 8 7 ♍
♌ Feb 12 10:39
D Mar 29 18 ♌
♍ May 18 21:00
♎ Jul 17 05:31
♏ Sep 3 13:51
♐ Oct 17 05:49
♑ Nov 26 21:55

Jupiter

Jan 1 15 ♐
R Apr 15 28 ♐
D Aug 16 19 ♐
♑ Nov 15 09:47

Saturn

Jan 1 21 ♌
D Apr 17 15 ♌
♍ Sep 19 05:36
R Dec 17 6 ♍

Uranus

Jan 1 23 ♊
D Feb 29 22 ♊
♋ Aug 30 13:37
R Oct 6 0 ♋
♊ Nov 12 14:43

Neptune

Jan 1 12 ♎
R Jan 14 12 ♎
D Jun 21 10 ♎

Pluto

Jan 1 14 ♌
D Apr 24 12 ♌
R Nov 17 16 ♌

1949

Sun

♒ Jan 20 09:08	♈ Mar 20 22:47	♊ May 21 09:48	♌ Jul 23 04:53	♎ Sep 23 09:03	♐ Nov 22 15:14
♓ Feb 18 23:27	♉ Apr 20 10:14	♋ Jun 21 18:00	♍ Aug 23 11:44	♏ Oct 23 18:00	♑ Dec 22 04:22

Moon

Jan 1 28♑	♈ Mar 1 15:35	♋ May 2 12:43	♎ Jul 2 13:22	♑ Sep 1 12:04	♈ Nov 2 05:34
♒ Jan 1 02:07	♉ Mar 4 04:32	♌ May 4 19:10	♏ Jul 4 16:22	♒ Sep 3 19:36	♉ Nov 4 18:37
♓ Jan 3 12:58	♊ Mar 6 16:05	♍ May 6 23:11	♐ Jul 6 19:45	♓ Sep 6 05:25	♊ Nov 7 06:54
♈ Jan 6 01:39	♋ Mar 9 00:21	♎ May 9 01:07	♑ Jul 9 00:01	♈ Sep 8 17:13	♋ Nov 9 17:35
♉ Jan 8 14:02	♌ Mar 11 04:32	♏ May 11 01:53	♒ Jul 11 06:08	♉ Sep 11 06:12	♌ Nov 12 01:59
♊ Jan 10 23:30	♍ Mar 13 05:22	♐ May 13 02:57	♓ Jul 13 15:00	♊ Sep 13 18:45	♍ Nov 14 07:42
♋ Jan 13 04:56	♎ Mar 15 04:38	♑ May 15 05:57	♈ Jul 16 02:41	♋ Sep 16 04:52	♎ Nov 16 10:35
♌ Jan 15 07:07	♏ Mar 17 04:25	♒ May 17 12:19	♉ Jul 18 15:35	♌ Sep 18 11:05	♏ Nov 18 11:17
♍ Jan 17 07:52	♐ Mar 19 06:29	♓ May 19 22:26	♊ Jul 21 02:57	♍ Sep 20 13:32	♐ Nov 20 11:15
♎ Jan 19 09:02	♑ Mar 21 12:03	♈ May 22 11:01	♋ Jul 23 10:52	♎ Sep 22 13:40	♑ Nov 22 12:20
♏ Jan 21 11:59	♒ Mar 23 21:09	♉ May 24 23:40	♌ Jul 25 15:19	♏ Sep 24 13:20	♒ Nov 24 16:24
♐ Jan 23 17:09	♓ Mar 26 08:50	♊ May 27 10:27	♍ Jul 27 17:36	♐ Sep 26 14:20	♓ Nov 27 00:35
♑ Jan 26 00:21	♈ Mar 28 21:41	♋ May 29 18:39	♎ Jul 29 19:19	♑ Sep 28 18:06	♈ Nov 29 12:18
♒ Jan 28 09:25	♉ Mar 31 10:29	♌ Jun 1 00:36	♏ Jul 31 21:44	♒ Oct 1 01:12	♉ Dec 2 01:22
♓ Jan 30 20:25	♊ Apr 2 22:03	♍ Jun 3 04:52	♐ Aug 3 01:25	♓ Oct 3 11:18	♊ Dec 4 13:29
♈ Feb 2 09:03	♋ Apr 5 07:09	♎ Jun 5 07:56	♑ Aug 5 06:36	♈ Oct 5 23:27	♋ Dec 6 23:31
♉ Feb 4 21:57	♌ Apr 7 12:59	♏ Jun 7 10:12	♒ Aug 7 13:33	♉ Oct 8 12:25	♌ Dec 9 07:28
♊ Feb 7 08:39	♍ Apr 9 15:30	♐ Jun 9 12:22	♓ Aug 9 22:45	♊ Oct 11 01:02	♍ Dec 11 13:30
♋ Feb 9 15:22	♎ Apr 11 15:46	♑ Jun 11 15:39	♈ Aug 12 10:20	♋ Oct 13 11:51	♎ Dec 13 17:44
♌ Feb 11 18:00	♏ Apr 13 15:26	♒ Jun 13 21:25	♉ Aug 14 23:17	♌ Oct 15 19:34	♏ Dec 15 20:13
♍ Feb 13 18:04	♐ Apr 15 16:23	♓ Jun 16 06:38	♊ Aug 17 11:21	♍ Oct 17 23:41	♐ Dec 17 21:31
♎ Feb 15 17:43	♑ Apr 17 20:15	♈ Jun 18 18:44	♋ Aug 19 20:15	♎ Oct 20 00:47	♑ Dec 19 22:59
♏ Feb 17 18:52	♒ Apr 20 03:59	♉ Jun 21 07:30	♌ Aug 22 01:07	♏ Oct 22 00:18	♒ Dec 22 02:23
♐ Feb 19 22:49	♓ Apr 22 15:06	♊ Jun 23 18:20	♍ Aug 24 02:55	♐ Oct 24 00:07	♓ Dec 24 09:20
♑ Feb 22 05:50	♈ Apr 25 04:01	♋ Jun 26 02:00	♎ Aug 26 03:23	♑ Oct 26 02:10	♈ Dec 26 20:04
♒ Feb 24 15:25	♉ Apr 27 16:39	♌ Jun 28 07:00	♏ Aug 28 04:19	♒ Oct 28 07:50	♉ Dec 29 08:57
♓ Feb 27 02:54	♊ Apr 30 03:47	♍ Jun 30 10:26	♐ Aug 30 07:00	♓ Oct 30 17:20	♊ Dec 31 21:13

Mercury

Jan 1 21♑	♋ Jul 10 03:01
♒ Jan 6 08:53	♌ Jul 25 05:18
R Jan 24 20♒	♍ Aug 9 09:02
D Feb 14 5♒	♎ Aug 28 15:43
♓ Mar 14 09:57	R Sep 21 18♎
♈ Apr 1 16:04	D Oct 12 3♎
♉ Apr 16 14:55	♏ Nov 3 18:58
♊ May 2 01:51	♐ Nov 22 09:06
R May 23 17♊	♑ Dec 11 13:35
D Jun 16 8♊	

Venus

Jan 1 14♐	♌ Jul 1 23:39
♑ Jan 13 09:00	♍ Jul 26 15:43
♒ Feb 6 09:05	♎ Aug 20 12:37
♓ Mar 2 09:39	♏ Sep 14 17:10
♈ Mar 26 11:54	♐ Oct 10 10:15
♉ Apr 19 16:44	♑ Nov 6 04:52
♊ May 14 00:26	♒ Dec 6 06:08
♋ Jun 7 10:48	

Mars

Jan 1 27♑	♋ Jul 23 05:56
♒ Jan 4 17:49	♌ Sep 7 04:49
♓ Feb 11 18:05	♍ Oct 27 01:00
♈ Mar 21 21:58	♎ Dec 26 05:25
♉ Apr 30 02:32	
♊ Jun 10 00:49	

Jupiter

Jan 1 10♑
♒ Apr 12 17:43
R May 20 2♒
♑ Jun 27 20:02
D Sep 18 22♑
♒ Nov 30 19:38

Saturn

Jan 1 5♍
♌ Apr 3 00:03
D May 1 29♌
♍ May 29 14:02
R Dec 30 19♍

Uranus

Jan 1 28♊
D Mar 5 26♊
♋ Jun 10 02:58
R Oct 11 5♋

Neptune

Jan 1 15♎
R Jan 16 15♎
D Jun 23 12♎

Pluto

Jan 1 16♌
D Apr 26 14♌
R Nov 19 18♌

1950

Sun

♒ Jan 20 15:00	♈ Mar 21 04:34	♊ May 21 15:27	♌ Jul 23 10:30	♎ Sep 23 14:43	♐ Nov 22 21:00
♓ Feb 19 05:17	♉ Apr 20 15:59	♋ Jun 21 23:37	♍ Aug 23 17:22	♏ Oct 23 23:43	♑ Dec 22 10:11

Moon

Jan 1 1 ♊	♍ Mar 3 12:23	♐ May 3 10:51	♓ Jul 3 13:51	♊ Sep 3 14:44	♍ Nov 4 14:20
♋ Jan 3 06:55	♎ Mar 5 13:59	♑ May 5 11:08	♈ Jul 5 22:24	♋ Sep 6 02:54	♎ Nov 6 19:09
♌ Jan 5 13:57	♏ Mar 7 14:55	♒ May 7 14:21	♉ Jul 8 10:12	♌ Sep 8 12:34	♏ Nov 8 20:29
♍ Jan 7 19:06	♐ Mar 9 16:36	♓ May 9 21:34	♊ Jul 10 23:00	♍ Sep 10 18:54	♐ Nov 10 19:51
♎ Jan 9 23:08	♑ Mar 11 20:07	♈ May 12 08:17	♋ Jul 13 10:32	♎ Sep 12 22:27	♑ Nov 12 19:25
♏ Jan 12 02:28	♒ Mar 14 01:52	♉ May 14 20:59	♌ Jul 15 19:52	♏ Sep 15 00:26	♒ Nov 14 21:14
♐ Jan 14 05:15	♓ Mar 16 09:59	♊ May 17 09:51	♍ Jul 18 03:04	♐ Sep 17 02:12	♓ Nov 17 02:37
♑ Jan 16 08:06	♈ Mar 18 20:20	♋ May 19 21:49	♎ Jul 20 08:34	♑ Sep 19 04:49	♈ Nov 19 11:38
♒ Jan 18 12:06	♉ Mar 21 08:32	♌ May 22 08:06	♏ Jul 22 12:26	♒ Sep 21 09:00	♉ Nov 21 23:07
♓ Jan 20 18:41	♊ Mar 23 21:27	♍ May 24 15:49	♐ Jul 24 14:55	♓ Sep 23 15:08	♊ Nov 24 11:37
♈ Jan 23 04:37	♋ Mar 26 09:17	♎ May 26 20:25	♑ Jul 26 16:38	♈ Sep 25 23:32	♋ Nov 27 00:13
♉ Jan 25 17:08	♌ Mar 28 18:03	♏ May 28 22:01	♒ Jul 28 18:54	♉ Sep 28 10:07	♌ Nov 29 12:01
♊ Jan 28 05:42	♍ Mar 30 23:00	♐ May 30 21:43	♓ Jul 30 23:17	♊ Sep 30 22:26	♍ Dec 1 21:52
♋ Jan 30 15:49	♎ Apr 2 00:40	♑ Jun 1 21:26	♈ Aug 2 07:03	♋ Oct 3 10:58	♎ Dec 4 04:29
♌ Feb 1 22:32	♏ Apr 4 00:36	♒ Jun 3 23:17	♉ Aug 4 18:04	♌ Oct 5 21:40	♏ Dec 6 07:19
♍ Feb 4 02:36	♐ Apr 6 00:37	♓ Jun 6 04:56	♊ Aug 7 06:44	♍ Oct 8 04:53	♐ Dec 8 07:16
♎ Feb 6 05:18	♑ Apr 8 02:29	♈ Jun 8 14:43	♋ Aug 9 18:26	♎ Oct 10 08:29	♑ Dec 10 06:16
♏ Feb 8 07:50	♒ Apr 10 07:24	♉ Jun 11 03:12	♌ Aug 12 03:36	♏ Oct 12 09:30	♒ Dec 12 06:34
♐ Feb 10 10:51	♓ Apr 12 15:38	♊ Jun 13 16:05	♍ Aug 14 10:03	♐ Oct 14 09:44	♓ Dec 14 10:09
♑ Feb 12 14:44	♈ Apr 15 02:31	♋ Jun 16 03:45	♎ Aug 16 14:31	♑ Oct 16 10:54	♈ Dec 16 17:58
♒ Feb 14 19:56	♉ Apr 17 15:00	♌ Jun 18 13:36	♏ Aug 18 17:49	♒ Oct 18 14:27	♉ Dec 19 05:09
♓ Feb 17 03:10	♊ Apr 20 03:53	♍ Jun 20 21:30	♐ Aug 20 20:36	♓ Oct 20 20:53	♊ Dec 21 17:49
♈ Feb 19 13:00	♋ Apr 22 16:02	♎ Jun 23 03:08	♑ Aug 22 23:22	♈ Oct 23 05:58	♋ Dec 24 06:18
♉ Feb 22 01:10	♌ Apr 25 01:56	♏ Jun 25 06:19	♒ Aug 25 02:53	♉ Oct 25 17:01	♌ Dec 26 17:44
♊ Feb 24 14:02	♍ Apr 27 08:30	♐ Jun 27 07:25	♓ Aug 27 08:01	♊ Oct 28 05:21	♍ Dec 29 03:41
♋ Feb 27 01:03	♎ Apr 29 11:24	♑ Jun 29 07:48	♈ Aug 29 15:45	♋ Oct 30 18:02	♎ Dec 31 11:19
♌ Mar 1 08:30	♏ May 1 11:37	♒ Jul 1 09:19	♉ Sep 1 02:18	♌ Nov 2 05:37	

Mercury

Jan 1 29 ♑	♋ Jul 2 14:59
♒ Jan 1 12:51	♌ Jul 16 17:10
R Jan 8 5 ♒	♍ Aug 2 02:57
♑ Jan 15 07:36	♎ Aug 27 14:07
D Jan 29 18 ♑	R Sep 4 2 ♎
♒ Feb 14 19:27	♍ Sep 10 19:30
♓ Mar 7 21:57	D Sep 26 17 ♍
♈ Mar 24 15:52	♎ Oct 9 14:39
♉ Apr 8 11:11	♏ Oct 27 10:34
R May 3 27 ♉	♐ Nov 15 03:08
D May 27 17 ♉	♑ Dec 5 01:43
♊ Jun 14 14:32	R Dec 23 19 ♑

Venus

Jan 1 16 ♒	♋ Jul 22 17:47
R Jan 10 18 ♒	♌ Aug 16 14:17
D Feb 20 3 ♒	♍ Sep 10 01:37
♓ Apr 6 15:05	♎ Oct 4 05:52
♈ May 5 19:16	♏ Oct 28 05:33
♉ Jun 1 14:17	♐ Nov 21 03:02
♊ Jun 27 10:43	♑ Dec 14 23:54

Mars

Jan 1 2 ♎
R Feb 12 11 ♎
♍ Mar 28 11:30
D May 3 21 ♍
♎ Jun 11 20:39
♏ Aug 10 16:46
♐ Sep 25 19:53
♑ Nov 6 06:31
♒ Dec 15 08:52

Jupiter

Jan 1 6 ♒
♓ Apr 15 08:25
R Jun 27 7 ♓
♒ Sep 15 03:53
D Oct 24 27 ♒
♓ Dec 1 18:49

Saturn

Jan 1 19 ♍
D May 15 12 ♍
♎ Nov 20 17:24

Uranus

Jan 1 2 ♋
D Mar 9 0 ♋
R Oct 16 9 ♋

Neptune

Jan 1 17 ♎
R Jan 18 17 ♎
D Jun 26 14 ♎

Pluto

Jan 1 17 ♌
D Apr 28 15 ♌
R Nov 21 19 ♌

1951

Sun

♒ Jan 20 20:52	♈ Mar 21 10:25	♊ May 21 21:15	♌ Jul 23 16:22	♎ Sep 23 20:39	♐ Nov 23 02:53
♓ Feb 19 11:10	♉ Apr 20 21:46	♋ Jun 22 05:25	♍ Aug 23 23:17	♏ Oct 24 05:38	♑ Dec 22 16:01

Moon

♎ Jan 1 7	♑ Mar 2 09:28	♈ May 2 11:25	♋ Jul 3 08:27	♎ Sep 3 05:32	♑ Nov 3 06:40
♏ Jan 2 15:58	♒ Mar 4 12:10	♉ May 4 20:45	♌ Jul 5 21:00	♏ Sep 5 11:49	♒ Nov 5 08:41
♐ Jan 4 17:37	♓ Mar 6 15:45	♊ May 7 07:51	♍ Jul 8 08:36	♐ Sep 7 16:10	♓ Nov 7 12:22
♑ Jan 6 17:31	♈ Mar 8 21:16	♋ May 9 20:13	♎ Jul 10 18:03	♑ Sep 9 19:06	♈ Nov 9 17:52
♒ Jan 8 17:35	♉ Mar 11 05:32	♌ May 12 08:49	♏ Jul 13 00:19	♒ Sep 11 21:10	♉ Nov 12 01:07
♓ Jan 10 19:55	♊ Mar 13 16:35	♍ May 14 19:43	♐ Jul 15 03:02	♓ Sep 13 23:21	♊ Nov 14 10:41
♈ Jan 13 02:05	♋ Mar 16 05:06	♎ May 17 03:04	♑ Jul 17 03:14	♈ Sep 16 02:46	♋ Nov 16 21:26
♉ Jan 15 12:09	♌ Mar 18 16:44	♏ May 19 06:22	♒ Jul 19 02:40	♉ Sep 18 08:40	♌ Nov 19 10:11
♊ Jan 18 00:36	♍ Mar 21 01:38	♐ May 21 06:44	♓ Jul 21 03:27	♊ Sep 20 17:45	♍ Nov 21 22:34
♋ Jan 20 13:06	♎ Mar 23 07:21	♑ May 23 06:06	♈ Jul 23 07:21	♋ Sep 23 05:34	♎ Nov 24 08:09
♌ Jan 23 00:10	♏ Mar 25 10:34	♒ May 25 06:41	♉ Jul 25 15:06	♌ Sep 25 18:06	♏ Nov 26 13:31
♍ Jan 25 09:25	♐ Mar 27 12:40	♓ May 27 10:05	♊ Jul 28 02:07	♍ Sep 28 05:05	♐ Nov 28 15:20
♎ Jan 27 16:46	♑ Mar 29 14:51	♈ May 29 16:52	♋ Jul 30 14:41	♎ Sep 30 13:07	♑ Nov 30 15:22
♏ Jan 29 22:03	♒ Mar 31 18:01	♉ Jun 1 02:33	♌ Aug 2 03:06	♏ Oct 2 18:22	♒ Dec 2 15:45
♐ Feb 1 01:15	♓ Apr 2 22:44	♊ Jun 3 14:02	♍ Aug 4 14:17	♐ Oct 4 21:47	♓ Dec 4 18:06
♑ Feb 3 02:52	♈ Apr 5 05:15	♋ Jun 6 02:31	♎ Aug 6 23:34	♑ Oct 7 00:29	♈ Dec 6 23:17
♒ Feb 5 04:04	♉ Apr 7 13:52	♌ Jun 8 15:10	♏ Aug 9 06:23	♒ Oct 9 03:19	♉ Dec 9 07:04
♓ Feb 7 06:28	♊ Apr 10 00:40	♍ Jun 11 02:45	♐ Aug 11 10:30	♓ Oct 11 06:45	♊ Dec 11 16:53
♈ Feb 9 11:41	♋ Apr 12 13:04	♎ Jun 13 11:31	♑ Aug 13 12:18	♈ Oct 13 11:18	♋ Dec 14 04:22
♉ Feb 11 20:33	♌ Apr 15 01:17	♏ Jun 15 16:16	♒ Aug 15 12:52	♉ Oct 15 17:37	♌ Dec 16 17:04
♊ Feb 14 08:17	♍ Apr 17 11:07	♐ Jun 17 17:25	♓ Aug 17 13:52	♊ Oct 18 02:21	♍ Dec 19 05:52
♋ Feb 16 20:51	♎ Apr 19 17:13	♑ Jun 19 16:37	♈ Aug 19 16:57	♋ Oct 20 13:42	♎ Dec 21 16:39
♌ Feb 19 08:00	♏ Apr 21 19:54	♒ Jun 21 16:04	♉ Aug 21 23:25	♌ Oct 23 02:23	♏ Dec 23 23:37
♍ Feb 21 16:42	♐ Apr 23 20:38	♓ Jun 23 17:49	♊ Aug 24 09:26	♍ Oct 25 14:00	♐ Dec 26 02:27
♎ Feb 23 23:00	♑ Apr 25 21:20	♈ Jun 25 23:13	♋ Aug 26 21:44	♎ Oct 27 22:25	♑ Dec 28 02:23
♏ Feb 26 03:30	♒ Apr 27 23:32	♉ Jun 28 08:16	♌ Aug 29 10:09	♏ Oct 30 03:08	♒ Dec 30 01:35
♐ Feb 28 06:48	♓ Apr 30 04:12	♊ Jun 30 19:51	♍ Aug 31 21:00	♐ Nov 1 05:19	

Mercury

Jan 1 11♑	♌ Jul 8 13:37
D Jan 12 2♑	♍ Jul 27 15:06
♒ Feb 9 17:52	R Aug 17 14♍
♓ Feb 28 13:03	D Sep 9 2♍
♈ Mar 16 11:53	♎ Oct 2 14:25
♉ Apr 2 02:52	♏ Oct 19 21:45
R Apr 14 7♉	♐ Nov 8 04:53
♈ May 1 20:04	♑ Dec 1 19:56
D May 8 28♈	R Dec 7 2♑
♉ May 15 02:40	♐ Dec 12 12:40
♊ Jun 9 08:37	D Dec 27 16♐
♋ Jun 24 03:13	

Venus

Jan 1 21♑	♌ Jun 7 05:13
♒ Jan 7 21:08	♍ Jul 8 04:56
♓ Jan 31 20:13	R Aug 13 18♍
♈ Feb 24 23:25	D Sep 25 2♍
♉ Mar 21 10:06	♎ Nov 9 18:47
♊ Apr 15 08:33	♏ Dec 8 00:19
♋ May 11 01:42	

Mars

Jan 1 13♒	
♓ Jan 22 13:05	
♈ Mar 1 22:01	
♉ Apr 10 09:39	
♊ May 21 15:28	
♋ Jul 3 23:42	
♌ Aug 18 10:52	
♍ Oct 5 00:21	
♎ Nov 24 06:21	

Jupiter

Jan 1 4♓
♈ Apr 21 14:35
R Aug 4 14♈
D Nov 30 4♈

Saturn

Jan 1 2♎
R Jan 12 2♎
♍ Mar 7 11:37
D May 29 25♍
♎ Aug 13 17:11

Uranus

Jan 1 7♋
D Mar 14 5♋
R Oct 20 13♋

Neptune

Jan 1 19♎
R Jan 21 19♎
D Jun 28 16♎

Pluto

Jan 1 19♌
D Apr 30 17♌
R Nov 23 21♌

1952

Sun

♒ Jan 21 02:39	♈ Mar 20 16:11	♊ May 21 03:01	♌ Jul 22 22:06	♎ Sep 23 02:22	♐ Nov 22 08:35
♓ Feb 19 16:56	♉ Apr 20 03:34	♋ Jun 21 11:11	♍ Aug 23 05:01	♏ Oct 23 11:21	♑ Dec 21 21:43

Moon

Jan 1 28♒	♉ Feb 29 05:00	♌ May 1 04:11	♏ Jul 2 05:24	♒ Sep 1 09:01	♉ Nov 1 06:58
♓ Jan 1 02:10	♊ Mar 2 12:36	♍ May 3 16:56	♐ Jul 4 10:27	♓ Sep 3 09:00	♊ Nov 3 11:01
♈ Jan 3 05:40	♋ Mar 4 23:39	♎ May 6 03:38	♑ Jul 6 12:01	♈ Sep 5 08:57	♋ Nov 5 18:12
♉ Jan 5 12:43	♌ Mar 7 12:29	♏ May 8 10:49	♒ Jul 8 11:54	♉ Sep 7 10:48	♌ Nov 8 04:55
♊ Jan 7 22:42	♍ Mar 10 00:50	♐ May 10 14:50	♓ Jul 10 11:59	♊ Sep 9 16:06	♍ Nov 10 17:46
♋ Jan 10 10:33	♎ Mar 12 11:15	♑ May 12 17:09	♈ Jul 12 13:55	♋ Sep 12 01:24	♎ Nov 13 05:57
♌ Jan 12 23:18	♏ Mar 14 19:20	♒ May 14 19:13	♉ Jul 14 18:45	♌ Sep 14 13:37	♏ Nov 15 15:18
♍ Jan 15 12:00	♐ Mar 17 01:14	♓ May 16 22:06	♊ Jul 17 02:37	♍ Sep 17 02:41	♐ Nov 17 21:32
♎ Jan 17 23:18	♑ Mar 19 05:18	♈ May 19 02:07	♋ Jul 19 13:05	♎ Sep 19 14:40	♑ Nov 20 01:39
♏ Jan 20 07:44	♒ Mar 21 07:54	♉ May 21 07:29	♌ Jul 22 01:20	♏ Sep 22 00:43	♒ Nov 22 04:51
♐ Jan 22 12:22	♓ Mar 23 09:39	♊ May 23 14:37	♍ Jul 24 14:23	♐ Sep 24 08:33	♓ Nov 24 07:54
♑ Jan 24 13:38	♈ Mar 25 11:34	♋ May 26 00:04	♎ Jul 27 02:54	♑ Sep 26 14:06	♈ Nov 26 11:09
♒ Jan 26 13:06	♉ Mar 27 15:04	♌ May 28 11:59	♏ Jul 29 13:04	♒ Sep 28 17:23	♉ Nov 28 14:54
♓ Jan 28 12:45	♊ Mar 29 21:35	♍ May 31 00:57	♐ Jul 31 19:36	♓ Sep 30 18:52	♊ Nov 30 19:52
♈ Jan 30 14:33	♋ Apr 1 07:38	♎ Jun 2 12:25	♑ Aug 2 22:27	♈ Oct 2 19:33	♋ Dec 3 03:07
♉ Feb 1 19:50	♌ Apr 3 20:09	♏ Jun 4 20:18	♒ Aug 4 22:40	♉ Oct 4 21:04	♌ Dec 5 13:22
♊ Feb 4 04:54	♍ Apr 6 08:39	♐ Jun 7 00:21	♓ Aug 6 22:05	♊ Oct 7 01:14	♍ Dec 8 01:56
♋ Feb 6 16:44	♎ Apr 8 18:54	♑ Jun 9 01:46	♈ Aug 8 22:33	♋ Oct 9 09:16	♎ Dec 10 14:35
♌ Feb 9 05:36	♏ Apr 11 02:13	♒ Jun 11 02:27	♉ Aug 11 01:45	♌ Oct 11 20:50	♏ Dec 13 00:39
♍ Feb 11 18:00	♐ Apr 13 07:07	♓ Jun 13 04:01	♊ Aug 13 08:36	♍ Oct 14 09:41	♐ Dec 15 07:00
♎ Feb 14 04:59	♑ Apr 15 10:40	♈ Jun 15 07:29	♋ Aug 15 18:51	♎ Oct 16 21:44	♑ Dec 17 10:16
♏ Feb 16 13:45	♒ Apr 17 13:43	♉ Jun 17 13:10	♌ Aug 18 07:19	♏ Oct 19 07:09	♒ Dec 19 12:01
♐ Feb 18 19:42	♓ Apr 19 16:39	♊ Jun 19 21:02	♍ Aug 20 20:21	♐ Oct 21 14:12	♓ Dec 21 13:45
♑ Feb 20 22:50	♈ Apr 21 19:55	♋ Jun 22 07:04	♎ Aug 23 08:40	♑ Oct 23 19:28	♈ Dec 23 16:30
♒ Feb 22 23:47	♉ Apr 24 00:14	♌ Jun 24 19:02	♏ Aug 25 19:09	♒ Oct 25 23:28	♉ Dec 25 20:45
♓ Feb 25 00:00	♊ Apr 26 06:40	♍ Jun 27 08:06	♐ Aug 28 02:53	♓ Oct 28 02:22	♊ Dec 28 02:47
♈ Feb 27 01:11	♋ Apr 28 16:05	♎ Jun 29 20:17	♑ Aug 30 07:24	♈ Oct 30 04:34	♋ Dec 30 10:52

Mercury

Jan 1 18♐	♌ Jun 30 10:28
♑ Jan 13 06:36	R Jul 29 27♌
♒ Feb 3 01:43	D Aug 22 15♌
♓ Feb 20 18:57	♍ Sep 7 12:02
♈ Mar 7 17:01	♎ Sep 23 18:46
R Mar 26 20♈	♏ Oct 11 13:02
D Apr 19 8♈	♐ Nov 1 05:22
♉ May 14 14:32	R Nov 20 16♐
♊ May 31 15:25	D Dec 10 0♐
♋ Jun 14 12:22	

Venus

Jan 1 27♏	♋ Jun 22 05:45
♐ Jan 2 18:45	♌ Jul 16 15:22
♑ Jan 27 15:59	♍ Aug 9 23:57
♒ Feb 21 04:43	♎ Sep 3 08:16
♓ Mar 16 14:16	♏ Sep 27 17:34
♈ Apr 9 23:15	♐ Oct 22 04:58
♉ May 4 08:53	♑ Nov 15 19:57
♊ May 28 19:17	♒ Dec 10 18:27

Mars

Jan 1 20♎
♏ Jan 20 01:45
R Mar 25 18♏
D Jun 10 0♏
♐ Aug 27 18:45
♑ Oct 12 04:47
♒ Nov 21 19:36
♓ Dec 30 21:36

Jupiter

Jan 1 5♈
♉ Apr 28 20:56
R Sep 9 20♉

Saturn

Jan 1 14♎
R Jan 24 14♎
D Jun 10 8♎

Uranus

Jan 1 12♋
D Mar 18 9♋
R Oct 24 18♋

Neptune

Jan 1 21♎
R Jan 23 21♎
D Jun 30 18♎

Pluto

Jan 1 21♌
D Apr 30 19♌
R Nov 24 23♌

1953

Sun

♒ Jan 20 08:21	♈ Mar 20 22:01	♊ May 21 08:52	♌ Jul 23 03:50	♎ Sep 23 08:06	♐ Nov 22 14:20
♓ Feb 18 22:42	♉ Apr 20 09:24	♋ Jun 21 16:58	♍ Aug 23 10:45	♏ Oct 23 17:06	♑ Dec 22 03:30

Moon

Jan 1 19♋	♎ Mar 2 11:40	♑ May 3 03:54	♈ Jul 3 02:23	♋ Sep 2 03:29	♎ Nov 3 01:51
♌ Jan 1 21:17	♏ Mar 4 23:31	♒ May 5 09:12	♉ Jul 5 05:22	♌ Sep 4 13:04	♏ Nov 5 14:12
♍ Jan 4 09:41	♐ Mar 7 09:20	♓ May 7 12:46	♊ Jul 7 09:42	♍ Sep 7 00:46	♐ Nov 8 01:06
♎ Jan 6 22:35	♑ Mar 9 16:09	♈ May 9 14:49	♋ Jul 9 15:53	♎ Sep 9 13:27	♑ Nov 10 10:17
♏ Jan 9 09:44	♒ Mar 11 19:36	♉ May 11 16:11	♌ Jul 12 00:27	♏ Sep 12 02:05	♒ Nov 12 17:31
♐ Jan 11 17:14	♓ Mar 13 20:16	♊ May 13 18:26	♍ Jul 14 11:28	♐ Sep 14 13:31	♓ Nov 14 22:16
♑ Jan 13 20:55	♈ Mar 15 19:38	♋ May 15 23:11	♎ Jul 17 00:02	♑ Sep 16 22:20	♈ Nov 17 00:35
♒ Jan 15 21:57	♉ Mar 17 19:44	♌ May 18 07:47	♏ Jul 19 12:17	♒ Sep 19 03:29	♉ Nov 19 01:14
♓ Jan 17 22:07	♊ Mar 19 22:34	♍ May 20 19:30	♐ Jul 21 21:59	♓ Sep 21 05:06	♊ Nov 21 01:54
♈ Jan 19 23:08	♋ Mar 22 05:29	♎ May 23 08:15	♑ Jul 24 04:07	♈ Sep 23 04:30	♋ Nov 23 04:30
♉ Jan 22 02:19	♌ Mar 24 16:13	♏ May 25 19:31	♒ Jul 26 07:03	♉ Sep 25 03:45	♌ Nov 25 10:39
♊ Jan 24 08:20	♍ Mar 27 05:04	♐ May 28 04:07	♓ Jul 28 08:07	♊ Sep 27 04:59	♍ Nov 27 20:40
♋ Jan 26 17:06	♎ Mar 29 17:51	♑ May 30 10:16	♈ Jul 30 08:56	♋ Sep 29 09:55	♎ Nov 30 09:05
♌ Jan 29 04:06	♏ Apr 1 05:18	♒ Jun 1 14:44	♉ Aug 1 10:56	♌ Oct 1 18:52	♏ Dec 2 21:29
♍ Jan 31 16:34	♐ Apr 3 14:58	♓ Jun 3 18:12	♊ Aug 3 15:09	♍ Oct 4 06:40	♐ Dec 5 08:09
♎ Feb 3 05:31	♑ Apr 5 22:29	♈ Jun 5 21:00	♋ Aug 5 21:59	♎ Oct 6 19:28	♑ Dec 7 16:32
♏ Feb 5 17:19	♒ Apr 8 03:27	♉ Jun 7 23:40	♌ Aug 8 07:14	♏ Oct 9 07:55	♒ Dec 9 22:58
♐ Feb 8 02:19	♓ Apr 10 05:50	♊ Jun 10 03:02	♍ Aug 10 18:32	♐ Oct 11 19:19	♓ Dec 12 03:45
♑ Feb 10 07:31	♈ Apr 12 06:19	♋ Jun 12 08:16	♎ Aug 13 07:07	♑ Oct 14 04:51	♈ Dec 14 07:06
♒ Feb 12 09:17	♉ Apr 14 06:30	♌ Jun 14 16:27	♏ Aug 15 19:43	♒ Oct 16 11:34	♉ Dec 16 09:22
♓ Feb 14 08:58	♊ Apr 16 08:27	♍ Jun 17 03:36	♐ Aug 18 06:29	♓ Oct 18 14:55	♊ Dec 18 11:27
♈ Feb 16 08:31	♋ Apr 18 13:52	♎ Jun 19 16:15	♑ Aug 20 13:52	♈ Oct 20 15:26	♋ Dec 20 14:39
♉ Feb 18 09:49	♌ Apr 20 23:27	♏ Jun 22 03:57	♒ Aug 22 17:28	♉ Oct 22 14:46	♌ Dec 22 20:21
♊ Feb 20 14:27	♍ Apr 23 11:52	♐ Jun 24 12:47	♓ Aug 24 18:12	♊ Oct 24 15:03	♍ Dec 25 05:23
♋ Feb 22 22:47	♎ Apr 26 00:40	♑ Jun 26 18:28	♈ Aug 26 17:45	♋ Oct 26 18:22	♎ Dec 27 17:11
♌ Feb 25 10:05	♏ Apr 28 11:52	♒ Jun 28 21:51	♉ Aug 28 18:09	♌ Oct 29 01:54	♏ Dec 30 05:42
♍ Feb 27 22:51	♐ Apr 30 20:52	♓ Jul 1 00:07	♊ Aug 30 21:05	♍ Oct 31 13:04	

Mercury

Jan 1 21♐	R Jul 11 8♌
♑ Jan 6 13:26	♋ Jul 28 13:51
♒ Jan 25 19:07	D Aug 4 28♋
♓ Feb 11 23:55	♌ Aug 11 14:27
♈ Mar 2 19:42	♍ Aug 30 22:51
R Mar 9 2♈	♎ Sep 15 21:43
♓ Mar 15 21:21	♏ Oct 4 16:39
D Apr 1 20♓	♐ Oct 31 15:27
♈ Apr 17 16:45	R Nov 3 29♏
♉ May 8 06:18	♏ Nov 7 00:17
♊ May 23 03:59	D Nov 23 14♏
♋ Jun 6 08:19	♐ Dec 10 14:51
♌ Jun 26 11:06	♑ Dec 30 17:15

Venus

Jan 1 24♒	♊ Jul 7 10:27
♓ Jan 5 11:13	♋ Aug 4 01:05
♈ Feb 2 05:57	♌ Aug 30 01:31
♉ Mar 14 18:37	♍ Sep 24 03:45
R Mar 23 1♉	♎ Oct 18 15:25
♈ Mar 31 05:20	♏ Nov 11 18:12
D May 4 14♈	♐ Dec 5 16:23
♉ Jun 5 10:30	♑ Dec 29 12:52

Mars

Jan 1 0♓
♈ Feb 8 00:58
♉ Mar 20 06:49
♊ May 1 06:02
♋ Jun 14 03:45
♌ Jul 29 19:17
♍ Sep 14 17:54
♎ Nov 1 14:16
♏ Dec 20 11:18

Jupiter

Jan 1 11♉
D Jan 5 10♉
♊ May 9 15:53
R Oct 15 26♊

Saturn

Jan 1 26♎
R Feb 5 27♎
D Jun 23 20♎
♏ Oct 22 15:52

Uranus

Jan 1 16♋
D Mar 22 14♋
R Oct 29 23♋

Neptune

Jan 1 23♎
R Jan 25 23♎
D Jul 2 21♎

Pluto

Jan 1 22♌
D May 2 20♌
R Nov 26 25♌

1954

Sun

♒ Jan 20 14:12	♈ Mar 21 03:53	♊ May 21 14:46	♌ Jul 23 09:43	♎ Sep 23 13:55	♐ Nov 22 20:15
♓ Feb 19 04:32	♉ Apr 20 15:19	♋ Jun 21 22:52	♍ Aug 23 16:33	♏ Oct 23 22:57	♑ Dec 22 09:24

Moon

Jan 1 21 ♏	♒ Mar 2 02:07	♉ May 2 01:43	♌ Jul 2 02:15	♏ Sep 1 22:48	♒ Nov 3 00:21
♐ Jan 1 16:38	♓ Mar 4 04:31	♊ May 4 01:07	♍ Jul 4 08:56	♐ Sep 4 11:32	♓ Nov 5 07:33
♑ Jan 4 00:45	♈ Mar 6 04:39	♋ May 6 02:30	♎ Jul 6 18:52	♑ Sep 6 23:10	♈ Nov 7 10:42
♒ Jan 6 06:08	♉ Mar 8 04:31	♌ May 8 07:29	♏ Jul 9 07:04	♒ Sep 9 07:30	♉ Nov 9 10:48
♓ Jan 8 09:43	♊ Mar 10 06:05	♍ May 10 16:23	♐ Jul 11 19:19	♓ Sep 11 11:55	♊ Nov 11 09:50
♈ Jan 10 12:26	♋ Mar 12 10:36	♎ May 13 04:03	♑ Jul 14 05:39	♈ Sep 13 13:22	♋ Nov 13 09:59
♉ Jan 12 15:09	♌ Mar 14 18:17	♏ May 15 16:42	♒ Jul 16 13:19	♉ Sep 15 13:44	♌ Nov 15 13:02
♊ Jan 14 18:28	♍ Mar 17 04:21	♐ May 18 04:52	♓ Jul 18 18:32	♊ Sep 17 14:55	♍ Nov 17 19:52
♋ Jan 16 23:00	♎ Mar 19 15:57	♑ May 20 15:48	♈ Jul 20 22:07	♋ Sep 19 18:13	♎ Nov 20 06:01
♌ Jan 19 05:23	♏ Mar 22 04:26	♒ May 23 00:48	♉ Jul 23 00:51	♌ Sep 22 00:03	♏ Nov 22 18:13
♍ Jan 21 14:13	♐ Mar 24 16:55	♓ May 25 07:08	♊ Jul 25 03:29	♍ Sep 24 08:10	♐ Nov 25 07:01
♎ Jan 24 01:30	♑ Mar 27 03:54	♈ May 27 10:31	♋ Jul 27 06:41	♎ Sep 26 18:10	♑ Nov 27 19:24
♏ Jan 26 14:02	♒ Mar 29 11:37	♉ May 29 11:34	♌ Jul 29 11:10	♏ Sep 29 05:52	♒ Nov 30 06:19
♐ Jan 29 01:42	♓ Mar 31 15:17	♊ May 31 11:40	♍ Jul 31 17:49	♐ Oct 1 18:41	♓ Dec 2 14:37
♑ Jan 31 10:27	♈ Apr 2 15:40	♋ Jun 2 12:45	♎ Aug 3 03:14	♑ Oct 4 07:04	♈ Dec 4 19:34
♒ Feb 2 15:38	♉ Apr 4 14:42	♌ Jun 4 16:33	♏ Aug 5 15:01	♒ Oct 6 16:45	♉ Dec 6 21:22
♓ Feb 4 18:02	♊ Apr 6 14:39	♍ Jun 7 00:05	♐ Aug 8 03:31	♓ Oct 8 22:16	♊ Dec 8 21:16
♈ Feb 6 19:13	♋ Apr 8 17:28	♎ Jun 9 10:58	♑ Aug 10 14:19	♈ Oct 10 23:58	♋ Dec 10 21:05
♉ Feb 8 20:46	♌ Apr 11 00:05	♏ Jun 11 23:29	♒ Aug 12 21:53	♉ Oct 12 23:32	♌ Dec 12 22:48
♊ Feb 10 23:54	♍ Apr 13 10:03	♐ Jun 14 11:37	♓ Aug 15 02:15	♊ Oct 14 23:10	♍ Dec 15 03:52
♋ Feb 13 05:10	♎ Apr 15 21:58	♑ Jun 16 22:05	♈ Aug 17 04:36	♋ Oct 17 00:49	♎ Dec 17 12:50
♌ Feb 15 12:35	♏ Apr 18 10:31	♒ Jun 19 06:25	♉ Aug 19 06:25	♌ Oct 19 05:40	♏ Dec 20 00:43
♍ Feb 17 22:00	♐ Apr 20 22:54	♓ Jun 21 12:37	♊ Aug 21 08:56	♍ Oct 21 13:44	♐ Dec 22 13:34
♎ Feb 20 09:14	♑ Apr 23 10:10	♈ Jun 23 16:44	♋ Aug 23 12:49	♎ Oct 24 00:12	♑ Dec 25 01:39
♏ Feb 22 21:43	♒ Apr 25 19:02	♉ Jun 25 19:08	♌ Aug 25 18:22	♏ Oct 26 12:09	♒ Dec 27 12:00
♐ Feb 25 10:00	♓ Apr 28 00:21	♊ Jun 27 20:40	♍ Aug 28 01:43	♐ Oct 29 00:58	♓ Dec 29 20:09
♑ Feb 27 19:57	♈ Apr 30 02:09	♋ Jun 29 22:35	♎ Aug 30 11:12	♑ Oct 31 13:35	

Mercury

Jan 1 1 ♑	♌ Aug 7 14:43
♒ Jan 18 07:42	♍ Aug 22 17:41
♓ Feb 4 17:56	♎ Sep 8 08:14
R Feb 20 16 ♓	♏ Sep 29 03:45
D Mar 14 2 ♓	R Oct 18 13 ♏
♈ Apr 13 11:36	♎ Nov 4 12:26
♉ Apr 30 11:27	D Nov 7 28 ♎
♊ May 14 13:55	♏ Nov 11 10:13
♋ May 30 16:17	♐ Dec 4 07:01
R Jun 23 18 ♋	♑ Dec 23 12:10
D Jul 17 10 ♋	

Venus

Jan 1 3 ♑	♍ Jul 13 08:44
♒ Jan 22 09:21	♎ Aug 9 00:35
♓ Feb 15 07:02	♏ Sep 6 23:28
♈ Mar 11 07:22	♐ Oct 23 21:41
♉ Apr 4 11:55	R Oct 25 0 ♐
♊ Apr 28 22:02	♏ Oct 27 11:06
♋ May 23 15:02	D Dec 5 14 ♏
♌ Jun 17 17:05	

Mars

Jan 1 6 ♏	
♐ Feb 9 19:28	
♑ Apr 12 16:58	
R May 23 9 ♑	
♐ Jul 3 07:39	
D Jul 29 25 ♐	
♑ Aug 24 12:45	
♒ Oct 21 11:55	
♓ Dec 4 07:51	

Jupiter

Jan 1 19 ♊
D Feb 10 16 ♊
♋ May 24 05:38
R Nov 17 29 ♋

Saturn

Jan 1 7 ♏
R Feb 17 9 ♏
D Jul 6 2 ♏

Uranus

Jan 1 21 ♋
D Mar 27 18 ♋
R Nov 3 27 ♋

Neptune

Jan 1 25 ♎
R Jan 27 26 ♎
D Jul 5 23 ♎

Pluto

Jan 1 24 ♌
D May 4 22 ♌
R Nov 28 26 ♌

1955

Sun

♒ Jan 20 20:04	♈ Mar 21 09:39	♊ May 21 20:28	♌ Jul 23 15:24	♎ Sep 23 19:40	♐ Nov 23 02:00
♓ Feb 19 10:22	♉ Apr 20 21:00	♋ Jun 22 04:33	♍ Aug 23 22:19	♏ Oct 24 04:43	♑ Dec 22 15:10

Moon

Jan 1 28 ♓	♊ Feb 28 19:24	♍ Apr 30 19:57	♐ Jul 1 15:34	♓ Sep 1 15:22	♊ Nov 1 19:22
♈ Jan 1 01:55	♋ Mar 2 22:39	♎ May 3 04:26	♑ Jul 4 04:29	♈ Sep 3 21:22	♋ Nov 3 20:11
♉ Jan 3 05:23	♌ Mar 5 02:47	♏ May 5 15:03	♒ Jul 6 16:17	♉ Sep 6 01:35	♌ Nov 5 22:20
♊ Jan 5 07:04	♍ Mar 7 08:09	♐ May 8 03:18	♓ Jul 9 02:08	♊ Sep 8 04:57	♍ Nov 8 02:37
♋ Jan 7 07:59	♎ Mar 9 15:20	♑ May 10 16:19	♈ Jul 11 09:32	♋ Sep 10 08:00	♎ Nov 10 09:15
♌ Jan 9 09:41	♏ Mar 12 01:04	♒ May 13 04:29	♉ Jul 13 14:19	♌ Sep 12 11:01	♏ Nov 12 18:12
♍ Jan 11 13:42	♐ Mar 14 13:12	♓ May 15 13:52	♊ Jul 15 16:43	♍ Sep 14 14:33	♐ Nov 15 05:16
♎ Jan 13 21:15	♑ Mar 17 02:00	♈ May 17 19:21	♋ Jul 17 17:29	♎ Sep 16 19:34	♑ Nov 17 17:59
♏ Jan 16 08:14	♒ Mar 19 12:45	♉ May 19 21:12	♌ Jul 19 18:02	♏ Sep 19 03:18	♒ Nov 20 06:58
♐ Jan 18 21:00	♓ Mar 21 19:45	♊ May 21 20:56	♍ Jul 21 20:06	♐ Sep 21 14:11	♓ Nov 22 18:09
♑ Jan 21 09:08	♈ Mar 23 23:09	♋ May 23 20:33	♎ Jul 24 01:15	♑ Sep 24 03:00	♈ Nov 25 01:48
♒ Jan 23 18:58	♉ Mar 26 00:30	♌ May 25 21:51	♏ Jul 26 10:19	♒ Sep 26 15:06	♉ Nov 27 05:27
♓ Jan 26 02:11	♊ Mar 28 01:42	♍ May 28 02:15	♐ Jul 28 22:24	♓ Sep 29 00:12	♊ Nov 29 06:10
♈ Jan 28 07:19	♋ Mar 30 04:05	♎ May 30 10:07	♑ Jul 31 11:18	♈ Oct 1 05:46	♋ Dec 1 05:46
♉ Jan 30 11:06	♌ Apr 1 08:20	♏ Jun 1 20:54	♒ Aug 2 22:52	♉ Oct 3 08:52	♌ Dec 3 06:06
♊ Feb 1 14:02	♍ Apr 3 14:31	♐ Jun 4 09:22	♓ Aug 5 08:04	♊ Oct 5 10:58	♍ Dec 5 08:50
♋ Feb 3 16:35	♎ Apr 5 22:33	♑ Jun 6 22:21	♈ Aug 7 14:59	♋ Oct 7 13:23	♎ Dec 7 14:47
♌ Feb 5 19:28	♏ Apr 8 08:37	♒ Jun 9 10:30	♉ Aug 9 20:02	♌ Oct 9 16:40	♏ Dec 9 23:59
♍ Feb 7 23:42	♐ Apr 10 20:40	♓ Jun 11 20:32	♊ Aug 11 23:33	♍ Oct 11 21:10	♐ Dec 12 11:34
♎ Feb 10 06:32	♑ Apr 13 09:40	♈ Jun 14 03:23	♋ Aug 14 01:50	♎ Oct 14 03:13	♑ Dec 15 00:22
♏ Feb 12 16:37	♒ Apr 15 21:19	♉ Jun 16 06:49	♌ Aug 16 03:34	♏ Oct 16 11:22	♒ Dec 17 13:19
♐ Feb 15 05:07	♓ Apr 18 05:28	♊ Jun 18 07:35	♍ Aug 18 05:57	♐ Oct 18 22:07	♓ Dec 20 01:02
♑ Feb 17 17:34	♈ Apr 20 09:28	♋ Jun 20 07:14	♎ Aug 20 10:32	♑ Oct 21 10:51	♈ Dec 22 10:05
♒ Feb 20 03:32	♉ Apr 22 10:29	♌ Jun 22 07:35	♏ Aug 22 18:37	♒ Oct 23 23:32	♉ Dec 24 15:32
♓ Feb 22 10:08	♊ Apr 24 10:24	♍ Jun 24 10:26	♐ Aug 25 06:02	♓ Oct 26 09:37	♊ Dec 26 17:33
♈ Feb 24 14:06	♋ Apr 26 11:09	♎ Jun 26 16:54	♑ Aug 27 18:55	♈ Oct 28 15:45	♋ Dec 28 17:16
♉ Feb 26 16:46	♌ Apr 28 14:09	♏ Jun 29 03:04	♒ Aug 30 06:35	♉ Oct 30 18:29	♌ Dec 30 16:35

Mercury

Jan 1 13 ♑	♋ Jul 13 14:53
♒ Jan 10 23:14	♌ Jul 30 17:21
R Feb 3 0 ♓	♍ Aug 14 13:07
D Feb 25 15 ♒	♎ Sep 1 12:07
♓ Mar 17 20:51	R Oct 1 28 ♎
♈ Apr 6 16:13	D Oct 22 12 ♎
♉ Apr 22 03:00	♏ Nov 8 07:03
♊ May 6 13:06	♐ Nov 27 04:36
R Jun 3 28 ♊	♑ Dec 16 06:05
D Jun 27 20 ♊	

Venus

Jan 1 25 ♏	♋ Jul 8 00:15
♐ Jan 6 06:48	♌ Aug 1 11:41
♑ Feb 6 01:12	♍ Aug 25 18:51
♒ Mar 4 20:19	♎ Sep 18 22:40
♓ Mar 30 11:32	♏ Oct 13 00:38
♈ Apr 24 15:16	♐ Nov 6 01:59
♉ May 19 13:36	♑ Nov 30 03:39
♊ Jun 13 08:37	♒ Dec 24 06:49

Mars

Jan 1 19 ♓
♈ Jan 15 04:38
♉ Feb 26 10:31
♊ Apr 10 23:13
♋ May 26 00:52
♌ Jul 11 09:21
♍ Aug 27 10:07
♎ Oct 13 11:15
♏ Nov 29 01:25

Jupiter

Jan 1 26 ♋
D Mar 16 19 ♋
♌ Jun 13 01:00
♍ Nov 17 05:31
R Dec 18 1 ♍

Saturn

Jan 1 18 ♏
R Mar 1 21 ♏
D Jul 19 14 ♏

Uranus

Jan 1 26 ♋
D Apr 1 23 ♋
♌ Aug 24 17:14
R Nov 8 2 ♌

Neptune

Jan 1 28 ♎
R Jan 29 28 ♎
D Jul 7 25 ♎
♏ Dec 24 14:59

Pluto

Jan 1 26 ♌
D May 6 24 ♌
R Dec 1 28 ♌

1956

Sun

| ♒ Jan 21 01:50 | ♈ Mar 20 15:22 | ♊ May 21 02:16 | ♌ Jul 22 21:22 | ♎ Sep 23 01:35 | ♐ Nov 22 07:49 |
| ♓ Feb 19 16:07 | ♉ Apr 20 02:46 | ♋ Jun 21 10:28 | ♍ Aug 23 04:15 | ♏ Oct 23 10:33 | ♑ Dec 21 20:58 |

Moon

Jan 1 19♌	♏ Feb 29 22:45	♒ May 2 01:27	♉ Jul 2 22:26	♌ Sep 1 23:14	♏ Nov 1 22:24
♍ Jan 1 17:31	♐ Mar 3 08:09	♓ May 4 13:14	♊ Jul 5 02:25	♍ Sep 3 23:19	♐ Nov 4 04:55
♎ Jan 3 21:44	♑ Mar 5 22:32	♈ May 6 22:05	♋ Jul 7 03:20	♎ Sep 6 00:03	♑ Nov 6 14:23
♏ Jan 6 06:00	♒ Mar 8 09:19	♉ May 9 03:23	♌ Jul 9 02:41	♏ Sep 8 03:25	♒ Nov 9 02:18
♐ Jan 8 17:33	♓ Mar 10 20:11	♊ May 11 06:00	♍ Jul 11 02:34	♐ Sep 10 10:46	♓ Nov 11 14:51
♑ Jan 11 06:34	♈ Mar 13 04:26	♋ May 13 07:21	♎ Jul 13 04:53	♑ Sep 12 21:45	♈ Nov 14 01:35
♒ Jan 13 19:19	♉ Mar 15 10:31	♌ May 15 08:52	♏ Jul 15 10:55	♒ Sep 15 10:28	♉ Nov 16 09:12
♓ Jan 16 06:46	♊ Mar 17 15:12	♍ May 17 11:39	♐ Jul 17 20:37	♓ Sep 17 22:32	♊ Nov 18 13:45
♈ Jan 18 16:16	♋ Mar 19 18:47	♎ May 19 16:25	♑ Jul 20 08:39	♈ Sep 20 08:46	♋ Nov 20 16:16
♉ Jan 20 23:11	♌ Mar 21 21:30	♏ May 21 23:25	♒ Jul 22 21:27	♉ Sep 22 17:00	♌ Nov 22 18:09
♊ Jan 23 03:05	♍ Mar 23 23:53	♐ May 24 08:45	♓ Jul 25 09:49	♊ Sep 24 23:24	♍ Nov 24 20:32
♋ Jan 25 04:20	♎ Mar 26 03:00	♑ May 26 20:11	♈ Jul 27 20:53	♋ Sep 27 04:00	♎ Nov 27 00:10
♌ Jan 27 04:06	♏ Mar 28 08:18	♒ May 29 08:52	♉ Jul 30 05:39	♌ Sep 29 06:48	♏ Nov 29 05:34
♍ Jan 29 04:16	♐ Mar 30 16:54	♓ May 31 21:08	♊ Aug 1 11:15	♍ Oct 1 08:23	♐ Dec 1 12:59
♎ Jan 31 06:55	♑ Apr 2 04:37	♈ Jun 3 07:04	♋ Aug 3 13:31	♎ Oct 3 10:01	♑ Dec 3 22:35
♏ Feb 2 13:32	♒ Apr 4 17:23	♉ Jun 5 13:22	♌ Aug 5 13:27	♏ Oct 5 13:19	♒ Dec 6 10:15
♐ Feb 5 00:13	♓ Apr 7 04:36	♊ Jun 7 16:09	♍ Aug 7 12:48	♐ Oct 7 19:46	♓ Dec 8 22:56
♑ Feb 7 13:07	♈ Apr 9 12:46	♋ Jun 9 16:42	♎ Aug 9 13:50	♑ Oct 10 05:47	♈ Dec 11 10:36
♒ Feb 10 01:52	♉ Apr 11 18:02	♌ Jun 11 16:45	♏ Aug 11 18:20	♒ Oct 12 18:08	♉ Dec 13 19:15
♓ Feb 12 12:51	♊ Apr 13 21:30	♍ Jun 13 18:02	♐ Aug 14 03:00	♓ Oct 15 06:23	♊ Dec 16 00:05
♈ Feb 14 21:47	♋ Apr 16 00:15	♎ Jun 15 21:59	♑ Aug 16 14:46	♈ Oct 17 16:34	♋ Dec 18 01:52
♉ Feb 17 04:48	♌ Apr 18 03:00	♏ Jun 18 05:02	♒ Aug 19 03:38	♉ Oct 20 00:06	♌ Dec 20 02:11
♊ Feb 19 09:50	♍ Apr 20 06:17	♐ Jun 20 14:55	♓ Aug 21 15:46	♊ Oct 22 05:28	♍ Dec 22 02:56
♋ Feb 21 12:49	♎ Apr 22 10:35	♑ Jun 23 02:42	♈ Aug 24 02:29	♋ Oct 24 09:22	♎ Dec 24 05:37
♌ Feb 23 14:11	♏ Apr 24 16:44	♒ Jun 25 15:24	♉ Aug 26 11:23	♌ Oct 26 12:26	♏ Dec 26 11:09
♍ Feb 25 15:04	♐ Apr 27 01:25	♓ Jun 28 03:53	♊ Aug 28 17:59	♍ Oct 28 15:08	♐ Dec 28 19:20
♎ Feb 27 17:19	♑ Apr 29 12:44	♈ Jun 30 14:42	♋ Aug 30 21:50	♎ Oct 30 18:09	♑ Dec 31 05:37

Mercury

Jan 1 24♑	♋ Jul 6 19:11
♒ Jan 4 09:18	♌ Jul 21 05:33
R Jan 18 14♒	♍ Aug 5 19:05
♑ Feb 2 12:09	♎ Aug 26 13:33
D Feb 8 27♑	R Sep 13 12♎
♒ Feb 15 06:03	♍ Sep 29 20:45
♓ Mar 11 10:30	D Oct 5 26♍
♈ Mar 28 22:48	♎ Oct 11 07:42
♉ Apr 12 17:06	♏ Oct 31 08:16
♊ Apr 29 23:20	♐ Nov 18 21:41
R May 14 9♊	♑ Dec 8 07:07
D Jun 7 29♉	

Venus

Jan 1 9♒	D Jul 13 22♊
♓ Jan 17 14:19	♋ Aug 4 10:00
♈ Feb 11 07:47	♌ Sep 8 09:21
♉ Mar 7 21:32	♍ Oct 6 03:12
♊ Apr 4 07:26	♎ Oct 31 19:39
♋ May 8 02:27	♏ Nov 25 13:00
R May 31 9♋	♐ Dec 19 19:05
♊ Jun 23 11:42	

Mars

Jan 1 21♏
♐ Jan 14 02:23
♑ Feb 28 19:51
♒ Apr 14 23:43
♓ Jun 3 07:29
R Aug 10 23♓
D Oct 10 13♓
♈ Dec 6 10:44

Jupiter

Jan 1 1♍
♌ Jan 18 01:17
D Apr 17 21♌
♍ Jul 7 19:33
♎ Dec 13 02:43

Saturn

Jan 1 28♏
♐ Jan 12 19:05
R Mar 12 2♐
♏ May 14 02:52
D Jul 30 26♏
♐ Oct 10 15:53

Uranus

Jan 1 1♌
♋ Jan 28 01:54
D Apr 5 28♋
♌ Jun 10 00:55
R Nov 12 6♌

Neptune

Jan 1 0♏
R Feb 1 0♏
♎ Mar 12 02:15
D Jul 9 27♎
♏ Oct 19 09:04

Pluto

Jan 1 28♌
D May 7 26♌
♍ Oct 20 05:33
R Dec 2 0♍

1957

Sun

♒ Jan 20 07:37	♈ Mar 20 21:15	♊ May 21 08:10	♌ Jul 23 03:15	♎ Sep 23 07:26	♐ Nov 22 13:37
♓ Feb 18 21:57	♉ Apr 20 08:39	♋ Jun 21 16:21	♍ Aug 23 10:07	♏ Oct 23 16:24	♑ Dec 22 02:49

Moon

Jan 1 9♑	♈ Mar 3 06:29	♋ May 3 19:07	♎ Jul 3 15:16	♑ Sep 2 21:04	♈ Nov 3 22:00
♒ Jan 2 17:23	♉ Mar 5 17:19	♌ May 5 22:53	♏ Jul 5 19:09	♒ Sep 5 07:50	♉ Nov 6 09:38
♓ Jan 5 06:03	♊ Mar 8 02:02	♍ May 8 01:36	♐ Jul 8 01:20	♓ Sep 7 20:04	♊ Nov 8 19:08
♈ Jan 7 18:22	♋ Mar 10 07:45	♎ May 10 03:58	♑ Jul 10 09:35	♈ Sep 10 08:43	♋ Nov 11 02:23
♉ Jan 10 04:26	♌ Mar 12 10:11	♏ May 12 06:47	♒ Jul 12 19:43	♉ Sep 12 20:57	♌ Nov 13 07:35
♊ Jan 12 10:44	♍ Mar 14 10:20	♐ May 14 11:13	♓ Jul 15 07:31	♊ Sep 15 07:26	♍ Nov 15 11:07
♋ Jan 14 13:06	♎ Mar 16 09:59	♑ May 16 18:13	♈ Jul 17 20:14	♋ Sep 17 14:50	♎ Nov 17 13:25
♌ Jan 16 12:50	♏ Mar 18 11:15	♒ May 19 04:11	♉ Jul 20 07:57	♌ Sep 19 18:30	♏ Nov 19 15:17
♍ Jan 18 12:03	♐ Mar 20 15:53	♓ May 21 16:20	♊ Jul 22 16:33	♍ Sep 21 19:10	♐ Nov 21 17:52
♎ Jan 20 12:54	♑ Mar 23 00:34	♈ May 24 04:33	♋ Jul 24 21:04	♎ Sep 23 18:31	♑ Nov 23 22:29
♏ Jan 22 17:01	♒ Mar 25 12:17	♉ May 26 14:42	♌ Jul 26 22:16	♏ Sep 25 18:40	♒ Nov 26 01:40
♐ Jan 25 00:51	♓ Mar 28 01:00	♊ May 28 21:46	♍ Jul 28 21:59	♐ Sep 27 21:26	♓ Nov 28 17:15
♑ Jan 27 11:32	♈ Mar 30 12:53	♋ May 31 02:06	♎ Jul 30 22:20	♑ Sep 30 03:59	♈ Dec 1 05:56
♒ Jan 29 23:41	♉ Apr 1 23:11	♌ Jun 2 04:45	♏ Aug 2 01:00	♒ Oct 2 14:04	♉ Dec 3 17:47
♓ Feb 1 12:20	♊ Apr 4 07:30	♍ Jun 4 06:59	♐ Aug 4 06:46	♓ Oct 5 02:16	♊ Dec 6 03:00
♈ Feb 4 00:42	♋ Apr 6 13:36	♎ Jun 6 09:45	♑ Aug 6 15:22	♈ Oct 7 14:57	♋ Dec 8 09:16
♉ Feb 6 11:37	♌ Apr 8 17:23	♏ Jun 8 13:40	♒ Aug 9 02:07	♉ Oct 10 02:47	♌ Dec 10 13:23
♊ Feb 8 19:34	♍ Apr 10 19:12	♐ Jun 10 19:08	♓ Aug 11 14:01	♊ Oct 12 13:01	♍ Dec 12 16:28
♋ Feb 10 23:38	♎ Apr 12 20:09	♑ Jun 13 02:36	♈ Aug 14 02:45	♋ Oct 14 20:54	♎ Dec 14 19:23
♌ Feb 13 00:18	♏ Apr 14 21:45	♒ Jun 15 12:22	♉ Aug 16 15:00	♌ Oct 17 01:58	♏ Dec 16 22:34
♍ Feb 14 23:16	♐ Apr 17 01:43	♓ Jun 18 00:15	♊ Aug 19 00:50	♍ Oct 19 04:23	♐ Dec 19 02:30
♎ Feb 16 22:50	♑ Apr 19 09:07	♈ Jun 20 12:45	♋ Aug 21 06:48	♎ Oct 21 05:02	♑ Dec 21 07:47
♏ Feb 19 01:06	♒ Apr 21 19:52	♉ Jun 22 23:37	♌ Aug 23 08:51	♏ Oct 23 05:31	♒ Dec 23 15:18
♐ Feb 21 07:23	♓ Apr 24 08:22	♊ Jun 25 07:07	♍ Aug 25 08:25	♐ Oct 25 07:32	♓ Dec 26 01:40
♑ Feb 23 17:27	♈ Apr 26 20:20	♋ Jun 27 11:00	♎ Aug 27 07:40	♑ Oct 27 12:41	♈ Dec 28 14:12
♒ Feb 26 05:41	♉ Apr 29 06:18	♌ Jun 29 12:30	♏ Aug 29 08:44	♒ Oct 29 21:31	♉ Dec 31 02:37
♓ Feb 28 18:24	♊ May 1 13:47	♍ Jul 1 13:23	♐ Aug 31 13:07	♓ Nov 1 09:18	

Mercury

Jan 1 28♑	♌ Jul 12 19:50
R Jan 1 27♑	♍ Jul 30 02:05
D Jan 21 12♑	R Aug 27 24♍
♒ Feb 12 14:30	D Sep 19 11♍
♓ Mar 4 11:32	♎ Oct 6 11:05
♈ Mar 20 19:47	♏ Oct 23 20:47
♉ Apr 4 23:41	♐ Nov 11 18:00
R Apr 25 18♉	♑ Dec 2 11:16
D May 19 9♉	R Dec 16 11♑
♊ Jun 12 13:40	♐ Dec 28 17:43
♋ Jun 28 17:10	

Venus

Jan 1 15♐	♌ Jul 1 10:43
♑ Jan 12 20:21	♍ Jul 26 03:09
♒ Feb 5 20:15	♎ Aug 20 00:43
♓ Mar 1 20:39	♏ Sep 14 06:20
♈ Mar 25 22:46	♐ Oct 10 01:15
♉ Apr 19 03:29	♑ Nov 5 23:46
♊ May 13 11:10	♒ Dec 6 15:27
♋ Jun 6 21:36	

Mars

Jan 1 13♈
♉ Jan 28 14:09
♊ Mar 17 21:35
♋ May 4 15:25
♌ Jun 21 12:22
♍ Aug 8 05:30
♎ Sep 24 04:31
♏ Nov 8 20:59
♐ Dec 23 01:29

Jupiter

Jan 1 1♎
R Jan 16 1♎
♍ Feb 19 15:10
D May 19 21♍
♎ Aug 7 02:20

Saturn

Jan 1 9♐
R Mar 24 14♐
D Aug 11 7♐

Uranus

Jan 1 5♌
D Apr 10 2♌
R Nov 17 11♌

Neptune

Jan 1 2♏
R Feb 2 2♏
♎ Jun 15 20:22
D Jul 11 29♎
♏ Aug 6 08:07

Pluto

Jan 1 0♍
♌ Jan 15 03:45
D May 9 27♌
♍ Aug 19 03:26
R Dec 4 2♍

1958

Sun

♒ Jan 20 13:29	♈ Mar 21 03:05	♊ May 21 13:52	♌ Jul 23 08:53	♎ Sep 23 13:11	♐ Nov 22 19:30
♓ Feb 19 03:48	♉ Apr 20 14:28	♋ Jun 21 22:00	♍ Aug 23 15:48	♏ Oct 23 22:12	♑ Dec 22 08:39

Moon

Jan 1 10 ♉	♌ Mar 2 18:26	♏ May 2 16:13	♒ Jul 2 19:44	♉ Sep 2 19:24	♌ Nov 3 17:01
♊ Jan 2 12:21	♍ Mar 4 19:14	♐ May 4 16:43	♓ Jul 5 03:55	♊ Sep 5 08:06	♍ Nov 5 22:45
♋ Jan 4 18:22	♎ Mar 6 18:36	♑ May 6 19:20	♈ Jul 7 15:17	♋ Sep 7 18:22	♎ Nov 8 01:15
♌ Jan 6 21:22	♏ Mar 8 18:34	♒ May 9 01:29	♉ Jul 10 04:08	♌ Sep 10 00:42	♏ Nov 10 01:30
♍ Jan 8 22:58	♐ Mar 10 20:56	♓ May 11 11:27	♊ Jul 12 15:45	♍ Sep 12 03:19	♐ Nov 12 01:03
♎ Jan 11 00:50	♑ Mar 13 02:36	♈ May 13 23:58	♋ Jul 15 00:16	♎ Sep 14 03:44	♑ Nov 14 01:53
♏ Jan 13 04:02	♒ Mar 15 11:28	♉ May 16 12:40	♌ Jul 17 05:31	♏ Sep 16 03:48	♒ Nov 16 05:52
♐ Jan 15 08:49	♓ Mar 17 22:40	♊ May 19 00:14	♍ Jul 19 08:41	♐ Sep 18 05:15	♓ Nov 18 13:55
♑ Jan 17 15:12	♈ Mar 20 11:16	♋ May 21 09:22	♎ Jul 21 11:11	♑ Sep 20 09:13	♈ Nov 21 01:28
♒ Jan 19 23:21	♉ Mar 23 00:15	♌ May 23 16:14	♏ Jul 23 13:56	♒ Sep 22 16:03	♉ Nov 23 14:30
♓ Jan 22 09:41	♊ Mar 25 12:19	♍ May 25 21:00	♐ Jul 25 17:24	♓ Sep 25 01:32	♊ Nov 26 03:00
♈ Jan 24 22:03	♋ Mar 27 21:52	♎ May 27 23:55	♑ Jul 27 21:52	♈ Sep 27 13:07	♋ Nov 28 13:51
♉ Jan 27 10:55	♌ Mar 30 03:45	♏ May 30 01:32	♒ Jul 30 03:51	♉ Sep 30 01:57	♌ Nov 30 22:40
♊ Jan 29 21:46	♍ Apr 1 06:00	♐ Jun 1 02:53	♓ Aug 1 12:10	♊ Oct 2 14:50	♍ Dec 3 05:17
♋ Feb 1 04:40	♎ Apr 3 05:54	♑ Jun 3 05:22	♈ Aug 3 23:14	♋ Oct 5 01:59	♎ Dec 5 09:30
♌ Feb 3 07:37	♏ Apr 5 05:16	♒ Jun 5 10:32	♉ Aug 6 12:03	♌ Oct 7 09:50	♏ Dec 7 11:28
♍ Feb 5 08:11	♐ Apr 7 06:06	♓ Jun 7 19:23	♊ Aug 9 00:16	♍ Oct 9 13:49	♐ Dec 9 12:01
♎ Feb 7 08:22	♑ Apr 9 10:01	♈ Jun 10 07:20	♋ Aug 11 09:24	♎ Oct 11 14:43	♑ Dec 11 12:45
♏ Feb 9 10:03	♒ Apr 11 17:40	♉ Jun 12 20:12	♌ Aug 13 14:42	♏ Oct 13 14:12	♒ Dec 13 15:37
♐ Feb 11 14:11	♓ Apr 14 04:37	♊ Jun 15 07:30	♍ Aug 15 17:07	♐ Oct 15 14:09	♓ Dec 15 22:11
♑ Feb 13 20:55	♈ Apr 16 17:22	♋ Jun 17 16:04	♎ Aug 17 18:17	♑ Oct 17 16:22	♈ Dec 18 08:44
♒ Feb 16 05:51	♉ Apr 19 06:16	♌ Jun 19 22:04	♏ Aug 19 19:50	♒ Oct 19 22:04	♉ Dec 20 21:37
♓ Feb 18 16:38	♊ Apr 21 18:02	♍ Jun 22 02:21	♐ Aug 21 22:48	♓ Oct 22 07:20	♊ Dec 23 10:08
♈ Feb 21 05:00	♋ Apr 24 03:45	♎ Jun 24 05:41	♑ Aug 24 03:38	♈ Oct 24 19:09	♋ Dec 25 20:33
♉ Feb 23 18:04	♌ Apr 26 10:14	♏ Jun 26 08:38	♒ Aug 26 10:28	♉ Oct 27 08:07	♌ Dec 28 04:32
♊ Feb 26 05:52	♍ Apr 28 14:39	♐ Jun 28 11:11	♓ Aug 28 19:25	♊ Oct 29 20:49	♍ Dec 30 10:39
♋ Feb 28 14:16	♎ Apr 30 16:06	♑ Jun 30 14:32	♈ Aug 31 06:35	♋ Nov 1 08:09	

Mercury

Jan 1 27 ♐	♋ Jun 20 02:18
D Jan 5 25 ♐	♌ Jul 4 23:58
♑ Jan 14 09:55	♍ Jul 26 10:09
♒ Feb 6 15:21	R Aug 9 7 ♍
♓ Feb 24 21:45	♌ Aug 23 14:34
♈ Mar 12 17:27	D Sep 2 24 ♌
♉ Apr 2 20:37	♍ Sep 11 01:00
R Apr 6 0 ♉	♎ Sep 28 22:45
♈ Apr 10 13:45	♏ Oct 16 08:55
D Apr 30 19 ♈	♐ Nov 5 02:22
♉ May 17 02:31	R Nov 30 25 ♐
♊ Jun 5 21:07	D Dec 20 9 ♐

Venus

Jan 1 15 ♒	♋ Jul 22 05:27
R Jan 8 16 ♒	♌ Aug 16 01:30
D Feb 18 0 ♒	♍ Sep 9 12:37
♓ Apr 6 15:53	♎ Oct 3 16:45
♈ May 5 11:57	♏ Oct 27 16:27
♉ Jun 1 04:07	♐ Nov 20 13:58
♊ Jun 26 23:08	♑ Dec 14 10:54

Mars

Jan 1 6 ♐
♑ Feb 3 18:48
♒ Mar 17 07:06
♓ Apr 27 02:11
♈ Jun 7 06:07
♉ Jul 21 07:08
♊ Sep 21 06:29
R Oct 10 2 ♊
♉ Oct 28 22:38
D Dec 20 16 ♉

Jupiter

Jan 1 28 ♎
♏ Jan 13 12:36
R Feb 15 1 ♏
♎ Mar 20 19:21
D Jun 19 21 ♎
♏ Sep 7 08:44

Saturn

Jan 1 19 ♐
R Apr 4 25 ♐
D Aug 24 19 ♐

Uranus

Jan 1 10 ♌
D Apr 15 7 ♌
R Nov 22 16 ♌

Neptune

Jan 1 4 ♏
R Feb 5 4 ♏
D Jul 14 2 ♏

Pluto

Jan 1 2 ♍
♌ Apr 11 19:28
D May 11 29 ♌
♍ Jun 10 15:30
R Dec 6 4 ♍

1959

Sun

♒ Jan 20 19:20	♈ Mar 21 08:55	♊ May 21 19:43	♌ Jul 23 14:47	♎ Sep 23 19:11	♐ Nov 23 01:30
♓ Feb 19 09:39	♉ Apr 20 20:16	♋ Jun 22 03:51	♍ Aug 23 21:45	♏ Oct 24 04:14	♑ Dec 22 14:37

Moon

Jan 1 21 ♍	♐ Mar 1 08:33	♓ May 1 11:59	♊ Jul 2 12:05	♍ Sep 2 08:31	♐ Nov 2 10:02
♎ Jan 1 15:21	♑ Mar 3 12:04	♈ May 3 22:19	♋ Jul 5 00:02	♎ Sep 4 12:57	♑ Nov 4 10:05
♏ Jan 3 18:42	♒ Mar 5 17:15	♉ May 6 10:38	♌ Jul 7 10:07	♏ Sep 6 15:52	♒ Nov 6 12:13
♐ Jan 5 20:56	♓ Mar 8 00:24	♊ May 8 23:34	♍ Jul 9 18:15	♐ Sep 8 18:20	♓ Nov 8 17:36
♑ Jan 7 22:50	♈ Mar 10 09:52	♋ May 11 11:57	♎ Jul 12 00:26	♑ Sep 10 21:04	♈ Nov 11 02:10
♒ Jan 10 01:52	♉ Mar 12 21:37	♌ May 13 22:39	♏ Jul 14 04:32	♒ Sep 13 00:43	♉ Nov 13 13:04
♓ Jan 12 07:38	♊ Mar 15 10:30	♍ May 16 06:38	♐ Jul 16 06:42	♓ Sep 15 05:54	♊ Nov 16 01:15
♈ Jan 14 17:09	♋ Mar 17 22:28	♎ May 18 11:07	♑ Jul 18 07:42	♈ Sep 17 13:15	♋ Nov 18 13:55
♉ Jan 17 05:32	♌ Mar 20 07:22	♏ May 20 12:23	♒ Jul 20 09:04	♉ Sep 19 23:12	♌ Nov 21 02:04
♊ Jan 19 18:16	♍ Mar 22 12:27	♐ May 22 11:51	♓ Jul 22 12:41	♊ Sep 22 11:15	♍ Nov 23 12:07
♋ Jan 22 04:47	♎ Mar 24 14:27	♑ May 24 11:23	♈ Jul 24 19:52	♋ Sep 24 23:49	♎ Nov 25 18:41
♌ Jan 24 12:13	♏ Mar 26 14:54	♒ May 26 12:54	♉ Jul 27 06:43	♌ Sep 27 10:35	♏ Nov 27 21:22
♍ Jan 26 17:13	♐ Mar 28 15:30	♓ May 28 18:42	♊ Jul 29 19:23	♍ Sep 29 18:03	♐ Nov 29 21:12
♎ Jan 28 20:54	♑ Mar 30 17:49	♈ May 31 04:17	♋ Aug 1 07:23	♎ Oct 1 22:07	♑ Dec 1 20:11
♏ Jan 31 00:04	♒ Apr 1 22:42	♉ Jun 2 16:36	♌ Aug 3 17:09	♏ Oct 3 23:54	♒ Dec 3 20:35
♐ Feb 2 03:10	♓ Apr 4 06:22	♊ Jun 5 05:35	♍ Aug 6 00:28	♐ Oct 6 00:53	♓ Dec 6 00:16
♑ Feb 4 06:28	♈ Apr 6 16:31	♋ Jun 7 17:43	♎ Aug 8 05:56	♑ Oct 8 02:37	♈ Dec 8 07:58
♒ Feb 6 10:40	♉ Apr 9 04:31	♌ Jun 10 04:19	♏ Aug 10 10:00	♒ Oct 10 06:12	♉ Dec 10 18:55
♓ Feb 8 16:50	♊ Apr 11 17:24	♍ Jun 12 12:49	♐ Aug 12 12:58	♓ Oct 12 12:05	♊ Dec 13 07:24
♈ Feb 11 01:53	♋ Apr 14 05:47	♎ Jun 14 18:42	♑ Aug 14 15:19	♈ Oct 14 20:19	♋ Dec 15 19:59
♉ Feb 13 13:47	♌ Apr 16 15:54	♏ Jun 16 21:38	♒ Aug 16 17:53	♉ Oct 17 06:40	♌ Dec 18 07:57
♊ Feb 16 02:38	♍ Apr 18 22:27	♐ Jun 18 22:13	♓ Aug 18 21:59	♊ Oct 19 18:40	♍ Dec 20 18:29
♋ Feb 18 13:50	♎ Apr 21 01:19	♑ Jun 20 22:01	♈ Aug 21 04:52	♋ Oct 22 07:22	♎ Dec 23 02:29
♌ Feb 20 21:38	♏ Apr 23 01:33	♒ Jun 22 23:00	♉ Aug 23 14:58	♌ Oct 24 19:04	♏ Dec 25 07:01
♍ Feb 23 02:06	♐ Apr 25 00:59	♓ Jun 25 03:08	♊ Aug 26 03:18	♍ Oct 27 03:48	♐ Dec 27 08:15
♎ Feb 25 04:29	♑ Apr 27 01:32	♈ Jun 27 11:28	♋ Aug 28 15:34	♎ Oct 29 08:41	♑ Dec 29 07:37
♏ Feb 27 06:15	♒ Apr 29 04:55	♉ Jun 29 23:11	♌ Aug 31 01:32	♏ Oct 31 10:13	♒ Dec 31 07:14

Mercury

Jan 1 18 ♐	R Jul 22 20 ♌
♑ Jan 10 16:52	D Aug 15 7 ♌
♒ Jan 30 15:41	♍ Sep 5 02:38
♓ Feb 17 02:12	♎ Sep 21 01:19
♈ Mar 5 11:51	♏ Oct 9 04:07
R Mar 19 13 ♈	♐ Oct 31 00:55
D Apr 12 29 ♓	R Nov 14 10 ♐
♉ May 12 19:46	♏ Nov 25 11:47
♊ May 28 17:37	D Dec 3 22 ♏
♋ Jun 11 14:15	♐ Dec 13 15:39
♌ Jun 28 16:32	

Venus

Jan 1 22 ♑	♍ Jul 8 12:14
♒ Jan 7 08:15	R Aug 10 16 ♍
♓ Jan 31 07:26	♌ Sep 20 01:07
♈ Feb 24 10:52	D Sep 22 29 ♌
♉ Mar 20 21:54	♍ Sep 25 10:12
♊ Apr 14 21:06	♎ Nov 9 18:10
♋ May 10 15:45	♏ Dec 7 16:42
♌ Jun 6 22:47	

Mars

Jan 1 17 ♉	
♊ Feb 10 13:39	
♋ Apr 10 09:45	
♌ Jun 1 02:31	
♍ Jul 20 11:11	
♎ Sep 5 22:54	
♏ Oct 21 09:45	
♐ Dec 3 18:17	

Jupiter

Jan 1 23 ♐
♐ Feb 10 13:24
R Mar 18 1 ♐
♏ Apr 24 14:34
D Jul 20 22 ♏
♐ Oct 5 14:25

Saturn

Jan 1 29 ♐
♑ Jan 5 13:36
R Apr 16 7 ♑
D Sep 5 0 ♑

Uranus

Jan 1 15 ♌
D Apr 20 12 ♌
R Nov 27 21 ♌

Neptune

Jan 1 6 ♏
R Feb 7 6 ♏
D Jul 16 4 ♏

Pluto

Jan 1 4 ♍
D May 13 1 ♍
R Dec 8 6 ♍

1960

Sun

♒ Jan 21 01:11	♈ Mar 20 14:42	♊ May 21 01:32	♌ Jul 22 20:37	♎ Sep 23 01:00	♐ Nov 22 07:17
♓ Feb 19 15:26	♉ Apr 20 02:05	♋ Jun 21 09:43	♍ Aug 23 03:35	♏ Oct 23 10:02	♑ Dec 21 20:25

Moon

Jan 1 10♒	♉ Mar 1 18:18	♌ May 2 21:59	♏ Jul 3 15:08	♒ Sep 2 12:35	♉ Nov 2 15:26
♓ Jan 2 09:19	♊ Mar 4 05:07	♍ May 5 08:59	♐ Jul 5 17:41	♓ Sep 4 13:51	♊ Nov 4 23:43
♈ Jan 4 15:21	♋ Mar 6 17:36	♎ May 7 16:30	♑ Jul 7 17:34	♈ Sep 6 16:26	♋ Nov 7 10:26
♉ Jan 7 01:22	♌ Mar 9 05:24	♏ May 9 20:07	♒ Jul 9 16:43	♉ Sep 8 21:45	♌ Nov 9 22:58
♊ Jan 9 13:45	♍ Mar 11 14:46	♐ May 11 20:55	♓ Jul 11 17:18	♊ Sep 11 06:30	♍ Nov 12 11:23
♋ Jan 12 02:22	♎ Mar 13 21:19	♑ May 13 20:50	♈ Jul 13 21:06	♋ Sep 13 18:09	♎ Nov 14 21:07
♌ Jan 14 13:58	♏ Mar 16 01:36	♒ May 15 21:50	♉ Jul 16 04:48	♌ Sep 16 06:46	♏ Nov 17 02:53
♍ Jan 17 00:02	♐ Mar 18 04:36	♓ May 18 01:23	♊ Jul 18 15:40	♍ Sep 18 18:06	♐ Nov 19 05:16
♎ Jan 19 08:14	♑ Mar 20 07:13	♈ May 20 07:54	♋ Jul 21 04:08	♎ Sep 21 02:58	♑ Nov 21 06:01
♏ Jan 21 13:58	♒ Mar 22 10:09	♉ May 22 16:59	♌ Jul 23 16:45	♏ Sep 23 09:18	♒ Nov 23 07:04
♐ Jan 23 17:02	♓ Mar 24 14:01	♊ May 25 03:54	♍ Jul 26 04:30	♐ Sep 25 13:42	♓ Nov 25 09:49
♑ Jan 25 17:59	♈ Mar 26 19:29	♋ May 27 16:06	♎ Jul 28 14:33	♑ Sep 27 16:53	♈ Nov 27 14:51
♒ Jan 27 18:19	♉ Mar 29 03:13	♌ May 30 04:50	♏ Jul 30 21:54	♒ Sep 29 19:31	♉ Nov 29 21:59
♓ Jan 29 19:56	♊ Mar 31 13:31	♍ Jun 1 16:37	♐ Aug 2 02:04	♓ Oct 1 22:13	♊ Dec 2 07:01
♈ Feb 1 00:39	♋ Apr 3 01:46	♎ Jun 4 01:30	♑ Aug 4 03:24	♈ Oct 4 01:46	♋ Dec 4 17:52
♉ Feb 3 09:16	♌ Apr 5 14:00	♏ Jun 6 06:20	♒ Aug 6 03:21	♉ Oct 6 07:08	♌ Dec 7 06:21
♊ Feb 5 20:58	♍ Apr 8 00:01	♐ Jun 8 07:30	♓ Aug 8 03:42	♊ Oct 8 15:16	♍ Dec 9 19:12
♋ Feb 8 09:37	♎ Apr 10 06:35	♑ Jun 10 06:47	♈ Aug 10 06:21	♋ Oct 11 02:17	♎ Dec 12 06:09
♌ Feb 10 21:07	♏ Apr 12 10:01	♒ Jun 12 06:22	♉ Aug 12 12:36	♌ Oct 13 14:55	♏ Dec 14 13:12
♍ Feb 13 06:35	♐ Apr 14 11:37	♓ Jun 14 08:16	♊ Aug 14 22:29	♍ Oct 16 02:39	♐ Dec 16 16:07
♎ Feb 15 13:54	♑ Apr 16 13:01	♈ Jun 16 13:42	♋ Aug 17 10:43	♎ Oct 18 11:32	♑ Dec 18 16:15
♏ Feb 17 19:24	♒ Apr 18 15:31	♉ Jun 18 22:32	♌ Aug 19 23:17	♏ Oct 20 17:06	♒ Dec 20 15:48
♐ Feb 19 23:12	♓ Apr 20 19:54	♊ Jun 21 09:45	♍ Aug 22 10:42	♐ Oct 22 20:15	♓ Dec 22 16:47
♑ Feb 22 01:39	♈ Apr 23 02:22	♋ Jun 23 22:08	♎ Aug 24 20:10	♑ Oct 24 22:28	♈ Dec 24 20:34
♒ Feb 24 03:31	♉ Apr 25 10:50	♌ Jun 26 10:51	♏ Aug 27 03:23	♒ Oct 27 00:58	♉ Dec 27 03:29
♓ Feb 26 06:03	♊ Apr 27 21:16	♍ Jun 28 22:52	♐ Aug 29 08:18	♓ Oct 29 04:26	♊ Dec 29 13:01
♈ Feb 28 10:36	♋ Apr 30 09:22	♎ Jul 1 08:45	♑ Aug 31 11:09	♈ Oct 31 09:10	

Mercury

Jan 1 24♐	R Jul 3 0♌
♑ Jan 4 08:24	♋ Jul 6 01:37
♒ Jan 23 06:18	D Jul 27 20♋
♓ Feb 9 10:12	♌ Aug 10 18:07
R Mar 1 25♓	♍ Aug 27 03:15
D Mar 24 12♓	♎ Sep 12 06:32
♈ Apr 16 02:53	♏ Oct 1 17:20
♉ May 4 16:52	R Oct 27 23♏
♊ May 19 03:26	D Nov 16 7♏
♋ Jun 2 20:46	♐ Dec 7 17:34
♌ Jul 1 02:44	♑ Dec 27 07:21

Venus

Jan 1 28♏	♋ Jun 21 16:34
♐ Jan 2 08:43	♌ Jul 16 02:12
♑ Jan 27 04:46	♍ Aug 9 10:54
♒ Feb 20 16:47	♎ Sep 2 19:30
♓ Mar 16 01:53	♏ Sep 27 05:12
♈ Apr 9 10:31	♐ Oct 21 17:09
♉ May 3 19:54	♑ Nov 15 08:54
♊ May 28 06:12	♒ Dec 10 08:34

Mars

Jan 1 20♐
♑ Jan 14 05:01
♒ Feb 23 04:16
♓ Apr 2 06:21
♈ May 11 07:14
♉ Jun 20 09:05
♊ Aug 2 04:30
♋ Sep 21 04:22
R Nov 20 18♋

Jupiter

Jan 1 18♐
♑ Mar 1 12:49
R Apr 20 3♑
♐ Jun 10 03:04
D Aug 20 23♐
♑ Oct 26 02:42

Saturn

Jan 1 9♑
R Apr 27 18♑
D Sep 15 11♑

Uranus

Jan 1 20♌
D Apr 24 16♌
R Dec 1 25♌

Neptune

Jan 1 8♏
R Feb 10 9♏
D Jul 18 6♏

Pluto

Jan 1 6♍
D May 15 3♍
R Dec 10 8♍

1961

Sun
♒ Jan 20 07:02	♈ Mar 20 20:33	♊ May 21 07:23	♌ Jul 23 02:24	♎ Sep 23 06:44	♐ Nov 22 13:07
♓ Feb 18 21:18	♉ Apr 20 07:54	♋ Jun 21 15:30	♍ Aug 23 09:20	♏ Oct 23 15:47	♑ Dec 22 02:18

Moon
Jan 1 29 ♊	♍ Mar 1 14:12	♐ May 2 05:24	♓ Jul 2 02:53	♊ Sep 1 05:53	♍ Nov 2 06:17
♋ Jan 1 00:22	♎ Mar 4 01:21	♑ May 4 08:39	♈ Jul 4 05:12	♋ Sep 3 15:00	♎ Nov 4 18:42
♌ Jan 3 12:52	♏ Mar 6 10:24	♒ May 6 11:23	♉ Jul 6 10:02	♌ Sep 6 03:00	♏ Nov 7 04:39
♍ Jan 6 01:48	♐ Mar 8 17:02	♓ May 8 14:22	♊ Jul 8 17:27	♍ Sep 8 16:05	♐ Nov 9 11:51
♎ Jan 8 13:30	♑ Mar 10 21:19	♈ May 10 17:56	♋ Jul 11 03:13	♎ Sep 11 04:32	♑ Nov 11 16:58
♏ Jan 10 22:08	♒ Mar 12 23:29	♉ May 12 22:25	♌ Jul 13 14:56	♏ Sep 13 15:22	♒ Nov 13 20:59
♐ Jan 12 02:40	♓ Mar 15 00:25	♊ May 15 04:33	♍ Jul 16 03:53	♐ Sep 15 23:54	♓ Nov 16 00:18
♑ Jan 15 03:41	♈ Mar 17 01:32	♋ May 17 13:15	♎ Jul 18 16:38	♑ Sep 18 05:41	♈ Nov 18 03:10
♒ Jan 17 02:56	♉ Mar 19 04:25	♌ May 20 00:45	♏ Jul 21 03:03	♒ Sep 20 08:42	♉ Nov 20 06:02
♓ Jan 19 02:32	♊ Mar 21 10:31	♍ May 22 13:37	♐ Jul 23 09:42	♓ Sep 22 09:36	♊ Nov 22 09:59
♈ Jan 21 04:26	♋ Mar 23 20:21	♎ May 25 01:17	♑ Jul 25 12:28	♈ Sep 24 09:40	♋ Nov 24 16:20
♉ Jan 23 09:50	♌ Mar 26 08:47	♏ May 27 09:34	♒ Jul 27 12:41	♉ Sep 26 10:42	♌ Nov 27 02:00
♊ Jan 25 18:49	♍ Mar 28 21:28	♐ May 29 14:11	♓ Jul 29 12:13	♊ Sep 28 14:31	♍ Nov 29 14:24
♋ Jan 28 06:22	♎ Mar 31 08:20	♑ May 31 16:20	♈ Jul 31 12:55	♋ Sep 30 22:19	♎ Dec 2 03:07
♌ Jan 30 19:05	♏ Apr 2 16:35	♒ Jun 2 17:44	♉ Aug 2 16:19	♌ Oct 3 09:43	♏ Dec 4 13:30
♍ Feb 2 07:48	♐ Apr 4 22:33	♓ Jun 4 19:50	♊ Aug 4 23:04	♍ Oct 5 22:45	♐ Dec 6 22:04
♎ Feb 4 19:27	♑ Apr 7 02:52	♈ Jun 6 23:23	♋ Aug 7 08:56	♎ Oct 8 11:04	♑ Dec 9 00:29
♏ Feb 7 04:51	♒ Apr 9 06:02	♉ Jun 9 04:37	♌ Aug 9 20:59	♏ Oct 10 21:19	♒ Dec 11 03:10
♐ Feb 9 11:00	♓ Apr 11 08:31	♊ Jun 11 11:39	♍ Aug 12 10:00	♐ Oct 13 05:20	♓ Dec 13 05:41
♑ Feb 11 13:51	♈ Apr 13 10:55	♋ Jun 13 20:45	♎ Aug 14 22:44	♑ Oct 15 11:23	♈ Dec 15 08:43
♒ Feb 13 14:14	♉ Apr 15 14:16	♌ Jun 16 08:15	♏ Aug 17 09:44	♒ Oct 17 15:37	♉ Dec 17 12:39
♓ Feb 15 13:52	♊ Apr 17 19:54	♍ Jun 18 21:12	♐ Aug 19 17:42	♓ Oct 19 18:09	♊ Dec 19 17:46
♈ Feb 17 14:40	♋ Apr 20 04:50	♎ Jun 21 09:31	♑ Aug 21 22:07	♈ Oct 21 19:35	♋ Dec 22 00:49
♉ Feb 19 18:21	♌ Apr 22 16:43	♏ Jun 23 18:50	♒ Aug 23 23:24	♉ Oct 23 21:06	♌ Dec 24 10:25
♊ Feb 22 01:51	♍ Apr 25 05:31	♐ Jun 26 00:05	♓ Aug 25 23:02	♊ Oct 25 00:23	♋ Dec 26 22:29
♋ Feb 24 12:47	♎ Apr 27 16:33	♑ Jun 28 01:59	♈ Aug 27 22:49	♋ Oct 28 07:03	♎ Dec 29 11:25
♌ Feb 27 01:33	♏ Apr 30 00:26	♒ Jun 30 02:17	♉ Aug 30 00:37	♌ Oct 30 17:29	♏ Dec 31 22:42

Mercury
Jan 1 7 ♑	D Jul 8 1 ♋
♒ Jan 14 19:03	♌ Aug 4 01:15
♓ Feb 1 21:08	♍ Aug 18 20:55
R Feb 12 9 ♓	♎ Sep 4 22:13
♒ Feb 24 20:31	♏ Sep 27 12:22
D Mar 6 25 ♒	R Oct 10 7 ♏
♓ Mar 18 10:08	♎ Oct 22 02:39
♈ Apr 10 09:25	D Oct 31 21 ♎
♉ Apr 26 14:34	♏ Nov 11 00:35
♊ May 10 16:37	♐ Nov 30 22:53
♋ May 28 17:22	♑ Dec 20 01:03
R Jun 14 10 ♋	

Venus
Jan 1 25 ♒	♋ Aug 3 15:24
♓ Jan 5 03:35	♌ Aug 29 14:15
♈ Feb 2 04:52	♍ Sep 23 15:43
R Mar 20 29 ♈	♎ Oct 18 02:59
D May 2 12 ♈	♏ Nov 11 05:34
♉ Jun 5 19:26	♐ Dec 5 03:40
♊ Jul 7 04:31	♑ Dec 29 00:06

Mars
Jan 1 8 ♋
♊ Feb 4 22:21
D Feb 6 0 ♋
♋ Feb 7 05:19
♌ May 6 01:11
♍ Jun 28 23:46
♎ Aug 17 00:41
♏ Oct 1 20:04
♐ Nov 13 21:53
♑ Dec 24 17:50

Jupiter
Jan 1 14 ♑
♒ Mar 15 07:03
R May 25 7 ♒
♑ Aug 12 11:15
D Sep 23 27 ♑
♒ Nov 4 01:05

Saturn
Jan 1 19 ♑
R May 9 29 ♑
D Sep 27 23 ♑

Uranus
Jan 1 25 ♌
D Apr 29 21 ♌
♍ Nov 1 15:05
R Dec 6 0 ♍

Neptune
Jan 1 10 ♏
R Feb 11 11 ♏
D Jul 20 8 ♏

Pluto
Jan 1 8 ♍
D May 17 5 ♍
R Dec 12 10 ♍

1962

Sun

♒ Jan 20 12:58	♈ Mar 21 02:29	♊ May 21 13:15	♌ Jul 23 08:18	♎ Sep 23 12:39	♐ Nov 22 19:04
♓ Feb 19 03:15	♉ Apr 20 13:50	♋ Jun 21 21:23	♍ Aug 23 15:14	♏ Oct 23 21:43	♑ Dec 22 08:16

Moon

Jan 1 0♏	♒ Mar 3 09:51	♉ May 3 06:48	♌ Jul 3 13:54	♏ Sep 3 15:45	♒ Nov 4 09:01
♐ Jan 3 06:22	♓ Mar 5 10:15	♊ May 5 08:15	♍ Jul 6 00:22	♐ Sep 6 03:25	♓ Nov 6 13:52
♑ Jan 5 10:24	♈ Mar 7 09:31	♋ May 7 12:27	♎ Jul 8 12:47	♑ Sep 8 12:20	♈ Nov 8 15:45
♒ Jan 7 12:00	♉ Mar 9 09:40	♌ May 9 20:36	♏ Jul 11 01:06	♒ Sep 10 17:25	♉ Nov 10 15:45
♓ Jan 9 12:52	♊ Mar 11 12:35	♍ May 12 08:11	♐ Jul 13 11:00	♓ Sep 12 19:02	♊ Nov 12 15:44
♈ Jan 11 14:34	♋ Mar 13 19:26	♎ May 14 21:02	♑ Jul 15 17:32	♈ Sep 14 18:32	♋ Nov 14 17:49
♉ Jan 13 18:01	♌ Mar 16 05:56	♏ May 17 08:42	♒ Jul 17 21:06	♉ Sep 16 18:00	♌ Nov 16 23:39
♊ Jan 15 23:41	♍ Mar 18 18:32	♐ May 19 18:01	♓ Jul 19 22:59	♊ Sep 18 19:29	♍ Nov 19 09:32
♋ Jan 18 07:38	♎ Mar 21 07:29	♑ May 22 01:07	♈ Jul 22 00:34	♋ Sep 21 00:25	♎ Nov 21 21:58
♌ Jan 20 17:50	♏ Mar 23 19:28	♒ May 24 06:30	♉ Jul 24 02:57	♌ Sep 23 09:06	♏ Nov 24 10:32
♍ Jan 23 05:53	♐ Mar 26 05:49	♓ May 26 10:30	♊ Jul 26 06:57	♍ Sep 25 20:31	♐ Nov 26 21:43
♎ Jan 25 18:51	♑ Mar 28 13:46	♈ May 28 13:14	♋ Jul 28 13:00	♎ Sep 28 09:07	♑ Nov 29 07:00
♏ Jan 28 06:53	♒ Mar 30 18:44	♉ May 30 15:17	♌ Jul 30 21:21	♏ Sep 30 21:47	♒ Dec 1 14:25
♐ Jan 30 15:59	♓ Apr 1 20:42	♊ Jun 1 17:40	♍ Aug 2 07:56	♐ Oct 3 09:40	♓ Dec 3 19:53
♑ Feb 1 21:09	♈ Apr 3 20:40	♋ Jun 3 21:57	♎ Aug 4 20:16	♑ Oct 5 19:34	♈ Dec 5 23:16
♒ Feb 3 22:56	♉ Apr 5 20:24	♌ Jun 6 05:22	♏ Aug 7 08:56	♒ Oct 8 02:21	♉ Dec 8 00:59
♓ Feb 5 22:52	♊ Apr 7 22:00	♍ Jun 8 16:11	♐ Aug 9 19:48	♓ Oct 10 05:29	♊ Dec 10 02:08
♈ Feb 7 22:51	♋ Apr 10 03:12	♎ Jun 11 04:51	♑ Aug 12 03:18	♈ Oct 12 05:40	♋ Dec 12 04:21
♉ Feb 10 00:35	♌ Apr 12 12:36	♏ Jun 13 16:45	♒ Aug 14 07:07	♉ Oct 14 04:44	♌ Dec 14 09:20
♊ Feb 12 05:17	♍ Apr 15 00:57	♐ Jun 16 02:04	♓ Aug 16 08:16	♊ Oct 16 04:50	♍ Dec 16 17:59
♋ Feb 14 13:19	♎ Apr 17 13:53	♑ Jun 18 08:30	♈ Aug 18 08:24	♋ Oct 18 08:05	♎ Dec 19 05:40
♌ Feb 17 00:03	♏ Apr 20 01:36	♒ Jun 20 12:48	♉ Aug 20 09:20	♌ Oct 20 15:29	♏ Dec 21 18:18
♍ Feb 19 12:25	♐ Apr 22 11:27	♓ Jun 22 15:59	♊ Aug 22 12:27	♍ Oct 23 02:31	♐ Dec 24 05:33
♎ Feb 22 01:22	♑ Apr 24 19:20	♈ Jun 24 18:43	♋ Aug 24 18:32	♎ Oct 25 15:14	♑ Dec 26 14:18
♏ Feb 24 13:35	♒ Apr 27 01:07	♉ Jun 26 21:34	♌ Aug 27 03:28	♏ Oct 28 03:48	♒ Dec 28 20:42
♐ Feb 26 23:45	♓ Apr 29 04:39	♊ Jun 29 01:08	♍ Aug 29 14:36	♐ Oct 30 15:20	♓ Dec 31 01:20
♑ Mar 1 06:38	♈ May 1 06:12	♋ Jul 1 06:18	♎ Sep 1 03:00	♑ Nov 2 01:16	

Mercury

Jan 1 19♑	♋ Jul 11 07:21
♒ Jan 7 15:06	♌ Jul 26 18:48
R Jan 27 23♒	♍ Aug 10 19:30
D Feb 17 7♒	♎ Aug 29 15:41
♓ Mar 15 11:42	R Sep 24 21♎
♈ Apr 3 02:28	D Oct 15 5♎
♉ Apr 18 04:12	♏ Nov 5 02:20
♊ May 3 05:42	♐ Nov 23 17:29
R May 26 20♊	♑ Dec 12 20:56
D Jun 19 11♊	

Venus

Jan 1 3♑	♌ Jun 17 05:32
♒ Jan 21 20:32	♍ Jul 12 22:34
♓ Feb 14 18:08	♎ Aug 8 17:16
♈ Mar 10 18:27	♏ Sep 7 00:13
♉ Apr 3 23:04	R Oct 23 27♏
♊ Apr 28 09:22	D Dec 3 12♏
♋ May 23 02:44	

Mars

Jan 1 5♑	
♒ Feb 1 23:12	
♓ Mar 12 08:05	
♈ Apr 19 17:05	
♉ May 28 23:58	
♊ Jul 9 03:55	
♋ Aug 22 11:41	
♌ Oct 11 23:51	
R Dec 26 24♌	

Jupiter

Jan 1 10♒	
♓ Mar 25 21:23	
R Jul 2 12♓	
D Oct 29 2♓	

Saturn

Jan 1 29♑	
♒ Jan 3 18:29	
R May 21 11♒	
D Oct 9 4♒	

Uranus

Jan 1 0♍	
♌ Jan 10 06:24	
D May 4 26♌	
♍ Aug 10 00:57	
R Dec 11 5♍	

Neptune

Jan 1 12♏	
R Feb 13 13♏	
D Jul 23 10♏	

Pluto

Jan 1 10♍	
D May 19 7♍	
R Dec 14 12♍	

1963

Sun

♒ Jan 20 18:55	♈ Mar 21 08:20	♊ May 21 18:59	♌ Jul 23 13:59	♎ Sep 23 18:25	♐ Nov 23 00:50
♓ Feb 19 09:10	♉ Apr 20 19:36	♋ Jun 22 03:04	♍ Aug 23 20:59	♏ Oct 24 03:30	♑ Dec 22 14:02

Moon

Jan 1 13♓	♊ Mar 1 21:39	♍ May 2 06:13	♐ Jul 3 08:11	♓ Sep 3 01:36	♊ Nov 2 23:49
♈ Jan 2 04:48	♋ Mar 4 02:08	♎ May 4 17:42	♑ Jul 5 19:03	♈ Sep 5 03:51	♋ Nov 5 00:07
♉ Jan 4 07:33	♌ Mar 6 09:15	♏ May 7 06:16	♒ Jul 8 03:36	♉ Sep 7 05:01	♌ Nov 7 03:28
♊ Jan 6 10:13	♍ Mar 8 18:34	♐ May 9 18:43	♓ Jul 10 09:52	♊ Sep 9 06:45	♍ Nov 9 10:13
♋ Jan 8 13:40	♎ Mar 11 05:35	♑ May 12 06:14	♈ Jul 12 14:15	♋ Sep 11 10:07	♎ Nov 11 20:07
♌ Jan 10 19:01	♏ Mar 13 17:51	♒ May 14 15:50	♉ Jul 14 17:15	♌ Sep 13 15:29	♏ Nov 14 07:56
♍ Jan 13 03:06	♐ Mar 16 06:26	♓ May 16 22:31	♊ Jul 16 19:27	♍ Sep 15 22:47	♐ Nov 16 20:38
♎ Jan 15 14:05	♑ Mar 18 17:34	♈ May 19 01:48	♋ Jul 18 21:45	♎ Sep 18 07:59	♑ Nov 19 09:22
♏ Jan 18 02:36	♒ Mar 21 01:22	♉ May 21 02:20	♌ Jul 21 01:14	♏ Sep 20 19:10	♒ Nov 21 20:52
♐ Jan 20 14:19	♓ Mar 23 05:05	♊ May 23 01:52	♍ Jul 23 07:06	♐ Sep 23 07:50	♓ Nov 24 05:32
♑ Jan 22 23:23	♈ Mar 25 05:37	♋ May 25 02:29	♎ Jul 25 16:02	♑ Sep 25 20:15	♈ Nov 26 10:25
♒ Jan 25 05:14	♉ Mar 27 04:56	♌ May 27 05:59	♏ Jul 28 03:36	♒ Sep 28 06:02	♉ Nov 28 11:49
♓ Jan 27 08:35	♊ Mar 29 05:13	♍ May 29 13:22	♐ Jul 30 16:07	♓ Sep 30 11:46	♊ Nov 30 11:15
♈ Jan 29 10:44	♋ Mar 31 08:14	♎ Jun 1 00:08	♑ Aug 2 03:12	♈ Oct 2 13:48	♋ Dec 2 10:45
♉ Jan 31 12:54	♌ Apr 2 14:44	♏ Jun 3 12:38	♒ Aug 4 11:25	♉ Oct 4 13:50	♌ Dec 4 12:20
♊ Feb 2 16:03	♍ Apr 5 00:20	♐ Jun 6 01:01	♓ Aug 6 16:46	♊ Oct 6 13:57	♍ Dec 6 17:25
♋ Feb 4 20:39	♎ Apr 7 11:50	♑ Jun 8 12:06	♈ Aug 8 20:07	♋ Oct 8 16:01	♎ Dec 9 02:07
♌ Feb 7 03:05	♏ Apr 10 00:14	♒ Jun 10 21:22	♉ Aug 10 22:37	♌ Oct 10 20:54	♏ Dec 11 14:04
♍ Feb 9 11:36	♐ Apr 12 12:47	♓ Jun 13 04:21	♊ Aug 13 01:15	♍ Oct 13 04:33	♐ Dec 14 02:53
♎ Feb 11 22:17	♑ Apr 15 00:26	♈ Jun 15 08:46	♋ Aug 15 04:38	♎ Oct 15 14:23	♑ Dec 16 15:21
♏ Feb 14 10:38	♒ Apr 17 09:34	♉ Jun 17 10:53	♌ Aug 17 09:17	♏ Oct 18 01:52	♒ Dec 19 02:29
♐ Feb 16 22:56	♓ Apr 19 14:54	♊ Jun 19 11:43	♍ Aug 19 15:40	♐ Oct 20 14:32	♓ Dec 21 11:29
♑ Feb 19 09:00	♈ Apr 21 16:30	♋ Jun 21 12:45	♎ Aug 22 00:25	♑ Oct 23 03:20	♈ Dec 23 17:40
♒ Feb 21 15:23	♉ Apr 23 16:01	♌ Jun 23 15:44	♏ Aug 24 11:38	♒ Oct 25 14:19	♉ Dec 25 20:57
♓ Feb 23 18:18	♊ Apr 25 15:05	♍ Jun 25 21:55	♐ Aug 27 00:15	♓ Oct 27 21:36	♊ Dec 27 21:58
♈ Feb 25 19:05	♋ Apr 27 16:27	♎ Jun 28 07:39	♑ Aug 29 11:57	♈ Oct 30 00:40	♋ Dec 29 22:07
♉ Feb 27 19:38	♌ Apr 29 21:24	♏ Jun 30 19:47	♒ Aug 31 20:37	♉ Nov 1 00:43	♌ Dec 31 23:09

Mercury

Jan 1 28♑
♒ Jan 2 01:49
R Jan 11 7♒
♑ Jan 20 04:53
D Feb 1 20♑
♒ Feb 15 10:09
♓ Mar 9 05:34
♈ Mar 26 03:48
♉ Apr 9 21:59
♊ May 3 05:01
R May 6 0♊
♉ May 10 20:44
D May 30 21♉
♊ Jun 14 22:52
♋ Jul 4 02:54
♌ Jul 18 06:17
♍ Aug 3 09:26
♎ Aug 26 20:54
R Sep 6 5♎
♍ Sep 16 20:46
D Sep 29 19 ♍
♎ Oct 10 16:33
♏ Oct 28 19:54
♐ Nov 16 11:08
♑ Dec 6 05:12
R Dec 26 21♑

Venus

Jan 1 25♏
♐ Jan 6 17:38
♑ Feb 5 20:34
♒ Mar 4 11:38
♓ Mar 30 01:00
♈ Apr 24 03:41
♉ May 19 01:21
♊ Jun 12 19:55
♋ Jul 7 11:16
♌ Jul 31 22:37
♍ Aug 25 05:47
♎ Sep 18 09:44
♏ Oct 12 11:50
♐ Nov 5 13:25
♑ Nov 29 15:20
♒ Dec 23 18:49

Mars

Jan 1 24♌
D Mar 16 5♌
♍ Jun 3 06:21
♎ Jul 27 04:07
♏ Sep 12 09:00
♐ Oct 25 17:28
♑ Dec 5 08:59

Jupiter

Jan 1 9♓
♈ Apr 4 03:19
R Aug 9 19♈
D Dec 5 9♈

Saturn

Jan 1 9♒
R Jun 3 23♒
D Oct 21 16♒

Uranus

Jan 1 5♍
D May 9 1♍
R Dec 16 10♍

Neptune

Jan 1 15♏
R Feb 16 15♏
D Jul 25 12♏

Pluto

Jan 1 12♍
D May 21 9♍
R Dec 17 14♍

1964

Sun

♒ Jan 21 00:42	♈ Mar 20 14:10	♊ May 21 00:49	♌ Jul 22 19:52	♎ Sep 23 00:18	♐ Nov 22 06:39
♓ Feb 19 14:58	♉ Apr 20 01:27	♋ Jun 21 08:57	♍ Aug 23 02:52	♏ Oct 23 09:22	♑ Dec 21 19:50

Moon

Jan 1 0 ♌	♏ Mar 2 13:53	♒ May 3 18:05	♉ Jul 4 05:42	♌ Sep 3 02:36	♏ Nov 3 08:24
♍ Jan 3 02:47	♐ Mar 5 01:47	♓ May 6 03:43	♊ Jul 6 07:43	♍ Sep 5 05:12	♐ Nov 5 18:43
♎ Jan 5 10:09	♑ Mar 7 14:35	♈ May 8 09:16	♋ Jul 8 07:56	♎ Sep 7 09:19	♑ Nov 8 07:06
♏ Jan 7 21:03	♒ Mar 10 01:35	♉ May 10 11:09	♌ Jul 10 08:00	♏ Sep 9 16:20	♒ Nov 10 20:08
♐ Jan 10 09:48	♓ Mar 12 09:04	♊ May 12 11:01	♍ Jul 12 09:44	♐ Sep 12 02:47	♓ Nov 13 07:28
♑ Jan 12 22:13	♈ Mar 14 13:14	♋ May 14 10:52	♎ Jul 14 14:40	♑ Sep 14 15:29	♈ Nov 15 15:09
♒ Jan 15 08:47	♉ Mar 16 15:29	♌ May 16 12:30	♏ Jul 16 23:33	♒ Sep 17 03:46	♉ Nov 17 18:57
♓ Jan 17 17:04	♊ Mar 18 17:25	♍ May 18 17:01	♐ Jul 19 11:28	♓ Sep 19 13:22	♊ Nov 19 19:58
♈ Jan 19 23:10	♋ Mar 20 20:12	♎ May 21 00:41	♑ Jul 22 00:26	♈ Sep 21 19:44	♋ Nov 21 20:04
♉ Jan 22 03:22	♌ Mar 23 00:15	♏ May 23 10:57	♒ Jul 24 12:30	♉ Sep 23 23:45	♌ Nov 23 20:59
♊ Jan 24 06:04	♍ Mar 25 05:41	♐ May 25 23:02	♓ Jul 26 22:34	♊ Sep 26 02:45	♍ Nov 26 00:02
♋ Jan 26 07:51	♎ Mar 27 12:47	♑ May 28 12:00	♈ Jul 29 06:24	♋ Sep 28 05:38	♎ Nov 28 05:54
♌ Jan 28 09:45	♏ Mar 29 22:03	♒ May 31 00:31	♉ Jul 31 12:00	♌ Sep 30 08:53	♏ Nov 30 14:31
♍ Jan 30 13:08	♐ Apr 1 09:41	♓ Jun 2 11:00	♊ Aug 2 15:27	♍ Oct 2 12:42	♐ Dec 3 01:24
♎ Feb 1 19:25	♑ Apr 3 22:35	♈ Jun 4 18:42	♋ Aug 4 17:13	♎ Oct 4 17:44	♑ Dec 5 13:52
♏ Feb 4 05:12	♒ Apr 6 10:24	♉ Jun 6 21:20	♌ Aug 6 18:10	♏ Oct 7 00:57	♒ Dec 8 02:57
♐ Feb 6 17:35	♓ Apr 8 18:46	♊ Jun 8 21:49	♍ Aug 8 19:50	♐ Oct 9 11:01	♓ Dec 10 15:00
♑ Feb 9 06:10	♈ Apr 10 23:08	♋ Jun 10 21:17	♎ Aug 10 23:51	♑ Oct 11 23:32	♈ Dec 13 00:12
♒ Feb 11 16:39	♉ Apr 13 00:37	♌ Jun 12 21:35	♏ Aug 13 07:30	♒ Oct 14 12:15	♉ Dec 15 05:33
♓ Feb 14 00:08	♊ Apr 15 01:06	♍ Jun 15 00:26	♐ Aug 15 18:44	♓ Oct 16 22:32	♊ Dec 17 07:22
♈ Feb 16 05:10	♋ Apr 17 02:23	♎ Jun 17 06:53	♑ Aug 18 07:37	♈ Oct 19 05:05	♋ Dec 19 07:02
♉ Feb 18 08:44	♌ Apr 19 05:39	♏ Jun 19 16:49	♒ Aug 20 19:38	♉ Oct 21 08:23	♌ Dec 21 06:30
♊ Feb 20 11:47	♍ Apr 21 11:16	♐ Jun 22 05:02	♓ Aug 23 05:13	♊ Oct 23 10:03	♍ Dec 23 07:40
♋ Feb 22 14:50	♎ Apr 23 19:07	♑ Jun 24 18:01	♈ Aug 25 12:15	♋ Oct 25 11:37	♎ Dec 25 12:03
♌ Feb 24 18:10	♏ Apr 26 05:00	♒ Jun 27 06:21	♉ Aug 27 17:22	♌ Oct 27 14:14	♏ Dec 27 20:11
♍ Feb 26 22:30	♐ Apr 28 16:46	♓ Jun 29 16:55	♊ Aug 29 21:16	♍ Oct 29 18:24	♐ Dec 30 07:20
♎ Feb 29 04:46	♑ May 1 05:42	♈ Jul 2 00:51	♋ Sep 1 00:13	♎ Nov 1 00:23	

Mercury

Jan 1 18 ♑	♍ Jul 27 11:37
D Jan 15 5 ♑	R Aug 19 17 ♍
♒ Feb 10 21:37	D Sep 11 4 ♍
♓ Feb 29 22:44	♎ Oct 3 00:22
♈ Mar 16 23:49	♏ Oct 20 07:15
♉ Apr 2 00:34	♐ Nov 8 11:01
R Apr 16 10 ♉	♑ Nov 30 19:15
D May 10 1 ♉	R Dec 9 4 ♑
♊ Jun 9 15:55	♐ Dec 16 14:35
♋ Jun 24 17:17	D Dec 29 19 ♐
♌ Jul 9 00:27	

Venus

Jan 1 10 ♒	D Jul 11 20 ♊
♓ Jan 17 02:51	♋ Aug 5 08:58
♈ Feb 10 21:08	♌ Sep 8 04:52
♉ Mar 7 12:39	♍ Oct 5 18:09
♊ Apr 4 03:05	♎ Oct 31 08:54
♋ May 9 03:21	♏ Nov 25 01:25
R May 29 6 ♋	♐ Dec 19 07:01
♊ Jun 17 18:20	

Mars

Jan 1 20 ♑
♒ Jan 13 06:10
♓ Feb 20 07:30
♈ Mar 29 11:20
♉ May 7 14:42
♊ Jun 17 11:40
♋ Jul 30 18:27
♌ Sep 15 05:24
♍ Nov 6 03:22

Jupiter

Jan 1 10 ♈
♉ Apr 12 07:06
R Sep 14 26 ♉

Saturn

Jan 1 20 ♒
♓ Mar 24 03:26
R Jun 15 5 ♓
♒ Sep 16 22:03
D Nov 1 28 ♒
♓ Dec 16 04:01

Uranus

Jan 1 9 ♍
D May 13 5 ♍
R Dec 20 14 ♍

Neptune

Jan 1 17 ♏
R Feb 18 17 ♏
D Jul 27 15 ♏

Pluto

Jan 1 14 ♍
D May 22 11 ♍
R Dec 18 16 ♍

1965

Sun

♒ Jan 20 06:28	♈ Mar 20 20:02	♊ May 21 06:47	♌ Jul 23 01:45	♎ Sep 23 06:04	♐ Nov 22 12:27
♓ Feb 18 20:46	♉ Apr 20 07:24	♋ Jun 21 14:53	♍ Aug 23 08:39	♏ Oct 23 15:08	♑ Dec 22 01:40

Moon

Jan 1 20 ♐	♓ Mar 2 09:38	♊ May 2 20:27	♍ Jul 2 17:11	≏ Aug 1 03:53	♐ Sep 2 00:00	♓ Nov 3 03:22
♑ Jan 1 20:07	♈ Mar 4 18:45	♋ May 4 22:38	≏ Jul 4 19:43	♏ Aug 3 08:19	♑ Sep 4 10:51	♈ Nov 5 14:21
♒ Jan 4 09:03	♉ Mar 7 01:50	♌ May 7 00:49	♏ Jul 6 01:37	♐ Aug 5 16:49	♒ Sep 6 23:33	♉ Nov 7 22:30
♓ Jan 6 21:05	♊ Mar 9 07:13	♍ May 9 03:46	♐ Jul 9 10:52	♑ Aug 8 04:22	♓ Sep 9 11:57	♊ Nov 10 03:53
♈ Jan 9 07:07	♋ Mar 11 11:02	≏ May 11 08:04	♑ Jul 11 22:29	♒ Aug 10 17:09	♈ Sep 11 22:50	♋ Nov 12 07:29
♉ Jan 11 14:11	♌ Mar 13 13:23	♏ May 13 14:10	♒ Jul 14 11:08	♓ Aug 13 05:37	♉ Sep 14 07:55	♌ Nov 14 10:13
♊ Jan 13 17:49	♍ Mar 15 14:56	♐ May 15 22:31	♓ Jul 16 23:43	♈ Aug 15 16:56	♊ Sep 16 15:05	♍ Nov 16 12:54
♋ Jan 15 18:35	≏ Mar 17 17:04	♑ May 18 09:19	♈ Jul 19 11:13	♉ Aug 18 02:28	♋ Sep 18 20:00	≏ Nov 18 16:09
♌ Jan 17 17:57	♏ Mar 19 21:31	♒ May 20 21:50	♉ Jul 21 20:14	♊ Aug 20 09:21	♌ Sep 20 22:34	♏ Nov 20 20:37
♍ Jan 19 17:55	♐ Mar 22 05:37	♓ May 23 10:13	♊ Jul 24 01:48	♋ Aug 22 13:05	♍ Sep 22 23:30	♐ Nov 23 02:57
≏ Jan 21 20:28	♑ Mar 24 17:07	♈ May 25 20:18	♋ Jul 26 03:52	♌ Aug 24 14:00	≏ Sep 25 00:16	♑ Nov 25 11:45
♏ Jan 24 03:00	♒ Mar 27 05:59	♉ May 28 02:49	♌ Jul 28 03:37	♍ Aug 26 13:35	♏ Sep 27 02:46	♒ Nov 27 23:02
♐ Jan 26 13:31	♓ Mar 29 17:32	♊ May 30 05:59	♍ Jul 30 02:55	≏ Aug 28 13:52	♐ Sep 29 08:41	♓ Nov 30 11:39
♑ Jan 29 02:21	♈ Apr 1 02:18	♋ Jun 1 07:06		♏ Aug 30 16:53	♑ Oct 1 18:28	♈ Dec 2 23:22
♒ Jan 31 15:18	♉ Apr 3 08:29	♌ Jun 3 07:47			♒ Oct 4 06:47	♉ Dec 5 08:11
♓ Feb 2 02:56	♊ Apr 5 12:54	♍ Jun 5 09:32			♓ Oct 6 19:13	♊ Dec 7 13:28
♈ Feb 5 12:43	♋ Apr 7 16:24	≏ Jun 7 13:30			♈ Oct 9 05:54	♋ Dec 9 15:57
♉ Feb 7 20:23	♌ Apr 9 19:24	♏ Jun 9 20:04			♉ Oct 11 14:15	♌ Dec 11 17:08
♊ Feb 10 01:35	♍ Apr 11 22:14	♐ Jun 12 05:10			♊ Oct 13 20:39	♍ Dec 13 18:36
♋ Feb 12 04:13	≏ Apr 14 01:38	♑ Jun 14 16:20			♋ Oct 16 01:27	≏ Dec 15 21:34
♌ Feb 14 04:53	♏ Apr 16 06:42	♒ Jun 17 04:51			♌ Oct 18 04:51	♏ Dec 18 02:39
♍ Feb 16 05:05	♐ Apr 18 14:31	♓ Jun 19 17:29			♍ Oct 20 07:12	♐ Dec 20 10:01
≏ Feb 18 06:45	♑ Apr 21 01:24	♈ Jun 22 04:29			≏ Oct 22 09:21	♑ Dec 22 19:27
♏ Feb 20 11:44	♒ Apr 23 14:04	♉ Jun 24 12:16			♏ Oct 24 12:31	♒ Dec 25 06:44
♐ Feb 22 20:57	♓ Apr 26 02:01	♊ Jun 26 16:17			♐ Oct 26 18:08	♓ Dec 27 19:16
♑ Feb 25 09:17	♈ Apr 28 11:12	♋ Jun 28 17:19			♑ Oct 29 03:04	♈ Dec 30 07:39
♒ Feb 27 22:14	♉ Apr 30 17:04	♌ Jun 30 16:58			♒ Oct 31 14:50	

Mercury

Jan 1 20 ♐	♍ Jul 31 09:40
♑ Jan 13 02:50	R Aug 1 0 ♍
♒ Feb 3 09:04	♌ Aug 3 09:36
♓ Feb 21 05:37	D Aug 25 17 ♌
♈ Mar 9 02:35	♍ Sep 8 17:13
R Mar 29 23 ♈	≏ Sep 25 05:47
D Apr 22 11 ♈	♏ Oct 12 21:06
♉ May 15 13:12	♐ Nov 2 05:50
♊ Jun 2 03:37	R Nov 23 19 ♐
♋ Jun 16 01:56	D Dec 12 2 ♐
♌ Jul 1 15:53	

Venus

Jan 1 15 ♐	♌ Jun 30 21:58
♑ Jan 12 07:59	♍ Jul 25 14:49
♒ Feb 5 07:43	≏ Aug 19 13:04
♓ Mar 1 07:56	♏ Sep 13 19:48
♈ Mar 25 09:53	♐ Oct 9 16:45
♉ Apr 18 14:31	♑ Nov 5 19:35
♊ May 12 22:08	♒ Dec 7 04:39
♋ Jun 6 08:38	

Mars

Jan 1 23 ♍
R Jan 28 28 ♍
D Apr 19 8 ♍
≏ Jun 29 00:50
♏ Aug 20 12:00
♐ Oct 4 06:38
♑ Nov 14 07:12
♒ Dec 23 05:34

Jupiter

Jan 1 16 ♉
D Jan 10 16 ♉
♊ Apr 22 15:15
♋ Sep 21 06:51
R Oct 19 1 ♋
♊ Nov 17 02:55

Saturn

Jan 1 1 ♓
R Jun 28 17 ♓
D Nov 14 10 ♓

Uranus

Jan 1 14 ♍
D May 18 10 ♍
R Dec 25 19 ♍

Neptune

Jan 1 19 ♏
R Feb 20 20 ♏
D Jul 29 17 ♏

Pluto

Jan 1 16 ♍
D May 25 13 ♍
R Dec 21 18 ♍

1966

Sun

♒ Jan 20 12:21	♈ Mar 21 01:52	♊ May 21 12:32	♌ Jul 23 07:22	♎ Sep 23 11:42	♐ Nov 22 18:14
♓ Feb 19 02:38	♉ Apr 20 13:11	♋ Jun 21 20:34	♍ Aug 23 14:16	♏ Oct 23 20:51	♑ Dec 22 07:28

Moon

Jan 1 20 ♈	♋ Mar 1 22:49	♎ May 1 19:30	♑ Jul 1 23:51	♈ Sep 1 22:27	♋ Nov 2 17:42
♉ Jan 1 17:45	♌ Mar 4 00:57	♏ May 3 21:22	♒ Jul 4 09:14	♉ Sep 4 10:58	♌ Nov 4 23:36
♊ Jan 4 00:06	♍ Mar 6 00:36	♐ May 6 00:51	♓ Jul 6 20:38	♊ Sep 6 21:51	♍ Nov 7 03:09
♋ Jan 6 02:40	♎ Mar 7 23:49	♑ May 8 07:11	♈ Jul 9 09:16	♋ Sep 9 05:25	♎ Nov 9 04:53
♌ Jan 8 02:50	♏ Mar 10 00:46	♒ May 10 16:51	♉ Jul 11 21:02	♌ Sep 11 09:00	♏ Nov 11 05:53
♍ Jan 10 02:35	♐ Mar 12 05:17	♓ May 13 04:54	♊ Jul 14 05:51	♍ Sep 13 09:25	♐ Nov 13 07:35
♎ Jan 12 03:52	♑ Mar 14 13:55	♈ May 15 17:15	♋ Jul 16 10:44	♎ Sep 15 08:33	♑ Nov 15 11:37
♏ Jan 14 08:09	♒ Mar 17 01:34	♉ May 18 03:48	♌ Jul 18 12:26	♏ Sep 17 08:34	♒ Nov 17 19:03
♐ Jan 16 15:40	♓ Mar 19 14:18	♊ May 20 11:39	♍ Jul 20 12:46	♐ Sep 19 11:20	♓ Nov 20 05:53
♑ Jan 19 01:45	♈ Mar 22 02:33	♋ May 22 16:59	♎ Jul 22 13:37	♑ Sep 21 17:53	♈ Nov 22 18:30
♒ Jan 21 13:26	♉ Mar 24 13:31	♌ May 24 20:37	♏ Jul 24 16:31	♒ Sep 24 03:47	♉ Nov 25 06:37
♓ Jan 24 01:57	♊ Mar 26 22:40	♍ May 26 23:21	♐ Jul 26 22:04	♓ Sep 26 15:47	♊ Nov 27 16:30
♈ Jan 26 14:33	♋ Mar 29 05:22	♎ May 29 01:59	♑ Jul 29 06:03	♈ Sep 29 04:29	♋ Nov 29 23:49
♉ Jan 29 01:43	♌ Mar 31 09:12	♏ May 31 05:11	♒ Jul 31 16:02	♉ Oct 1 16:47	♌ Dec 2 05:00
♊ Jan 31 09:44	♍ Apr 2 10:30	♐ Jun 2 09:39	♓ Aug 3 03:35	♊ Oct 4 03:43	♍ Dec 4 08:49
♋ Feb 2 13:40	♎ Apr 4 10:39	♑ Jun 4 16:09	♈ Aug 5 16:14	♋ Oct 6 12:12	♎ Dec 6 11:42
♌ Feb 4 14:13	♏ Apr 6 11:30	♒ Jun 7 01:21	♉ Aug 8 04:37	♌ Oct 8 17:24	♏ Dec 8 14:17
♍ Feb 6 13:10	♐ Apr 8 14:54	♓ Jun 9 12:57	♊ Aug 10 14:37	♍ Oct 10 19:27	♐ Dec 10 17:13
♎ Feb 8 12:50	♑ Apr 10 22:02	♈ Jun 12 01:26	♋ Aug 12 20:40	♎ Oct 12 19:29	♑ Dec 12 21:30
♏ Feb 10 15:15	♒ Apr 13 08:41	♉ Jun 14 12:29	♌ Aug 14 22:50	♏ Oct 14 19:21	♒ Dec 15 05:00
♐ Feb 12 21:32	♓ Apr 15 21:13	♊ Jun 16 20:25	♍ Aug 16 22:34	♐ Oct 16 20:59	♓ Dec 17 14:16
♑ Feb 15 07:26	♈ Apr 18 09:26	♋ Jun 19 01:05	♎ Aug 18 22:05	♑ Oct 19 01:55	♈ Dec 20 02:38
♒ Feb 17 19:26	♉ Apr 20 19:59	♌ Jun 21 03:28	♏ Aug 20 23:23	♒ Oct 21 10:40	♉ Dec 22 15:06
♓ Feb 20 08:05	♊ Apr 23 04:27	♍ Jun 23 05:08	♐ Aug 23 03:50	♓ Oct 23 22:20	♊ Dec 25 01:13
♈ Feb 22 20:30	♋ Apr 25 10:48	♎ Jun 25 07:23	♑ Aug 25 11:37	♈ Oct 26 11:02	♋ Dec 27 07:57
♉ Feb 25 07:52	♌ Apr 27 15:08	♏ Jun 27 11:04	♒ Aug 27 21:55	♉ Oct 28 23:06	♌ Dec 29 11:57
♊ Feb 27 17:02	♍ Apr 29 17:50	♐ Jun 29 16:30	♓ Aug 30 09:47	♊ Oct 31 09:27	♍ Dec 31 14:33

Mercury

Jan 1 20 ♐	♌ Jun 26 18:43
♑ Jan 7 18:29	R Jul 14 12 ♌
♒ Jan 27 04:16	D Aug 7 0 ♌
♓ Feb 13 10:17	♍ Sep 1 10:35
♈ Mar 3 02:45	♎ Sep 17 08:18
R Mar 12 6 ♈	♏ Oct 5 22:01
♓ Mar 22 02:17	♐ Oct 30 07:36
D Apr 4 22 ♓	R Nov 6 3 ♐
♈ Apr 17 21:18	♏ Nov 13 03:12
♉ May 9 14:50	D Nov 26 16 ♏
♊ May 24 17:59	♐ Dec 11 15:28
♋ Jun 7 19:20	

Venus

Jan 1 13 ♒	♊ Jun 26 11:37
R Jan 5 13 ♒	♋ Jul 21 17:10
♑ Feb 6 12:47	♌ Aug 15 12:45
D Feb 15 28 ♑	♍ Sep 8 23:39
♒ Feb 25 11:04	♎ Oct 3 03:44
♓ Apr 6 15:48	♏ Oct 27 03:27
♈ May 5 04:31	♐ Nov 20 01:06
♉ May 31 17:59	♑ Dec 13 22:07

Mars

Jan 1 6 ♒	
♓ Jan 30 07:04	
♈ Mar 9 12:55	
♉ Apr 17 20:37	
♊ May 28 22:02	
♋ Jul 11 03:13	
♌ Aug 25 15:45	
♍ Oct 12 18:36	
♎ Dec 4 00:57	

Jupiter

Jan 1 24 ♊
D Feb 15 21 ♊
♋ May 5 15:26
♌ Sep 27 13:37
R Nov 21 4 ♌

Saturn

Jan 1 12 ♓
R Jul 11 29 ♓
D Nov 26 22 ♓

Uranus

Jan 1 19 ♍
D May 23 15 ♍
R Dec 30 24 ♍

Neptune

Jan 1 21 ♏
R Feb 22 22 ♏
D Aug 1 19 ♏

Pluto

Jan 1 18 ♍
D May 27 15 ♍
R Dec 23 20 ♍

1967

Sun

♒ Jan 20 18:07	♈ Mar 21 07:36	♊ May 21 18:19	♌ Jul 23 13:16	♎ Sep 23 17:38	♐ Nov 23 00:05
♓ Feb 19 08:23	♉ Apr 20 18:55	♋ Jun 22 02:23	♍ Aug 23 20:13	♏ Oct 24 02:44	♑ Dec 22 13:17

Moon

Jan 1 5 ♍	♐ Mar 2 11:53	♓ May 3 00:46	♊ Jul 4 04:38	♍ Sep 3 17:07	♐ Nov 3 14:51
♎ Jan 2 17:04	♑ Mar 4 17:35	♈ May 5 13:09	♋ Jul 6 13:47	♎ Sep 5 18:02	♑ Nov 5 15:44
♏ Jan 4 20:15	♒ Mar 7 02:02	♉ May 8 02:10	♌ Jul 8 19:58	♏ Sep 7 18:44	♒ Nov 7 19:45
♐ Jan 7 00:27	♓ Mar 9 12:41	♊ May 10 14:08	♍ Jul 11 00:06	♐ Sep 9 20:39	♓ Nov 10 03:43
♑ Jan 9 05:53	♈ Mar 12 00:52	♋ May 13 00:10	♎ Jul 13 03:20	♑ Sep 12 00:43	♈ Nov 12 14:59
♒ Jan 11 13:05	♉ Mar 14 13:53	♌ May 15 07:49	♏ Jul 15 06:17	♒ Sep 14 07:07	♉ Nov 15 03:51
♓ Jan 13 22:45	♊ Mar 17 02:18	♍ May 17 12:51	♐ Jul 17 09:22	♓ Sep 16 15:52	♊ Nov 17 16:39
♈ Jan 16 10:48	♋ Mar 19 12:09	♎ May 19 15:30	♑ Jul 19 12:59	♈ Sep 19 02:45	♋ Nov 20 04:12
♉ Jan 18 23:38	♌ Mar 21 18:03	♏ May 21 16:30	♒ Jul 21 17:59	♉ Sep 21 15:20	♌ Nov 22 13:47
♊ Jan 21 10:37	♍ Mar 23 20:08	♐ May 23 17:06	♓ Jul 24 01:28	♊ Sep 24 04:21	♍ Nov 24 20:45
♋ Jan 23 17:51	♎ Mar 25 19:50	♑ May 25 18:58	♈ Jul 26 12:00	♋ Sep 26 15:45	♎ Nov 27 00:47
♌ Jan 25 21:20	♏ Mar 27 19:09	♒ May 27 23:43	♉ Jul 29 00:40	♌ Sep 28 23:40	♏ Nov 29 02:14
♍ Jan 27 22:35	♐ Mar 29 20:09	♓ May 30 08:17	♊ Jul 31 13:01	♍ Oct 1 03:38	♐ Dec 1 02:10
♎ Jan 29 23:33	♑ Apr 1 00:10	♈ Jun 1 20:07	♋ Aug 2 22:31	♎ Oct 3 04:33	♑ Dec 3 02:24
♏ Feb 1 01:44	♒ Apr 3 07:49	♉ Jun 4 09:03	♌ Aug 5 04:26	♏ Oct 5 04:13	♒ Dec 5 04:56
♐ Feb 3 05:56	♓ Apr 5 18:28	♊ Jun 6 20:52	♍ Aug 7 07:35	♐ Oct 7 04:14	♓ Dec 7 11:18
♑ Feb 5 12:09	♈ Apr 8 06:57	♋ Jun 9 06:18	♎ Aug 9 09:34	♑ Oct 9 07:04	♈ Dec 9 21:43
♒ Feb 7 20:16	♉ Apr 10 19:55	♌ Jun 11 13:19	♏ Aug 11 11:43	♒ Oct 11 12:45	♉ Dec 12 10:31
♓ Feb 10 06:19	♊ Apr 13 08:15	♍ Jun 13 18:23	♐ Aug 13 14:52	♓ Oct 13 21:38	♊ Dec 14 23:17
♈ Feb 12 18:17	♋ Apr 15 18:37	♎ Jun 15 21:58	♑ Aug 15 19:17	♈ Oct 16 08:58	♋ Dec 17 10:23
♉ Feb 15 07:19	♌ Apr 18 01:53	♏ Jun 18 00:24	♒ Aug 18 01:16	♉ Oct 18 21:41	♌ Dec 19 19:21
♊ Feb 17 19:14	♍ Apr 20 05:42	♐ Jun 20 02:19	♓ Aug 20 09:18	♊ Oct 21 10:37	♍ Dec 22 02:20
♋ Feb 20 03:47	♎ Apr 22 06:41	♑ Jun 22 04:46	♈ Aug 22 19:47	♋ Oct 23 22:27	♎ Dec 24 07:27
♌ Feb 22 08:04	♏ Apr 24 06:19	♒ Jun 24 09:10	♉ Aug 25 08:20	♌ Oct 26 07:39	♏ Dec 26 10:35
♍ Feb 24 09:03	♐ Apr 26 06:26	♓ Jun 26 16:49	♊ Aug 27 21:07	♍ Oct 28 13:19	♐ Dec 28 12:08
♎ Feb 26 08:43	♑ Apr 28 08:54	♈ Jun 29 03:51	♋ Aug 30 07:34	♎ Oct 30 15:30	♑ Dec 30 13:10
♏ Feb 28 09:09	♒ Apr 30 14:57	♉ Jul 1 16:43	♌ Sep 1 14:08	♏ Nov 1 15:26	

Mercury

Jan 1 29 ♐	R Jun 26 21 ♋
♑ Jan 1 00:49	D Jul 20 13 ♋
♒ Jan 19 17:06	♌ Aug 8 22:21
♓ Feb 6 00:57	♍ Aug 24 06:17
R Feb 23 18 ♓	♎ Sep 9 16:49
D Mar 17 5 ♓	♏ Sep 30 01:31
♈ Apr 14 14:29	R Oct 21 16 ♏
♉ May 1 23:35	D Nov 10 1 ♏
♊ May 16 03:25	♐ Dec 5 13:43
♋ May 31 18:08	♑ Dec 24 20:35

Venus

Jan 1 22 ♑	♍ Jul 8 22:17
♒ Jan 6 19:33	R Aug 8 13 ♍
♓ Jan 30 18:51	♌ Sep 9 11:41
♈ Feb 23 22:29	D Sep 20 27 ♌
♉ Mar 20 09:55	♍ Oct 1 18:13
♊ Apr 14 09:53	♎ Nov 9 16:31
♋ May 10 06:05	♏ Dec 7 08:49
♌ Jun 6 16:52	

Mars

Jan 1 14 ♎	D May 26 14 ♎
♏ Feb 12 12:22	♏ Jul 19 22:54
R Mar 8 3 ♏	♐ Sep 10 01:32
♎ Mar 31 06:17	♑ Oct 23 01:59
	♒ Dec 1 20:01

Jupiter

Jan 1 1 ♌
♋ Jan 16 02:01
D Mar 21 24 ♋
♌ May 23 08:47
♍ Oct 19 11:23
R Dec 22 5 ♍

Saturn

Jan 1 24 ♓
♈ Mar 3 20:18
R Jul 25 12 ♈
D Dec 9 5 ♈

Uranus

Jan 1 24 ♍
D May 28 20 ♍

Neptune

Jan 1 23 ♏
R Feb 24 24 ♏
D Aug 3 21 ♏

Pluto

Jan 1 20 ♍
D May 29 17 ♍
R Dec 26 22 ♍

1968

Sun

♒ Jan 20 23:55	♈ Mar 20 13:21	♊ May 21 00:04	♌ Jul 22 19:07	♎ Sep 22 23:25	♐ Nov 22 05:46
♓ Feb 19 14:10	♉ Apr 20 00:40	♋ Jun 21 08:13	♍ Aug 23 02:01	♏ Oct 23 08:29	♑ Dec 21 18:59

Moon

Jan 1 20♑	♈ Feb 29 23:14	♋ May 2 01:50	♎ Jul 2 16:09	♑ Sep 1 13:22	♈ Nov 1 16:51
♒ Jan 1 15:23	♉ Mar 3 10:27	♌ May 4 12:53	♏ Jul 4 20:20	♒ Sep 3 16:19	♉ Nov 4 03:00
♓ Jan 3 20:35	♊ Mar 5 13:16	♍ May 6 20:58	♐ Jul 6 22:05	♓ Sep 5 20:28	♊ Nov 6 14:47
♈ Jan 6 05:44	♋ Mar 8 11:20	♎ May 9 01:21	♐ Jul 8 22:24	♈ Sep 8 02:49	♊ Nov 9 03:26
♉ Jan 8 18:01	♌ Mar 10 20:27	♏ May 11 02:30	♒ Jul 10 23:02	♉ Sep 10 12:05	♌ Nov 11 15:45
♊ Jan 11 06:53	♍ Mar 13 01:51	♐ May 13 01:52	♓ Jul 13 02:02	♊ Sep 12 23:55	♍ Nov 14 01:54
♋ Jan 13 17:54	♎ Mar 15 04:23	♑ May 15 01:30	♈ Jul 15 08:52	♋ Sep 15 12:28	♎ Nov 16 08:25
♌ Jan 16 02:09	♏ Mar 17 05:33	♒ May 17 03:22	♉ Jul 17 19:30	♌ Sep 17 23:25	♏ Nov 18 11:06
♍ Jan 18 08:11	♐ Mar 19 06:53	♓ May 19 08:53	♊ Jul 20 08:13	♍ Sep 20 07:15	♐ Nov 20 11:04
♎ Jan 20 12:46	♑ Mar 21 09:35	♈ May 21 18:15	♋ Jul 22 20:31	♎ Sep 22 12:00	♑ Nov 22 10:20
♏ Jan 22 16:28	♒ Mar 23 14:16	♉ May 24 06:16	♌ Jul 25 06:54	♏ Sep 24 14:38	♒ Nov 24 11:01
♐ Jan 24 19:24	♓ Mar 25 21:15	♊ May 26 19:11	♍ Jul 27 15:09	♐ Sep 26 16:30	♓ Nov 26 14:52
♑ Jan 26 21:57	♈ Mar 28 06:31	♋ May 29 07:43	♎ Jul 29 21:31	♑ Sep 28 18:44	♈ Nov 28 22:26
♒ Jan 29 01:06	♉ Mar 30 17:55	♌ May 31 18:52	♏ Aug 1 02:11	♒ Sep 30 22:10	♉ Dec 1 08:58
♓ Jan 31 06:16	♊ Apr 2 06:40	♍ Jun 3 03:51	♐ Aug 3 05:11	♓ Oct 3 03:21	♊ Dec 3 21:05
♈ Feb 2 14:39	♋ Apr 4 19:12	♎ Jun 5 09:48	♑ Aug 5 06:58	♈ Oct 5 10:34	♋ Dec 6 09:43
♉ Feb 5 02:15	♌ Apr 7 05:28	♏ Jun 7 12:29	♒ Aug 7 08:37	♉ Oct 7 20:07	♌ Dec 8 22:02
♊ Feb 7 15:08	♍ Apr 9 12:03	♐ Jun 9 12:42	♓ Aug 9 11:45	♊ Oct 10 07:44	♍ Dec 11 08:59
♋ Feb 10 02:34	♎ Apr 11 15:00	♑ Jun 11 12:05	♈ Aug 11 17:53	♋ Oct 12 20:23	♎ Dec 13 17:09
♌ Feb 12 10:50	♏ Apr 13 15:31	♒ Jun 13 12:45	♉ Aug 14 03:36	♌ Oct 15 08:08	♏ Dec 15 21:30
♍ Feb 14 16:03	♐ Apr 15 15:22	♓ Jun 15 16:42	♊ Aug 16 15:50	♍ Oct 17 16:58	♐ Dec 17 22:27
♎ Feb 16 19:21	♑ Apr 17 16:23	♈ Jun 18 00:49	♋ Aug 19 04:15	♎ Oct 19 22:05	♑ Dec 19 21:31
♏ Feb 18 22:00	♒ Apr 19 19:56	♉ Jun 20 12:24	♌ Aug 21 14:39	♏ Oct 22 00:05	♒ Dec 21 20:59
♐ Feb 21 00:47	♓ Apr 22 02:45	♊ Jun 23 01:22	♍ Aug 23 22:21	♐ Oct 24 00:32	♓ Dec 23 23:00
♑ Feb 23 04:11	♈ Apr 24 12:31	♋ Jun 25 13:43	♎ Aug 26 03:45	♑ Oct 26 01:13	♈ Dec 26 05:01
♒ Feb 25 08:37	♉ Apr 27 00:22	♌ Jun 28 00:30	♏ Aug 28 07:37	♒ Oct 28 03:43	♉ Dec 28 14:57
♓ Feb 27 14:41	♊ Apr 29 13:10	♍ Jun 30 09:25	♐ Aug 30 10:40	♓ Oct 30 08:54	♊ Dec 31 03:10

Mercury

Jan 1 11♑	D Jun 30 23♊
♒ Jan 12 07:15	♋ Jul 13 00:46
♓ Feb 1 12:44	♌ Jul 31 06:10
R Feb 6 2♓	♍ Aug 15 00:45
♒ Feb 11 18:22	♎ Sep 1 16:48
D Feb 28 17♒	♏ Sep 28 14:54
♓ Mar 17 14:43	R Oct 3 0♏
♈ Apr 7 01:05	♎ Oct 8 00:00
♉ Apr 22 16:17	D Oct 24 15♎
♊ May 6 23:12	♏ Nov 8 10:57
♋ May 29 21:41	♐ Nov 27 12:45
R Jun 6 2♋	♑ Dec 16 14:10
♊ Jun 13 22:47	

Venus

Jan 1 28♏	♋ Jun 21 03:22
♐ Jan 1 22:39	♌ Jul 15 13:00
♑ Jan 26 17:35	♍ Aug 8 21:49
♒ Feb 20 04:54	♎ Sep 2 06:40
♓ Mar 15 13:31	♏ Sep 26 16:44
♈ Apr 8 21:47	♐ Oct 21 05:13
♉ May 3 06:55	♑ Nov 14 21:43
♊ May 27 17:02	♒ Dec 9 22:37

Mars

Jan 1 23♒
♓ Jan 9 09:44
♈ Feb 17 03:14
♉ Mar 27 23:41
♊ May 8 14:12
♋ Jun 21 05:00
♌ Aug 5 17:02
♍ Sep 21 18:32
♎ Nov 9 06:05
♏ Dec 29 21:58

Jupiter

Jan 1 5♍
♌ Feb 27 02:12
D Apr 21 25♌
♍ Jun 15 15:23
♎ Nov 15 22:57

Saturn

Jan 1 6♈
R Aug 7 25♈
D Dec 21 18♈

Uranus

Jan 1 29♍
R Jan 4 29♍
D Jun 2 25♍

Neptune

Jan 1 25♏
R Feb 27 26♏
D Aug 5 23♏
♎ Sep 28 16:25

Pluto

Jan 1 22♍
D May 31 20♍
R Dec 27 25♍

1969

Sun

♒ Jan 20 05:38	♈ Mar 20 19:07	♊ May 21 05:49	♌ Jul 23 00:47	♎ Sep 23 05:07	♐ Nov 22 11:30
♓ Feb 18 19:54	♉ Apr 20 06:25	♋ Jun 21 13:54	♍ Aug 23 07:44	♏ Oct 23 14:10	♑ Dec 22 00:43

Moon

Jan 1 10 ♊	♍ Mar 3 04:07	♐ May 3 11:18	♓ Jul 3 07:27	♊ Sep 2 19:24	♍ Nov 4 00:00
♋ Jan 2 15:52	♎ Mar 5 11:34	♑ May 5 11:57	♈ Jul 5 11:16	♋ Sep 5 06:57	♎ Nov 6 09:59
♌ Jan 5 03:54	♏ Mar 7 16:55	♒ May 7 13:28	♉ Jul 7 18:52	♌ Sep 7 19:35	♏ Nov 8 16:17
♍ Jan 7 14:41	♐ Mar 9 20:47	♓ May 9 17:04	♊ Jul 10 05:31	♍ Sep 10 07:21	♐ Nov 10 19:30
♎ Jan 9 23:33	♑ Mar 11 23:39	♈ May 11 23:09	♋ Jul 12 17:47	♎ Sep 12 17:01	♑ Nov 12 21:07
♏ Jan 12 05:32	♒ Mar 14 02:09	♉ May 14 07:28	♌ Jul 15 06:28	♏ Sep 15 00:24	♒ Nov 14 22:52
♐ Jan 14 08:18	♓ Mar 16 05:04	♊ May 16 17:41	♍ Jul 17 18:42	♐ Sep 17 05:41	♓ Nov 17 01:52
♑ Jan 16 08:38	♈ Mar 18 09:26	♋ May 19 05:30	♎ Jul 20 05:18	♑ Sep 19 09:14	♈ Nov 19 06:31
♒ Jan 18 08:15	♉ Mar 20 16:20	♌ May 21 18:12	♏ Jul 22 13:04	♒ Sep 21 11:31	♉ Nov 21 12:51
♓ Jan 20 09:21	♊ Mar 23 02:13	♍ May 24 06:06	♐ Jul 24 17:10	♓ Sep 23 13:23	♊ Nov 23 20:59
♈ Jan 22 13:43	♋ Mar 25 14:18	♎ May 26 15:06	♑ Jul 26 18:08	♈ Sep 25 15:55	♋ Nov 26 07:09
♉ Jan 24 22:12	♌ Mar 28 02:37	♏ May 28 20:05	♒ Jul 28 17:35	♉ Sep 27 20:29	♌ Nov 28 19:22
♊ Jan 27 09:52	♍ Mar 30 12:52	♐ May 30 21:29	♓ Jul 30 17:31	♊ Sep 30 04:06	♍ Dec 1 08:14
♋ Jan 29 22:36	♎ Apr 1 20:02	♑ Jun 1 21:06	♈ Aug 1 19:54	♋ Oct 2 14:52	♎ Dec 3 19:16
♌ Feb 1 10:29	♏ Apr 4 00:22	♒ Jun 3 21:03	♉ Aug 4 02:01	♌ Oct 5 03:24	♏ Dec 6 02:30
♍ Feb 3 20:40	♐ Apr 6 02:57	♓ Jun 5 23:15	♊ Aug 6 11:49	♍ Oct 7 15:21	♐ Dec 8 05:42
♎ Feb 6 04:59	♑ Apr 8 05:05	♈ Jun 8 04:36	♋ Aug 8 23:57	♎ Oct 10 00:47	♑ Dec 10 06:20
♏ Feb 8 11:17	♒ Apr 10 07:46	♉ Jun 10 13:06	♌ Aug 11 12:38	♏ Oct 12 07:19	♒ Dec 12 06:06
♐ Feb 10 15:23	♓ Apr 12 11:40	♊ Jun 12 23:49	♍ Aug 14 00:32	♐ Oct 14 11:33	♓ Dec 14 07:55
♑ Feb 12 17:28	♈ Apr 15 11:52	♋ Jun 15 11:52	♎ Aug 16 10:51	♑ Oct 16 14:35	♈ Dec 16 11:56
♒ Feb 14 18:29	♉ Apr 17 00:43	♌ Jun 18 00:35	♏ Aug 18 18:53	♒ Oct 18 17:20	♉ Dec 18 18:35
♓ Feb 16 20:02	♊ Apr 19 10:29	♍ Jun 20 12:53	♐ Aug 21 00:12	♓ Oct 20 20:25	♊ Dec 21 03:27
♈ Feb 18 23:49	♋ Apr 21 22:16	♎ Jun 22 23:02	♑ Aug 23 02:49	♈ Oct 23 00:17	♋ Dec 23 14:08
♉ Feb 21 07:02	♌ Apr 24 10:51	♏ Jun 25 05:31	♒ Aug 25 03:36	♉ Oct 25 05:33	♌ Dec 26 02:20
♊ Feb 23 17:40	♍ Apr 26 21:57	♐ Jun 27 07:59	♓ Aug 27 04:03	♊ Oct 27 13:00	♍ Dec 28 15:20
♋ Feb 26 06:10	♎ Apr 29 05:43	♑ Jun 29 07:44	♈ Aug 29 05:57	♋ Oct 29 23:13	♎ Dec 31 03:18
♌ Feb 28 18:12	♏ May 1 09:49	♒ Jul 1 06:49	♉ Aug 31 10:50	♌ Nov 1 11:35	

Mercury

Jan 1 24 ♑	♌ Jul 22 19:11
♒ Jan 4 12:18	♍ Aug 7 04:24
R Jan 20 16 ♒	♎ Aug 27 06:54
D Feb 10 0 ♒	R Sep 16 14 ♎
♓ Mar 12 15:18	♍ Oct 7 04:48
♈ Mar 30 09:57	D Oct 8 29 ♍
♉ Apr 14 05:59	♎ Oct 9 18:18
♊ Apr 30 15:39	♏ Nov 1 16:53
R May 17 12 ♊	♐ Nov 20 06:00
D Jun 10 3 ♊	♑ Dec 9 13:20
♋ Jul 8 03:41	

Venus

Jan 1 25 ♒	♋ Aug 3 05:25
♓ Jan 4 20:09	♌ Aug 29 02:44
♈ Feb 2 04:48	♍ Sep 23 03:23
R Mar 18 26 ♈	♎ Oct 17 14:16
D Apr 29 10 ♈	♏ Nov 10 16:39
♉ Jun 6 01:48	♐ Dec 4 14:39
♊ Jul 6 22:02	♑ Dec 28 11:02

Mars

Jan 1 1 ♏	♊ Sep 2 19:24
♐ Feb 25 06:07	
R Apr 27 17 ♐	
D Jul 8 1 ♐	
♑ Sep 21 06:36	
♒ Nov 4 18:46	
♓ Dec 15 14:16	

Jupiter

Jan 1 5 ♎
R Jan 20 6 ♎
♍ Mar 30 21:13
D May 23 26 ♍
♎ Jul 15 13:43
♏ Dec 16 15:44

Saturn

Jan 1 18 ♈
♉ Apr 29 21:20
R Aug 21 8 ♉

Uranus

Jan 1 3 ♎
R Jan 8 4 ♎
♍ May 20 19:27
D Jun 7 29 ♍
♎ Jun 24 12:00

Neptune

Jan 1 27 ♏
R Feb 28 28 ♏
D Aug 7 25 ♏

Pluto

Jan 1 25 ♍
D Jun 2 22 ♍
R Dec 30 27 ♍

1970

Sun

♒ Jan 20 11:23	♈ Mar 21 00:55	♊ May 21 11:37	♌ Jul 23 06:36	♎ Sep 23 11:00	♐ Nov 22 17:25
♓ Feb 19 01:42	♉ Apr 20 12:14	♋ Jun 21 19:42	♍ Aug 23 13:33	♏ Oct 23 20:07	♑ Dec 22 06:38

Moon

Jan 1 10 ♎	♑ Mar 2 12:53	♈ May 2 09:32	♋ Jul 2 17:20	♎ Sep 2 18:24	♑ Nov 3 08:32
♏ Jan 2 12:03	♒ Mar 4 14:35	♉ May 4 13:06	♌ Jul 5 04:26	♏ Sep 5 05:54	♒ Nov 5 13:10
♐ Jan 4 16:32	♓ Mar 6 14:49	♊ May 6 18:18	♍ Jul 7 17:11	♐ Sep 7 14:58	♓ Nov 7 16:32
♑ Jan 6 17:29	♈ Mar 8 15:16	♋ May 9 02:16	♎ Jul 10 06:02	♑ Sep 9 20:52	♈ Nov 9 18:51
♒ Jan 8 16:47	♉ Mar 10 17:43	♌ May 11 13:22	♏ Jul 12 16:40	♒ Sep 11 23:34	♉ Nov 11 20:50
♓ Jan 10 16:35	♊ Mar 12 23:37	♍ May 14 02:11	♐ Jul 14 23:25	♓ Sep 13 23:57	♊ Nov 13 23:47
♈ Jan 12 18:47	♋ Mar 15 09:19	♎ May 16 14:02	♑ Jul 17 02:18	♈ Sep 15 23:35	♋ Nov 16 05:22
♉ Jan 15 00:20	♌ Mar 17 21:40	♏ May 18 22:49	♒ Jul 19 02:44	♉ Sep 18 00:21	♌ Nov 18 14:36
♊ Jan 17 09:06	♍ Mar 20 10:30	♐ May 21 04:10	♓ Jul 21 02:37	♊ Sep 20 04:02	♍ Nov 21 02:50
♋ Jan 19 20:14	♎ Mar 22 21:57	♑ May 23 07:12	♈ Jul 23 03:43	♋ Sep 22 11:40	♎ Nov 23 15:39
♌ Jan 22 08:39	♏ Mar 25 07:09	♒ May 25 09:25	♉ Jul 25 05:17	♌ Sep 25 22:53	♏ Nov 26 02:24
♍ Jan 24 21:32	♐ Mar 27 14:07	♓ May 27 11:59	♊ Jul 27 13:52	♍ Sep 27 11:54	♐ Nov 28 10:02
♎ Jan 27 09:42	♑ Mar 29 19:00	♈ May 29 15:26	♋ Jul 29 23:14	♎ Sep 30 00:32	♑ Nov 30 15:05
♏ Jan 29 19:33	♒ Mar 31 22:08	♉ May 31 20:02	♌ Aug 1 10:44	♏ Oct 2 11:36	♒ Dec 2 18:45
♐ Feb 1 01:50	♓ Apr 3 00:00	♊ Jun 3 02:10	♍ Aug 3 23:34	♐ Oct 4 20:31	♓ Dec 4 21:54
♑ Feb 3 04:22	♈ Apr 5 01:31	♋ Jun 5 10:26	♎ Aug 6 12:32	♑ Oct 7 03:09	♈ Dec 7 01:03
♒ Feb 5 04:19	♉ Apr 7 04:02	♌ Jun 7 21:17	♏ Aug 8 23:56	♒ Oct 9 07:26	♉ Dec 9 04:04
♓ Feb 7 03:37	♊ Apr 9 09:01	♍ Jun 10 10:02	♐ Aug 11 08:07	♓ Oct 11 09:29	♊ Dec 11 08:33
♈ Feb 9 04:16	♋ Apr 11 17:33	♎ Jun 12 22:28	♑ Aug 13 12:24	♈ Oct 13 10:11	♋ Dec 13 14:32
♉ Feb 11 07:58	♌ Apr 14 05:15	♏ Jun 15 08:01	♒ Aug 15 13:30	♉ Oct 15 10:59	♌ Dec 15 23:20
♊ Feb 13 15:28	♍ Apr 16 18:06	♐ Jun 17 13:38	♓ Aug 17 13:01	♊ Oct 17 13:43	♍ Dec 18 11:05
♋ Feb 16 02:16	♎ Apr 19 05:35	♑ Jun 19 16:05	♈ Aug 19 12:50	♋ Oct 19 19:58	♎ Dec 21 00:00
♌ Feb 18 14:53	♏ Apr 21 14:15	♒ Jun 21 17:00	♉ Aug 21 14:45	♌ Oct 22 06:12	♏ Dec 23 11:27
♍ Feb 21 03:42	♐ Apr 23 20:15	♓ Jun 23 18:13	♊ Aug 23 20:04	♍ Oct 24 18:57	♐ Dec 25 19:28
♎ Feb 23 15:29	♑ Apr 26 00:25	♈ Jun 25 20:52	♋ Aug 26 04:57	♎ Oct 27 07:36	♑ Dec 28 00:00
♏ Feb 26 01:23	♒ Apr 28 03:43	♉ Jun 28 01:34	♌ Aug 28 16:37	♏ Oct 29 18:15	♒ Dec 30 02:23
♐ Feb 28 08:37	♓ Apr 30 06:38	♊ Jun 30 08:23	♍ Aug 31 05:36	♐ Nov 1 02:23	

Mercury

Jan 1 29 ♑	♋ Jun 30 06:21
R Jan 4 0 ♒	♌ Jul 14 08:04
D Jan 24 13 ♑	♍ Jul 31 05:38
♒ Feb 13 13:12	R Aug 30 28 ♍
♓ Mar 5 20:04	D Sep 22 13 ♍
♈ Mar 22 07:58	♎ Oct 7 17:55
♉ Apr 6 07:35	♏ Oct 25 06:18
R Apr 28 22 ♉	♐ Nov 13 01:14
D May 22 12 ♉	♑ Dec 3 10:14
♊ Jun 13 12:47	R Dec 19 14 ♑

Venus

Jan 1 4 ♑	♌ Jun 16 17:50
♒ Jan 21 07:27	♍ Jul 12 12:18
♓ Feb 14 05:04	♎ Aug 8 10:01
♈ Mar 10 05:23	♏ Sep 7 01:53
♉ Apr 3 10:05	R Oct 20 25 ♏
♊ Apr 27 20:33	D Nov 30 9 ♏
♋ May 22 14:18	

Mars

Jan 1 12 ♓
♈ Jan 24 21:23
♉ Mar 7 01:28
♊ Apr 18 18:59
♋ Jun 2 06:50
♌ Jul 18 06:40
♍ Sep 3 04:53
♎ Oct 20 10:54
♏ Dec 6 16:25

Jupiter

Jan 1 2 ♏
R Feb 19 5 ♏
♎ Apr 30 07:07
D Jun 23 26 ♎
♏ Aug 15 17:45

Saturn

Jan 1 2 ♉
D Jan 3 2 ♉
R Sep 4 22 ♉

Uranus

Jan 1 8 ♎
R Jan 13 8 ♎
D Jun 12 4 ♎

Neptune

Jan 1 29 ♏
♐ Jan 4 18:42
R Mar 3 0 ♐
♏ May 3 02:50
D Aug 10 28 ♏
♐ Nov 6 15:45

Pluto

Jan 1 27 ♍
D Jun 5 24 ♍

1971

Sun

♒ Jan 20 17:15	♈ Mar 21 06:41	♊ May 21 17:16	♌ Jul 23 12:15	♎ Sep 23 16:45	♐ Nov 22 23:14
♓ Feb 19 07:30	♉ Apr 20 17:57	♋ Jun 22 01:20	♍ Aug 23 19:13	♏ Oct 24 01:52	♑ Dec 22 12:23

Moon

Jan 1 27♒	♉ Feb 28 23:54	♌ May 1 09:35	♏ Jul 2 13:46	♒ Sep 2 07:04	♉ Nov 2 05:55
♓ Jan 1 04:07	♊ Mar 3 03:01	♍ May 3 21:02	♐ Jul 4 23:59	♓ Sep 4 08:51	♊ Nov 4 05:27
♈ Jan 3 06:26	♋ Mar 5 09:47	♎ May 6 09:59	♑ Jul 7 07:04	♈ Sep 6 08:43	♋ Nov 6 07:14
♉ Jan 5 10:00	♌ Mar 7 19:54	♏ May 8 22:03	♒ Jul 9 11:27	♉ Sep 8 08:37	♌ Nov 8 12:57
♊ Jan 7 15:07	♍ Mar 10 08:11	♐ May 11 08:08	♓ Jul 11 14:15	♊ Sep 10 10:25	♍ Nov 10 22:44
♋ Jan 9 22:08	♎ Mar 12 21:05	♑ May 13 16:08	♈ Jul 13 16:31	♋ Sep 12 15:21	♎ Nov 13 11:06
♌ Jan 12 07:24	♏ Mar 15 09:30	♒ May 15 22:20	♉ Jul 15 19:10	♌ Sep 14 23:37	♏ Nov 15 23:50
♍ Jan 14 18:57	♐ Mar 17 20:23	♓ May 18 02:39	♊ Jul 17 22:47	♍ Sep 17 10:29	♐ Nov 18 11:30
♎ Jan 17 07:52	♑ Mar 20 04:37	♈ May 20 05:11	♋ Jul 20 03:57	♎ Sep 19 22:47	♑ Nov 20 21:37
♏ Jan 19 20:04	♒ Mar 22 09:28	♉ May 22 06:31	♌ Jul 22 11:16	♏ Sep 22 11:32	♒ Nov 23 05:52
♐ Jan 22 05:15	♓ Mar 24 11:00	♊ May 24 08:00	♍ Jul 24 21:08	♐ Sep 24 23:42	♓ Nov 25 11:47
♑ Jan 24 10:32	♈ Mar 26 10:46	♋ May 26 11:25	♎ Jul 27 09:12	♑ Sep 27 09:51	♈ Nov 27 15:03
♒ Jan 26 12:36	♉ Mar 28 10:15	♌ May 28 18:16	♏ Jul 29 21:49	♒ Sep 29 16:38	♉ Nov 29 16:07
♓ Jan 28 13:02	♊ Mar 30 11:43	♍ May 31 04:48	♐ Aug 1 08:50	♓ Oct 1 19:36	♊ Dec 1 16:26
♈ Jan 30 13:33	♋ Apr 1 16:51	♐ Jun 2 17:27	♑ Aug 3 16:01	♈ Oct 3 19:40	♋ Dec 3 17:51
♉ Feb 1 15:48	♌ Apr 4 02:06	♏ Jun 5 05:36	♒ Aug 5 20:46	♉ Oct 5 18:42	♌ Dec 5 22:16
♊ Feb 3 20:35	♍ Apr 6 14:15	♐ Jun 7 15:27	♓ Aug 7 22:34	♊ Oct 7 18:52	♍ Dec 8 06:41
♋ Feb 6 04:07	♎ Apr 9 03:17	♑ Jun 9 22:45	♈ Aug 9 23:27	♋ Oct 9 22:09	♎ Dec 10 18:19
♌ Feb 8 14:06	♏ Apr 11 15:27	♒ Jun 12 04:03	♉ Aug 12 00:55	♌ Oct 12 05:31	♏ Dec 13 07:02
♍ Feb 11 01:57	♐ Apr 14 02:02	♓ Jun 14 08:01	♊ Aug 14 04:10	♍ Oct 14 16:15	♐ Dec 15 18:37
♎ Feb 13 14:50	♑ Apr 16 10:37	♈ Jun 16 11:06	♋ Aug 16 09:49	♎ Oct 17 04:48	♑ Dec 18 04:07
♏ Feb 16 03:22	♒ Apr 18 16:46	♉ Jun 18 13:38	♌ Aug 18 17:57	♏ Oct 19 17:31	♒ Dec 20 11:33
♐ Feb 18 13:46	♓ Apr 20 20:08	♊ Jun 20 16:24	♍ Aug 21 04:19	♐ Oct 22 05:31	♓ Dec 22 17:10
♑ Feb 20 20:37	♈ Apr 22 21:08	♋ Jun 22 20:30	♎ Aug 23 16:23	♑ Oct 24 16:05	♈ Dec 24 21:08
♒ Feb 22 23:42	♉ Apr 24 21:06	♌ Jun 25 03:12	♏ Aug 26 05:09	♒ Oct 27 00:10	♉ Dec 26 23:44
♓ Feb 25 00:05	♊ Apr 26 21:59	♍ Jun 27 13:06	♐ Aug 28 16:56	♓ Oct 29 04:56	♊ Dec 29 01:38
♈ Feb 26 23:30	♋ Apr 29 01:44	♎ Jun 30 01:23	♑ Aug 31 01:53	♈ Oct 31 06:25	♋ Dec 31 04:01

Mercury

Jan 1 1♑	♋ Jun 21 16:26
♐ Jan 3 00:35	♌ Jul 6 08:50
D Jan 8 28♐	♍ Jul 26 16:50
♑ Jan 14 02:24	R Aug 12 10♍
♒ Feb 7 20:54	♌ Aug 29 20:42
♓ Feb 26 07:57	D Sep 5 27♌
♈ Mar 14 04:52	♍ Sep 11 06:26
♉ Apr 1 14:37	♎ Sep 30 09:21
R Apr 9 3♉	♏ Oct 17 17:41
♈ Apr 18 21:42	♐ Nov 6 06:54
D May 3 22♈	R Dec 3 28♐
♉ May 17 04:04	D Dec 22 12♐
♊ Jun 7 06:40	

Venus

Jan 1 24♏	♋ Jul 6 22:02
♐ Jan 7 01:01	♌ Jul 31 09:15
♑ Feb 5 14:57	♍ Aug 24 16:25
♒ Mar 4 02:24	♎ Sep 17 20:27
♓ Mar 29 14:04	♏ Oct 11 22:43
♈ Apr 23 15:46	♐ Nov 5 00:29
♉ May 18 12:47	♑ Nov 29 02:39
♊ Jun 12 06:57	♒ Dec 23 06:29

Mars

Jan 1 16♏
♐ Jan 23 01:32
♑ Mar 12 10:04
♒ May 3 21:00
R Jul 11 21♒
D Sep 9 12♒
♓ Nov 6 12:37
♈ Dec 26 18:05

Jupiter

Jan 1 27♏
♐ Jan 14 08:10
R Mar 23 6♐
♏ Jun 5 03:32
D Jul 24 26♏
♐ Sep 11 14:21

Saturn

Jan 1 15♉
D Jan 17 15♉
♊ Jun 18 15:38
R Sep 19 6♊

Uranus

Jan 1 13♎
R Jan 18 13♎
D Jun 17 9♎

Neptune

Jan 1 1♐
R Mar 5 3♐
D Aug 12 0♐

Pluto

Jan 1 29♍
R Jan 1 29♍
D Jun 7 26♍
♎ Oct 5 06:15

1972

Sun

♒ Jan 20 22:59	♈ Mar 20 12:22	♊ May 20 23:01	♌ Jul 22 18:03	♎ Sep 22 22:32	♐ Nov 22 05:00
♓ Feb 19 13:11	♉ Apr 19 23:38	♋ Jun 21 07:07	♍ Aug 23 01:03	♏ Oct 23 07:40	♑ Dec 21 18:12

Moon

Jan 1 11♋	♎ Mar 1 19:00	♑ May 2 20:29	♈ Jul 3 06:22	♋ Sep 2 02:11	♎ Nov 2 10:27
♌ Jan 2 08:21	♏ Mar 4 07:00	♒ May 5 06:35	♉ Jul 5 09:24	♌ Sep 4 06:53	♏ Nov 4 21:46
♍ Jan 4 12:25	♐ Mar 6 19:36	♓ May 7 13:28	♊ Jul 7 11:05	♍ Sep 6 13:14	♐ Nov 7 10:15
♎ Jan 7 02:33	♑ Mar 9 06:48	♈ May 9 16:34	♋ Jul 9 12:28	♎ Sep 8 21:37	♑ Nov 9 23:11
♏ Jan 9 15:02	♒ Mar 11 14:42	♉ May 11 16:48	♌ Jul 11 15:04	♏ Sep 11 08:15	♒ Nov 12 11:01
♐ Jan 12 02:57	♓ Mar 13 18:40	♊ May 13 15:58	♍ Jul 13 20:15	♐ Sep 13 20:41	♓ Nov 14 19:55
♑ Jan 14 12:25	♈ Mar 15 19:36	♋ May 15 16:15	♎ Jul 16 04:49	♑ Sep 16 09:06	♈ Nov 17 00:44
♒ Jan 16 19:04	♉ Mar 17 19:28	♌ May 17 19:37	♏ Jul 18 16:14	♒ Sep 18 19:05	♉ Nov 19 01:52
♓ Jan 18 23:28	♊ Mar 19 20:13	♍ May 20 02:56	♐ Jul 21 04:47	♓ Sep 21 01:08	♊ Nov 21 01:05
♈ Jan 21 02:36	♋ Mar 21 23:27	♎ May 22 13:36	♑ Jul 23 16:09	♈ Sep 23 03:45	♋ Nov 23 00:30
♉ Jan 23 05:16	♌ Mar 24 05:16	♏ May 25 02:00	♒ Jul 26 01:07	♉ Sep 25 04:27	♌ Nov 25 02:11
♊ Jan 25 08:14	♍ Mar 26 14:47	♐ May 27 14:33	♓ Jul 28 07:29	♊ Sep 27 05:14	♍ Nov 27 07:25
♋ Jan 27 12:01	♎ Mar 29 01:42	♑ May 30 02:13	♈ Jul 30 11:50	♋ Sep 29 07:38	♎ Nov 29 16:14
♌ Jan 29 17:20	♏ Mar 31 13:48	♒ Jun 1 12:16	♉ Aug 1 14:58	♌ Oct 1 12:24	♏ Dec 2 03:42
♍ Feb 1 00:55	♐ Apr 3 02:27	♓ Jun 3 19:52	♊ Aug 3 17:34	♍ Oct 3 19:30	♐ Dec 4 16:23
♎ Feb 3 11:07	♑ Apr 5 14:19	♈ Jun 6 00:27	♋ Aug 5 20:17	♎ Oct 6 04:34	♑ Dec 7 05:06
♏ Feb 5 23:17	♒ Apr 7 23:37	♉ Jun 8 02:15	♌ Aug 7 23:56	♏ Oct 8 15:26	♒ Dec 9 16:53
♐ Feb 8 11:37	♓ Apr 10 04:57	♊ Jun 10 02:23	♍ Aug 10 05:22	♐ Oct 11 03:51	♓ Dec 12 02:33
♑ Feb 10 21:49	♈ Apr 12 06:32	♋ Jun 12 02:44	♎ Aug 12 13:28	♑ Oct 13 16:44	♈ Dec 14 09:00
♒ Feb 13 04:35	♉ Apr 14 05:55	♌ Jun 14 05:10	♏ Aug 15 00:19	♒ Oct 16 03:50	♉ Dec 16 11:59
♓ Feb 15 08:11	♊ Apr 16 05:16	♍ Jun 16 11:02	♐ Aug 17 12:48	♓ Oct 18 11:13	♊ Dec 18 12:24
♈ Feb 17 09:50	♋ Apr 18 06:45	♎ Jun 18 20:38	♑ Aug 20 00:38	♈ Oct 20 14:22	♋ Dec 20 11:57
♉ Feb 19 11:12	♌ Apr 20 11:46	♏ Jun 21 08:42	♒ Aug 22 09:43	♉ Oct 22 14:37	♌ Dec 22 12:35
♊ Feb 21 13:35	♍ Apr 22 20:23	♐ Jun 23 21:15	♓ Aug 24 15:27	♊ Oct 24 14:02	♍ Dec 24 16:03
♋ Feb 23 17:52	♎ Apr 25 07:34	♑ Jun 26 08:36	♈ Aug 26 18:41	♋ Oct 26 14:43	♎ Dec 26 23:21
♌ Feb 26 00:15	♏ Apr 27 19:55	♒ Jun 28 18:02	♉ Aug 28 20:42	♌ Oct 28 18:14	♏ Dec 29 10:09
♍ Feb 28 08:38	♐ Apr 30 08:31	♓ Jul 1 01:19	♊ Aug 30 22:55	♍ Oct 31 01:00	♐ Dec 31 22:52

Mercury

Jan 1 17♐	R Jul 24 22♌
♑ Jan 11 18:27	D Aug 17 10♌
♒ Jan 31 23:40	♍ Sep 5 11:35
♓ Feb 18 12:53	♎ Sep 21 12:12
♈ Mar 5 16:49	♏ Oct 9 11:13
R Mar 21 15♈	♐ Oct 30 19:51
D Apr 14 3♈	R Nov 15 12♐
♉ May 12 23:38	♏ Nov 29 07:03
♊ May 29 06:45	D Dec 5 25♏
♋ Jun 12 02:45	♐ Dec 12 22:33
♌ Jun 28 16:51	

Venus

Jan 1 10♒	D Jul 9 18♊
♓ Jan 16 14:59	♋ Aug 6 01:32
♈ Feb 10 10:08	♌ Sep 7 23:27
♉ Mar 7 03:26	♍ Oct 5 08:34
♊ Apr 3 22:52	♎ Oct 30 21:40
♋ May 10 13:56	♏ Nov 24 13:23
R May 27 4♋	♐ Dec 18 18:32
♊ Jun 11 20:02	

Mars

Jan 1 3♈
♉ Feb 10 14:09
♊ Mar 27 04:36
♋ May 12 13:21
♌ Jun 28 16:14
♍ Aug 15 01:01
♎ Sep 30 23:22
♏ Nov 15 22:11
♐ Dec 30 16:11

Jupiter

Jan 1 22♐
♑ Feb 6 18:39
R Apr 25 8♑
♐ Jul 24 19:21
D Aug 25 28♐
♑ Sep 25 16:22

Saturn

Jan 1 0♊
♉ Jan 10 05:55
D Jan 31 29♉
♊ Feb 21 13:37
R Oct 2 20♊

Uranus

Jan 1 18♎
R Jan 23 18♎
D Jun 21 14♎

Neptune

Jan 1 4♐
R Mar 7 5♐
D Aug 14 2♐

Pluto

Jan 1 2♎
R Jan 4 2♎
♍ Apr 17 09:59
D Jun 9 29♍
♎ Jul 30 11:18

1973

Sun

≈ Jan 20 04:48	♈ Mar 20 18:12	♊ May 21 04:54	♌ Jul 22 23:56	♎ Sep 23 04:21	♐ Nov 22 10:52
♓ Feb 18 19:01	♉ Apr 20 05:30	♋ Jun 21 13:02	♍ Aug 23 06:52	♏ Oct 23 13:29	♑ Dec 22 00:05

Moon

Jan 1 0 ♐	♓ Mar 3 22:30	♊ May 4 01:15	♍ Jul 3 23:31	♐ Sep 3 15:23	♓ Nov 4 20:25
♑ Jan 3 11:30	♈ Mar 6 03:37	♋ May 6 01:34	♎ Jul 6 04:24	♑ Sep 6 04:01	♈ Nov 7 04:20
≈ Jan 5 22:47	♉ Mar 8 06:50	♌ May 8 03:36	♏ Jul 8 13:06	≈ Sep 8 16:30	♉ Nov 9 08:25
♓ Jan 8 08:02	♊ Mar 10 09:30	♍ May 10 08:13	♐ Jul 11 00:47	♓ Sep 11 02:39	♊ Nov 11 10:00
♈ Jan 10 14:58	♋ Mar 12 12:28	♎ May 12 15:30	♑ Jul 13 13:46	♈ Sep 13 09:54	♋ Nov 13 10:47
♉ Jan 12 19:25	♌ Mar 14 16:07	♏ May 15 01:08	≈ Jul 16 02:15	♉ Sep 15 14:59	♌ Nov 15 12:20
♊ Jan 14 21:41	♍ Mar 16 20:41	♐ May 17 12:42	♓ Jul 18 13:07	♊ Sep 17 18:47	♍ Nov 17 15:41
♋ Jan 16 22:38	♎ Mar 19 02:47	♑ May 20 01:30	♈ Jul 20 21:44	♋ Sep 19 22:01	♎ Nov 19 21:16
♌ Jan 18 23:39	♏ Mar 21 11:15	≈ May 22 14:16	♉ Jul 23 03:41	♌ Sep 22 00:55	♏ Nov 22 05:07
♍ Jan 21 02:22	♐ Mar 23 22:26	♓ May 25 01:05	♊ Jul 25 06:59	♍ Sep 24 03:59	♐ Nov 24 15:10
♎ Jan 23 08:15	♑ Mar 26 11:15	♈ May 27 08:15	♋ Jul 27 08:10	♎ Sep 26 08:00	♑ Nov 27 03:13
♏ Jan 25 17:52	≈ Mar 28 23:12	♉ May 29 11:28	♌ Jul 29 08:29	♏ Sep 28 14:17	≈ Nov 29 16:19
♐ Jan 28 06:10	♓ Mar 31 07:54	♊ May 31 11:53	♍ Jul 31 09:35	♐ Sep 30 23:47	♓ Dec 2 04:31
♑ Jan 30 18:53	♈ Apr 2 12:47	♋ Jun 2 11:20	♎ Aug 2 13:11	♑ Oct 3 12:01	♈ Dec 4 13:50
≈ Feb 2 05:56	♉ Apr 4 14:58	♌ Jun 4 11:49	♏ Aug 4 20:36	≈ Oct 6 00:48	♉ Dec 6 19:08
♓ Feb 4 14:21	♊ Apr 6 16:11	♍ Jun 6 14:52	♐ Aug 7 07:36	♓ Oct 8 11:23	♊ Dec 8 20:59
♈ Feb 6 20:29	♋ Apr 8 18:03	♎ Jun 8 21:16	♑ Aug 9 20:30	♈ Oct 10 18:28	♋ Dec 10 20:52
♉ Feb 9 00:53	♌ Apr 10 21:31	♏ Jun 11 06:51	≈ Aug 12 08:53	♉ Oct 12 22:35	♌ Dec 12 20:44
♊ Feb 11 04:09	♍ Apr 13 02:46	♐ Jun 13 18:43	♓ Aug 14 19:13	♊ Oct 15 01:08	♍ Dec 14 22:21
♋ Feb 13 06:44	♎ Apr 15 09:49	♑ Jun 16 07:36	♈ Aug 17 03:16	♋ Oct 17 03:28	♎ Dec 17 02:54
♌ Feb 15 09:13	♏ Apr 17 18:50	≈ Jun 18 20:18	♉ Aug 19 09:14	♌ Oct 19 06:24	♏ Dec 19 10:44
♍ Feb 17 12:30	♐ Apr 20 06:01	♓ Jun 21 07:29	♊ Aug 21 13:26	♍ Oct 21 10:19	♐ Dec 21 21:20
♎ Feb 19 17:58	♑ Apr 22 18:48	♈ Jun 23 15:47	♋ Aug 23 16:07	♎ Oct 23 15:27	♑ Dec 24 09:42
♏ Feb 22 02:35	≈ Apr 25 07:21	♉ Jun 25 20:37	♌ Aug 25 17:49	♏ Oct 25 22:28	≈ Dec 26 22:43
♐ Feb 24 14:15	♓ Apr 27 17:10	♊ Jun 27 22:17	♍ Aug 27 19:32	♐ Oct 28 07:57	♓ Dec 29 11:10
♑ Feb 27 03:03	♈ Apr 29 22:53	♋ Jun 29 22:07	♎ Aug 29 22:52	♑ Oct 30 19:56	♈ Dec 31 21:34
≈ Mar 1 14:21	♉ May 2 01:02	♌ Jul 1 21:55	♏ Sep 1 05:17	≈ Nov 2 08:58	

Mercury

Jan 1 24 ♐	R Jul 6 3 ♌
♑ Jan 4 14:41	♋ Jul 16 08:13
≈ Jan 23 15:21	D Jul 30 23 ♋
♓ Feb 9 19:25	♌ Aug 11 12:12
R Mar 4 28 ♓	♍ Aug 28 15:19
D Mar 27 15 ♓	♎ Sep 13 16:14
♈ Apr 16 20:59	♏ Oct 2 20:14
♉ May 6 02:45	R Oct 30 25 ♏
♊ May 20 17:22	D Nov 19 10 ♏
♋ Jun 4 04:24	♐ Dec 8 21:32
♌ Jun 27 07:08	♑ Dec 28 15:15

Venus

Jan 1 16 ♐	♋ Jun 30 08:56
♑ Jan 11 19:14	♍ Jul 25 02:14
≈ Feb 4 18:44	♎ Aug 19 01:10
♓ Feb 28 18:46	♏ Sep 13 09:04
♈ Mar 24 20:35	♐ Oct 9 08:06
♉ Apr 18 01:07	♑ Nov 5 15:37
♊ May 12 08:44	≈ Dec 7 21:37
♋ Jun 5 19:22	

Mars

Jan 1 0 ♐
♑ Feb 12 05:47
≈ Mar 26 21:05
♓ May 8 04:06
♈ Jun 20 21:08
♉ Aug 12 15:09
R Sep 19 8 ♉
♈ Oct 29 23:09
D Nov 26 25 ♈
♉ Dec 24 07:28

Jupiter

Jan 1 17 ♑
≈ Feb 23 08:52
R May 30 12 ≈
D Sep 28 2 ≈

Saturn

Jan 1 15 ♊
D Feb 13 13 ♊
♋ Aug 1 22:19
R Oct 17 4 ♋

Uranus

Jan 1 22 ♎
R Jan 27 23 ♎
D Jun 26 18 ♎

Neptune

Jan 1 6 ♐
R Mar 9 7 ♐
D Aug 16 4 ♐

Pluto

Jan 1 4 ♎
R Jan 6 4 ♎
D Jun 11 1 ♎

1974

Sun

♒ Jan 20 10:45	♈ Mar 21 00:05	♊ May 21 10:37	♌ Jul 23 05:33	♎ Sep 23 10:01	♐ Nov 22 16:37
♓ Feb 19 00:58	♉ Apr 20 11:19	♋ Jun 21 18:41	♍ Aug 23 12:30	♏ Oct 23 19:11	♑ Dec 22 05:55

Moon

Jan 1 1 ♈	♋ Mar 3 03:00	♎ May 2 23:38	♑ Jul 3 12:19	♈ Sep 3 12:58	♋ Nov 3 23:00
♉ Jan 3 04:37	♌ Mar 5 04:49	♏ May 5 04:43	♒ Jul 6 00:41	♉ Sep 5 22:50	♌ Nov 6 02:30
♊ Jan 5 07:59	♍ Mar 7 05:33	♐ May 7 12:05	♓ Jul 8 13:26	♊ Sep 8 06:36	♍ Nov 8 05:17
♋ Jan 7 08:28	♎ Mar 9 06:51	♑ May 9 22:14	♈ Jul 11 01:10	♋ Sep 10 11:39	♎ Nov 10 07:58
♌ Jan 9 07:42	♏ Mar 11 10:39	♒ May 12 10:33	♉ Jul 13 10:21	♌ Sep 12 13:53	♏ Nov 12 11:23
♍ Jan 11 07:42	♐ Mar 13 18:20	♓ May 14 23:02	♊ Jul 15 15:53	♍ Sep 14 14:12	♐ Nov 14 16:38
♎ Jan 13 10:21	♑ Mar 16 05:41	♈ May 17 09:20	♋ Jul 17 17:56	♎ Sep 16 14:16	♑ Nov 17 00:42
♏ Jan 15 16:53	♒ Mar 18 18:39	♉ May 19 16:09	♌ Jul 19 17:42	♏ Sep 18 16:13	♒ Nov 19 11:38
♐ Jan 18 03:12	♓ Mar 21 06:34	♊ May 21 19:53	♍ Jul 21 17:10	♐ Sep 20 21:45	♓ Nov 22 00:10
♑ Jan 20 15:47	♈ Mar 23 16:03	♋ May 23 21:45	♎ Jul 23 18:18	♑ Sep 23 07:22	♈ Nov 24 11:59
♒ Jan 23 04:50	♉ Mar 25 23:10	♌ May 25 23:12	♏ Jul 25 22:46	♒ Sep 25 19:37	♉ Nov 26 21:04
♓ Jan 25 17:00	♊ Mar 28 04:32	♍ May 28 01:26	♐ Jul 28 07:00	♓ Sep 28 08:15	♊ Nov 29 02:58
♈ Jan 28 03:31	♋ Mar 30 08:39	♎ May 30 05:15	♑ Jul 30 18:10	♈ Sep 30 19:25	♋ Dec 1 06:22
♉ Jan 30 11:41	♌ Apr 1 11:40	♏ Jun 1 11:10	♒ Aug 2 06:46	♉ Oct 3 04:38	♌ Dec 3 08:32
♊ Feb 1 16:53	♍ Apr 3 13:56	♐ Jun 3 19:22	♓ Aug 4 19:27	♊ Oct 5 12:00	♍ Dec 5 10:39
♋ Feb 3 19:06	♎ Apr 5 16:23	♑ Jun 6 05:47	♈ Aug 7 07:14	♋ Oct 7 17:30	♎ Dec 7 13:43
♌ Feb 5 19:11	♏ Apr 7 20:24	♒ Jun 8 18:01	♉ Aug 9 17:13	♌ Oct 9 21:02	♏ Dec 9 18:14
♍ Feb 7 18:51	♐ Apr 10 03:26	♓ Jun 11 06:43	♊ Aug 12 00:15	♍ Oct 11 22:55	♐ Dec 12 00:34
♎ Feb 9 20:10	♑ Apr 12 13:56	♈ Jun 13 17:52	♋ Aug 14 03:48	♎ Oct 14 00:10	♑ Dec 14 09:03
♏ Feb 12 00:58	♒ Apr 15 02:34	♉ Jun 16 01:47	♌ Aug 16 04:26	♏ Oct 16 02:22	♒ Dec 16 19:48
♐ Feb 14 10:01	♓ Apr 17 14:43	♊ Jun 18 05:59	♍ Aug 18 03:43	♐ Oct 18 07:13	♓ Dec 19 08:12
♑ Feb 16 22:15	♈ Apr 20 00:20	♋ Jun 20 07:21	♎ Aug 20 03:44	♑ Oct 20 15:44	♈ Dec 21 20:35
♒ Feb 19 11:20	♉ Apr 22 06:53	♌ Jun 22 07:30	♏ Aug 22 06:37	♒ Oct 23 03:20	♉ Dec 24 06:45
♓ Feb 21 23:15	♊ Apr 24 11:11	♍ Jun 24 08:11	♐ Aug 24 13:33	♓ Oct 25 15:57	♊ Dec 26 13:15
♈ Feb 24 09:13	♋ Apr 26 14:17	♎ Jun 26 10:56	♑ Aug 27 00:15	♈ Oct 28 03:13	♋ Dec 28 16:15
♉ Feb 26 17:11	♌ Apr 28 17:04	♏ Jun 28 16:39	♒ Aug 29 12:52	♉ Oct 30 12:00	♌ Dec 30 17:05
♊ Feb 28 23:10	♍ Apr 30 20:00	♐ Jul 1 01:20	♓ Sep 1 01:29	♊ Nov 1 18:22	

Mercury

Jan 1 5 ♑	D Jul 12 5 ♋
♒ Jan 16 03:53	♌ Aug 5 11:42
♓ Feb 2 22:17	♍ Aug 20 09:03
R Feb 15 11 ♓	♎ Sep 6 06:00
♒ Mar 2 17:52	♏ Sep 27 23:46
D Mar 9 27 ♒	R Oct 13 9 ♏
♓ Mar 17 21:05	♎ Oct 26 23:04
♈ Apr 11 15:12	D Nov 3 24 ♎
♉ Apr 28 03:06	♏ Nov 11 15:49
♊ May 12 04:51	♐ Dec 2 06:17
♋ May 29 08:02	♑ Dec 21 09:16
R Jun 17 13 ♋	

Venus

Jan 1 11 ♒	♊ Jun 25 23:43
R Jan 3 11 ♒	♋ Jul 21 04:34
♑ Jan 29 20:11	♌ Aug 14 23:47
D Feb 13 25 ♑	♍ Sep 8 10:29
♒ Feb 28 14:08	♎ Oct 2 14:29
♓ Apr 6 14:09	♏ Oct 26 14:14
♈ May 4 20:19	♐ Nov 19 11:57
♉ May 31 07:20	♑ Dec 13 09:04

Mars

Jan 1 2 ♉
♊ Feb 27 10:13
♋ Apr 20 08:22
♌ Jun 9 01:05
♍ Jul 27 14:07
♎ Sep 12 19:10
♏ Oct 28 07:03
♐ Dec 10 22:06

Jupiter

Jan 1 14 ♒
♓ Mar 8 11:01
R Jul 7 17 ♓
D Nov 3 7 ♓

Saturn

Jan 1 0 ♋
♊ Jan 7 20:11
D Feb 27 27 ♊
♋ Apr 18 22:42
R Oct 31 18 ♋

Uranus

Jan 1 27 ♎
R Feb 1 27 ♎
D Jul 2 23 ♎
♏ Nov 21 10:30

Neptune

Jan 1 8 ♐
R Mar 12 9 ♐
D Aug 19 6 ♐

Pluto

Jan 1 6 ♎
R Jan 9 6 ♎
D Jun 14 4 ♎

1975

Sun

♒ Jan 20 16:34	♈ Mar 21 05:56	♊ May 21 16:25	♌ Jul 23 11:25	♎ Sep 23 16:00	♐ Nov 22 22:33
♓ Feb 19 06:48	♉ Apr 20 17:07	♋ Jun 22 00:28	♍ Aug 23 18:27	♏ Oct 24 01:09	♑ Dec 22 11:47

Moon

♍ Jan 1 19♌	♏ Mar 1 14:34	♒ May 2 05:34	♉ Jul 3 09:53	♌ Sep 2 23:08	♏ Nov 2 20:08
♍ Jan 1 17:33	♐ Mar 3 19:06	♓ May 4 17:34	♊ Jul 5 18:59	♍ Sep 4 23:29	♐ Nov 4 21:09
♎ Jan 3 19:22	♑ Mar 6 03:40	♈ May 7 06:02	♋ Jul 8 00:22	♎ Sep 6 22:37	♑ Nov 7 00:45
♏ Jan 5 23:38	♒ Mar 8 15:09	♉ May 9 17:02	♌ Jul 10 02:50	♏ Sep 8 22:45	♒ Nov 9 07:58
♐ Jan 8 06:39	♓ Mar 11 03:49	♊ May 12 01:45	♍ Jul 12 03:55	♐ Sep 11 01:39	♓ Nov 11 18:42
♑ Jan 10 15:58	♈ Mar 13 16:17	♋ May 14 08:08	♎ Jul 14 05:20	♑ Sep 13 08:11	♈ Nov 14 07:16
♒ Jan 13 03:02	♉ Mar 16 03:52	♌ May 16 12:39	♏ Jul 16 08:22	♒ Sep 15 17:51	♉ Nov 16 19:37
♓ Jan 15 15:22	♊ Mar 18 13:43	♍ May 18 15:45	♐ Jul 18 13:31	♓ Sep 18 05:32	♊ Nov 19 06:15
♈ Jan 18 04:04	♋ Mar 20 20:47	♎ May 20 18:04	♑ Jul 20 20:45	♈ Sep 20 18:06	♋ Nov 21 14:37
♉ Jan 20 15:21	♌ Mar 23 00:31	♏ May 22 20:25	♒ Jul 23 05:56	♉ Sep 23 06:43	♌ Nov 23 20:47
♊ Jan 22 23:22	♍ Mar 25 01:21	♐ May 24 23:51	♓ Jul 25 16:57	♊ Sep 25 18:13	♍ Nov 26 01:04
♋ Jan 25 03:21	♎ Mar 27 00:50	♑ May 27 05:31	♈ Jul 28 05:27	♋ Sep 28 03:06	♎ Nov 28 03:47
♌ Jan 27 04:00	♏ Mar 29 01:07	♒ May 29 14:09	♉ Jul 30 17:54	♌ Sep 30 08:20	♏ Nov 30 05:37
♍ Jan 29 03:14	♐ Mar 31 04:09	♓ Jun 1 01:31	♊ Aug 2 04:02	♍ Oct 2 10:03	♐ Dec 2 07:32
♎ Jan 31 03:14	♑ Apr 2 11:09	♈ Jun 3 14:00	♋ Aug 4 10:16	♎ Oct 4 09:39	♑ Dec 4 10:58
♏ Feb 2 05:53	♒ Apr 4 21:45	♉ Jun 6 01:17	♌ Aug 6 12:44	♏ Oct 6 09:07	♒ Dec 6 17:12
♐ Feb 4 12:09	♓ Apr 7 10:16	♊ Jun 8 09:48	♍ Aug 8 12:53	♐ Oct 8 08:20	♓ Dec 9 02:52
♑ Feb 6 21:42	♈ Apr 9 22:44	♋ Jun 10 15:22	♎ Aug 10 12:50	♑ Oct 10 15:28	♈ Dec 11 15:05
♒ Feb 9 09:17	♉ Apr 12 09:53	♌ Jun 12 18:45	♏ Aug 12 14:30	♒ Oct 13 00:09	♉ Dec 14 03:39
♓ Feb 11 21:45	♊ Apr 14 19:14	♍ Jun 14 21:10	♐ Aug 14 18:59	♓ Oct 15 11:39	♊ Dec 16 14:13
♈ Feb 14 10:22	♋ Apr 17 02:27	♎ Jun 16 23:40	♑ Aug 17 02:24	♈ Oct 18 00:20	♋ Dec 18 21:44
♉ Feb 16 22:08	♌ Apr 19 07:14	♏ Jun 19 02:59	♒ Aug 19 12:08	♉ Oct 20 12:43	♌ Dec 21 02:54
♊ Feb 19 07:34	♍ Apr 21 09:43	♐ Jun 21 07:34	♓ Aug 21 23:32	♊ Oct 22 23:51	♍ Dec 23 06:27
♋ Feb 21 13:20	♎ Apr 23 10:42	♑ Jun 23 13:55	♈ Aug 24 12:02	♋ Oct 25 08:57	♎ Dec 25 09:27
♌ Feb 23 15:13	♏ Apr 25 11:39	♒ Jun 25 22:32	♉ Aug 27 00:45	♌ Oct 27 15:20	♏ Dec 27 12:27
♍ Feb 25 14:37	♐ Apr 27 14:19	♓ Jun 28 09:32	♊ Aug 29 11:53	♍ Oct 29 18:46	♐ Dec 29 15:52
♎ Feb 27 13:38	♑ Apr 29 20:09	♈ Jun 30 22:02	♋ Aug 31 19:34	♎ Oct 31 19:54	♑ Dec 31 20:16

Mercury

Jan 1 16♑	♋ Jul 12 08:55
♒ Jan 8 22:03	♌ Jul 28 08:07
R Jan 30 26♒	♍ Aug 12 06:12
D Feb 20 10♒	♎ Aug 30 17:14
♓ Mar 16 11:50	R Sep 26 23♎
♈ Apr 4 12:26	D Oct 18 8♎
♉ Apr 19 17:18	♏ Nov 6 09:01
♊ May 4 11:57	♐ Nov 25 01:48
R May 29 23♊	♑ Dec 14 04:07
D Jun 22 15♊	

Venus

Jan 1 23♑	♍ Jul 9 11:13
♒ Jan 6 06:38	R Aug 6 11♍
♓ Jan 30 06:02	♌ Sep 2 15:01
♈ Feb 23 09:52	D Sep 18 25♌
♉ Mar 19 21:42	♍ Oct 4 05:37
♊ Apr 13 22:25	♎ Nov 9 13:55
♋ May 9 20:14	♏ Dec 7 00:31
♌ Jun 6 11:00	

Mars

Jan 1 14♐	
♑ Jan 21 18:45	
♒ Mar 3 05:28	
♓ Apr 11 19:10	
♈ May 21 08:08	
♉ Jul 1 04:02	
♊ Aug 14 20:40	
♋ Oct 17 09:20	
R Nov 6 2♋	
♊ Nov 25 18:31	

Jupiter

Jan 1 13♓
♈ Mar 18 16:34
R Aug 14 24♈
D Dec 10 14♈

Saturn

Jan 1 15♋
D Mar 14 11♋
♌ Sep 17 05:10
R Nov 14 2♌

Uranus

Jan 1 1♏
R Feb 6 2♏
♎ May 1 17:18
D Jul 7 28♎
♏ Sep 8 06:24

Neptune

Jan 1 10♐
R Mar 14 11♐
D Aug 21 9♐

Pluto

Jan 1 9♎
R Jan 11 9♎
D Jun 17 6♎

1976

Sun

♒ Jan 20 22:26	♈ Mar 20 11:47	♊ May 20 22:19	♌ Jul 22 17:18	♎ Sep 22 21:49	♐ Nov 22 04:22
♓ Feb 19 12:40	♉ Apr 19 22:59	♋ Jun 21 06:22	♍ Aug 23 00:20	♏ Oct 23 06:59	♑ Dec 21 17:36

Moon

Jan 1 2♑	♈ Mar 2 14:21	♋ May 3 14:54	♎ Jul 3 19:34	♑ Sep 2 16:29	♈ Nov 3 04:46
♒ Jan 3 02:33	♉ Mar 5 03:18	♌ May 5 23:09	♏ Jul 5 22:33	♒ Sep 4 22:20	♉ Nov 5 17:22
♓ Jan 5 11:35	♊ Mar 7 15:55	♍ May 8 04:21	♐ Jul 8 01:05	♓ Sep 7 06:12	♊ Nov 8 06:21
♈ Jan 7 23:20	♋ Mar 10 01:58	♎ May 10 06:40	♑ Jul 10 03:49	♈ Sep 9 16:17	♋ Nov 10 18:27
♉ Jan 10 12:09	♌ Mar 12 07:55	♏ May 12 07:03	♒ Jul 12 07:52	♉ Sep 12 04:30	♌ Nov 13 04:36
♊ Jan 12 23:19	♍ Mar 14 09:59	♐ May 14 07:04	♓ Jul 14 14:36	♊ Sep 14 17:32	♍ Nov 15 11:46
♋ Jan 15 07:01	♎ Mar 16 09:44	♑ May 16 08:32	♈ Jul 17 00:40	♋ Sep 17 05:07	♎ Nov 17 15:34
♌ Jan 17 11:15	♏ Mar 18 09:18	♒ May 18 13:03	♉ Jul 19 13:11	♌ Sep 19 13:10	♏ Nov 19 16:31
♍ Jan 19 13:25	♐ Mar 20 10:33	♓ May 20 21:26	♊ Jul 22 01:39	♍ Sep 21 17:15	♐ Nov 21 16:04
♎ Jan 21 15:10	♑ Mar 22 14:47	♈ May 23 09:06	♋ Jul 24 11:39	♎ Sep 23 18:27	♑ Nov 23 16:04
♏ Jan 23 17:47	♒ Mar 24 22:20	♉ May 25 22:07	♌ Jul 26 18:19	♏ Sep 25 18:34	♒ Nov 25 18:29
♐ Jan 25 21:50	♓ Mar 27 08:34	♊ May 28 10:22	♍ Jul 28 22:24	♐ Sep 27 19:21	♓ Nov 30 11:01
♑ Jan 28 03:23	♈ Mar 29 20:37	♋ May 30 20:38	♎ Jul 31 01:13	♑ Sep 29 22:12	♉ Dec 2 23:40
♒ Jan 30 10:33	♉ Apr 1 09:34	♌ Jun 2 04:37	♏ Aug 2 03:54	♒ Oct 2 03:49	♊ Dec 5 12:39
♓ Feb 1 19:47	♊ Apr 3 22:15	♍ Jun 4 10:21	♐ Aug 4 07:04	♓ Oct 4 12:09	♋ Dec 8 00:21
♈ Feb 4 07:16	♋ Apr 6 09:05	♎ Jun 6 13:59	♑ Aug 6 10:54	♈ Oct 6 22:50	♌ Dec 10 10:11
♉ Feb 6 20:13	♌ Apr 8 16:36	♏ Jun 8 15:58	♒ Aug 8 15:57	♉ Oct 9 11:11	♍ Dec 12 17:55
♊ Feb 9 08:15	♍ Apr 10 20:15	♐ Jun 10 17:07	♓ Aug 10 23:00	♊ Oct 12 00:15	♎ Dec 14 23:13
♋ Feb 11 16:58	♎ Apr 12 20:54	♑ Jun 12 18:45	♈ Aug 13 08:49	♋ Oct 14 12:23	♏ Dec 17 02:01
♌ Feb 13 21:32	♏ Apr 14 20:14	♒ Jun 14 22:30	♉ Aug 15 21:05	♌ Oct 16 21:49	♐ Dec 19 02:54
♍ Feb 15 22:58	♐ Apr 16 20:07	♓ Jun 17 05:42	♊ Aug 18 09:53	♍ Oct 19 03:24	♑ Dec 21 03:12
♎ Feb 17 23:14	♑ Apr 18 22:43	♈ Jun 19 16:31	♋ Aug 20 20:34	♎ Oct 21 05:27	♒ Dec 23 04:49
♏ Feb 20 00:14	♒ Apr 21 04:48	♉ Jun 22 05:20	♌ Aug 23 03:30	♏ Oct 23 05:16	♓ Dec 25 09:36
♐ Feb 22 03:18	♓ Apr 23 14:28	♊ Jun 24 17:37	♍ Aug 25 07:04	♐ Oct 25 04:49	♈ Dec 27 18:31
♑ Feb 24 08:55	♈ Apr 26 02:37	♋ Jun 27 03:28	♎ Aug 27 08:41	♑ Oct 27 05:55	♉ Dec 30 06:43
♒ Feb 26 16:49	♉ Apr 28 15:38	♌ Jun 29 10:39	♏ Aug 29 10:05	♒ Oct 29 10:05	
♓ Feb 29 02:41	♊ May 1 04:05	♍ Jul 1 15:46	♐ Aug 31 12:27	♓ Oct 31 17:53	

Mercury

Jan 1 27♑	♊ Jun 13 18:52
♒ Jan 2 19:54	♋ Jul 4 14:22
R Jan 14 10♒	♌ Jul 18 19:37
♑ Jan 25 01:14	♍ Aug 3 16:37
D Feb 3 23♑	♎ Aug 25 21:06
♒ Feb 15 19:16	R Sep 8 7♎
♓ Mar 9 12:05	♍ Sep 21 07:10
♈ Mar 26 15:39	D Oct 1 22♍
♉ Apr 10 09:29	♎ Oct 10 14:47
♊ Apr 29 23:38	♏ Oct 29 04:53
R May 9 3♊	♐ Nov 16 19:02
♉ May 19 19:05	♑ Dec 6 09:21
D Jun 2 24♉	R Dec 28 24♑

Venus

Jan 1 29♏	♋ Jun 20 13:56
♐ Jan 1 12:18	♌ Jul 14 23:37
♑ Jan 26 06:09	♍ Aug 8 08:37
♒ Feb 19 16:50	♎ Sep 1 17:45
♓ Mar 15 00:59	♏ Sep 26 04:15
♈ Apr 8 08:55	♐ Oct 20 17:19
♉ May 2 17:46	♑ Nov 14 10:38
♊ May 27 03:43	♒ Dec 9 12:51

Mars

Jan 1 17♊
D Jan 20 14♊
♋ Mar 18 13:24
♌ May 16 11:18
♍ Jul 6 23:30
♎ Aug 24 05:59
♏ Oct 8 20:21
♐ Nov 20 23:55

Jupiter

Jan 1 15♈
♉ Mar 26 10:40
♊ Aug 23 11:36
R Sep 19 1♊
♉ Oct 16 19:13

Saturn

Jan 1 1♌
♋ Jan 14 12:13
D Mar 27 26♋
♌ Jun 5 06:02
R Nov 27 16♌

Uranus

Jan 1 6♏
R Feb 10 7♏
D Jul 11 3♏

Neptune

Jan 1 12♐
R Mar 15 13♐
D Aug 23 11♐

Pluto

Jan 1 11♎
R Jan 14 11♎
D Jun 18 8♎

1977

Sun

♒ Jan 20 04:14	♈ Mar 20 17:41	♊ May 21 04:12	♌ Jul 22 23:04	♎ Sep 23 03:31	♐ Nov 22 10:07
♓ Feb 18 18:30	♉ Apr 20 04:55 .	♋ Jun 21 12:13	♍ Aug 23 06:01	♏ Oct 23 12:43	♑ Dec 21 23:23

Moon

Jan 1 20♉	♌ Mar 2 09:24	♏ May 2 16:24	♌ Jul 2 12:55	♉ Sep 2 00:51	♌ Nov 3 05:04
♊ Jan 1 19:43	♍ Mar 4 15:19	♐ May 4 15:59	♓ Jul 4 15:30	♊ Sep 4 12:26	♍ Nov 5 15:17
♋ Jan 4 07:12	♎ Mar 6 18:35	♑ May 6 15:54	♈ Jul 6 22:03	♋ Sep 7 01:03	♎ Nov 7 21:50
♌ Jan 6 16:21	♏ Mar 8 20:37	♒ May 8 18:00	♉ Jul 9 08:33	♌ Sep 9 12:15	♏ Nov 10 00:42
♍ Jan 8 23:22	♐ Mar 10 22:42	♓ May 10 23:30	♊ Jul 11 21:15	♍ Sep 11 20:35	♐ Nov 12 01:04
♎ Jan 11 04:48	♑ Mar 13 01:39	♈ May 13 08:30	♋ Jul 14 09:49	♎ Sep 14 02:08	♑ Nov 14 00:50
♏ Jan 13 08:44	♒ Mar 15 06:00	♉ May 15 20:05	♌ Jul 16 20:51	♏ Sep 16 05:45	♒ Nov 16 01:59
♐ Jan 15 11:17	♓ Mar 17 12:05	♊ May 18 08:51	♍ Jul 19 05:59	♐ Sep 18 08:28	♓ Nov 18 05:59
♑ Jan 17 13:02	♈ Mar 19 20:22	♋ May 20 21:36	♎ Jul 21 13:09	♑ Sep 20 11:04	♈ Nov 20 13:12
♒ Jan 19 15:12	♉ Mar 22 07:06	♌ May 23 09:14	♏ Jul 23 18:14	♒ Sep 22 14:12	♉ Nov 22 23:10
♓ Jan 21 19:30	♊ Mar 24 19:38	♍ May 25 18:30	♐ Jul 25 21:44	♓ Sep 24 18:29	♊ Nov 25 10:49
♈ Jan 24 03:20	♋ Mar 27 08:16	♎ May 28 00:28	♑ Jul 27 22:14	♈ Sep 27 00:41	♋ Nov 27 23:19
♉ Jan 26 14:40	♌ Mar 29 18:41	♏ May 30 02:57	♒ Jul 29 23:05	♉ Sep 29 09:22	♌ Nov 30 11:53
♊ Jan 29 03:37	♍ Apr 1 01:25	♐ Jun 1 02:54	♓ Aug 1 01:24	♊ Oct 1 20:34	♍ Dec 2 23:06
♋ Jan 31 15:20	♎ Apr 3 04:39	♑ Jun 3 02:08	♈ Aug 3 06:54	♋ Oct 4 09:08	♎ Dec 5 07:17
♌ Feb 3 00:12	♏ Apr 5 05:39	♒ Jun 5 02:43	♉ Aug 5 16:17	♌ Oct 6 20:58	♏ Dec 7 11:34
♍ Feb 5 06:17	♐ Apr 7 06:08	♓ Jun 7 06:36	♊ Aug 8 04:30	♍ Oct 9 05:59	♐ Dec 9 12:22
♎ Feb 7 10:35	♑ Apr 9 07:40	♈ Jun 9 14:35	♋ Aug 10 17:04	♎ Oct 11 11:30	♑ Dec 11 11:25
♏ Feb 9 14:04	♒ Apr 11 11:23	♉ Jun 12 01:56	♌ Aug 13 03:57	♏ Oct 13 14:11	♒ Dec 13 10:59
♐ Feb 11 17:11	♓ Apr 13 17:50	♊ Jun 14 14:50	♍ Aug 15 12:25	♐ Oct 15 15:26	♓ Dec 15 12:05
♑ Feb 13 20:14	♈ Apr 16 02:52	♋ Jun 17 03:28	♎ Aug 17 18:48	♑ Oct 17 16:51	♈ Dec 17 19:10
♒ Feb 15 23:44	♉ Apr 18 14:02	♌ Jun 19 14:54	♏ Aug 19 23:36	♒ Oct 19 19:35	♉ Dec 20 04:53
♓ Feb 18 04:45	♊ Apr 21 02:37	♍ Jun 22 00:28	♐ Aug 22 03:02	♓ Oct 22 00:26	♊ Dec 22 16:52
♈ Feb 20 12:22	♋ Apr 23 15:24	♎ Jun 24 07:35	♑ Aug 24 05:31	♈ Oct 24 07:33	♋ Dec 25 05:30
♉ Feb 22 23:07	♌ Apr 26 02:42	♏ Jun 26 11:41	♒ Aug 26 07:40	♉ Oct 26 16:52	♌ Dec 27 17:52
♊ Feb 25 11:50	♍ Apr 28 10:52	♐ Jun 28 13:02	♓ Aug 28 10:47	♊ Oct 29 04:07	♍ Dec 30 05:14
♋ Feb 28 00:02	♎ Apr 30 15:13	♑ Jun 30 12:47	♈ Aug 30 16:11	♋ Oct 31 16:39	

Mercury

Jan 1 22♑	♍ Jul 28 10:15
D Jan 17 8♑	R Aug 22 20♍
♒ Feb 11 00:03	D Sep 14 7♍
♓ Mar 2 08:12	♎ Oct 4 09:22
♈ Mar 18 11:56	♏ Oct 21 16:22
♉ Apr 3 02:27	♐ Nov 9 17:22
R Apr 20 13♉	♑ Dec 1 06:45
D May 13 4♉	R Dec 12 7♑
♊ Jun 10 21:20	♐ Dec 21 07:15
♋ Jun 26 07:07	D Dec 31 21♐
♌ Jul 10 11:58	

Venus

Jan 1 26♒	♌ Aug 2 19:13
♓ Jan 4 13:04	♌ Aug 28 15:06
♈ Feb 2 05:57	♍ Sep 22 15:05
R Mar 16 24♈	♎ Oct 17 01:38
D Apr 27 8♈	♏ Nov 10 03:52
♉ Jun 6 06:04	♐ Dec 4 01:49
♊ Jul 6 15:04	♑ Dec 27 22:09

Mars

Jan 1 29♐	
♑ Jan 1 00:43	
♒ Feb 9 12:01	
♓ Mar 20 02:24	
♈ Apr 27 15:47	
♉ Jun 6 03:00	
♊ Jul 17 15:05	
♋ Sep 1 00:17	
♌ Oct 26 18:46	
R Dec 12 11♌	

Jupiter

Jan 1 21♉
D Jan 15 21♉
♊ Apr 3 15:50
♋ Aug 20 13:39
R Oct 24 6♋
♊ Dec 30 21:52

Saturn

Jan 1 15♌
D Apr 11 9♌
♍ Nov 17 03:59
R Dec 11 0♍

Uranus

Jan 1 10♏
R Feb 14 11♏
D Jul 16 7♏

Neptune

Jan 1 14♐
R Mar 18 16♐
D Aug 25 13♐

Pluto

Jan 1 14♎
R Jan 16 14♎
D Jun 21 11♎

1978

Sun

♒ Jan 20 10:05	♈ Mar 20 23:33	♊ May 21 10:07	♌ Jul 23 04:58	♎ Sep 23 09:27	♐ Nov 22 16:07
♓ Feb 19 00:22	♉ Apr 20 10:49	♋ Jun 21 18:08	♍ Aug 23 11:57	♏ Oct 23 18:41	♑ Dec 22 05:23

Moon

Jan 1 22 ♍	♐ Mar 1 13:02	♓ May 1 09:00	♊ Jul 1 19:37	♍ Sep 1 20:46	♐ Nov 2 10:03
♎ Jan 1 14:32	♑ Mar 3 15:58	♈ May 3 14:27	♋ Jul 4 07:33	♎ Sep 4 07:15	♑ Nov 4 12:41
♏ Jan 3 20:36	♒ Mar 5 17:51	♉ May 5 21:52	♌ Jul 6 20:13	♏ Sep 6 15:38	♒ Nov 6 15:03
♐ Jan 5 23:04	♓ Mar 7 19:46	♊ May 8 07:19	♍ Jul 9 08:44	♐ Sep 8 21:39	♓ Nov 8 18:05
♑ Jan 7 22:54	♈ Mar 9 23:09	♋ May 10 18:42	♎ Jul 11 19:48	♑ Sep 11 01:20	♈ Nov 10 22:11
♒ Jan 9 22:05	♉ Mar 12 05:17	♌ May 13 07:16	♏ Jul 14 03:46	♒ Sep 13 03:08	♉ Nov 13 03:35
♓ Jan 11 22:51	♊ Mar 14 14:49	♍ May 15 19:14	♐ Jul 16 07:50	♓ Sep 15 04:09	♊ Nov 15 10:45
♈ Jan 14 03:04	♋ Mar 17 02:49	♎ May 18 04:24	♑ Jul 18 08:33	♈ Sep 17 05:50	♋ Nov 17 20:15
♉ Jan 16 11:31	♌ Mar 19 15:13	♏ May 20 09:39	♒ Jul 20 07:42	♉ Sep 19 09:43	♌ Nov 20 08:09
♊ Jan 18 23:07	♍ Mar 22 01:50	♐ May 22 11:31	♓ Jul 22 07:26	♊ Sep 21 16:55	♍ Nov 22 20:57
♋ Jan 21 11:51	♎ Mar 24 09:42	♑ May 24 11:41	♈ Jul 24 09:45	♋ Sep 24 03:31	♎ Nov 25 08:07
♌ Jan 24 00:02	♏ Mar 26 15:00	♒ May 26 12:09	♉ Jul 26 15:50	♌ Sep 26 16:02	♏ Nov 27 15:39
♍ Jan 26 10:55	♐ Mar 28 18:37	♓ May 28 14:37	♊ Jul 29 01:30	♍ Sep 29 04:10	♐ Nov 29 19:24
♎ Jan 28 20:08	♑ Mar 30 21:23	♈ May 30 19:52	♋ Jul 31 13:29	♎ Oct 1 14:16	♑ Dec 1 20:43
♏ Jan 31 03:03	♒ Apr 2 00:04	♉ Jun 2 03:49	♌ Aug 3 02:10	♏ Oct 3 21:47	♒ Dec 3 21:36
♐ Feb 2 07:13	♓ Apr 4 03:21	♊ Jun 4 13:53	♍ Aug 5 14:29	♐ Oct 6 03:06	♓ Dec 5 23:37
♑ Feb 4 08:50	♈ Apr 6 07:51	♋ Jun 7 01:30	♎ Aug 8 01:30	♑ Oct 8 06:52	♈ Dec 8 03:40
♒ Feb 6 09:04	♉ Apr 8 14:21	♌ Jun 9 14:07	♏ Aug 10 10:11	♒ Oct 10 09:43	♉ Dec 10 09:50
♓ Feb 8 09:47	♊ Apr 10 23:28	♍ Jun 12 02:35	♐ Aug 12 15:43	♓ Oct 12 12:13	♊ Dec 12 17:55
♈ Feb 10 12:57	♋ Apr 13 10:58	♎ Jun 14 12:55	♑ Aug 14 18:02	♈ Oct 14 15:05	♋ Dec 15 03:49
♉ Feb 12 19:51	♌ Apr 15 23:31	♏ Jun 16 19:29	♒ Aug 16 18:15	♉ Oct 16 19:22	♌ Dec 17 15:38
♊ Feb 15 06:23	♍ Apr 18 10:44	♐ Jun 18 22:01	♓ Aug 18 18:04	♊ Oct 19 02:06	♍ Dec 20 04:34
♋ Feb 17 18:55	♎ Apr 20 18:52	♑ Jun 20 21:51	♈ Aug 20 19:30	♋ Oct 21 11:53	♎ Dec 22 16:39
♌ Feb 20 07:09	♏ Apr 22 23:38	♒ Jun 22 21:07	♉ Aug 23 00:05	♌ Oct 24 00:03	♏ Dec 25 01:32
♍ Feb 22 17:39	♐ Apr 25 01:59	♓ Jun 24 21:57	♊ Aug 25 08:32	♍ Oct 26 12:31	♐ Dec 27 06:07
♎ Feb 25 02:04	♑ Apr 27 03:27	♈ Jun 27 01:52	♋ Aug 27 19:58	♎ Oct 28 22:51	♑ Dec 29 07:15
♏ Feb 27 08:28	♒ Apr 29 05:28	♉ Jun 29 09:21	♌ Aug 30 08:39	♏ Oct 31 05:53	♒ Dec 31 06:52

Mercury

Jan 1 21 ♐	♍ Jul 27 06:21
♑ Jan 13 20:20	R Aug 4 3 ♍
♒ Feb 4 15:54	♌ Aug 13 07:11
♓ Feb 22 16:11	D Aug 28 20 ♌
♈ Mar 10 12:08	♍ Sep 9 19:27
R Apr 1 25 ♈	♎ Sep 26 16:42
D Apr 25 14 ♈	♏ Oct 14 05:35
♉ May 16 08:19	♐ Nov 3 07:43
♊ Jun 3 15:27	R Nov 25 21 ♐
♋ Jun 17 15:49	D Dec 15 5 ♐
♌ Jul 2 22:30	

Venus

Jan 1 5 ♑
♒ Jan 20 18:30
♓ Feb 13 16:07
♈ Mar 9 16:29
♉ Apr 2 21:14
♊ Apr 27 07:52
♋ May 22 02:04
♌ Jun 16 06:21
♍ Jul 12 02:16
♎ Aug 8 03:09
♏ Sep 7 05:07
R Oct 18 22 ♏
D Nov 28 7 ♏

Mars

Jan 1 8 ♌
♋ Jan 26 02:12
D Mar 2 22 ♋
♌ Apr 10 19:07
♍ Jun 14 02:43
♎ Aug 4 09:03
♏ Sep 19 20:51
♐ Nov 2 01:19
♑ Dec 12 17:33

Jupiter

Jan 1 29 ♊
D Feb 20 26 ♊
♋ Apr 12 01:34
♌ Sep 5 09:28
R Nov 25 9 ♌

Saturn

Jan 1 0 ♍
♌ Jan 4 22:09
D Apr 25 23 ♌
♍ Jul 26 13:15
R Dec 24 13 ♍

Uranus

Jan 1 15 ♏
R Feb 19 16 ♏
D Jul 21 12 ♏

Neptune

Jan 1 16 ♐
R Mar 20 18 ♐
D Aug 28 15 ♐

Pluto

Jan 1 16 ♎
R Jan 19 16 ♎
D Jun 24 13 ♎

1979

Sun

♒ Jan 20 16:03	♈ Mar 21 05:23	♊ May 21 15:54	♌ Jul 23 10:49	♎ Sep 23 15:17	♐ Nov 22 21:54
♓ Feb 19 06:16	♉ Apr 20 16:36	♋ Jun 21 23:57	♍ Aug 23 17:46	♏ Oct 24 00:28	♑ Dec 22 11:11

Moon

Jan 1 10♒	♉ Mar 2 07:08	♌ May 3 01:56	♏ Jul 4 05:58	♒ Sep 3 13:58	♉ Nov 3 11:15
♓ Jan 2 07:07	♊ Mar 4 12:58	♍ May 5 14:41	♐ Jul 6 12:55	♓ Sep 5 14:02	♊ Nov 5 13:26
♈ Jan 4 09:41	♋ Mar 6 22:34	♎ May 8 02:47	♑ Jul 8 16:07	♈ Sep 7 13:29	♋ Nov 7 18:23
♉ Jan 6 15:18	♌ Mar 9 10:48	♏ May 10 12:09	♒ Jul 10 16:58	♉ Sep 9 14:13	♌ Nov 10 03:15
♊ Jan 8 23:42	♍ Mar 11 23:42	♐ May 12 18:24	♓ Jul 12 17:22	♊ Sep 11 17:54	♍ Nov 12 15:20
♋ Jan 11 10:14	♎ Mar 14 11:41	♑ May 14 22:26	♈ Jul 14 18:57	♋ Sep 14 01:27	♎ Nov 15 04:16
♌ Jan 13 22:15	♏ Mar 16 21:49	♒ May 17 01:26	♉ Jul 16 22:43	♌ Sep 16 12:25	♏ Nov 17 15:29
♍ Jan 16 11:10	♐ Mar 19 05:37	♓ May 19 04:19	♊ Jul 19 04:59	♍ Sep 19 01:15	♐ Nov 19 23:57
♎ Jan 18 23:40	♑ Mar 21 10:55	♈ May 21 07:30	♋ Jul 21 13:39	♎ Sep 21 14:11	♑ Nov 22 06:01
♏ Jan 21 09:50	♒ Mar 23 13:52	♉ May 23 11:20	♌ Jul 24 00:29	♏ Sep 24 01:53	♒ Nov 24 10:36
♐ Jan 23 16:07	♓ Mar 25 16:29	♊ May 25 16:29	♍ Jul 26 13:01	♐ Sep 26 11:36	♓ Nov 26 14:17
♑ Jan 25 18:27	♈ Mar 27 15:47	♋ May 27 23:51	♎ Jul 29 02:06	♑ Sep 28 18:40	♈ Nov 28 17:16
♒ Jan 27 18:12	♉ Mar 29 17:37	♌ May 30 10:07	♏ Jul 31 13:47	♒ Sep 30 22:49	♉ Nov 30 19:54
♓ Jan 29 17:25	♊ Mar 31 22:07	♍ Jun 1 22:40	♐ Aug 2 22:06	♓ Oct 3 00:23	♊ Dec 2 23:02
♈ Jan 31 18:10	♋ Apr 3 06:23	♎ Jun 4 11:12	♑ Aug 5 02:22	♈ Oct 5 00:27	♋ Dec 5 04:02
♉ Feb 2 22:03	♌ Apr 5 17:58	♏ Jun 6 21:04	♒ Aug 7 03:28	♉ Oct 7 00:45	♌ Dec 7 12:08
♊ Feb 5 05:33	♍ Apr 8 06:51	♐ Jun 9 03:15	♓ Aug 9 03:05	♊ Oct 9 03:06	♍ Dec 9 23:33
♋ Feb 7 16:06	♎ Apr 10 18:45	♑ Jun 11 06:23	♈ Aug 11 03:10	♋ Oct 11 09:08	♎ Dec 12 12:28
♌ Feb 10 04:26	♏ Apr 13 04:15	♒ Jun 13 08:07	♉ Aug 13 05:21	♌ Oct 13 19:11	♏ Dec 15 00:07
♍ Feb 12 17:17	♐ Apr 15 11:17	♓ Jun 15 09:55	♊ Aug 15 10:42	♍ Oct 16 07:51	♐ Dec 17 08:37
♎ Feb 15 05:37	♑ Apr 17 16:23	♈ Jun 17 12:52	♋ Aug 17 19:16	♎ Oct 18 20:44	♑ Dec 19 13:54
♏ Feb 17 16:11	♒ Apr 19 20:01	♉ Jun 19 17:17	♌ Aug 20 06:28	♏ Oct 21 08:02	♒ Dec 21 17:13
♐ Feb 19 23:51	♓ Apr 21 22:42	♊ Jun 21 23:22	♍ Aug 22 19:11	♐ Oct 23 17:10	♓ Dec 23 19:51
♑ Feb 22 04:01	♈ Apr 24 00:51	♋ Jun 24 07:25	♎ Aug 25 08:14	♑ Oct 26 00:12	♈ Dec 25 22:40
♒ Feb 24 05:12	♉ Apr 26 03:27	♌ Jun 26 17:46	♏ Aug 27 20:13	♒ Oct 28 05:16	♉ Dec 28 02:08
♓ Feb 26 04:52	♊ Apr 28 07:49	♍ Jun 29 06:14	♐ Aug 30 05:38	♓ Oct 30 08:29	♊ Dec 30 06:31
♈ Feb 28 04:54	♋ Apr 30 15:10	♎ Jul 1 19:07	♑ Sep 1 11:34	♈ Nov 1 10:08	

Mercury

Jan 1 19♐	♌ Jun 27 10:01
♑ Jan 8 22:45	R Jul 17 15♌
♒ Jan 28 12:51	D Aug 11 3♌
♓ Feb 14 20:40	♍ Sep 2 21:28
♈ Mar 3 21:24	♎ Sep 18 18:59
R Mar 15 8♈	♏ Oct 7 03:58
♓ Mar 28 10:40	♐ Oct 30 07:04
D Apr 7 25♓	R Nov 9 6♐
♈ Apr 17 12:44	♏ Nov 18 03:05
♉ May 10 22:06	D Nov 29 18♏
♊ May 26 07:44	♐ Dec 12 13:35
♋ Jun 9 06:27	

Venus

Jan 1 24♏	♋ Jul 6 09:01
♐ Jan 7 06:42	♌ Jul 30 20:07
♑ Feb 5 09:16	♍ Aug 24 03:16
♒ Mar 3 17:18	♎ Sep 17 07:22
♓ Mar 29 03:20	♏ Oct 11 09:47
♈ Apr 23 04:05	♐ Nov 4 11:49
♉ May 18 00:29	♑ Nov 28 14:16
♊ Jun 11 18:13	♒ Dec 22 18:30

Mars

Jan 1 14♑
♒ Jan 20 17:07
♓ Feb 27 20:29
♈ Apr 7 01:12
♉ May 16 04:32
♊ Jun 26 01:53
♋ Aug 8 13:28
♌ Sep 24 21:16
♍ Nov 19 21:29

Jupiter

Jan 1 6♌
♋ Feb 28 20:56
D Mar 26 29♋
♌ Apr 20 10:40
♍ Sep 29 10:57
R Dec 26 10♍

Saturn

Jan 1 13♍
D May 9 7♍

Uranus

Jan 1 19♏
R Feb 24 20♏
D Jul 26 16♏

Neptune

Jan 1 18♐
R Mar 23 20♐
D Aug 30 17♐

Pluto

Jan 1 19♎
R Jan 21 19♎
D Jun 27 16♎

1980

Sun

♒ Jan 20 21:49	♈ Mar 20 11:10	♊ May 20 21:43	♌ Jul 22 16:43	♎ Sep 22 21:09	♐ Nov 22 03:41
♓ Feb 19 12:01	♉ Apr 19 22:23	♋ Jun 21 05:47	♍ Aug 22 23:40	♏ Oct 23 06:18	♑ Dec 21 16:55

Moon

Jan 1 23♊	♍ Feb 29 21:52	♐ May 1 22:22	♓ Jul 2 05:49	♊ Sep 1 01:50	♍ Nov 1 12:19
♋ Jan 1 12:29	♎ Mar 3 10:39	♑ May 4 07:14	♈ Jul 4 08:46	♋ Sep 3 06:40	♎ Nov 4 00:31
♌ Jan 3 20:46	♏ Mar 5 23:22	♒ May 6 14:04	♉ Jul 6 11:31	♌ Sep 5 14:21	♏ Nov 6 13:19
♍ Jan 6 07:49	♐ Mar 8 10:38	♓ May 8 18:34	♊ Jul 8 14:34	♍ Sep 8 00:30	♐ Nov 9 01:26
♎ Jan 8 20:37	♑ Mar 10 19:02	♈ May 10 20:45	♋ Jul 10 18:45	♎ Sep 10 12:22	♑ Nov 11 12:16
♏ Jan 11 08:56	♒ Mar 12 23:45	♉ May 12 21:24	♌ Jul 13 01:03	♏ Sep 13 01:06	♒ Nov 13 21:09
♐ Jan 13 18:18	♓ Mar 15 01:10	♊ May 14 22:07	♍ Jul 15 10:11	♐ Sep 15 13:28	♓ Nov 16 03:21
♑ Jan 15 23:52	♈ Mar 17 00:42	♋ May 17 00:52	♎ Jul 17 21:54	♑ Sep 17 23:44	♈ Nov 18 06:22
♒ Jan 18 02:24	♉ Mar 19 00:14	♌ May 19 07:14	♏ Jul 20 10:33	♒ Sep 20 06:30	♉ Nov 20 06:50
♓ Jan 20 03:34	♊ Mar 21 01:48	♍ May 21 17:33	♐ Jul 22 21:43	♓ Sep 22 09:26	♊ Nov 22 06:06
♈ Jan 22 04:52	♋ Mar 23 06:55	♎ May 24 06:10	♑ Jul 25 05:45	♈ Sep 24 09:38	♋ Nov 24 07:19
♉ Jan 24 07:31	♌ Mar 25 15:59	♏ May 26 18:37	♒ Jul 27 10:34	♉ Sep 26 08:54	♌ Nov 26 11:22
♊ Jan 26 12:10	♍ Mar 28 03:51	♐ May 29 05:05	♓ Jul 29 13:10	♊ Sep 28 09:21	♍ Nov 28 19:37
♋ Jan 28 19:03	♎ Mar 30 16:50	♑ May 31 13:14	♈ Jul 31 14:54	♋ Sep 30 12:46	♎ Dec 1 07:13
♌ Jan 31 04:08	♏ Apr 2 05:21	♒ Jun 2 19:30	♉ Aug 2 16:54	♌ Oct 2 19:56	♏ Dec 3 20:00
♍ Feb 2 15:21	♐ Apr 4 16:34	♓ Jun 5 00:09	♊ Aug 4 20:10	♍ Oct 5 06:19	♐ Dec 6 07:57
♎ Feb 5 04:05	♑ Apr 7 01:43	♈ Jun 7 03:23	♋ Aug 7 01:11	♎ Oct 7 18:30	♑ Dec 8 18:12
♏ Feb 7 16:46	♒ Apr 9 07:59	♉ Jun 9 05:30	♌ Aug 9 08:23	♏ Oct 10 07:14	♒ Dec 11 02:36
♐ Feb 10 03:20	♓ Apr 11 11:08	♊ Jun 11 07:23	♍ Aug 11 17:55	♐ Oct 12 19:36	♓ Dec 13 09:03
♑ Feb 12 10:12	♈ Apr 13 11:40	♋ Jun 13 10:30	♎ Aug 14 05:32	♑ Oct 15 06:37	♈ Dec 15 13:22
♒ Feb 14 13:20	♉ Apr 15 11:11	♌ Jun 15 16:22	♏ Aug 16 18:15	♒ Oct 17 14:54	♉ Dec 17 15:36
♓ Feb 16 13:54	♊ Apr 17 11:41	♍ Jun 18 01:47	♐ Aug 19 06:07	♓ Oct 19 19:31	♊ Dec 19 16:39
♈ Feb 18 13:43	♋ Apr 19 15:12	♎ Jun 20 13:55	♑ Aug 21 15:12	♈ Oct 21 20:42	♋ Dec 21 18:03
♉ Feb 20 14:35	♌ Apr 21 22:52	♏ Jun 23 02:27	♒ Aug 23 20:33	♉ Oct 23 19:55	♌ Dec 23 21:34
♊ Feb 22 17:59	♍ Apr 24 10:12	♐ Jun 25 13:03	♓ Aug 25 22:44	♊ Oct 25 19:17	♍ Dec 26 04:32
♋ Feb 25 00:35	♎ Apr 26 23:10	♑ Jun 27 20:45	♈ Aug 27 23:11	♋ Oct 27 21:00	♎ Dec 28 15:04
♌ Feb 27 10:10	♏ Apr 29 11:35	♒ Jun 30 02:04	♉ Aug 29 23:40	♌ Oct 30 02:38	♏ Dec 31 03:36

Mercury

Jan 1 27♐	R Jun 28 25♋
♑ Jan 2 08:02	D Jul 22 16♋
♒ Jan 21 02:18	♌ Aug 9 03:16
♓ Feb 7 08:15	♍ Aug 24 18:45
R Feb 26 21♓	♎ Sep 10 02:13
D Mar 19 8♓	♏ Sep 30 01:09
♈ Apr 14 15:53	R Oct 23 19♏
♉ May 2 10:52	D Nov 12 3♏
♊ May 16 17:07	♐ Dec 5 19:47
♋ May 31 22:28	♑ Dec 25 04:46

Venus

Jan 1 11♒	D Jul 6 16♊
♓ Jan 16 03:34	♋ Aug 6 14:25
♈ Feb 9 23:39	♌ Sep 7 17:54
♉ Mar 6 18:55	♍ Oct 4 23:06
♊ Apr 3 19:50	♎ Oct 30 10:36
♋ May 12 20:56	♏ Nov 24 01:34
R May 24 2♋	♐ Dec 18 06:21
♊ Jun 5 05:33	

Mars

Jan 1 13♍
R Jan 16 15♍
♌ Mar 11 20:36
D Apr 6 25♌
♍ May 4 02:52
♎ Jul 10 18:03
♏ Aug 29 05:53
♐ Oct 12 06:29
♑ Nov 22 01:34
♒ Dec 30 22:23

Jupiter

Jan 1 10♍
D Apr 26 0♍
♎ Oct 27 10:19

Saturn

Jan 1 26♍
R Jan 6 27♍
D May 22 20♍
♎ Sep 21 12:00

Uranus

Jan 1 24♏
R Feb 29 25♏
D Jul 30 21♏

Neptune

Jan 1 20♐
R Mar 24 22♐
D Aug 31 19♐

Pluto

Jan 1 21♎
R Jan 24 21♎
D Jun 28 18♎

1981

Sun

♒ Jan 20 03:36	♈ Mar 20 17:00	♊ May 21 03:37	♌ Jul 22 22:36	♎ Sep 23 03:03	♐ Nov 22 09:35	
♓ Feb 18 17:51	♉ Apr 20 04:15	♋ Jun 21 11:41	♍ Aug 23 05:36	♏ Oct 23 12:12	♑ Dec 21 22:50	

Moon

♏ Jan 1 10	♒ Mar 3 03:50	♉ May 3 07:00	♌ Jul 3 04:47	♏ Sep 2 21:10	♒ Nov 4 00:50
♐ Jan 2 15:42	♓ Mar 5 08:13	♊ May 5 06:01	♍ Jul 5 09:25	♐ Sep 5 09:23	♓ Nov 6 09:51
♑ Jan 5 01:40	♈ Mar 7 09:48	♋ May 7 06:18	♎ Jul 7 17:42	♑ Sep 7 21:48	♈ Nov 8 14:38
♒ Jan 7 09:13	♉ Mar 9 10:23	♌ May 9 09:41	♏ Jul 10 05:01	♒ Sep 10 07:58	♉ Nov 10 15:45
♓ Jan 9 14:42	♊ Mar 11 11:42	♍ May 11 16:55	♐ Jul 12 17:35	♓ Sep 12 14:34	♊ Nov 12 15:00
♈ Jan 11 18:44	♋ Mar 13 15:05	♎ May 14 03:24	♑ Jul 15 05:19	♈ Sep 14 17:56	♋ Nov 14 14:37
♉ Jan 13 21:45	♌ Mar 15 21:02	♏ May 16 15:38	♒ Jul 17 15:01	♉ Sep 16 19:30	♌ Nov 16 16:31
♊ Jan 16 00:17	♍ Mar 18 05:19	♐ May 19 04:13	♓ Jul 19 22:26	♊ Sep 18 20:59	♍ Nov 18 21:52
♋ Jan 18 03:07	♎ Mar 20 15:30	♑ May 21 16:21	♈ Jul 22 03:44	♋ Sep 20 23:39	♎ Nov 21 06:32
♌ Jan 20 07:21	♏ Mar 23 03:14	♒ May 24 03:00	♉ Jul 24 07:19	♌ Sep 23 04:08	♏ Nov 23 17:37
♍ Jan 22 14:02	♐ Mar 25 15:51	♓ May 26 11:06	♊ Jul 26 09:42	♍ Sep 25 10:29	♐ Nov 26 06:00
♎ Jan 24 23:44	♑ Mar 28 03:52	♈ May 28 15:45	♋ Jul 28 11:40	♎ Sep 27 18:41	♑ Nov 28 18:52
♏ Jan 27 11:49	♒ Mar 30 13:15	♉ May 30 17:11	♌ Jul 30 14:20	♏ Sep 30 04:52	♒ Dec 1 07:09
♐ Jan 30 00:12	♓ Apr 1 18:42	♊ Jun 1 16:49	♍ Aug 1 18:54	♐ Oct 2 16:59	♓ Dec 3 17:15
♑ Feb 1 10:36	♈ Apr 3 20:25	♋ Jun 3 16:38	♎ Aug 4 02:23	♑ Oct 5 05:49	♈ Dec 5 23:49
♒ Feb 3 17:56	♉ Apr 5 20:05	♌ Jun 5 18:43	♏ Aug 6 12:58	♒ Oct 7 17:00	♉ Dec 8 02:32
♓ Feb 5 22:22	♊ Apr 7 19:48	♍ Jun 8 00:25	♐ Aug 9 01:23	♓ Oct 10 00:32	♊ Dec 10 02:30
♈ Feb 8 01:02	♋ Apr 9 21:34	♎ Jun 10 09:54	♑ Aug 11 13:21	♈ Oct 12 04:01	♋ Dec 12 01:40
♉ Feb 10 03:10	♌ Apr 12 02:37	♏ Jun 12 21:54	♒ Aug 13 22:56	♉ Oct 14 04:44	♌ Dec 14 02:09
♊ Feb 12 05:51	♍ Apr 14 10:56	♐ Jun 15 10:31	♓ Aug 16 05:35	♊ Oct 16 04:40	♍ Dec 16 05:37
♋ Feb 14 09:43	♎ Apr 16 21:38	♑ Jun 17 22:21	♈ Aug 18 09:48	♋ Oct 18 05:52	♎ Dec 18 12:58
♌ Feb 16 15:09	♏ Apr 19 09:40	♒ Jun 20 08:37	♉ Aug 20 12:44	♌ Oct 20 09:35	♏ Dec 20 23:38
♍ Feb 18 22:33	♐ Apr 21 22:14	♓ Jun 22 16:45	♊ Aug 22 15:19	♍ Oct 22 16:05	♐ Dec 23 12:12
♎ Feb 21 08:12	♑ Apr 24 10:31	♈ Jun 24 22:19	♋ Aug 24 18:17	♎ Oct 25 00:57	♑ Dec 26 00:59
♏ Feb 23 19:54	♒ Apr 26 20:57	♉ Jun 27 01:16	♌ Aug 26 22:09	♏ Oct 27 11:37	♒ Dec 28 12:53
♐ Feb 26 08:30	♓ Apr 29 03:57	♊ Jun 29 02:21	♍ Aug 29 03:31	♐ Oct 29 23:49	♓ Dec 30 23:00
♑ Feb 28 19:46	♈ May 1 06:58	♋ Jul 1 02:57	♎ Aug 31 11:02	♑ Nov 1 12:45	

Mercury

Jan 1 10 ♑	D Jul 3 26 ♊
♒ Jan 12 15:50	♋ Jul 12 21:15
♓ Jan 31 17:18	♌ Aug 1 18:30
R Feb 8 5 ♓	♍ Aug 16 12:47
♒ Feb 16 08:06	♎ Sep 2 22:25
D Mar 2 20 ♒	♏ Sep 27 10:54
♓ Mar 18 04:22	R Oct 6 3 ♏
♈ Apr 8 09:10	♎ Oct 14 01:55
♉ Apr 24 05:31	D Oct 27 17 ♎
♊ May 8 09:38	♏ Nov 9 13:12
♋ May 28 16:58	♐ Nov 28 20:50
R Jun 9 5 ♋	♑ Dec 17 22:21
♊ Jun 22 23:01	

Venus

Jan 1 17 ♐	♌ Jun 29 20:18
♑ Jan 11 06:48	♍ Jul 24 14:04
♒ Feb 4 06:08	♎ Aug 18 13:45
♓ Feb 28 06:01	♏ Sep 12 22:51
♈ Mar 24 07:43	♐ Oct 9 00:03
♉ Apr 17 12:08	♑ Nov 5 12:39
♊ May 11 19:47	♒ Dec 8 20:51
♋ Jun 5 06:29	R Dec 31 8 ♒

Mars

Jan 1 0 ♒
♓ Feb 6 22:45
♈ Mar 17 02:35
♉ Apr 25 07:19
♊ Jun 5 05:25
♋ Jul 18 08:56
♌ Sep 2 01:49
♍ Oct 21 01:45
♎ Dec 16 00:10

Jupiter

Jan 1 9 ♎
R Jan 24 10 ♎
D May 27 0 ♎
♏ Nov 27 02:14

Saturn

Jan 1 9 ♎
R Jan 18 9 ♎
D Jun 5 2 ♎

Uranus

Jan 1 28 ♏
♐ Feb 17 14:22
R Mar 5 0 ♐
♏ Mar 20 18:32
D Aug 4 26 ♏
♐ Nov 16 13:09

Neptune

Jan 1 23 ♐
R Mar 27 24 ♐
D Sep 3 22 ♐

Pluto

Jan 1 24 ♎
R Jan 26 24 ♎
D Jul 1 21 ♎

1982

Sun

♒ Jan 20 09:30	♈ Mar 20 22:54	♊ May 21 09:22	♌ Jul 23 04:13	♎ Sep 23 08:45	♐ Nov 22 15:22
♓ Feb 18 23:45	♉ Apr 20 10:06	♋ Jun 21 17:21	♍ Aug 23 11:15	♏ Oct 23 17:58	♑ Dec 22 04:37

Moon

Jan 1 13 ♓	♊ Mar 2 01:50	♍ May 1 23:44	♐ Jul 2 14:25	♓ Sep 2 16:10	♊ Nov 3 00:22
♈ Jan 2 06:32	♋ Mar 4 04:49	♎ May 4 06:32	♑ Jul 5 03:15	♈ Sep 5 00:23	♋ Nov 5 01:58
♉ Jan 4 11:02	♌ Mar 6 07:51	♏ May 6 15:24	♒ Jul 7 16:03	♉ Sep 7 06:26	♌ Nov 7 04:09
♊ Jan 6 12:48	♍ Mar 8 11:27	♐ May 9 02:16	♓ Jul 10 03:35	♊ Sep 9 10:57	♍ Nov 9 07:39
♋ Jan 8 13:01	♎ Mar 10 16:33	♑ May 11 14:50	♈ Jul 12 12:48	♋ Sep 11 14:18	♎ Nov 11 12:45
♌ Jan 10 13:21	♏ Mar 13 00:17	♒ May 14 03:45	♉ Jul 14 19:00	♌ Sep 13 16:46	♏ Nov 13 19:43
♍ Jan 12 15:37	♐ Mar 15 11:04	♓ May 16 14:46	♊ Jul 16 22:04	♍ Sep 15 18:58	♐ Nov 16 04:52
♎ Jan 14 21:17	♑ Mar 17 23:46	♈ May 18 22:05	♋ Jul 18 22:46	♎ Sep 17 22:03	♑ Nov 18 16:22
♏ Jan 17 06:46	♒ Mar 20 11:53	♉ May 21 01:22	♌ Jul 20 22:35	♏ Sep 20 03:32	♒ Nov 21 05:20
♐ Jan 19 19:01	♓ Mar 22 21:01	♊ May 23 01:54	♍ Jul 22 23:19	♐ Sep 22 12:30	♓ Nov 23 17:42
♑ Jan 22 07:51	♈ Mar 25 02:37	♋ May 25 01:38	♎ Jul 25 02:44	♑ Sep 25 00:31	♈ Nov 26 03:07
♒ Jan 24 19:25	♉ Mar 27 05:39	♌ May 27 02:27	♏ Jul 27 09:58	♒ Sep 27 13:22	♉ Nov 28 08:32
♓ Jan 27 04:50	♊ Mar 29 07:44	♍ May 29 05:43	♐ Jul 29 20:47	♓ Sep 30 00:19	♊ Nov 30 10:35
♈ Jan 29 11:59	♋ Mar 31 10:09	♎ May 31 12:01	♑ Aug 1 09:36	♈ Oct 2 08:06	♋ Dec 2 10:57
♉ Jan 31 17:04	♌ Apr 2 13:36	♏ Jun 2 21:12	♒ Aug 3 22:17	♉ Oct 4 13:08	♌ Dec 4 11:27
♊ Feb 2 20:19	♍ Apr 4 18:19	♐ Jun 5 08:32	♓ Aug 6 09:23	♊ Oct 6 16:38	♍ Dec 6 13:32
♋ Feb 4 22:17	♎ Apr 7 00:26	♑ Jun 7 21:12	♈ Aug 8 18:21	♋ Oct 8 19:39	♎ Dec 8 18:10
♌ Feb 6 23:51	♏ Apr 9 08:34	♒ Jun 10 10:08	♉ Aug 11 01:00	♌ Oct 10 22:45	♏ Dec 11 01:34
♍ Feb 9 02:15	♐ Apr 11 19:07	♓ Jun 12 21:44	♊ Aug 13 05:22	♍ Oct 13 02:09	♐ Dec 13 11:27
♎ Feb 11 07:02	♑ Apr 14 07:42	♈ Jun 15 06:21	♋ Aug 15 07:40	♎ Oct 15 06:22	♑ Dec 15 23:15
♏ Feb 13 15:16	♒ Apr 16 20:17	♉ Jun 17 11:07	♌ Aug 17 08:39	♏ Oct 17 12:21	♒ Dec 18 12:13
♐ Feb 16 02:44	♓ Apr 19 06:20	♊ Jun 19 12:35	♍ Aug 19 09:40	♐ Oct 19 21:02	♓ Dec 21 00:55
♑ Feb 18 15:36	♈ Apr 21 12:22	♋ Jun 21 12:13	♎ Aug 21 12:22	♑ Oct 22 08:37	♈ Dec 23 11:34
♒ Feb 21 03:15	♉ Apr 23 14:59	♌ Jun 23 11:57	♏ Aug 23 18:21	♒ Oct 24 21:36	♉ Dec 25 18:37
♓ Feb 23 12:08	♊ Apr 25 15:48	♍ Jun 25 13:35	♐ Aug 26 04:10	♓ Oct 27 09:13	♊ Dec 27 21:48
♈ Feb 25 18:17	♋ Apr 27 16:44	♎ Jun 27 18:30	♑ Aug 28 16:42	♈ Oct 29 17:25	♋ Dec 29 22:11
♉ Feb 27 22:31	♌ Apr 29 19:09	♏ Jun 30 03:01	♒ Aug 31 05:23	♉ Oct 31 22:04	♌ Dec 31 21:34

Mercury

Jan 1 22 ♑	♋ Jul 9 11:24	
♒ Jan 5 16:47	♌ Jul 24 08:49	
R Jan 23 19 ♒	♍ Aug 8 14:07	
D Feb 13 3 ♒	♎ Aug 28 03:30	
♓ Mar 13 19:02	R Sep 19 17 ♎	
♈ Mar 31 21:03	D Oct 11 1 ♎	
♉ Apr 15 18:47	♏ Nov 3 01:07	
♊ May 1 13:33	♐ Nov 21 14:27	
R May 21 15 ♊	♑ Dec 10 20:10	
D Jun 13 6 ♊		

Venus

Jan 1 8 ♒	♋ Jul 20 16:21
♑ Jan 23 03:21	♌ Aug 14 11:09
D Feb 10 23 ♑	♍ Sep 7 21:38
♒ Mar 2 11:18	♎ Oct 2 01:33
♓ Apr 6 12:15	♏ Oct 26 01:20
♈ May 4 12:24	♐ Nov 18 23:07
♉ May 30 21:01	♑ Dec 12 20:18
♊ Jun 25 12:13	

Mars

Jan 1 7 ♎
R Feb 20 19 ♎
D May 11 29 ♍
♏ Aug 3 11:52
♐ Sep 20 01:30
♑ Oct 31 22:55
♒ Dec 10 06:08

Jupiter

Jan 1 6 ♏
R Feb 24 10 ♏
D Jun 27 0 ♏
♐ Dec 26 01:45

Saturn

Jan 1 21 ♎
R Jan 31 22 ♎
D Jun 18 15 ♎
♏ Nov 29 11:34

Uranus

Jan 1 2 ♐
R Mar 9 4 ♐
D Aug 9 0 ♐

Neptune

Jan 1 25 ♐
R Mar 29 27 ♐
D Sep 5 24 ♐

Pluto

Jan 1 26 ♎
R Jan 29 26 ♎
D Jul 4 24 ♎

1983

Sun

♒ Jan 20 15:18	♈ Mar 21 04:37	♊ May 21 15:05	♌ Jul 23 10:04	♎ Sep 23 14:42	♐ Nov 22 21:20
♓ Feb 19 05:31	♉ Apr 20 15:49	♋ Jun 21 23:08	♍ Aug 23 17:07	♏ Oct 23 23:56	♑ Dec 22 10:31

Moon

Jan 1 1♌	♏ Mar 2 23:51	♒ May 3 23:10	♉ Jul 5 00:05	♌ Sep 4 04:48	♏ Nov 4 01:53
♍ Jan 2 21:49	♐ Mar 5 07:14	♓ May 6 11:43	♊ Jul 7 05:41	♍ Sep 6 04:35	♐ Nov 6 06:08
♎ Jan 5 00:45	♑ Mar 7 18:29	♈ May 8 22:16	♋ Jul 9 07:51	♎ Sep 8 04:13	♑ Nov 8 13:31
♏ Jan 7 07:16	♒ Mar 10 07:30	♉ May 11 05:36	♌ Jul 11 07:53	♏ Sep 10 05:49	♒ Nov 11 00:10
♐ Jan 9 17:14	♓ Mar 12 19:48	♊ May 13 10:04	♍ Jul 13 07:43	♐ Sep 12 11:08	♓ Nov 13 12:41
♑ Jan 12 05:25	♈ Mar 15 06:00	♋ May 15 12:47	♎ Jul 15 09:09	♑ Sep 14 20:34	♈ Nov 16 00:37
♒ Jan 14 18:26	♉ Mar 17 14:05	♌ May 17 15:00	♏ Jul 17 13:37	♒ Sep 17 08:45	♉ Nov 18 10:07
♓ Jan 17 07:03	♊ Mar 19 20:19	♍ May 19 17:37	♐ Jul 19 21:31	♓ Sep 19 21:29	♊ Nov 20 16:46
♈ Jan 19 18:07	♋ Mar 22 00:52	♎ May 21 21:12	♑ Jul 22 08:11	♈ Sep 22 09:09	♋ Nov 22 21:10
♉ Jan 22 02:36	♌ Mar 24 03:44	♏ May 24 02:17	♒ Jul 24 20:27	♉ Sep 24 19:12	♌ Nov 25 00:20
♊ Jan 24 07:40	♍ Mar 26 05:18	♐ May 26 09:27	♓ Jul 27 09:10	♊ Sep 27 03:24	♍ Nov 27 03:01
♋ Jan 26 09:28	♎ Mar 28 06:48	♑ May 28 19:07	♈ Jul 29 21:21	♋ Sep 29 09:24	♎ Nov 29 05:57
♌ Jan 28 09:09	♏ Mar 30 09:57	♒ May 31 07:00	♉ Aug 1 07:36	♌ Oct 1 12:54	♏ Dec 1 09:41
♍ Jan 30 08:35	♐ Apr 1 16:20	♓ Jun 2 19:42	♊ Aug 3 14:42	♍ Oct 3 14:15	♐ Dec 3 14:56
♎ Feb 1 09:46	♑ Apr 4 02:30	♈ Jun 5 07:00	♋ Aug 5 18:08	♎ Oct 5 14:41	♑ Dec 5 22:28
♏ Feb 3 14:33	♒ Apr 6 15:06	♉ Jun 7 15:04	♌ Aug 7 18:38	♏ Oct 7 16:06	♒ Dec 8 08:39
♐ Feb 5 23:29	♓ Apr 9 03:30	♊ Jun 9 19:37	♍ Aug 9 17:49	♐ Oct 9 20:20	♓ Dec 10 20:53
♑ Feb 8 11:34	♈ Apr 11 13:36	♋ Jun 11 21:32	♎ Aug 11 17:52	♑ Oct 12 04:30	♈ Dec 13 09:17
♒ Feb 11 00:41	♉ Apr 13 20:59	♌ Jun 13 22:22	♏ Aug 13 20:43	♒ Oct 14 16:00	♉ Dec 15 19:32
♓ Feb 13 13:02	♊ Apr 16 02:15	♍ Jun 15 23:37	♐ Aug 16 03:34	♓ Oct 17 04:42	♊ Dec 18 02:23
♈ Feb 15 23:45	♋ Apr 18 06:14	♎ Jun 18 02:37	♑ Aug 18 13:59	♈ Oct 19 16:19	♋ Dec 20 06:02
♉ Feb 18 08:31	♌ Apr 20 09:26	♏ Jun 20 07:59	♒ Aug 21 02:25	♉ Oct 22 01:48	♌ Dec 22 07:44
♊ Feb 20 14:52	♍ Apr 22 12:12	♐ Jun 22 15:55	♓ Aug 23 15:09	♊ Oct 24 09:10	♍ Dec 24 09:01
♋ Feb 22 18:31	♎ Apr 24 15:04	♑ Jun 25 02:09	♈ Aug 26 03:07	♋ Oct 26 14:47	♎ Dec 26 11:18
♌ Feb 24 19:47	♏ Apr 26 19:05	♒ Jun 27 14:07	♉ Aug 28 13:37	♌ Oct 28 18:50	♏ Dec 28 15:26
♍ Feb 26 19:50	♐ Apr 29 01:29	♓ Jun 30 02:52	♊ Aug 30 21:48	♍ Oct 30 21:32	♐ Dec 30 21:44
♎ Feb 28 20:30	♑ May 1 11:00	♈ Jul 2 14:47	♋ Sep 2 02:53	♎ Nov 1 23:31	

Mercury

Jan 1 29♑	♋ Jul 1 19:21
♒ Jan 1 13:12	♌ Jul 15 21:03
R Jan 7 3♒	♍ Aug 1 10:26
♑ Jan 12 07:04	♎ Aug 29 04:01
D Jan 27 16♑	R Sep 2 0♎
♒ Feb 14 09:30	♍ Sep 6 02:44
♓ Mar 7 04:29	D Sep 24 15♍
♈ Mar 23 20:11	♎ Oct 8 23:17
♉ Apr 7 17:00	♏ Oct 26 15:47
R May 1 25♉	♐ Nov 14 08:57
D May 25 15♉	♑ Dec 4 11:21
♊ Jun 14 08:06	R Dec 22 17♑

Venus

Jan 1 24♑	♍ Jul 10 05:22
♒ Jan 5 17:57	R Aug 3 9♍
♓ Jan 29 17:30	♌ Aug 27 11:44
♈ Feb 22 21:34	D Sep 15 23♌
♉ Mar 19 09:50	♍ Oct 5 19:37
♊ Apr 13 11:24	♎ Nov 9 10:52
♋ May 9 10:57	♏ Dec 6 16:15
♌ Jun 6 06:08	

Mars

- Jan 1 16♒
- ♓ Jan 17 13:06
- ♈ Feb 25 00:12
- ♉ Apr 5 14:01
- ♊ May 16 21:42
- ♋ Jun 29 06:54
- ♌ Aug 13 16:55
- ♍ Sep 30 00:10
- ♎ Nov 18 10:28

Jupiter

- Jan 1 1♐
- R Mar 27 10♐
- D Jul 29 1♐

Saturn

- Jan 1 2♏
- R Feb 12 4♏
- ♎ May 6 17:30
- D Jul 1 27♎
- ♏ Aug 24 12:18

Uranus

- Jan 1 6♐
- R Mar 14 9♐
- D Aug 14 5♐

Neptune

- Jan 1 27♐
- R Apr 1 29♐
- D Sep 8 26♐

Pluto

- Jan 1 29♎
- R Feb 1 29♎
- D Jul 7 26♎
- ♏ Nov 5 21:25

1984

Sun

♒ Jan 20 21:06	♈ Mar 20 10:23	♊ May 20 20:56	♌ Jul 22 15:54
♓ Feb 19 11:16	♉ Apr 19 21:36	♋ Jun 21 04:59	♍ Aug 22 22:56
♎ Sep 22 20:30	♐ Nov 22 03:07		
♏ Oct 23 05:42	♑ Dec 21 16:22		

Moon

♐ Jan 1 14	♓ Mar 1 17:30	♊ May 2 16:03	♍ Jul 2 19:28	♐ Sep 1 16:30	♓ Nov 2 07:50
♑ Jan 2 06:07	♈ Mar 4 06:06	♋ May 4 23:25	♎ Jul 4 21:26	♑ Sep 3 22:54	♈ Nov 4 20:20
♒ Jan 4 16:30	♉ Mar 6 18:08	♌ May 7 04:44	♏ Jul 7 00:28	♒ Sep 6 08:12	♉ Nov 7 08:54
♓ Jan 7 04:33	♊ Mar 9 04:30	♍ May 9 08:01	♐ Jul 9 05:02	♓ Sep 8 19:25	♊ Nov 9 20:11
♈ Jan 9 17:15	♋ Mar 11 11:49	♎ May 11 09:53	♑ Jul 11 11:22	♈ Sep 11 07:47	♋ Nov 12 05:32
♉ Jan 12 04:36	♌ Mar 13 15:22	♏ May 13 11:22	♒ Jul 13 19:42	♉ Sep 13 20:33	♌ Nov 14 12:34
♊ Jan 14 12:41	♍ Mar 15 15:46	♐ May 15 13:50	♓ Jul 16 06:10	♊ Sep 16 08:25	♍ Nov 16 17:08
♋ Jan 16 16:48	♎ Mar 17 14:52	♑ May 17 18:44	♈ Jul 18 18:25	♋ Sep 18 17:36	♎ Nov 18 19:30
♌ Jan 18 17:50	♏ Mar 19 14:49	♒ May 20 02:56	♉ Jul 21 06:52	♌ Sep 20 22:49	♏ Nov 20 20:31
♍ Jan 20 17:36	♐ Mar 21 17:40	♓ May 22 14:09	♊ Jul 23 17:11	♍ Sep 23 00:19	♐ Nov 22 21:35
♎ Jan 22 18:06	♑ Mar 24 00:37	♈ May 25 02:39	♋ Jul 25 23:43	♎ Sep 24 23:40	♑ Nov 25 00:18
♏ Jan 24 21:03	♒ Mar 26 11:09	♉ May 27 14:14	♌ Jul 28 02:41	♏ Sep 26 23:04	♒ Nov 27 06:05
♐ Jan 27 03:13	♓ Mar 28 23:37	♊ May 29 23:22	♍ Jul 30 03:29	♐ Sep 29 00:31	♓ Nov 29 15:34
♑ Jan 29 12:13	♈ Mar 31 12:14	♋ Jun 1 05:54	♎ Aug 1 04:03	♑ Oct 1 05:28	♈ Dec 2 03:42
♒ Jan 31 23:12	♉ Apr 2 23:56	♌ Jun 3 10:20	♏ Aug 3 06:03	♒ Oct 3 14:04	♉ Dec 4 16:21
♓ Feb 3 11:21	♊ Apr 5 10:05	♍ Jun 5 13:28	♐ Aug 5 10:30	♓ Oct 6 01:20	♊ Dec 7 03:23
♈ Feb 6 00:03	♋ Apr 7 18:00	♎ Jun 7 16:04	♑ Aug 7 17:24	♈ Oct 8 13:51	♋ Dec 9 11:57
♉ Feb 8 12:05	♌ Apr 9 23:01	♏ Jun 9 18:48	♒ Aug 10 02:25	♉ Oct 11 02:28	♌ Dec 11 18:08
♊ Feb 10 21:40	♍ Apr 12 01:10	♐ Jun 11 22:27	♓ Aug 12 13:12	♊ Oct 13 14:14	♍ Dec 13 22:35
♋ Feb 13 03:21	♎ Apr 14 01:30	♑ Jun 14 03:47	♈ Aug 15 01:28	♋ Oct 16 00:00	♎ Dec 16 01:52
♌ Feb 15 05:10	♏ Apr 16 01:42	♒ Jun 16 11:40	♉ Aug 17 14:14	♌ Oct 18 06:42	♏ Dec 18 04:28
♍ Feb 17 04:32	♐ Apr 18 03:44	♓ Jun 18 22:17	♊ Aug 20 01:31	♍ Oct 20 09:55	♐ Dec 20 06:59
♎ Feb 19 03:40	♑ Apr 20 09:10	♈ Jun 21 10:39	♋ Aug 22 09:21	♎ Oct 22 10:31	♑ Dec 22 10:21
♏ Feb 21 04:45	♒ Apr 22 18:26	♉ Jun 23 22:37	♌ Aug 24 13:00	♏ Oct 24 10:07	♒ Dec 24 15:47
♐ Feb 23 09:22	♓ Apr 25 06:26	♊ Jun 26 08:04	♍ Aug 26 13:32	♐ Oct 26 10:43	♓ Dec 27 00:19
♑ Feb 25 17:50	♈ Apr 27 19:03	♋ Jun 28 14:10	♎ Aug 28 12:57	♑ Oct 28 14:05	♈ Dec 29 11:50
♒ Feb 28 05:01	♉ Apr 30 06:30	♌ Jun 30 17:30	♏ Aug 30 13:23	♒ Oct 30 21:14	

Mercury

Jan 1 7♑	♌ Jul 6 19:04
D Jan 11 1♑	♍ Jul 26 06:52
♒ Feb 9 01:48	R Aug 14 13♍
♓ Feb 27 18:03	D Sep 7 0♍
♈ Mar 14 16:23	♎ Sep 30 19:38
♉ Mar 31 20:46	♏ Oct 18 03:07
R Apr 11 6♉	♐ Nov 6 12:06
♈ Apr 25 12:01	♑ Dec 1 15:46
D May 5 26♈	R Dec 4 0♑
♉ May 15 12:40	♐ Dec 7 22:32
♊ Jun 7 15:46	D Dec 24 14♐
♋ Jun 22 06:38	

Venus

Jan 1 29♏	♋ Jun 20 00:49
♐ Jan 1 02:01	♌ Jul 14 10:31
♑ Jan 25 18:50	♍ Aug 7 19:40
♒ Feb 19 04:52	♎ Sep 1 05:07
♓ Mar 14 12:36	♏ Sep 25 16:02
♈ Apr 7 20:13	♐ Oct 20 05:40
♉ May 2 04:52	♑ Nov 13 23:51
♊ May 26 14:39	♒ Dec 9 03:25

Mars

Jan 1 24♎	
♏ Jan 11 03:18	
R Apr 5 28♏	
D Jun 19 11♏	
♐ Aug 17 19:54	
♑ Oct 5 06:01	
♒ Nov 15 18:09	
♓ Dec 25 06:39	

Jupiter

Jan 1 25♐
♑ Jan 19 15:00
R Apr 29 12♑
D Aug 29 3♑

Saturn

Jan 1 13♏
R Feb 24 16♏
D Jul 13 9♏

Uranus

Jan 1 11♐
R Mar 18 13♐
D Aug 18 9♐

Neptune

Jan 1 29♐
♑ Jan 19 01:33
R Apr 2 1♑
♐ Jun 23 03:12
D Sep 9 28♐
♑ Nov 21 11:27

Pluto

Jan 1 1♏
R Feb 4 2♏
♎ May 18 13:36
D Jul 9 29♎
♏ Aug 28 05:16

1985

Sun

♒ Jan 20 02:58	♈ Mar 20 16:13	♊ May 21 02:42	♌ Jul 22 21:36	♎ Sep 23 02:07	♐ Nov 22 08:49
♓ Feb 18 17:08	♉ Apr 20 03:24	♋ Jun 21 10:44	♍ Aug 23 04:34	♏ Oct 23 11:19	♑ Dec 21 22:06

Moon

Jan 1 29 ♈	♍ Mar 1 15:23	♎ May 1 21:22	♑ Jul 1 18:22	♈ Sep 1 05:41	♋ Nov 2 08:31
♉ Jan 1 00:36	♌ Mar 3 21:28	♏ May 3 21:17	♒ Jul 3 21:36	♉ Sep 3 17:28	♌ Nov 4 19:04
♊ Jan 3 12:00	♍ Mar 5 23:42	♐ May 5 20:56	♓ Jul 6 03:40	♊ Sep 6 06:27	♍ Nov 7 02:18
♋ Jan 5 20:17	♎ Mar 7 23:47	♑ May 7 22:11	♈ Jul 8 13:21	♋ Sep 8 18:09	♎ Nov 9 05:53
♌ Jan 8 01:28	♏ Mar 9 23:47	♒ May 10 02:37	♉ Jul 11 01:44	♌ Sep 11 02:28	♏ Nov 11 06:31
♍ Jan 10 04:39	♐ Mar 12 01:29	♓ May 12 10:55	♊ Jul 13 14:23	♍ Sep 13 06:52	♐ Nov 13 05:53
♎ Jan 12 07:13	♑ Mar 14 05:55	♈ May 14 22:26	♋ Jul 16 00:54	♎ Sep 15 08:34	♑ Nov 15 05:54
♏ Jan 14 10:07	♒ Mar 16 13:10	♉ May 17 11:23	♌ Jul 18 08:25	♏ Sep 17 09:17	♒ Nov 17 08:25
♐ Jan 16 13:49	♓ Mar 18 22:51	♊ May 20 00:00	♍ Jul 20 13:30	♐ Sep 19 10:39	♓ Nov 19 14:42
♑ Jan 18 18:28	♈ Mar 21 10:21	♋ May 22 11:06	♎ Jul 22 17:10	♑ Sep 21 13:50	♈ Nov 22 00:43
♒ Jan 21 00:39	♉ Mar 23 23:07	♌ May 24 19:54	♏ Jul 24 20:15	♒ Sep 23 19:11	♉ Nov 24 13:07
♓ Jan 23 09:01	♊ Mar 26 12:02	♍ May 27 02:07	♐ Jul 26 23:13	♓ Sep 26 02:51	♊ Nov 27 02:09
♈ Jan 25 20:06	♋ Mar 28 23:14	♎ May 29 05:40	♑ Jul 29 02:20	♈ Sep 28 12:43	♋ Nov 29 14:23
♉ Jan 28 08:54	♌ Mar 31 06:51	♏ May 31 07:07	♒ Jul 31 06:25	♉ Oct 1 00:35	♌ Dec 2 01:00
♊ Jan 30 21:00	♎ Apr 2 10:25	♐ Jun 2 07:33	♓ Aug 2 12:34	♊ Oct 3 13:05	♍ Dec 4 09:15
♋ Feb 2 06:00	♏ Apr 4 10:53	♑ Jun 4 08:34	♈ Aug 4 21:43	♋ Oct 6 01:58	♎ Dec 6 14:34
♌ Feb 4 11:01	♐ Apr 6 10:10	♒ Jun 6 11:52	♉ Aug 7 09:41	♌ Oct 8 11:34	♏ Dec 8 16:56
♍ Feb 6 13:09	♐ Apr 8 10:17	♓ Jun 8 18:46	♊ Aug 9 22:31	♍ Oct 10 17:10	♐ Dec 10 17:14
♎ Feb 8 14:11	♑ Apr 10 12:58	♈ Jun 11 05:23	♋ Aug 12 09:28	♎ Oct 12 19:11	♑ Dec 12 16:59
♏ Feb 10 15:48	♒ Apr 12 19:04	♉ Jun 13 18:12	♌ Aug 14 16:57	♏ Oct 14 19:12	♒ Dec 14 18:16
♐ Feb 12 19:08	♓ Apr 15 04:30	♊ Jun 16 06:45	♍ Aug 16 21:15	♐ Oct 16 19:06	♓ Dec 16 22:50
♑ Feb 15 00:26	♈ Apr 17 16:19	♋ Jun 18 17:21	♎ Aug 18 23:43	♑ Oct 18 20:35	♈ Dec 19 07:36
♒ Feb 17 07:35	♉ Apr 20 05:13	♌ Jun 21 01:32	♏ Aug 21 01:51	♒ Oct 21 00:54	♉ Dec 21 19:40
♓ Feb 19 16:37	♊ Apr 22 18:00	♍ Jun 23 07:32	♐ Aug 23 04:35	♓ Oct 23 08:28	♊ Dec 24 08:45
♈ Feb 22 03:43	♋ Apr 25 05:27	♎ Jun 25 11:47	♑ Aug 25 08:24	♈ Oct 25 18:47	♋ Dec 26 20:44
♉ Feb 24 16:28	♌ Apr 27 14:10	♏ Jun 27 14:37	♒ Aug 27 13:31	♉ Oct 28 07:00	♌ Dec 29 06:45
♊ Feb 27 05:12	♍ Apr 29 19:25	♐ Jun 29 16:30	♓ Aug 29 20:24	♊ Oct 30 19:59	♍ Dec 31 14:43

Mercury

Jan 1 18 ♐	R Jul 28 25 ♌
♑ Jan 11 18:31	D Aug 20 13 ♌
♒ Feb 1 07:47	♍ Sep 6 19:33
♓ Feb 18 23:50	♎ Sep 22 23:16
♈ Mar 7 00:22	♏ Oct 10 18:43
R Mar 24 18 ♈	♐ Oct 31 16:52
D Apr 17 6 ♈	R Nov 18 15 ♐
♉ May 14 02:15	♏ Dec 4 20:08
♊ May 30 19:46	D Dec 8 28 ♏
♋ Jun 13 16:13	♐ Dec 12 11:17
♌ Jun 29 19:33	

Venus

Jan 1 26 ♒	♋ Aug 2 09:04
♓ Jan 4 06:27	♌ Aug 28 03:36
♈ Feb 2 08:34	♍ Sep 22 02:52
R Mar 13 22 ♈	♎ Oct 16 13:04
D Apr 25 6 ♈	♏ Nov 9 15:08
♉ Jun 6 08:52	♐ Dec 3 13:00
♊ Jul 6 07:58	♑ Dec 27 09:18

Mars

Jan 1 5 ♓
♈ Feb 2 17:15
♉ Mar 15 05:05
♊ Apr 26 09:07
♋ Jun 9 10:39
♌ Jul 25 04:00
♍ Sep 10 01:27
♎ Oct 27 15:07
♏ Dec 14 18:51

Jupiter

Jan 1 21 ♑
♒ Feb 6 15:02
R Jun 4 16 ♒
D Oct 3 7 ♒

Saturn

Jan 1 24 ♏
R Mar 7 28 ♏
D Jul 25 21 ♏
♐ Nov 17 02:28

Uranus

Jan 1 15 ♐
R Mar 22 17 ♐
D Aug 23 13 ♐

Neptune

Jan 1 1 ♑
R Apr 5 3 ♑
D Sep 12 0 ♑

Pluto

Jan 1 4 ♏
R Feb 6 4 ♏
D Jul 12 1 ♏

1986

Sun

♒ Jan 20 08:45	♈ Mar 20 22:03	♊ May 21 08:28	♌ Jul 23 03:23	♎ Sep 23 07:59	♐ Nov 22 14:44
♓ Feb 18 22:57	♉ Apr 20 09:12	♋ Jun 21 16:30	♍ Aug 23 10:26	♏ Oct 23 17:15	♑ Dec 22 04:03

Moon

Jan 1 5 ♍	♐ Mar 2 14:52	♓ May 2 14:31	♊ Jul 3 10:31	♍ Sep 3 10:06	♐ Nov 3 15:20
♎ Jan 2 20:45	♑ Mar 4 17:56	♈ May 4 23:00	♋ Jul 5 23:19	♎ Sep 5 16:33	♑ Nov 5 15:48
♏ Jan 5 00:45	♒ Mar 6 21:43	♉ May 7 09:59	♌ Jul 8 10:55	♏ Sep 7 21:12	♒ Nov 7 17:29
♐ Jan 7 02:47	♓ Mar 9 02:49	♊ May 9 22:27	♍ Jul 10 20:51	♐ Sep 10 00:41	♓ Nov 9 21:29
♑ Jan 9 03:42	♈ Mar 11 10:04	♋ May 12 11:17	♎ Jul 13 04:39	♑ Sep 12 03:27	♈ Nov 12 04:14
♒ Jan 11 05:01	♉ Mar 13 20:04	♌ May 14 23:15	♏ Jul 15 09:59	♒ Sep 14 06:07	♉ Nov 14 13:25
♓ Jan 13 08:38	♊ Mar 16 08:22	♍ May 17 08:44	♐ Jul 17 12:35	♓ Sep 16 09:27	♊ Nov 17 00:26
♈ Jan 15 16:04	♋ Mar 18 21:04	♎ May 19 14:41	♑ Jul 19 13:09	♈ Sep 18 14:34	♋ Nov 19 12:45
♉ Jan 18 03:14	♌ Mar 21 07:38	♏ May 21 17:02	♒ Jul 21 13:17	♉ Sep 20 22:26	♌ Nov 22 01:26
♊ Jan 20 16:11	♍ Mar 23 14:39	♐ May 23 16:56	♓ Jul 23 14:59	♊ Sep 23 09:14	♍ Nov 24 12:46
♋ Jan 23 04:14	♎ Mar 25 18:22	♑ May 25 16:15	♈ Jul 25 20:02	♋ Sep 25 21:45	♏ Nov 29 01:13
♌ Jan 25 13:48	♏ Mar 27 20:06	♒ May 27 16:59	♉ Jul 28 05:12	♌ Sep 28 09:40	♐ Dec 1 02:09
♍ Jan 27 20:52	♐ Mar 29 21:21	♓ May 29 20:55	♊ Jul 30 17:18	♍ Sep 30 18:58	♑ Dec 3 01:29
♎ Jan 30 02:10	♑ Mar 31 23:25	♈ Jun 1 04:43	♋ Aug 2 06:03	♎ Oct 3 01:03	♒ Dec 5 01:24
♏ Feb 1 06:20	♒ Apr 3 03:12	♉ Jun 3 15:45	♌ Aug 4 17:27	♏ Oct 5 04:05	♓ Dec 7 03:47
♐ Feb 3 09:32	♓ Apr 5 09:03	♊ Jun 6 04:28	♍ Aug 7 02:44	♐ Oct 7 06:47	♈ Dec 9 09:48
♑ Feb 5 12:01	♈ Apr 7 17:12	♋ Jun 8 17:16	♎ Aug 9 10:05	♑ Oct 9 08:53	♉ Dec 11 19:10
♒ Feb 7 14:36	♉ Apr 10 03:36	♌ Jun 11 05:12	♏ Aug 11 15:36	♒ Oct 11 11:45	♊ Dec 14 06:42
♓ Feb 9 18:32	♊ Apr 12 15:50	♍ Jun 13 15:18	♐ Aug 13 19:16	♓ Oct 13 16:04	♋ Dec 16 19:09
♈ Feb 12 01:21	♋ Apr 15 04:43	♎ Jun 15 22:37	♑ Aug 15 21:22	♈ Oct 15 22:13	♌ Dec 19 07:44
♉ Feb 14 11:38	♌ Apr 17 16:09	♏ Jun 18 02:37	♒ Aug 17 22:45	♉ Oct 18 06:36	♍ Dec 21 19:30
♊ Feb 17 00:18	♍ Apr 20 00:23	♐ Jun 20 03:36	♓ Aug 20 00:52	♊ Oct 20 17:15	♎ Dec 24 05:05
♋ Feb 19 12:40	♎ Apr 22 04:51	♑ Jun 22 03:00	♈ Aug 22 05:28	♋ Oct 23 05:05	♏ Dec 26 11:07
♌ Feb 21 22:25	♏ Apr 24 06:16	♒ Jun 24 02:51	♉ Aug 24 13:36	♌ Oct 25 18:02	♐ Dec 28 13:20
♍ Feb 24 04:57	♐ Apr 26 06:17	♓ Jun 26 05:13	♊ Aug 27 01:01	♍ Oct 28 04:21	♑ Dec 30 12:54
♎ Feb 26 09:06	♑ Apr 28 06:42	♈ Jun 28 11:35	♋ Aug 29 13:39	♎ Oct 30 11:05	
♏ Feb 28 12:05	♒ Apr 30 09:05	♉ Jun 30 21:54	♌ Sep 1 01:08	♏ Nov 1 14:19	

Mercury

Jan 1 22 ♐	♌ Jun 26 14:08
♑ Jan 5 20:45	R Jul 9 6 ♌
♒ Jan 25 00:39	♋ Jul 23 21:50
♓ Feb 11 05:22	D Aug 3 26 ♋
♈ Mar 3 07:04	♌ Aug 11 22:05
R Mar 7 1 ♈	♍ Aug 30 03:32
♓ Mar 11 17:15	♎ Sep 15 02:31
D Mar 30 18 ♓	♏ Oct 4 00:19
♈ Apr 17 12:26	R Nov 2 28 ♏
♉ May 7 12:37	D Nov 22 13 ♏
♊ May 22 07:27	♐ Dec 10 00:25
♋ Jun 5 14:10	♑ Dec 29 23:12

Venus

Jan 1 5 ♑	♌ Jun 15 18:52
♒ Jan 20 05:37	♍ Jul 11 16:25
♓ Feb 13 03:10	♎ Aug 7 20:45
♈ Mar 9 03:31	♏ Sep 7 10:10
♉ Apr 2 08:19	R Oct 15 20 ♏
♊ Apr 26 19:09	D Nov 26 4 ♏
♋ May 21 13:46	

Mars

Jan 1 10 ♏
♐ Feb 2 06:22
♑ Mar 28 03:31
R Jun 8 23 ♑
D Aug 12 11 ♑
♒ Oct 9 00:34
♓ Nov 26 02:37

Jupiter

Jan 1 18 ♒
♓ Feb 20 15:28
R Jul 12 22 ♓
D Nov 8 12 ♓

Saturn

Jan 1 5 ♐
R Mar 19 9 ♐
D Aug 7 3 ♐

Uranus

Jan 1 19 ♐
R Mar 27 22 ♐
D Aug 27 18 ♐

Neptune

Jan 1 3 ♑
R Apr 7 5 ♑
D Sep 14 3 ♑

Pluto

Jan 1 6 ♏
R Feb 8 7 ♏
D Jul 15 4 ♏

1987

Sun

♒ Jan 20 14:41	♈ Mar 21 03:53	♊ May 21 14:12	♌ Jul 23 09:06	♎ Sep 23 13:46	♐ Nov 22 20:29
♓ Feb 19 04:52	♉ Apr 20 14:59	♋ Jun 21 22:11	♍ Aug 23 16:09	♏ Oct 23 23:00	♑ Dec 22 09:45

Moon

Jan 1 22♑	♈ Mar 1 12:37	♋ May 2 07:38	♎ Jul 3 09:54	♑ Sep 2 17:04	♈ Nov 2 13:40
♒ Jan 1 11:54	♉ Mar 3 18:12	♌ May 4 20:07	♏ Jul 5 18:03	♒ Sep 4 18:22	♉ Nov 4 18:02
♓ Jan 3 12:36	♊ Mar 6 03:26	♍ May 7 08:08	♐ Jul 7 22:05	♓ Sep 6 18:37	♊ Nov 7 00:17
♈ Jan 5 16:51	♋ Mar 8 15:24	♎ May 9 17:29	♑ Jul 9 22:43	♈ Sep 8 19:33	♋ Nov 9 09:10
♉ Jan 8 01:12	♌ Mar 11 03:54	♏ May 11 23:10	♒ Jul 11 21:49	♉ Sep 10 22:57	♌ Nov 11 20:45
♊ Jan 10 12:40	♍ Mar 13 14:55	♐ May 14 01:40	♓ Jul 13 21:37	♊ Sep 13 05:55	♍ Nov 14 09:29
♋ Jan 13 01:19	♎ Mar 15 23:35	♑ May 16 02:37	♈ Jul 16 00:00	♋ Sep 15 16:23	♎ Nov 16 20:49
♌ Jan 15 13:45	♏ Mar 18 05:57	♒ May 18 03:43	♉ Jul 18 06:04	♌ Sep 18 04:51	♏ Nov 19 04:47
♍ Jan 18 01:14	♐ Mar 20 10:31	♓ May 20 06:23	♊ Jul 20 15:32	♍ Sep 20 17:14	♐ Nov 21 09:17
♎ Jan 20 11:10	♑ Mar 22 13:49	♈ May 22 11:22	♋ Jul 23 03:14	♎ Sep 23 03:59	♑ Nov 23 11:32
♏ Jan 22 18:30	♒ Mar 24 16:19	♉ May 24 18:39	♌ Jul 25 15:49	♏ Sep 25 12:30	♒ Nov 25 13:12
♐ Jan 24 22:35	♓ Mar 26 18:45	♊ May 27 03:55	♍ Jul 28 04:26	♐ Sep 27 18:48	♓ Nov 27 15:41
♑ Jan 26 23:42	♈ Mar 28 22:12	♋ May 29 15:00	♎ Jul 30 16:00	♑ Sep 29 23:09	♈ Nov 29 19:35
♒ Jan 28 23:16	♉ Mar 31 03:45	♌ Jun 1 03:25	♏ Aug 2 01:09	♒ Oct 2 01:52	♉ Dec 2 01:06
♓ Jan 30 23:24	♊ Apr 2 12:17	♍ Jun 3 15:57	♐ Aug 4 06:47	♓ Oct 4 03:40	♊ Dec 4 08:14
♈ Feb 2 02:10	♋ Apr 4 23:34	♎ Jun 6 02:24	♑ Aug 6 08:52	♈ Oct 6 05:35	♋ Dec 6 17:19
♉ Feb 4 08:53	♌ Apr 7 12:03	♏ Jun 8 09:06	♒ Aug 8 08:37	♉ Oct 8 08:58	♌ Dec 9 04:40
♊ Feb 6 19:24	♍ Apr 9 23:28	♐ Jun 10 11:53	♓ Aug 10 08:01	♊ Oct 10 15:03	♍ Dec 11 17:31
♋ Feb 9 07:54	♎ Apr 12 08:06	♑ Jun 12 12:04	♈ Aug 12 09:08	♋ Oct 13 00:30	♎ Dec 14 05:39
♌ Feb 11 20:21	♏ Apr 14 13:40	♒ Jun 14 11:44	♉ Aug 14 13:38	♌ Oct 15 12:35	♏ Dec 16 14:41
♍ Feb 14 07:26	♐ Apr 16 17:01	♓ Jun 16 12:54	♊ Aug 16 21:59	♍ Oct 18 01:06	♐ Dec 18 19:32
♎ Feb 16 16:45	♑ Apr 18 19:21	♈ Jun 18 16:56	♋ Aug 19 09:19	♎ Oct 20 11:51	♑ Dec 20 21:07
♏ Feb 19 00:04	♒ Apr 20 21:45	♉ Jun 21 00:08	♌ Aug 21 21:58	♏ Oct 22 19:42	♒ Dec 22 21:20
♐ Feb 21 05:09	♓ Apr 23 01:02	♊ Jun 23 09:54	♍ Aug 24 10:24	♐ Oct 25 00:57	♓ Dec 24 22:09
♑ Feb 23 07:56	♈ Apr 25 05:40	♋ Jun 25 21:22	♎ Aug 26 21:36	♑ Oct 27 04:32	♈ Dec 27 01:06
♒ Feb 25 09:08	♉ Apr 27 12:05	♌ Jun 28 09:51	♏ Aug 29 06:49	♒ Oct 29 07:27	♉ Dec 29 06:37
♓ Feb 27 10:07	♊ Apr 29 20:42	♍ Jun 30 22:34	♐ Aug 31 13:24	♓ Oct 31 10:20	♊ Dec 31 14:29

Mercury

Jan 1 3♑	D Jul 15 8♋
♒ Jan 17 13:08	♌ Aug 6 21:27
♓ Feb 4 03:02	♍ Aug 21 21:38
R Feb 18 14♓	♎ Sep 7 13:47
♒ Mar 11 19:27	♏ Sep 28 17:32
♒ Mar 12 20:22	R Oct 16 12♏
D Mar 12 0♓	♎ Nov 1 02:14
♈ Apr 12 20:12	D Nov 6 27♎
♉ Apr 29 15:43	♏ Nov 11 20:52
♊ May 13 17:52	♐ Dec 3 13:32
♋ May 30 04:13	♑ Dec 22 17:39
R Jun 21 16♋	

Venus

Jan 1 24♏	♋ Jul 5 19:50
♐ Jan 7 10:22	♌ Jul 30 06:48
♑ Feb 5 03:02	♍ Aug 23 13:59
♒ Mar 3 07:55	♎ Sep 16 18:13
♓ Mar 28 16:22	♏ Oct 10 20:49
♈ Apr 22 16:08	♐ Nov 3 23:02
♉ May 17 11:56	♑ Nov 28 01:49
♊ Jun 11 05:15	♒ Dec 22 06:24

Mars

Jan 1 24♓
♈ Jan 8 12:20
♉ Feb 20 14:53
♊ Apr 5 16:44
♋ May 21 03:07
♌ Jul 6 16:50
♍ Aug 22 19:50
♎ Oct 8 19:26
♏ Nov 24 03:15

Jupiter

Jan 1 17♓
♈ Mar 2 18:36
R Aug 19 29♈
D Dec 15 19♈

Saturn

Jan 1 15♐
R Mar 31 21♐
D Aug 19 14♐

Uranus

Jan 1 23♐
R Apr 1 26♐
D Sep 1 22♐

Neptune

Jan 1 5♑
R Apr 10 8♑
D Sep 17 5♑

Pluto

Jan 1 9♏
R Feb 11 9♏
D Jul 18 7♏

1988

Sun

♒ Jan 20 20:25 | ♈ Mar 20 09:40 | ♊ May 20 19:58 | ♌ Jul 22 14:53 | ♎ Sep 22 19:30 | ♐ Nov 22 02:11
♓ Feb 19 10:36 | ♉ Apr 19 20:46 | ♋ Jun 21 03:59 | ♍ Aug 22 21:55 | ♏ Oct 23 04:45 | ♑ Dec 21 15:26

Moon

Jan 1 5♊	♍ Mar 2 13:07	♐ May 3 08:53	♓ Jul 3 08:34
♋ Jan 3 00:17	♎ Mar 5 01:32	♑ May 5 13:53	♈ Jul 5 10:37
♌ Jan 5 11:46	♏ Mar 7 12:26	♒ May 7 17:37	♉ Jul 7 14:27
♍ Jan 8 00:36	♐ Mar 9 20:59	♓ May 9 20:39	♊ Jul 9 20:16
♎ Jan 10 13:17	♑ Mar 12 02:32	♈ May 11 23:23	♋ Jul 12 04:08
♏ Jan 12 23:39	♒ Mar 14 05:08	♉ May 14 02:21	♌ Jul 14 14:12
♐ Jan 15 05:59	♓ Mar 16 05:42	♊ May 16 06:31	♍ Jul 17 02:17
♑ Jan 17 08:15	♈ Mar 18 05:45	♋ May 18 13:06	♎ Jul 19 15:22
♒ Jan 19 08:02	♉ Mar 20 07:06	♌ May 20 22:52	♏ Jul 22 03:13
♓ Jan 21 07:27	♊ Mar 22 11:20	♍ May 23 11:13	♐ Jul 24 11:42
♈ Jan 23 08:31	♋ Mar 24 19:28	♎ May 25 23:50	♑ Jul 26 16:07
♉ Jan 25 12:37	♌ Mar 27 06:53	♏ May 28 10:07	♒ Jul 28 17:24
♊ Jan 27 20:02	♍ Mar 29 19:49	♐ May 30 16:57	♓ Jul 30 17:22
♋ Jan 30 06:12	♎ Apr 1 08:06	♑ Jun 1 20:59	♈ Aug 1 17:54
♌ Feb 1 18:06	♏ Apr 3 18:25	♒ Jun 3 23:34	♉ Aug 3 20:24
♍ Feb 4 06:54	♐ Apr 6 02:29	♓ Jun 6 02:00	♊ Aug 6 01:43
♎ Feb 6 19:36	♑ Apr 8 08:19	♈ Jun 8 05:04	♋ Aug 8 09:51
♏ Feb 9 06:42	♒ Apr 10 12:10	♉ Jun 10 09:02	♌ Aug 10 20:27
♐ Feb 11 14:36	♓ Apr 12 14:24	♊ Jun 12 14:15	♍ Aug 13 08:45
♑ Feb 13 18:37	♈ Apr 14 15:47	♋ Jun 14 21:19	♎ Aug 15 21:51
♒ Feb 15 19:26	♉ Apr 16 17:32	♌ Jun 17 06:58	♏ Aug 18 10:11
♓ Feb 17 18:44	♊ Apr 18 21:09	♍ Jun 19 19:04	♐ Aug 20 19:54
♈ Feb 19 18:36	♋ Apr 21 04:05	♎ Jun 22 07:57	♑ Aug 23 01:50
♉ Feb 21 20:51	♌ Apr 23 14:35	♏ Jun 24 18:59	♒ Aug 25 04:05
♊ Feb 24 02:42	♎ Apr 26 03:16	♐ Jun 27 02:17	♓ Aug 27 04:02
♋ Feb 26 12:12	♏ Apr 28 15:38	♑ Jun 29 06:00	♈ Aug 29 03:29
♌ Feb 29 00:13	♐ May 1 01:39	♒ Jul 1 07:30	♉ Aug 31 04:23

♊ Sep 2 08:12	♍ Nov 3 04:02
♋ Sep 4 15:38	♎ Nov 5 17:04
♌ Sep 7 02:14	♏ Nov 8 04:47
♍ Sep 9 14:47	♐ Nov 10 14:06
♎ Sep 12 03:50	♑ Nov 12 21:13
♏ Sep 14 16:07	♒ Nov 15 02:37
♐ Sep 17 02:24	♓ Nov 17 06:34
♑ Sep 19 09:45	♈ Nov 19 09:13
♒ Sep 21 13:43	♉ Nov 21 11:02
♓ Sep 23 14:51	♊ Nov 23 13:11
♈ Sep 25 14:30	♋ Nov 25 17:19
♉ Sep 27 14:29	♌ Nov 28 00:51
♊ Sep 29 16:43	♍ Nov 30 12:00
♋ Oct 1 22:38	♎ Dec 3 00:55
♌ Oct 4 08:31	♏ Dec 5 12:51
♍ Oct 6 21:01	♐ Dec 7 21:55
♎ Oct 9 10:04	♑ Dec 10 04:07
♏ Oct 11 21:58	♒ Dec 12 08:25
♐ Oct 14 07:57	♓ Dec 14 11:53
♑ Oct 16 15:03	♈ Dec 16 15:03
♒ Oct 18 21:04	♉ Dec 18 18:12
♓ Oct 20 23:59	♊ Dec 20 21:43
♈ Oct 23 00:59	♋ Dec 23 02:35
♉ Oct 25 01:23	♌ Dec 25 09:58
♊ Oct 27 02:56	♍ Dec 27 20:28
♋ Oct 29 07:29	♎ Dec 30 09:09
♌ Oct 31 16:04	

Mercury

Jan 1 14♑	♋ Jul 12 06:22
♒ Jan 10 05:24	♌ Jul 28 21:18
R Feb 2 28♒	♍ Aug 12 17:31
D Feb 23 13♒	♎ Aug 30 20:09
♓ Mar 16 10:09	R Sep 28 26♎
♈ Apr 4 22:03	D Oct 20 11♎
♉ Apr 20 06:45	♏ Nov 6 14:58
♊ May 4 19:52	♐ Nov 25 10:06
R May 31 26♊	♑ Dec 14 11:53
D Jun 24 18♊	

Venus

Jan 1 12♒	D Jul 4 13♊
♓ Jan 15 16:02	♋ Aug 6 23:27
♈ Feb 9 13:06	♌ Sep 7 11:37
♉ Mar 6 10:26	♍ Oct 4 13:13
♊ Apr 3 17:16	♎ Oct 29 23:18
♋ May 17 17:07	♏ Nov 23 13:32
R May 22 0♋	♐ Dec 17 17:55
♊ May 27 06:35	

Mars

Jan 1 24♏
♐ Jan 8 15:20
♑ Feb 22 10:07
♒ Apr 6 21:38
♓ May 22 07:19
♈ Jul 13 19:54
R Aug 26 11♈
♓ Oct 24 03:27
D Oct 28 29♓
♈ Nov 1 08:23

Jupiter

Jan 1 20♈
♉ Mar 8 15:54
♊ Jul 22 00:46
R Sep 24 6♊
♉ Nov 30 19:46

Saturn

Jan 1 25♐
♑ Feb 14 00:05
R Apr 11 2♑
♐ Jun 10 05:11
D Aug 30 25♐
♑ Nov 12 09:32

Uranus

Jan 1 27♐
♑ Feb 15 02:22
R Apr 4 1♑
♐ May 27 00:17
D Sep 5 27♐
♑ Dec 2 16:59

Neptune

Jan 1 7♑
R Apr 11 10♑
D Sep 18 7♑

Pluto

Jan 1 11♏
R Feb 14 12♏
D Jul 20 9♏

1989

Sun

♒ Jan 20 02:07	♈ Mar 20 15:27	♊ May 21 01:52	♌ Jul 22 20:43	♎ Sep 23 01:19	♐ Nov 22 08:04
♓ Feb 18 16:20	♉ Apr 20 02:37	♋ Jun 21 09:52	♍ Aug 23 03:45	♏ Oct 23 10:34	♑ Dec 21 21:22

Moon

Jan 1 19♎	♑ Mar 2 08:59	♈ May 2 11:52	♋ Jul 2 09:19	♎ Sep 2 01:48	♑ Nov 3 02:46
♏ Jan 1 21:34	♒ Mar 4 13:36	♉ May 4 11:56	♌ Jul 4 14:37	♏ Sep 4 14:22	♒ Nov 5 12:09
♐ Jan 4 07:11	♓ Mar 6 15:00	♊ May 6 12:03	♍ Jul 6 23:05	♐ Sep 7 02:51	♓ Nov 7 18:24
♑ Jan 6 13:13	♈ Mar 8 14:37	♋ May 8 14:19	♎ Jul 9 10:30	♑ Sep 9 13:13	♈ Nov 9 21:07
♒ Jan 8 16:30	♉ Mar 10 14:25	♌ May 10 20:22	♏ Jul 11 23:10	♒ Sep 11 20:01	♉ Nov 11 21:09
♓ Jan 10 18:31	♊ Mar 12 16:16	♍ May 13 06:30	♐ Jul 14 10:31	♓ Sep 13 23:08	♊ Nov 13 20:19
♈ Jan 12 20:36	♋ Mar 14 21:27	♎ May 15 19:07	♑ Jul 16 19:02	♈ Sep 15 23:38	♋ Nov 15 20:51
♉ Jan 14 23:37	♌ Mar 17 06:11	♏ May 18 07:48	♒ Jul 19 00:36	♉ Sep 17 23:22	♌ Nov 18 00:45
♊ Jan 17 03:57	♍ Mar 19 17:39	♐ May 20 18:51	♓ Jul 21 04:07	♊ Sep 20 00:17	♍ Nov 20 08:55
♋ Jan 19 09:57	♎ Mar 22 06:23	♑ May 23 03:54	♈ Jul 23 06:41	♋ Sep 22 03:50	♎ Nov 22 20:24
♌ Jan 21 18:02	♏ Mar 24 19:10	♒ May 25 11:01	♉ Jul 25 09:10	♌ Sep 24 10:45	♏ Nov 25 09:14
♍ Jan 24 04:32	♐ Mar 27 06:54	♓ May 27 16:13	♊ Jul 27 12:15	♍ Sep 26 20:33	♐ Nov 27 21:29
♎ Jan 26 17:01	♑ Mar 29 16:26	♈ May 29 19:26	♋ Jul 29 16:31	♎ Sep 29 08:15	♑ Nov 30 08:27
♏ Jan 29 05:49	♒ Mar 31 22:46	♉ May 31 21:00	♌ Jul 31 22:40	♏ Oct 1 20:53	♒ Dec 2 17:41
♐ Jan 31 16:30	♓ Apr 3 01:37	♊ Jun 2 22:03	♍ Aug 3 07:19	♐ Oct 4 09:29	♓ Dec 5 00:47
♑ Feb 2 23:30	♈ Apr 5 01:52	♋ Jun 5 00:18	♎ Aug 5 18:28	♑ Oct 6 20:45	♈ Dec 7 05:12
♒ Feb 5 02:51	♉ Apr 7 01:07	♌ Jun 7 05:28	♏ Aug 8 07:05	♒ Oct 9 05:07	♉ Dec 9 06:59
♓ Feb 7 03:52	♊ Apr 9 01:31	♍ Jun 9 14:30	♐ Aug 10 19:03	♓ Oct 11 09:38	♊ Dec 11 07:14
♈ Feb 9 04:17	♋ Apr 11 04:58	♎ Jun 12 02:32	♑ Aug 13 04:16	♈ Oct 13 10:42	♋ Dec 13 07:50
♉ Feb 11 05:44	♌ Apr 13 12:31	♏ Jun 14 15:12	♒ Aug 15 10:00	♉ Oct 15 09:52	♌ Dec 15 10:42
♊ Feb 13 09:22	♍ Apr 15 23:39	♐ Jun 17 02:13	♓ Aug 17 12:45	♊ Oct 17 09:20	♍ Dec 17 17:19
♋ Feb 15 15:40	♎ Apr 18 12:31	♑ Jun 19 10:42	♈ Aug 19 13:59	♋ Oct 19 11:10	♎ Dec 20 03:45
♌ Feb 18 00:32	♏ Apr 21 01:13	♒ Jun 21 16:56	♉ Aug 21 15:10	♌ Oct 21 16:48	♏ Dec 22 16:19
♍ Feb 20 11:35	♐ Apr 23 12:39	♓ Jun 23 21:37	♊ Aug 23 17:38	♍ Oct 24 02:15	♐ Dec 25 04:37
♎ Feb 23 00:04	♑ Apr 25 22:13	♈ Jun 26 01:07	♋ Aug 25 22:13	♎ Oct 26 14:12	♑ Dec 27 15:10
♏ Feb 25 12:57	♒ Apr 28 05:34	♉ Jun 28 03:45	♌ Aug 28 05:12	♏ Oct 28 02:57	♒ Dec 29 23:37
♐ Feb 28 00:29	♓ Apr 30 10:04	♊ Jun 30 06:08	♍ Aug 30 14:30	♐ Oct 31 15:22	

Mercury

Jan 1 26♑	♊ Jun 12 09:15
♒ Jan 2 19:26	♋ Jul 6 00:42
R Jan 16 12♒	♌ Jul 20 09:03
♑ Jan 29 03:46	♍ Aug 5 01:03
D Feb 5 26♑	♎ Aug 26 06:13
♒ Feb 14 18:36	R Sep 11 10♎
♓ Mar 10 18:00	♍ Sep 26 15:23
♈ Mar 28 03:10	D Oct 3 25♍
♉ Apr 11 21:28	♎ Oct 11 06:24
♊ Apr 29 20:14	♏ Oct 30 13:52
R May 12 7♊	♐ Nov 18 03:10
♉ May 28 23:28	♑ Dec 7 14:34
D Jun 5 27♉	R Dec 30 26♑

Venus

Jan 1 17♐	♌ Jun 29 07:21
♑ Jan 10 18:08	♍ Jul 24 01:31
♒ Feb 3 17:16	♎ Aug 18 01:57
♓ Feb 27 17:00	♏ Sep 12 12:22
♈ Mar 23 18:32	♐ Oct 8 15:57
♉ Apr 16 22:53	♑ Nov 5 10:08
♊ May 11 06:30	♒ Dec 10 04:50
♋ Jun 4 17:18	R Dec 29 6♒

Mars

Jan 1 20♈
♉ Jan 19 07:54
♊ Mar 11 08:47
♋ Apr 29 04:43
♌ Jun 16 14:15
♍ Aug 3 13:40
♎ Sep 19 14:42
♏ Nov 4 05:31
♐ Dec 18 05:01

Jupiter

Jan 1 26♉
D Jan 20 26♉
♊ Mar 11 04:34
♋ Jul 31 00:27
R Oct 29 10♋

Saturn

Jan 1 5♑
R Apr 22 13♑
D Sep 11 7♑

Uranus

Jan 1 1♑
R Apr 9 5♑
D Sep 10 1♑

Neptune

Jan 1 9♑
R Apr 13 12♑
D Sep 21 9♑

Pluto

Jan 1 14♏
R Feb 16 15♏
D Jul 23 12♏

1990

Sun

♒ Jan 20 08:01	♈ Mar 20 21:21	♊ May 21 07:40	♌ Jul 23 02:23	♎ Sep 23 06:58	♐ Nov 22 13:47
♓ Feb 18 22:14	♉ Apr 20 08:29	♋ Jun 21 15:36	♍ Aug 23 09:22	♏ Oct 23 16:15	♑ Dec 22 03:06

Moon

Jan 1 26♒	♉ Mar 1 01:44	♌ May 1 00:08	♏ Jul 1 18:00	♒ Sep 1 20:52	♉ Nov 2 05:32
♓ Jan 1 06:10	♊ Mar 3 03:38	♍ May 3 07:19	♐ Jul 4 06:36	♓ Sep 4 04:06	♊ Nov 4 05:07
♈ Jan 3 10:56	♋ Mar 5 07:03	♎ May 5 17:29	♑ Jul 6 18:40	♈ Sep 6 08:23	♋ Nov 6 05:08
♉ Jan 5 14:04	♌ Mar 7 12:24	♏ May 8 05:22	♒ Jul 9 05:07	♉ Sep 8 10:55	♌ Nov 8 07:24
♊ Jan 7 16:02	♍ Mar 9 19:48	♐ May 10 17:57	♓ Jul 11 13:30	♊ Sep 10 13:05	♍ Nov 10 12:48
♋ Jan 9 17:53	♎ Mar 12 05:09	♑ May 13 06:21	♈ Jul 13 19:36	♋ Sep 12 15:52	♎ Nov 12 21:08
♌ Jan 11 21:02	♏ Mar 14 16:25	♒ May 15 17:31	♉ Jul 15 23:29	♌ Sep 14 19:52	♏ Nov 15 07:39
♍ Jan 14 02:58	♐ Mar 17 04:56	♓ May 18 01:53	♊ Jul 18 01:31	♍ Sep 17 01:19	♐ Nov 17 19:39
♎ Jan 16 12:18	♑ Mar 19 17:01	♈ May 20 06:31	♋ Jul 20 02:43	♎ Sep 19 08:34	♑ Nov 20 08:32
♏ Jan 19 00:17	♒ Mar 22 02:32	♉ May 22 07:43	♌ Jul 22 04:29	♏ Sep 21 18:06	♒ Nov 22 21:06
♐ Jan 21 12:44	♓ Mar 24 08:09	♊ May 24 07:00	♍ Jul 24 08:17	♐ Sep 24 05:53	♓ Nov 25 07:31
♑ Jan 23 23:28	♈ Mar 26 10:15	♋ May 26 06:34	♎ Jul 26 15:19	♑ Sep 26 18:37	♈ Nov 27 14:07
♒ Jan 26 07:26	♉ Mar 28 10:27	♌ May 28 08:30	♏ Jul 29 01:38	♒ Sep 29 05:54	♉ Nov 29 16:37
♓ Jan 28 12:50	♊ Mar 30 10:43	♍ May 30 14:08	♐ Jul 31 13:59	♓ Oct 1 13:43	♊ Dec 1 16:23
♈ Jan 30 16:34	♋ Apr 1 12:49	♎ Jun 1 23:31	♑ Aug 3 02:09	♈ Oct 3 17:41	♋ Dec 3 15:27
♉ Feb 1 19:28	♌ Apr 3 17:50	♏ Jun 4 11:21	♒ Aug 5 12:20	♉ Oct 5 19:07	♌ Dec 5 16:00
♊ Feb 3 22:12	♍ Apr 6 01:42	♐ Jun 7 00:00	♓ Aug 7 19:54	♊ Oct 7 19:47	♍ Dec 7 19:38
♋ Feb 6 01:28	♎ Apr 8 11:44	♑ Jun 9 12:12	♈ Aug 10 01:12	♋ Oct 9 21:29	♎ Dec 10 03:00
♌ Feb 8 05:52	♏ Apr 10 23:17	♒ Jun 11 23:09	♉ Aug 12 04:54	♌ Oct 12 01:16	♏ Dec 12 13:28
♍ Feb 10 12:14	♐ Apr 13 11:47	♓ Jun 14 08:00	♊ Aug 14 07:42	♍ Oct 14 07:21	♐ Dec 15 01:45
♎ Feb 12 21:09	♑ Apr 16 00:15	♈ Jun 16 13:54	♋ Aug 16 10:12	♎ Oct 16 15:26	♑ Dec 17 14:35
♏ Feb 15 08:35	♒ Apr 18 10:52	♉ Jun 18 16:43	♌ Aug 18 13:10	♏ Oct 19 01:24	♒ Dec 20 03:00
♐ Feb 17 21:06	♓ Apr 20 17:58	♊ Jun 20 17:15	♍ Aug 20 17:33	♐ Oct 21 13:08	♓ Dec 22 13:48
♑ Feb 20 08:30	♈ Apr 22 20:59	♋ Jun 22 17:10	♎ Aug 22 23:02	♑ Oct 24 02:02	♈ Dec 24 21:45
♒ Feb 22 16:52	♉ Apr 24 21:03	♌ Jun 24 18:24	♏ Aug 25 09:57	♒ Oct 26 14:14	♉ Dec 27 02:10
♓ Feb 24 21:49	♊ Apr 26 20:13	♍ Jun 26 22:42	♐ Aug 27 21:58	♓ Oct 28 23:21	♊ Dec 29 03:25
♈ Feb 27 00:17	♋ Apr 28 20:39	♎ Jun 29 06:47	♑ Aug 30 10:24	♈ Oct 31 04:14	♋ Dec 31 03:02

Mercury

Jan 1 26♑	♌ Jul 12 00:01
D Jan 20 10♑	♍ Jul 29 11:15
♒ Feb 12 01:07	R Aug 25 22♍
♓ Mar 3 17:11	D Sep 17 9♍
♈ Mar 20 00:08	♎ Oct 5 17:35
♉ Apr 4 07:30	♏ Oct 23 01:51
R Apr 23 16♉	♐ Nov 11 00:00
D May 17 7♉	♑ Dec 2 00:09
♊ Jun 12 00:09	R Dec 14 9♑
♋ Jun 27 20:47	♐ Dec 25 23:07

Venus

Jan 1 6♋	♋ Jul 20 03:41
♑ Jan 16 15:42	♌ Aug 13 22:05
D Feb 8 20♑	♍ Sep 7 08:20
♒ Mar 3 17:50	♎ Oct 1 12:14
♓ Apr 6 09:10	♏ Oct 25 12:03
♈ May 4 03:53	♐ Nov 18 09:58
♉ May 30 10:15	♑ Dec 12 07:16
♊ Jun 25 00:15	

Mars

Jan 1 9♐
♑ Jan 29 14:14
♒ Mar 11 16:00
♓ Apr 20 22:13
♈ May 31 07:17
♉ Jul 12 14:53
♊ Aug 31 11:10
R Oct 20 14♊
♉ Dec 14 08:40

Jupiter

Jan 1 5♋
D Feb 24 0♋
♌ Aug 18 07:35
R Nov 30 13♌

Saturn

Jan 1 15♑
R May 4 25♑
D Sep 23 18♑

Uranus

Jan 1 5♑
R Apr 13 9♑
D Sep 14 5♑

Neptune

Jan 1 12♑
R Apr 16 14♑
D Sep 23 11♑

Pluto

Jan 1 17♏
R Feb 19 17♏
D Jul 26 14♏

1991

Sun

♒ Jan 20 13:47	♈ Mar 21 03:01	♊ May 21 13:23	♌ Jul 23 08:15	♎ Sep 23 12:51	♐ Nov 22 19:37
♓ Feb 19 03:58	♉ Apr 20 14:10	♋ Jun 21 21:22	♍ Aug 23 15:17	♏ Oct 23 22:07	♑ Dec 22 08:55

Moon

Jan 1 13♋	♎ Mar 2 06:03	♑ May 3 03:54	♈ Jul 4 03:34	♋ Sep 3 06:20	♎ Nov 3 04:12
♌ Jan 2 02:55	♏ Mar 4 13:08	♒ May 5 16:52	♉ Jul 6 09:52	♌ Sep 5 08:14	♏ Nov 5 10:08
♍ Jan 4 04:56	♐ Mar 6 23:35	♓ May 8 04:05	♊ Jul 8 12:42	♍ Sep 7 09:35	♐ Nov 7 18:22
♎ Jan 6 10:33	♑ Mar 9 12:14	♈ May 10 11:35	♋ Jul 10 13:03	♎ Sep 9 11:52	♑ Nov 10 05:16
♏ Jan 8 19:59	♒ Mar 12 00:30	♉ May 12 15:07	♌ Jul 12 12:36	♏ Sep 11 16:43	♒ Nov 12 18:06
♐ Jan 11 08:07	♓ Mar 14 10:10	♊ May 14 16:03	♍ Jul 14 13:11	♐ Sep 14 01:14	♓ Nov 15 06:34
♑ Jan 13 21:00	♈ Mar 16 16:37	♋ May 16 16:14	♎ Jul 16 16:34	♑ Sep 16 13:04	♈ Nov 17 16:07
♒ Jan 16 09:04	♉ Mar 18 20:40	♌ May 18 17:31	♏ Jul 18 23:40	♒ Sep 19 01:57	♉ Nov 19 21:49
♓ Jan 18 19:24	♊ Mar 20 23:37	♍ May 20 21:00	♐ Jul 21 10:16	♓ Sep 21 13:21	♊ Nov 22 00:22
♈ Jan 21 03:27	♋ Mar 23 02:28	♎ May 23 03:07	♑ Jul 23 22:55	♈ Sep 23 21:55	♋ Nov 24 01:26
♉ Jan 23 09:01	♌ Mar 25 05:44	♏ May 25 11:41	♒ Jul 26 11:50	♉ Sep 26 04:00	♌ Nov 26 02:37
♊ Jan 25 12:06	♍ Mar 27 09:41	♐ May 27 22:22	♓ Jul 28 23:35	♊ Sep 28 08:25	♍ Nov 28 05:13
♋ Jan 27 13:24	♎ Mar 29 14:50	♑ May 30 10:40	♈ Jul 31 09:21	♋ Sep 30 11:59	♎ Nov 30 09:46
♌ Jan 29 14:04	♏ Mar 31 22:01	♒ Jun 1 23:41	♉ Aug 2 16:31	♌ Oct 2 14:59	♏ Dec 2 16:33
♍ Jan 31 15:45	♐ Apr 3 07:58	♓ Jun 4 11:37	♊ Aug 4 20:55	♍ Oct 4 17:44	♐ Dec 5 01:32
♎ Feb 2 20:02	♑ Apr 5 20:19	♈ Jun 6 20:25	♋ Aug 6 22:47	♎ Oct 6 21:00	♑ Dec 7 12:41
♏ Feb 5 04:02	♒ Apr 8 09:00	♉ Jun 9 01:12	♌ Aug 8 23:10	♏ Oct 9 01:59	♒ Dec 10 01:27
♐ Feb 7 15:23	♓ Apr 10 19:17	♊ Jun 11 02:37	♍ Aug 10 23:35	♐ Oct 11 09:58	♓ Dec 12 14:19
♑ Feb 10 04:15	♈ Apr 13 01:50	♋ Jun 13 02:16	♎ Aug 13 01:52	♑ Oct 13 21:10	♈ Dec 15 01:07
♒ Feb 12 16:16	♉ Apr 15 05:06	♌ Jun 15 02:11	♏ Aug 15 07:33	♒ Oct 16 10:05	♉ Dec 17 08:11
♓ Feb 15 01:58	♊ Apr 17 06:42	♍ Jun 17 04:04	♐ Aug 17 17:11	♓ Oct 18 21:52	♊ Dec 19 11:21
♈ Feb 17 09:12	♋ Apr 19 08:17	♎ Jun 19 09:01	♑ Aug 20 05:34	♈ Oct 21 06:34	♋ Dec 21 11:56
♉ Feb 19 14:24	♌ Apr 21 11:05	♏ Jun 21 17:18	♒ Aug 22 18:26	♉ Oct 23 11:56	♌ Dec 23 11:38
♊ Feb 21 18:10	♍ Apr 23 15:29	♐ Jun 24 04:16	♓ Aug 25 05:52	♊ Oct 25 15:08	♍ Dec 25 12:23
♋ Feb 23 20:57	♎ Apr 25 21:37	♑ Jun 26 16:50	♈ Aug 27 15:00	♋ Oct 27 17:37	♎ Dec 27 15:38
♌ Feb 25 23:13	♏ Apr 28 05:35	♒ Jun 29 05:47	♉ Aug 29 22:00	♌ Oct 29 20:20	♏ Dec 29 22:04
♍ Feb 28 01:51	♐ Apr 30 15:42	♓ Jul 1 17:51	♊ Sep 1 03:01	♍ Oct 31 23:46	

Mercury

Jan 1 24♐	♌ Jul 4 06:04
D Jan 3 24♐	♍ Jul 26 13:04
♑ Jan 14 07:59	R Aug 7 5♍
♒ Feb 5 22:20	♌ Aug 19 21:49
♓ Feb 24 02:33	D Aug 31 23♌
♈ Mar 11 22:29	♍ Sep 10 17:21
R Apr 4 28♈	♎ Sep 28 03:27
D Apr 28 17♈	♏ Oct 15 14:00
♉ May 16 22:17	♐ Nov 4 10:35
♊ Jun 5 02:10	R Nov 28 24♐
♋ Jun 19 05:39	D Dec 18 7♐

Venus

Jan 1 24♑	♍ Jul 11 05:19
♒ Jan 5 05:01	R Aug 1 7♍
♓ Jan 29 04:43	♌ Aug 21 14:49
♈ Feb 22 09:01	D Sep 13 20♌
♉ Mar 18 21:45	♍ Oct 6 21:21
♊ Apr 13 00:10	♎ Nov 9 06:40
♋ May 9 01:32	♏ Dec 6 07:24
♌ Jun 6 01:27	

Mars

Jan 1 27♉	
D Jan 1 27♉	
♊ Jan 21 01:22	
♋ Apr 3 00:58	
♌ May 26 12:31	
♍ Jul 15 12:44	
♎ Sep 1 06:47	
♏ Oct 16 19:08	
♐ Nov 29 02:24	

Jupiter

Jan 1 11♌
D Mar 30 3♌
♍ Sep 12 06:16
R Dec 30 14♍

Saturn

Jan 1 25♑
♒ Feb 6 18:45
R May 17 6♒
D Oct 5 0♒

Uranus

Jan 1 9♑
R Apr 18 13♑
D Sep 19 9♑

Neptune

Jan 1 14♑
R Apr 19 16♑
D Sep 26 13♑

Pluto

Jan 1 19♏
R Feb 22 20♏
D Jul 28 17♏

1992

Sun

♒ Jan 20 19:32	♈ Mar 20 08:46	♊ May 20 19:11	♌ Jul 22 14:11	♎ Sep 22 18:45	♐ Nov 22 01:26
♓ Feb 19 09:43	♉ Apr 19 19:54	♋ Jun 21 03:15	♍ Aug 22 21:12	♏ Oct 23 03:58	♑ Dec 21 14:42

Moon

Jan 1 26♏	♒ Feb 29 20:35	♉ May 1 19:09	♌ Jul 1 22:15	♏ Aug 31 19:38	♒ Nov 1 12:44
♐ Jan 1 07:30	♓ Mar 3 09:12	♊ May 4 00:28	♍ Jul 3 22:37	♐ Sep 3 00:50	♓ Nov 4 01:12
♑ Jan 3 19:08	♈ Mar 5 20:07	♋ May 6 04:09	♎ Jul 6 00:27	♑ Sep 5 10:07	♈ Nov 6 13:20
♒ Jan 6 07:59	♉ Mar 8 05:06	♌ May 8 07:07	♏ Jul 8 04:53	♒ Sep 7 22:08	♉ Nov 8 23:18
♓ Jan 8 20:52	♊ Mar 10 12:03	♍ May 10 09:57	♐ Jul 10 12:18	♓ Sep 10 10:56	♊ Nov 11 06:49
♈ Jan 11 08:22	♋ Mar 12 16:50	♎ May 12 13:06	♑ Jul 12 22:15	♈ Sep 12 23:02	♋ Nov 13 12:19
♉ Jan 13 17:00	♌ Mar 14 19:21	♏ May 14 17:15	♒ Jul 15 10:03	♉ Sep 15 09:46	♌ Nov 15 16:24
♊ Jan 15 21:54	♍ Mar 16 20:14	♐ May 16 23:21	♓ Jul 17 22:45	♊ Sep 17 18:41	♍ Nov 17 19:29
♋ Jan 17 23:27	♎ Mar 18 20:55	♑ May 19 08:13	♈ Jul 20 11:08	♋ Sep 20 00:59	♎ Nov 19 22:03
♌ Jan 19 22:57	♏ Mar 20 23:19	♒ May 21 19:44	♉ Jul 22 21:36	♌ Sep 22 04:20	♏ Nov 22 00:51
♍ Jan 21 22:22	♐ Mar 23 05:14	♓ May 24 08:25	♊ Jul 25 05:45	♍ Sep 24 05:08	♐ Nov 24 05:00
♎ Jan 23 23:42	♑ Mar 25 15:08	♈ May 26 19:52	♋ Jul 27 08:09	♎ Sep 26 04:55	♑ Nov 26 11:38
♏ Jan 26 04:32	♒ Mar 28 03:45	♉ May 29 04:16	♌ Jul 29 08:39	♏ Sep 28 05:43	♒ Nov 28 21:20
♐ Jan 28 13:21	♓ Mar 30 16:24	♊ May 31 09:20	♍ Jul 31 08:01	♐ Sep 30 09:34	♓ Dec 1 09:23
♑ Jan 31 01:07	♈ Apr 2 03:03	♋ Jun 2 11:59	♎ Aug 2 08:16	♑ Oct 2 17:30	♈ Dec 3 21:48
♒ Feb 2 14:09	♉ Apr 4 11:18	♌ Jun 4 13:35	♏ Aug 4 11:16	♒ Oct 5 04:52	♉ Dec 6 08:16
♓ Feb 5 02:51	♊ Apr 6 17:33	♍ Jun 6 15:27	♐ Aug 6 17:57	♓ Oct 7 17:37	♊ Dec 8 15:37
♈ Feb 7 14:15	♋ Apr 8 22:19	♎ Jun 8 18:34	♑ Aug 9 04:00	♈ Oct 10 05:36	♋ Dec 10 20:06
♉ Feb 9 23:36	♌ Apr 11 01:47	♏ Jun 10 23:27	♒ Aug 11 16:07	♉ Oct 12 15:48	♌ Dec 12 22:48
♊ Feb 12 06:08	♍ Apr 13 04:09	♐ Jun 13 06:28	♓ Aug 14 04:51	♊ Oct 15 00:08	♍ Dec 15 00:55
♋ Feb 14 09:31	♎ Apr 15 06:10	♑ Jun 15 15:49	♈ Aug 16 17:12	♋ Oct 17 06:36	♎ Dec 17 03:34
♌ Feb 16 10:15	♏ Apr 17 09:09	♒ Jun 18 03:19	♉ Aug 19 04:09	♌ Oct 19 11:01	♏ Dec 19 07:20
♍ Feb 18 09:46	♐ Apr 19 14:40	♓ Jun 20 16:00	♊ Aug 21 12:37	♍ Oct 21 13:28	♐ Dec 21 12:43
♎ Feb 20 10:05	♑ Apr 21 23:40	♈ Jun 23 04:04	♋ Aug 23 17:37	♎ Oct 23 14:39	♑ Dec 23 20:05
♏ Feb 22 13:11	♒ Apr 24 11:38	♉ Jun 25 13:29	♌ Aug 25 19:15	♏ Oct 25 16:05	♒ Dec 26 05:43
♐ Feb 24 20:27	♓ Apr 27 00:20	♊ Jun 27 19:14	♍ Aug 27 18:46	♐ Oct 27 19:30	♓ Dec 28 17:28
♑ Feb 27 07:33	♈ Apr 29 11:14	♋ Jun 29 21:43	♎ Aug 29 18:10	♑ Oct 30 02:17	♈ Dec 31 06:06

Mercury

Jan 1 18♐	♌ Jun 27 05:22
♑ Jan 10 01:37	R Jul 20 18♌
♒ Jan 29 21:12	D Aug 13 5♌
♓ Feb 16 07:03	♍ Sep 3 08:09
♈ Mar 3 21:34	♎ Sep 19 05:40
R Mar 17 11♈	♏ Oct 7 10:15
♓ Apr 4 01:53	♐ Oct 29 17:15
D Apr 9 28♓	R Nov 11 8♐
♈ Apr 14 17:44	♏ Nov 21 19:43
♉ May 11 04:09	D Dec 1 21♏
♊ May 26 21:19	♐ Dec 12 08:10
♋ Jun 9 18:34	

Venus

Jan 1 0♐	♌ Jul 13 21:08
♑ Jan 25 07:13	♍ Aug 7 06:27
♒ Feb 18 16:39	♎ Aug 31 16:09
♓ Mar 13 23:57	♏ Sep 25 03:30
♈ Apr 7 07:15	♐ Oct 19 17:43
♉ May 1 15:41	♑ Nov 13 12:45
♊ May 26 01:19	♒ Dec 8 17:47
♋ Jun 19 11:24	

Mars

Jan 1 23♐
♑ Jan 9 09:48
♒ Feb 18 04:42
♓ Mar 28 02:06
♈ May 5 21:45
♉ Jun 14 16:11
♊ Jul 26 19:12
♋ Sep 12 06:20
R Nov 28 27♋

Jupiter

Jan 1 14♍
D Apr 30 4♍
♎ Oct 10 13:36

Saturn

Jan 1 5♒
R May 28 18♒
D Oct 16 11♒

Uranus

Jan 1 13♑
R Apr 21 18♑
D Sep 22 14♑

Neptune

Jan 1 16♑
R Apr 20 18♑
D Sep 27 16♑

Pluto

Jan 1 22♏
R Feb 24 22♏
D Jul 30 20♏

1993

Sun

♒ Jan 20 01:23	♈ Mar 20 14:39	♊ May 21 01:01	♌ Jul 22 19:52	♎ Sep 23 00:25	♐ Nov 22 07:07
♓ Feb 18 15:35	♉ Apr 20 01:47	♋ Jun 21 09:00	♍ Aug 23 02:53	♏ Oct 23 09:39	♑ Dec 21 20:25

Moon

Jan 1 8♈	♋ Mar 3 02:16	♎ May 3 01:21	♑ Jul 3 01:49	♈ Sep 2 21:21	♋ Nov 3 20:24
♉ Jan 2 17:31	♌ Mar 5 05:40	♏ May 5 01:57	♒ Jul 5 09:15	♉ Sep 5 10:09	♌ Nov 6 04:07
♊ Jan 5 01:43	♍ Mar 7 05:52	♐ May 7 03:35	♓ Jul 7 19:09	♊ Sep 7 22:15	♍ Nov 8 08:47
♋ Jan 7 06:10	♎ Mar 9 04:47	♑ May 9 07:52	♈ Jul 10 07:11	♋ Sep 10 07:36	♎ Nov 10 10:43
♌ Jan 9 07:50	♏ Mar 11 04:39	♒ May 11 15:45	♉ Jul 12 19:37	♌ Sep 12 12:51	♏ Nov 12 10:59
♍ Jan 11 08:20	♐ Mar 13 07:33	♓ May 14 02:51	♊ Jul 15 06:07	♍ Sep 14 14:20	♐ Nov 14 11:20
♎ Jan 13 09:30	♑ Mar 15 14:29	♈ May 16 15:24	♋ Jul 17 13:07	♎ Sep 16 13:44	♑ Nov 16 13:33
♏ Jan 15 12:42	♒ Mar 18 00:52	♉ May 19 03:17	♌ Jul 19 16:48	♏ Sep 18 13:14	♒ Nov 18 19:07
♐ Jan 17 18:30	♓ Mar 20 13:11	♊ May 21 13:07	♍ Jul 21 18:24	♐ Sep 20 14:53	♓ Nov 21 04:28
♑ Jan 20 02:46	♈ Mar 23 01:52	♋ May 23 20:38	♎ Jul 23 19:39	♑ Sep 22 19:53	♈ Nov 23 16:30
♒ Jan 22 13:01	♉ Mar 25 13:59	♌ May 26 02:04	♏ Jul 25 22:00	♒ Sep 25 04:19	♉ Nov 26 05:15
♓ Jan 25 00:47	♊ Mar 28 00:48	♍ May 28 05:46	♐ Jul 28 02:13	♓ Sep 27 15:13	♊ Nov 28 16:48
♈ Jan 27 13:28	♋ Mar 30 09:15	♎ May 30 08:18	♑ Jul 30 08:27	♈ Sep 30 03:28	♋ Dec 1 02:17
♉ Jan 30 01:37	♌ Apr 1 14:21	♏ Jun 1 10:23	♒ Aug 1 16:36	♉ Oct 2 16:12	♌ Dec 3 09:34
♊ Feb 1 11:15	♍ Apr 3 16:10	♐ Jun 3 13:02	♓ Aug 4 02:43	♊ Oct 5 04:28	♍ Dec 5 14:43
♋ Feb 3 16:57	♎ Apr 5 15:54	♑ Jun 5 17:27	♈ Aug 6 14:39	♋ Oct 7 14:42	♎ Dec 7 18:03
♌ Feb 5 18:51	♏ Apr 7 15:32	♒ Jun 8 00:40	♉ Aug 9 03:22	♌ Oct 9 21:34	♏ Dec 9 20:05
♍ Feb 7 18:28	♐ Apr 9 17:10	♓ Jun 10 10:56	♊ Aug 11 14:46	♍ Oct 12 00:36	♐ Dec 11 21:40
♎ Feb 9 17:59	♑ Apr 11 22:25	♈ Jun 12 23:15	♋ Aug 13 22:47	♎ Oct 14 00:47	♑ Dec 14 00:06
♏ Feb 11 19:24	♒ Apr 14 07:36	♉ Jun 15 11:19	♌ Aug 16 02:43	♏ Oct 16 00:00	♒ Dec 16 04:52
♐ Feb 14 00:07	♓ Apr 16 19:32	♊ Jun 17 21:13	♍ Aug 18 03:41	♐ Oct 18 00:22	♓ Dec 18 12:59
♑ Feb 16 08:20	♈ Apr 19 08:15	♋ Jun 20 04:06	♎ Aug 20 03:36	♑ Oct 20 03:42	♈ Dec 21 00:19
♒ Feb 18 19:06	♉ Apr 21 20:08	♌ Jun 22 08:27	♏ Aug 22 04:28	♒ Oct 22 10:50	♉ Dec 23 13:05
♓ Feb 21 07:12	♊ Apr 24 06:27	♍ Jun 24 11:18	♐ Aug 24 07:46	♓ Oct 24 21:18	♊ Dec 26
♈ Feb 23 19:51	♋ Apr 26 14:45	♎ Jun 26 13:46	♑ Aug 26 13:57	♈ Oct 27 09:39	♋ Dec 28 09:46
♉ Feb 26 08:12	♌ Apr 28 20:39	♏ Jun 28 16:37	♒ Aug 28 22:42	♉ Oct 29 22:21	♌ Dec 30 16:00
♊ Feb 28 18:52	♍ May 1 00:00	♐ Jun 30 20:29	♓ Aug 31 09:19	♊ Nov 1 10:12	

Mercury

Jan 1 27♐	R Jul 1 28♋
♑ Jan 2 14:47	D Jul 25 19♋
♒ Jan 21 11:25	♌ Aug 10 05:38
♓ Feb 7 16:13	♍ Aug 26 07:08
R Feb 27 24♓	♎ Sep 11 11:20
D Mar 22 11♓	♏ Oct 1 02:06
♈ Apr 15 15:08	R Oct 25 21♏
♉ May 3 22:03	D Nov 15 6♏
♊ May 18 06:53	♐ Dec 7 00:55
♋ Jun 2 03:38	♑ Dec 26 12:46

Venus

Jan 1 26♒	♋ Aug 1 22:34
♓ Jan 3 23:55	♌ Aug 27 15:46
♈ Feb 2 12:37	♍ Sep 21 14:22
R Mar 11 20♈	♎ Oct 16 00:15
D Apr 22 3♈	♏ Nov 9 02:08
♉ Jun 6 10:01	♐ Dec 2 23:54
♊ Jul 6 00:19	♑ Dec 26 20:10

Mars

Jan 1 20♋
D Feb 15 8♋
♌ Apr 27 23:49
♍ Jun 23 07:40
♎ Aug 12 01:10
♏ Sep 27 02:13
♐ Nov 9 05:29
♑ Dec 20 00:31

Jupiter

Jan 1 13♎
R Jan 28 14♎
D Jun 1 4♎
♏ Nov 10 08:09

Saturn

Jan 1 16♒
♓ May 21 02:02
R Jun 10 0♓
♒ Jun 30 12:24
D Oct 28 23♒

Uranus

Jan 1 17♑
R Apr 26 22♑
D Sep 27 18♑

Neptune

Jan 1 18♑
R Apr 22 21♑
D Sep 30 18♑

Pluto

Jan 1 24♏
R Feb 26 25♏
D Aug 2 22♏

1994

Sun

♒ Jan 20 07:07	♈ Mar 20 20:27	♊ May 21 06:46	♌ Jul 23 01:40	♎ Sep 23 06:22	♐ Nov 22 13:08
♓ Feb 18 21:22	♉ Apr 20 07:33	♋ Jun 21 14:45	♍ Aug 23 08:44	♏ Oct 23 15:40	♑ Dec 22 02:25

Moon

Jan 1 18 ♌	♏ Mar 1 14:43	♒ May 1 16:34	♉ Jul 2 14:23	♌ Sep 2 15:38	♏ Nov 2 20:19
♍ Jan 1 20:15	♐ Mar 3 16:53	♓ May 4 00:46	♊ Jul 5 03:13	♍ Sep 4 20:34	♐ Nov 4 19:47
♎ Jan 3 23:31	♑ Mar 5 21:24	♈ May 6 12:01	♋ Jul 7 14:17	♎ Sep 6 22:56	♑ Nov 6 20:01
♏ Jan 6 02:29	♒ Mar 8 04:14	♉ May 9 00:50	♌ Jul 9 22:44	♏ Sep 9 00:25	♒ Nov 8 22:49
♐ Jan 8 05:34	♓ Mar 10 13:09	♊ May 11 13:44	♍ Jul 12 04:49	♐ Sep 11 02:24	♓ Nov 11 05:05
♑ Jan 10 09:16	♈ Mar 12 23:59	♋ May 14 01:28	♎ Jul 14 09:15	♑ Sep 13 05:44	♈ Nov 13 14:43
♒ Jan 12 14:24	♉ Mar 15 12:27	♌ May 16 10:58	♏ Jul 16 12:35	♒ Sep 15 10:43	♉ Nov 16 02:43
♓ Jan 14 22:04	♊ Mar 18 01:30	♍ May 18 17:31	♐ Jul 18 15:09	♓ Sep 17 17:32	♊ Nov 18 15:42
♈ Jan 17 08:41	♋ Mar 20 12:53	♎ May 20 20:55	♑ Jul 20 17:31	♈ Sep 20 02:30	♋ Nov 21 04:21
♉ Jan 19 21:22	♌ Mar 22 20:39	♏ May 22 21:50	♒ Jul 22 20:38	♉ Sep 22 13:48	♌ Nov 23 15:34
♊ Jan 22 09:35	♍ Mar 25 00:15	♐ May 24 21:44	♓ Jul 25 01:36	♊ Sep 25 02:41	♍ Nov 26 00:08
♋ Jan 24 18:55	♎ Mar 27 00:46	♑ May 26 22:17	♈ Jul 27 10:30	♋ Sep 27 15:12	♎ Nov 28 05:22
♌ Jan 27 00:39	♏ Mar 29 00:15	♒ May 29 01:19	♉ Jul 29 22:12	♌ Sep 30 00:55	♏ Nov 30 07:22
♍ Jan 29 03:39	♐ Mar 31 00:42	♓ May 31 08:04	♊ Aug 1 11:05	♍ Oct 2 06:40	♐ Dec 2 07:13
♎ Jan 31 05:34	♑ Apr 2 03:38	♈ Jun 2 18:31	♋ Aug 3 22:23	♎ Oct 4 08:57	♑ Dec 4 06:43
♏ Feb 2 07:50	♒ Apr 4 09:45	♉ Jun 5 07:14	♌ Aug 6 06:31	♏ Oct 6 09:22	♒ Dec 6 07:52
♐ Feb 4 11:15	♓ Apr 6 18:50	♊ Jun 7 20:04	♍ Aug 8 11:42	♐ Oct 8 09:46	♓ Dec 8 12:24
♑ Feb 6 16:02	♈ Apr 9 06:08	♋ Jun 10 07:23	♎ Aug 10 15:06	♑ Oct 10 11:44	♈ Dec 10 21:03
♒ Feb 8 22:16	♉ Apr 11 18:47	♌ Jun 12 16:30	♏ Aug 12 17:56	♒ Oct 12 16:09	♉ Dec 13 08:56
♓ Feb 11 06:22	♊ Apr 14 07:48	♍ Jun 14 23:16	♐ Aug 14 20:54	♓ Oct 14 23:18	♊ Dec 15 22:01
♈ Feb 13 16:50	♋ Apr 16 19:42	♎ Jun 17 03:48	♑ Aug 17 00:19	♈ Oct 17 08:57	♋ Dec 18 10:25
♉ Feb 16 05:19	♌ Apr 19 04:46	♏ Jun 19 06:20	♒ Aug 19 04:33	♉ Oct 19 20:35	♌ Dec 20 21:14
♊ Feb 18 18:05	♍ Apr 21 09:59	♐ Jun 21 07:32	♓ Aug 21 10:28	♊ Oct 22 09:27	♎ Dec 23 06:01
♋ Feb 21 04:28	♎ Apr 23 11:40	♑ Jun 23 08:37	♈ Aug 23 18:54	♋ Oct 24 22:15	♏ Dec 25 12:27
♌ Feb 23 10:48	♏ Apr 25 11:18	♒ Jun 25 11:10	♉ Aug 26 06:14	♌ Oct 27 09:04	♏ Dec 27 16:17
♍ Feb 25 13:28	♐ Apr 27 10:49	♓ Jun 27 16:45	♊ Aug 28 19:07	♍ Oct 29 16:22	♐ Dec 29 17:45
♎ Feb 27 14:06	♑ Apr 29 12:05	♈ Jun 30 02:07	♋ Aug 31 07:01	♎ Oct 31 19:47	♑ Dec 31 17:58

Mercury

Jan 1 8 ♑	D Jul 6 29 ♊
♒ Jan 14 00:17	♋ Jul 10 12:16
♓ Feb 1 10:27	♌ Aug 3 06:10
R Feb 11 7 ♓	♍ Aug 18 00:40
♒ Feb 21 15:22	♎ Sep 4 05:05
D Mar 5 23 ♒	♏ Sep 27 08:49
♓ Mar 18 11:58	R Oct 9 5 ♏
♈ Apr 9 16:27	♎ Oct 19 06:16
♉ Apr 25 18:26	D Oct 30 20 ♎
♊ May 9 21:16	♏ Nov 10 12:41
♋ May 28 14:52	♐ Nov 30 04:40
R Jun 12 8 ♋	♑ Dec 19 06:26
♊ Jul 3 01:33	

Venus

Jan 1 6 ♑	♌ Jun 15 07:25
♒ Jan 19 16:29	♍ Jul 11 06:35
♓ Feb 12 14:04	♎ Aug 7 14:37
♈ Mar 8 14:27	♏ Sep 7 17:11
♉ Apr 1 19:20	R Oct 13 18 ♏
♊ Apr 26 06:23	D Nov 23 2 ♏
♋ May 21 01:27	

Mars

Jan 1 9 ♑	♉ May 23 22:43
♒ Jan 28 04:04	♊ Jul 3 22:30
♓ Mar 7 11:00	♋ Aug 16 19:25
♈ Apr 14 18:02	♌ Oct 4 16:06
	♍ Dec 12 11:38

Jupiter

Jan 1 9 ♏
R Feb 28 14 ♏
D Jul 2 4 ♏
♐ Dec 9 10:32

Saturn

Jan 1 27 ♒
♓ Jan 28 23:19
R Jun 23 12 ♓
D Nov 9 5 ♓

Uranus

Jan 1 21 ♑
R Apr 30 26 ♑
D Oct 2 22 ♑

Neptune

Jan 1 20 ♑
R Apr 25 23 ♑
D Oct 2 20 ♑

Pluto

Jan 1 27 ♏
R Mar 1 28 ♏
D Aug 5 25 ♏

1995

Sun

♒ Jan 20 13:04	♈ Mar 21 02:16	♊ May 21 12:35	♌ Jul 23 07:28	♎ Sep 23 12:14	♐ Nov 22 19:02
♓ Feb 19 03:14	♉ Apr 20 13:23	♋ Jun 21 20:34	♍ Aug 23 14:34	♏ Oct 23 21:32	♑ Dec 22 08:17

Moon

♑ Jan 1 3	♈ Mar 2 23:31	♋ May 4 00:45	♎ Jul 4 19:55	♑ Sep 3 19:46	♈ Nov 3 19:21
♒ Jan 2 18:39	♉ Mar 5 08:51	♌ May 6 12:55	♏ Jul 7 01:20	♒ Sep 5 21:47	♉ Nov 6 03:36
♓ Jan 4 21:48	♊ Mar 7 20:56	♍ May 8 22:33	♐ Jul 9 03:38	♓ Sep 8 00:08	♊ Nov 8 13:54
♈ Jan 7 04:56	♋ Mar 10 09:41	♎ May 11 04:30	♑ Jul 11 03:44	♈ Sep 10 04:14	♋ Nov 11 01:56
♉ Jan 9 15:59	♌ Mar 12 20:29	♏ May 13 06:53	♒ Jul 13 03:21	♉ Sep 12 11:21	♌ Nov 13 14:37
♊ Jan 12 04:57	♍ Mar 15 03:54	♐ May 15 06:59	♓ Jul 15 04:36	♊ Sep 14 21:48	♍ Nov 16 02:02
♋ Jan 14 17:20	♎ Mar 17 08:17	♑ May 17 06:36	♈ Jul 17 09:23	♋ Sep 17 10:15	♎ Nov 18 10:19
♌ Jan 17 03:37	♏ Mar 19 10:52	♒ May 19 07:39	♉ Jul 19 18:21	♌ Sep 19 22:20	♏ Nov 20 14:40
♍ Jan 19 11:39	♐ Mar 21 12:58	♓ May 21 11:40	♊ Jul 22 06:23	♍ Sep 22 08:01	♐ Nov 22 15:57
♎ Jan 21 17:54	♑ Mar 23 15:31	♈ May 23 19:13	♋ Jul 24 19:16	♎ Sep 24 14:51	♑ Nov 24 15:48
♏ Jan 23 22:32	♒ Mar 25 19:09	♉ May 26 05:46	♌ Jul 27 07:07	♏ Sep 26 19:20	♒ Nov 26 16:15
♐ Jan 26 01:36	♓ Mar 28 00:18	♊ May 28 18:07	♍ Jul 29 17:13	♐ Sep 28 22:30	♓ Nov 28 18:59
♑ Jan 28 03:26	♈ Mar 30 07:26	♋ May 31 07:00	♎ Aug 1 01:24	♑ Oct 1 01:10	♈ Dec 1 00:51
♒ Jan 30 05:04	♉ Apr 1 16:58	♌ Jun 2 19:17	♏ Aug 3 07:30	♒ Oct 3 04:00	♉ Dec 3 09:41
♓ Feb 1 08:06	♊ Apr 4 04:50	♍ Jun 5 05:46	♐ Aug 5 11:15	♓ Oct 5 07:35	♊ Dec 5 20:35
♈ Feb 3 14:13	♋ Apr 6 17:39	♎ Jun 7 13:13	♑ Aug 7 12:51	♈ Oct 7 12:42	♋ Dec 8 08:44
♉ Feb 6 00:08	♌ Apr 9 05:15	♏ Jun 9 17:04	♒ Aug 9 13:28	♉ Oct 9 20:06	♌ Dec 10 21:24
♊ Feb 8 12:44	♍ Apr 11 13:39	♐ Jun 11 17:50	♓ Aug 11 14:46	♊ Oct 12 06:09	♍ Dec 13 09:26
♋ Feb 11 01:17	♎ Apr 13 18:21	♑ Jun 13 17:06	♈ Aug 13 18:41	♋ Oct 14 18:21	♎ Dec 15 19:09
♌ Feb 13 11:32	♏ Apr 15 20:13	♒ Jun 15 16:52	♉ Aug 16 02:25	♌ Oct 17 06:46	♏ Dec 18 01:07
♍ Feb 15 18:51	♐ Apr 17 20:52	♓ Jun 17 19:12	♊ Aug 18 13:39	♍ Oct 19 17:12	♐ Dec 20 03:14
♎ Feb 18 00:00	♑ Apr 19 21:53	♈ Jun 20 01:30	♋ Aug 21 02:23	♎ Oct 22 00:16	♑ Dec 22 02:45
♏ Feb 20 03:55	♒ Apr 22 00:39	♉ Jun 22 11:36	♌ Aug 23 14:13	♏ Oct 24 04:07	♒ Dec 24 01:52
♐ Feb 22 07:12	♓ Apr 24 05:51	♊ Jun 25 00:02	♍ Aug 25 23:52	♐ Oct 26 05:57	♓ Dec 26 02:44
♑ Feb 24 10:10	♈ Apr 26 13:42	♋ Jun 27 12:57	♎ Aug 28 07:15	♑ Oct 28 07:14	♈ Dec 28 07:06
♒ Feb 26 13:13	♉ Apr 28 23:54	♌ Jun 30 01:02	♏ Aug 30 12:51	♒ Oct 30 09:23	♉ Dec 30 15:21
♓ Feb 28 17:15	♊ May 1 11:54	♍ Jul 2 11:36	♐ Sep 1 16:57	♓ Nov 1 13:17	

Mercury

Jan 1 20 ♑
♒ Jan 6 22:19
R Jan 26 21 ♒
D Feb 16 6 ♒
♓ Mar 14 21:28
♈ Apr 2 07:28
♉ Apr 17 07:56
♊ May 2 15:35
R May 24 18 ♊
D Jun 17 9 ♊

♋ Jul 10 17:01
♌ Jul 25 22:17
♍ Aug 10 00:10
♎ Aug 29 02:14
R Sep 22 19 ♎
D Oct 14 4 ♎
♏ Nov 4 08:51
♐ Nov 22 22:44
♑ Dec 12 02:53

Venus

Jan 1 23 ♏
♐ Jan 7 12:10
♑ Feb 4 20:15
♒ Mar 2 22:13
♓ Mar 28 05:13
♈ Apr 22 04:08
♉ May 16 23:21
♊ Jun 10 16:17

♋ Jul 5 06:39
♌ Jul 29 17:32
♍ Aug 23 00:44
♎ Sep 16 05:01
♏ Oct 10 07:49
♐ Nov 3 10:17
♑ Nov 27 13:22
♒ Dec 21 18:20

Mars

Jan 1 2 ♍
R Jan 2 2 ♍
♌ Jan 23 00:36
D Mar 24 13 ♌
♍ May 25 16:16
♎ Jul 21 09:21
♏ Sep 7 06:54
♐ Oct 20 21:03
♑ Nov 30 13:52

Jupiter

Jan 1 4 ♐
R Apr 1 15 ♐
D Aug 2 5 ♐

Saturn

Jan 1 7 ♓
R Jul 6 24 ♓
D Nov 21 17 ♓

Uranus

Jan 1 25 ♑
♒ Apr 1 14:23
R May 5 0 ♒
♑ Jun 9 00:26
D Oct 6 26 ♑

Neptune

Jan 1 22 ♑
R Apr 27 25 ♑
D Oct 5 22 ♑

Pluto

Jan 1 29 ♏
♐ Jan 17 12:28
R Mar 4 0 ♐
♏ Apr 21 00:14
D Aug 8 27 ♏
♐ Nov 10 21:18

1996

Sun

♒ Jan 20 18:53	♈ Mar 20 08:04	♊ May 20 18:23	♌ Jul 22 13:17	♎ Sep 22 18:00	♐ Nov 22 00:47
♓ Feb 19 09:01	♉ Apr 19 19:10	♋ Jun 21 02:23	♍ Aug 22 20:21	♏ Oct 23 03:18	♑ Dec 21 14:05

Moon

Jan 1 16♉	♌ Mar 1 16:48	♏ May 2 12:43	♒ Jul 2 12:05	♉ Sep 1 12:20	♌ Nov 2 09:17
♊ Jan 2 02:30	♍ Mar 4 04:13	♐ May 4 16:05	♓ Jul 4 12:07	♊ Sep 3 19:08	♍ Nov 4 21:58
♋ Jan 4 14:56	♎ Mar 6 13:40	♑ May 6 17:54	♈ Jul 6 14:41	♋ Sep 5 05:30	♎ Nov 7 09:28
♌ Jan 7 03:30	♏ Mar 8 21:05	♒ May 8 19:39	♉ Jul 8 20:43	♌ Sep 8 17:55	♏ Nov 9 18:02
♍ Jan 9 15:29	♐ Mar 11 02:33	♓ May 10 22:30	♊ Jul 11 05:53	♍ Sep 11 06:28	♐ Nov 11 23:27
♎ Jan 12 01:55	♑ Mar 13 06:08	♈ May 13 03:00	♋ Jul 13 17:08	♎ Sep 13 17:52	♑ Nov 14 02:43
♏ Jan 14 09:30	♒ Mar 15 08:15	♉ May 15 09:24	♌ Jul 16 05:32	♏ Sep 16 03:21	♒ Nov 16 05:15
♐ Jan 16 13:26	♓ Mar 17 09:50	♊ May 17 17:47	♍ Jul 18 18:17	♐ Sep 18 10:30	♓ Nov 18 08:00
♑ Jan 18 14:08	♈ Mar 19 12:16	♋ May 20 04:16	♎ Jul 21 06:14	♑ Sep 20 15:13	♈ Nov 20 11:34
♒ Jan 20 13:15	♉ Mar 21 16:58	♌ May 22 16:29	♏ Jul 23 15:43	♒ Sep 22 17:39	♉ Nov 22 16:12
♓ Jan 22 13:02	♊ Mar 24 01:00	♍ May 25 04:58	♐ Jul 25 21:24	♓ Sep 24 18:43	♊ Nov 24 22:20
♈ Jan 24 15:37	♋ Mar 26 12:05	♎ May 27 15:34	♑ Jul 27 23:17	♈ Sep 26 19:46	♋ Nov 27 06:38
♉ Jan 26 22:16	♌ Mar 29 00:37	♏ May 29 22:30	♒ Jul 29 22:48	♉ Sep 28 22:24	♌ Nov 29 17:30
♊ Jan 29 08:42	♍ Mar 31 12:15	♐ Jun 1 01:43	♓ Jul 31 22:01	♊ Oct 1 04:02	♍ Dec 2 06:12
♋ Jan 31 21:10	♎ Apr 2 21:26	♑ Jun 3 02:30	♈ Aug 2 23:05	♋ Oct 3 13:14	♎ Dec 4 18:23
♌ Feb 3 09:46	♏ Apr 5 03:58	♒ Jun 5 02:44	♉ Aug 5 03:34	♌ Oct 6 01:11	♏ Dec 7 03:39
♍ Feb 5 21:22	♐ Apr 7 08:21	♓ Jun 7 04:20	♊ Aug 7 11:49	♍ Oct 8 13:50	♐ Dec 9 08:59
♎ Feb 8 07:30	♑ Apr 9 11:31	♈ Jun 9 08:22	♋ Aug 9 22:57	♎ Oct 11 01:01	♑ Dec 11 11:15
♏ Feb 10 15:36	♒ Apr 11 14:10	♉ Jun 11 15:10	♌ Aug 12 11:30	♏ Oct 13 09:46	♒ Dec 13 12:14
♐ Feb 12 20:59	♓ Apr 13 17:00	♊ Jun 14 00:16	♍ Aug 15 00:07	♐ Oct 15 16:07	♓ Dec 15 13:44
♑ Feb 14 23:30	♈ Apr 15 20:42	♋ Jun 16 11:09	♎ Aug 17 11:56	♑ Oct 17 20:37	♈ Dec 17 16:55
♒ Feb 17 00:00	♉ Apr 18 02:06	♌ Jun 18 23:21	♏ Aug 19 21:50	♒ Oct 19 23:52	♉ Dec 19 22:09
♓ Feb 19 00:09	♊ Apr 20 09:54	♍ Jun 21 12:06	♐ Aug 22 04:49	♓ Oct 22 02:22	♊ Dec 22 05:17
♈ Feb 21 01:58	♋ Apr 22 20:24	♎ Jun 23 23:37	♑ Aug 24 08:21	♈ Oct 24 04:51	♋ Dec 24 14:15
♉ Feb 23 07:08	♌ Apr 25 08:44	♏ Jun 26 07:53	♒ Aug 26 09:10	♉ Oct 26 08:12	♌ Dec 27 01:08
♊ Feb 25 16:13	♍ Apr 27 20:49	♐ Jun 28 12:01	♓ Aug 28 08:50	♊ Oct 28 13:34	♍ Dec 29 13:46
♋ Feb 28 04:10	♎ Apr 30 06:27	♑ Jun 30 12:47	♈ Aug 30 09:16	♋ Oct 30 21:57	

Mercury

Jan 1 29♑	♋ Jul 2 07:32
♒ Jan 1 17:49	♌ Jul 16 09:54
R Jan 9 6♒	♍ Aug 1 16:16
♑ Jan 17 09:37	♎ Aug 26 04:37
D Jan 30 19♑	R Sep 4 3♎
♒ Feb 15 02:29	♍ Sep 12 09:30
♓ Mar 7 11:55	D Sep 26 18♍
♈ Mar 24 08:01	♎ Oct 9 03:31
♉ Apr 8 03:17	♏ Oct 27 00:59
R May 3 28♉	♐ Nov 14 16:36
D May 27 18♉	♑ Dec 4 13:52
♊ Jun 13 21:31	R Dec 23 20♑

Venus

Jan 1 12♒	♋ Aug 7 06:13
♓ Jan 15 04:29	♌ Sep 7 05:04
♈ Feb 9 02:33	♍ Oct 4 03:20
♉ Mar 6 02:05	♎ Oct 29 12:00
♊ Apr 3 15:30	♏ Nov 23 01:33
R May 20 28♊	♐ Dec 17 05:34
D Jul 2 11♊	

Mars

Jan 1 24♑	♊ Jun 12 14:37
♒ Jan 8 10:59	♋ Jul 25 18:34
♓ Feb 15 11:49	♌ Sep 9 20:07
♈ Mar 24 15:08	♍ Oct 30 07:04
♉ May 2 18:15	

Jupiter

Jan 1 29♐
♑ Jan 3 06:38
R May 4 17♑
D Sep 3 7♑

Saturn

Jan 1 19♓
♈ Apr 7 08:18
R Jul 18 7♈
D Dec 3 0♈

Uranus

Jan 1 29♑
♒ Jan 12 08:29
R May 8 4♒
D Oct 10 0♒

Neptune

Jan 1 24♑
R Apr 29 27♑
D Oct 6 24♑

Pluto

Jan 1 1♐
R Mar 5 3♐
D Aug 10 0♐

1997

Sun

♒ Jan 20 00:42	♈ Mar 20 13:53	♊ May 21 00:17	♌ Jul 22 19:12	♎ Sep 22 23:54	♐ Nov 22 06:45
♓ Feb 18 14:51	♉ Apr 20 01:02	♋ Jun 21 08:17	♍ Aug 23 02:15	♏ Oct 23 09:13	♑ Dec 21 20:06

Moon

Jan 1 28 ♍	♐ Mar 1 12:01	♓ May 1 12:50	♊ Jul 1 11:36	♍ Sep 1 04:27	♐ Nov 2 04:27
♎ Jan 1 02:33	♑ Mar 3 17:38	♈ May 3 15:00	♋ Jul 3 18:32	♎ Sep 3 17:30	♑ Nov 4 12:31
♏ Jan 3 13:03	♒ Mar 5 19:54	♉ May 5 17:05	♌ Jul 6 03:45	♏ Sep 6 06:10	♒ Nov 6 18:34
♐ Jan 5 19:28	♓ Mar 7 19:57	♊ May 7 20:20	♍ Jul 8 15:22	♐ Sep 8 16:54	♓ Nov 8 22:34
♑ Jan 7 21:55	♈ Mar 9 19:32	♋ May 10 02:13	♎ Jul 11 04:21	♑ Sep 11 00:23	♈ Nov 11 00:44
♒ Jan 9 22:01	♉ Mar 11 20:37	♌ May 12 11:34	♏ Jul 13 16:21	♒ Sep 13 04:10	♉ Nov 13 01:46
♓ Jan 11 21:51	♊ Mar 14 00:48	♍ May 14 23:43	♐ Jul 16 01:03	♓ Sep 15 04:59	♊ Nov 15 03:05
♈ Jan 13 23:21	♋ Mar 16 08:51	♎ May 17 12:27	♑ Jul 18 05:45	♈ Sep 17 04:25	♋ Nov 17 06:32
♉ Jan 16 03:41	♌ Mar 18 20:09	♏ May 19 23:12	♒ Jul 20 07:30	♉ Sep 19 04:22	♌ Nov 19 13:38
♊ Jan 18 10:53	♍ Mar 21 09:00	♐ May 22 06:50	♓ Jul 22 07:59	♊ Sep 21 06:39	♍ Nov 22 00:32
♋ Jan 20 20:29	♎ Mar 23 21:36	♑ May 24 11:52	♈ Jul 24 09:03	♋ Sep 23 12:34	♎ Nov 24 13:30
♌ Jan 23 07:50	♏ Mar 26 08:42	♒ May 26 15:21	♉ Jul 26 11:54	♌ Sep 25 22:12	♏ Nov 27 01:44
♍ Jan 25 20:27	♐ Mar 28 17:40	♓ May 28 18:19	♊ Jul 28 17:05	♍ Sep 28 10:28	♐ Nov 29 11:29
♎ Jan 28 09:22	♑ Mar 31 00:06	♈ May 30 21:18	♋ Jul 31 00:39	♎ Sep 30 23:33	♑ Dec 1 18:39
♏ Jan 30 20:49	♒ Apr 2 03:59	♉ Jun 2 00:39	♌ Aug 2 10:28	♏ Oct 3 11:58	♒ Dec 3 23:58
♐ Feb 2 04:52	♓ Apr 4 05:42	♊ Jun 4 04:54	♍ Aug 4 22:15	♐ Oct 5 22:44	♓ Dec 6 02:25
♑ Feb 4 08:44	♈ Apr 6 06:20	♋ Jun 6 11:01	♎ Aug 7 11:17	♑ Oct 8 07:04	♈ Dec 8 07:25
♒ Feb 6 09:22	♉ Apr 8 07:21	♌ Jun 8 19:58	♏ Aug 9 23:51	♒ Oct 10 12:28	♉ Dec 10 10:01
♓ Feb 8 08:35	♊ Apr 10 10:29	♍ Jun 11 07:44	♐ Aug 12 09:45	♓ Oct 12 15:00	♊ Dec 12 12:36
♈ Feb 10 08:30	♋ Apr 12 17:04	♎ Jun 13 20:36	♑ Aug 14 15:43	♈ Oct 14 15:25	♋ Dec 14 16:26
♉ Feb 12 10:56	♌ Apr 15 03:22	♏ Jun 16 07:52	♒ Aug 16 17:59	♉ Oct 16 15:16	♌ Dec 16 22:57
♊ Feb 14 16:53	♍ Apr 17 16:01	♐ Jun 18 15:40	♓ Aug 18 18:01	♊ Oct 18 16:27	♍ Dec 19 09:00
♋ Feb 17 02:13	♎ Apr 20 04:36	♑ Jun 20 20:02	♈ Aug 20 17:45	♋ Oct 20 20:45	♎ Dec 21 21:36
♌ Feb 19 13:52	♏ Apr 22 15:20	♒ Jun 22 22:21	♉ Aug 22 18:58	♌ Oct 23 05:11	♏ Dec 24 10:07
♍ Feb 22 02:38	♐ Apr 24 23:33	♓ Jun 25 00:09	♊ Aug 24 22:56	♍ Oct 25 16:59	♐ Dec 26 20:08
♎ Feb 24 15:23	♑ Apr 27 05:33	♈ Jun 27 02:38	♋ Aug 27 06:12	♎ Oct 28 06:05	♑ Dec 29 02:49
♏ Feb 27 02:58	♒ Apr 29 09:50	♉ Jun 29 06:23	♌ Aug 29 16:19	♏ Oct 30 18:16	♒ Dec 31 06:59

Mercury

Jan 1 13 ♑	♌ Jul 8 05:19
D Jan 12 3 ♑	♍ Jul 27 01:09
♒ Feb 9 05:52	R Aug 17 15 ♍
♓ Feb 28 03:55	D Sep 10 3 ♍
♈ Mar 16 04:21	♎ Oct 2 05:41
♉ Apr 1 13:48	♏ Oct 19 12:08
R Apr 15 8 ♉	♐ Nov 7 17:44
♈ May 5 02:58	♑ Nov 30 18:32
D May 8 29 ♈	R Dec 7 3 ♑
♉ May 12 10:29	♐ Dec 13 18:15
♊ Jun 8 23:45	D Dec 27 17 ♐
♋ Jun 23 20:40	

Venus

Jan 1 18 ♐	♌ Jun 28 18:38
♑ Jan 10 05:33	♍ Jul 23 13:16
♒ Feb 3 04:29	♎ Aug 17 14:32
♓ Feb 27 04:02	♏ Sep 12 02:15
♈ Mar 23 05:27	♐ Oct 8 08:20
♉ Apr 16 09:44	♑ Nov 5 08:43
♊ May 10 17:21	♒ Dec 12 04:31
♋ Jun 4 04:17	R Dec 26 3 ♒

Mars

Jan 1 29 ♍
♎ Jan 3 08:07
R Feb 6 5 ♎
♍ Mar 8 19:52
D Apr 27 16 ♍
♎ Jun 19 08:53
♏ Aug 14 08:38
♐ Sep 28 22:19
♑ Nov 9 05:24
♒ Dec 18 06:31

Jupiter

Jan 1 25 ♑
♒ Jan 21 14:27
R Jun 10 21 ♒
D Oct 8 12 ♒

Saturn

Jan 1 1 ♈
R Aug 1 20 ♈
D Dec 16 13 ♈

Uranus

Jan 1 3 ♒
R May 13 8 ♒
D Oct 14 4 ♒

Neptune

Jan 1 26 ♑
R May 1 29 ♑
D Oct 9 27 ♑

Pluto

Jan 1 4 ♐
R Mar 8 5 ♐
D Aug 13 2 ♐

1998

Sun

♒ Jan 20 06:45	♈ Mar 20 19:53	♊ May 21 06:06	♌ Jul 23 00:55	♎ Sep 23 05:37	♐ Nov 22 12:34
♓ Feb 18 20:55	♉ Apr 20 06:57	♋ Jun 21 14:04	♍ Aug 23 07:58	♏ Oct 23 14:59	♑ Dec 22 01:54

Moon

Jan 1 9♒	♉ Mar 2 05:00	♌ May 2 09:49	♏ Jul 3 11:45	♒ Sep 3 09:22	♉ Nov 3 11:13
♓ Jan 2 09:57	♊ Mar 4 07:14	♍ May 4 19:48	♐ Jul 5 23:24	♓ Sep 5 12:47	♊ Nov 5 10:11
♈ Jan 4 12:44	♋ Mar 6 12:26	♎ May 7 08:18	♑ Jul 8 08:18	♈ Sep 7 13:52	♋ Nov 7 10:39
♉ Jan 6 15:52	♌ Mar 8 20:45	♏ May 9 21:10	♒ Jul 10 14:53	♉ Sep 9 14:16	♌ Nov 9 14:33
♊ Jan 8 19:43	♍ Mar 11 07:35	♐ May 12 08:47	♓ Jul 12 19:23	♊ Sep 11 15:41	♍ Nov 11 22:37
♋ Jan 11 00:44	♎ Mar 13 19:58	♑ May 14 18:40	♈ Jul 14 22:46	♋ Sep 13 19:21	♎ Nov 14 09:58
♌ Jan 13 07:46	♏ Mar 16 08:52	♒ May 17 02:31	♉ Jul 17 01:33	♌ Sep 16 01:48	♏ Nov 16 22:42
♍ Jan 15 17:32	♐ Mar 18 20:57	♓ May 19 08:04	♊ Jul 19 04:19	♍ Sep 18 10:52	♐ Nov 19 11:13
♎ Jan 18 05:44	♑ Mar 21 06:44	♈ May 21 11:07	♋ Jul 21 07:43	♎ Sep 20 21:58	♑ Nov 21 22:46
♏ Jan 20 18:35	♒ Mar 23 13:02	♉ May 23 12:06	♌ Jul 23 12:48	♏ Sep 23 10:22	♒ Nov 24 08:43
♐ Jan 23 05:25	♓ Mar 25 15:44	♊ May 25 12:25	♍ Jul 25 23:05	♐ Sep 25 23:05	♓ Nov 26 16:14
♑ Jan 25 12:40	♈ Mar 27 15:48	♋ May 27 13:58	♎ Jul 28 07:14	♑ Sep 28 10:30	♈ Nov 28 20:35
♒ Jan 27 16:28	♉ Mar 29 15:06	♌ May 29 18:38	♏ Jul 30 19:45	♒ Sep 30 18:53	♉ Nov 30 21:52
♓ Jan 29 18:08	♊ Mar 31 15:38	♍ Jun 1 03:22	♐ Aug 2 07:49	♓ Oct 2 23:23	♊ Dec 2 21:30
♈ Jan 31 19:22	♋ Apr 2 19:09	♎ Jun 3 15:18	♑ Aug 4 17:18	♈ Oct 5 00:31	♋ Dec 4 21:28
♉ Feb 2 21:24	♌ Apr 5 02:36	♏ Jun 6 04:06	♒ Aug 6 23:32	♉ Oct 6 23:58	♌ Dec 6 23:56
♊ Feb 5 01:09	♍ Apr 7 13:26	♐ Jun 8 15:35	♓ Aug 9 03:04	♊ Oct 8 23:44	♍ Dec 9 06:22
♋ Feb 7 06:58	♎ Apr 10 02:06	♑ Jun 11 00:50	♈ Aug 11 05:11	♋ Oct 11 01:49	♎ Dec 11 16:44
♌ Feb 9 14:57	♏ Apr 12 14:56	♒ Jun 13 08:04	♉ Aug 13 07:05	♌ Oct 13 07:26	♏ Dec 14 05:16
♍ Feb 11 01:09	♐ Apr 15 02:53	♓ Jun 15 13:31	♊ Aug 15 09:45	♍ Oct 15 16:32	♐ Dec 16 17:47
♎ Feb 14 13:17	♑ Apr 17 13:06	♈ Jun 17 17:23	♋ Aug 17 13:55	♎ Oct 18 04:03	♑ Dec 19 04:55
♏ Feb 17 02:14	♒ Apr 19 20:41	♉ Jun 19 19:48	♌ Aug 19 20:00	♏ Oct 20 16:36	♒ Dec 21 14:17
♐ Feb 19 13:56	♓ Apr 22 01:07	♊ Jun 21 21:26	♍ Aug 22 04:22	♐ Oct 23 05:16	♓ Dec 23 21:45
♑ Feb 21 22:30	♈ Apr 24 02:49	♋ Jun 23 23:39	♎ Aug 24 15:02	♑ Oct 25 17:06	♈ Dec 26 03:04
♒ Feb 24 03:10	♉ Apr 26 02:09	♌ Jun 26 04:04	♏ Aug 27 03:25	♒ Oct 28 02:44	♉ Dec 28 06:04
♓ Feb 26 04:43	♊ Apr 28 01:55	♍ Jun 28 11:55	♐ Aug 29 15:55	♓ Oct 30 08:59	♊ Dec 30 07:23
♈ Feb 28 04:43	♋ Apr 30 03:58	♎ Jun 30 23:06	♑ Sep 1 02:23	♈ Nov 1 11:28	

Mercury

Jan 1 19♐	♌ Jun 30 23:53
♑ Jan 12 16:30	R Jul 31 28♌
♒ Feb 2 15:14	D Aug 23 16♌
♓ Feb 20 10:22	♍ Sep 8 02:04
♈ Mar 8 08:32	♎ Sep 24 10:11
R Mar 27 21♈	♏ Oct 12 02:53
D Apr 20 9♈	♐ Nov 1 16:11
♉ May 15 02:24	R Nov 21 17♐
♊ Jun 1 08:06	D Dec 11 1♐
♋ Jun 15 05:29	

Venus

Jan 1 3♒	♋ Jul 19 15:17
♑ Jan 9 21:23	♌ Aug 13 09:19
D Feb 5 18♑	♍ Sep 6 19:24
♒ Mar 4 16:06	♎ Sep 30 23:15
♓ Apr 6 05:34	♏ Oct 24 23:08
♈ May 3 19:16	♐ Nov 17 21:06
♉ May 29 23:34	♑ Dec 11 18:32
♊ Jun 24 12:27	

Mars

Jan 1 10♒
♓ Jan 25 09:26
♈ Mar 4 16:17
♉ Apr 13 01:07
♊ May 24 03:41
♋ Jul 6 09:00
♌ Aug 20 19:13
♍ Oct 7 12:25
♎ Nov 27 10:19

Jupiter

Jan 1 22♒
♓ Feb 4 10:35
R Jul 18 28♓
D Nov 13 18♓

Saturn

Jan 1 13♈
♉ Jun 9 05:19
R Aug 15 3♉
♈ Oct 25 20:19
D Dec 29 26♈

Uranus

Jan 1 7♒
R May 17 12♒
D Oct 18 8♒

Neptune

Jan 1 28♑
♒ Jan 29 00:51
R May 4 2♒
♑ Aug 23 04:14
D Oct 11 29♑
♒ Nov 27 21:17

Pluto

Jan 1 6♐
R Mar 11 8♐
D Aug 16 5♐

1999

Sun

♒ Jan 20 12:37	♈ Mar 21 01:44	♊ May 21 11:53	♌ Jul 23 06:45	♎ Sep 23 11:34	♐ Nov 22 18:25
♓ Feb 19 02:45	♉ Apr 20 12:45	♋ Jun 21 19:50	♍ Aug 23 13:52	♏ Oct 23 20:54	♑ Dec 22 07:45

Moon

Jan 1 24♊	♍ Mar 1 10:06	♐ May 2 07:36	♓ Jul 3 04:35	♊ Sep 2 05:24	♍ Nov 2 04:07
♋ Jan 1 08:15	♎ Mar 3 18:35	♑ May 4 20:13	♈ Jul 5 11:21	♋ Sep 4 08:10	♎ Nov 4 11:57
♌ Jan 3 10:31	♏ Mar 6 05:22	♒ May 7 07:40	♉ Jul 7 15:22	♌ Sep 6 11:29	♏ Nov 6 21:45
♍ Jan 5 15:49	♐ Mar 8 17:46	♓ May 9 16:16	♊ Jul 9 17:00	♍ Sep 8 15:57	♐ Nov 9 09:16
♎ Jan 8 00:53	♑ Mar 11 05:54	♈ May 11 20:55	♋ Jul 11 17:28	♎ Sep 10 22:16	♑ Nov 11 22:00
♏ Jan 10 12:49	♒ Mar 13 15:32	♉ May 13 21:57	♌ Jul 13 18:25	♏ Sep 13 07:08	♒ Nov 14 10:46
♐ Jan 13 01:24	♓ Mar 15 21:30	♊ May 15 21:07	♍ Jul 15 21:39	♐ Sep 15 18:36	♓ Nov 16 21:21
♑ Jan 15 12:28	♈ Mar 18 00:14	♋ May 17 20:39	♎ Jul 18 04:20	♑ Sep 18 07:13	♈ Nov 19 03:58
♒ Jan 17 21:12	♉ Mar 20 01:08	♌ May 19 22:37	♏ Jul 20 14:31	♒ Sep 20 18:39	♉ Nov 21 06:26
♓ Jan 20 03:41	♊ Mar 22 02:06	♍ May 22 04:15	♐ Jul 23 02:49	♓ Sep 23 02:52	♊ Nov 23 06:15
♈ Jan 22 08:25	♋ Mar 24 04:33	♎ May 24 13:30	♑ Jul 25 15:08	♈ Sep 25 07:33	♋ Nov 25 05:30
♉ Jan 24 11:53	♌ Mar 26 09:22	♏ May 27 01:06	♒ Jul 28 01:54	♉ Sep 27 09:50	♌ Nov 27 06:19
♊ Jan 26 14:30	♍ Mar 28 16:34	♐ May 29 13:37	♓ Jul 30 10:28	♊ Sep 29 11:20	♍ Nov 29 10:11
♋ Jan 28 16:57	♎ Mar 31 01:50	♑ Jun 1 02:06	♈ Aug 1 16:48	♋ Oct 1 13:31	♎ Dec 1 17:30
♌ Jan 30 20:15	♏ Apr 2 12:48	♒ Jun 3 13:37	♉ Aug 3 21:08	♌ Oct 3 17:14	♏ Dec 4 03:36
♍ Feb 2 01:37	♐ Apr 5 01:07	♓ Jun 5 23:00	♊ Aug 5 23:58	♍ Oct 5 22:40	♐ Dec 6 15:27
♎ Feb 4 09:55	♑ Apr 7 13:39	♈ Jun 8 05:09	♋ Aug 8 01:52	♎ Oct 8 05:52	♑ Dec 9 04:13
♏ Feb 6 21:06	♒ Apr 10 00:24	♉ Jun 10 07:45	♌ Aug 10 03:55	♏ Oct 10 15:01	♒ Dec 11 16:59
♐ Feb 9 09:39	♓ Apr 12 07:35	♊ Jun 12 07:49	♍ Aug 12 07:22	♐ Oct 13 02:18	♓ Dec 14 04:17
♑ Feb 11 21:10	♈ Apr 14 10:47	♋ Jun 14 07:14	♎ Aug 14 13:25	♑ Oct 15 15:03	♈ Dec 16 12:30
♒ Feb 14 05:58	♉ Apr 16 11:08	♌ Jun 16 08:08	♏ Aug 16 22:40	♒ Oct 18 03:18	♉ Dec 18 16:46
♓ Feb 16 11:40	♊ Apr 18 10:39	♍ Jun 18 12:13	♐ Aug 19 10:31	♓ Oct 20 12:32	♊ Dec 20 17:39
♈ Feb 18 15:06	♋ Apr 20 11:28	♎ Jun 20 20:11	♑ Aug 21 22:59	♈ Oct 22 17:41	♋ Dec 22 16:53
♉ Feb 20 17:30	♌ Apr 22 14:19	♏ Jun 23 07:19	♒ Aug 24 09:49	♉ Oct 24 19:26	♌ Dec 24 16:31
♊ Feb 22 19:53	♍ Apr 24 22:05	♐ Jun 25 19:52	♓ Aug 26 17:50	♊ Oct 26 19:33	♍ Dec 26 18:35
♋ Feb 24 23:09	♎ Apr 27 07:47	♑ Jun 28 08:13	♈ Aug 28 23:10	♋ Oct 28 20:10	♎ Dec 29 00:15
♌ Feb 27 03:45	♏ Apr 29 19:13	♒ Jun 30 19:20	♉ Aug 31 02:40	♌ Oct 30 22:47	♏ Dec 31 09:37

Mercury

Jan 1 21♐	R Jul 12 10♌
♑ Jan 7 01:57	♋ Jul 31 19:16
♒ Jan 26 09:31	D Aug 6 28♋
♓ Feb 12 15:26	♌ Aug 11 02:40
♈ Mar 2 22:58	♍ Aug 31 15:09
R Mar 10 4♈	♎ Sep 16 12:53
♓ Mar 18 09:29	♏ Oct 5 05:15
D Apr 2 20♓	♐ Oct 30 20:04
♈ Apr 17 21:51	R Nov 5 1♐
♉ May 8 21:28	♏ Nov 9 20:41
♊ May 23 21:22	D Nov 25 14♏
♋ Jun 6 23:59	♐ Dec 11 02:04
♌ Jun 26 15:26	

Venus

Jan 1 25♑	♍ Jul 12 15:14
♒ Jan 4 16:24	R Jul 30 5♍
♓ Jan 28 16:14	♌ Aug 15 14:20
♈ Feb 21 20:47	D Sep 11 18♌
♉ Mar 18 09:59	♍ Oct 7 16:52
♊ Apr 12 13:16	♎ Nov 9 02:20
♋ May 8 16:32	♏ Dec 5 22:44
♌ Jun 5 21:34	

Mars

Jan 1 18♎
♏ Jan 26 12:01
R Mar 18 12♏
♎ May 5 21:25
D Jun 4 23♎
♏ Jul 5 04:02
♐ Sep 2 19:34
♑ Oct 17 01:34
♒ Nov 26 06:49

Jupiter

Jan 1 21♓
♈ Feb 13 01:10
♉ Jun 28 09:39
R Aug 25 4♉
♈ Oct 23 05:41
D Dec 20 25♈

Saturn

Jan 1 26♈
♉ Mar 1 00:09
R Aug 30 17♉

Uranus

Jan 1 10♒
R May 21 16♒
D Oct 23 12♒

Neptune

Jan 1 1♒
R May 7 4♒
D Oct 14 1♒

Pluto

Jan 1 9♐
R Mar 13 10♐
D Aug 19 7♐

Astrological Software and Chart Services

ASTROLOGICAL SOFTWARE

Time Cycles Research, 27 Dimmock Road, Waterford, CT 06385
   Voice: (203) 444-6641
   Fax: (203) 442-0625
   1-800-827-2240

CHART SERVICES

Note: The chart services listed below provide a natal chart for $5.00. Send check or money order along with your birth information—Name, Date of Birth, Time of Birth, and Place of Birth (city and state or city and country if outside USA). If you do not have a time of birth, request either a midnight, noon, or sunrise chart.

- Paisley Charts, 26 Four Mile River Road, Old Lyme, CT 06371
- KNS Chart Services, 1315 St. Joseph's Ct., Crownsville, MD 21032
- Llewellyn Chart Services, P.O. Box 64383, St. Paul, MN 55164-0383

Appendix C

Birth Data Sources

THEODORE ROOSEVELT

William DeGregorio's book, *The Complete Book of U. S. Presidents*, states on p. 376 that
Roosevelt was born on October 27, 1858 at 7:45 PM, at the family brownstone on
East 20th Street, New York City. The same data is given on p. 29 in Nathan Miller's
book, *Theodore Roosevelt: A Life*.

GRACE KELLY

The Circle Book of Charts, compiled by Stephen Erlewine, #1123 states birth data as
November 12, 1929; 5:31 AM EST; Philadelphia, Pennsylvania, from "*Astrology
Magazine* article by H. Paquette: 'from birth certificate.' "

TED BUNDY

Birth data of November 24, 1946 at 10:35 PM EST is credited to T. Patrick Davis from the
birth certificate. The same data appeared in *Mercury Hour*, credited to astrologer
Dorothy Hughes.

MATA HARI

T. Patrick Davis quotes birth data from Douglas Lannark of Copenhagen for 12:34 PM.

Endnotes

PREFACE

1. Oppenheim, A. Leo. *Ancient Mesopotamia: Portrait of a Dead Civilization.* Chicago: The University of Chicago Press, 1977, p. 224.

CHAPTER ONE

1. Gleick, James. "Fermat's Theorem," *The New York Times Magazine.* October 3, 1993, p. 53.

CHAPTER ELEVEN

1. Miller, Nathan. *Theodore Roosevelt: A Life.* New York: William Morrow and Company, Inc., 1992, p. 436.

2. Wadler, Joyce, et al. "The President's Astrologers," *People Weekly,* May 23, 1988, p. 112.

3. DeGregorio, William A. *The Complete Book of U. S. Presidents—From George Washington to Bill Clinton.* Avenel, New Jersey: Wings Books, 1993, p. 373.

4. Miller, *Theodore Roosevelt: A Life.* p. 46.

5. Ibid., p. 47.

6. Ibid., p. 50.

7. Ibid., p. 530.

8. Ibid., p. 61-62.

9. Bishop, Joseph Bucklin, ed. *Theodore Roosevelt's Letters to His Children.* New York: Charles Scribner's Sons, 1919, p. 7.

10. Miller, *Theodore Roosevelt: A Life,* p.413–414.

11. Ibid., p. 18.

12. Morris, Edmund. *The Rise of Theodore Roosevelt.* New York: Ballantine Books, 1979, p. 706.

13. Miller, *Theodore Roosevelt: A Life,* p. 205.

14. Morris, *The Rise of Theodore Roosevelt,* p. 18.

15. Miller, *Theodore Roosevelt: A Life,* p. 413.

16. Ibid., p. 358.

17. Ibid., p. 230.

18. Ibid., p. 226.

19. Miller, Nathan. *The Roosevelt Chronicles: The Story of a Great American Family*. Garden City, New York: Doubleday and Company, Inc., 1979. p. 186.

20. Miller, *Theodore Roosevelt: A Life*, p. 19.

21. Ibid., p. 412.

22. Miller, *The Roosevelt Chronicles: The Story of a Great American Family*, p. 166.

23. Miller, *Theodore Roosevelt: A Life*, p. 154.

24. Ibid., p. 203.

25. Ibid., p. 399.

26. Morris, p. 11.

27. Miller, *Theodore Roosevelt: A Life*, p. 412.

28. Ibid., p. 136.

29. Ibid., p. 412.

30. Ibid., p. 152.

31. Ibid., p. 473.

32. Miller, *The Roosevelt Chronicles: The Story of a Great American Family*, p. 213–214.

33. Miller, *Theodore Roosevelt: A Life*, p. 9.

34. Ibid., p. 18.

35. Ibid., p. 50.

36. Morris, p. 18.

37. Miller, *Theodore Roosevelt: A Life*, p. 535.

38. Edwards, Anne. *The Grimaldis of Monaco: The Centuries of Scandal—The Years of Grace*. New York: William Morrow and Company, Inc., 1992, p. 302.

39. Spada, James. *Grace: The Secret Lives of a Princess*. New York: Dell Publishing, 1987, p. 109–110.

40. Ibid., p. 308.

41. Quine, Judith Balaban. *The Bridesmaids: Grace Kelly, Princess of Monaco and Six Intimate Friends*. New York: Weidenfeld & Nicholson, 1989, p.45.

42. Spada, p. 55.

43. Ibid., p. 4.

44. Ibid., p. 31.

45. Ibid., p. 30.

46. Ibid., p. 36.

47. Ibid., p. 4.

48. Ibid., p. 17.

49. Ibid., p. 18.

50. Quine, p. 378.

51. Ibid., p. 366.

52. Spada, p. 27.

53. Ibid., p. 44.

54. Ibid., p. 16.

55. Rule, Ann. *The Stranger Beside Me.* New York: W.W. Norton & Co., 1980, p. 145.

56. Ibid., p. 31.

57. Michaud, Steven G. and Hugh Aynesworth. *Ted Bundy: Conversations With a Killer.* New York: Signet, 1989, p. v, Foreword.

58. Ibid., p. 32-33.

59. Rule, p. 119.

60. Ibid., p. 38.

61. Ibid., p. 23.

62. Ibid., p. 337.

63. Ibid., p. 338.

64. Michaud, p. 283.

65. Rule, p. 25-26.

66. Ibid., p. 29.

67. Ibid., p. 31.

68. Michaud, p. 13.

69. Ibid., p. 15.

70. Rule, p. 24.

71. Michaud, p. 10.

72. Ibid., p. 14.

73. Ibid., p. 73

74. Ibid., p. 202.

75. Rule, p. 144.

76. Ibid., p. 114.

77. Ostrovsky, Erika. *Eye of Dawn: The Rise and Fall of Mata Hari.* New York: Dorset Press, 1978, p. 70.

78. Ibid., p. 73.

79. Ibid., p. 2.

80. Ibid., p. 3.

81. Ibid., p. 77.

Bibliography

Bishop, Joseph Bucklin, ed. *Theodore Roosevelt's Letters to His Children.* New York: Charles Scribner's Sons, 1919.

DeGregorio, William A. *The Complete Book of U. S. Presidents—From George Washington to Bill Clinton.* Avenel, New Jersey: Wings Books, 1993.

Edwards, Anne. *The Grimaldis of Monaco: The Centuries of Scandal—The Years of Grace.* New York: William Morrow and Company, Inc., 1992.

Gleick, James. "Fermat's Theorem," *The New York Times Magazine.* October 3, 1993, p. 52–53.

Michaud, Steven G. and Hugh Aynesworth. *Ted Bundy: Conversations With a Killer.* New York: Signet, 1989.

Miller, Nathan. *The Roosevelt Chronicles: The Story of a Great American Family.* Garden City, New York: Doubleday and Company, Inc., 1979.

Miller, Nathan. *Theodore Roosevelt: A Life.* New York: William Morrow and Company, Inc., 1992.

Morris, Edmund. *The Rise of Theodore Roosevelt.* New York: Ballantine Books, 1979.

Nissen, Hans J. (translation by Elizabeth Lutzeier with Kenneth J. Norcott). *The Early History of the Ancient Near East: 9000–2000 BC.* Chicago: The University of Chicago Press, 1988.

Oppenheim, A. Leo. *Ancient Mesopotamia: Portrait of a Dead Civilization.* Chicago: The University of Chicago Press, 1977.

Ostrovsky, Erika. *Eye of Dawn: The Rise and Fall of Mata Hari*. New York: Dorset Press, 1978.

Quine, Judith Balaban. *The Bridesmaids: Grace Kelly, Princess of Monaco and Six Intimate Friends*. New York: Weidenfeld & Nicholson, 1989.

Roux, Georges. *Ancient Iraq*. England: Penguin Books, 1992.

Rule, Ann. *The Stranger Beside Me*. New York: W.W. Norton & Co., 1980.

Saggs, H.W.F. *Civilization Before Greece and Rome*. New Haven: Yale University Press, 1989.

Sherman, Dan. *The Man Who Loved Mata Hari*. New York: Donald I. Fine, Inc., 1985.

Spada, James. *Grace: The Secret Lives of a Princess*. New York: Dell Publishing, 1987.

Wadler, Joyce, et al., "The President's Astrologers," *People Weekly*, May 23, 1988, p. 107–113.

Wheelwright, Julie. *The Fatal Lover: Mata Hari and the Myth of Women in Espionage*. London: Collins and Brown Ltd., 1992.

ASTROLOGY BOOKS

Adams, Evangeline. *Astrology For Everyone: What It is and How It Works*. New York: Dell Publishing Company, Inc., 1972.

Adams, Evangeline. *Astrology: Your Place Among the Stars*. New York: Dell Publishing Company, Inc., 1972.

Escobar, Thyrza. *Essentials of Natal Interpretation with Study Guide*. Hollywood, California: Golden Seal Research Headquarters, 1972.

George, Llewellyn. *A to Z Horoscope Maker and Delineator*. St. Paul, Minnesota: Llewellyn Publications, 1973.

Gettings, Fred. *The Arkana Dictionary of Astrology*. London: Arkana, 1990.

Michelsen, Neil F. *The American Ephemeris for the 20th Century 1900 to 2000 at Midnight*. San Diego, California: ACS Publications, Inc., 1988.

Michelsen, Neil F. *The American Ephemeris for the 21st Century 2000 to 2050 at Midnight*. San Diego, California: ACS Publications, Inc., 1990.

Sakoian, Frances and Louis S. Acker. *The Astrologer's Handbook*. New York: Harper and Row, Publishers, Inc., 1973.

Shanks, Thomas G. *The American Atlas: US Latitudes and Longitudes—Time Changes and Time Zones*. San Diego, California: ACS Publications, Inc., 1978.

Shanks, Thomas G. *The International Atlas: World Latitudes, Longitudes and Time Changes.* San Diego, California: ACS Publications, Inc., 1985.

TEXTS TO CONSULT FOR BASIC CHART CALCULATIONS

McCaffery, Ellen. *Graphic Astrology: The Astrological Home Study Course.* Richmond, Virginia: Macoy Publishing Company, 1952.

Oken, Alan. *Alan Oken's Complete Astrology.* New York: Bantam Books, Inc., 1980.

Index

mutable signs, 5, 8–9, 220

rising sign (also see ascendant), 33–35, 38, 41, 52, 299–300, 307, 317

Sagittarius

fire sign, 6, 9–11

mutable sign, 9, 11

mutable fire sign, 11

Saturn

aspects in natal chart, 231, 233, 235–38, 241, 243, 245, 247, 249, 251, 253–54, 256–258, 260–61, 263, 265–68, 270–72, 274–83

through the houses, 188–195

through the signs, 128–132

Scorpio

fixed sign, 8–9, 11

fixed water sign, 11

water sign, 7, 12

Sun

apparent position, 37–38

aspects in natal chart, 229–239

degree on a given date, 37

through the houses, 151–157

through the signs, 60–82

Taurus

earth sign, 6–7, 10–11, 139

fixed sign, 8–11

fixed earth sign, 10–11

Uranus

aspects in natal chart, 231–233, 235, 237, 239, 241, 243, 245, 247, 249, 251–56, 258, 260, 262–63, 265, 267, 269–71, 273–86

through the houses, 195–202

through the signs, 132–135

Venus

aspects in natal chart, 230, 240, 242, 244, 246, 248, 250, 252, 259–67

through the houses, 169–175

through the signs, 106–114

vernal equinox, 14–15

Virgo

earth sign, 6–7, 10–11, 139

mutable sign, 9

mutable earth sign, 11

zodiac, 2–3, 13–20, 24–25, 27, 29, 31–34, 37–38, 41, 49, 79, 107, 123, 217